Literacy Deve

in Early Chil

Literacy Development in Early Childhood

Reflective Teaching for Birth to Age Eight

Beverly Otto

Northeastern Illinois University

WAVELAND

PRESS, INC.

Long Grove, Illinois

For information about this book, contact:
Waveland Press, Inc.
4180 IL Route 83, Suite 101
Long Grove, IL 60047-9580
(847) 634-0081
info@waveland.com
www.waveland.com

10-digit ISBN 1-4786-3020-5
13-digit ISBN 978-1-4786-3020-3

Printed in the United States of America

7   6   5   4   3   2

To my parents: Thanks for starting me on the path to literacy.

About the Author

Beverly Otto, Ph.D., an early childhood educator for more than 25 years, is a professor in the Teacher Education Department at Northeastern Illinois University. She earned her doctorate at Northwestern University in Teaching and Learning Processes with a focus on emergent literacy. Dr. Otto teaches courses in language and literacy development for preservice and inservice teachers, along with research for classroom teachers. She also serves as adviser for the Master of Arts in Teaching: Language Arts–Elementary Education and Master of Science in Instruction: Language Arts–Elementary programs. Her major professional goal is preparing teachers to support children's lifelong learning through language and literacy development. Dr. Otto has also served as department chair as well as associate dean in the College of Education.

Dr. Otto is the author of *Language Development in Early Childhood,* Second Edition (Merrill/Prentice Hall) and has also authored articles published in international, national, and state professional journals. Her field-based research on emergent literacy has been presented at international, national, state, and local conferences. She has also served as a consultant to early childhood centers and school districts, as well as to the Illinois State Board of Education.

Preface

Learning to read and write are major educational achievements for children in a literate society. Developing these competencies positively affects each child's cognitive, social-emotional, and economic future. As an early childhood educator, you are in a unique position to provide key experiences to young children that will significantly enhance their literacy development. Through the design and implementation of literacy-rich curricula in your early childhood classroom, and through partnership with parents, you can create a positive environment that will foster children's literacy development.

Your success as a teacher of young children depends not only on your implementation of learning activities, but also on your understanding of why specific learning activities are valuable and your ability to determine whether your curriculum is meeting the needs of the children in your classroom. This text has been designed to provide you with the knowledge base you will need to understand how children develop reading and writing competencies, what learning activities enhance the development of these competencies, and how to determine children's progress in developing literacy.

My goal in writing this text was to provide you with a foundation of professional knowledge about literacy-related theoretical perspectives, research, teaching strategies, and assessments, beginning with infancy and continuing through the early elementary years, so that you will be prepared to make instructional decisions for each child in your classroom. To prepare you to meet the challenges of working with children from culturally and linguistically diverse backgrounds, this text also provides background knowledge and related guidelines for literacy development among English language learners.

Book Organization

The first three chapters provide a conceptual and theoretical foundation for understanding reading and writing processes as well as the relationship of oral language to literacy development. Beginning with Chapter 4, companion chapters describe the signs of emergent literacy for each specific developmental level, followed by a chapter that focuses on developmentally appropriate instructional strategies. Assessment of student performance and specific strategies for working with special needs and at-risk students are also presented.

For the Professor

At the end of each chapter, there are two sections that will be useful for you and your students. The chapter review focuses on major concepts and terminology presented in each chapter. Chapter extension activities provide opportunities to apply the concepts through observation, research, curriculum development, or discussion. At the end of the text, a glossary and 12 appendices also provide useful information for the beginning early childhood educator.

This text includes a final chapter that focuses on fourth grade. While most states and NAEYC define early childhood in terms of infancy through third grade/age 8, there are other states that include fourth grade as part of their early childhood education teaching certification. Therefore, we have tried to be as inclusive as possible. In addition, all primary teachers need to be aware of the context and academic expectations of fourth grade in order to appropriately prepare their students for success at that level. Finally, third-grade teachers who have students who are academically talented will also want to be aware of ways to challenge these students with more complex literacy experiences.

An online instructor's manual and an online test bank are also available for downloading at waveland.com/Extra_Material/30203/. Also included on this site are more than 70 PowerPoint® slides that present the main concepts from each chapter.

Acknowledgments

To my colleagues at Northeastern Illinois University/NEIU, thank you for your support and encouragement. I am indebted to Dr. Parul Raval, assistant professor at NEIU, for sharing her knowledge of Gujarati and Urdu for Table 7.1. A special thanks is also extended to my undergraduate and graduate students at NEIU who provided questions and insightful comments that encouraged me to pursue this project.

I also would like to thank the children and their family members who appear in the photos, as well as those who are featured in the examples and vignettes. Your participation has brought the concepts of this book to life.

A special appreciation is extended to Julie Peters, acquisitions editor in early childhood education, who provided key insights in the design and development of this text. I would also like to thank the following reviewers for their comments and suggestions: Alida Anderson, University of Maryland; Adrienne Herrell, Florida State University; Bonnie L. Hoewing, University of Northern Iowa; Nancy Lauter, Montclair State University; Rose Anne Mott, West Texas A&M University; Nancy L. Petersen, Utah Valley State College; Muriel K. Rand, New Jersey City University; Elizabeth Rowell, Rhode Island College; Judith Schillo, The State University of New York, Cortland; Patricia Scully, University of Maryland, Baltimore County; Sandra J. Stone, Northern Arizona University; and Kaveri Subrahmanyam, California State University, Los Angeles.

Beverly Otto

Brief Contents

Contents

6　Signs of Emergent Literacy Among Preschoolers　111

7　Enhancing Emergent Literacy Among Preschoolers　131

11 Literacy Instruction in Second and Third Grade: Transitioning to Fluent Reading and Writing   272

Note: Every effort has been made to provide accurate and current Internet information in this book. However, the Internet and information posted on it are constantly changing, so it is inevitable that some of the Internet addresses listed in this textbook will change.

Chapter 1

Literacy and Learning

In their preschool room, Maria and Jennifer are looking through books in the library corner. Maria has selected *The Very Quiet Cricket* (Carle, 1990) and is paging through the book and telling a story while she looks at the illustrations. Jennifer is looking at *Winnie the Pooh's A to Zzzz* (Ferguson, 1992). As she looks at each page, she points to each illustration and names the items pictured. She does not point to the print.

In the art/writing center, Marc and Eduardo are using felt-tip markers to create books. Marc announces, "My book's gonna be about my dog." Eduardo responds by saying, "I'm gonna make a book about bugs." As they create their books, they use both drawing and letter-like forms to express their stories.

Imagine you are an observer in this classroom. How would you interpret these events? Are these children simply "playing" and having fun or do their behaviors indicate they are developing important knowledge about reading and writing? Do early childhood teachers need to be concerned about literacy development, or is that only a concern for elementary school teachers? As we begin to address these questions, we first need to consider what it means to be literate and why learning to read and write is important. It will also be beneficial to take a look at the current movements in the United States that focus on the importance and quality of literacy education.

What Does It Mean to Be Literate?

Defining Literacy

Many years ago, being "literate" meant only that one could read or write one's own name (Soltow & Stevens, 1981, cited in *NCTE/IRA Standards for the English Language Arts*, 1996). This definition has expanded considerably over the past few decades. Technological advances have affected the ways in which we now communicate, spend our leisure time, and engage in work-related tasks. The use of email, the Internet, DVDs, laptop computers, text messaging, videos, and digital imaging each have required new aspects of literacy. Literacy now demands a wider range of language competencies. To be literate in our contemporary society means

being active, critical, and creative users not only of print and spoken language but also of the visual language of film and television, commercial and political advertising, photography, and more. . . . Visual communication is part of the fabric of contemporary life.

(NCTE/IRA, 1996, pp. 5, 6)

This expanded definition of literacy emphasizes the role of literacy throughout our lives. Literacy development is not simply an academic goal; it is a lifelong necessity. Literacy has often been defined in a narrow way, restricting the goal of literacy development to academic achievement. For example, in this view a good reader is someone who can read and comprehend stories as well as content-area textbooks and school reference materials. Similarly, writing competency is defined as being able to create written responses to comprehension questions and creating reports, essays, poems, or short stories.

Literacy development does affect academic achievement in direct and significant ways; however, it should not be viewed as only a school-based achievement. Instead, a broader definition of literacy challenges educators and children's families to view literacy as a lifelong skill that contributes significantly to the ways in which children will be able to interact in community and social contexts as well as in academic and occupational settings.

Cultural-social aspects of literacy. A broader definition of literacy also challenges educators to recognize the ways literacy is used outside of the classroom in the real world of diverse cultural-social settings. Through this understanding teachers will be better able to prepare students for using literacy throughout their lives.

From birth on, children are enveloped in their home culture and observe the ways in which written language is used in that setting. For example, writing and reading may be used in religious services, business transactions, cultural events, and personal communication, in addition to academic-related activities (Heath, 1983; Teale, 1986). When teachers define literacy in a manner that incorporates the ways in which reading and writing are used in children's homes and communities, children are better able to see the value of literacy in their lives. They begin to realize that being able to read and write is not something you learn to do simply for school; it is something you can use outside of school every day of your life.

Why Is Literacy Important in School and in Life?

As an early childhood educator, you will be children's first school teacher. You will be giving young children opportunities to develop their knowledge about reading and writing. Your role in children's literacy development is a very important one because the early childhood years are a critical time for the development of literacy.

School Achievement

Developing reading ability is a major goal for the early grades from kindergarten through grade 3. Most school curricula are based on the expectation that the K–3 years involve "learning to read" and the upper elementary grades involve "reading to learn." This means that once a child enters fourth grade, it is assumed that he will be able to read books independently and use written texts in content-area learning (for example, science, math, and social studies). Children who do not learn to read before the end of third grade are at-risk for school failure because they are unable to keep up with their classmates who can read and they cannot effectively learn from the instructional materials that are used in their classrooms.

Researchers have documented the difficulty children have in overcoming their lack of success in developing reading competencies in the early elementary grades. This difficulty

Beginning in fourth grade, children are expected to read and comprehend nonfiction text.

Monkey Business Images

may show up as early as first grade. Struggling first-grade readers have a 90 percent chance of still experiencing reading difficulties three years later (Juel, 1988, cited in Chard & Kame'enui, 2000). Children who are struggling readers in third grade are still likely to have difficulties in reading when they are eighth graders (Felton & Wood, 1992). Another study found that sixth graders who had a combination of poor attendance (below 80 percent), behavior problems, and failing English grades or failing math grades had only a 10 percent chance of graduating from high school on schedule (Philadelphia Education Fund, 2005, cited in Reimer & Smink, 2005). It is possible that low-level literacy skills also contribute to poor school attendance and behavior problems. If a student is not able to participate in the learning activities at school, motivation to attend school decreases and behavior problems may develop.

Although there are other factors associated with becoming a high school dropout, reading and writing competencies remain key factors (Reimer & Smink, 2005). Indications that children may become at-risk for dropping out of high school are often seen as early as first grade (Education Commission of the States, 2006; Griffin, 1987). When children experience difficulty developing reading and writing competencies and begin to fall behind, they are at-risk for becoming high school dropouts (Jordan-Davis, 1984; Manzo, 2005; Self, 1985; Vanderslice, 2004). Because they cannot read and write effectively, they cannot successfully participate in most, if not all, of the learning activities at school. This results in their dropping out of school.

Lifelong Effects

Because reading and writing competencies are required for daily living skills as well as to meet job and career responsibilities (NCTE/IRA, 1996), high school dropouts also have less chance of later success (Education Commission of the States, 2006; Focus Adolescent Services, 2000; Reimer & Smink, 2005; Schwartz, 1996). Consequently, dropouts are also "more likely to become dependent on public assistance, have health problems and engage in criminal activity" (Education Commission of the States, 2006, p. 1).

Generational Effects

Adults who lack literacy skills may also affect their children's development of literacy. According to the 2003 National Assessment of Adult Literacy (U.S. Department of Education, 2006), 30 million adults were reported to have "no more than the most simple and concrete literacy skills." Many of these adults did not graduate from high school (55 percent).

Parents who are not comfortable reading are less likely to have reading and writing materials in the home and to engage their children in literacy-related activities (Cooter, 2006). Parents' low-level literacy skills may also affect employment and family income: They may be unemployed or be working at low-paying jobs, which affects the time they can spend with their families. All of these factors contribute to the situation where parents' illiteracy impacts the next generation.

Implications

The implications of these statistics for early childhood teachers are very clear: The development of literacy competencies is a critical accomplishment for all children in their first years of schooling. Early childhood educators need to be knowledgeable and prepared to create and implement curricula that foster literacy development (Strickland & Riley-Ayers, 2006).

What Is Your Role as a Teacher of Young Children?

From birth on, children's learning and development are greatly influenced by the people with whom they interact. Parents play a major role in their children's learning and development. They are their children's first teachers. As an early childhood teacher, you also have a major role in the learning and development of the children in your classroom. It is important to remember that the single most important factor that influences the learning that occurs in your classroom is *you*.

Your role as an early childhood teacher is characterized by three specific responsibilities: (a) Making instructional decisions, (b) creating a positive learning environment, and (c) using effective interaction strategies. The decisions you make about instruction, the ways in which you create and maintain a positive learning environment, and the interaction strategies you use will reflect your teaching approach, professional knowledge, and philosophy.

Making Instructional Decisions

For many decades now, researchers have sought to determine the best way to teach all children how to read and write. While many research studies reported success with specific methods, widespread implementation of those methods did not bring universal success in children's development of reading and writing (see further discussion in Chapter 2). What does this mean? Do researchers need to still keep searching for the *one* best method or strategy? Or are there other important factors to consider? One such factor is the role of the teacher and the way in which teachers make instructional decisions in their classrooms (Learning First Alliance, 2000).

In fulfilling your responsibilities as a teacher, you will be making many decisions. You will need to decide which learning activities will be used in your classroom, what materials you will use, and how you will interact with children as you implement these activities. The decisions you make in planning and implementing the learning activities, and how children's learning is evaluated will have a major impact on the learning process that takes place in your classroom.

For example, in the vignette that opened this chapter, the way the teacher responds to the children will affect their future learning. Will their teacher carefully observe this "free play" time for indications of learning, or use the time to organize more formal lessons involving direct instruction, or prepare for the snack time that follows free play? The answers to these questions are found in not only the teacher's understanding of how children learn but also the way that this teacher observes these events. The answers are also found in the way she uses her professional knowledge to make critical decisions about the classroom activities, how they will be implemented, and how children's learning will be evaluated.

As a teacher, you will need to be able to explain your decisions and instructional approaches to administrators, fellow teachers, and parents. You will need to be able to explain clearly why you are teaching what you teach, why you are using a particular strategy or approach, how you are meeting the instructional needs of each child, and how you are determining each child's learning progress.

The acquisition of reading and writing skills is a critical achievement for children to prepare them to participate in literate cultures. You can expect that parents, school board members, administrators, and colleagues will be highly interested in your approach to the development of reading and writing in your early childhood classroom. The way in which you make instructional decisions will have a major influence on your classroom and the children's learning. Some of the decisions you make will be made deliberately in planning prior to entering your classroom; other decisions will be made while you are engaged in teaching.

Factors influencing instructional decisions. The decisions teachers make are influenced by four major factors: the presence of a formally adopted curriculum, the teacher's intuition about how children learn, the teacher's professional knowledge and training, and the teacher's observations of student learning. These factors serve as sources of information to consider when you make decisions about what to teach and how to teach it in your classroom.

Formal curriculum. The term **curriculum** is used to refer to a written set of specific instructional plans for teaching children at a particular level of development. A specific curriculum might consist of a framework with general instructional goals, activities, and ways of assessing student progress. A curriculum might also be highly scripted and specify not only the instructional goals and content of what is taught in a set sequence but also include exactly what the teacher should say when teaching each segment.

Teachers in school settings where a formal curriculum has been adopted by their school may be strongly influenced by this curriculum when making their instructional decisions. They may believe that if the curriculum is followed closely, all students will learn what they are supposed to learn. When asked to justify why a teaching strategy is used in the classroom, the teacher might reply, "That's what the curriculum guide said is appropriate."

For example, the teacher in the opening vignette might justify her decision to have the library center and the writing center in her classroom because her district's preschool curriculum guide specifies that each classroom should have these two centers.

Teacher's intuition. Another factor that influences teachers' decision is their intuition about children's learning. This intuition involves a teacher's unconscious beliefs about the ways in which children learn and the ways in which teachers should teach. Many of our intuitions are formed based upon our prior experiences as students when we were in school. From these experiences we form ideas about learning and teaching. Teachers who rely heavily on their intuition when making decisions might justify using a particular teaching strategy by stating, "It just seemed like the right thing to do." For example, if the teacher in the opening vignette used an intuitive approach to decision making, she would justify her decision to have a library center and writing center by saying, "The children seem to enjoy these centers. Both centers keep them busy for quite a while."

Professional knowledge and experiences. A third factor influencing a teacher's decisions is her extensive professional knowledge and training. For example, in the opening vignette, let's see how a classroom teacher might use her professional knowledge and experiences to explain her teaching decision to provide a writing center and a library corner in her classroom. Here's the teacher's response:

> Preschoolers need lots of opportunities to explore and experiment with reading and writing. It is during this exploration and experimentation that they begin to see how written language is used to communicate. By providing them with opportunities to use paper and markers and by sharing many interesting and colorful storybooks with them, they will begin to develop specific knowledge of how reading and writing can be used for personal purposes.

Teacher's observations of student learning. A fourth factor that influences teachers' decisions is their observations of children's responses to the learning activities and contexts. As teachers interact with their students, they observe how students respond and become engaged in the various learning activities. These observations then become part of a teacher's considerations when making instructional decisions (Risko, Roskos, & Vukelich, 2002).

An important part of observing students' responses to learning is to be aware of the uniqueness that each student brings to the learning process. Generic learners do not exist; instead, each learner has a unique combination of prior experiences, conceptual knowledge, and personal characteristics that becomes part of the learning transaction that takes place. Thus, teachers need to carefully observe each student's interactions and incorporate this information into their decisions.

Becoming a reflective teacher. Teachers who make instructional decisions based only on their school's adopted curriculum or only on their intuitions about teaching and learning will find that they have a more difficult time responding to administrators' and parents' questions about student learning and their instructional decisions. Although it is important to take into consideration the formal curriculum as well as your personal intuitions about learning and teaching, it is also important to be able to incorporate your professional knowledge and experiences, as well as your observations of students' learning when you make instructional decisions.

Teachers who consider each of the four factors when making their instructional decisions will be engaging in **reflective practice.** This means that they will be consciously considering each source of information (curriculum, intuition, professional knowledge, and student observation) in making their decisions. A diagram representing the relationship between these four factors and reflective decision making is shown in Figure 1.1.

Here's how a reflective teacher might describe her teaching decisions in providing the learning environment described in the opening vignette:

> In creating the storybook center and the writing center in my classroom, I wanted to have an environment where preschoolers could explore and experiment with reading and

Figure 1.1 Reflective Teaching Decisions

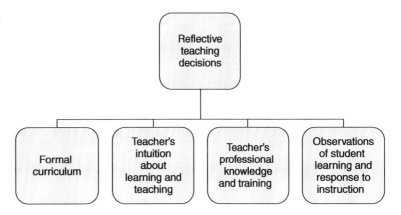

writing. I can see how this is benefiting to my students because they are developing many signs of emergent literacy. While Maria and Jennifer are not yet reading the print, their interactions with storybooks indicate they are learning how to go about the reading process. Marc and Eduardo are emerging as writers. Although they are not yet writing in the conventional sense, they are eagerly creating their "stories" by drawing what they want to communicate. Their use of letter-like forms indicates they know that print carries meaning, although they are still acquiring knowledge of how written language actually works. When I asked them to share their stories, Marc and Eduardo confidently "read" the meaning of what they had illustrated. This tells me that they are learning that print has meaning and that they can communicate through their symbol-making (drawing and writing) attempts.

Through this teacher's reflective decision making and ability to articulate her rationale to others, she is providing critical support to her students in their development of early literacy competencies. She is able to explain her instructional decisions as well as describe how she determines the growth and learning of her students.

As you proceed in this text, use the content of this text to develop your professional knowledge of children's literacy development. This professional knowledge will provide a basis for you to become an early childhood educator who is also a reflective decision-maker. This professional knowledge will also provide a basis for you to create a positive learning environment.

Creating a Positive Learning Environment

In addition to making reflective instructional decisions, teachers need to consciously create learning environments in which the activities and interactions are designed to meet the developmental needs of the children.

Developmentally appropriate practice. An overriding principle of early childhood education is that of **developmentally appropriate practice.** In the field of early childhood education, the concept of developmentally appropriate practice is often used to describe optimal learning environments for young children. Developmentally appropriate practice refers to the belief that a learning environment and learning tasks for young children should be directly related to the developmental level of each child rather than his or her chronological age (National Association for the Education of Young Children/NAEYC, 1997). Developmentally appropriate practice also represents an understanding of how young children best learn based on decades of research and key theoretical perspectives

(for example, Piaget, Vygotsky, and Bruner). Developmentally appropriate practice is founded in the following understandings of how young children learn and develop (NAEYC, 1997):

- ❖ A close relationship exists among the physical, social, emotional, and cognitive development of children.
- ❖ The rate of development varies between children as well as within each of the areas of development for each child.
- ❖ Learning and development are influenced by the social and cultural contexts in which children interact.
- ❖ Children actively construct their own knowledge from their direct and indirect experiences.
- ❖ Children's play provides a context to learn new things and to practice what has been learned.

These principles of developmentally appropriate practice guide our understanding of the critical aspects of young children's home and early childhood learning environments. This understanding informs the ways we plan and implement learning activities and the ways that we interact with children's parents and families.

Learning contexts: Independent and teacher-guided activities. From birth on, children interact with their environments through their five senses—tasting, touching, smelling, hearing, and seeing. Through these sensorimotor experiences (Piaget, 1962), concepts and schemas of action are developed. Home and school learning environments that provide settings in which children can safely explore and learn about their surroundings will facilitate children's conceptual knowledge and cognitive development (Bredekamp & Copple, 1997).

Children benefit from two types of activities: self-initiated, independent, exploratory activities and teacher-guided activities (Bredekamp & Copple, 1997). As reflective teachers we make decisions as to which learning activities are most appropriate for each child based on their developmental level. Most early childhood settings will have a combination of both types of activities.

Independent activities. Children are born with a high motivation to learn (Puckett & Black, 2001; Trawick-Smith, 2003). They are constantly seeking to figure things out. By providing opportunities for young children to engage in self-initiated, exploratory activities you will be encouraging them to use their natural curiosity to construct their knowledge about the world. These activities allow each child to decide how he wants to participate and interact. Your role as a teacher is to prepare a safe environment with independent activities that motivate children to explore at their own pace. Hands-on, experiential learning provides important opportunities for young children to develop conceptual knowledge. This knowledge provides a basis for language and literacy.

Besides providing the setting for the independent activities, your role also involves monitoring children's engagement in the activity and providing encouragement that will keep them involved. You may also need to briefly show them ways of using the resources provided in the activity, such as how to use a funnel at the water table to fill up a plastic bottle.

Teacher-guided activities. In addition to having activities that allow them to explore independently, children need to have activities that involve interaction with adults who guide their learning and support their interactions. The ways in which you interact with young children in your classroom will have an influence on what skills and competencies they learn and develop. In your role as a reflective decision-maker in your classroom, you will find the following interaction patterns are especially beneficial: Shared reference and

Children's play provides a context to learn new things and practice what has been learned.

eye contact; communication loops, verbal mapping, child-directed speech, linguistic scaffold, and mediation (Otto, 2002, 2006).

By consciously using these interaction patterns you will be able to support children's development of new knowledge and skills. Although these interaction patterns can be used throughout the early childhood curriculum, they are particularly beneficial for enhancing children's language and literacy development.

1. *Shared reference and eye contact.* This interaction pattern is basic to communication because it involves a joint attention between the adult and child on a particular object or event. For example, when sharing a book with a toddler, the adult will often point to a part of the picture and then monitor the child's gaze to be sure she is looking at the same picture. This is essential to communication as well as to learning the names of objects.

2. *Communication loops.* Conversation requires that listeners and speakers take turns, forming a communication loop. Adults begin creating these communication loops during a child's infancy as they talk to the infant and then pause for a response (verbal or nonverbal) from the infant. This turn-taking routine forms a foundation for later, more complex conversations.

3. *Verbal mapping.* When adults verbally describe an ongoing event to a child, they are creating a verbal map for that event. For example, when a mother is dressing her infant daughter for bedtime, she might create the following verbal map:

> Oh, here's your pink sleeper. Let's see, first I'll put it underneath you. There you go. Now, your foot goes in here, and your other foot over here. Now let's put this arm in here, and your other arm over here. Now it's time to snap you up. One, two, three, four, five. You're all dressed! You look so snuggly and warm!

The use of verbal mapping with young children provides a description of what is occurring and thus provides an association between actions and language. Over time, this interaction pattern provides children with the words and language structures to use to understand events and actions.

A linguistic scaffold is created when adults structure their verbal interactions with children to encourage them to participate verbally.

Diego Cervo

4. *Child-directed speech.* There are many ways in which adults change the way in which they are speaking when they are talking to children. While the specific features of child-directed speech vary with the age of the child being addressed, the major features of child-directed speech include the following: less complex grammar in sentence and phrases ("Let's go bye-bye"), more expressive intonation, more general vocabulary (*car* not *Cadillac*), slower pace of speech, a focus on the immediate context (not what is happening tomorrow or next month), and repetition of key words or phrases. These features serve to increase children's comprehension of language and encourage children's verbal participation.

5. *Linguistic scaffold.* Adults create language support when they structure their interaction with a child to encourage the child to participate. This is referred to as a **linguistic scaffold.** Through the adult's use of questioning, expanding upon what the child has said, and using repetition to clarify what the child said, the child is able to participate in conversations and to increase his learning and language development. For example, in the following conversation with Marc (age three and a half), the teacher's questions and use of repetition and expanding the child's responses provide a linguistic scaffold that supports the child's continued participation.

Marc:	Hi, Ms. Brown.
Teacher:	Good morning, Marc. I see you brought something for show and tell.
Marc:	New toy (takes it out of the bag).
Teacher:	Oh, a new truck. What kind of a truck is it?
Marc:	Dump truck.
Teacher:	Wow, a big, red, dump truck. What do you put in the back of the dump truck?
Marc:	Dirt and stones and stuff.
Teacher:	Yes, it looks like you can put a lot of dirt and stones and other things in the back.

6. *Mediation.* This interaction pattern occurs when adults simplify the learning setting or task to allow the child to participate in that event. For example, when sharing a story book with a toddler, an adult might change the story text or omit it completely and

Adults often mediate, or change, the text of a story book to make it more understandable and to encourage children's active participation.

Dmitri Maruta

instead focus on labeling and talking about the objects pictured. Knowing that a child would not be developmentally able to comprehend the story text if read word for word, the adult decided to create a text or conversation about the illustrations that would encourage the child to participate at his developmental level.

Throughout this text, these interaction patterns will be further defined as specific learning activities are described for each developmental level. It is also important to remember that each culture has its own ways of communicating with children and supporting their development. These interaction patterns reflect the basic ways in which teachers in the United States communicate with young children in learning activities. You will want to be aware that children from diverse cultures may not have experienced some of these interaction patterns in their home and communities. For example, in some cultures, children are not encouraged to establish direct eye contact with adults. Thus, you will need to consider cultural differences when you interact with children from diverse backgrounds and provide additional opportunities for them to respond to you as you engage in a particular interaction pattern.

What Recent Initiatives Have Addressed Literacy in the United States?

Literacy education has been a national concern for many decades, and remains a major concern today. As an early childhood teacher, you need to be aware of the work of educational organizations, federal agencies, and state boards of education that has focused on enhancing children's literacy development through a range of recent initiatives. These initiatives have been influenced by concerns about student achievement while in school as well as lifelong success (Brynildssen, 2002).

In this section, an overview is presented of the major initiatives that have occurred during the past two decades. It is important to remember, however, that part of your continued professional development as an educator will be to stay aware of new initiatives that occur and impact children's educational settings and curriculum. The recent initiatives described in this section include the development of position statements, standards for literacy education, and federal- and state-funded reports and programs. Each of these initiatives did not develop in isolation but was influenced by a national consciousness among educational leaders, concerned elected officials, parents, community leaders, and educational agencies of the need to focus more specifically on children's literacy development. In the overview that follows, several key initiatives are described. A timeline summary of these initiatives is located in Figure 1.2. Additional resources are provided in Appendix A.

The initiatives listed above the timeline in Figure 1.2 are specific to literacy acquisition, while the initiatives listed below the timeline focus on the development of educational standards for curriculum and assessment in all areas of study.

A Call for Education Reform

In 1983, the National Commission on Excellence in Education released their report, *A Nation at Risk: The Imperative for Educational Reform*. This report, directed to the nation and the U.S. Secretary of Education, emphasized the need for significant changes in the education of children in all areas: language arts, science, social studies, mathematics, and the arts. Educational institutions and educators were challenged to become more accountable for the achievement of the students they served.

A major part of the report's recommendations focused on the need to develop standards and expectations for student performance in each area and for each grade level. The need for children to develop literacy-related competencies was emphasized throughout this report as a key to achievement in school and in adult life.

Standards Movement

Since the release of *A Nation at Risk*, national educational summits have been held on a periodic basis to develop standards for student achievement and performance (Department of Education, 2005; Gottlieb, 2001). In addition, state-level meetings of educational leaders have also focused on the development of standards. Through the involvement of teachers, school administrators, and state boards of education, nearly all of the individual states have now articulated their standards for reading achievement in preschool and K–12 classrooms (see Appendix A for resources).

Figure 1.2 Timeline of Recent National Literacy-Related Initiatives

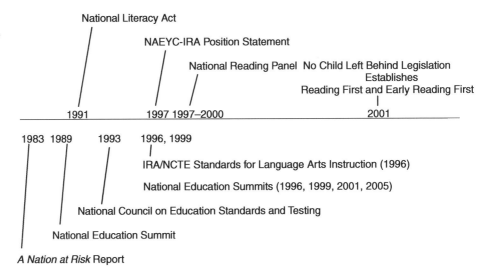

In addition, professional education organizations have also played an active role in the drive to improve reading instruction and children's reading achievement through the articulation of standards for instruction and student learning. The International Reading Association (IRA) and the National Council for Teachers of English (NCTE) have established standards for language arts instruction (NCTE-IRA, 1996). These standards identify specific literacy-related competencies that students need in order to "pursue life's goals and to participate as informed, productive members of society" (p. 3). For example, Standard 11 reads:

> Students participate as knowledgeable, reflective, creative, and critical members of a variety of literacy communities (p. 3).

Standards for the educational preparation of teachers of young children in the areas of literacy development have also been developed and adopted as part of the criteria for national and state accreditation of teacher certification programs (for example, The National Association for the Education of Young Children [NAEYC] and the Association for Childhood Education International [ACEI]; see Resource List in Appendix A). For example, ACEI's standard for the English language arts area specifies that beginning teachers should

> demonstrate a high level of competence in use of English language arts and know, understand, and use concepts from reading, language, and child development to teach reading, writing, speaking, viewing, listening, and thinking skills, and to help students successfully apply their developing skills to many different situations, materials and ideas.
> (Association for Childhood Education International, 2003)

Many school districts have also developed or adopted specific standards for reading achievement. While these various state and local standards draw from the national standards and research-based publications, the individual state and district standards reflect local concerns and educational issues. Teachers are expected to address these standards in their daily lesson plans and instructional units.

Federal- and State-Funded Reports and Programs

Concurrent with the standards movement, federal and state governments initiated specific programs to enhance literacy development. In 1991, the National Literacy Act was passed, which established the National Institute for Literacy as a center for research and research dissemination (National Literacy Act, 1991). In 1997, Congress requested the formation of a national panel to review research on reading and the effectiveness of various instructional approaches. Subsequently the National Reading Panel was convened.

The National Reading Panel. The National Reading Panel was composed of leading researchers and professionals in literacy education. Their report, issued in 2000, summarized research-based knowledge on the effectiveness of various reading approaches as well as current understandings of the reading process and how reading instruction might be improved through teachers' professional development (National Reading Panel/NRP, 2000). In beginning their work, the NRP held regional hearings throughout the United States as a way of developing a thorough awareness of the literacy-related issues experienced by teachers, parents, students, higher education faculty, educational policy experts and scientists. Based on these hearings, five topic areas were identified for intensive study and research review. These areas included: alphabetics (phonemic awareness instruction, phonics instruction), fluency, comprehension, teacher education and reading instruction, and computer technology and reading instruction.

The NRP report has served to focus and redefine reading instruction and professional development for teachers of reading. (Specific details of this report will be included in subsequent chapters as the individual topics relate to chapter content.)

Based on this comprehensive report issued by the National Reading Panel/NRP (2000), several professional organizations collaborated to present the findings of the NRP report in a format for teacher training and professional development. This collaboration resulted in the report entitled, "Put Reading First: The Research Building Blocks for Teaching Children to Read" (National Institute for Literacy, 2001). The professional organizations involved in issuing this document included the National Institute for Literacy, the National Institute of Child Health and Human Development, the U.S. Department of Education, and the Center for the Improvement of Early Reading Achievement (CIERA).

The No Child Left Behind Act. The NRP report also served as a basis for the reading initiatives contained in the No Child Left Behind Act (NCLB) passed by Congress in 2001. The No Child Left Behind legislation (U.S. Education Department, 2001a) emphasized the importance of making sure that every child would be able to read by the end of third grade. Since its initial passage in 2001, funding has been renewed annually. As part of this legislation, the Reading First initiative provides grants to school districts to identify children in K–3 grades who are at-risk for failure and for grants that focus on the professional development of K–3 teachers in reading instruction. At the preschool level, the Early Reading First program provides for grants to "support early language, literacy, and pre-reading development of preschool-age children, particularly those from low-income families" (U.S. Education Department, 2001a, p. 2). Throughout Reading First and Early Reading First, the emphasis is on the strategies and knowledge of reading development that are found in scientifically based reading research.

Professional Organizations' Position Statements

During the past two decades, professional educational organizations have also issued position statements that articulated their commitment to literacy development. The members and leaders of these professional organizations conducted extensive reviews of research and reached consensus on the position statements that best represented their organizations.

The National Association for the Education of Young Children (NAEYC) and the International Reading Association (IRA) are two major organizations involved in early childhood and literacy development. Their joint position statement on literacy development (NAEYC/IRA, 1997) focused on goals and expectations for reading and writing achievement as well as the need for developmentally appropriate teaching practices, and the professional development of early childhood educators. A primary commitment of these two organizations expressed in this position statement is to help "children learn to read well enough by the end of third grade so that they can read to learn in all curriculum areas" (p. 30). Key aspects of this position statement are located in Figure 1.3.

This position statement subsequently was endorsed by eleven other professional education organizations, including the Association for Childhood Education International, the Association of Teacher Educators, and the Zero to Three/National Center for Infants, Toddlers, & Families.

Throughout this text, position statements, standards for literacy education, and federal and/or state-funded reports and programs will be referred to as the various aspects of literacy education are introduced.

Figure 1.3 Learning to Read and Write: Developmentally Appropriate Practices for Young Children

Key Points

❖ Teachers of young children play a key role in promoting children's literacy development.

❖ Learning to read and write is a multidimensional, complex process and requires diverse instructional approaches to meet all children's needs.

❖ Children are active learners, constructing their knowledge from their social and physical experiences along with culturally transmitted knowledge.

❖ Expectations for young children's development of reading and writing competencies should be developmentally appropriate and accompanied by support from caring, engaged adults (e.g., teachers and parents).

Source: Young Children, July 1998, 53(4), 30–46. A Joint Position Statement of the International Reading Association (IRA) and the National Association for the Education of Young Children (NAEYC).

Continuing Your Professional Development

As an early childhood educator, the professional knowledge you develop, the way in which you implement that knowledge, and the way in which you make instructional decisions determines the nature of the transactions that occur between your students, the learning context, and you as their teacher. It is also important to remember that the development of your professional knowledge will involve continued learning and refinement throughout your career in early childhood education. Whether you choose to engage in professional development formally through advanced degrees or more informally through workshops, attending conferences, and other avenues, continued acquisition and refinement of your professional knowledge is critical to the learning environment of your classroom and to your students.

Chapter Summary

The definition of literacy has expanded beyond simply being able to read or write one's own name. It now involves being able to read and comprehend a variety of different types of texts. It also involves being able to create written texts for a variety of purposes. Literacy also includes being able to comprehend and use other types of visual communication such as video, film, and television. Children's development of literacy competencies impacts not only their school achievement, but also later in their lives as adults. The social and cultural contexts in which young children interact in literacy-related events have a significant role in the opportunities and support provided for developing literacy. Definitions of literacy have influenced the ways in which researchers and educators have considered culturally and linguistically diverse settings.

Your role as an early childhood teacher is characterized by three specific responsibilities: making instructional decisions, creating a positive learning environment, and using effective interaction strategies. The decisions you make about instruction, the ways in which you create and maintain a positive learning environment, and the interaction strategies you use will reflect your teaching approach, professional knowledge, and philosophy. Your decisions will also determine the quality of the learning environment in your classroom.

The decisions teachers make are influenced by four major factors: the presence of a formally adopted curriculum, the teacher's intuition about how children learn, the teacher's professional knowledge and training, and the teacher's observations of student learning. These factors serve as sources of information to consider when you make decisions about what to teach and how to teach it in your classroom. Reflective decision making provides a responsive and professionally sound approach to meeting the educational needs of children in your classroom.

National concerns for children's literacy development have been reflected in the standards movement as well as in specific national and state programs that focus on enhancing children's literacy development.

Chapter Review

1. Terms to know:

   literacy
   curriculum
   reflective practice

   developmentally
   appropriate practice
   linguistic scaffold

2. How has literacy traditionally been defined in educational settings? What impact might this have on children from diverse cultural and social contexts?

3. In what ways do children's literacy competencies influence their lives?

4. What advantage does a reflective approach to decision making have over focusing only on either curricular or intuitive information? Explain your answer.

5. In what ways has the National Reading Panel's report influenced reading instruction and other reading initiatives?

6. True or false: Developmentally appropriate practice applies only to preschool settings. Explain your answer.

7. How do the following interaction patterns enhance children's development of language and literacy?
   a. eye contact–shared reference
   b. verbal mapping
   c. communication loops
   d. child-directed speech
   e. linguistic scaffolding
   f. mediated learning

Chapter Extension Activities

Discussion: Keep a literacy journal for several days, noting the ways that you and others around you are involved in literacy-related events. Include all instances where reading and writing occur during daily events. Come to class prepared to share your journal entries. Also reflect on the limitations faced by someone who is not able to read and write.

Observation: Observe a parent sharing a story book with a young child (3–5 years old). Prepare a written description of what you observed and respond to the following questions:

1. How does the parent encourage the child to participate in the story book sharing? For example, does the parent comment on the illustrations, ask questions, or repeat what was read?

2. How does the child respond to this story book sharing? Include both verbal and nonverbal responses.

Research: Locate the standards for language arts instruction developed by a local school district or your state. Share an oral summary of your review in your class. Bring in a copy of the standards to class.

Chapter 2

Theoretical Perspectives of Literacy Development

> **W**hen asked if her students could "sound out" unknown words when reading, the first-grade teacher replied, "I know they can sound out the consonants, because I've taught them the consonant sounds. We won't cover the vowel sounds until next spring."

How do children become readers and writers? What is the best way to support children's literacy development? Based on the teacher's comments in this opening vignette, she thought that because she had not taught the vowel sounds, her students could not begin to "sound out" vowels. This perspective reflects the belief that children only learn about reading (or writing) when they have received formal instruction. Thus, according to this teacher, the most appropriate way to teach reading would be through direct instruction in the separate skills related to reading.

Throughout the past 50 years, there has been continuous debate about the best way to teach children to read. The fervor surrounding this issue has been referred to as the "reading wars" (Roller, 2002). Early in this search, Bond and Dykstra (1967, 1997; Spiegel, 1999) reported that while some approaches "worked" for some children, it was also apparent that none of the approaches were effective for every child. Further, differences in reading achievement appeared to be influenced by factors present in the learning environment and not the method or the materials of instruction. Bond and Dykstra concluded, "To improve reading instruction, it is necessary to train better teachers of reading rather than to expect a panacea in the form of materials" (1997, p. 416).

Thus, while not answering the question of what method was best, the Bond and Dykstra research initiated a significant and evolving awareness of the complexity of the reading process, as well as recognition of factors in the learning environment that influence children's reading achievement. One of these factors, according to Bond and Dykstra, is the classroom teacher. As seen in the opening vignette, the beliefs and professional knowledge of a teacher influence not only the way in which reading is defined, but also the assumptions that are made about how children learn and how they are best taught.

The focus of this chapter is on describing four major instructional approaches to literacy development that have been practiced over the past 50 years. Each of these instructional approaches is based on a specific theoretical perspective that describes how children learn to read and write as well as a particular way in which reading and writing are defined. Additionally, the way in which reading and writing are defined in a classroom also influences how reading and writing achievement is assessed. By becoming familiar with these approaches and their respective theoretical and historical foundations, you will be developing a core of professional knowledge that you will find useful as you support children's literacy development and as you engage in reflective teaching.

The four major approaches to literacy instruction include: Subskills/Readiness, Whole Language, Balanced, and Comprehensive Literacy. The Subskills/Readiness Approach was prevalent in the 1950s through the early 1980s. During the 1980s and early 1990s, the Whole Language Approach was adopted by many schools. Beginning in the mid-1990s, the Balanced Approach to literacy instruction was a focus of both research and curricular materials (Blair-Larsen & Williams, 1999; Cassidy & Wenrich, 1998; Hammond, 1999). At this time, Comprehensive Literacy Instruction is being promoted as the most effective way to enhance literacy development (Reutzel & Fawson, 2002; Reutzel & Cooter, 2005; Roller, 2002). Table 2.1 presents an overview of these four approaches.

It is important to keep in mind that although there has been a movement from one approach to another, it is still possible to find classrooms and schools where an earlier approach, such as Subskills/Readiness, dominates the literacy curriculum. In the sections that follow, these theoretical perspectives are described along with their related definitions of reading and writing, descriptions of how children learn to read and write, and instructional approaches.

With the successive development of each perspective and implementation of the corresponding approach, our collective understanding of how children develop reading and writing competencies has increased. In each instance, continued research has provided evidence of the usefulness of that perspective and instructional approach in enhancing literacy development. Continued research also promises to increase further our understandings of the cognitive and social-cultural processes involved in reading and writing development.

As you read the following overviews of the theoretical perspectives and approaches, reflect on your own experiences as you learned to read and write in your early school years. Which one represents the way in which you remember learning to read and write?

Table 2.1 Overview of Major Perspectives on Literacy Development

Time of Prevalence	Theoretical Perspective	How Children Learn to Read and Write	Instructional Approach
1950s–1970s	Behaviorist	Children must first learn individual skills in a specific sequence.	Reading/Subskills/Readiness
1980s–1990s	Naturalist	Children learn to read and write through everyday experiences involving literacy events.	Whole Language
Mid-1990s to early 2000s	Interactive	Children learn to read and write through a combination of skill and holistic, everyday experiences.	Balanced
Early 2000s to present	Transactional	Children learn to read and write through transactions involving their knowledge of language, the texts they encounter, and social-cultural contexts.	Comprehensive Literacy Instruction

Behaviorist Perspective

Historical and Theoretical Foundations

This perspective is based in the behaviorist theory of how children learn (Skinner, 1974; Watson, 1924). According to this theory, learning occurs as associations develop among stimuli, responses, and reinforcements or rewards. For example, if a parent gives a toddler a ball and says "ball," and the toddler responds by attempting to say the word *ball,* the parent smiles and appears happy and excited and says "You're right. That's a ball!" The parent's positive response to the child's attempt to say the word provides reinforcement and increases the chance that the child will respond in a similar manner when he sees a ball another time. Spontaneous behaviors may also be associated with specific reinforcements. For example, when an infant spontaneously babbles "dada" when his parent is in the room, he will quickly be rewarded for this attempt to say "Daddy." This reinforcement increases the likelihood the infant will repeat "dada" and results in the infant's learning. This reinforcement is **contingent** because it depends upon the child's responses. If the child's utterance does not resemble "dada," the reinforcement will be different.

Reinforcement also may be used to shape or gradually encourage a particular behavior. For example, a mother is trying to encourage her young child to say "mama." She begins to shape this behavior by first reinforcing her child's attempts at producing the beginning sound /m/. After the child can produce this sound, the mother then encourages the child to say /ma/ by using reinforcement in response to the child's attempts. When the pronunciation of /ma/ is mastered, the mother introduces the repeated syllable, creating *mama.* Again contingent reinforcement is used in response to the child's attempts to say the whole word. In this way the child's production of the word "mama" is gradually shaped through the use of reinforcement.

How Reading and Writing Are Defined

In the Behaviorist perspective, reading is considered to be a process of visually perceiving the written symbols (letters and words) and associating the written symbols with spoken words (Adams, 1990; Gough, 1972; LaBerge & Samuels, 1974; Pearson & Stephens, 1994; and Weaver, 2002). Writing involves being able to produce the symbols (the letters of the written language and to combine them to create conventionally spelled words.

In this perspective, reading has been also described as a **bottom-up process** in which reading results from the processing of separate pieces of visual information (see Figure 2.1). The perception of these discrete pieces of visual information (print) has been explored through various research studies (Gough, 1972; Just & Carpenter, 1980). Topics of this research include how people read using their knowledge of letter–sound relationships, letter recognition, movement of the eyes during reading, and orthographic (spelling) pattern recognition.

In a bottom-up perspective, writing is defined as being able to form the individual letters. It is thought that children must learn to form each letter of the alphabet and have knowledge of how to spell words conventionally prior to being able to "write."

How Children Learn to Read and Write

According to Behaviorism, children learn through the associations established among stimuli, responses, and contingent reinforcements (Alexander & Fox, 2004). This

Figure 2.1 Bottom-Up Model of Reading

Source: Based on Adams, 1990; Gough, 1972; LaBerge and Samuels, 1974; Weaver, 2002.

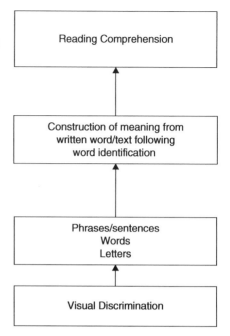

perspective assumes that for a child to learn to read or write, they must be directly and formally "taught" the subskills or basic concepts separately prior to trying to read or write. These individual skills or concepts include letter recognition, auditory discrimination, visual memory, and letter–sound relationships (Palardy, 1991). Once they have mastered all of the subskills, they then are considered ready to begin to read and write.

Reading readiness refers to the idea that at a particular point each child is ready to learn to read, having acquired all of the necessary subskills. Readiness concepts and skills are considered to be hierarchical in nature. There is a specific sequence in which these skills are to be learned. Reading readiness is also considered a prerequisite for beginning to learn how to write. Thus, children are not encouraged to begin to write until they have reached a certain level of reading, usually sometime in first grade.

Learning to write is also thought to require the mastery of specific concepts and subskills (Barbe, Lucas, & Wasylyk, 1984). Handwriting instruction is predicated upon the development of specific subskills involving motor coordination, such as those involving controlled finger movements. In this perspective, readiness to write also includes specific perceptual, cognitive, and integrative skills (Harries & Yost, 1981). Once children reach a level of readiness for writing instruction, a specific sequence is also followed. For example, first children must learn how to print the individual letters of the alphabet. Uppercase letters are taught first, followed by lowercase letters. Great emphasis is placed on the correct formation of the letters. The teacher carefully demonstrates the appropriate way to form letters and children practice making each letter until they successfully have learned how to print each letter of the alphabet in both upper- and lowercase. In this viewpoint, systematic practice is considered critical to the development of good penmanship (Freeman, 1954). Specially lined paper with visual guidelines and model letters are used to teach children how to write (Harries & Yost, 1981; Pasternicki, 1987). (See Figure 2.2).

At school, children are directed to first follow as the teacher models the correct way to make the letters, and then practice making letters on their own (Barbe, Lucas, & Wasylyk, 1984; Thurber, 1984). Often this involves filling a whole page with a certain

Figure 2.2 This Specially Lined Paper, Sample Letters, and Specific Directions for Writing each Letter Characterize a Subskill Approach to Writing

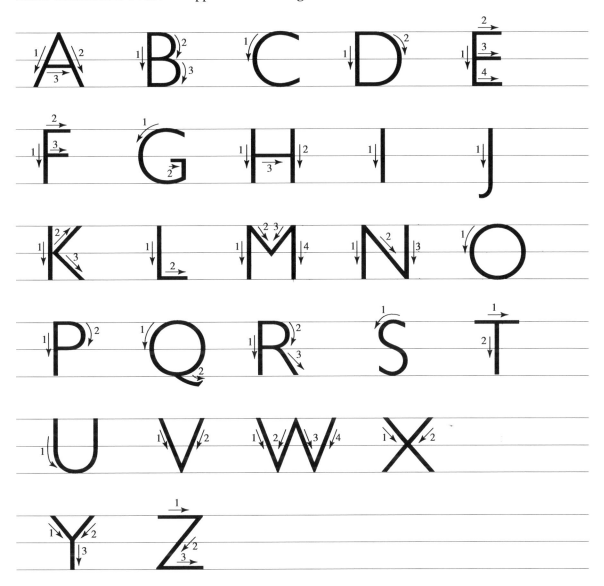

letter, for example, "B," and repeating the activity with the rest of the alphabet until each letter meets a certain standard of legibility and form.

After all of the letters are learned, spelling lessons are introduced and lessons in basic punctuation are taught. Only after a certain level of spelling accuracy is achieved are children encouraged to "write" on their own. In many instances, children first learn to copy a text that the teacher has written on the classroom chalkboard. After children have successfully engaged in these copying activities, they may be given opportunities to write their own texts or messages; however, the emphasis is on the correct spelling of words and the correct formation of letters and punctuation instead of the meaningful message created.

In many instances, parents are discouraged from introducing any type of reading- or writing-related activities during the preschool years at home because it is thought that children need to be formally taught to read and write in a set sequence of subskills and this teaching is best done by teachers at school.

Instructional Approach: Subskills/Readiness

Conceptualizing reading and writing as involving a discrete hierarchy of subskills has led to specific types of instructional activities and curricular materials designed to establish children's reading readiness. This hierarchy is evident in the established sequence in which the concepts and subskills are presented in curricular materials and subsequently taught. For example, in order to be ready to read, a child must first know the alphabet, the individual sounds associated with alphabetic letters, and how to combine or blend sounds as represented by the letters. Additionally, consonant sounds are to be taught before any of the vowels are taught.

Classrooms with a Subskills/Readiness approach will have the following characteristics:

1. The curriculum has a predetermined sequence of learning activities involving the identified subskills or basic concepts through which each child must pass, achieving mastery. There is no recognition or attention paid to what the child may know upon entry to the classroom. The assumption is that if the subskill was not taught, then the child cannot have achieved mastery of it. Thus, a child who enters kindergarten already reading would still be expected to complete all of the prereading or readiness subskills activities and be tested for mastery along with the other children who are not yet reading conventionally.

2. The curriculum is represented by materials specifically developed to teach the hierarchy of subskills through isolated practice in workbooks, worksheets, and specially designed beginning reader texts (primers) and penmanship workbooks. Teachers are expected to closely follow the set curriculum and to be sure that every activity is completed.

3. Although there may still be time in the subskills curriculum for the teacher to read stories aloud to the whole class, this approach does not encourage children

In the readiness/subskill approach, the emphasis is on learning letter–sound relationships.

Hurst Photo

to interact with books or attempt to create print on their own. This is because it is thought children cannot begin to read or write until they have mastered all of the identified subskills.

4. A major emphasis of the subskill lessons is on letter–sound relationships or phonics. Specific phonetic concepts and patterns are taught in a predetermined order. When reading orally, children are encouraged to "sound-out" words they do not know.

5. Evaluation of students' readiness for reading and writing is by formal assessments developed by publishers of commercial instructional materials or by publishers of standardized tests, for example, the Metropolitan Readiness Test (Nurss & McGauvran, 1986).

Naturalist Perspective

Historical and Theoretical Foundations

The Naturalist perspective stems from the Nativist perspective in language development. The Nativist perspective emphasizes the natural capacity of humans to acquire language (Chomsky, 1975, in Alexander & Fox, 2004; Pearson & Stephens, 1994). With respect to literacy acquisition, the Naturalist perspective believes that all children have this natural capacity to not only develop oral language, but to develop competencies in written language as well (Goodman, 1986; Smith, 1988).

The Naturalist perspective of literacy acquisition was fueled by three types of research: (a) Emergent literacy research that documented the acquisition of reading and writing behaviors prior to any type of formal instruction in reading and writing subskills (Baghban, 1984; Bissex, 1980; Briggs & Elkind, 1977; Durkin, 1966; Liston, 1980; Sulzby, 1985, 1986; Taylor, 1983; Temple, Nathan, Temple, & Burris, 1993); (b) reports documenting children's difficulty in becoming fluent readers and motivated writers even though they had succeeded in learning the specific subskills (Goodman, 2002; Harlin, Lipa, & Lonberger, 1991; Manning & Manning, 1989); and (c) research that focused on the innate cognitive processes involved in reading and writing (Goodman, 1965, 1967; Smith, 1978, 1988; Temple et al., 1993).

How Reading and Writing Are Defined

Emphasis on reading for meaning and communication. Just as the purpose of oral language is for communication of meaning, the Naturalist perspective emphasizes that the purpose of reading is to communicate meaning. For example, in our daily lives reading is used not only to communicate in our family and social interactions but also to conduct business, to entertain, to record past events, to plan for future events, and numerous other purposes. Thus, reading is defined in ways that emphasize its communicative, meaning-constructive nature. This perspective places its primary focus on the construction of meaning in reading and contends that this focus dominates the cognitive processes of reading.

Two key theorists and researchers in this perspective are Ken Goodman (1967) and Frank Smith (1988). Both Goodman and Smith emphasize the role of the brain in the reading process. Their studies of the cognitive processes in reading have created a greater awareness of the complexity of the reading process as a meaning-making process.

During the process of reading, the eyes send information to the brain; however, it is the interpretation of that information by the brain that determines what is actually "read" and what meaning is constructed from the written symbols. Goodman considers reading as a "psycholinguistic guessing game" in which the brain actively interprets the visual and nonvisual information to bring meaning to what is read (1993, p. 53).

Critical role of prior knowledge in reading. Smith (1988) emphasizes that "the brain's perceptual decisions are based only partly on information from the eyes, greatly augmented by knowledge that the brain already possesses" (p. 64). Reading is described as a **top-down process** that is meaning-driven (Boothe, Walter, & Waters, 1999). This search for meaning is driven by a person's nonvisual information (that is, prior knowledge of language, conceptual knowledge, and past experiences). While the actual print is also perceived, Smith (1997) contends that not every letter and every word are processed or "read" during the reading process. In other words, the brain is in control of the reading process and only selects the needed visual information in order to create meaning from what is read. (See Figure 2.3 for a diagram of the top-down model of reading.)

Reading is not simply a perception of print. Instead it is a process in which the individual's brain actively constructs meaning from print through both visual and nonvisual information. For example, read the following paragraph aloud:

> A tetrahedral amine with three different substituents (and a lone pair) is non superimposable on its mirror image. We might hope to resolve such an amine into two enantiomers. In most cases, however, such a resolution is not possible, because the enantiomers interconvert rapidly. This interconversion takes place by nitrogen inversion, in which the lone pair moves from one face of the molecule to the other.
>
> (Wade, 1995, p. 871)

Were you able to "read" this paragraph? Now, close this book, and tell someone what you have just read. Did you find it difficult to summarize this segment? In reading the above segment of text, you probably were able to fluently recognize and pronounce the words; however, unless you have a background in science and more specifically organic

Figure 2.3 Top-Down Model of Reading

Source: Based on Goodman, 1967; Smith, 1988, 1997.

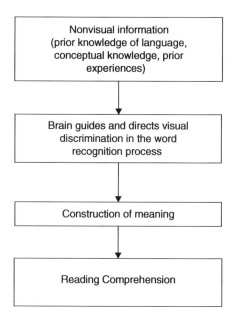

chemistry, you probably did not fully comprehend what you read. As we read, our brains actively work to make meaning of what we read. Not only do we make use of the visual cues found in the written symbols (letter–sound relationships), we use our prior conceptual knowledge of the subject as well as our knowledge of the different aspects of written language (for example, grammar and type of texts). If you had previously taken a course in organic chemistry and had been told prior to reading the paragraph above that it was from an organic chemistry text and from the chapter on amines, you might have been able to comprehend it more successfully.

Emphasis on meaning in children's early writing. In the Naturalist perspective, young children's attempts to communicate graphically on paper are interpreted as "writing." Drawing is considered a precursor to writing. Perhaps this writing takes the form of scribbles or random marks on paper. Children may present their graphic representations to adults and ask "What does that say?" Later on as they begin to use letter forms, their writings may be identified as notes to a friend or family member, a caption for their own drawing, a sign for their bedroom door, or an original story book.

These early writing attempts are not evaluated in terms of conventional spelling or even conventional formation of letters; instead, the focus is on what meaning the young child is trying to communicate. Thus, the focus of early writing attempts is on the meaning rather than on whether the form of the writing is conventional letters and words.

How Children Learn to Read and Write

In the Naturalist perspective, the acquisition of reading and writing is considered to be the result of a general ability to learn. According to Frank Smith (1988), "Reading does not make any exclusive or esoteric demands on the brain . . . reading requires no special talent or unique brain development" (p. 1).

In this perspective it is assumed that children will begin to develop literacy through repeated opportunities to interact with written language in their homes, communities, and informal preschool settings. Research has documented this development of reading and writing prior to explicit instruction (Alexander & Fox, 2004; Bissex, 1980; Clay, 1975, 1991; Ferreiro, 1986; Heath, 1983; Teale and Sulzby, 1986; Temple et. al., 1993; Wren, 2001). Much of this research has focused on children's interactions with story books (Bissex, 1980; Crago & Crago, 1983; Otto, 1996, 1997; Sulzby, 1985). In a longitudinal study, Sulzby (1985) described preschool children's emergent reading behaviors as they interacted independently with familiar story books. She described a continuum of emergent reading that began with labeling and commenting and continued to accurately reading the text. (This continuum will be described further in Chapter 6.)

Just as emergent reading develops when children have opportunities to interact with story books, so do children develop knowledge of writing in their early attempts to communicate through drawing, scribbling, and letter-like units (Temple et al., 1993). Because young children have not yet acquired conventional spelling, these early attempts to communicate in writing will involve their own versions of specific words, or **invented spellings**. For example, a young child might write "SW" and say it reads "Snow White." Another child might write "S Wyte" for "Snow White." Yet another child might write "DMPR" and say it also spells "Snow White." In this Naturalist perspective, children's invented spellings are not considered mistakes to be immediately corrected, but are considered as evidence children are beginning to associate specific sounds with specific letters and letter combinations.

Figure 2.4 Mairead's
Snow Story

When a child spontaneously and independently writes "THAR.WL.B.SHAWERS.IN. THE.AFTR.NUN" (Bissex, 1980, p. 27), ("There will be showers in the afternoon"), he has effortfully used his knowledge of the letters of the alphabet to represent the sounds he hears in each word. This naturalist approach also assumes that with frequent, informal opportunities to begin to explore writing, children will gradually progress to developing conventional or standard spelling without explicit instruction (see Figure 2.4).

Research has also described the home and school settings in which children acquired early literacy (Goodman & Goodman, 1979; Heath, 1983; Hiebert, 1993; Teale, 1986; Vernon-Feagans, Hammer, Miccio, & Manlove, 2002). This research has shown that children learned to read and write in settings where they were encouraged to begin exploring and experimenting with written language to communicate. In these settings, children were part of a community where reading and writing were engaged in for authentic purposes. This awareness of the importance of authentic purposes for reading and writing tasks in natural literacy development then fostered the idea that written language should not be fragmented or separated into isolated skill lessons in educational settings, but should be kept "whole."

Instructional Approach: Whole Language

Based upon this Naturalist perspective, literacy instruction materials, methods, and strategies were designed to keep language "whole" and to provide opportunities for children to actively engage in literacy-related activities. As concepts about emergent reading and invented spelling were translated into educational approaches and materials, the Whole Language approach evolved. The concept of **whole language** initially referred to an instructional philosophy in which "meaning and 'natural language' are the basis of literacy learning" (Smith, 1988, p. 301); however, it quickly became associated with a particular instructional approach and specific types of learning activities (Neuman, 1985). This approach has also been defined as "a child-centered, literature-based approach . . . that immerses students in real communication situations whenever possible" (Froese, 1996, p. 2). The Whole Language approach emphasizes the idea that reading instruction should not involve attention to the discrete language concepts or subskills. The teaching of reading and writing is not separated into discrete skills for isolated direct instruction; instead, the language is kept "whole" (Altwerger, Edelsky, & Flores, 1989; Edelsky, Altwerger, & Flores, 1991). The focus is on learning how to read and write by being immersed in reading and literacy-related activities. Instead of direct instruction in letter–sound relationships, this approach assumes students will acquire this knowledge through "meaningful reading and writing activities" (Froese, 1996, p. 219). For example, Figure 2.5 shows Ariel's early distinction between writing and drawing.

Figure 2.5 Ariel's Story

In the Whole Language approach, young children are encouraged to write their own stories.

Dmitri Kalinovsky

Teachers who adopt the Whole Language approach to literacy acquisition will be likely to have classrooms with the following characteristics (Edelsky, Altwerger, & Flores, 1991; Froese, 1996; Harlin, Lipa, & Lonberger, 1991; Smullin, 1989):

1. Children are encouraged to interact in authentic reading- and writing-related activities from the first day of school. Instead of skills workbooks, children have opportunities to write their own stories and spend time in the classroom library.
2. Real literature is used rather than texts that have been designed for a specific reading level. Trade books are used instead of a basal reader.
3. The curriculum is child-centered rather than textbook-centered. The teacher develops learning activities based on his knowledge of students' reading levels and instructional needs. Commercial instructional/curricular materials are used as a flexible resource, not as a mandatory curriculum.
4. The emphasis is on the construction and comprehension of written language. There is a consistent emphasis on reading for comprehension as well as writing to communicate. Thus, oral reading performance and standard penmanship receive little emphasis.
5. Language concepts and skills are learned within the context of authentic tasks. For example, learning about word syllables takes place within the context of reading a story and looking at particular words in the story. Letter formation is demonstrated by the teacher as she writes children's dictated stories.
6. Instructional activities are characterized by informal, collaborative learning rather than direct instruction. Children are encouraged to read to each other in pairs or small groups. Story vocabulary may be enhanced through a learning center display of objects or artifacts represented in the story.
7. The classroom teacher serves as a model user of literacy as well as a facilitator of children's interactions with written language. For example, after a fireman's

visit to a kindergarten classroom, the teacher would engage the children in a group activity to dictate a thank-you note to the fireman and also demonstrate how the note would be sent by mail.

Interactive Perspective

Historical and Theoretical Foundations

The evolution of the Interactive perspective was influenced by the continued research that occurred as the Whole Language approach was implemented. There were two main lines of research that facilitated or contributed to this evolution: (a) Research on the effectiveness of the Whole Language approach, and (b) research on the processes of reading and writing.

Research on the effectiveness of the Whole Language approach. As research on the effectiveness of Whole Language instruction was conducted, it became apparent that while the approach was successful in some classrooms (Dahl & Freppon, 1994; Freppon, 1993; Stice & Bertrand, 1990), the Whole Language approach was not always successful. Not all children were able to benefit from a curriculum that primarily focused on reading literature and creative writing. Some children who had been in whole-language classrooms during the primary years experienced problems in the upper grades due to a lack of conventional spelling skills, a lack of knowledge of grammar, and an inability to fluently read content-area texts. Some school districts reported that reading achievement scores declined with the implementation of the Whole Language approach. Standardized test scores indicated low achievement in tasks related to reading (Johns & Elish-Piper, 1997). A major controversy developed in California when the Whole Language approach was deemed responsible for the statewide decline in reading achievement (Farris, Fuhler, & Walther, 2004; Innes, 2002; Johns & Elish-Piper, 1997; Krashen, 2002; Matson, 1996).

While the validity of this claim was questioned (Krashen, 2002), researchers and school districts began to study the ways in which Whole Language was being implemented. Researchers conducting observations in Whole Language classrooms reported that not all teachers were implementing the approach in the same way: in fact, there seemed to be many different definitions of what constituted the Whole Language approach (McIntyre, 1996). For example, although the Whole Language approach encouraged the embedding of instruction in specific language skills such as phonemic awareness in the context of reading a story, some teachers interpreted the Whole Language approach as prohibiting any attention to separate language skills.

The implementation of the Whole Language approach also resulted in whole class oral reading and the disappearance of reading ability groups. Because this approach assumed that children would learn to read by reading and that no explicit instruction in separate reading skills was needed, there was no need to have ability reading groups. This practice was also supported by research in classrooms using the subskill approach which documented the negative effects of reading ability groups on children's motivation and long-term achievement (Allington, 1982; Davis, 1991; Grant, 1981; Phillips, 1990; Wilkinson & Spinelli, 1981). Unfortunately, this practice of whole class oral reading made it very difficult for individual children to receive the additional guidance they needed to learn to read.

Research on Reading and Writing Processes. As this research on the effectiveness (or lack thereof) of the Whole Language approach accumulated, continued research on the cognitive processes involved in reading and writing provided new insights on what happens when we read. In his description of the process of reading, Rummelhart (1985) emphasized the roles of both perception and cognition, and the interaction that occurs between visual perception and cognitive processes that results in comprehension of written language. According to Rummelhart's Interactive Model of Reading, skilled readers use various sources of information (such as visual discrimination, grammar, and vocabulary) when reading. These sources of information interact in complex ways during the process of reading. It is not a bottom-up or top-down process, but instead an interactive process where the reader's prior knowledge of language and conceptual knowledge interacts dynamically with the visual information on the written page (see Figure 2.6).

How Reading and Writing Are Defined

Based on Rummelhart's model, the Interactive perspective defines reading and writing as meaning-making processes that involve both bottom-up and top-down aspects. When reading, a person's brain processes the visual-sensory information (written words) along with prior knowledge of language (grammar, vocabulary, and word parts) in the construction of meaning, resulting in the comprehension of text. When writing, a person's brain constructs a message through a dynamic interaction between what he wants the message to communicate and what he knows about using language (grammar and vocabulary) to express this message in writing.

How Children Learn to Read and Write

Because the Interactive perspective defines reading and writing as meaning-making processes involving both top-down and bottom-up aspects, it follows that this perspective's description of how children develop literacy focuses on children's experiences in both informal reading and writing activities (such as story book sharing and invented spelling) and formal, direct instruction (such as lessons on letter–sound relationships). Thus, it is assumed that children need to have both types of learning experiences in order to acquire literacy (Cassidy & Wenrich, 1998; Hammond, 1999; Morrow & Asbury, 1999; Pressley, 1998; Williams & Blair-Larsen, 1999).

Figure 2.6 Interactive Model of Reading

Source: Based on Rummelhart, 2004; Ruddell and Speaker, 1985.

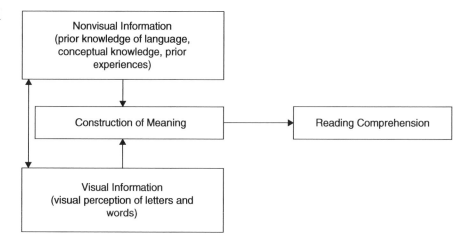

The Interactive perspective also recognizes that the dynamic interactions that occur during reading and writing are not the same for each person, nor will all children benefit from experiencing the same learning activities. Thus, a learning environment should provide a wide range of informal and formal literacy-related experiences so that individual children's needs are met. This approach to instruction is referred to as a "balanced approach."

Instructional Approach: Balanced

The Balanced approach has been referred to as a "middle of the road approach" to instruction (Matson, 1996), as well as being seen as a compromise between two approaches (Subskills/Readiness and Whole Language), because it integrates both subskills and whole-language instructional activities (Reutzel & Cooter, 2004).

Guidelines for implementing this Balanced approach suggest a wide range of learning activities. Components of this range include the following (Fitzgerald, 1999; Hammond, 1999; Pressley, 1998; Strickland, 1996; Williams & Blair-Larsen, 1999; Wren, 2001):

1. *Direct instruction and independent, discovery learning.* Reading activities include direct instruction by the teacher, opportunities for children to use independent learning centers, and opportunities to work with one another in pairs or small groups.
2. *Isolated skill emphasis and meaning-construction emphasis.* Workbooks may be used that focus on developing phonics skills. At other times, activities focus on reading and writing as forms of meaningful, personal communication, such as writing notes to family or friends or acting out a favorite story.
3. *Pre-planned formal instruction and flexible instruction in response to children's questions or immediate needs.* While specific lessons are planned around instructional goals, the learning activities are changed or modified in response to children's questions or interactions.
4. *Use of trade books and use of commercially developed, ability-leveled reading texts.* In addition to a well-stocked classroom library that children use during designated times of the day, there are times when children engage in reading texts that are designed for specific reading levels.
5. *Formal standardized assessments and informal assessments.* Student progress is evaluated through teachers' daily observations and students' work examples, along with commercially prepared tests that are part of a formal reading curriculum.
6. *Focus on language arts within a communicative context as well as a separate emphasis on activities in each area: reading, writing, listening, and speaking.* For example, there are times when instructional activities focus only on a reading skill, such as word recognition. At other times, the learning activities emphasize several language arts, such as when a small group of children create a play of a favorite story, writing their own script and then presenting it in front of the class.
7. *Heterogeneous, flexible grouping of students and homogeneous, ability grouping.* Within the literacy curriculum, children have opportunities to work in a variety of groups. Some groups are formed by interest and other groups are determined by instructional needs or general reading ability; however, the groupings are flexible or temporary, rather than static or permanent.

According to Fitzgerald (1999), there is no one balanced approach. While there is agreement on the general philosophy and theoretical perspective of this approach, the ways in which "balance" is achieved in the curriculum of individual classrooms and at different levels of literacy development is still being researched and debated. A determining factor in the literacy curriculum that is implemented in individual classrooms is each teacher's knowledge of her students and their particular instructional needs.

Transactional Perspective

Historical and Theoretical Foundations

As the Balanced approach was implemented in many schools, questions about the merits of this approach arose. This was due in part to the lack of a common definition of "balance" in literacy instruction (Fitzgerald, 1999; Serafini, 2003). This lack of consensus often led to implementation that simply combined skill-based activities and Whole Language–based activities into a literacy curriculum without an understanding of how these separate instructional approaches should be integrated in real classrooms (Pearson & Raphael, 1999). Commercial curricular materials promoted as following the Balanced approach varied in content and instructional strategies. Some emphasized holistic strategies; others were more focused on a skills approach with a heavy emphasis on phonics (Pressley, Roehrig, Bogner, Raphael, & Dolezal, 2002).

In addition to this concern over the ways in which instructional strategies were to be "balanced," additional research and theoretical explanations of literacy learning have provided further awareness of the complex transactions that occur in learning environments among learners, teachers, and the learning environment or context, as well as the important role teachers have as decision-makers in that learning environment (Hammond, 1999; Morrow & Asbury, 1999; Pressley et al., 2002).

While the Interactive perspective and its respective Balanced instructional approach did acknowledge the integration of top-down and bottom-up processes, there was no recognition of the complex transactions that occur within the learning environment as children experience literacy-related activities.

Detailed descriptions of teacher–student interactions, along with teachers' reflections on their instructional decisions, have contributed to our understanding of the critical role teachers have in the learning transactions that occur in their classrooms (Dickenson & Sprague, 2002; Hiebert, 1999; Morrow & Asbury, 1999; Roskos & Neuman, 2002). These new understandings of learning transactions and teachers' roles as decision-makers have provided a greater awareness of why specific methods or strategies do not work in every classroom. Each classroom is unique. There are no generic classrooms or generic students. The increasing diversity of children's cultural, social, and linguistic backgrounds in many schools also contributes to the dynamic and variable learning transactions that take place in classrooms. Not only are the reading and writing processes complex, the transactions which facilitate literacy development are also complex, involving the learner, the learning task, and the learning environment. Within this learning environment, the teacher plays a critical role.

To be useful, a theoretical perspective on literacy development needs to address all of these complexities. The **Transactional perspective** provides this framework for understanding the complexities of literacy development. A key distinguishing feature of the Transactional perspective is the emphasis on transactions that occur as children participate in a learning community and develop literacy competencies.

The roots of the Transactional perspective are found in the work of four seminal researchers/theorists: Bronfenbrenner, Vygotsky, Rosenblatt, and Heath.

Bronfenbrenner's (1979, 1989, 2000, 2005) work centered on an ecological theory that identified the "conditions and processes that shape human development" (2000, p. 9).

He identified complex settings that influence human development such as family, school, peers, and community, along with the interactions between these settings with respect to cultural, social, political, and historical factors. His work encouraged educators to look at the larger picture of human development rather than focusing only on the individual's growth and development. This means that in order to create appropriate learning settings, educators need to consider children's home and community environments and the direct and vicarious experiences of children within those environments (Bronfenbrenner & Evans, 2000; Swick & Williams, 2006).

Vygotsky's (1978, 1981, 1986) work also contributed to our understanding of the influence of social interaction on cognitive development. Vygotsky described the importance of adult mediation in the learning process. Specifically, this adult mediation was beneficial when it took place within a child's **zone of proximal development**. The zone of proximal development is the area of potential growth between what a child can do independently and what the child can do with adult mediation. This adult mediation supports the child's continued development, thus facilitating gradual and higher levels of independent performance. Applying this concept to classroom instruction, it means that a teacher must be aware of each child's prior knowledge and skills and then design and implement instruction which supports each child's development of increased competencies.

Several decades ago, Louise Rosenblatt's (1978, 1983) work identified reading as a transactional process between the reader, the text, and the context in which the reading occurs. Since that time, her work was mainly applied to understanding how comprehension of text occurs in secondary classrooms (Rosenblatt, 1994, 2004).

According to Rosenblatt, as one reads, a dynamic interaction or transaction occurs between the reader's knowledge of language and concepts, the text content and characteristics, as well as the social setting or context in which the reading is taking place. As a result of this dynamic interaction, the reader constructs meaning of what is read. Rosenblatt's work increased our awareness that different readers would be likely to construct different interpretations of what they had read, even though they had read the same text, because their individual transactions with the text would differ. This approach to the reading and teaching of literature in secondary schools was referred to as the "reader-response method" (Rosenblatt, 2004, p. 1394). For an overview of the components of the Transactional perspective of literacy development, see Figure 2.7.

More recently, Rosenblatt applied this Transactional theory to both reading and writing processes (1994). In doing so, Rosenblatt emphasized:

- ❖ The total context in which learning transactions occur, including not only the classroom, but also the entire school and larger social-cultural context of the family and community.
- ❖ The Transactional view of reading and writing is not represented by a set of stages that are strictly followed; instead, the process engaged in by individual learners is acknowledged and supported as an avenue to continued growth in literacy competencies.
- ❖ A primary concern is the creation of learning environments and activities that are motivating and encourage students to construct their own meaningful interactions with language and literacy.
- ❖ The dialogue between a teacher and his students, as well as the interactions between students, is a critical component of the transactions that occur. The teacher's role is to facilitate this transactional process for students as they interact with texts and each other.

Figure 2.7 Transactional Perspective of Literacy Development

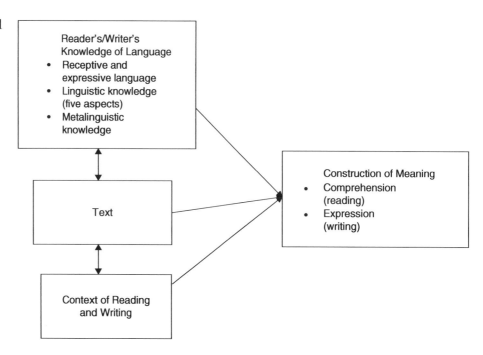

Evidence of the importance of interactions between texts and the contexts of home, community, and school settings is found in Heath's (1983) ethnographic study of children in two working-class communities in the Piedmont Carolinas. Heath's work clarified the important roles of teachers and parents as mediators of children's literacy learning in varied social-cultural groups.

The patterns of language use in the two communities Heath studied reflected the ways in which language was used orally and in writing by parents and community residents. In these communities, teachers' knowledge of home and community contexts served as a basis for these teachers to create school learning environments that supported children's success in literacy transactions.

The importance of mediation by teachers and parents has more recently been documented by researchers in the longitudinal Home-School Study of Language and Literacy Development by Tabors, Snow, and Dickinson (2001). Their examination of how children's homes and schools supported language and literacy development indicated the important role of parents. They concluded that parents' awareness of the total context of their children's everyday language interactions was a determining factor in children's language and literacy abilities in kindergarten. Key factors identified were the frequency of book reading at home and the quality of the book-talk language that occurred.

How Reading and Writing Are Defined

Transactions between reader/writer, text, and context. In the Transactional perspective, reading and writing are defined as involving a "transaction" between the reader-writer, text, and context that results in the construction of a meaningful message (Rosenblatt, 1994; Ruddell & Unrau, 2004). These three components of the transaction interact in a dynamic, synergistic manner.

The reader-writer component. The reader-writer's knowledge of language is based on his knowledge of oral language as well as his knowledge of written language and prior conceptual knowledge. Reflected also in this prior knowledge is the "reader's cultural, social, and personal history" (Rosenblatt, 1994, p. 1064). (The role of oral language as a foundation for literacy development is the focus of Chapter 3.)

The text component. The second component of the transaction involves the text, specifically the type of text and its characteristics. The characteristics of the text influence the transaction that occurs based on a reader's/writer's prior experiences with that type of text. When a reader begins to interact with the written text on a page, he has some expectations or ideas, however vague, of the meaning that will be constructed during the reading process. When writing, a writer first decides his purpose for writing and this determines the text that will be created. For example, is it going to be a note to a friend, a shopping list, or a creative story?

Rosenblatt describes this interaction with text as stemming from one's past experience with language and with other texts, along with his present setting and interests (Rosenblatt, 1994). For example, if the text to be read is an alphabet book, prior experiences with alphabet books would create the expectation that a different letter of the alphabet would be featured on each page along with words beginning with that letter of the alphabet.

In addition, the way in which a text is structured to introduce new concepts and vocabulary also influences the transaction with the reader and the meaning that is constructed. The meaning of a text is embedded in the vocabulary or semantic knowledge represented in the text. Researchers have documented the important role of vocabulary in the comprehension of text (Graves & Watts-Taffe, 2002; National Institute of Child Health & Human Development, 2000; National Reading Panel, 2000; Ruddell, 1994). Children with larger listening vocabularies are more likely to be successful in developing reading competencies than are children with smaller listening vocabularies. Word recognition is easier for children with extensive listening vocabularies because they are already familiar with more words and their related meanings. Children with larger vocabularies also have more conceptual knowledge and this contributes to increased comprehension when reading.

When writing, a person's vocabulary (and conceptual knowledge) also determines the text that evolves during the writing process. Meaning is constructed through the vocabulary that becomes part of the writing product as well as the way in which the text is organized.

The context component. The third component of the reading/writing transaction involves the context. This refers to the social-cultural setting in which the reading and/or writing occurs. For example, is the literacy activity part of a social-studies lesson at school or is it taking place in the community as part of a religious service? Is the reading activity a solitary one for personal leisure? Perhaps the writing activity is a personal journal or a school essay assignment. Each of these social-cultural settings influence the reader-text-context transactions and the resulting construction of meaning.

Comprehension of text occurs as the reader constructs meaning from the dynamic interplay between reader, text, and context. The writing process also involves a transaction between the writer, the text and the context. As a writer writes, the transactions between his knowledge of language, the text he is creating, and the context of his environment (for example, personal, social, and cultural) are continuous and interactive (Rosenblatt, 1994).

How Children Learn to Read and Write

A key idea in the Transactional perspective is that literacy development occurs as transactions take place in social-cultural settings where language and literacy are used in authentic, meaningful tasks (Au, 1997). In these settings adults (parents and teachers) mediate literacy-related activities and events within a child's zone of proximal development. Emphasis is placed on the role of adults in facilitating children's experiences in reading and writing at all levels of literacy acquisition. More specifically, this perspective recognizes the role of teachers in assessing the prior knowledge and skills of children in their classrooms. Based on their awareness of children's prior knowledge and skills, teachers determine the appropriate instruction that will meet the needs of the children, thus teaching within children's individual zones of proximal development.

Instructional Approach: Comprehensive Literacy Instruction

While the Balanced instruction approach provided a compromise in the controversy between explicit, skills-based instruction and whole-language instruction, clarification was needed as to how to include both types of learning activities in classrooms. Clarification was also needed as to the ways in which teachers would interact with children within their zones of proximal development. Teachers also needed to be more aware of the way in which instructional decisions are made and the way teachers' resources are used. The Transactional perspective has provided the theoretical orientation for addressing these issues, clearly identifying the complex interactions that occur between readers, texts, and social-cultural contexts. This perspective also acknowledges the dynamic role of teachers in children's interactions during literacy-related activities.

The instructional approach that has been identified with the Transactional perspective is Comprehensive Literacy Instruction (Reutzel & Fawson, 2002; Reutzel & Cooter, 2005; Roller, 2002). This approach is focused on using a wide range of strategies, and recognizes that the strategies will vary with each level of literacy development (preschool, primary, elementary, middle, and high school). This approach is "comprehensive" in several respects because it:

1. recognizes the complex processes involved in reading and writing,
2. includes a broad range of learning activities incorporating authentic literacy tasks and embedded skill lessons,
3. recognizes the social-cultural contexts of literacy acquisition, and
4. acknowledges the key role of teachers in facilitating children's learning.

Comprehensive Literacy Instruction incorporates the three main areas of transaction identified by Rosenblatt (1978) as contributing to the construction of meaning during reading and writing, that is, the reader, the text, and the context. In addition, this approach explicitly acknowledges the role of the teacher in mediating readers' and writers' transactions. This teacher-mediated instruction reflects the teachers' decisions, knowledge base, resources, and interactions with students in their zones of proximal development (Ruddell & Unrau, 2004). (See Figure 2.8.)

Critical role of classroom teacher. At the center of this approach is the classroom teacher. The teacher is the key to the learning that occurs in her classroom; the curriculum is secondary (Bond & Dykstra, 1967, 1997). This recognizes the dynamic role played by teachers in their interactions with their students in deciding what is to be taught and how it is to be taught. Their reflective decision making involves an awareness of the unique and complex transactions that occur as children learn (Corcoran & Leahy, 2003; Glazer, 2004; Parsons & Stephenson, 2005; Schön, 1983; Zeichner & Liston, 1996).

Implementation of Comprehensive Literacy Instruction involves developing and implementing learning activities that will facilitate readers' and writers' knowledge of language. This approach also facilitates students' developing competencies in engaging,

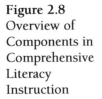

Figure 2.8
Overview of
Components in
Comprehensive
Literacy
Instruction

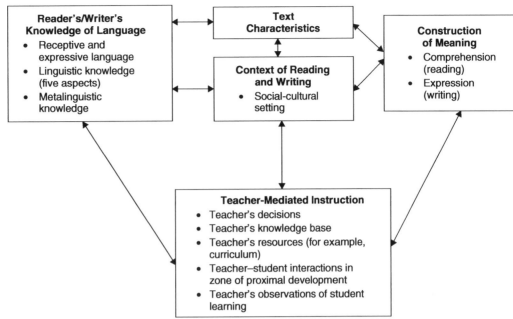

comprehending, and creating texts in a variety of social-cultural settings. A teacher's knowledge and professional skills are critical to the decisions that are made in the classroom (Cox & Hopkins, 2006), and to the ways children are encouraged to interact with the instructional resources, as well as the ways in which children's zones of proximal development are identified and engaged.

Categories of instructional activities. Roller (2002) identified three main categories of instructional activities in Comprehensive Literacy Instruction: word-level knowledge, comprehension, and motivation. Activities that focus on word-level knowledge include an emphasis on letter–sound relationships, vocabulary, and grammar within meaningful, authentic learning contexts. Emphasis is also on comprehension as the construction of meaning across many types of texts that are read for different purposes. Motivation is another key area of instructional strategies and activities. Children's ownership of reading and writing is emphasized and children are encouraged to use literacy for personal purposes in their daily lives (Au, 2002). This ownership provides a motivating force in children's literacy development.

Components of Comprehensive Literacy Instruction. While more specific learning activities involved in Comprehensive Literacy Instruction are detailed in later chapters, the components around which this approach is organized can be summarized in the following (Reutzel & Cooter, 2004; Roller, 2002; Weaver, 2002):

❖ Teachers' extensive, evidence-based knowledge of reading processes and children's development provides the underlying foundation for enhancing children's development of literacy through reflective, contingent decision making.

❖ Instructional activities incorporate authentic literacy tasks in a whole-to-part-to-whole perspective. Reading and writing are considered meaning-making, communicative activities. Additionally, word study activities increase children's awareness of the features of written language.

Special visitor programs
provide opportunities to read
with older, more fluent readers.

Gayle Perrin

❖ A variety of informal and formal assessments provide a comprehensive view of children's progress in literacy acquisition. Daily, ongoing observations of children's development as well as periodic, formal tests provide a picture of children's literacy growth.

❖ Children are engaged in being read to, reading with and to adults, and reading to each other. Teacher read-alouds occur on a regular basis as do opportunities for children to read to each other informally. Children are encouraged to read to and with their parents and extended family members. Special visitor programs may be developed to provide additional opportunities for children to read with older students or adults in their classrooms.

❖ Reading and writing instruction are integrated throughout the curriculum. Units of study in science, mathematics, and social studies involve activities where reading and writing competencies are further developed. In addition, subject-related literature such as historical fiction and nonfiction trade books is incorporated into units of study.

❖ Children participate in a variety of groupings for instruction and collaboration as well as independently and in one-on-one tutoring. Throughout each day, children have opportunities to work alone and with others.

❖ A learning community is formed which creates home–school partnerships and also focuses on meeting the needs of all students in the classroom. These partnerships include frequent communication between home and school as well as many opportunities for parents and other family members to become involved in school activities. A key element in this learning community is the mutual respect for all participants and an appreciation for social-cultural diversities.

Summary. Building upon the earlier theoretical perspectives, the Transactional perspective provides a broader and more extensive framework for understanding the complex interactions that occur between readers, texts, and contexts. Comprehensive Literacy Instruction implements that perspective and provides guidelines for reading and writing instruction for all children.

A major shortcoming of each of the earlier theoretical perspectives on literacy development was that they did not acknowledge the complex and dynamic social-cultural-linguistic contexts in which children live and learn. Because the Transactional perspective acknowledges the learning context and the teacher's role in that context as critical components in literacy development, it has the potential to increase teachers' awareness of how to meet the instructional needs of all learners, such as English language learners, children with learning difficulties, and children from culturally and socially diverse settings.

In this text, the Transactional perspective provides the framework for describing children's literacy development from infancy to age eight. The critical role of early childhood educators as reflective decision-makers and mediators of learning in their classrooms is also addressed, along with strategies for implementing Comprehensive Literacy Instruction throughout the early childhood years.

Chapter Summary

Since the 1950s, four theoretical perspectives have provided the underlying framework for literacy education. These theoretical perspectives include the following: Behaviorist, Naturalist, Interactive, and Transactional. Each of these theoretical perspectives describes how children learn to read and write as well as a particular way in which reading and writing are defined. From each perspective specific instructional approaches have developed. These include: Subskills/Readiness, Whole Language, Balanced, and Comprehensive Literacy instruction.

With the successive development of each perspective and implementation of the corresponding approach, our collective understanding of literacy development has increased. In each instance, continued research has provided evidence of the usefulness of that perspective and approach to determining the best way to enhance literacy development in young children. Continued research also promises to increase further our understandings of the processes involved in all areas of literacy. At the time of this writing, comprehensive reading instruction is evolving as a highly recommended approach that addresses current concerns and incorporates best practice in literacy instruction. This approach is "comprehensive" in several respects: (a) Recognition of the complex processes involved in reading and writing, (b) a broad range of learning activities incorporating authentic literacy tasks and embedded skill lessons, (c) recognition of social-cultural contexts of literacy acquisition, and (d) acknowledgment of the key role of teachers in facilitating children's learning.

Chapter Review

1. Terms to know:

contingent	invented spelling
reinforcement	whole language
bottom-up process	Transactional
reading	perspective
readiness	zone of proximal
top-down process	development

2. How does a teacher's theoretical perspective on the process of reading and writing influence his or her classroom?

3. What is the significance of the study by Bond and Dykstra (1967)?

4. Compare the ways that reading and writing are defined in the Behaviorist perspective with the Naturalist perspective.

5. Compare the focus on direct instruction of letter–sound relations found in the Whole Language approach and the Balanced approach.

6. In what ways has the Balanced approach proved difficult to implement?

7. What are the "transactions" in the Transactional theory of reading? Recall the last book you read. Using this theory's three components, list several transactions that occurred during your reading.

8. How has our understanding of the reading process changed in the last four decades?
9. List three characteristics of each of the following instructional approaches: Subskills/Readiness, Whole Language, Balanced, Comprehensive Literacy.
10. In what ways is Comprehensive Literacy Instruction "comprehensive"?

Chapter Extension Activities

Observation: Visit a preschool or kindergarten class session. Prepare a written description of the ways in which you observe reading and writing activities are incorporated throughout the class time. Identify the instructional approach toward literacy development represented by the specific activities.

In-class or Online Discussion: Reflect on your experiences as a beginning reader and writer. Describe the learning activities that were part of your classroom. Identify the theoretical perspective and instructional approach related to those learning activities.

Research: Locate a current professional journal article on a recommended literacy-related instructional activity. Review the main points of the article. Identify the theoretical perspective and instructional approach embedded in the instructional activity. Explain your reasoning in classifying this activity into the theoretical perspective and instructional approach.

Chapter 3

Oral Language Development: Foundation for Literacy

> Eric (2½ years old) was in his stroller, going for a ride in the neighborhood with his mom. She noticed a small dog and its owner who were also out for a walk and coming toward them on the sidewalk. She said, "Look, Eric! Here comes a little dog. A little black dog." Eric responded by looking directly at the dog and smiling. As they passed by the little dog, Eric turned to his mom and exclaimed, "Mom! No tail!" Eric's mom replied, "You're right! That puppy dog doesn't have a tail." Eric laughed and smiled as they continued on their way.

Eric's conversation with his mother provides dramatic evidence of his oral language development. He is able to understand his mother's initial message, focus on the unfolding event, and then express his thoughts. Even though Eric speaks only three words, the message he communicates is clear. Eric is well on his way to developing effective oral language skills.

The development of oral language competencies is a major accomplishment during the preschool years. Unless there are developmental delays, cognitive impairment, or physical speech impediments, all children will become relatively fluent in their home language during the first four years. The ability to use language to communicate affects children's learning and social-cultural interactions. Oral language knowledge also provides a foundation for children's later development of reading and writing. According to Moats (2000), "What children bring to the printed page, and to the task of writing, is knowledge of spoken language" (p. 16).

The importance of children's oral language is recognized in the Transactional perspective described in Chapter 2. In this perspective, a child's knowledge of language, along with their prior experiences, is considered a major component of all literacy transactions. By understanding children's oral language development, early childhood teachers are better able to facilitate this development and thus, also understand children's transactions with literacy.

In this chapter we will explore children's oral language development and the relationship of oral language development to children's literacy development. This knowledge establishes a basis for the subsequent chapters which provide research-based descriptions of children's literacy development and the ways in which this knowledge informs our teaching interactions. In addition, this chapter also focuses on the ways early childhood teachers can support language and literacy transactions among children from diverse home and community environments. This diversity includes differences in social-economic status, culture, and ethnicity, as well as language.

Role of Adults in Children's Language Development: Overview

In the opening vignette to this chapter, Eric's mother initiated the conversation and engaged him in a dialogue about the little dog. Social interaction is a key factor in language development. Language does not develop in isolation. This is true for oral language development as well as for the development of knowledge about written language. There are two key components in this social interaction. First, the child needs to be engaged as a "partner in communication" and second, the adult/fluent speaker needs to use effective interaction strategies that facilitate communication and keep the child engaged in the interaction.

Partners in Communication

Language development begins when a child is considered a conversational partner. This can occur even before the child can participate verbally. For many children, this occurs shortly after birth as the parents begin to talk to their newborn. In these conversations, parents engage their infants in a dialogue-like interaction and look for nonverbal behaviors as signs of response. For example, in the short dialogue below, the mother responds to her newborn child's hiccup as if it was a conversational response, and continues on with the conversation:

Mother:	Hello little one. I'm so glad you are here.
	Look at your little hands (*touches fingers*).
	You are so beautiful!
Newborn:	(*hiccups*)
Mother:	Oh, my goodness. You have the hiccups! Let's see if you need a pat on the back (*lifts infant to her shoulder, pats her on the back*).
Newborn:	(*hiccups stop*)
Mother:	There you go. You're better now.

When adults (or older siblings) consider young children conversational partners, it creates a setting in which the very young child begins to participate in a communicative exchange. This is where language development begins.

Effective Interaction Patterns

The specific ways in which parents and other family members engage young children in communicating also influence oral language development. The six interaction patterns were described in Chapter 1 as characterizing a developmentally appropriate setting in early childhood. These interaction patterns are also descriptive of the ways in which many parents and other family members intuitively and effectively encourage young children's language development. These six interaction patterns include: (a) shared reference and eye contact, (b) communication loops, (c) verbal mapping, (d) child-directed speech, (e) linguistic scaffolding and (f) mediation (Otto, 2002, 2006). (For examples of each pattern, refer to Chapter 1.) Through these social interactions, young children gradually develop the ability to use language to communicate. In the next section, the major stages of language development are described. Each of these stages is facilitated when parents and other fluent speakers engage children as conversational partners.

Stages of Oral Language Development

From birth on, children begin to learn about their environments and to communicate with family members. What they are learning is reflected in the ways in which they vocalize.

Cooing

As early as six weeks, infants will begin to spontaneously make cooing sounds (Reich, 1986; Wolff, 1969). These extended sounds resemble vowel sounds, such as /aaa/, /ooo/, /ahhh/. (Note that the slash marks surrounding the letters refer to the sound associated with the letters.) At this stage children are learning to make sounds by manipulating their tongues, mouths, and breathing. This cooing behavior may occur when the child is alone and clearly indicates the child is experimenting with making sounds.

These vowel-like sounds occur earlier than do the consonant-like sounds because the vowel-like sounds are produced with less articulation than are the consonant sounds. For example, when you produce an /aaa/ sound your mouth and throat are more open; when you produce a /p/ sound, you need to coordinate your lips and breath to produce the sound.

Babbling

Infants' sound production becomes more varied and complex around 4–6 months of age. At this time they begin to babble, making repeated consonant–vowel sounds, such as *ba-ba-ba* (Clark & Clark, 1977; Stoel-Gammon, 1998). A more complex type of babbling develops around 8–10 months. This type of babbling varies in intonation and rhythm and sounds like the child is talking. It is called **echolalic babbling** because it reflects the intonation and rhythm of the speech of the adults in the child's environment (Sachs, 1989).

One-Word Stage

Around one year of age, children begin to produce word-like units. These word-like units may be invented words, also known as **idiomorphs** (Reich, 1986). For example, a child may have a special invented word that refers to a toy or to his personal blanket. This idiomorph is a "word" in the sense that it is stable and used to refer to a particular object on a consistent basis. In addition to these invented words, children also produce more conventional words that resemble adult pronunciation and meaning.

The one-word stage is a significant development because the child is now using a stable language unit to communicate meaning. Often parents and family members will adopt the child's invented words or pronunciations as a way of encouraging the child to talk.

Telegraphic Stage

As toddlers develop their speaking vocabulary, they begin to string several words together. Like Eric in the chapter's opening vignette, children typically enter their preschool years speaking in several word utterances or short sentence-like segments. This is referred to as **telegraphic speech** because utterance includes only content words with no conjunctions, articles, prepositions, or word endings (for example, plural endings) (Tager-Flusberg, 1997), such as "daddy shoe," "go bye-bye," or "cookie all gone." This stage is significant because now the child is arranging the words in ways that communicate more complex messages.

Beginning Oral Fluency

By ages 3–4, most children will be moderately fluent in the language used at home. They use this oral language for a variety of purposes, such as asking questions, responding to others' questions, and expressing their thoughts. Throughout the remaining preschool years, as well as in elementary school, children's oral language continues to become more complex in grammar and vocabulary, and more varied in the ways that they use language to communicate with others, both in their family and in their community.

In the next section, the specific areas of language knowledge that begin to develop during the preschool years are described. Each of these areas provides a foundation for reading and writing.

Oral Language Foundations for Literacy

Areas of Language Knowledge

Children's language development involves learning the sounds and symbols of language, learning how language communicates meaning, and how language is structured during communication. More specifically, language knowledge develops in these five areas: (a) Knowledge of the symbols and sounds of language, (b) knowledge of word meanings, (c) knowledge of grammar or word order, (d) knowledge of word structure, and (e) knowledge of how language is used differently in different situations (Emmitt, Pollock, & Komesaroff, 2006; Otto, 2002, 2006). Table 3.1 provides an overview of these areas along with identifying the specific linguistic term associated with each area.

Table 3.1 Overview of Five Areas of Language Knowledge

Area of Knowledge	Description	Example	Linguistic Term
Sound System of Language	Production and perception of speech sounds and sound–symbol relationships	*Car* and *cat* are recognized as different words	Phonetic knowledge
Vocabulary	Word meanings	Ball = spherical object that rolls and bounces	Semantic knowledge
Grammar	The order in which words are used in sentences and utterances	"The ball is round" vs. "the is ball round"	Syntactic knowledge
Word Structure	Words can be changed by adding or changing parts of the word	*Verb tense:* Want Wanted Wanting *Possessive:* Matt Matt's hat *Plurality:* cat cats	Morphemic knowledge
Use of Language in Different Settings	Awareness that language use varies with the social-cultural setting	Talking on the playground vs. in classroom discussions	Pragmatic knowledge

Language development begins when an infant is considered a partner in conversation.

Solis Images

In each of these areas, this knowledge first develops receptively through listening and comprehending others' language in meaningful interactions. Based upon their comprehension of others' language, known as **receptive language,** children begin to express themselves verbally, with **expressive language.** For example, an infant first develops an awareness of what "bottle" means as he is being fed and as he hears the word used to refer to the object. Later on in infancy, he may attempt to make the speech sounds in the word "bottle" to communicate his wish to be fed. In this instance the infant is making use of his awareness of speech sounds and his knowledge of the meaning of the oral symbol, for example, "bottle."

Children acquire knowledge about written language as they are continuing to develop their knowledge of oral language. This is particularly evident in environments where children can observe and participate in activities involving reading and writing. This knowledge plays a major role in children's transactions with text, both as readers and writers. These five areas of knowledge about oral language become the "cueing systems" that children will use as they begin to actually read and write.

In the sections that follow, each of the five areas of language knowledge is described. In addition, the connections between oral language knowledge and the development of written language knowledge are described. It is important to keep in mind that these five areas of language knowledge do not develop in isolation from each other, but interact concurrently as they develop; however, they are presented separately here for the purposes of this chapter.

Knowledge of the Sound System: Phonetic

During infancy, children begin to acquire knowledge of the sounds of language and are able to discriminate between similar sounds, such as /b/ as in bat, /p/ as in pat, and /k/ as in cat. More specifically, children acquire the sounds of language that are part of their home language. They learn which sounds are important in that language. For example, in Japanese, there is no distinction made between /r/ and /l/ sounds, so those sounds are not considered different.

Children's knowledge of the sound system also includes awareness of the rhythm, tempo, intonation, and volume of speech. Young children, not yet a year old, respond differently to speech that varies in one or more of these ways. Children learn that the way in which something is said carries meaning. Their ability to perceive these differences allows them to infer the meaning of what is said. This is often observed when adults share favorite story books with toddlers who protest if a book's text is not "read" the same each time; for example, when a parent first reads *Goldilocks and the Three Bears* using different voices for the three bears and then on a different occasion does not use the same voices.

Phonetic knowledge and literacy.   Children's awareness of the sounds in spoken words contributes directly to their developing knowledge of how those sounds are represented in written language (Foy & Mann, 2006; Huba & Ramisetty-Mikler, 1995; Mann & Foy, 2003; Notari, 1996; Sensenbaugh, 1996).

The sounds of a language are transferred to print through a symbolic system or code. In alphabetic languages such as English, reading and writing involve figuring out and manipulating the sound–symbol relationships represented by the 26 letters of the alphabet. Sound–symbol relationships are *decoded* during reading and *encoded* during writing. When **decoding**, a reader will use his knowledge of individual sounds represented by letters in the words to pronounce and recognize words. Although the other areas of language knowledge are also used in the reading process, a reader needs to know the sound system in order to be successful and fluent in the decoding process.

Knowledge of sound–symbol relationships is also important in the writing process, when it is used to encode, or write, the message. During the **encoding** process, the writer determines what letters to use to represent the sounds in the words he wants to write down in his message.

The foundation for this knowledge appears to be the awareness that speech units, words, can be separated into distinct sounds, called **phonemic awareness**. Separate speech sounds are called phonemes. A **phoneme** is the smallest unit of meaningful sound in a language. For example, the word *cat* has three specific phonemes or speech sounds, /k/ /a/ /t/. It is important here to remember that the term *phoneme* refers to the speech sound and does not refer to the letters representing that sound. (**Phonics** refers to the teaching of the relationships between alphabet letters and the sounds associated with the letters and letter clusters. See further discussion in Chapter 8).

Phonemic awareness is a part of a more general concept of **phonological awareness**, which refers to awareness of the general sound structure of language and includes not only phonemes, but also syllables and other segments of sounds in words (Yopp & Yopp, 2000). Awareness of these larger units of sounds within words is acquired before the awareness of the separate phonemes (Goswami, 2002).

Researchers have documented the important role of phonological awareness in the development of literacy among young children (Foy & Mann, 2006; Goswami, 2002; Huba & Ramisetty-Mikler, 1995; Mann & Foy, 2003; Maclean, Bryant, & Bradley, 1987; National Reading Panel, 2000; Ramos-Sanchez & Cuadrado-Gordillo, 2004, Savin, 1972; Silva & Martens, 2003). This body of research has documented the role of phonological awareness as a precursor for both invented spelling and actual reading of print. Children who performed at higher levels on tasks requiring phonological awareness, such as rhyming, also performed at higher levels on early reading and writing measures.

Knowledge of Word Meanings: Semantic

Another area of language development involves vocabulary or semantic knowledge. Semantic knowledge is based in one's **conceptual knowledge**, or knowledge about the world. Conceptual knowledge develops through direct experiences interacting in home and community environments. As specific words or labels become associated with each concept, semantic knowledge of vocabulary develops. The names of persons, places, or objects (nouns) are typically learned before words representing actions (verbs) or descriptors (adjectives and adverbs). Concrete nouns such as "milk," "car," and "dog" are learned before abstract nouns such as "peace" and "happiness." As young children begin to use words to represent their thoughts and the events in the world around them, they learn that these oral symbols are powerful in communicating their ideas, thoughts, and wishes.

In addition to children's direct experiences, vicarious experiences contribute to concept and vocabulary development. **Vicarious experiences** are those in which the actual event is not directly participated in but is experienced through reading a book, watching a video, or hearing someone tell a story. For example, children's early experiences sharing picture books with parents and other adults are associated with children's increased conceptual development and vocabulary growth (Sénéchal, 1997; Wood, 2002).

Vocabulary development and literacy. When a child begins to read, his oral vocabulary provides him with a basis for figuring out and comprehending words he sees in print. For example, if a child has the concept and word for "firefly" in his oral vocabulary, he will be more successful in figuring out the word when he encounters it in a story or nonfiction text. This prior concept knowledge and vocabulary increases a child's ability to decode because of the meaning implied in the text. If a child has no prior experience with the concept and spoken word for firefly, then when he comes to the word in a text, he will need to rely on his knowledge of letter–sound relationships to decode the word.

Knowledge of Word Order: Syntactic

Young children learn that when they communicate there is a system of rules, or **syntax**, for putting words together in phrases and sentences. Meaning is not communicated when words are randomly strung together. For example, "let's read a storybook" clearly communicates a message; however, "storybook a read let's" does not. This rule system for structuring oral and written language is also referred to as **grammar**.

Each language has its own specific grammar, or syntax. For example, in English, adjectives precede the noun that they modify: The *big, blue* truck went up the hill. In Spanish, adjectives may follow the noun that they modify: *mesa* (table) *redonda* (round).

Children also learn that meaning is dependent on word order. In English for example, "The cat chased the dog" has a meaning different from "The dog chased the cat." As oral language is acquired, children learn how to use words in a certain order to make statements, ask questions, and answer questions.

Knowledge of word order and literacy. Children's knowledge of how words are arranged in phrases and sentences to create meaning contributes to their ability to comprehend when they read (Groth & Darling, 2001). In addition, children's knowledge of the ways that larger units of speech, such as oral stories, are organized is also related to literacy development.

Oral stories, also known as **narratives**, involve descriptions of the order in which events have happened and require that the speaker follow the rules of grammar associated with their language. Evidence of the early beginnings of this narrative organization of experiences occurs during toddlerhood (Baghban, 1984; Bruner, 1990; Im, Parlakian, & Osborn, 2007) and continues to develop during the preschool years (Glaubman, Kashi, & Koresh, 2001; Paley, 1981, 1990). According to Bruner (1990), narrative thought is a primary way in which we organize and interpret our experiences.

Many of our daily interactions with others are narrative-like when we describe what happened and what we experienced. Oral narratives require more complex grammar than simple conversations because telling about events that have already happened to someone who was not present when the event happened requires more precise vocabulary, clear use of pronouns, and a sequence of events in order to make our story comprehensible to our listener(s). In order to effectively use language in this more precise way, we use more complex grammar (that is, syntactic knowledge) to communicate what happened. When language is used in this way, it becomes **decontextualized language** because we are describing what happened apart from the context in which it occurred.

Children's ability to use decontextualized language in storytelling directly contributes to their comprehension of stories in text and their ability to create stories through writing (Groth & Darling, 2001). Many of children's early experiences with print in school will involve narratives or stories (Beals, 2001; Gilliam, McFadden, & van Kleeck, 1995). Thus, their experiences with storytelling during the preschool years provide them with syntactic knowledge that will help them comprehend stories when they begin the primary grades.

The decontextualization of language can be represented as a continuum that begins with conversations and continues to written stories (see Figure 3.1).

This continuum illustrates the connections between children's early experiences with storytelling and their later competencies in reading texts. In conversations, meaning is coconstructed by the participants alternating between speaker and listener roles through questioning, repetition, and elaborations. Telephone conversations require more decontextualization because the participants are not present in the same setting (Wang & Cameron, 1996).

Storytelling requires even more decontextualization than telephone conversations because it is a monologue rather than a dialogue. In storytelling, the speaker tells a story with little or no verbal interaction with the listener(s). Oral stories are less decontextualized than written stories because they are spoken language, accompanied by variations in intonation, facial expression, and gesture that provide additional meaning. When stories are written down, the language needs to be further decontextualized. This means that the language used must be comprehensible regardless of the ongoing setting: The meaning must be contained within the text itself.

Knowledge of Word Structure: Morphemic

As they develop oral language, children learn that a word's meaning can be changed by changing the word in some way. For example, in English, the plural of regular nouns is created by adding /s/ or /z/ to the singular noun form. *Dog* becomes *dogs*. *Dish* becomes *dishes*. If you want to indicate that a hat belongs to Matt, you say "that is Matt's hat" by adding /s/ to *Matt*.

Children's knowledge of how to change words can be noted in their speech. During the preschool years they begin to master the use of past tense in verbs and plural endings for regular words. Children's errors provide evidence that they are learning these regular patterns of word use (Gopnik, Meltzoff, & Kuhl, 1999). For example, the past tense of the irregular verb *fall* is *fell*; however, a preschooler might create the word *falled* instead: "He

Figure 3.1 Continuum of Decontextualization

Continuum				
Dialogue	Oral Story	Telephone Conversation	Dictated Story	Written Story

Increasing decontextualized language

falled down." Words that are irregular in forming past tense, such as *go–went–gone,* and irregular plural forms, such as *child–children,* are learned later.

Morphemic knowledge and literacy. Children's awareness of how words can be changed when speaking provides a basis for their decoding and comprehension of words when they begin to read. Through their understanding of how words are changed to show plurality, verb tense, or possession, they will be able to transfer that knowledge to their early spelling and composing attempts. Children will also rely on their oral experiences as they begin to participate in more formalized word study during the primary years. For example, a lesson which focuses on word prefixes might first require that selected words be sorted by the specific prefix and then examine how the prefix changes the word meaning; for example, the prefix *un-* in *unhappy.*

Knowledge of How to Use Language in Different Settings: Pragmatic

When acquiring oral language, children learn that language is used differently in different situations. They learn how to be socially polite by saying "please" and "thank you." They learn that language can be used in different ways to achieve different purposes in seeking information, asserting oneself, giving directions, entertaining others, or asking questions. Children may even learn which adult is most responsive to whining. Young children's conversations during dramatic play often indicate their awareness of the different ways in which language is used to communicate in different settings. For example, they will use different language if they are playing the role of a bus driver or a post office clerk.

During the preschool years, children also become aware of the ways in which language is used during shared story book time. This is especially true when children experience different types of story books, such as alphabet books, poetry, fairy tales, and nonfiction books. These experiences create awareness that language is used differently in different types of books.

Pragmatic knowledge and literacy. Based on their awareness of how language is used differently in different settings, children may use that knowledge when they begin to

Young children's conversations during dramatic play show their awareness of how language is used in different settings.

Dragon Images

interact with books. For example, in the excerpt below, Glynnis (age 3 years) and her mom are sharing an alphabet book (Otto, 1994; 1996).

> *Mom:* That one's "R."
> *Glynnis:* Well, what's "R" for?
> *Mom:* "R" is for that big flower, that rose.

Glynnis' question indicates that she is aware that the text in alphabet books has a particular format; that language is used in a particular way in alphabet books. A similar understanding of the alphabet format comes from Sharbani (Otto, 1986–1987). When asked to read the book she had created, Sharbani replied, "It's not going to be in words or anything. H for Hawaiian, another H for Hawaiian, W for water fountain." Although her book did not have any writing except for the alphabet letter on each page, her verbal response indicated that she was aware of the way language was used in alphabet books.

Children's knowledge of how language is used in books is important because it is part of their prior knowledge that supports their transactions with texts. The earlier section in this chapter on syntactic knowledge focused on children's understanding of the more complex grammar that is used in decontextualizing language in storytelling and in story texts. Decontextualized language is also present in nonfiction. For example, if you were going to explain how to pack a suitcase, you would use language differently if you were handling the suitcase and giving directions directly to a person, or if you were writing out directions for someone to follow when you were not present. Your written directions would have to be much more specific in vocabulary, more grammatically complex, and more temporal in sequence.

Book language is different from conversational language. Children's awareness of these differences comprises their pragmatic language knowledge. Book language has been referred to by several terms: **academic English, literate register**, and **academic register** (Chamot & O'Malley, 1994; Cox, Fang, & Otto, 1997; Delpit, 1992; Grant, 1995; Wong Fillmore, 1999). The term *academic English* refers to the literate or academic register in the English language. Other languages will also have a "literate" or "academic" register. Because the focus of this text is on literacy development in English-speaking classrooms, the term *academic English* will be used in this text. This specialized form of language differs in several ways from the language used in informal, everyday conversations. Wong Fillmore (1999) describes academic English as having the following distinguishing characteristics: (a) A more precise and technical vocabulary, (b) specific grammatical features, and (c) specific types of text.

Academic English is used in educational materials and is also embedded in the oral interactions that occur in classroom-learning activities (Grant, 1995). Not only is academic English used when interacting with peers and teachers during learning activities, it is also used to structure and guide one's own thoughts when engaged in academic activities (Chamot & O'Malley, 1994). The prevalence of academic English is not limited to children's educational settings, but extends to the adult world in the fields of commerce, business, law, science, and government, where specialized vocabulary, specific grammatical structures, and types of texts are used. Because academic English is so embedded in educational materials and settings, it has not always been recognized as a specialized form of language, and its importance to children's success at school has been overlooked.

Children who have not had opportunities to interact with story books or other forms of decontextualized language prior to arriving in your classroom may need to have more support in learning how to comprehend book language. Specific strategies for providing this support will be described in the later chapters of this text.

Metalinguistic Knowledge

In addition to developing knowledge in each of the five areas, children also develop a conscious awareness of specific features of language, its structure, and how language units (sounds, words, text segments) can be manipulated (Clark, 1978; Ely, Gleason, MacGibbon, & Zaretsky, 2001; Lazo, Pumfrey, & Peers, 1997; Read, 1978). This knowledge is referred to as **metalinguistic knowledge**. It means that a person is able to consciously reflect on language as an object of thought. Phonemic awareness and phonological awareness are forms of metalinguistic knowledge.

Evidence of metalinguistic knowledge may be present in children's responses around the age of four or five years. Metalinguistic knowledge appears to be influenced by children's experiences and contexts in which language is used (Rowe & Harste, 1986). A more complex form of metalinguistic knowledge is evident when children can explain their language concepts or use comparison and contrast in talking about language-related concepts. For example, when Julie (age 5 years, 7 months) was asked, "What is a word?" she did not respond. When she was asked, "What's your favorite word?" she replied, "Red. That was my first word" (Otto, 1979).

Younger children are usually not able to respond to such metalinguistic questions. For example, Julie's younger brother, Robbie (age 3 years, 3 months) gave the following responses to the same questions. When asked, "What is a word?" he responded, "I'll tell you numbers, nine." When then asked, "What is a favorite word of yours?" he responded by saying, "I don't like questions".

Metalinguistic knowledge is an important development because beginning reading and writing instruction may explicitly focus on specific language concepts such as letters, sounds, and words. Tasks eliciting children's phonemic and phonological awareness require that children communicate their metalinguistic knowledge because they are asked to consciously manipulate the sound elements or units in a word (Yopp & Yopp, 2000).

When children are able to respond to a request to recognize or identify certain language-related concepts such as "word," "rhyme," "sound," or "letter", they are using their metalinguistic knowledge. For example, being aware that *pat* and *cat* rhyme, a child then uses that knowledge to select a similar rhyming word from several choices, for example, *man, mat,* or *map.* In a lesson on word prefixes in third grade, children will need to verbalize their awareness of how words change when specific prefixes are used, such as *un-* in *unhappy, untrue,* and *undone.* This ability to verbalize will also be evident when children explain how they figured out an unknown word based on their knowledge of word structure, such as the word *remarkable* (*re*—to do again; *mark*—to take note; *able*—capable of; see Herrell & Jordan, 2006, p. 14).

Children's ability to talk about their language concepts also contributes to reading and writing development, because it allows them to talk about the ways in which they are reading and writing. When teachers observe children's metalinguistic comments as they interact with reading and writing, it provides a window to children's thought processes and experimentation with written language. Children's comments about language show the ways in which they are reflecting on their use of language and the decisions they are making (Rowe & Harste, 1986).

Diversity in Early Childhood Settings

Early childhood settings today serve a population that is increasingly diverse. This diversity includes differences in social-economic status, culture, and ethnicity, as well as language.

While most of the emphasis has been on recognizing language diversity, it is also important to recognize the complex relationships among language, culture, and social interactions. In this section, we will focus on eight key guidelines for supporting the development of language and literacy among children from diverse settings. Future chapters will present additional guidelines related to specific developmental levels and literacy activities.

Key Guidelines for Teachers in Diverse Settings

1. Become familiar with the children's individual diversities. As an early childhood teacher, you will have children who come to your classroom who represent a range of diversities with respect to social-cultural characteristics, as well as ethnicities and language. Each child has his own unique combination of diversities. To effectively prepare learning experiences you need to become familiar with your children's diverse backgrounds and settings.

A first step in becoming familiar with children's diversities is to recognize each child's home-language setting. Children acquire the language that is spoken in their homes and communities (Emmitt, Pollock, & Komesaroff, 2003). This may be a language distinctly different from English or it may be a dialect of English, such as African American English. Variations of a language that develop within a specific population or geographic region are referred to as **dialects**. For example, in the United States there are regional dialects, such as Central Midland, Southwest, and Middle Atlantic (Owens, 2005). Each dialect has specific linguistic features, such as the way words are pronounced and how words are combined into sentences and phrases, as well as specific vocabulary, morphemes, and uses of the dialect in different interactions. For example, different areas of the United States use different words to refer to the same concept. In the Chicago area, multilane roads are called *expressways*; in New York, they are called *thruways*; in New Jersey, *parkways*; and in other dialect areas, *turnpikes* (Fromkin & Rodman, 1998).

The concept of linguistic diversity applies not only to the ways in which oral language is used in different cultural-social contexts; it also refers to the ways in which written language is used in children's homes and communities. Through their experiences in their homes and communities, children learn how reading and writing are used. Emmitt, Pollock, and Komesaroff (2003) point out that reading and writing instruction cannot be isolated from the ways in which written language is used in homes and communities.

Within these different home and community contexts, young children begin to develop their language and literacy competencies. These cultural-social contexts influence not only the language that is learned but the ways in which language is used to communicate and interact (Delpit, 2002; Faltis, 1998; Hart & Risley, 1995; Heath, 1983). For example, different cultures have different storytelling traditions (Heath, 1983; Karmiloff & Karmiloff-Smith, 2001; McCabe, 1997; Shiro, 1995). Thus, children from diverse cultures and home languages may have different narrative experiences and expectations. Narratives created by young children from diverse cultures have been found to differ in content as well as structure (McCabe, 1992; Muñoz, Gillam, Peña, & Gulley-Faehnle, 2003).

When children attend early childhood settings outside of their homes, they may encounter a different social-cultural-linguistic setting than they experienced at home. With this in mind, it is important for early childhood teachers to recognize and validate the ways in which children experience reading and writing in their communities and homes. While reading and writing activities are important ways in which learning occurs in academic settings, they also are ways in which social, cultural, and economic communication takes place (Owocki, 2001).

2. Acknowledge, accept, and value children's diversities. A child's personal identity and culture are closely tied to the child's home language (Delpit, 1990). A teacher's attitude toward linguistic and cultural-social diversity impacts children's learning interactions and motivation to learn (Cary, 2000; Saracho & Spodek, 1995; Scott, 1995). For example, if a teacher implies that a child's home language is not acceptable or valued, this negative feeling also extends to the family and affects the child's responsiveness in the classroom, as well as the parents' involvement and rapport with the teacher. The realization that children are developing different language competencies and use different languages or dialects does not mean that these differences represent deficiencies. The way in which language differences (dialect or second language) are interpreted by teachers and administrators in the educational setting will determine whether the differences become a negative factor in children's literacy development. Teachers need to create positive learning environments where children's diversities are accepted and celebrated.

3. Recognize and value children's prior experiences. In many educational settings, reading and writing competencies have been narrowly defined to focus only on the skills needed for success in school. This narrow perspective excludes and devalues the literacy-related competencies found in a broader range of social and cultural situations present in more diverse communities. Research on inner-city families by Purcell-Gates (1996) described a wide range of literacy-related activities that were embedded in everyday activities among the families studied, for example, board games, religious materials, newspapers, food coupons, movie ads, job-related reading and writing, newspapers, and magazines.

Where differences exist between the home setting and the school setting with respect to language and literacy use, children will be faced with adjustments at school. These adjustments may be with language; with the definitions of, and uses for, literacy; as well as with the structure of narratives. Language differences do not necessarily mean that children are deficient in language.

When these social-cultural literacy-related experiences are ignored and not validated, young children see the tasks of schooling as completely separate from their home culture and community. This may affect their interest in school and their level of participation in the academic learning community. In addition, the failure of the educational system to understand and value diverse cultural and linguistic contexts contributes to the belief that children of diversity cannot succeed. This becomes a self-fulfilling prophecy for many children. As an early childhood teacher, you have an important role in providing experiences that enhance children's learning and development in ways that build upon children's prior language and literacy experiences (Ogbu, 1999).

4. Avoid making assumptions based on children's diversities. Even though children may have similar ethnicities or home languages, teachers should recognize each child as having a unique combination of social-cultural-linguistic experiences. Research has identified complex interrelationships between literacy development, culture, and diversity (Heath, 1983; Taylor & Dorsey-Gaines, 1988; Teale, 1986; Tindall & Nisbet, 2004). Simply because a child comes from a particular social-cultural and/or linguistic diversity does not mean that she will have the same learning style or prior knowledge as other children from that same grouping.

While researchers have noted associations between social-economic status (SES) and children's early academic skills, parent–child interactions, and literacy-related events (Dodici, Draper, & Peterson, 2003; Ninio, 1980; Walker, Greenwood, Hart, & Carta, 1994), other researchers have concluded that SES alone does not explain differences in children's literacy development (Baghban, 1984; Heath, 1983; Teale, 1986).

More recently, Hart and Risley (1995) conducted longitudinal research on language development among families ranging in SES (upper, middle, lower, and welfare level).

Of all of the factors they studied in relation to subsequent language (and early literacy) competencies, the "most important difference among families was in the amount of talking that went on" (p. 192). The "increased amounts of talking provided some children vastly more experience with nearly every quality feature of language and interaction" (p. 192). The longitudinal data showed that children of parents with a higher amount of talking had more developed language competencies that were also associated with higher language and literacy skills in elementary school.

While there are some patterns identified in research, it is important for teachers to remember that not all children and families are the same. Within your classroom, you will want to focus on each child's individual characteristics rather than on their membership in a specific social, cultural, or linguistic group.

5. Acknowledge and build on children's prior knowledge (Moll & González, 2004). Children from culturally and linguistically diverse settings will bring to your classroom knowledge they have gained through their families and their own personal experiences. By acknowledging children's prior knowledge and building on it, learning activities at school will be more relevant and encourage more active, engaged learning from all children. For example, when you select learning materials that represent concepts and vocabulary that are present in children's respective social-cultural settings, they will be able to participate more fully due to their prior experiences and knowledge.

6. Encourage children to continue to use their home languages and dialects (NAEYC, 1996). Children who develop fluency in two or more languages have higher levels of metalinguistic awareness, increased awareness of language structure, more diverse perspectives, and increased social skills (Ben Zeev, 1977; Genesee, Tucker, & Lambert, 1975; Goodz, Legare, & Bilodeau, 1987; Ianco-Worrall, 1972). Because language is an inherent part of one's culture, children who lose the ability to speak in their home language experience a loss in the ability to communicate effectively with their families (Wong Fillmore, 1991).

7. Encourage all children to develop academic English. While it is important to support children's linguistic and cultural diversity, it is also important to encourage children to develop the knowledge of how language is used in academic settings as well as other contexts of literacy (for example, business, government, and politics). In other words, encourage children to be linguistically flexible, so that they can interact effectively in a wide range of social, educational, and cultural contexts.

In Delpit's (1988) pioneering work in understanding linguistic diversity in educational settings, she emphasized the importance of teaching all children "the codes needed to participate fully in the mainstream of American life" (p. 296). Among the codes that Delpit refers to is academic English. To fail to prepare children to develop competencies in interacting with academic English is to limit their current and future participation in the larger society.

8. Recognize and support English language learners (ELLs). Your support of ELLs will need to be focused in three main areas: (1) their acquisition of English, (2) their interactions with texts, and (3) their interactions with the contexts of literacy.

Supporting ELLs' acquisition of English. Children whose home language is different from English will be faced with learning a new language, English, when they begin to interact in early childhood classrooms. For an English language learner, his home language provides a basis for understanding how language works and is used in his home and community environments. This knowledge base includes knowledge of oral language as well as knowledge of written language. ELLs use knowledge of their home language and how it works as they begin to interact in settings where the new or target language, such as English, is used (Bruer, 1999; Collier, 1995; Cummins, 1979; Drucker, 2003; Krashen, 1997, 2003a). Children whose home languages have similarities to English with respect to letter–sound relations, grammar, or vocabulary will be able to learn English easier (Pang & Kamil, 2004). For example, Spanish and English have more similarities with respect to letter–sound correspondences than do Russian and English.

Expect ELLs to acquire their second language (such as English) in the same developmental stages as native speakers of English. Learning another language involves distinguishing between two different language systems. Each language system involves the five areas of language knowledge: phonetic, semantic, syntactic, morphemic, and pragmatic. There will be times when children may mix up the two systems, for example, mixing Spanish vocabulary words with English words. This is to be expected.

It is also typical for English language learners to have a "silent period" while they are developing receptive language through listening (Krashen, 1981, 1982; Santos & Ostrosky, 2002; Tabors, 1997). During this time they will rarely participate verbally but appear to be observing others and comprehending what others say.

English language learners develop conversational skills in English before they develop academic English. ELLs are usually able to develop conversational English, also referred to as Basic Interpersonal Communication Skills (or BICS), in two to three years (Collier, 1995; Cummins, 1994). In contrast, it will take five to seven years to develop academic English, also referred to as Cognitive Academic Proficiency Skills (or CALPS). The acquisition of academic English may even take longer if the child does not have any formal schooling in their home language before they come to the United States (Collier, 1995). Because of this extended time needed to develop academic English, ELLs need to have extra language and literacy support long after they have developed conversational fluency in English.

Supporting ELLs' interactions with text. In their interactions with text, ELLs are influenced by their prior experiences with various types of texts. Because each social-cultural group has specific ways in which literacy and language are used (for example, Dyson, 2003; Hart & Risley, 1995; Heath, 1983; Teale, 1986; Zentella, 2005), it is important for teachers to provide texts for ELLs that acknowledge their prior experiences with different types of text in their home and community social-cultural settings as well as texts that build upon their prior knowledge (Brisk & Harrington, 2000; Cappellini, 2005). For example, *A Day's Work* (Bunting, 1994) is about an immigrant grandfather and grandson and their first job. This book might be relevant for children who have recently arrived in the United States.

Because comprehension is a key aspect of both reading and writing, vocabulary development has a critical role in the acquisition of literacy competencies for English language learners. You can support their interactions with text by emphasizing vocabulary development. Children who are learning English as their second language experience two types of vocabulary development. The first type occurs when they have the necessary conceptual knowledge but do not have the actual word in their English vocabulary, only in their home vocabulary. For this type of vocabulary learning, you will need to provide opportunities for them to associate the English word with their existing concept and home-language word. For example, the concept of a dog is represented in Spanish with the word *perro*. To learn the English vocabulary for this concept would involve activities that associate the word *dog* with their concept for *perro*.

The second type of vocabulary development for ELLs occurs when they do not have the conceptual knowledge for a particular vocabulary word and must develop both the concept and the English vocabulary. Thus, the learning process for this type of vocabulary development is much more complex. For this type of vocabulary development you will want to provide hands-on direct experiences with the concepts as well as vicarious experiences.

Supporting ELLs' interactions in literacy contexts. The contexts of reading and writing within the school environment may reflect similar settings for literacy-related activities experienced by ELL children, or there may be dramatic differences. In instances where there are differences between ELL children's prior experiences and the classroom context, you will need to focus on creating an appropriate learning environment for reading and writing that draws on children's prior experiences in their social-cultural contexts (George, Raphael, & Florio-Ruane, 2003; Grant & Wong, 2003). For example, instead of assigning a standard topic for children's individual essays, you could encourage them to write about their own experiences in their home country or after they arrived in the United States (Tindall & Nisbet, 2004).

Supporting ELLs through reflective teaching. A key aspect of Comprehensive Literacy Instruction involves teachers' professional knowledge and decision-making along with their interaction strategies. As teachers provide mediated instruction, their decisions, knowledge base, resources, and interactions with students need to reflect knowledge and awareness of the complex transactions that are occurring between each ELL reader, the text, and the context (see Figure 2.7). According to Valdes (1998),

> a critical practice of English-language teaching must begin by critically examining and exploring students' knowledges, histories, and cultures in ways that are both affirming and supportive. (p. 16)

Your mediated instruction with ELL children must also reflect an awareness of each learner's zone of proximal development (Cummins, 2003; Vygotsky, 1978). Unless you consider each child's prior knowledge and experiences and their level of independent learning, you will not be able to structure and implement appropriate learning activities that support and guide ELL children's literacy development. In mediating their learning, you also need to provide **comprehensible input** (Krashen, 1995, 2003a). This means that you use English that is at a level that the ELL can comprehend. This level is usually just beyond the learner's current independent level for using English.

Continuum of Literacy Development

Just as children progress through different phases when they are developing oral language, they also progress through different phases as they are developing knowledge of written language. During the past three decades, research on literacy development has increased our awareness that knowledge about reading and writing develops during the preschool years before children begin to read and write in the conventional sense, and prior to formal reading or writing instruction. This recognition of children's gradual development of knowledge about reading and writing is called **emergent literacy** (Clay, 1966; Teale & Sulzby, 1986). This gradual development of literacy can be represented in a continuum (see Figure 3.2).

This continuum incorporates four phases of emergent literacy: observation, exploration, experimentation, and communication, and leads to a final phase in which children are reading and writing conventionally. Throughout this text, each of these phases will be described in terms of specific characteristics and language knowledge as well as developmentally

Figure 3.2
Emergent Literacy
Continuum

Phase I	Phase II →	Phase III →	Phase IV →	Phase V
				Conventional
Observation	Exploration	Experimentation	Communication	Reading/Writing

appropriate instructional practices that enhance children's development of literacy-related knowledge and skills.

Phase I: Observation

In this initial phase of emergent literacy, children observe family members and others in their community as they interact with written language in the course of their daily lives. For example, children observe others (adults and older siblings) interacting with newspapers, magazines, and books. Children may notice signs in the neighborhood and associate meaning with the signs (such as McDonald's restaurant signs). Children observe the ways in which others write letters, notes, and lists. Children who have home environments where literacy interactions occur on a regular basis may begin this observation phase during infancy.

Phase II: Exploration

The second phase of emergent literacy begins when children begin to interact with and manipulate written materials. In literate environments, this behavior typically occurs among older toddlers and early preschoolers (2½ to 4 years of age). They begin to pick up and interact with junk mail, books, and magazines used by family members; story books used in shared reading with a caregiver; and product packaging (such as cereal boxes).

In the initial phase of emergent literacy, children observe others' interactions with books and other printed materials.

Anna Jurkovska

Sometimes they pretend to read and other times they ask an adult to read to them. Children in this phase also seem fascinated with making marks on paper (as well as walls, tablecloths, and furniture). They may take their writing to an adult and ask "What dis say?" These emergent literacy behaviors indicate children are aware that written language carries meaning and want to explore this meaning.

Phase III: Experimentation

In this third phase of emergent literacy, children are active experimenters in using their developing knowledge about reading and writing to create written messages through drawing, scribbling, invented letters, and invented spelling. Children in this phase attempt to recreate story book texts that have been read to them by following clues in the illustrations. Through this experimentation children begin to see patterns in the way language is used to read and write and begin to predict how language is used in different contexts. This phase is typically seen among older preschool children and kindergartners.

Phase IV: Communication

In phase four, children are beginning to read and write. They are able to use writing to create simple messages using a combination of invented spelling and conventional spelling. For example, when Katie (age 6) wrote about her experience climbing on rocks during a hike, she wrote: "DEAR JRNL I HAD A TUF DA" ("Dear Journal, I had a tough day.") (Baghban, 2007, p. 22). Along with her writing, she drew a picture of her experiences. (See also Figure 3.3 for a sample from a kindergartner's writing journal.)

Children in this phase are beginning to recognize and accurately pronounce high-frequency words. In addition, they can comprehend more complex stories during shared story book time. In literate settings, these competencies will be typical of kindergarten and early primary children.

In the third phase of emergent literacy, children experiment with ways of "reading" a familiar book.

Oksana Kuzmina

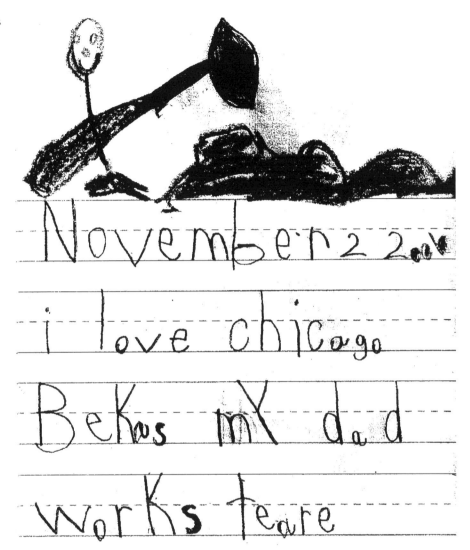

Figure 3.3 Child's
Emergent Writing

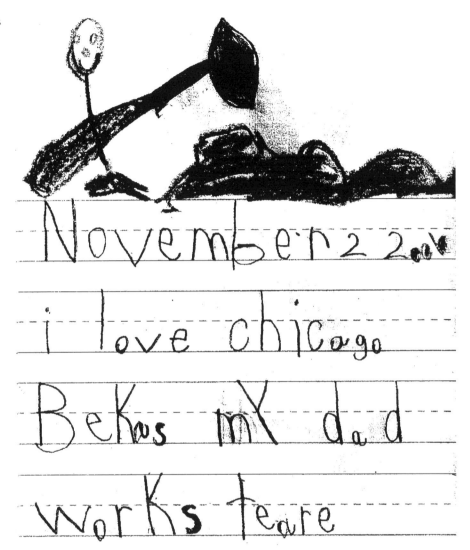

November 2 2

i love chicago

Bekos mY dad

works teare

Phase V: Conventional Reading and Writing

This phase marks the transition to writing conventionally and independent reading. This phase typically begins in late first grade and second grade. As children progress through the elementary grades they continue to develop competencies in using reading and writing for communication as well as for learning.

As an early childhood teacher, you will probably be assigned to a particular age level or grade level. You might be teaching in a room for toddlers or in a kindergarten. Although your instructional efforts will be focused on a specific developmental level within the early childhood years, it is important that you are aware of the entire sequence of literacy development. Children who are at the same age level will not all be in the same phase of literacy development. You will need to be able to carefully observe each child's language and literacy interactions and determine each child's zone of proximal development. Then you will be able to determine which experiences will facilitate each child's literacy development.

Chapter Summary

Children's development of reading and writing begins with their development of oral language in social-cultural settings. Children's early explorations with oral communication involve cooing and babbling. Their oral expressions become more complex as they begin to engage in echolalic babbling, creating their own words, and developing telegraphic speech. Around the age of four years, they develop more fluency in speaking and increase the grammatical complexity of their speech.

Language knowledge is developed in five areas: phonetic, semantic, syntactic, morphemic, and pragmatic. From this oral language foundation, children gradually develop knowledge of written language. When children begin to interact with written language, they use their knowledge in these five areas to comprehend texts and to create their own written messages. Children also develop metalinguistic knowledge which contributes to their ability to consciously manipulate language and to reflect on the ways in which they are using language.

Early childhood settings are increasingly diverse. Children's linguistic diversities also involve social-cultural and ethnic diversities. These varied contexts influence not only the language that is learned but the ways in which language is used to communicate and interact. Early childhood teachers have an important role in providing experiences that enhance all children's learning and development by building upon their prior language and literacy experiences.

Chapter Review

1. Terms to know:

echolalic babbling	syntax
idiomorphs	grammar
telegraphic speech	narratives
receptive language	decontextualized
expressive language	language
decoding	academic English
encoding	literate register
phonemic awareness	academic register
phoneme	metalinguistic knowledge
phonics	BICS
phonological knowledge	CALPS
conceptual knowledge	comprehensible input
vicarious experiences	emergent literacy

2. What are the five areas of language knowledge? Provide an example of each.

3. When does language development begin?

4. How do intonation, rhythm, and volume contribute to the comprehension of another's speech?

5. In what ways do the five areas of language knowledge provide a foundation for learning to read and write? Give specific examples.

6. How is academic register different from the language used in everyday, informal conversations? Why do children need to learn to use academic register?

7. Select one of the eight key guidelines for teachers in diverse settings. Describe a specific classroom activity that follows this guideline.

Chapter Extension Activities

In-class or Online Discussion: Describe your experiences in a setting where a dialect or language was spoken that was different from your home language or dialect. Indicate how old you were and describe the setting. How did this experience increase your awareness of the role of language in cultural-social settings?

Observation: Observe two children during free-play time in a toddler classroom. Describe the ways in which each child communicates verbally and nonverbally. Relate your observations to the stages of language development. Include specific examples.

Research:

a. Select a professional journal article on linguistic diversity that was published in the past five years. Prepare a written summary of the article and describe how the article relates to chapter content. Suggested journals include: *Childhood Education, Young Children, Early Childhood Research Quarterly, Early Childhood Care and Development*, and *Child Development*.

b. Audiotape a child's talk while he or she is looking at a story book. Transcribe the tape and analyze the child's use of language in terms of pronunciation, vocabulary, grammar, and use of plural endings and past tense. Present your analysis in class.

Chapter 4

Signs of Emergent Literacy Among Infants and Toddlers: Observation and Exploration

> Ellie (5 months old) is sitting on her father's lap. He is reading *The Wall Street Journal*. Occasionally he reads aloud. Ellie gazes at the paper in front of her and occasionally brushes the paper with her hand as she randomly moves her arm.
>
> Glynnis (11 months old) is seated on the floor with several story books around her. She picks up one book, opens it, and begins to vocalize speechlike sounds of varied intonations. She turns the pages one by one and continues her vocalizations as she looks at each page.

Each of these vignettes describes young children observing and exploring literacy-related events. In Ellie's setting, she is observing her father as he interacts with a newspaper. In Glynnis' exploration of books, she is showing that she already knows how to interact with story books. She knows that speech accompanies story book experiences and that varied intonations are used during these interactions. Both of these children are from homes where their parents have high levels of literacy. From early on these children will have many opportunities to experience literacy-related events. These experiences contribute to their emergent literacy and support their development of later, more complex literacy-related knowledge and competencies.

In this chapter, we will focus on describing young children as they observe and explore literacy-related events in their home and community environments. Evidence for this emergent literacy has been documented in descriptive, longitudinal, and case-study research with infants and toddlers in home or homelike settings and tasks (Baghban, 1984; Doake, 1986; Joyner & Ray, 1987; Lamme & Packer, 1986; Ninio & Bruner, 1978; Otto, 1994, 1996, 1997). Although this research has involved only limited samples of young children and its findings cannot be generalized to all infants and toddlers, the detailed and descriptive nature of this research is valuable because it contributes to our understanding of the beginnings of emergent literacy.

As reflective teachers of young children, we can then use this knowledge of infants' and toddlers' emergent literacy behaviors to more appropriately develop and implement valuable literacy-related experiences in early childhood settings. The following chapter (Chapter 5) focuses on the specific ways in which this knowledge of emergent literacy can be used to plan and implement developmentally appropriate experiences for infants and toddlers.

Oral Language and Emergent Literacy

Children's development of oral language provides a foundation for the development of emergent literacy. As infants and toddlers acquire their home languages, they learn from the daily routine activities of their families as well as from the special events that occur. Young children's waking hours are characterized by constant learning as the brain processes the events that take place. As described in Chapter 3, young children's oral language development is characterized by the development of language knowledge in these five areas: phonetic, semantic, syntactic, morphemic, and pragmatic. This language knowledge provides a foundation for the development of their knowledge of written language.

Family and community experiences provide the context in which infants and toddlers not only acquire oral language but also observe their parents and family members interacting with written language. As young children develop communication skills and begin to explore their home environments, their curiosity about their surroundings and the events taking place draws them into literacy-related transactions with family members. For example, these experiences may involve reading a child's story book aloud, reading a magazine or a newspaper, using a computer, writing a check, or composing a grocery list. In homes where these types of literacy-related activities occur, children first observe how written language is used. Then they begin to explore it on their own and when they interact with family members. Early literacy-related behaviors documented in the research described here contribute to our awareness of how these experiences may nurture and enhance development of written language knowledge.

Observing and Exploring Written Language

This section offers evidence from emergent literacy research that documents young children's early observations and explorations of written language; however, it is important to keep in mind that children will respond differently to literacy-related events in their home and in community environments. Some young children exhibit an intense interest in reading and writing activities. Others appear to be interested in learning about other aspects of their environments. These individual differences among children are to be expected. According to Owocki (2001), "Children's unique interests, ways of knowing, and dispositions influence how and to what extent they participate in early literacy events, and in turn, the knowledge they construct" (p. 5).

Research on emergent literacy among infants and toddlers has focused on two specific contexts of interactions between parent and child: picture-book sharing and explorations of environmental print. In each of these contexts, research has begun to describe young children's developing literacy. Another area of research, though limited, involves toddlers' early writing attempts.

Picture-Book Sharing

When parents share picture books with their young children, they are introducing them to the ways in which written language and illustrations are used to communicate meaning.

In this interaction, the book is the focal point for both the parent and the young child. Young children's interactions with picture books provide a context for oral language development (Evans, 1978; Karrass & Braungart-Rieker, 2005), as well as for developing knowledge of written language, because this book sharing involves oral language that mediates the written story.

In this section, infants' and toddlers' literacy-related behaviors during story book sharing are described. These behaviors have been documented by researchers who carefully observed infants' and toddlers' verbal and nonverbal behaviors during story book sharing (Baghban, 1984; Doake, 1986; Joyner & Ray, 1987; Lamme & Packer, 1986; Ninio & Bruner, 1978; Otto, 1996, 1997). Most of the research documenting these interactions has focused on parents, mainly mothers, and their young children. There is very little research documenting these early literacy interactions in child care settings.

Among children who have frequent opportunities to engage in story book sharing, there is a gradual progression from receptive observer to active participant (Campbell, 2001; Joyner & Ray, 1987; Lamme & Packer, 1986; Makin, 2006; Murphy, 1978; Otto, 1994; Schickedanz, 1981).

Early infancy (birth–7 months): Observing. Parents may begin story book interactions long before young children can talk or even begin to verbalize (Joyner & Ray, 1987; Im, Parlakian, & Osborn, 2007; Lamme & Packer, 1986; Makin, 2006; McKechnie, 2006). In this first level of interaction, very young infants (birth–3 months) simply listened to their parents' voices as the picture books were shared. Cuddling their infants in their arms, parents engaged their infants' attention by pointing at the illustrations and labeling them, making up short textlike segments or reading segments of text. Lulled by their parents' voices, young infants appeared to enjoy the rhythms and varied intonation as books were shared. These interactions occurred as part of everyday life, were relatively spontaneous, and were contingent upon the attentiveness and interest of the infant. At the first sign of disinterest, observant parents discontinued the particular book or the book sharing session. Many interactions lasted only a few minutes before infants became distracted or inattentive (Honig & Shin, 2001).

These young infants may also begin to show an interest in the physical properties of the book. They begin to reach out to touch or pat it, or may wave their arms toward it. Further exploration may occur as infants attempt to chew or suck on the book.

Late infancy (8–12 months): Early responding. During this time, two specific developmental achievements relate to picture-book sharing events: object permanence (Trawick-Smith, 2003) and symbolic thought (Frost, Wortham, & Reifel, 2001 in Trawick-Smith, 2003). With the acquisition of object permanence, children understand that objects still exist when they are not seen or heard. Symbolic thought occurs as they begin to associate verbal labels with real objects and with pictures of objects. These two developments are accompanied by more active responses during book sharing events.

Older infants now showed more specific book-related knowledge, such as knowing how to orient the book, beginning the book reading at the front, with the right side up, and then turning the pages from front to back. They were able to join in by babbling or making sounds to go along with the actions or animal characters in the story. They also pointed to the illustrations and occasionally used rising intonation along with the pointing, as if asking a question. As attention span increased during later infancy, they became more active verbally and nonverbally in the book sharing by attempting to help turn the pages, imitating parents' gestures, and laughing, smiling, or giggling in anticipation of upcoming story events.

In the following two examples, Glynnis' (11 months old) gestures and vocalizations indicated she was predicting upcoming story events (Otto, 1994).

> Glynnis and her mother, Suzanne, were looking at a picture book that had been shared at numerous story times. As they shared the book, Glynnis appeared to be anticipating book content through her gestures. As Suzanne turned the page on which the text said, "pat your head," and before Suzanne read the page, Glynnis reached up and patted her head. Then as Suzanne turned to the page that said, "wiggle your toes," Glynnis wiggled her toes just moments before her mother read the text.

> During another picture book interaction, Glynnis indicated further her memory for book content when she responded with animal sounds simultaneously with her mother as the page and hidden animals were viewed. In this particular book, the illustrations of animals were hidden under flaps. Suzanne did not read the text word for word, but instead had created a "text" for each page that focused on the hidden animals. Glynnis eagerly manipulated each flap to see the animal pictured underneath while enthusiastically making the animal's sound. After they had reached the end of the book, Glynnis flipped several pages back and repeated her interaction with the page on which the roaring lion was hidden under the flap, by lifting the flap and making a roaring sound.

Glynnis' parents indicated they had begun to share story books with her when she was four months old. At the time of the above observations, Glynnis was 11 months old. Although she was not yet speaking in words, she was participating and verbalizing in ways that indicated she was remembering book content, predicting upcoming book events, and attempting to participate in the story sharing.

Infants' independent picture-book interactions. Some older infants may also seek out picture books and interact with them independently. One such instance involved an 11-month-old infant (Otto, 1994), who over the course of a five-minute observation spontaneously interacted independently with three different picture books. As she paged through each book, her gaze went from page to page, accompanied by babbling that appeared to imitate the dramatic intonations her mother had used during earlier picture-book sharing. In addition, the infant held the book so that it was right-side-up and began at the front of the book. In another instance, a nine-month-old was observed for a 10-minute period during which she silently paged through several books, appearing to focus intently on the illustrations, and repeatedly paged through a part of a book.

Toddlerhood (12–30 months): Actively participating. When children enter toddlerhood, they are beginning to walk independently. For this reason, picture-book sharing with young toddlers may decrease in length and frequency, due to children's new mobility and interest in exploring their surroundings (Lamme & Packer, 1986; Joyner & Ray, 1987). Though each session may be only a few minutes, the daily opportunities for story sharing results in a cumulative effect in the preschool years, enhancing the acquisition of knowledge about written language (Adams, 1990; Literacy Partners of Manitoba, 1999).

Toddlers' story sharing sessions became more interactive as they began to participate more verbally as well as nonverbally, especially with favorite or familiar books. As their attention span increased, longer story book sharing sessions took place.

Labeling, commenting, and asking questions. Toddlers now became engaged in labeling and in opportunities to fill in a character's name, rhyming word, or predictable refrain. Children's participation in this labeling was encouraged by parents who interpreted their child's nonverbal behaviors (smiling, reaching, and pointing) as well as her babbling as either a request for a label or an attempt to provide a label for the picture in the book (Ninio and Bruner, 1978).

Older toddlers began to spontaneously point to illustrations (Murphy, 1978) and ask questions and make comments, as well as label actions or objects. When children engage in labeling or commenting, it indicates their awareness that books have meaning and that meaning is stable across repeated interactions with that text.

Attending to print. Toddlers may also begin to explore print by focusing on it during shared book interactions. In the following example, Ryan (1 year, 9 months old) indicated his curiosity with individual letters that were part of the inside cover design in *Richard Scarry's Best Word Book Ever* (1963). As the picture-book interaction began, Ryan spontaneously pointed to letters of the alphabet on the inside cover pages and made sounds. His mother then started to pronounce the correct letter name as he pointed to each letter. He occasionally took her finger and used it to point to the letters. Each time, she said the letter name. This interaction continued for about two minutes.

Toddlers' independent interactions. In addition to enjoying picture-book interactions, toddlers may also seek opportunities to engage in story books independently. In these instances, they are likely to select a picture book that is very familiar and will page through the book, labeling the actions or objects pictured or making the sounds associated with illustrations. For example, Ryan (1 year, 8 months) picked up a book that had a cat featured in it. He opened up the book, pointed to the cat and said, "me-ow." He then continued for several pages, repeating "me-ow, me-ow."

Implications of research. Infants and toddlers who have had frequent opportunities to engage in story book sharing with their parents have shown progressively more verbal and

Toddlers who have had frequent opportunities to explore books learn how to handle books and turn pages.

Zaikina

Figure 4.1 Key Emergent Literacy Behaviors During Picture-Book Sharing with Adults

❖ Shared gaze, looking at illustrations to which the parent is pointing

❖ Facial expressions indicating comprehension or prediction of book content

❖ Attempts to turn pages and assist in holding the book

❖ Shows memory for story content by verbal and nonverbal behaviors (gestures, verbalization, or sounds) in predicting upcoming events portrayed in the picture/story book

❖ Uses gestures or questionlike verbalizations to elicit responses from parent

❖ Participates in labeling objects or actions pictured, or in asking for the parent to provide the label, indicating listening vocabulary and expressive vocabulary

nonverbal involvement. Figure 4.1 provides a list of specific emergent literacy behaviors observed in older infants and toddlers.

While additional research is needed to clarify more clearly the developmental progression of infants' and toddlers' picture-book interactions, these detailed descriptions have furthered our awareness of the importance of providing opportunities for very young children to observe and explore picture books with adults as well as time to explore books independently.

Does this mean that we should expect that all infants and toddlers will or should show these emergent literacy behaviors? No, it does not. There are several reasons for this. First, these emergent literacy behaviors have been documented in only a relatively small sample of young children. Additional research is needed that will focus on larger populations of infants and toddlers, and also include more diverse settings. Second, young children vary in their interests in story book sharing. Not all infants and toddlers will show the same interest in story book sharing activities. Thus, parents and teachers will want to be sensitive to the interests and developmental needs of each child. Providing opportunities for shared book time is important. Insisting that every child participate is not developmentally appropriate. Third, although we are beginning to understand the interaction patterns and mediation that support story book sharing with infants and toddlers, much more research needs to be done.

Exploring Environmental Print

In addition to observing and exploring written language during picture-book interactions, infants and toddlers begin to observe and explore written language in other daily events at home and in their communities. Children may observe their parents interacting with a wide variety of print found in their environment. Examples of **environmental print** include newspapers, business letters, advertisements, magazines, road signs, business signs, product logos and labels, personal correspondence, and shopping lists. As these encounters with environmental print occur, young children observe and then begin to explore what these various forms of printed material mean and how they work. These explorations contribute to children's developing pragmatic knowledge of language—knowledge about the ways in which language is used in different settings and contexts.

For example, in one of the opening vignettes to this chapter, Ellie's early experiences of sitting on her father's lap while he read the newspaper provided opportunities to begin to learn about ways in which written language is used during the day. Seeing the pages turned and hearing her father read aloud added to her experience.

While Ellie's participation in these early experiences during infancy was at the level of passive observation, examples of active exploration of environmental print are seen

The daily event of receiving the mail can provide opportunity for young children to interact with varied forms of print.

Olesya Feketa

among children later on during the toddler and preschool years. When children's level of oral language development is at the telegraphic stage of two to three words per utterance, they may begin to ask questions about ongoing events and also may begin to ask questions about print in their environment or attempt to read it (Walton, 1989).

For example, the daily event of receiving the mail can provide an opportunity for young children to interact with environmental print (Baghban, 1984). When Jon was a year and a half old, his mother described his involvement in receiving and "reading" the mail:

> Usually when the mailman comes, there is some junk mail that I give to Jon to open and play with. Today when the mail came, I gave him a couple pieces of junk mail. He opened them and then came over and grabbed the letter I had just received from his grandmother (and was silently reading). I said, "Jon, sit on my lap and I'll read Grandma's letter to you." He then sat on my lap and held the letter while I read it aloud. After I finished reading, he got up, picked up another piece of mail (which just happened to be a form letter from a political candidate) and brought it over and sat on my lap. I read a couple of sentences to him. Then he lost interest and got up and went to play. Today was the first time he showed any interest in having the mail read to him.

A couple of months later, Jon's mom noted that he had picked up another handwritten letter from his grandmother and started to verbalize while looking at it. She also reported that he verbalized when he saw the printed card that came in his father's new billfold.

In Baghban's (1984) detailed case study of her daughter's exploration of reading and writing, she notes that her daughter was very interested in environmental print. At 20 months of age, her daughter identified the "broad yellow *M* as /onaw/ (for McDonald's) whether it stood alone or appeared on a billboard or cup" (p. 29).

Toddlers who are interested in exploring print will do so in a wide variety of settings. For example, Shatz (1994) describes a toddler's attempt to read (by babbling) the fortune printed on a slip of paper in a fortune cookie. Sinclair and Golan (2002) describe a toddler, Luc, who showed interest in environmental print that was found on "shop fronts, posters, house numbers, print on trucks . . . packages of manufactured goods, . . . and newspapers" (p. 588), and focused his efforts on identifying the letters found in the environmental print.

At two years, 10 months of age, Jon was asking his mother questions about print ("What dat?" and "What dat say?") that he saw in numerous locations. These included print embossed on a plastic card box, the printed directions on the spout area of a milk carton, the price and code number on the upper corner of the front cover of a story book, a label on an umbrella, the letters *H* and *C* on the water faucet, and writing on a family shopping list. In each instance, Jon's mom explained what the print "said." Toddlers attending religious services with their parents have also been observed paging through the worship booklets and babbling when the pages showed text, and humming when the pages showed musical notation.

Further evidence of toddlers' attention to environmental print is seen in this example: When she was 15 months old, Suzanne was attending a library program for toddlers and their moms (McKechnie, 2006). Holding a nametag in her hand, she took it over to another child's mom, looked at the nametag in her hand and then pointed to the nametag worn by the other mother.

Implications of research. In each of these instances, toddlers are showing their interest in written language found in their home and community environments. Not only do they notice the environmental print, but there is a clear interest in trying to make sense of the print. Parents and teachers of toddlers can encourage children's emergent literacy by carefully observing and mediating their interactions with environmental print. It is important for these interactions to be child-initiated rather than elicited by an adult.

Early Writing Attempts

Young children may also show an interest in watching an adult write and attempt to write on their own. Toddlers' early explorations of writing begin with making marks on paper (as well as other surfaces!). They seem to enjoy seeing that they are creating a visual mark (Baghban, 2007).

In the following example, Christopher, 18 months old, explores how to use a pen and then crayons to make marks on paper and other surfaces. This interaction is described by Christopher's caregiver. As the caregiver was writing with a pen, Christopher stopped his play, came over to where she was and took her pen. He then began to mark on the paper.

> As he did so, he squealed, looking at the line he had drawn. He then smiled and looked at his caregiver. He fingered the pen, turned it over in his hand, and made some more marks on the paper, giggling. He looked at each end of the pen and then turned it point down to use it. Then the caregiver gave Christopher a box of crayons and a large sheet of paper. He then took the crayons out of the box and began to select different colors and mark on the paper. Throughout this time he would draw and then laugh or squeal in delight at what he had done. When trying out the different colors, he appeared to note which ones did not leave a clearly visible mark (e.g., pink), and then picked a darker color. He also tried marking on a plastic pencil case, but when no mark appeared, he went back to making marks on the paper.

This phase of random scribbling is followed by scribbling that is more purposeful. As they become aware that written marks can "stand for something" they may take their scribbling to an adult and ask "Wha dis say?" Later on, children will begin to give their own label or meaning to their scribbles (Baghban, 2007).

This progression of scribbling is noted in the following example of a child's fascination with the writing process (Baghban, 1984). At 18 months, Giti appeared to carefully observe when her parents were writing and then would seek opportunities to write on her own. While her initial writing appeared to be random scribbling, her writing gradually did not "sprawl over the page to such an extent" (p. 47) and she began to incorporate smaller circles and wavy lines. At 23 months, she began to practice "book babbling" on her own writing as if she was reading what she had written (p. 52). By 27 months, Giti's writing contained letter-like units in addition to scribbling. At this time, she was also now labeling what she had written.

Another example of a child's interest in writing comes from Ryan when he was two years, 11 months of age. At this time his mother reported that he showed interest in helping to make the family grocery list (see Figure 4.2 for the grocery list). Here is her description:

> When writing my grocery list, I asked Ryan what he wanted from the store, he said "raisins." I wrote it down. A few moments later I asked him if there was anything else we needed from the store, he said "raisins" again. I said that I'd already written it down. He took the pencil from my hand and said, "me write raisins." He then made some pencil marks (lines) on the grocery list along with some dots. Then he handed the paper back to me.

Implications of research. Although some toddlers, such as those highlighted in the previous examples, are exploring writing and drawing, not all toddlers will be interested. We are only beginning to accumulate research that will provide more descriptions of toddlers' early writing attempts. Research with toddlers from diverse linguistic and cultural settings is also

Figure 4.2 Shopping List Artifact

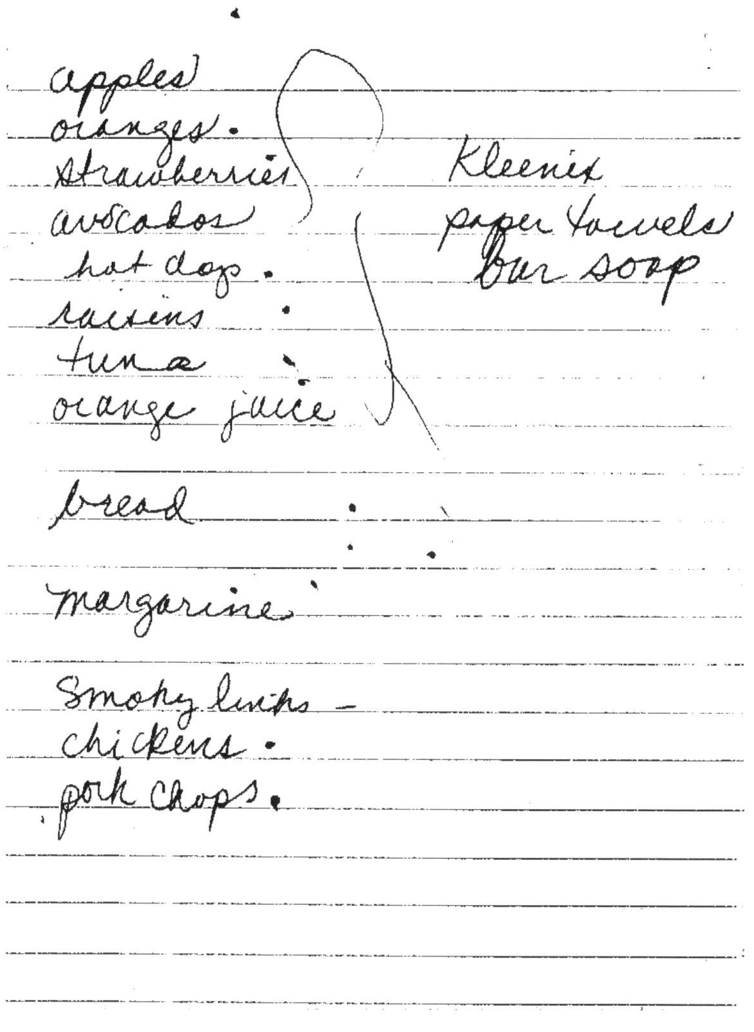

needed. Most of the research on early drawing and writing has been with older children of preschool or kindergarten age. It is important to also keep in mind that these toddlers' early writing behaviors developed during interactions with caring adults in home and community settings. In each instance, these adults provided the opportunities for children to be engaged in literacy-related events and interacted in a way that promoted children's involvement. The ways that specific characteristics of family environments have been associated with infants' and toddlers' emergent literacy are described in the next section of this chapter.

Critical Role of Family Setting

The family setting plays a critical role in providing literacy-related experiences for infants' and toddlers' observation and exploration. Home environments where young children have shown evidence of emergent literacy knowledge can be characterized by the following nine characteristics. These characteristics highlight the ways in which the contexts of literacy and the interaction with adults are associated with children's early literacy transactions. A summary of these nine characteristics is located in Figure 4.3.

Parents Value Literacy

Parents who expressed pleasure in reading and writing were more likely to encourage their children's interest in books (Bus, 2002). In contrast, parents who did not enjoy reading and writing activities themselves were less likely to encourage reading activities for their children. Additionally, when they shared story books with their children, their interactions involved less complex discussions and showed less consideration of children's developmental levels. For example, some mothers simply read the text and did not appear to consider their child's ability to comprehend what was being read.

Parents Use Reading and Writing in Their Daily Activities

In homes associated with emergent literacy of infants and toddlers, there were many opportunities for children to observe their parents' interactions with written language on a daily basis (Baghban, 1984; Crago & Crago, 1983; Lujan & Wooden, 1984; Sinclair & Golan, 2002). Throughout each day infants and toddlers had the opportunity to observe parents making shopping lists; reading a newspaper, magazine, or book, using a cookbook; writing a letter; and completing work-related documents. As infants and toddlers accompanied

 Figure 4.3 Characteristics of Home Environments Associated with Infants' and Toddlers' Emergent Literacy

1. Parents value literacy.
2. Parents use reading and writing in their daily activities.
3. Parents engage children in frequent book sharing.
4. Parents encourage children's early literacy explorations.
5. Parents respond positively to children's questions.
6. Parents value children's early attempts to draw or write.
7. Parents engage children in frequent conversations.
8. Parents are sensitive to their children's developmental level and prior experiences.
9. Parents use scaffolding and mediation.

parents on their activities and errands in their communities, they may have observed further literacy-related events as groceries were purchased, packages were mailed at the post office, or magazines were read in medical waiting rooms, and as families participated in religious services.

Parents Engage Children in Frequent Book Sharing

From early in their children's lives, parents have made picture-book sharing a part of their daily routines (Baghban, 1984; Crago & Crago, 1983; Joyner, 1987). This picture-book sharing is not simply motivated by the desire for their children to get a head start on reading. In fact, parents of young children are quite aware that it will be several years before their children will actually read in the conventional sense. Instead, this daily routine of sharing picture books stems from parents' strong orientation to literacy and their past and ongoing personal satisfaction with their own experiences with books, as well as their personal pleasure in sharing books with their young children. The sharing of picture books builds upon the attachment bond between parent and child (Bus, 2002) and provides opportunity for parents to teach their children about the world around them.

Parents Encourage Children's Early Literacy Explorations

As children observe their parents in daily literacy-related events, and as they experience frequent picture-book sharing events, they begin to show an interest in participating in these events. Children's responses may involve nonverbal behaviors (pointing, gesturing, facial expressions, helping to turn the pages of the book) or verbal behaviors (babbling, laughing, and making animal sounds). These early explorations are encouraged by their parents. Parents carefully observe children's interest in these language and literacy-related events and begin to nurture this interest by facilitating their children's explorations. Perhaps this involves providing paper and markers to the toddler who is interested in "writing," that is, drawing and scribbling (Baghban, 1984; Schickedanz, 1986). Or it may involve providing a range of developmentally appropriate picture books that are easily accessible and then responding positively when their toddlers select a book and ask for it to be read to them. It

The sharing of picture books builds upon the attachment bond between parent and child.

TAGSTOCK1

may also involve understanding that toddlers may like to sit and look at their books independently, but are not yet able to put the books away consistently.

Parents also encourage literacy explorations when they respond positively to their children's attempts to participate in other literacy-related events, such as reading the mail, making a shopping list, writing a letter to a relative, locating the desired box of cereal at the grocery store, or singing in a religious service.

Parents Respond Positively to Children's Questions

Children's early explorations and participation in literacy-related events are often accompanied by questions directed to their parents. Parents' positive responses focus on answering their children's questions at a level they can comprehend and letting their children take the lead in continuing with the questioning or moving on to another activity. For example, when Ryan was two years, 10 months of age, his mother noted the following behaviors over a five-day period:

> Episode 1: "Ryan brought a plastic box to me that had embossed print on it and said, "what dat?" I read the words for him. He turned the box over, found more print and said: "what dat?" I also read it to him. He then turned and went off to play.

> Episode 2: Ryan spontaneously pointed to some words in a storybook and said to me, "what dat write?" I read it to him. He asked no further questions.

> Episode 3: At the breakfast table, Ryan spontaneously pointed to the words on the spout area of the milk carton and asked me, "what dat say?" I read him the words and showed him how to open it up. He smiled, and wanted to try opening it up himself.

These three episodes illustrate the curiosity young children express while exploring their world. As shown above, Ryan asked questions about print he noticed in various places in his environment: print on a plastic box, print in a story book, and print on the milk carton. In each of these instances, Ryan's mother responded to his questions, continuing the interaction as long as he was interested. This type of interaction also occurs during picture-book sharing when children begin to ask questions about the events or concepts in the book.

Parents' positive responsiveness to children's explorations and questions is also characterized by an attitude of "acceptance and non-correction" (Lujan & Wooden, 1984, p. 5). This is especially important because parents have a significant role in nurturing their children's general development as well as their opportunities to interact with literacy-related events. When parents attempt to rigidly control the interaction during story book time by insisting that their children just listen as the text is read and are not sensitive to their child's nonverbal behaviors or interests, their children may show less interest in book interactions (Bus, 2002).

Parents Value Children's Early Attempts to Draw or Write

In families where toddlers and early preschoolers are given opportunities to draw and scribble on paper, parents interpret these attempts as meaningful communication and respond to children's questions and comments about the meaning of what they just "wrote" (Baghban, 1984). In these instances, children's comments and labels for what was written (or drawn) are accepted without correction or question from their parents. Children's early writing is also likely to be posted on the refrigerator along with other family notes and communications, indicating its value and meaningfulness to the family.

Parents Engage Children in Frequent Conversations

Families of young emergent readers and writers are also characterized by lots of talk between parents and children (Hart & Risley, 1995). Parents' conversations with children show changes over time that mirror and enhance their children's developing language competencies. Through these conversations, parents use a range of interaction patterns, such as eye contact and shared reference, verbal mapping, communication loops, and child-directed speech. For infants and toddlers, the focus of these conversations is on developing language that represents the objects, situations, pictures, and activities they encounter and experience. Picture-book sharing provides a context for many of these conversations (Moerk, 1974).

Parents Are Sensitive to Their Children's Developmental Level and Prior Experiences

Successful literacy-related interactions with infants and toddlers involve parents' awareness of their children's developmental level. This knowledge includes awareness of their children's physical, emotional, social, and cognitive development. For example, parents will have an awareness of their child's experiences and developing concepts, such as their experiences with the family pet, a recent visit from a relative, or a trip to the zoo. Parents will also be aware of the child's physical abilities, such as holding onto the book, pointing, and turning pages, as well as their developing attention span.

Based on their intuitive awareness, parents structure their interactions to provide opportunity for their children to participate as fully as possible. Parents carefully observe their children's interest in and response to the specific literacy-related event and know when to continue the interaction, or when it is time to move on to another activity.

Positive learning interactions occur in settings that are relaxed and comfortable for young children. In these settings children feel secure and are able to become engaged (Berk & Winsler, 1995; Greenspan, 1997, 1999). Young children base their responses to an interaction upon their perception of the adult's expressions (Trawick-Smith, 2006). If there is emotional or physical tension, young children will sense it and this will impact the learning interaction (Puckett & Black, 2001).

Adults' sensitivity to children's interest in the picture-book sharing is critical to the mutual enjoyment of the interaction (Dodici, Draper, & Peterson, 2003; Honig & Brophy, 1996; Lamme & Packer, 1986; Martin & Reutzel, 1999). In picture-book sharing events, "parents need to be sensitive to the infant's signals of readiness and cooperation, sensitivity to behaviors that signal when the infant has had enough, awareness of the times most suitable to the infant's daily routine, and receptiveness to the reading sessions in general" (Joyner, 1987, p. 22).

Parents Use Scaffolding and Mediation

The way in which parents engage their children successfully in conversation about a picture book is referred to as **scaffolding**. As parents share the book with their young children, they use a variety of strategies to keep their children involved, such as asking questions, labeling pictures, elaborating on actions that are illustrated, praising children's responses, and responding to children's questions (DeLoache, 1984; Loughner, 1993; Martin & Reutzel, 1999; Whitehurst, Falco, Lonigan, Fischel, DeBaryshe, Valdes-Menchaca, & Caulfield, 1988). Successful scaffolding is based upon parents' knowledge of their individual child's prior knowledge and competencies (DeLoache & DeMendoza, 1985). This knowledge informs the way in which parents then create the scaffold to support their child's participation and learning.

This scaffolding may vary depending on whether the book read was a narrative story or an informational book (Potter & Haynes, 2000). While this scaffolding serves to guide a child's participation (Dixon-Krauss, 1996; Martin & Reutzel, 1999), it also is dynamic and unfolds based on the specific responses of the child. Parents will use their child's preceding responses to make a related comment or question that serves to keep the interaction going (Snow, 1983). For example, see Figure 4.4 for the interaction between Allison, one and a half years old, and her mother as they shared an alphabet book (Otto, 1996). Based on Allison's responses, her mother used labeling and elaboration to keep the interaction going. With each new page, Allison's mom appeared to wait to see what her daughter's response or interest would be. Based on this, she would provide a comment or label to expand or confirm her daughter's response.

This scaffolding also changes with the age of young children. With infants, parents use more attention-getting strategies (Martin & Reutzel, 1999), such as saying "Oh, look!" while pointing to an illustration. Parents also use more verbal elaborations (Sénéchal, Cornell, & Broda, 1995). For example, when sharing *The Very Quiet Cricket* (Carle, 1990) with an infant, the parent might say, "Oh, look at the worm! He's peeking out of the apple. (*Points to apple*) He's saying, 'hello.'" With older infants, more questioning was used and more feedback was given to children's responses (Honig & Shin, 2001; Sénéchal, Cornell, &

 Figure 4.4 Example of Parent's Scaffolding During Picture-Book Sharing
Allison (1½ years old) and her mother are sharing an alphabet book

Mom:	(*holding book in front of Allison.*) What are those?
Allison:	/a/
Mom:	/a/, Uh-huh (*points to letters A-B-C on the cover; Allison's eye contact follows and she also points to the letters*), /b/, ABCs.
Allison:	apple
Mom:	apple
Allison:	/buh/ (*points to illustration*)
Mom:	bug
Allison:	(*points to letter A*)
Mom:	and there's the A.
Allison:	/a/ (*pointing to letter*)
Mom:	that's A
Allison:	/a/
Mom:	big A and a little a
Allison:	/a/ apple (*pauses, points to airplane*)
Mom:	that's an airplane
Allison:	(*looks at page with bear picture*) mama
Mom:	oh, that's the mama bear, that's a B, mama bear
Allison:	bear (*points to picture*)
Mom:	giving the baby bear a bath. Baby bear has a bath.
Allison:	(*points to picture of bug*)
Mom:	and that's a little bug
Allison:	(*points to letter C*)
Mom:	C, that's for candle

Source: Otto, 1996.

Broda, 1995). For example, a parent reading *The Very Quiet Cricket* might ask, "Where's the little worm? Show me where he is. (*Child points accurately*) That's right! There he is wiggling out of the apple. What is he saying?"

In addition to using scaffolding, parents adapt the literacy event to fit their child's developmental level (Bus, 2002; Honig & Brophy, 1996; Martin & Reutzel, 1999). The ways in which parents adapt picture-book sharing to their individual children's level of comprehension is referred to as **mediation**. In this mediation, parents simplify the task to a level at which their children can participate.

For example, when a parent begins to use a particular picture book with a young child, the parent may become aware that the actual story text is too complex for the child to understand, or that the specific words used in the text are too advanced. Perhaps the child is at a level where he is interested in only the pictures. At this point, parents may focus on only the illustrations. Bus (2002) described parents' mediation of illustrations as involving an emphasis on the illustrations that represent some emotional or conceptual tie to the child's life experiences. This personalizes the book content and builds upon the child's prior knowledge and experiences. For example, reading *The Very Quiet Cricket*, a mother would draw on her child's experience of seeing a dragonfly in their backyard as they looked at the illustrations of the dragonfly. This mother might say, "Oh, look! There's a dragonfly. Remember we saw a dragonfly in our garden today. Look at the big wings!"

Parents also adapt the text to fit the comprehension and interests of their children. This "oral text" may have little relation to the actual text of the book, but results in a story that has more appeal to the child, increasing the child's interest and participation (Bus, 2002; Honig & Brophy, 1996; Martin & Reutzel, 1999). In this way parental knowledge of children's concepts and experiences are used in mediating and integrating book illustrations and text with children's experiences and developing concepts. This mediation provides a bridge between the real world and the world represented in books.

Research implications. These nine characteristics of home environments where young children have shown evidence of emergent literacy knowledge provide examples that could be transferred and integrated into early childhood settings. For example, because research has indicated emergent literacy in home settings that have opportunities for frequent story book sharing, early childhood settings should incorporate multiple opportunities for story book sharing throughout each day. Further implications of this body of research for infants and toddlers in early childhood settings are described in Chapter 5.

Emergent Literacy Among Observers and Explorers in Diverse Contexts

Earlier sections of this chapter described emergent literacy transactions among infants and toddlers with picture-book sharing, environmental print, and early writing/drawing attempts. In addition, characteristics of environments that supported children's emergent literacy during infancy and toddlerhood were described. Without exception, the research from which these descriptions came was based in middle-class, English-speaking, Caucasian homes or early childhood settings. Unfortunately, there is only a limited amount of early literacy research that has been conducted with infants and toddlers who come from home settings with social-cultural-linguistic diversity. While this research on infants and toddlers in diverse settings is limited and thus does not yet support conclusions about the relation of these diverse environments to literacy development, several studies will be described here to provide a look at this existing body of knowledge.

Low Social-Economic Status (SES) Settings

In their research involving infants and toddlers from low-income homes, Fletcher and Jean-Francois (1998) focused on two- and three-year-olds' responses to repeated story book readings. This study showed that low-income children's responses were similar to children from mainstream environments in three ways: (1) children's responses were characterized by labeling pictures and making comments about the illustration or the story; (2) children sometimes repeated what the reader had said (echolike responses); and (3) while individual differences were noted between low-income children, over the repeated readings there was an increase in verbal responses and the variety of those responses. This result has also been documented among middle–SES children. Thus, this research shows that low–SES children exhibit some of the same emergent literacy behaviors and benefit from increased story book sharing as do middle–SES children.

Dodici, Draper, and Peterson (2003) also focused on children from low-income homes. They explored the relationship between story book interactions of parents and their infants/toddlers and early literacy skills. This research documented a relationship between parental interaction style and children's emergent literacy. When parents used developmentally appropriate language, a positive emotional tone, and were responsive listeners, their children were found to have larger listening vocabularies, greater understanding of symbols, and more phonemic awareness.

Culturally and Linguistically Diverse Settings

The importance of story book sharing for second language learners was emphasized in Patterson's (2002) study of bilingual children who were between 21 and 27 months of age. Patterson reported that children's oral vocabulary in each language (Spanish and English) was larger when they were read to more frequently in that same language. This research also highlights the value of story book-reading experiences in both the home language and the new language.

In their research with African American and white middle-class and working-class mothers and their toddlers, Haynes and colleagues (Anderson-Yockel & Haynes, 1994; Haynes & Saunders, 1999) focused on the interaction styles of parents during picture-book sharing. They reported both similarities and differences between the interaction styles of these parents during picture-book sharing. African American working-class mothers did not use questioning as much as white working-class mothers, while "white children produced more question-related communications," and African American children verbalized more spontaneously (Anderson-Yockel & Haynes, 1994, p. 590). Fewer differences in book-reading behaviors were found between the middle-class white and African American mother–toddler pairs. This finding indicates the need to consider social-economic status as well as cultural diversity when conducting research in emergent literacy (Haynes & Saunders, 1999).

Research implications. The relationship between children's acquisition of literacy and the social-cultural-linguistic contexts in which learning takes place is a complex one involving a range of factors and settings. Although this body of research on infants and toddlers is limited, it is important because it contributes to our knowledge of the critical role of the home environment in encouraging the development of literacy-related knowledge. Additional research on early literacy-related interactions is needed within a wide range of social-cultural and linguistic settings to better understand the ways in which interaction patterns and styles impact children's early literacy knowledge.

Figure 4.5 Revisiting the Transactional Perspective: Infants' and Toddlers' Emergent Literacy

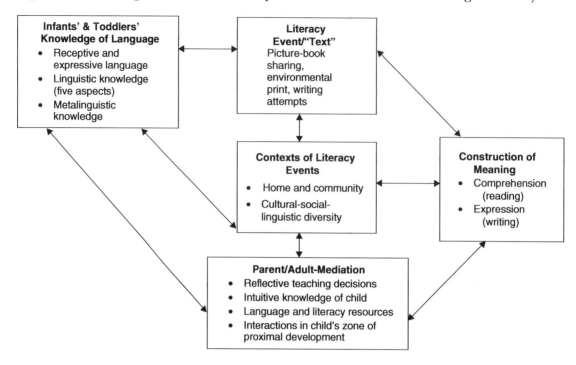

Revisiting the Transactional Perspective

This chapter has described infants' and toddlers' emergent literacy knowledge expressed through their interactions in literacy-related events. It has also described the settings in which this emergent literacy has occurred as well as the types of interaction strategies used by caring adults. These four components (child's emergent literacy, literacy events, contexts of literacy events, and adult mediation) interact in complex ways. This complexity is represented in the Transactional perspective of literacy development. These interactions are represented graphically in Figure 4.5.

As reflective teachers of infants and toddlers, we can use this research-based knowledge of children's emergent literacy and the characteristics of environments associated with emergent literacy to develop and implement activities and experiences that will enhance young children's development. The next chapter describes the ways in which this research-based knowledge of early literacy can be used to create literacy-rich early childhood classrooms. Chapter 5 also incorporates an emphasis on reflective teaching within a transactional perspective.

Chapter Summary

This chapter focused on infants and toddlers as they observe and explore literacy-related events in their home and community environments. From birth, children begin to learn about their environments. As they each acquire their home language, they learn from the daily activities of their families as well as from the special events that occur. Family and community experiences provide the contexts in which infants and toddlers not only develop oral language but also observe their parents and family members interacting with written language. When infants and toddlers have frequent and voluntary opportunities to interact with picture books, they begin to develop concepts and vocabulary related to these experiences. As they interact with picture books, their verbal and nonverbal behaviors may indicate their emerging literacy knowledge. Older toddlers' behaviors may indicate a memory for story or picture content.

In addition to observing and exploring written language during picture-book interactions, infants and toddlers begin to observe and explore written language in other daily events at home and in their communities. Young children may also show an interest in an adult's writing and attempt to write on their own.

The social-cultural-linguistic contexts in which infants and toddlers observe and explore reading and writing have a significant role in the opportunities and support provided for developing emergent literacy knowledge; however, it is important to remember that young children will respond differently to literacy-related events. A key aspect of these social and cultural contexts of emergent literacy is found in the ways in which adults interact with young children within their zones of proximal development.

Chapter Review

1. Terms to know:
   environmental print   mediation
   scaffolding

2. In what ways does oral language provide a foundation for emergent literacy? Give several examples.

3. Describe specific verbal and nonverbal responses during picture-book sharing that indicate emergent literacy among infants and toddlers. Relate these responses to children's developing knowledge in each of these areas: phonetic, semantic, syntactic, and pragmatic.

4. In what ways do toddlers show an interest or curiosity about written language in their environment? As their teacher, describe how you would respond to these emergent literacy-related behaviors.

5. Describe four characteristics of home environments where infants and toddlers have shown evidence of emergent literacy knowledge. Indicate the ways in which these characteristics may support children's early literacy development.

Chapter Extension Activities

Observation: Observe toddlers and their parents in community activities for interaction with environmental print (for example, shopping, religious services, and restaurants). Describe the interaction that occurred and the environmental print involved.

In-Class Discussion: Survey your local library for young children's books that are available in languages other than English. Are there books available that use two languages side-by-side? Bring an example book to your class to share. Explain how the book could be shared with an infant or toddler.

Research: Review a professional journal article on oral language development or picture-book sharing among parents and their infants or toddlers. Participate in a small group discussion in your class, relating the journal article to chapter content.

Chapter 5

Enhancing Emergent Literacy Among Infants and Toddlers

In a quiet corner of the infant room, the teacher, Alicia, is sitting in a rocking chair, holding Kari, six months old. They are looking at a board book, *Farm Animals* (Dorling Kindersley, 2001). As Alicia begins to turn pages in the book, she points to the animals pictured on each page and makes a comment. "Oh, here are the chicks. Peep, peep, peep." "See the little lambs. Baaa, baaa." Kari looks intently at the pictures and waves her arms, touching the book. When Alicia pauses after saying "baaa," Kari responds by making a /b/ sound.

Early Childhood Settings for Infants and Toddlers

Alicia and Kari are in an early childhood setting that has provided the materials, space, and time for picture-book sharing. Not all infants will show the same interest in book sharing, so Alicia takes her cues from each infant. She individualizes these book interactions to meet each infant's interest and attention span. Some book interactions last only a minute or so. Alicia is careful to provide additional times during the day for picture-book sharing so that she can engage each infant at a time when they are rested and alert. Although infants in Alicia's classroom are not yet speaking, she is aware of the importance of book-sharing experiences in enhancing young children's emergent literacy. As she plans the curriculum for her infant room, Alicia incorporates language and literacy-related experiences along with the needed physical-care routines and opportunities for motor and social development.

Infants and toddlers may be in group-care settings for ten or more hours a day (Soundy, 1997). Because this time span represents the majority of infants' and toddlers' wakeful hours each day, the quality of their care and learning experiences are critical to their future development. Although infant and toddler rooms are often dominated by routines for meeting children's physical needs, such as feeding, sleeping, and diapering, it is important to provide opportunities for children to engage in social interaction and language development as well as times of independent exploration. High-quality infant and toddler rooms will have low child-to-teacher ratios, such as three infants per teacher and six toddlers per teacher (Bredekamp & Copple, 1997).

Infants and toddlers are in the beginning phases of emergent literacy. Initially, they are observers of the ways that language and literacy are used by people in their environments. Gradually, they become explorers who are actively involved in participating in literacy-related events. In both infant and toddler classrooms, activities and routines will be individualized in order to meet each child's needs. As toddlers begin to interact with one another, they may be able to participate in small group activities of short duration.

This chapter focuses on providing descriptions of activities and interaction strategies that will enhance and mediate infants' and toddlers' transactions with literacy in early childhood settings and at home. Throughout this chapter, emphasis is placed on becoming a careful observer of infants' and toddlers' responses during language and literacy-related activities. Your careful observations will provide you with knowledge and awareness of individual children's needs so that you can make reflective decisions about your classroom curriculum and the ways in which you interact with infants and toddlers.

General Classroom Guidelines

As you plan the ways in which you will enhance infants' and toddlers' observations and explorations of language and literacy in your classroom, you will find these two general guidelines useful: (1) Observe each child's ways of communicating, and (2) create a language and literacy-rich setting.

Observe Each Child's Ways of Communicating

Chapter 1 described the importance of creating a developmentally appropriate learning environment for young children. As a reflective teacher, you will want to provide a developmentally appropriate environment for the infants and toddlers in your classroom. The first step you will take in determining which language and literacy-related activities will be developmentally appropriate is to closely observe the ways in which each child communicates. This involves observing each child for the following behaviors: (a) Attention to others' speech, (b) eye contact and shared reference, (c) turn-taking/dialogic participation, (d) attention to ongoing events, (e) level of oral language, and (f) home language or dialect. (See Figure 5.1 for a sample observation format).

Attention to others' speech. When very young children pay attention to speech in their environment, it indicates that they are hearing the speech sounds. Observe the child as others are talking in the classroom. Does the child look for who is talking? Does the child turn to face the speaker? Does the child stop what they are doing and look to see who is talking? Attending to others' speech is a primary requirement for becoming involved in communication.

Newborns appear to be prewired to pay attention to speech in their environment. In fact, infants will pay more attention to the human voice than they will any other sound in their environment (Condon & Sandler, 1974; Eisenberg, 1976; Jensen, Williams, & Bzoch, 1975). Within a few days after birth, infants also can distinguish their mother's voice from other female voices (DeCasper & Fifer, 1980; Karmiloff & Karmiloff-Smith, 2001).

Eye contact and shared reference. In addition to attending to others' speech, another key aspect of early communication is a child's eye contact with the adult. An infant's eye contact with an adult represents a very basic interaction pattern that provides a foundation for communication (Carlson & Bricker, 1982; Wells, 1986). Once eye contact and mutual attention have been established, the infant learns to follow the adult's gaze and focus on a specific object or event. This shared reference then becomes the center of their interaction.

Figure 5.1 Observation of Infants' and Toddlers' Ways of Communicating

Child's name: _____ Age: _____ Date(s) observed: _____

Focus of Observation	Questions to Consider	Consistently	Occasionally	Not at this time
Attention to adult's speech	1. Does child look to speaker? 2. Does child turn to face the speaker? 3. Does child stop what they are doing and look to see who is talking?			
Eye contact, shared reference	1. Does child respond to adult's request to "look"? 2. Does child follow adult's pointing gestures? 3. Does child make eye contact with adult when adult is talking and directly in front of, or holding the child? 4. When presented with an object, does child first look at adult and then at object?			
Turn-taking/dialogic participation	1. When adult speaks to child and then pauses, does the child respond nonverbally? 2. When adult speaks to child and then pauses, does child respond verbally? 3. Does child "take turns" in listening and responding?			
Attention to ongoing events	1. Does child notice a new event in classroom? 2. Does child continue to watch ongoing event?			
Level of language	Which level characterizes child's expressive language? 1. cooing 2. babbling 3. echolalic babbling 4. one-word (invented and conventional) 5. two- to three-word phrases			
Home use of language	1. Non–English speaking 2. Standard English–speaking 3. Dialect of English			

Figure 5.2 Sample of Eye Contact and Shared Reference

Setting: Adult is holding an infant of seven months of age. They are near a window. Infant is looking around the room, not out the window. The adult sees a squirrel running across the grass outside.

Adult: Look! Look! (*points out the window and looks at child*)

Infant: (*first looks to adult's face and then to adult's pointing gesture, then turns to face the window, and looks out*)

Adult: Look! A squirrel! (*points to squirrel as it is running; gesture follows path of squirrel; looks to child to determine child's gaze*)

Infant: (*eyes follow squirrel; smiles and giggles*)

Adult: Look at him run! He's going up the tree!

Infant: (*squeals with delight, waves arms; squirrel goes out of sight; classroom door opens and child hears door open and turns toward door*)

Adult: OK, let's go see who just came in.

Look at the sample interaction between an infant and an adult located in Figure 5.2. In what ways did the adult begin the interaction and monitor the child's eye contact and shared reference?

In Figure 5.2 the adult first secured the child's attention by exclaiming "Look!" Then gestures were used to introduce the focus of shared reference (such as a squirrel outside the window) to the child. Then the adult continued to monitor the child's gaze and attention, while the interaction continued. This particular interaction ended when the squirrel ran out of sight and the child's attention was drawn back into the room.

In determining a child's use of eye contact and shared reference, you will be asking the following questions: Does the child respond to adult's request to "Look" and follow the adult's pointing gestures? Does the child make eye contact with the adult when the adult is talking and directly in front of or holding the child? When the adult presents an object to the child or engages in an activity involving the child, does the child look directly at the object or activity? By determining each child's ability to engage in this type of interaction you will acquire the information you need in order to interact effectively and plan appropriate learning activities.

Turn-taking/dialogic participation. When we carry on a conversation with someone, we alternate between listening and speaking. This pattern of turn-taking or dialogue has its foundation in infants' early interactions with those around them. As you are determining the ways a child communicates, observe whether the child participates in this turn-taking pattern of interaction. When an adult speaks to an infant or toddler, and then pauses, does the child respond either verbally or nonverbally? Is a pattern established where the adult and child take turns listening and responding? For example, in Figure 5.2, the infant responded to the adult's speech with both verbal (squealing) and nonverbal behaviors (waving arms). Once the initial dialogue was started, the adult extended the interaction and responded to the child's participation with additional comments and gestures.

Attention to ongoing events. A child's awareness of ongoing events indicates his level of mental alertness as well as his interest in that event. An observant adult then can use the child's focus of attention to begin communicating about that event. This focus of attention may then begin an interaction involving eye contact and shared reference as well as a dialogic turn-taking. Read the example located in Figure 5.3. Note how the child's attention to an ongoing event develops into a conversation with his teacher.

Eye contact and shared reference are key aspects of communication that are established during infancy.

Olesya Feketa

When you observe a young child's interest in ongoing events, you will be able to then engage the child in conversations that further involve the child in learning about his environment. In making these observations, you may find that a child shows particular interest in certain types of events involving people or objects. You can also use this knowledge to determine which picture books or other activities the child would find engaging.

Level of oral language. As described in Chapter 3, young children's oral or expressive language develops over a series of stages, beginning with cooing around six to eight weeks of age. At around four to six months, most infants will begin to babble. Later on, their babbling reflects or echoes the intonation and expressive prosody of their home language (echolalic babbling). At around one year of age, most infants will use single words and then develop two- to three-word utterances, known as telegraphic speech, during toddlerhood. In order to appropriately develop learning activities for infants and toddlers, you need to be aware of each child's level of oral language.

 Figure 5.3 Example of Toddler's Attention to Ongoing Event

Setting: The toddler class from the child care center is outdoors. Marco, a two-year-old, is playing by himself in the sandbox. Maria, one of his teachers, is seated nearby on a bench. A robin starts singing from a tree close to the outdoor area. Maria notices that when the robin started to sing, Marco stopped his play.

Marco: (*stops play and looks up at the tree and the robin*)
Maria: Marco, what was that sound?
Marco: (*smiles, looks at his teacher and then looks and points at the tree*) Bird!
Maria: Yes, Marco. There's a bird singing in the tree. He sounds happy. He's a happy bird.
Marco: happy bird (*bird flies away; Marco goes back to playing in the sandbox*)

Home language. Infants and toddlers will arrive in your classroom having had many communication experiences with their families. It is important that you are aware of their home language as well as the social-cultural setting of the family environment. In order to do this, you will need to carefully observe family members interactions with the young child when he arrives at school and when he is picked up at the end of the day. If a different language or dialect is spoken at home from that spoken at school, you will need to keep this in mind when planning learning activities. (See later section in this chapter for additional information on interacting with English language learners.)

By carefully observing the infants and toddlers in your classroom, you can determine the ways in which they communicate and then use this knowledge to plan activities. In this way your classroom curriculum will encourage each child to participate as well as enhance active learning and development.

Create a Language- and Literacy-Rich Environment

A developmentally appropriate classroom for infants and toddlers provides a safe and secure environment for each child. In addition to providing supportive opportunities for physical growth and development as well as emotional well-being and development, this environment also needs to provide opportunities to develop language competencies. A language- and literacy-rich environment will have the following five characteristics: (a) A special area of the room for book sharing, (b) a variety of language and literacy-related activities embedded throughout each day, (c) opportunities for interaction and conversation, (d) opportunities for conceptual development through exploration and interaction, and (e) developmentally-based learning materials.

Special area for book sharing. This area is best arranged to provide space for one-on-one experiences as well as for children's independent exploration of books. Toddler rooms also need space for spontaneous small group gatherings (Soundy, 1997). In addition to comfortable seating, such as a cushioned rocking chair, small sofa, or upholstered chair, you will want to provide some floor cushions for toddlers to use while sharing books. Books that are easily accessible from a low bookshelf, basket, or display shelf will encourage children to explore this area. If possible, the books should be displayed so the covers, and not only the book spines, can be seen by the child. Multiple copies of the same books will allow children to use the same story book without having to share or take turns, which is often difficult for children this age. A diversity of book types and topics should be available, including books representing different cultural and social settings.

Variety of language- and literacy-related activities embedded throughout each day. A language- and literacy-rich environment is one in which language activities are embedded or integrated throughout each day, not just isolated to a specific time of day. For infants and toddlers, this environment will focus on developing their ability to hear and understand oral language as well as to use oral language to communicate. With this oral language as a foundation, activities involving written language are introduced. A language- and literacy-rich environment will have the following characteristics.

Opportunities for interaction and conversation. Language develops through interaction. A language- and literacy-rich environment will provide infants and toddlers with many opportunities to engage in one-on-one interactions with their teachers. As a reflective teacher, you will use your knowledge of each child's ways of communicating to engage the child in eye contact and shared reference and dialogic turn-taking throughout each day. You will also use this knowledge to provide questioning and linguistic scaffolding to support each child's conversations and interactions.

Exploration and direct experiences provide critical interactions that enhance concept development.

Opportunities for conceptual development through exploration and interaction. During infancy and toddlerhood, children's direct experiences serve as a basis for their development of concepts. Concept development provides a foundation for vocabulary development. Exploration and direct experiences provide critical interactions that enhance concept development. Piaget (1955) described this stage of cognitive development as the **sensorimotor stage** because children are experiencing their environment and learning through their senses and movements or manipulation of objects they encounter. As these concepts are developed, words become attached to the concepts and symbol formation occurs (Werner & Kaplan, 1963). For example, Figure 5.4 describes an infant's encounter

 Figure 5.4 Example of an Infant's Encounter with a Ball

Setting: Kiesha, an eight-month-old girl, is lying on her stomach on the carpeted area of the infant room. Her arms are positioned in front of her and she is resting up on her arms. Caryl, her teacher, is seated nearby. Caryl reaches into the toy basket and takes out a red ball, about six inches in diameter.

    Caryl: (*Moves to orient herself directly in front of Kiesha; then places the ball on the floor and rolls it toward Kiesha*)

Kiesha: (*Looks at her teacher, then looks at the ball. As the ball nears her, Kiesha smiles. The ball touches her outstretched arm. Kiesha moves her arm and pushes the ball so that it goes away from her. She laughs.*)

    Caryl: (*Moves to reach the ball and again rolls it gently in Kiesha's direction*) Here you go. Here's the ball. Can you push the ball?

Kiesha: (*waits until the ball reaches her hand and then pushes it, smiles and laughs*)

with a soft, rubber ball. As you read this example, think about your concept of ball and what this experience might bring to Kiesha's concept of a ball.

Kiesha's experience with the ball was both visual and tactile. She could see the ball rolling toward and away from her. She also touched the ball. Additionally, she experienced what happens to a ball when it is pushed away. All of these experiences become part of her developing concept of a ball. These experiences contribute to her comprehension of the word *ball* during speech as well as her comprehension of the word when she encounters it during picture-book sharing. By providing opportunities for conceptual development through exploration and interaction, you are also enhancing children's language and emergent literacy development.

Developmentally-Based Learning Materials

A language- and literacy-rich classroom will have materials that have been chosen to fit the developmental needs of the particular children in the classroom. For example, in an infant and toddler classroom, the picture books will need to be very durable because these young children are just learning how to manipulate objects and often will mouth or chew on the object as they explore its features. Thus, you will need to select picture books made of cardboard and laminated because the pages are thicker and more easily manipulated by young children. (More examples of the features of developmentally appropriate picture books are included in the following section on picture-book sharing.)

When older toddlers begin to show interest in drawing and writing, they will need to have materials that fit their developmental needs. For example, because toddlers are just developing small-muscle coordination, they will need large pieces of thick paper for their early attempts at drawing and writing. They will also need nontoxic, water-based markers in case they end up marking on the table or themselves.

Language and literacy materials should also be selected that will engage and stimulate children's interest. In addition to a wide variety of appropriate books, stuffed animals and puppets that resemble story book characters will add interest to picture-book sharing (Soundy, 1997), and will encourage children to participate verbally.

Enhancing Emergent Literacy Through Specific Activities

In infant and toddler classrooms, emergent literacy can be encouraged through four specific types of activities: oral language activities, picture-book sharing, environmental print experiences, and symbol-making experiences.

Oral Language Activities

Oral language development is the foundation for emergent literacy as well as for continued cognitive development. Therefore it is important to carefully consider the oral language activities that occur in infant and toddler classrooms. In this section, three main categories of oral language activities will be described: conversations; labeling; and songs, rhymes, and finger plays.

Conversations. Because language is acquired through interaction with others, infants and toddlers need to have frequent opportunities for conversations with adults. Even before an infant is making speech sounds, he can be encouraged to participate as a conversational partner. As you talk to a young infant, pause frequently, and look for the infant's responses in the form of movements, eye contact, and facial expressions. When there is a response, continue on with the conversation as if the child's response fits into the context. In this setting, adults often provide a verbal answer as if they were the infant, especially if the infant has made only a limited response. By the adult's taking both parts of the verbal dialogue, this sets up the beginning of a back and forth turn-taking that will easily incorporate the infant's responses as they occur. This also sets the stage for more complex conversations later on.

For example, in Figure 5.5, notice how the adult interprets the infant's nonverbal behaviors as conversational turns, and also provides a verbal response on behalf of the infant.

Conversations with infants and toddlers should focus on events and objects in the immediate environment. This provides a focus or reference point for the conversation and enhances concept development and symbol formation. As a reflective teacher, you will use questioning and repetition as well as expansion to keep the conversation going. This is illustrated by the example in Figure 5.6.

Most of your conversations with toddlers will be individual, one-on-one conversations; however, snack time in a toddler classroom provides an important opportunity for children to begin to talk in a small group setting. In beginning this activity, you will need to take the lead in introducing a topic for conversation (Selman, 2001). As you begin a conversation at snack time, keep in mind that the goals for this activity are for the children to listen and take turns when speaking. Your role is to provide the linguistic scaffold that supports the dialogue between children and you by using questioning, repetition, and expansion (see further discussion in Chapter 1). One particular type of question that is effective in encouraging continued participation is the **tag question**. In this type of question, you restate what the child said and then add a question that asks for confirmation. For example, during the talk time in Rick's classroom, he asked Jean what she wanted to talk about (Selman, 2001). When she replied "Mommy," this dialogue followed:

> *Rick:* Your mommy?
> *Jean:* (*nods head yes*) Mommy work
> *Rick:* Yes, your mommy works. She works, doesn't she? (p. 15)

In this interaction, Rick's use of a tag question ("doesn't she?") encouraged Jean to continue talking about her mother. Toddlers are just beginning to develop their conversation skills and will need many opportunities to become listeners and know how to take turns in speaking. If you find that your toddlers are not able to participate while they are focused on eating their snack, you may want to wait until the children are almost finished eating before you begin a group conversation.

 Figure 5.5 Example of Early Conversation with Infant

Setting: Infant classroom of child care center. Maggie, a three-month-old, has just awakened from a nap. Sara, her teacher, approaches the crib and leans over to Maggie.

Sara:	Hi there, Maggie! Did you have a good nap?
Maggie:	(*looks at Sara. Waves her arms and legs*)
Sara:	Oh, you did? I'm glad you had a good nap. Let's get you up and give you a fresh diaper. Are you ready to get up?
Maggie:	(*looks at Sara and smiles, gurgles*)
Sara:	OK, let's go. (*begins to lift Maggie from the crib*) Up you go. What a great nap you had! Let's go to the changing table to get a fresh diaper! (*walks to changing table and places Maggie gently down on the table*) There you go. Are you ready?
Maggie:	(*smiles and waves both arms and legs*)
Sara:	Here we go. Off with the old diaper. And on with the new. (*proceeds to change diaper, continues with conversation*)

Figure 5.6 Example of a Teacher's Use of Questioning, Repitition, and Expansion with a Toddler

---

Setting: Toddler classroom. Sam, 30 months old, is walking around in the playhouse area. He is the only one in the area at this time. His teacher, Melanie, approaches the house area and sits down in one of the chairs.

Melanie: Hi Sam. What shall we have for breakfast?

Sam: Cheerios. Juice.

Melanie: Great idea. Let's have Cheerios and juice. What kind of juice shall we have?

Sam: Apple.

Melanie: Oh, I like apple juice. Shall we look for the cereal bowls?

Sam: (*Nods his head*)

Melanie: (*looks around the area*) Oh, I think the cereal bowls are over there on the shelf. (*points*)

Labeling. As young children approach the age of one year, they become very interested in learning the names of things in their environment (Wells, 1986). By learning labels, children can better communicate their intents and wishes. Toddlers frequently will ask adults "Wha dis?" and "Wha dat?" Teachers can encourage children's learning of labels by providing consistent labels for objects in the classroom environment as well as by encouraging toddlers to provide the name of the object by asking them "What's this?" and then confirming the label provided by the child. It is also important to provide the most common label for an entity or object. For example, rather than using the specific label for a bird, such as "blue jay," simply refer to it as a "bird." This provides children with a way of categorizing all similar entities into the same conceptual group.

Song, rhymes, and finger plays. Infants and toddlers enjoy the rhythms and variations in sound that are present in songs, rhymes, and finger plays. These experiences contribute to children's awareness of the sounds of language. When actions are combined with the song or rhyme, it helps children understand the meaning of the words. For example, the action rhyme "Open them, Shut them" involves opening and shutting their hands, giving a clap, and then putting their hands in their laps. By the pairing of actions and words, children learn the concepts involved. "Itsy Bitsy Spider," another traditional favorite, combines actions and words that help children understand the concepts of up and down, along with concepts related to rain and sunshine.

When young children have frequent opportunities to enjoy the rhythmic language and repetition found in songs, rhymes, and finger plays, they become aware of the patterns and predictability found in each. This predictability encourages children to become involved verbally and nonverbally in these activities. For example, when a song like "Old MacDonald Had a Farm" becomes familiar to young children they are able to predict the animal sounds that accompany the song and may eagerly participate in making these sounds. It is also important to remember that infants and young toddlers will be able to participate in the action part of the song or rhymes before they will participate verbally. This indicates they are able to predict the upcoming actions and perform them as well as comprehend the words, although they are not yet able to produce the speech that goes along with the actions.

Songs, rhymes, and finger plays can be incorporated throughout the day during caregiving routines (diapering, dressing) as well as special times of one-on-one interaction. Songs and rhymes can be created by teachers for individual children or situations. (See Appendix B for a listing of resources for songs, rhymes, and finger plays for infants and toddlers).

Picture Book Sharing

Although picture-book sharing involves oral interaction, it is more than just an oral language activity. Because the object of joint reference between the adult and child is a book, and therefore includes written language as well as illustrations, there is a more complex dimension to this language activity. The book serves as the joint "object of contemplation" for the adult and child. In this contemplation, the language that occurs is much more complex than the language of other conversations. These early picture-book sharing experiences help young children begin to learn about various symbol systems (National Association for the Education of Young Children, 1998). Reading to and with young children appears to be the "single most important activity" for building knowledge about literacy (p. 3).

Infants. Sharing books with infants may seem unusual because they are not yet able to talk; however, this experience is a very appropriate one for these young children. When books are shared, infants experience a warm, secure feeling as they are held and cuddled in the adult's lap (Honig & Brophy, 1996). Even very young infants will enjoy being held in a caring adult's lap and hearing the adult's voice reading expressively. When children are introduced to books in these warm and comforting settings, they begin to associate books with this feeling of pleasure and security (Rocklin, 2000). This association sets a foundation for future positive interactions with books.

Early on, it is the adult's expressive voice that provides enjoyment for the child and their close proximity to someone who cares for them. A newspaper or magazine article read expressively may provide as much interest for a young baby as would a story book; however, this phase passes and the specific features of the printed material that is shared are more important in keeping a child engaged in the book sharing. With older infants (6 to 12 months) the book sharing becomes a time of talking about what is pictured in the book. As the adult and child become engaged in sharing the book, the book becomes the object of contemplation around which their literacy-related interactions take place. It is important for teachers to know how to select appropriate books to share as well as how to engage infants in this interaction. Guidelines for book selection and interaction with infants are presented in the following two sections. (See Appendix B for suggested books.)

Sharing books with young children is strongly associated with developing literacy knowledge.

Nadezhda 1906

Book selection guidelines. In selecting a book to share with an infant, you will want to keep in mind these three main considerations: (a) Durability and ease of manipulation, (b) content, and (c) illustrations (Armbruster, Lehr, & Osborn, 2003; Brown, 2001; Dinsmore, 1988; Honig & Brophy, 1996; Honig, 2001; Honig & Shin, 2001; Soundy, 1997; Stevenson, 2006).

1. *Durability and ease of manipulation.* Books should have laminated coating on each page so that they are more durable and can be wiped clean. Select board books that have thick pages that are easily grasped. Cloth books are also appropriate but only if the cloth is stiffened and easy to manipulate. Older infants may also enjoy books that have tactile features, such as pages with smooth, bumpy, or wavy sections that can be touched and experienced.

2. *Book content.* Select books with content that reflects infants' experiences and environment. For example, if you know the infant's family has a pet dog, you might select *Find the Puppy* (Cox, 1999) to read. The book focuses on the puppy in his bed, being fed, drinking, knocking over the trash can, playing hide and seek, and going to sleep. *Peekaboo Baby* (Miller, 2001) would be a good choice to share with a child who has enjoyed playing peek-a-boo with her family or teachers.

Books for young infants usually will have a simple sequence of a daily event, such as getting dressed, or will provide an opportunity to label objects or actions. Book content that contains repetition, rhythm, and rhyme will provide a feeling of security to the infant because it soon becomes predictable. With that predictability is the security in knowing the book content is stable (Rocklin, 2000). Wordless picture books as well as books of photographs with limited text are good choices because they also provide opportunities for labeling.

Books that have content that is hidden under flaps will also encourage prediction through repeated readings. Knowing that the lion's picture is located under the flap is exciting and at the same time reassuring to the young child. Because infants are developing the concept of object permanence, their experiences in revealing the entity located under a flap confirms that the same object or animal will be there each time they look. Although this type of book is thoroughly enjoyed by infants, it is not usually very durable and may not withstand the exuberance of these very young children.

3. *Illustrations.* The quality of illustrations in books for infants is critical to the interactions that will occur. In book sharing, the adult first establishes shared or joint reference, and then monitors the child's gaze and attention to specific parts of the illustration that were the focus of the adult's speech. When illustrations are more complex or abstract, it is difficult to determine the child's gaze and also difficult for the child to focus on visually. Thus, books for infants need to have colorful, clear, simple illustrations or actual photographs, which are more related to their visual experiences and less abstracted from reality. For example, *Peekaboo Baby* (Miller, 2001) has photographs of different children playing peek-a-boo on each page. You will want to choose books for very young infants that have only one picture per page to avoid distractions from the main focus (Honig, 2001). Simple illustrations and photographs will also encourage older infants to participate in naming or labeling what is pictured.

Interaction strategies for teachers. In providing opportunities for infants to participate in book sharing, you will find these ten guidelines useful:

1. *Choose a time when the infant is content, rested, and happy* (Stevenson, 2006). Be sure the infant is comfortable and feels secure in your lap and embrace (Honig, 2001). It is also important to remember that book sharing with infants is always an individual activity between one teacher and one child. (Even with toddlers, one-on-one sharing is more beneficial and successful.) Book sharing should not be on an arbitrary schedule, but

should occur as children show interest throughout the day (Soundy, 1997). Multiple opportunities throughout the day for this book sharing also are beneficial because then you can respond to infants' interests and attentiveness.

2. *Be sensitive to the child's attention span and interests.* Book sharing with infants is typically very short. Perhaps it will last only one to three minutes before the child becomes distracted or loses interest. As you interact with an infant in book sharing, monitor her gaze and other nonverbal behaviors to determine whether she is attending to the book and to your interaction. For example, if after several pages, the older infant flips the book closed and looks around, that is a very clear indication that the interaction is over.

3. *Establish shared reference.* As a way of establishing joint or shared reference, you will need to use gestures and pointing to direct an infant's attention to the focus of your comments. You may find that you will point directly to objects and use a sweeping motion to direct the child to actions that are illustrated. You will also use your voice along with your gestures to establish this joint reference, such as saying "Look!"

4. *Establish a dialogue or turn-taking.* To do this you first briefly talk about the illustrations and then pause and wait for the infant to respond either nonverbally or verbally (Arnold, 2005). It is important to provide ample "wait time" to give the infant a chance to respond before you go ahead with your next turn in the conversation (Carlson & Bricker, 1982). Show your enthusiasm and delight with the child's responses. Do not be concerned with creating a story. Remember that the book and its contents serve as a focus for your joint contemplation. This interaction should not be hurried, but instead, sensitive to the interests and responses of the child.

5. *Vary your intonation, tempo, and volume.* Although you probably will not be actually reading the words of the text, it is important to use a range of intonation and expression as you talk (Armbruster, Lehr, & Osborn, 2003; Honig, 2001). Make your voice exciting by varying the volume, tempo, and rhythm. This creates a memorable experience and helps to sustain the child's attention. Varying your voice also contributes to the meaning

When you share a book with an infant, use gestures and pointing to focus the child's attention and to add meaning to your comments.

Catalin Petolea

of what you say. For example, "Prince George is a *big* dog. He is *soooo* tall!" In this way you are also expressing your delight in books and in the book-sharing experience (*Early Childhood Today*, 2004).

6. *Mediate the text to increase child's comprehension.* In sharing each book, you will probably need to adapt what you say to meet infants' interest and comprehension levels. This is especially true when you are sharing a new, unfamiliar book with an infant. For example, if you were sharing the board book, *Where's Spot?* (Hill, 1980; 2000), for the first time you might decide that certain adaptations are needed, such as those found in Figure 5.7. As you read this example, look for the ways in which the text was changed and think about the reasons this teacher might have made these changes.

7. *Share the same book on repeated occasions.* As you share books with infants, you may find that with repeated experiences with the same book you can begin to include more of the actual text in your reading because the infant is now able to comprehend more complex language.

8. *Remember children's individual favorites.* It is important to pay attention to which books are liked by which children. In this way you can motivate children to participate in story book sharing. Many young children will want to interact with the same book again and again. This repetition is important because it develops their memory for the book content and for the language associated with the book. You will need to be fairly consistent even with your adapted oral text so that they develop this sense of predictability and stability for book content.

9. *Encourage child's physical contact with book.* When you share books with infants, you will want to them to be active rather than passive. Encourage them to help hold the book and turn the pages. This will help them learn to manipulate books on their own. Older infants may also show interest in selecting a book to be shared and bringing it to you to be shared.

10. *Provide opportunities for book exploration on their own.* Older infants will also enjoy looking at familiar books independently. Take time to observe how they are learning to hold the book and turn the pages. Also note how they focus on the illustrations. You may find that older infants who have had frequent book-sharing experiences will begin to vocalize as they turn the pages and their intonation may resemble that of the adult who reads with them (Otto, 1994).

 Figure 5.7 Example of Text Adaptation When Book Sharing with an Infant

Book: *Where's Spot?* (Hill, 1980)

Page	What Teacher Reads/Says	Book Text	Book Illustration
1–2	Look! Here's Spot's mom. she's going to look for Spot. He did not eat his food.	Where's Spot? That Spot. He hasn't eaten his supper. Where can he be?	Spot's mom is walking away from two food bowls. Spot's bowl still has food in it.
3–4	Where is Spot? Oh, let's check behind this door— (moves flap) Oh, no. There's a bear eating honey!	Is he behind the door?	Spot's mom is looking behind a blue door (flap book feature)

Toddlers. Picture-book sharing with toddlers generally involves more active participation due to toddlers' increased fine-muscle coordination and their increased verbal skills. Young toddlers (13 to 24 months) are usually moving from the one-word stage to using multiple words (also known as telegraphic speech). They are also able to better coordinate their arm and hand movements, which facilitates book handling and page turning. Toddlers also are keenly interested in the "naming game" and begin to ask questions such as, "Wha dis?" and "Wha dat?" Such questions often become part of book sharing interactions.

Book selection guidelines. Many of the book selection guidelines presented in the prior section for infants are also relevant to selecting books for toddlers. As a reflective teacher, you will need to be able to determine the appropriateness of specific books for the individual children in your classroom. As you interact with toddlers during book sharing, you will develop a clearer understanding of each child's interests and language interactions that will guide you in selecting books for future sharing times. If you become aware that a particular toddler has not had many book-sharing experiences during infancy, you will need to begin your book sharing with books that reflect the characteristics of books appropriate for infants.

In this section, additional guidelines for selecting books are presented; however, it is your decision, based on your professional judgment, as to what book will be appropriate for which child. If you are still getting acquainted with a particular child, you may need to try out several different books to determine which type of book will be appropriate and engaging for that child. Carefully observe the child's responses to your book sharing to have a better idea of what types of books to use the next time.

For young toddlers, board books are still appropriate because they are easier to handle and page turning is easier. Toddlers will enjoy special-feature books with parts that move, such as flaps or tabs, or pages with a hole to peek through or put fingers through; however, these types may not be very durable (Bardige & Segal, 2005). Toddlers enjoy books of a range of sizes, from the small, personal-sized board books (for example, 5″ × 5″), which are easy to carry and manipulate, to the very large Big Books (for example, 14″ × 18″) that can be viewed alone or shared with other children.

Book and story content still need to focus on familiar concepts (Novick, 1999–2000); however, because toddlers' conceptual development and experiences have expanded, there is a greater range of topics that would be familiar to them. Be sure to have books that represent cultural and social diversity in your classroom to engage children who are from diverse settings. Toddlers will enjoy books that encourage labeling, such as *Richard Scarry's Best Word Book Ever* (1991). Also include books that focus on a particular concept through illustrations and text that present a wide variety of examples. For example, *Trucks—WHIZZ! Zoom! Rumble!* (Hubbell, 2003) provides opportunities to focus on many different kinds of trucks, such as dump trucks, tank trucks, fire trucks, ice cream trucks, and the noises each one makes. When selecting books for toddlers, choose books with simple texts, limited to a sentence or two on each page. Toddlers who have had many prior experiences with story book sharing may be ready for longer and more complex texts.

During the toddler years, children will continue to enjoy texts that have repetition, rhythm, and rhyme. These features create awareness that a text is predictable and stable and also increases awareness of the sounds of language. This predictability also encourages toddlers to begin to participate in the book sharing by joining in on a refrain or by supplying a word that rhymes.

Books for toddlers may have illustrations that are more complex and detailed than those found in books for infants. Be sure that the illustrations are accurate representations of the text that accompanies them. A good example of this is *Over in the Meadow* (Cabrera, 1999). The illustrations are vivid paintings that closely represent the lines of the rhyming text.

Books with photographs provide a clear connection to the real world, particularly for nonfiction topics: For example, the photographs of traffic signs in *I Read Symbols* (Hoban, 1983) or *Look Book* (Hoban, 1997), which provides clear, colorful photographs of animals, flowers, foods, and butterflies.

As a toddler teacher, you may decide to develop a themed approach to your curriculum and choose books that fit into that theme. For example, if the theme is on animals, you would select a group of books about animals and also have related activities that focus on animals. This creates connections between concepts, language, and literacy (Rosenquest, 2002). It also provides continuity throughout the curriculum and provides increased opportunities for children to develop vocabulary.

Interaction strategies for teachers. One of the first steps in sharing picture books with toddlers is to create an inviting area that encourages children to explore books. Place children's books on low bookshelves or in book baskets or bins. Children will be more interested in the books if the covers are visible. You also want to make it easy for toddlers to return the books after they are finished. You will find that they will want to interact with books that you have shared with them. Having multiple copies of favorite books is also a good idea. Toddlers often find it difficult to take turns or wait for another person to finish with the book that they want.

Provide comfortable cushions or small chairs for several children so that more than one child can explore this area at the same time, as well as seating that you and your aide can use when interacting with toddlers in this area.

Toddlers also have an increasing need for active involvement and a desire for autonomy (Bardige & Segal, 2005). This means that toddler book sharing will usually be on an individual, one-on-one basis because toddlers are not yet ready for group activities. Be sure to provide several opportunities throughout each day for book sharing (Novick, 1999–2000) and for independent exploration and experiences with books.

Toddler book sharing will often be very short in duration, perhaps only several minutes in length. Frequently, only a portion of a book will be shared. Be sensitive to each child's attention span and interest, and discontinue the sharing when the child loses interest or becomes distracted.

As toddlers approach three years of age, you may find that some are ready for book sharing in a small group setting.

Monkey Business Images

You may find that when you are sharing a book with one toddler, that others may come to join you for a moment or two, but then go on to other activities. This is to be expected. Toddlers still need to have the individualized attention from an adult when they are interacting with a book that will respond to their questions and comments. They are not yet ready to sit and listen and share the teacher with others.

As toddlers approach preschool age, around three years old, you may find that some are ready for small group sharing; however, you will still need to expect that some children will not be able to remain attentive throughout the complete book sharing. Those who become restless should be allowed to go on to another activity.

A key aspect of your book sharing with toddlers is the enthusiasm you share for books. You are a motivating factor in encouraging toddlers to engage in this shared activity. This enthusiasm is evident in the way you vary your intonation and rhythm of speech and by the way in which you encourage toddlers to interact with you and with the book content. Encourage verbal responses as well as nonverbal responses. When the text is predictable, encourage toddlers to chime in on a refrain or text segment.

You may need to mediate text and simplify it to meet a child's level of comprehension. This would involve simplifying the vocabulary (for example, substituting "work truck" for "cement-mixer truck") or making the sentence structure less complex.

When sharing a picture book with a toddler, you will want to not only mediate the text, but establish a turn-taking, conversation-like interaction. Arnold (2005) refers to this as **dialogic reading**. The three parts of dialogic reading include: (a) Asking a question that has a specific answer that can be found in the illustration or the text, (b) asking open-ended questions, and (c) expanding on children's responses. For example:

Adult:	What is that? (*pointing to the illustration*) [*book-based question*]
Child:	truck
Adult:	Yes! That's a truck. It's a blue truck. [*expansion of child's response*] What do you see in the back of the truck? [*book-based question*]
Child:	logs
Adult:	Yes, there are logs in the back. [*expansion of child's response*] What do you think they will do with the logs? [*open-ended question*]
Child:	make a house
Adult:	Yes, they could use the logs to build a house. [*expansion of child's response*]

Through the use of these dialogic reading strategies, toddlers' active participation is encouraged. As you gain experience in sharing books with toddlers, you will be able to consciously use questioning and expansion to actively engage children in book sharing.

You can also use an **oral cloze** strategy to encourage toddlers' verbal participation. For this strategy, you first select a child's favorite story book. Then as you read the text, you stop at a predictable part and encourage the child to fill in the gap. For example, when you read a book with a patterned text such as *Brown Bear, Brown Bear, What Do You See?* (Martin, 1996), you will pause just before you turn the page to encourage the child to tell you what happens next.

Older toddlers may want to read a familiar book to you (*Early Childhood Today*, 2001). This is a wonderful opportunity to sit back and listen to the verbal text that is created by the toddler. Be an active, interested listener and provide positive feedback even if the child's version varies from the original text. Toddlers who seek out these opportunities to read are showing not only their memory for book content and language, but also their enjoyment in sharing a book with someone special—you!

A key aspect of your book shaing with toddlers is the enthusiasm you share for books.

Robert Kneschke

Environmental Print Experiences

As children proceed through the toddler years, they may begin to notice print in their environment, begin to ask questions about it, and attempt to figure out its meaning. You can provide opportunities for them to see how print is used in everyday activities in the following ways: by using their name as a label, sending newsletters and notes to parents, and providing props for play that contain print. These activities will develop children's awareness of the ways in which written language is used in different settings.

Use the child's name as a label. A very personal experience with the use of print in the toddler environment is when toddlers' names are used to identify the location of their cubby or space where they hang their coat and store their personal possessions. When you use their names to identify their artwork or other projects, they will also see the way in which their ownership can be communicated. It is also beneficial to use a particular symbol along with the young child's name, such as a square, triangle, or flower (Epstein, 2002a). This will be easier for a young child to recognize and when the symbol is associated with their name day after day, they will also begin to recognize their written names. Be consistent in the way children's names are written. For example, always use uppercase for the initial letter and lowercase for the remaining letters. Be sure that you follow family preferences for name use: do not abbreviate or use another form of a child's name unless it is also used by the family, for example, Chris for Christopher, Frankie for Frank, Eddie for Eduardo. For children with names from other languages, you will also want to use the correct spelling and accent markings of that language, for example, José.

Send newsletters and notes to parents. When newsletters or notes are given to parents, older toddlers will also notice the use of print to communicate. They may ask to have the print read to them. Take time to share with them the general meaning communicated in the newsletter and/or note, such as, "This note is to your mommy. I'm asking her to bring in your shoes for gym."

Providing props for play that contain print. As you prepare the play environment in a toddler classroom, you can include different objects that incorporate environmental print (Bardige & Segal, 2005). For the dramatic play area, you could bring in empty cereal boxes and other cardboard food packages, along with copies of magazines and catalogs. You will want to select the types of items that children may have had experience with in their home settings. This will increase toddlers' engagement and interest in using these items in their play. In the block area, you could provide small versions of road signs that older toddlers could use when they are in this area.

Symbol-Making Experiences

In addition to providing infants and toddlers with experiences that focus on constructing meaning from written and graphic symbols in books and environmental print, it is important to have additional opportunities to participate in making symbols as well as engaging in symbolic or imaginative play. In this section, three types of symbol-making activities are described: personalized **caption books,** imaginative play, and drawing-scribbling. Each of these activities provides young children with opportunities to begin to understand how symbols and other representations are used to communicate.

Personalized caption books. These books are made especially for individual children with pictures of items or people that have special meaning for the child (Bardige & Segal, 2005; *Early Childhood Today*, 2001). For very young children, you will want to use photographs of the actual item or person in their environment. Enlist the help of their families to obtain pictures of family pets, siblings, parents, extended family members, their homes, or favorite toys. Then mount each photograph on a separate page and print a caption below the picture. Cover each page with clear plastic or laminate to increase durability. Older toddlers may want to dictate the captions for their special book. Be sure to put each child's name on the cover as the book's author.

Caption books can also be developed from magazine and catalog pictures. For infants and young toddlers, select pictures that represent the child's experiences. Older toddlers may want to select their own pictures, and may even select pictures that have some similar concept, such as "things that move," "food," or "my favorite things." Since toddlers are still developing small-muscle coordination, you will need to have the pictures precut from the magazines or catalogs. Ask the toddler what caption they want you to write on each page. Bind the book together using a ring or large, sturdy clip.

Imaginative play. Opportunities for pretend play are important because toddlers will begin to use objects in imaginative ways to represent ideas and events. In this way, they are using an object to symbolize or represent something else. In order to encourage imaginative play, you will need to provide basic materials that can be used to represent a variety of other objects, such as cardboard blocks or soft blocks. An oblong block may be used to represent a telephone, a hammer, or a guitar. A big, empty box suggests many possibilities to toddlers, such as using it as a house, car, train, or airplane.

Drawing and scribbling. Older toddlers may begin to show an interest in drawing or attempting to write. To encourage these early symbol-makers, provide an area where the basic materials are easily accessible and can be used independently. Some of the materials need to be available every day, such as felt-tip (washable) markers and crayons as well as smaller markers that have a finer tip, along with materials to write or draw on. Other materials, for finger painting and painting with brushes, can be made available on a less frequent basis.

Older toddlers may begin to show an interest in drawing or attempting to write.

dotshock

Because toddlers are in the early stages of fine muscle control, they will need to have larger pieces of paper for their early drawing and scribbling activities. You may find that a large piece of paper taped to a low table, a wall, or floor provides the space that toddlers will need (Bardige & Segal, 2005). Later on you might introduce smaller pieces of paper and different formats, including note cards and envelopes as well as simple books. Encourage children to talk with you about their creations and the meaning they have represented visually.

Guidelines for Teachers of English Language Learners (ELLs)

Infants and toddlers who are enrolled in English-speaking classrooms and who are from families who speak a different home language than English will develop **simultaneous bilingualism** (Weitzman & Greenberg, 2002). They will be learning their home language as well as learning English because it is the language used at the infant-toddler center.

As their teacher, it is important for you to focus on specific strategies to support their acquisition of English and to provide a foundation for their emergent literacy. This section will focus on five major guidelines: (a) Establish rapport with parents and family, (b) encourage and support use of first language at home, (c) focus on oral language development, (d) provide classroom materials in their home language and culture, and (e) provide language and literacy take-home activities.

Establish Rapport with Parents and Family

All children need to feel safe and secure. This is especially true for infants and toddlers. In establishing rapport with the children's parents and family, you are creating a connection between their home and your classroom. It is important to establish rapport with each child's family; however, it is particularly critical for families who have a non–English home language. Once you are aware of a child's specific home language, make an effort to learn the basic phrases in their language so that you can greet family members in their home language. In making this effort, you are indicating that you value their home language (National Association for the Education of Young Children, 1996).

It is especially important that you learn how to correctly pronounce the parents' names because this also is a sign of respect. Always address parents in a formal manner by using the courtesy title of Mr., Mrs., or Ms. and their family name. You could also learn the comparable courtesy title of their home language, such as Señor or Madame.

You will also need to be aware of the nonverbal communication customs of each child's home culture. In some groups, they greet each other with a slight nod of the head, while in other groups, adults shake hands when they meet. Learn the appropriate ways to greet the families of English language learners so that they will feel comfortable in interacting with you. By creating a welcoming environment in your classroom, the parents and families will pass on this level of comfort to their young children.

Even though the focus of your classroom will be on communicating in English, you can add to a child's feeling of comfort and security by learning some key phrases in their home language, such as "lunchtime," "come," and "bathroom." This is especially important during the first few weeks (Weitzman & Greenberg, 2002).

Encourage and Support Use of First Language at Home

When children are learning a language, they need to have interactions with fluent speakers of that language. By encouraging parents to use their first language at home, infants and toddlers will develop a strong foundation in that language (Tabors & Snow, 2002; Weitzman & Greenberg, 2002). Because the parents are fluent speakers of their home language, their children will experience a rich language environment and develop communication skills in that setting. For all children, a rich language environment is "the most important aspect of early literacy" (Vernon-Feagans, Hammer, Miccio, and Manlove, 2002). This rich language environment also provides a foundation for learning the second language, such as English.

When families want to encourage both languages at home, it is usually less confusing for the child if each parent focuses on using just one language rather than speaking in both languages (Piper, 1998). Or perhaps the grandparents could use the non–English language and the parents use English. This way, the child will be able to separate out the different language patterns by associating them with specific speakers.

Focus on Oral Language Development

Since oral language is the foundation for emergent literacy, the focus of teachers of English language learners in infant and toddler classrooms should be on oral language development. At this age, the process of learning the second language, English, is very similar to the way they are each learning their home language. Thus, you will use some of the same strategies for oral language development that you use with children from English-speaking homes, such as eye contact and shared reference, mediation, linguistic scaffolding, and labeling, as well as similar activities such as conversations, picture-book sharing, and symbol-making activities. As much as possible, use key phrases in their home language as well as in English. Learning two languages concurrently is a complex process. Infants and toddlers who are in settings that use different languages will probably mix the two languages until they are approaching preschool age (Weitzman & Greenberg, 2002). This mixing of languages is to be expected and should not be interpreted as evidence of a problem.

When you interact with infants and toddlers who are English language learners, you will need to carefully observe the ways in which they communicate, both nonverbally and verbally. As with first language acquisition, children's receptive knowledge of their second language develops before they are able to communicate orally in the new language. A silent period may occur while the child is developing his receptive knowledge and comprehension of oral language. This is a precursor to beginning to use that language when speaking (Krashen, 1981, 1982; Santos & Ostrosky, 2002; Tabors, 1997; Weitzman & Greenberg, 2002).

Provide Classroom Literacy Materials in Home Language

In addition to exposing young English language learners to stories, poems, and books that are in English, it is important to also have classroom materials that represent their home language and social-cultural setting. In this way, you will be providing experiences that build on their prior knowledge and strengthen their conceptual development as well as the development of their home language.

Some children's books have text written in two or more languages. For example, *En vacances: dictionnaire multilingue* (I Dioscuri, 1994) has four different languages: German, French, English, and Spanish. Bilingual books for infants and toddlers are now available in a wide range of languages, including Arabic, Bengali, Chinese, Gujarati, French, Hebrew, Italian, Portuguese, Russian, Somali, Turkish, Urdu, and Vietnamese (see Appendix B for a sample listing of titles along with useful Websites for locating additional books).

You can also ask families to help you make tapes of nursery rhymes or songs in their home languages (Bardige & Segal, 2005). Then you could use these tapes in your classroom in a listening center or during quiet times.

Provide Language and Literacy Take-Home Activities

Infants' and toddlers' experiences with literacy can be extended through take-home activities carried in book bags, and for toddlers, drawing/writing tote bags. In this way, you are providing the materials for children to continue their observations and explorations of literacy-related events at home. You are also encouraging parents and family members to interact with their children in literacy-related events.

These bags can be loaned for several days or for a week at a time. Create a check-out system and set aside time to check bags back in and assure the contents are ready for the next check-out. Select colorful and durable tote bags and add an identification tag with your school's name and phone number and your classroom designation. Be sure the bag is designed so materials are secure and will not slip out.

Book bags. For each book bag, select two to three books that you have used in your classroom. If possible, include titles that have the text written in both the child's home language and English as well as books written only in the child's home language. Prepare several book bags to increase availability to parents.

Drawing/writing tote bags. To encourage toddlers' exploration of drawing and writing, you will need to provide a variety of felt-tip markers (water-soluble) and big crayons. Place several sheets of paper in a folder. You could also include a roll of plain paper that will provide a larger surface to draw or write on. When the tote is returned, remove the child's drawing/writing and talk with the child about what was created. Be sure the child's name is on the paper and display it in your room for the day and then return it to the toddler so he can take it home.

Guidelines for Teachers of At-Risk Children

The definition of children who are at-risk frequently has focused families at poverty or low-income levels, parents with low-literacy skills, single parents, and language dialect use (Bus, 2002; Dickinson & Sprague, 2002; Storch & Whitehurst, 2001; Strickland, 2002). It is important to keep in mind, however, that not every child from an environment that appears to be at-risk will experience difficulties in literacy development. Not all families with similar at-risk characteristics are the same.

For example, not all low-SES homes will lack access to books. Some low-SES parents will borrow books from the library or obtain books from garage sales or resale shops. A low-SES child in these homes will have opportunities to develop emergent literacy and language competencies at home. Instead of basing your teaching decisions on assumptions about a child's home environment, you will want to make your instructional decisions after a careful observation of each child's ways of communicating. By using the observation format located in Figure 5.1, you will be able to have a clearer understanding of a child's ways of communicating. If, after this careful observation, you are concerned that a child actually is at-risk for difficulty in language development and emergent literacy, you will need to focus your efforts on providing repeated, individualized language and literacy-related experiences that the child may not have opportunity to experience at home.

The types of activities appropriate for children at-risk do not differ from those described earlier in the chapter. Your curriculum will still focus on oral language development and creating a language and literacy-rich environment; however, in order to more appropriately teach children whom you have identified as at-risk, you will need to keep these three guidelines in mind: increase one-on-one interactions, use repetition to strengthen learning, and observe each child's responses to plan future activities.

Increase One-on-One Interactions

Language is learned through interaction. Children who are at-risk need frequent opportunities to interact with an adult to develop ways of communicating. As you engage these young children in conversations, picture-book sharing, or symbol-making activities, you will need to monitor closely each child's eye contact and shared reference. You will also need to carefully observe how each child responds in dialogic turn-taking during conversations as well as in book sharing.

Use Repetition to Strengthen Learning

Children who are at-risk may need to have more repeated experiences in order to begin to participate more actively in book sharing, in singing a song, or becoming engaged in a finger play. For example, when you find a particular book that a toddler enjoys sharing, use that book several times during the week to increase his familiarity with the book. You may also find that toddlers will enjoy repeated readings during the same day. This high level of familiarity will encourage more active responses and participation.

Observe Each Child's Responses to Plan Future Activities

Although this guideline can be applied to all curricular decisions in infant-toddler classrooms, it is especially important for interactions with at-risk learners. As you observe each child's responses to the learning activities, notice which aspects of the activity appear to be beneficial for the child and which areas may need repetition or further mediation. When you reflect on each child's behavior, use this information to adjust ongoing activities as well as when planning future learning activities.

The decisions you make as a teacher of infants and toddlers, and the ways in which you provide a developmentally appropriate curriculum to all children, and especially to children who are at-risk, will have a very critical role in each child's growth and development.

Informal Assessment of Emergent Literacy Behaviors

As a reflective teacher, you will be making teaching decisions based on careful observations of your children's responses to the learning environment in your classroom. Some of your observations will be made on the spot and you will use them to modify your ongoing interactions with children; other observations will be more systematic and will involve a checklist or written format (Owocki, 1999; Owocki & Goodman, 2002). Systematic observations are descriptive records of behavior you have observed. Such observations will help you learn what the child knows and can do (Owocki & Goodman, 2002). Your observations may take the form of **anecdotal records**, which are descriptive notes of observed behaviors, or you may use some type of checklist or observation format. You will also want to develop some way of organizing your observations so that you can refer back to them. This will also help you be able to share your observations with children's families. Generally, teachers have found that some type of filing or portfolio organization is useful.

Key Areas for Informal Assessment

There are three areas of observations that are valuable in assessing infants' and toddlers' emergent literacy behaviors. These include (a) Ways of communicating, (b) book sharing, and (c) symbol-making. It is important to remember that infants' and toddlers' behaviors may vary from day-to-day as well as within different settings. Repeated and periodic observations will be needed to thoroughly describe each child's developing language and emergent literacy.

Ways of communicating. Because oral language development provides the foundation for learning about written language, it is important to first determine the ways in which a child communicates. The observation guide presented earlier in this chapter (see Figure 5.1) focuses on children's ways of communicating in six areas: attention to adult's speech, eye contact–shared reference, turn-taking/dialogic participation, attention to ongoing events, level of oral language, and home language. Periodic observations using this guide will provide you with an understanding of infants' and toddlers' oral language development.

Book-sharing interactions. When you share books with infants and toddlers, you have an opportunity to observe their responses, which can indicate their developing language and emergent literacy. Specific behaviors you will want to observe include the following: eye contact, shared reference, turn-taking/dialogic participation, book handling, memory for book content, attentiveness, and affective responses. In the remainder of this section, specific aspects of each of these behaviors are described. A format is provided in Figure 5.8 that will be useful in observing infants' and toddlers' interactions during book sharing.

When you begin to document your observation of book sharing, be sure that you also document the specific book you have chosen to share. The characteristics of the book as well as a child's familiarity with the book will be related to the ways in which the child responds during the book sharing.

Figure 5.8 Observation of Infant–Toddler Book Sharing

Child's name: _____ Age: _____ Date: _____

Book shared: _____

Focus of Observation	Questions to Consider	Consistently	Occasionally	Not at This Time
Eye contact	Makes eye contact with book? with adult?			
Shared reference	Follows adult's gestures/ pointing?			
Turn-taking/ dialogic participation	Responds nonverbally? Responds verbally?			
Book handling	Touches, pats, or hits book? Attempts to turn pages? Picks up book independently?			
Memory for book content	Anticipates book content: • Through gestures or facial expression? • Through verbal expression?			
Attentiveness	Maintains focus on book?			
Affective Response	Appears to enjoy book sharing? Initiates book-sharing interaction?			

Eye contact. During the picture-book interaction, monitor the child's eye contact. Does he look at you? Does he look at the book? Is the eye contact re-established as each page is turned? Or is the eye contact only momentary so that the child becomes distracted and looks around the room?

Shared reference. When you point to a picture or illustration, does the child's eye contact follow your gesture? Does the child attempt to imitate your gesture?

Turn-taking/dialogic participation. As you engage the child in book sharing and you pause after labeling or commenting about a picture, carefully observe the child's response. Does the child respond nonverbally? This response may involve a facial expression, a gesture, or eye contact with you. Older infants may respond verbally by making sounds, babbling, laughing, or even squealing in delight. Toddlers may respond with one or more word utterances and may even ask questions. If you find the child is not responding, you may want to increase the "wait time" before you speak. As you have repeated book-sharing experiences with children, you will develop an awareness of the wait time needed to encourage young children's responses.

Book handling. Another way of looking at children's responses to book sharing is to see if they are attempting to touch or physically interact with the book. Infants who are just beginning to develop physical control over their arm and hand movements may indicate their interest by just waving or moving their arms. Older infants and toddlers may begin to point to illustrations and attempt to turn pages. They may also begin to initiate a book sharing by picking up a book and taking it to an adult.

Memory for book content. Infants and toddlers will develop a memory for book content when books are shared repeatedly. This memory or content familiarity may be expressed verbally or nonverbally. The older infant who remembers that the lion's picture is hidden under the flap on a certain page and makes the sound of the lion's roar just prior to lifting up the flap is indicating her memory for book content. Similarly, the infant who touches her head just before the adult reads "Touch your head, baby" is also indicating her memory for book content. This evidence of memory for book content is part of emergent literacy because it shows that the child is aware that book content is stable and can be re-created or revisited during repeated interactions with a particular book.

Attentiveness. Infants and toddlers typically will have attention spans that are relatively short and will vary from day to day and even within one day. The length of book-sharing interactions needs to be totally determined by each child's attentiveness and interest in the activity. As soon as a child becomes disinterested, the book sharing should be discontinued.

There are many factors that influence young children's attentiveness during book sharing, such as their level of physical comfort and emotional security. Other factors involve the type of book that is shared along with the ways in which the teacher engages the child in the book sharing through eye contact, shared reference, dialogic participation, and mediation. Although considerable variation will be seen between children, and even for individual children from time to time, you will typically be able to document increased attentiveness over a period of several months when children have had many opportunities for book sharing.

Affective response. Children who express delight and curiosity during book sharing are more likely to seek out additional opportunities to share books with adults. Infants and toddlers express their delight and curiosity through their smiles, giggles, squeals, claps, and enthusiastic responses during book sharing, as well as by their requests to engage in book sharing. Positive affect is also indicated when a young child requests a familiar book be read or shared again and again.

Symbol-making. Another area for observing toddlers' emergent literacy involves symbol-making. During the toddler years, children develop more control of their hand and arm muscles as well as eye-hand coordination (Santrock, 2001). As this is occurring, children may be observing adults as they write and begin to ask questions or attempt to imitate adults' actions. Toddlers may also begin to notice environmental print and associate it with a particular meaning or message. There are six specific behaviors related to symbol-making that you will want to focus on as you observe toddlers. These include: interest in adults' writing, interest in environmental print, interest in graphic expression, forms of graphic expression, meaning attributed to graphic expression, and symbolic or abstract representation during imaginary play. Each of these behaviors is described in the remainder of this section. Through careful observation, you can begin to document these early symbol-making behaviors. See Figure 5.9 for an observation format.

Interest in adults' writing. When you or other teachers are writing in the classroom, observe whether toddlers show interest in this writing process. Perhaps you are writing a note to send home with the parents, making a list of materials needed for an activity, or taking attendance. A toddler may approach you and ask, "Wha da say?"

Interest in environmental print. A child's interest in environmental print indicates his awareness that print has a special purpose and carries meaning. Older toddlers may begin to pay attention to print in your classroom, in the school building, or outside the school. They may ask questions about the print or indicate they know what it says. Some toddlers

Figure 5.9 Observation of Toddler Symbol-Making Behaviors

Child's name: _____	Age: _____
Behaviors to Look For:	**Description of Behavior (include date observed)**
Interest in adult's writing	
Interest in environmental print	
Interest in graphic expression	
Forms of graphic expression (attach artifact or copy)	Drawing? Scribbling? Letter-like units? Letters?
Meaning attributed to graphic expression	
Symbolic or abstract representation during imaginary play	

may even focus on individual letters. As their individual names are used in the classroom to label their possessions or the location of their cubby or locker, children become aware of the ways in which print carries a very personal meaning of ownership and identity.

Interest in graphic expression. When toddlers have access to writing and drawing implements, they may begin to use them to make marks on paper (or any available surface!). As you make these materials available, notice which children use this opportunity to begin to express themselves graphically.

Forms of graphic expression. Initially, toddlers' graphic expression is usually random marks or wide, sweeping lines. As they experiment with the process of creating marks on paper, they also will be developing more fine-muscle control of the process. Over time, these random marks develop into graphic representations of objects as well as wavy lines, like scribbling. Older toddler's writing attempts may begin to resemble letter-like forms.

Meaning attributed to graphic expression. Toddlers may begin to indicate that what they have expressed graphically has some meaning. They may approach an adult with their drawing or scribbling and ask, "Read this" or "Wha dis say?"

Symbolic or abstract representation during imaginary play. As you observe toddlers during their imaginary play, notice the ways in which they use objects to represent other objects or actions. For example, a toddler holds a long spoon from the house play area like a guitar, strums it and hums. Another toddler pushes an oblong block across the floor and makes an enginelike roaring sound. Both of these children are showing their ability to take an object and imagine its function as a different object.

Home–School Connections

Children's parents and families are their first teachers and their most enduring teachers. Parents will meet you as their children's first nonfamily teacher. Early childhood teachers have a key role in establishing positive and mutually supportive relationships with children's families (Goldenberg, 2002; National Association for the Education of Young Children, 1996; McCaleb, 1994; Wright, Stegelin, & Hartle, 2007).

Because the focus of this text is on children's literacy development, the following sections will present three guidelines for establishing home–school connections related to language and literacy: (a) Acknowledge home and community language and literacy, (b) share information about children's language and emergent literacy, and (c) assist parents in providing literacy materials at home.

Acknowledge Home and Community Language and Literacy

The ways in which language and literacy are used will vary from family to family and may also be related to social and cultural settings. As an infant-toddler teacher, you need to acknowledge, accept, and value these diversities. This will facilitate the development of a mutual rapport between the children, their families, and you. This will also open up opportunities for you to encourage parents to recognize how language, reading, and writing are used in their everyday lives. Events such as grocery shopping, religious services, reading the mail, writing letters, reading food packages, and reading newspapers/magazines, as well as the sharing of oral stories, all incorporate various aspects of oral and written language. When you encourage parents to include their young children in these types of activities, they will be providing their children with important learning opportunities.

Share Information About Classroom Learning Activities

You are in a partnership role with parents that is centered on the development of their children. By sharing information with parents about the learning activities in your classroom, you are acknowledging their role in this partnership. This sharing also serves to increase parents' confidence in the value of these experiences for their children. For example, you might share the titles of books that have been enjoyed in your classroom as well as describing the frequent opportunities children have to explore books in your library corner.

The ways in which you share this information may vary from short, daily conversations to more formal communications through newsletters. If you choose to use a newsletter, be sure that you keep these three things in mind: (a) Avoid unnecessary educational terminology, (b) keep the newsletter brief (no more than one page), and (c) when you describe a learning activity they could use at home, always include a short explanation of why that activity is appropriate and valuable.

Share Information About Children's Language and Emergent Literacy

In addition to communicating with parents about the learning activities in your classroom, you also will need to share information with parents about their children's language and emergent literacy development. This is an important part of creating and nurturing your partnership with parents.

Although there will be times when you may have brief conversations about a child's development with parents as they bring their children in the morning and pick them up at the end of the day, these will be very general in nature. For example, "Hi, Mrs. Cortez. I just wanted to mention that José really enjoyed this book today (show the book to parent). He seemed to enjoy it so much that we read it together twice!"

In order to share more detailed and confidential information with parents, you will need to arrange for individual conferences. Scheduling these conferences can be a challenge if parents have demanding work schedules; however, be flexible so that every effort is made to arrange for a mutually acceptable time. In these conferences you will want to share information about children's developing oral language and conversation skills, the ways in which they respond during book sharing, and their interest in symbol-making activities. As you provide this information to parents, you will be helping them understand the ways in which their children are developing language and literacy. Be sure to provide parents with specific examples whenever possible. This will also give parents an awareness of the important behaviors to watch for when they interact with their children in similar activities at home. Individual conference time also gives parents an opportunity to share observations of their child in home and community settings as well as to ask specific questions.

Assist Parents in Providing Literacy Materials at Home

Helping parents provide literacy materials at home is also an important part of creating home–school connections. There are two reasons why you will want to help parents in this way. First of all, parents of children in infant-toddler centers are usually working in full-time positions and thus are very busy when they come home from work at night. They may not have time to visit the local library. In addition, parents may not be aware of the types of books and other materials that are appropriate for infants and toddlers.

One way you can help provide literacy materials for children and their families is through the use of take-home activity bags. A take-home activity bag for an infant could include several board books that have been enjoyed in your classroom. For toddlers, you could develop take-home bags that have several familiar picture books as well as paper and felt-tip markers for drawing and writing attempts. (Specific directions for developing and using these bags are located in the earlier section on English language learners in this chapter.)

Another way you can help parents provide literacy materials for their children is to work with parents in creating personalized caption books. As described earlier in this chapter, caption books may be personalized photo books or picture books. A personalized photo book is created from photos of the child, their family, and/or their favorite toys. Enlist the parents' help in securing the photos and then create a small book with one photo on each page and a caption for the photo. You may decide to provide one-use cameras to assist parents and families in obtaining these photos. To make these books more durable, laminate or cover each page with plastic film. Personalized picture books are created using pictures clipped from magazines and advertisements (Straub, 1999). For example, pictures from a grocery store ad can be used to create a book with the theme "foods I like to eat." These personalized books quickly become a child's favorite because they can easily identify with the objects and people pictured. This is also a way for parents to provide early books that are culturally and socially relevant to their children.

Looking Ahead to Preschool

Young children's literacy-related experiences during infancy and toddlerhood start them on the path to becoming readers and writers. In Chapter 6, signs of emergent literacy among preschool children are described. As you read this next chapter, keep in mind the three components of children's literacy transactions: their knowledge of language, the specific types of literacy events and texts, and the context of their learning, as well as the critical role played by adults (parents and teachers) in supporting and mediating children's literacy transactions.

Chapter Summary

As a reflective teacher, the first step you will take in determining which activities will be developmentally appropriate for infants and toddlers in your classroom is to closely observe the ways in which each child communicates. This involves observing children's attention to adult's speech, their eye contact and shared reference, dialogic participation, attention to ongoing events, level of oral language, and home language.

As you establish your language- and literacy-rich classroom, you will want to include a special area of the room for book sharing, a variety of language activities embedded throughout each day, opportunities for interaction and conversation, opportunities for conceptual development through exploration and interaction, along with developmentally-based learning materials.

Emergent literacy can also be enhanced through four specific types of activities: oral language interactions, picture-book sharing, environmental-print experiences, and symbol-making experiences. In each of these types of activities, you will need to carefully select the materials to be used as well as the ways in which children will be engaged and supported during the experiences.

As a teacher of English language learners, you will support their acquisition of English and emergent literacy by observing the following guidelines: (a) Establish rapport with parents and family, (b) encourage and support use of first language at home, (c) focus on oral language development, (d) provide classroom materials in home language and culture, and (e) provide language and literacy take-home activities.

When interacting with infants and toddlers who are identified as being at-risk for language and emergent literacy, your curriculum will still focus on oral language development and creating a language- and literacy-rich environment. In order to more appropriately teach children whom you have identified as at-risk, you will focus on increasing one-on-one interactions, using repetition to strengthen learning, and carefully observing each child's responses.

Informal assessment of infant' and toddlers' emergent literacy focuses on documenting their ways of communicating, their book-sharing interactions, and their involvement in symbol-making experiences. Anecdotal records and checklists serve as useful ways of documenting these emergent literacy behaviors.

Early childhood teachers have a key role in establishing positive and mutually supportive relationships with children's families. The acknowledgement of the value of the language used in children's homes and neighborhoods is critical to the establishment of this mutual respect and acceptance. When you share general information about your classroom curriculum with parents, as well as information on the individual development of their children, you are establishing important home–school connections. Assisting parents in providing literacy materials at home contributes further to the home–school partnership.

Chapter Review

1. Terms to know:

sensorimotor stage	caption books
dialogic reading	simultaneous
tag question	bilingualism
oral cloze	anecdotal records

2. Explain the importance of monitoring a young child's eye contact and shared reference during picture-book sharing.

3. How is turn-taking/dialogic participation enhanced by picture book sharing?

4. Explain the rationale for sharing books with infants who are not yet speaking.

5. Explain why one-on-one interactions with toddlers may be more beneficial than small group activities.

6. In what ways do oral language activities provide a basis for emergent literacy?

7. In what ways are books for toddlers more complex than books for infants?

8. What is the value of personalized caption books to emergent literacy?

9. As a teacher of English language learners, why should you become familiar with their home language and customs?

10. What is the relationship between informal assessment of emergent literacy and the curricular decisions that are made in infant-toddler classrooms?

Chapter Extension Activities

Observation: Observe a teacher sharing a book with an infant or toddler. Describe the interaction strategies used and the child's responses to the book sharing.

In-class or online discussion: Share a story book/picture book with an infant or toddler. Describe the interaction strategies you used and the child's responses during the book sharing.

Research: Explore your local public library for appropriate books to share with infants and toddlers. Bring five books to your class. Be prepared to describe the features of each book that make it appropriate to use with infants or toddlers.

Curriculum development: Make a personalized book for an infant or young toddler following the guidelines in this chapter. Share your book with a young child. Based on this interaction, evaluate the effectiveness of your book.

Chapter 6

Signs of Emergent Literacy Among Preschoolers

Katy loves to read and write. At 3½ years old, she could distinguish between letters and words, identify some letters, find words in texts that were interesting, retell stories accurately, make predictions, and correct words and ideas that didn't make sense. She "wrote" grocery lists, stories, and letters. Her written work moved from the left of the page to the right and from top to bottom. Certain letters appeared as distinct entities. She was confident that she could communicate through print. (Walton, 1989, p. 56)

In the vignette that opens this chapter, we are introduced to Katy, an emergent reader and writer. Although she was not yet reading and writing in the conventional sense, Katy's knowledge about written language was emerging and developing as she interacted with her parents and at her preschool (Walton, 1989). She was aware that written language carried a message and that it had a specific form. She was also aware that written language is used for different purposes, for example, grocery lists, stories, and letters.

Other preschool children, like Katy, are very interested in literacy-related events that take place at home, in their communities, and at preschool. There is, however, considerable variation between children. Children develop at their own rates. Children's interest in literacy-related interactions is influenced by their individual initiative and the opportunities provided in their home and school environments. Some preschoolers will still be in the observation and exploration phases. Others, like Katy, will be entering the experimentation phase when they engage in reading and writing attempts. As children begin to experiment with written language, they will also continue to observe and explore the ways in which written language is used.

Evidence of Preschoolers' Development of Emergent Literacy

Our knowledge of preschoolers' emergent literacy comes from descriptive and longitudinal studies of preschool children at home or in early childhood classrooms (Allor & McCathren, 2003; Clay, 1982, 1987; Doake, 1981; Haussler, 1985; Heath, 1983; Rubin & Carlan, 2005; Sulzby, 1985, 1991; Teale, 1986). Researchers have documented preschool

Preschoolers' interactions with familiar books provide evidence of their developing literacy.

Robert Kneschke

children's emergent literacy behaviors through careful observation of the ways in which they participate in literacy-related events with others as well as the ways in which they interact with reading and writing independently. Throughout these interactions, preschoolers use their oral language competencies when participating in book sharing, interpreting environmental print, and attempting to write and read what they write. In this way, children's oral language provides the basis for their comprehension as well as their own communication during these literacy-related events. It is also the foundation upon which their knowledge of written language develops.

Preschool children's emergent literacy behaviors can be categorized into eight specific areas: (a) Awareness of sound patterns and individual sounds in words, (b) associating sounds with letters of the alphabet, (c) focusing on specific features of letters and discriminating between the letters, (d) creating narratives, (e) developing a concept of book language, (f) developing a concept of how to read, (g) developing book-related concepts, and (h) developing a concept of how to write. In the following sections, preschoolers' emergent literacy behaviors in each of these areas are described. (See Figure 6.1.)

Awareness of Sound Patterns and Individual Sounds in Words

During the preschool years, children begin to show a more conscious awareness that words are composed of separate sounds (Adams, 1990; Maclean, Bryant, & Bradley, 1987; Savin, 1972; Schwartz, 1981; Stewart & Mason, 1989). Research studies have engaged preschoolers in sound games where they are asked by a puppet to change or delete initial or final sounds in nonsense words (Foy & Mann, 2006; Mann & Foy, 2003). Rhyming awareness is elicited by having children point to pictures of items that represent rhyming words. Rhyme production is determined by asking the child to name something that rhymes with a target word. In early childhood classrooms, preschoolers' phonological awareness is evident when they engage in spontaneous word play or rhyming. For example, spontaneous rhyming chants such as "fan, man, ran, pan, tan," show that preschoolers are engaged in sound play.

Figure 6.1 Signs of Emergent Literacy in Preschoolers

❖ Awareness of sound patterns and individual sounds in words
❖ Associating sounds with letters of the alphabet
❖ Focusing on specific features of letters and discriminating between the letters
❖ Creating narratives
❖ Developing a concept of "book language"
❖ Developing a concept of how to "read"
❖ Developing book-related concepts
❖ Developing a concept of how to "write"

In their study of phonological awareness, Maclean, Bryant, and Bradley (1987) reported that preschool children were aware of alliteration and rhyme and were able to respond to rhyming and alliteration requests. You can observe this awareness when you share books with preschoolers that have rhyming text or text with alliteration. Many favorite children's books have rhyming text, such as *Put Me in the Zoo* (Lopshire, 1988) and *The Cat in the Hat* (Seuss (Geisel), 1957). Preschool children also show their awareness of speech sounds through their enjoyment of teacher read-alouds of books with alliteration, such as *Dr. Seuss's ABC* (Seuss (Geisel), 1963), *Bugs in Boxes* (Carter, 1990), and *Six Sleepy Sheep* (Gordon, 1991).

Associating Sounds with Letters of the Alphabet

Preschool children are also beginning to associate sounds with letters (Bissex, 1980; Clay, 1987; Haussler, 1985). Sometimes children express this knowledge during book sharing or as they interact with environmental print. It may also be evident in their early writing attempts. In the excerpt below, Glynnis (age 3 years) and her mom are sharing an alphabet book (Otto, 1994, 1996). This interaction shows two segments where Glynnis is beginning to associate beginning sounds in words with letters of the alphabet.

Segment 1

    Mom: T is for? (pause)
    Glynnis: Turtle and toast!

Segment 2

    Mom: That's a yak. What's he eating? (illustration appears to show a cup of ice cream)
    Glynnis: Yogurt

Segment 2 illustrates the complex relationship that often occurs in the way letters represent sounds in words. The letter name for Y does not represent the sound in the words *yak* and *yogurt*. In the first segments, the letter name for T more closely resembled the pictured objects, that is, turtle and toast. This segment also shows Glynnis' awareness that the item pictured is not ice cream, but yogurt, because the initial sound of 'ice cream' would not fit with the sounds on the 'Y' page.

Preschoolers may also notice environmental print and associate individual letters with words or names they know. In the example below, Jon (3½ years old) notices the letter B on a bank's sign. Here is the dialogue that occurred:

    Jon: See that B, Mom? B for you, Mom. (*Her name is Barb*).
    Mom: Yes. There's a B in the bank's name. B, bank.

Another example comes from Anna (3 years old) (Haussler, 1985), who read TWA as "Tommy" and, when asked how she knew this, replied, "Because it is T like Tina" (her sister's name) (p. 78).

Invented spelling. Associating sounds with specific letters is also evident in children's early spelling attempts (Bissex, 1985; Clay, 1987; Temple, Nathan, Temple, & Burris, 1993). These early attempts have been referred to as **invented spelling** because children are experimenting with representing specific speech sounds by using the letters of the alphabet. There is a developmental pattern to these early spelling attempts (Temple et al., 1993). At first, children may attempt to spell by using random letters. This is referred to as **prephonemic spelling** because there is no phonetic relationship between the letters and the sounds in the word. At the next level, letters are used only for part of the sounds in a word. For example, "SW" is used to represent "Snow White" (Otto, 1986–87). This is referred to as **early phonemic spelling**. In the next stage, **letter-name spelling**, the sounds are represented by the name of the letter, as in "LADE" for "lady." Some preschoolers will also show more advanced awareness of letter–sound relationships and represent several phonemes in each word, for example "whyt" for "white" (Otto, 1986–87). This stage has been referred to as the **phonemic spelling** stage (Gentry, 1982, 2000) or **transitional spelling** stage (Temple et al., 1993). Early research also indicates that Spanish bilingual children's early writing is represented by similar categories (Rubin & Carlan, 2005). Representative examples of each of these types of invented spelling are found in Table 6.1.

Many children learn to recognize and write their own names during the preschool years. Some children learn to write their own name but do not learn the individual letter names. Other children may use their names to better understand letter–sound relationships (Bloodgood, 1999; Green, 1998; Martens, 1999). They use their knowledge of the letters in their name as a starting point for experimenting with how to form letters, how letters are sequenced in words, and how letters are oriented. This experimentation may also contribute to their understanding of the relationship between speech sounds and print. Learning to produce the letters in their names provides children with a repertoire of letters they can make. When these children write using random letter strings, many of the letters they use are letters found in their own individual names (Bloodgood, 1990). For example, when Brent wrote his story about a space ship, he repeatedly used letters in his name: n-E-n-E-Nt-nt.

Preschoolers' phonological awareness and knowledge of letter names have been found to predict later success in reading (Sensenbaugh, 1996; Stanovich, 1993–94); however, it

Table 6.1 Examples of Invented Spelling

Category	Child's Spelling	Words As Read by Child
Prephonemic	sptso	(*not read*)
	OFACDYEHTHI	I was walking down to the park
Early phonemic	SW	Snow White
	ROB	rowboat
Letter name	LADE	lady
Phonetic spelling/Transitional	spas	space
	RABT	rabbit
	THEEED	the end

is not yet clear what relationship exists between phonological awareness and letter-name knowledge (Foy & Mann, 2006). Does letter-name knowledge influence the development of phonological awareness? Is there a causal relationship between them or do these two emergent literacy knowledges develop concurrently? Additional research is necessary to determine an answer to these questions. It is important for preschool teachers to remember, however, that phonological awareness and knowledge of letter names are important aspects of literacy development.

Focusing on Specific Features of Letters

When children begin to focus on letters, they also may indicate their perception of letter similarities. This attention to letter features is expressed spontaneously by the child. It is not directly taught or elicited, but instead emerges from daily interactions with adults in literacy-related events. For example, Ryan (3 years, 5 months old) appeared to confuse a "3" with the letter "S." Below is the entry from his mother's journal.

> When we were looking at a newspaper, Ryan saw a 3 and said "that starts Suzanne's name" (his babysitter). I said, "Oh, that's a 3, the number. It kinda looks like an S but the top curve is different" and then I pointed to an S in the print on the same page and then back to the 3. Later that same day, he came into the kitchen, looked at the clock and said, "Where starts Suzanne's name?" I said, "Ryan, those are numbers not letters. Suzanne's name starts with the letter S." He looked at the clock again, said nothing, and then went back to his play.

Ryan's interaction indicates his attention to the features of letters and numbers as well as to how letters represent the sounds in a word. Another example of a preschooler's attention to the features of letters comes from Laura (Clay, 1987). After writing the letter "L" on paper, she commented, "That's a down and across 'L', just like Laura" (p. 15).

Creating Narratives

Preschool children are also developing in their abilities to create narratives. Preschool children's narrative abilities are evident in the different types of stories they tell. Many of their stories are personal narratives of experiences they have had (Beals, 2001; Heath, 1983; Kaderavek & Sulzby, 2000; Menig-Peterson & McCabe, 1977). Preschoolers' expression of personal narratives may occur as they talk with parents or teachers about daily events at mealtime or during other times of the day (Beals, 2001; Heath, 1983; Karmiloff & Karmiloff-Smith, 2001; Magee & Sutton-Smith, 1983). These narratives may be mediated by the adult listener who provides a scaffold by asking questions and prompting the child for further "storytelling" segments.

Preschool children may also create narratives to fit a sequence of pictures (Magee & Sutton-Smith, 1983; Wang & Cameron, 1996) or a wordless picture book (Curenton & Justice, 2004). Other forms of preschool narratives occur as they tell or dictate an original story (Cox, Fang, & Otto, 1997; Groth & Darling, 2001; Paley, 1981), or reconstruct a story while interacting independently with a familiar story book (Kaderavek & Sulzby, 2000; Marjanovič-Umek, Kranjc, & Fekonja, 2002) or with an adult (Magee & Sutton-Smith, 1983; Otto, 1984). They may also create narratives when making their own story books.

During the preschool years, children's narratives gradually become more coherent and more cohesive (Manovič-Umek, Kranjc, & Fekonja, 2002). Some preschoolers' narratives may have missing story parts, may not have clear pronoun reference, and may lack a

Figure 6.2 Kiki's Narratives

> **Story #1**
> Well, one day the three bears went for a walk. Later on, they came back to the house and um, and —— porridge, and baby bear, ——, "Somebody's been eating my porridge," said the daddy bear. And then they went upstairs, and found a little girl sleeping in the baby's bed, and then um, and then, they found out that someone had been sleeping in the papa's bed and the mom's bed. And that's it.
>
> **Story #2**
> Once upon a time there was a bad giraffe and she thought there was a house nearby and then she went in it and she sort of got a spanking, and then they saw there was a garbage can nearby and they spanked her some more, and then they went in the garbage, and then it was the end.
>
> **Story #3**
> One day I saw two rainbows, and then I went to a puppet show to see a mama bunny, and a baby bunny. At the end there was a big /U/ and a crash when it ended. And then the bunny said "Yes, I want to come to the party with you." So they walked across the street and then they saw a lion. And that was a case where the zoo animals are, were. And then they had a —— and that means they had to stop for the lower, because cars were crossing. And then, one day a car came along and this crashed the door, and then a big Kiki came, and then, a yellow /U/ came and a crash, a little crash, and zoomed it along, and colored it blue.

clear sequence of events. As they approach kindergarten, their narratives may become more complex and more clearly structured (Gilliam, McFadden, & van Kleeck, 1995; Otto, 1990). Three examples of Kiki's (age 4) stories are located in Figure 6.2. These stories were created over a two-month span when she was asked to "make a storybook" and then read it. As you read her transcribed story texts, notice the differences in the length, use of pronouns, and story complexity.

According to Stadler and Ward (2005), a developmental continuum of preschool children's storytelling skills with pictures and story books begins with simple labeling of picture content. At the next level, the child lists the actions or features of the pictured content. The remaining three levels of the continuum involve connecting actions or events, sequencing events in time while establishing cause and effect, and more complete narrations with more complex story plots. Stadler and Ward also noted that the type of narrative task was associated with the level of complexity of the story. In instances where children were retelling a familiar folktale, higher levels of narration were observed. Children's memory for the familiar folktale appeared to serve as a basis for the retelling and supported a more complete narration.

Cultural differences in narratives. Preschool children from diverse cultures and home languages may have different narrative experiences and expectations (Heath, 1983; Karmiloff & Karmiloff-Smith, 2001; McCabe, 1992, 1997; Shiro, 1995). In some cultural-social settings, narratives are encouraged only if they are true and actually happened, and imaginative stories are not part of the oral tradition. Even within some broader cultural groups, such as Native Americans, there are differences in storytelling between subgroups, such as Navajo, Pueblo, and Sioux (John-Steiner & Panofsky, 1992).

Narratives created by preschoolers from diverse cultures have been found to differ in content as well as structure (McCabe, 1992; Muñoz, Gillam, Peña, & Gulley-Faehnle, 2003). McCabe (1992) reported European American children's stories were personal narratives that had a fairy tale format while Japanese American children told stories that were a combination of several personal experiences. African American children's stories began and ended with a themed focus, and had several events in-between. Latino children's stories focused more on family relationships within events and places rather than on cause-and-effect sequencing of events.

Preschoolers who are learning a second language may create narratives that reflect not only their different narrative experiences and expectations, but also development of their second language. For example, in Figure 6.3, Story 1 was created by a four-year-old who was also learning to speak English while Story 2 was created by a four-year-old for whom English was the home and primary language. As you read these two stories, notice the differences in the grammar, story structure, and vocabulary/descriptive details.

Cultural differences in storytelling and narrative forms have implications for the early childhood classroom. Based on McCabe's (1997) review of research on the cultural differences in storytelling and narrative forms, she encourages teachers of young children to "recognize, appreciate, and value cultural differences in storytelling style" (p. 462). For example, the first child's story in Figure 6.3 should not be interpreted as evidence of a lack of knowledge of narrative and language skills, but should be seen as a reflection of the child's prior authentic experiences with narrative in her home language and culture.

McCabe (1997) also emphasizes that these different narrative experiences and expectations will influence children's comprehension and memory of stories they hear at school. Stories that have a structure similar to the stories they have heard at home will be comprehended and remembered more completely. Preschoolers who are able to comprehend stories that are read during book sharing and who are able to create their own oral stories will be able to use this language knowledge as a basis for later reading comprehension and story writing in kindergarten and the primary grades.

Developing a Concept of "Book Language"

Preschool children also begin to show awareness that the language found in books is different from the language used in narratives or in conversation. This awareness is evident in research settings where preschoolers were first asked to "tell" a story and then asked to "dictate" that story so it could be written down. When preschoolers' oral monologues were compared with their dictated stories, preschoolers used more precise vocabulary

Figure 6.3 Comparison of Narratives by an English Language Learner and a Native English Speaker

---

Narrative by 4-Year-Old English Language Learner
A little girl, her name is Hirsch, and she wants to go home, and take a ride to school. And if she want to, her mommy will take her to school. But she is dangerous, she always get up to the car, and she falls. She falls down the car because she is not setting well.

Narrative by 4-Year-Old Native English Speaker
Once there was a goldfish, and he swam all over the sea. And then there came a fisherman, and he took this fish into the net. And then, the net was something he could stay in to bring home. He does have something to hold the net with, and there's food for the fish to eat. The person goes home in his car, in the purple car. He rides off and calls home. And at home is where he eats dinner and then he goes back to fishing in the sea.

Preschoolers' comprehension during teacher read-alouds is influenced by their prior narrative experiences and expectations.

and text structures that were characteristic of written language (Cox, Fang, & Otto, 1997). An example of the differences between oral monologues and dictated stories is found in Figure 6.4.

When Shirley's two stories in Figure 6.4 are compared, the dictated story has more precise wording. For example, the Hershey Kisses are described more elaborately in the dictated story as well as the description of the "water with ice and lemon in it." Another difference was in the grammatical features of the two stories. In the dictated story, Shirley

 Figure 6.4 Shirley's Oral and Dictated Stories

Oral Monologue
And I had an Easter party on Easter. I found a Hershey Kisses and a basket with surprises but the Easter bunny didn't leave the basket, my Mom and Dad did. The basket had thin markers in there for us and lots of candy. I even dumped my Hershey Kisses in my basket. And I got to put on a dress that my gramma gave me. And I got to put on my pretty shoes and a shirt that I used to wear with the dress. And the guests came and we had an Easter dinner but it wasn't real dinner. It was sort of an Easter lunch with potatoes and meat and crustini. And that's all I can remember.

Shirley's Dictated Story
We woke up in the morning and I said, "Yippee" and just then Sam woke up and said, "What?" and stuff. We raced to wake up Papa but he wasn't in bed. And we asked Mom where he was and he was downstairs. We went to find the Easter eggs and Hershey Kisses were leading to a trail with different color wrappers like pink, blue, green, silver, and dark pink, and light pink. And then we found our Easter baskets with surprises. And then we went in and the guests came. And we had the water with the ice and lemon in it. And we went outside and we got out the crustini. And we let out the dogs. And Tony took a piece of crustini, that's my dog. . . ."

Source: From Cox, B. E., Fang, Z., & Otto, B. (1997, Jan/Feb/Mar). Preschoolers' developing ownership of the literate register. *Reading Research Quarterly, 32*(1), pp. 48–49.

included conversational aspects that were not present in the told story. Her dictated story also included a clarification of Tony's identity: "That's my dog."

Preschool children also may indicate their awareness that book language is different from oral language when they "pretend read" books. Kaderavek and Sulzby (2000) asked preschoolers who were developing normally and preschoolers who were language impaired to tell a story orally and then to "read" a familiar book. For both groups the children's "reading" of the familiar book contained more precise vocabulary, more direct quotations, and were longer when compared to their told stories.

Curenton and Justice (2004) also reported similar decontextualized language among African American and Caucasian children (3–5 years old) who were asked to create a story for a wordless picture book. Children's stories were analyzed for use of simple and complex nouns, adverbs, and conjunctions. Although age-related differences were noted, there were no differences in syntactic complexity between Caucasian and African American children.

Preschooler's use of booklike language may also be evident when they are asked to create their own story book and then "read" it. While they are not yet reading and writing conventionally, these pretend readings provide evidence that preschoolers are using more descriptive language as well as story structures and event sequencing. The three stories in Figure 6.5 show a four-year-old's knowledge of story structure and sequencing as well as her descriptive vocabulary.

All three of Gwen's stories in Figure 6.5 begin with the opening word, "Once. . . ." It is also interesting to note the difference in the language that she uses to describe learning to ride a bicycle from her two other, imaginative stories. The language used in the imaginative stories is more booklike and decontextualized, that is, more descriptive and more complex in its grammatical structures.

Developing Book-Related Concepts

Preschool children's emergent literacy also involves concepts about books and expectations for the texts found in books. These book-related concepts include: (a) Text is stable; (b) the text, not the picture, is "read"; and (c) there are different types of text.

Preschool children may also show their awareness of 'book language' when they 'pretend read.'

Tomisckova Tatayana

Figure 6.5 Gwen's Three Narratives (4 years old)

#1 Story Prompt: How I Learned to Ride My Big Wheel

Once I ride my bicycle on my driveway but my car was in my way so I, so I had to wait till the car was out of the way to bicycle.

#2 Story Prompt: Story about Animals

Once there was a elf. He, he had some presents. He delivered them.
All of a sudden a big lion jumped up on him and tried to eat him, and then he said, "Wait, wait." And then he didn't eat them. The children opened up the presents and lived happily ever after with the elf.

#3 Story Prompt: Fairy Tale, Magical Story

Once the fairy was getting very hot so she made, the volcano. The volcano was erupted and the sea divers didn't know the underwater volcano named Kalypsie erupted. When the sea divers didn't know, know what and the sea divers were all killed and then it stopped once second, and there was a big pool of saliva on the floor of the ocean.

Text is stable. The text in books does not change from reading to reading: It is stable. When preschool children are interacting with books they may indicate their awareness that texts are stable in several ways. For example, children may "correct" an adult reader who makes a change or error in a reading a familiar story text. One mother who purposely substituted different nouns for parts of a story reported that her son (3 years, 3 months) stopped her and said "you're giving wrong words." Children's attempts to "read" a story book may also indicate their awareness of stable text when they make self-corrections. Although a child can reconstruct the general meaning of the text during a pretend reading, their self-corrections indicate the child is attempting to retrieve or re-create the exact text wording. This indicates the child is aware that the text is stable (Sulzby, 1985).

Another indication that a child is aware that text is stable is found in his requests to have the same book read repeatedly. Within this request for repeated readings is the awareness and expectation that the "story" or "text" will be the same each time. These requests for repeated readings may occur over a period of days or weeks, or even during the same day. For example, Ryan (3½ years old) requested a book be read to him five times in one day, and three of those times were one after another.

Text is read, not pictures. Throughout the preschool years, children gradually begin to focus more on the print or text as what is "read" rather than the illustrations. This may occur during shared-book interactions or as children interact with environmental print. When Ryan was three years old, his mother reported that he spontaneously pointed to the print in *Richard Scarry's Hop Aboard, Here We Go!* (1972), and said "read that." After his mom read the print to which he had pointed, he repeated this request several times while pointing to other print sections. Children may also point to the print when attempting to figure out environmental print (Haussler, 1985).

Additional examples of children's awareness that the print is read comes from preschoolers' attempts to "read" familiar story books (Otto, 1984; Sulzby, 1985). Children who are aware that the print is what is read may refuse to attempt to read, saying, "I don't know what that word says." When preschoolers create their own stories by drawing, they may also refuse to attempt to read their story, indicating they don't have to read it, because it's just pictures (Otto, 1986–87).

Different types of text. Preschool children who have had many shared book experiences will be developing an awareness of different types of text or **genre**. In the following example of Anna's (age 5) story, it is clear that she is familiar with fairy tales (Otto, 1990; 1996) and uses that awareness in creating her own fairy tale.

> There once was a king that had a beautiful castle and he had a wonderful beard. It was yellow and his —— (*indecipherable*). And he always went (*pause*) to people's houses to ask them for a job. Whenever he had nothing to do, he went to the job and got tons of money. He was so rich than any other king. Also he had a beautiful queen. She always said, "My dear, why don't you go to the parlor to get your food?" He said, "No." So the queen didn't ask him anymore, because he said, "I love you." (*Aside:*) And this is the princess and her dog by the castle.

When children are creating their own story books, they may indicate what type of book they are creating, and thus indicate they are aware of different types of stories or texts. In the examples below, each child shared their ideas for creating a specific type of book (Otto, 1996, p. 14).

> *Jennifer:* Mine's going to be a picture book. (*She writes "Pat BH" on the front cover. The rest of her book is done by drawing and wavy scribbling. When asked to read it, she replies, "Pat the bunny."*)
>
> *Pam:* Mine's gonna spell something. (*She writes "The Lion" on the cover and announces "the title."*)
>
> *Joel:* Every page is going to be a different story.
>
> *Sharbani:* Mine's gonna be a reading book. (*She writes her name as "author" and writes "I Love You" as the title*).

Developing a Concept of How to Read

Although preschool children are not yet reading conventionally, they are developing knowledge about the process of reading. Their awareness that reading involves "constructing meaning while interacting with a book" is evident when they participate in shared book interactions and interact independently with books. It is also evident in children's metalinguistic comments when they share their ideas about how they are learning to read and what others do when they read.

Evidence from shared book interactions. When preschool children are involved in shared book experiences, their responses typically represent a wide range of participation, from nonverbal responses (for example, smiling and gesturing) to very active involvement in verbally reconstructing or re-enacting a familiar story (Cochran-Smith, 1984; Magee & Sutton-Smith, 1983; Otto, 1984, 1990). Their responses also vary in the way they contribute to the reconstruction of the original text. As the adult reads and pauses, some children will respond with conversational comments about the illustrations, others will provide verbal segments that are semantically equivalent to the text or may even be verbatim-like text segments. In this way, they are contributing to the reconstruction of the story text.

Semantically equivalent responses are those in which the general meaning of the text is constructed; however, the wording is not that of the actual text. (See Figure 6.6.)

Another type of response during assisted or shared book reading is verbatim-like. This response reconstructs the actual wording of the text. See the example in Figure 6.7. Verbatim-like responses are evidence of the child's memory for specific text wording and also evidence that the child knows texts are stable.

In both the semantically equivalent and verbatim responses, the child is focusing on the illustrations, not the print, and using his prior memory of the story and its text to participate in the shared reading.

Figure 6.6 Semantically Equivalent Reconstruction

Betsy (4 years, 9 months)

Book: *Pocket for Corduroy* (Freeman, 1978, p. 22)

Interaction	Text
Betsy: Then he came to, um, a, a laundry, um basket.	He landed paws first in an empty laundry basket.

Evidence from independent book interactions. During the preschool years, children also begin to interact with books on their own. They become more adept at orienting the book and turning pages from left to right, visually scanning from the top to the bottom of the page, and paging from front to back. They may silently page through a book looking closely at the illustrations or they may verbally reconstruct the story or text (Sulzby, 1985). They begin to sound and look like readers (Elster, 1994b).

In a developmental study of children's emergent reading of favorite story books, Sulzby (1985, 1991) described different categories of children's reading. This classification scheme is presented in Table 6.2. Key aspects of this system focus on whether the child is using the pictures or print to re-create the story, and the type of language used by the child (oral-like, writtenlike, or verbatim-like language). The least mature category involves labeling and commenting about the pictures. The most advanced category involves actually decoding the print. Sulzby's category system is useful in characterizing children's dominant strategies during emergent readings of story books.

Additional research by Elster (1994a) explored the variation in children's strategies that may be present within a single emergent reading. Elster describes children's emergent readings as "a sequence of reading and talk episodes, combining a variety of reading and talk strategies" (p. 413). During the child's reading, the ways in which these different strategies are used may be influenced by the book that is used and the child's personal memories and experiences, as well as their knowledge base and the social setting in which the emergent reading occurs (Elster, 1994a, 1998).

At times these story reconstructions may occur as children interact alone with a book. Other times, they may be sharing the book with another person (adult or peer) who

 Figure 6.7 Verbatim-like Responses

Book: *Are You My Mother?* (Eastman, 1960).
Child: Dennis (3 years, 11 months)

Interaction		Text
Adult:	How could I (*pause*)	(p. 33) "How could I
Child:	be your mother?	be your mother,"
Adult:	(*pause*) said the cow.	said the cow.
	I am (*pause*)	"I am
Child:	the cow.	a cow."

Table 6.2 Sulzby's Story Book Reading Classification Scheme

Broad Categories	Brief Explanation of Categories
1. Attending to Pictures, not Forming Stories	The child is "reading" by looking at the story book's pictures. The child's speech is *just* about the picture in view; the child is not "weaving a story" across the pages. (Subcategories are "labeling and commenting" and "following the action.")
2. Attending to Pictures, Forming ORAL Stories	The child is "reading" by looking at the story book's pictures. The child's speech weaves a story across the pages but the wording and intonation are like that of someone telling a story, either like a conversation about the pictures or like a fully recited story, in which the listener can see the pictures (and often *must* see them to understand the child's story). (Subcategories and "dialogic storytelling" and "monologic storytelling.")
3. Attending to Pictures, Reading and Storytelling mixed	This category for the simplified version was originally the first subcategory of (4). It fits between (2) and (4) and is easier to understand if it is treated separately. The child is "reading" by looking at the story book's pictures. The child's speech fluctuates between sounding like a storyteller, with oral intonation, and sounding like a reader, with reading intonation. To fit this category, the majority of the reading attempt must show fluctuations between storytelling and reading.
4. Attending to Pictures, Forming WRITTEN Stories	The child is "reading" by looking at the story book's pictures. The child's speech sounds as if the child is reading, both in the wording and intonation. The listener does not need to look at the pictures (or rarely does) in order to understand the story. If the listener closes his or her eyes, most of the time he or she would think the child is reading from print. Subcategories are "reading similar-to-original story", and "reading verbatim-like story.")
5. Attending to Print	There are four subcategories of attending to print. Only the *final* one is what is typically called "real reading." In the others the child is exploring the print by such strategies as refusing to read based on print-related reasons, or using only some of the aspects of print. (Subcategories are "refusing to read based on print awareness," "reading aspectually", "reading with strategies imbalanced," and "reading independently" or "conventional reading.")

Source: Table from Sulzby, E. (1991). "Assessment of Emergent Literacy: Storybook Reading." *The Reading Teacher,* *44* (7), pp. 498–500.

listens to their story/text reconstruction. When children interact with unfamiliar or new books, they usually focus on the illustrations as sources of "meaning" for the book content. If the books are familiar, they will also use their memory of prior interactions to reconstruct the story or text. For example, in Figure 6.8, Jon's mother describes his interaction with a new, unfamiliar book that they had just checked out from the public library.

Jon's independent interaction with this new story book was evidence of his confidence in being able to read in his own way by using the illustrations to construct meaning. Note that after he read by himself, he asked his mother to read. Perhaps he realized that there was more to the story than what he had read!

For some preschoolers, reading also has a dramatic component, especially when reading for an audience. In these settings, their independent story book interactions will not only reconstruct the original story but will also replicate the gestures and intonation of the adult(s) who shared the story book with them on previous occasions. For example, when

Figure 6.8 Jon's Interaction with a New Book

> When we arrived home from the library, Jon carried several books by himself into the house. Without taking off his coat, he carried the books into the living room and sat on the couch. He took a new book and said, "I read all by myself." He opened the book, orienting it correctly, and went to a story page near the beginning. He verbalized a story segment not related to the actual story but it included a boy in it. The actual book had a boy appearing in the illustrations. After he continued this "story" for about 10 seconds, he said, "Do you wanna read a story?"

Glynnis (3 years, 10 months) was "reading" "Goldilocks and the Three Bears" to her younger sister, she varied her intonation to indicate which character was speaking (Otto, 1996). For Papa Bear she used a loud, gruff, angry voice; for Mama Bear, she used a moderate and pleasant voice; and for Baby Bear, she used a high-pitched and whiny voice.

Talking about reading. As preschool children experiment with the reading process, they may talk about their experiences (Bissex, 1980; Butler & Clay, 1979; Elster, 1994a; Haussler, 1985; Otto, 1990; Stewart & Mason, 1989; Strommen & Mates, 1997; Sulzby, 1985, 1991). These metalinguistic comments provide a glimpse into children's thoughts and developing concepts. Ryan's (3 years, 5 months) concept of reading appeared to be based on his observations and experiences (Strommen & Mates, 1997). When asked what people do when they read, he proceeded to turn the story book pages from back to front, then from front to back, and then again from back to front, pausing to label illustrations.

Children may also make metalinguistic comments about reading when they are trying to figure out how speech and print relate. When Robbie (4 years old) attempted to read the title *Where the Wild Things Are* (Sendak, 1963) by pointing to each word, his speech did not match up with the individual words (Schickedanz, 1981). Realizing this, he commented, "This book's not working right" (p. 18).

When asked to pretend read, some children will refuse, indicating that they know they cannot read or that they "don't know the words" or that they need help to "sound out the words" (Sulzby, 1985, p. 471). These comments reflect children's developing metalinguistic knowledge and language concepts as well as their ideas about what they need to know to be able to read.

Developing a Concept of How to Write

Preschoolers who are developing a concept of what writing is and how one goes about writing appear to be acquiring several important understandings. These understandings include: (a) Writing is a form of communication; (b) writing involves letters and words, not drawing; and (c) writing has many purposes. These understandings are acquired through opportunities for observation, experimentation, and interaction with other writers (Fox & Saracho, 1990; Henderson, 1986).

Writing is a form of communication. Children who have observed adults' writing and who have begun to explore graphic forms will begin to express their awareness that these graphic representations (drawing, scribbling, adult's writing) have meaning (Clay, 1979, 1987; Temple et al., 1993). Sometimes, preschoolers will approach adults with their scribbled paper and ask them to "read" it. Other times, children will provide their own "reading" of what they have put on paper. For example, Casbergue (1998, p. 201) documented how three-year-old Brandon shared his page of random scribbles: "This is a letter for Santa Claus. I want this stuff." Then he went on to name what he wanted while looking at the paper and using reading intonation.

The meaning or communicative aspect of writing seems to predominate and motivate young children's exploration and experimentation. Instead of first learning how to make letters and then how to put letters together to make words, children appear to be first and foremost concerned with creating a message through graphic forms, such as drawing, scribbling, and emergent writing (Temple et al., 1993).

Preschoolers may incorporate writing-related events into their creative drama as a way of communicating in that specific setting. Vukelich (1990) describes children's dramatic play involving a post office–package delivery center. In this setting, preschoolers used their emergent writing to address packages, keep records, and write receipts.

Writing involves letters, not drawing. Older preschool children's awareness that writing involves letters, not drawing, may be evident when they create stories on paper. In addition to using drawing to communicate their stories, they may begin to incorporate letters and letter-like forms in their stories. Preschoolers' use of prephonemic spelling indicates they know that letters are used in writing, but they have not yet figured out the way that letters represent specific sounds.

Figure 6.9 shows a sample of a child's early distinction between writing and drawing. In this example, Ariel created a story of going to the zoo, using wavy scribbling to indicate writing. Note that the wavy scribbling was placed either as a caption beneath her illustrations or on pages separate from the illustrations. When asked to read her story, Ariel responded:

> (*Opens book*) Once upon a time they wanted to go to the zoo, so they did. (*turns page*) They saw lions, and (*turns page*) then, they looked at the giraffe, but they only had time to look at two of them, because they didn't want to miss their lunch. The end.

When Kiki created her story book (refer back to Figure 6.2, story 1) she used no illustrations, only prephonemic spelling. When she read her story, she used her finger to track the print. For each line of print she "read" one sentence. For example, the first sentence in her story was: "Well, one day the three bears went for a walk." This was represented in print by the following string of letters: T-H-O-K-I-W-M-O-T. This is a clear example of a preschool child's awareness that when you create a story book, you need to have print carry the message, though in this case her writing had no phonemic relationship to the story she created and "read."

Preschool children are beginning to create messages by drawing, scribbling, using letter-like forms, and letters.

Pozynakov

Figure 6.9 Ariel's Story Book

In the next example, Erica's use of invented spelling provides evidence that she is developing awareness that written language involves the use of letters. Her knowledge of letter–sound relationships is evident in her spelling of "space" as "spas."

Erica's invented spelling was a placeholder for her story, which she read as, "The space-ship was going up and then the spaceship starting to go upper. And that is the end." Thus, the story that she "read" was more complex than her written story; however, the inclusion of the one word, "spas" provides evidence that she is aware that books have written language and she is beginning to understand how letters represent sounds.

Even when children appear to understand that letters represent specific sounds, they may use a variety of strategies in creating their stories. Although they may use phonemic

Figure 6.10 Eva's Story

Eva's Reading of Her Story Book		
Cover	page 1	page 2
Eva:	See how I can make up a rowboat. I don't really know how to make one, but I know how to fish in a rowboat. *(turns page)*	My first rowboat The end.

spelling for some writing, they may also use other strategies to create their messages on paper, such as illustration, wavy scribble, letter-like forms, or random letters (Casbergue, 1998). An example of this range of strategies is found in Eva's story about a rowboat in Figure 6.10.

In creating her story book, Eva used her name, the numeral five, random letters (sptso, eduaowe), conventional spelling (My) and invented spelling (ROB for rowboat). Note that when she read her story, she did not refer to the numeral five. Also Eva's reading of the first two pages of the book had oral-like, conversational dialogue. Then when she came to the last page, she read it as if it were written text.

Writing has many purposes. Preschool children's awareness that writing has many purposes is evident in the ways that they use emergent writing in their daily activities, such as making lists, sharing stories, and writing notes (Casbergue, 1998; Temple et al., 1993).

For preschool children, learning how to write their name provides a very personal purpose to writing (Green, 1998; Martens, 1999). It contributes to their sense of self as well as allowing their property, such as artwork, to be labeled. Children's written names are used frequently in school settings to identify their belongings as well as their locker or cubby location. Once they know how to write their own name, they begin to find many different ways to use this new knowledge.

When preschool classrooms provide opportunity for children to sign in when they arrive, it allows children to see yet another purpose for written language. In a year-long study of a classroom's signing-in activity, Green (1998) noted the high level of motivation and attention preschoolers devoted to their name writing. When children were trying out a more complex way of signing their name, they sometimes spent 10 to 12 minutes engaged in this activity. They experimented with name writing in individual and unique ways, and gradually developed more advanced ways of writing their names. For example, Molly (age three) began the year making small scribble marks. Through the course of the school year, she began to use letter-like forms, then used the letters of her name but in scrambled order, and then upper- and lowercase letters. This purposeful activity of writing provided these young children with a setting in which their experimentation with writing forms fostered their emergent literacy.

Contexts of Preschoolers' Emergent Literacy

The focus in this chapter has been on preschool children's emergent literacy behaviors; however, it is also important to remember that preschoolers' transactions with written language are mediated through conversations and verbal interactions with their parents, family, and teachers. These emergent literacy behaviors do not develop in isolation; instead, their development occurs in social-cultural settings that are responsive to children's observation, exploration, and experimentation during literacy-related events (Weigel, Martin, & Bennett, 2005).

Key Characteristics of Preschool Contexts

Preschool children's literacy transactions take place in their homes and at school. For both home and school settings, three key characteristics are associated with preschoolers' emergent literacy: (a) Access to literacy materials, (b) frequency and type of literacy-related experiences, and (c) social interaction with adult involvement.

Access to books and literacy-related resources. In families where children were developing emergent literacy, there was a variety of books and other literacy-related materials for both parents and children. Children who have more books at home, whether library loaned or purchased, have more opportunities to interact with books than those who do not. Access to books and literacy-related resources is often affected by the family's financial resources and the accessibility to the local library. The size of public libraries' collections is also influenced by the economic resources of the community, with poorer neighborhoods having libraries with fewer books and reduced night hours (Neuman & Celano, 2001). Libraries may also lack sufficient books in other (non-English) languages. Parents who do not speak English may be hesitant to go to a public library because they anticipate difficulty communicating with the library staff (Diener, Wright, Julian, & Byington, 2003). Even when a library has a collection of bilingual books for children, it may be difficult to locate them because they are separated from the regular collection and may not be prominently displayed.

Access to literacy-related materials is embedded in families' social-economic status as well as their cultural and social activities. Families with greater income will likely purchase more products and services, as well as engage in more entertainment activities and travel. These differences expose middle- and upper-income children to additional literacy-related experiences in terms of environmental print and activity-related texts (such as travel brochures, product information, restaurant menus) (Teale, 1986). Although family income may influence the amount of literacy materials in the home, it is not appropriate to conclude that all children in low-income families do not have any opportunities for story book sharing or other literacy-related activities. There are variations among low-income families just as they are in any other social-economic group (Teale, 1986.).

School environments also may vary in quality and access to literacy-rich materials due to the financial resources available to schools in low-income areas. When child care centers in low-income neighborhoods were provided with additional books, preschoolers' verbal interactions in literacy-related activities and the time they spent reading and relating to books increased (Neuman, 1999).

Frequency and type of literacy-related experiences. Preschool children from homes with a higher frequency of literacy-related events had higher levels of emergent literacy (Nord, Lennon, Liu, & Chandler, 1999; Weigel et al., 2005). When children had frequent experiences with different types of narratives, such as story books, dramatic play, and dramatic re-enactments, their narrative abilities increased (Groth & Darling, 2001). Repeated readings of story books were also associated with increases in receptive and expressive vocabulary (Sénéchal, 1997).

Specific literacy-related activities also are associated with preschoolers' emergent literacy. These key activities include story book sharing, oral storytelling by adults, and visiting the public library (Durkin, 1966; Nord, Lennon, Liu, & Chandler, 1999, Sénéchal, Thomas, & Monker, 1995; Wood, 2002). Story-reading experiences have also been associated with gains in language complexity. Storytelling experiences have been associated with improved story comprehension in children's retelling of stories (Isbell, Sobol, Lindauer, & Lowrance, 2004).

Social interaction with adult involvement. In addition to having access to books and frequent opportunities to interact in literacy-related events, emergent literacy among preschoolers is also associated with social interactions and adult involvement. The amount of talk between parents and children and parents' responsive involvement in their children's daily activities is associated not only with language development but also with emergent literacy (Durkin, 1966; Hart & Risley, 1995; Rush, 1999). This has been documented in middle-class English-speaking homes as well as low-income homes of diverse ethnicities and languages (Britto, Brooks-Gunn, & Griffin, 2006; Bus, van IJzendoorn, & Pellegrini, 1995; Collins, 2005; Hart & Risley, 1995; Peterson, Jesso, & McCabe, 1999; Roberts, Jurgens, & Burchinal, 2005; Rush, 1999; Tabors, Snow, & Dickinson, 2001).

The specific ways that mothers read and interact during shared book experiences are associated with preschoolers' vocabulary growth. Preschoolers' vocabulary increased when their mothers actively encouraged their participation by asking questions during the book reading, making comments that extended the story, and relating the book's concepts to prior experiences (Britto, Brooks-Gunn, & Griffin, 2006). In preschool settings, active engagement in story book reading has also been associated with the development of vocabulary (Walsh & Blewitt, 2006). The type of questioning used by teachers does not appear to be as important as children's active participation in discussing the story (Walsh & Blewitt, 2006; Dickinson & Smith, 1994).

Revisiting the Transactional Perspective

The research findings highlighted in this chapter reflect the complex ways in which children's knowledge of language, the literacy-related events, and the contexts of those events interact in home and school environments in dynamic ways. Early childhood curricula need to provide settings for literacy development that will support and extend the experiences children have had in their homes and communities (Daniels, 2004). For children who have not had opportunities to participate in literacy-related events, the preschool setting needs to provide those critical opportunities. In Chapter 7 the focus will be on the ways you as a preschool teacher can create a literacy-rich classroom setting and implement effective strategies that will support your children's transactions with literacy. An important part of this implementation will be the ways that you use reflective decision-making to meet the needs of your preschool children.

Chapter Summary

Preschool children's participation in literacy-related events at home and at school provides opportunity for the development of emergent literacy. There is considerable variation between children in the ways that they become involved in literacy-related experiences. Children's interest in literacy is influenced by each child's own initiative and the opportunities provided in their home and school environments. Some preschoolers will still be in the observation and exploration phases;

others will be entering the experimentation phase when they engage in reading and writing attempts, experimenting with the ways in which written language is used to communicate.

Preschool children's emergent literacy behaviors can be categorized into eight specific areas: (a) Awareness of sound patterns and individual sounds in words, (b) associating sounds with letters of the alphabet, (c) focusing on specific features of letters and discriminating between the letters, (d) creating narratives, (e) developing a concept of "book language," (f) developing a concept of how to "read," (g) developing book-related concepts, and (h) developing a concept of how to "write." These emergent literacy behaviors do not develop in isolation, instead this development occurs in contexts at home and in early childhood settings that are responsive to children's observations, explorations, and experimentations with written language.

Chapter Review

1. Terms to know:

invented spelling	phonemic spelling
prephonemic spelling	transitional spelling
early phonemic spelling	genre
letter-name spelling	

2. In what ways does a child's enjoyment of rhyming texts indicate his phonological awareness?

3. Review the example on page 115. What other way could Ryan's mother have responded to his questions about the letter S?

4. How do children's attempts to "read" a familiar story book indicate their emergent literacy?

5. In what ways can shared story book interactions provide children with a linguistic scaffold?

6. Why is it important to ask preschoolers to "read" or talk about what they have written?

7. Why is a child's use of invented spelling an important emergent literacy behavior?

8. What emergent literacy opportunities are found in a preschool classroom's "signing in" activity?

Chapter Extension Activities

Discussion: What story books do you remember reading as a young child? Which ones were your favorites? Who read them with you?

Observation: Visit a preschool classroom's writing center. Observe children's early writing attempts and their reading of what they wrote. Review several samples of children's work. Analyze the type of writing used by the children and its relationship to what they "read."

Visit a preschool classroom's book/library center. Observe the ways in which children are interacting with books. Encourage several children to share the book with you or to "read it to you." Analyze their readings according to Sulzby's (1985) Story Book Reading Classification Scheme (Table 6.2).

Visit the children's section of your public library. Observe parents interacting with their children as they select and share books. Describe the ways in which parents support their children's interest in books and their comprehension of stories.

Research: Using your library's online professional journal database, select a journal article published within the last five years on any of the following topics: emergent literacy, phonemic awareness, phonological awareness, narratives, or invented spelling. Prepare a written summary and critique of the article. Share the main points of your review with your class.

Chapter 7

Enhancing Emergent Literacy Among Preschoolers

Ms. Clark's preschool room is a beehive of activity. In the library corner, Lizzie and Maria are engaged with their own copies of *Are You My Mother?* They are pointing to the illustrations and creating their own versions of the story. Maggie is at the easel. When she finishes her painting, she makes a big "M" in the lower corner, and announces, "That's my name." Frankie and Eduardo are in the block area, where they are involved in a "delivery service." Frankie tells Eduardo, "Here's your package (handing him a block). Now sign this (hands him a small clipboard containing a piece of paper and pencil)." Eduardo adds his signature and says "Thanks." Frankie responds with "No problem."

In each of these instances, preschool children are engaged in contexts where they are exploring and experimenting with the ways in which written language is used to communicate. In these contexts, children see reading and writing as activities that have meaning and purpose. Their teacher, Ms. Clark, carefully observes their interactions with each other and the literacy-related activity, noting how their transactions with written language develop over time and in different contexts. She uses these observations to plan and implement future activities in her preschool classroom.

Setting the Stage for Children's Literacy Transactions

According to the Transactional perspective, children's development of literacy occurs as they engage in reading- and writing-related events in their environment. This engagement involves transactions that incorporate their knowledge of language, the texts they encounter, and the contexts in which the interactions occur. As a preschool teacher, you will want to create a learning environment where children's transactions will support and enhance their literacy development. Your reflective decision making is an important part of creating and sustaining this literacy-rich environment.

General Guidelines

In establishing your literacy-rich environment, you will find the following four guidelines useful: (a) Provide a developmentally appropriate curriculum, (b) provide opportunities for multiple and frequent literacy-related experiences, (c) engage in reflective, responsive teaching, and (d) utilize staff and volunteer resources to increase support for children's literacy interactions.

Provide a developmentally appropriate curriculum. The preschool years are a time of continued exploration and experimentation. Preschool children are striving to learn about their world and the people around them. The motivation to learn and explore is very strong; however, each child's developmental path to literacy is unique (Neuman & Roskos, 2005). Thus, a developmentally appropriate curriculum will be flexible and provide many opportunities for independent, self-initiated activities as well as activities that are teacher-mediated (NAEYC, 1997, 1998).

It is also important that these activities involve reading and writing in meaningful and purposeful ways. For example, direct instruction on isolated letters and sounds should not "take center stage" (Neuman & Roskos, 2005, p. 25). Instead children's awareness of letters and sounds can be facilitated through word play, listening to rhyming texts, and dictated stories. Children's awareness of the meaning and purpose of written language can also be enhanced through a focus on environmental print (Neuharth-Prichett, Hamilton, & Schwanenflugel, 2005). As preschoolers interact with signs, posted schedules, and sign-in sheets, their transactions with written language have meaning and purpose (Roskos, Christie, & Richgels, 2003).

Your classroom may be part of a multiclassroom early childhood center, or it may be part of a universal pre-K program in a public school. In these settings, a particular commercial curriculum model may be adopted. There are three such models that have been widely recommended and proven successful in preschool settings: (a) *The Creative Curriculum®*, (b) *HIGH/SCOPE®*, and (c) *Success for All® Foundation's Curiosity Corner*. Each of these curriculum models maintains an online Website that will provide you with additional information. These Website addresses are located in the Extension Activities section at the end of this chapter. Whether you work in a system that has adopted a particular curriculum model or you are in a setting where you develop your own curriculum, it is important to ensure that your curriculum is developmentally appropriate for the children in your classroom. This chapter will provide you with a basis for making reflective teaching decisions as you implement a developmentally appropriate curriculum.

Utilize staff and volunteer resources to increase support for children's literacy interactions. Language and literacy development occur in settings where there is interaction with others—in conversation and in literacy-related events. In creating your literacy-rich classroom, you will want to also provide opportunities for children's development to be supported through interactions with other adults. Most preschool settings will have two adults in classrooms of 15–20 children (Bredekamp & Copple, 1997). This means you may work with a paraprofessional/teaching aide. In addition, you may be able to arrange for parent or community volunteers to assist in your classroom as well. Each of these adults is in reality a teacher of your children. It is important for you to share with them your reflective teaching approach as well as your rationale for the various activity areas of your classroom.

In the sections that follow, specific learning activities and strategies will be described. Because no teacher can be in two places at once, the teaching aide and classroom volunteer can provide supportive interactions with children in specific areas, such as the computer center, the writing center, or the library center as well as other center-based activities.

Although a developmentally appropriate curriculum will have the above four general characteristics, it is important to remember that whether a particular activity is developmentally appropriate will differ with each child in your classroom. As their teacher, your responsibility is to determine the appropriate learning activities for each child (Lin, 2001). In order to do this, you will need to become aware of each child's developmental level with respect to their knowledge of language, their conceptual knowledge, and their prior experiences. This includes becoming aware of children's home environment and cultural-social-linguistic setting (Weigel, Martin, & Bennett, 2005).

Provide opportunities for multiple, frequent literacy-related experiences. As children develop their knowledge of literacy, they need many opportunities to continue to observe, explore, and experiment with both oral and written language (Nord, Lennon, Liu, & Chandler, 1999; Yaden, Rowe, & MacGillivray, 1999). This means that reading- and writing–related activities should occur throughout each day's schedule, in addition to repeated opportunities over time to engage in similar activities, such as hearing a story book read again (Sénéchal, 1997) or spending time in the art/writing center at several points during the class schedule.

Engage in responsive and reflective teaching. In addition to planning, preparing, and implementing the literacy-related activities in your classroom, the ways in which you respond to and mediate children's involvement are critical to their literacy development. As you implement your curriculum, you will need to be observant of children's individual transactions with reading and writing, and use those observations to determine what future experiences will be appropriate. The effectiveness of each activity in enhancing children's development will depend upon each child's individual transaction with the task and context.

These four guidelines provide you with an overview of the key aspects of a literacy-rich environment in preschool; however, only you can decide what specific activities will be developmentally appropriate for children in your classroom. In the remaining parts of this chapter, specific activities for enhancing preschoolers' language knowledge are described. Your awareness of the objectives of each activity, its relationship to literacy development, and the general guidelines for implementing the activity will provide you with the professional knowledge you need to determine how the activity will meet the needs of your preschoolers.

Enhancing Emergent Literacy Through Specific Activities

Earlier chapters of this text described the ways in which oral language provides a foundation for the development of literacy. In planning your preschool classroom's curriculum, you will want to plan for many opportunities for children to use their oral language as well as to explore and experiment with written language.

Informal Conversations

When you are talking with children as they engage in different learning experiences in your classroom, make a special effort to engage each child in your classroom in a one-on-one conversation every day (Dickinson, 2001; Snow, Burns, & Griffin, 1998). This individualized attention and opportunity to communicate with an adult provides important practice for developing communication skills, for example, listening, vocabulary, and grammar. Opportunities for these conversations may occur during arrival or departure, outdoor time, independent activity time, or snack time. These conversations should have the character of a friendly visit rather than an instructional dialogue. Such extended conversations will involve several turns or communication loops (Dickinson, 2001). These longer conversations will provide opportunity for children to talk as well as allow you to respond specifically to their comments and questions. You may also be able to introduce new vocabulary words that are tied to ongoing events or your shared topic of conversation (Dickinson, 2001; Strickland, 2004).

Procedural Activities

Opportunities for embedding language and literacy also occur during the routine procedures in your classroom. These activities enhance children's awareness of how oral and written language are used to communicate throughout the day.

Attendance-taking.　You can structure your attendance-taking procedures to encourage children to begin to read their names as well as others' names. This might involve creating a photo card for each child that contains their name. You could then establish a routine in which children know that when they come in to school, they are to select their card and put it on the attendance bulletin board. (Use Velcro or a clip or hook system to attach it to the bulletin board.) These photos cards can also be used to encourage preschoolers to begin to focus on letters and their corresponding sounds. For example, you might ask each child to identify the letter that starts his or her name as well as other children's names.

You may decide to start out by using only the child's first name on the photo card. After the children have begun to recognize their first name, new photo cards can be made with both their first and last names.

Independent activities allow preschoolers to communicate with others and to develop conceptual knowledge and vocabulary.

Robert Kneschke

Another attendance-taking activity involves giving children the opportunity to sign-in (Green, 1998). This is an open-ended activity that allows each child to decide how he will sign his name. Children's participation in this activity should also be optional and self-directed. Start out the year by providing a large sheet of paper on a table (taped down) where each child will add their signature as they arrive, emphasizing they can sign in any way they want. Position yourself at the sign-in table so that you can respond to children's questions. You may also decide to place their name cards nearby, in case they want to consult their name card when they sign in; however, referring to the name card should be optional and child-initiated. You can expect that some children will sign in by scribbling, drawing, using letter-like forms, or writing only a letter or two. Over the course of the school year, you will be able to see development in children's awareness of letters, letter–sound relationships, letter sequencing and directionality. Remember that not all children will progress at the same rate and you may see children reverting to an earlier form of signing in for a short time.

Environmental print. The ways in which print is used in your classroom environment also provides important opportunities for children to observe how written language communicates meaning. For example, using their names on their locker spaces or on their artwork shows preschoolers how their ownership is indicated by their written names. Perhaps you have signs in each learning center that announce the learning center's focus, such as "Science Center," or you might have a sign-up sheet for children to indicate their desire to use a center.

Teachers can also use signs and lists as a way of solving children's conflicts in sharing or taking turns (Kantor, Miller, & Fernie, 1992). Listing the order in which children will have an opportunity to use a particular toy or activity reduces the conflict and validates their requests. A large class calendar with notations for upcoming events also provides preschoolers an opportunity to see how written language is useful in anticipating future activities. You may notice your preschoolers wanting to create signs of their own when they are in the block or dramatic play areas (Kantor, Miller, & Fernie, 1992).

Independent Activities

Preschool classrooms will typically have one or more blocks of time that provide an opportunity for children to choose from among several types of activities. It is important for all of these activities to be optional and self-selected. This independent activity time is often referred to as "free play"; however, parents and school administrators sometimes question the value of "play" and emphasize their concerns that this playtime does not provide educational outcomes (Nourot & Van Hoorn, 1991). Therefore, instead of referring to this time as "free play," you may decide to refer to it as "independent activity time" or "independent work time." In doing so, you are emphasizing the purposeful nature of children's interactions in the various activity centers.

These independent activities for preschoolers allow children to communicate with others and to develop conceptual knowledge and vocabulary. In addition, independent activities provide opportunities to begin to use symbols to represent ideas and objects. In the sections that follow, four specific types of activity centers will be described: art/writing center, library center, creative drama center, and concept center. In each of these areas, the emphasis will be on the ways in which the center can be developed to focus on literacy-related experiences.

Art/writing center. In this center, preschoolers have the opportunity to explore the use of different media in making graphic representations on paper. These graphic representations are the beginnings of their use of visual symbols that contribute to their later abilities to communicate through writing and illustration (Edwards & Willis, 2000).

You can expect to see a wide range of interest by preschoolers in using this center. Some children will focus on exploring different types of media. Other children may show interest in only one or two media, and will be more focused on creating a specific drawing, story, or message. Still other children may show little interest in becoming involved in this center. Because of these developmental differences and varied individual interests, it is important that this center, as well as the other centers, remain optional for children's participation. In developing this center to encourage visual communication and symbol-making, you will want to keep two guidelines in mind: (a) Provide a variety of materials and other media, and (b) include print-related reference materials.

Provide a variety of materials and media. It is important for this preschool art/writing center to be stocked with a wide range of materials and to be organized in a way that encourages children's independent and self-selected participation. Clear storage boxes with picture labels will allow easy access. Writing utensils such as washable felt-tip markers and crayons should be available in a variety of colors. You can encourage children's creativity and symbol-making by providing a wide range of different types and colors of paper, along with pieces of yarn, and papers of different textures. Blunt-nosed scissors will also allow children to cut out pictures or shapes to use in illustrating their books or making collages. Most preschool children will be just beginning to develop the small-muscle coordination needed to effectively use scissors; however, simply having the scissors available will encourage children to begin developing that coordination.

In addition to providing a wide range of writing implements and papers, you could include some simple, pre-made books. For this you will simply take several sheets of plain paper, fold them in half, and staple them together on the fold. Later on you can gradually introduce the ways in which children can use glue, tape, a stapler, and a hole punch in working in this center. These additional tools provide opportunities for children to create their own books and develop their own unique ways of communicating.

If space permits, include a mailbox system where each child has a separate slot or small box with their name on it. This will encourage children to communicate with each other. You will also want to provide small envelopes and an assortment of rubber stamps with a stamp pad.

You may also find that your preschool children will enjoy using a small magnetic board and plastic letters that attach easily. Not only will this support development of small-muscle control, it will encourage visual familiarity with letter shapes, and may encourage invented spelling.

It is also important for preschoolers to have opportunities to use paint, whether for easel painting, sponge painting, or finger painting. Painting activities will require more organization and supervision but they provide important opportunities for artistic and symbolic exploration and experimentation.

Include print-related reference materials. You can encourage children to focus on print and written language by including other specific materials and activities in the writing center. For example, provide a chart of the letters of the alphabet, each paired with an appropriate picture, for example, B paired with a picture of a ball. Preschoolers often show a fascination with learning to write and recognize their own names as well as the names of their friends and teachers. To encourage this, you could make a name and photo card for each child and teacher in your classroom. Place these in a box in the writing center (Kirk & Clark, 2005) or hole-punched and attached to a ring. This provides a handy reference for children who are interested in learning how to read and write their own name as well as others' names. Children who choose to begin writing their own names (and others' names) may also be developing phonetic knowledge of letter–sound correspondences (Temple et al., 1993). Because everyone's name is meaningful, learning to write names helps children understand how written language communicates.

In addition to providing the above materials and tools, you will want to include a writing table and chairs that allow several children to use this center at one time. This setting also encourages children to talk with each other about the stories and messages they are creating.

Library center. The classroom library center is a focal point in creating a literacy-rich preschool setting. The way in which you organize this center and provide interesting books will influence children's motivation to spend time interacting in this area.

Make your library center welcoming and easy to use. As adults, many of us enjoy relaxing with a good book in a soft chair or on the sofa. Preschoolers' interests in books can also be encouraged by providing comfortable seating such as soft chairs, benches, and floor pillows. It is also important to have seating arrangements that will accommodate several children so that they are encouraged to talk with each other as they enjoy books.

Books can be displayed in ways that add to the welcoming atmosphere of the library center. Provide low book shelves that allow books to be displayed with the covers visible. You could also use plastic bins or tubs to store books, being sure that the front cover of the book is visible. Because most preschoolers rely on the cover illustrations to predict book content, this type of display makes it easier for preschoolers to find a book that interests them. Be sure that it is easy for preschoolers to return the books to the display shelf or book-bin when they are finished with each book.

Provide developmentally appropriate books. When selecting books for your classroom's library corner, you will want to choose books that build on children's interests and language competencies. If you know that children in your classroom have not had many prior experiences with books at home, you will need to provide books that encourage

In the library center, you will want to provide low book shelves that allow books to be displayed with the covers visible.

SchubPhoto

labeling and commenting, as well as books that have simple story lines. (See Appendix B for sample titles of books for children who are just beginning to explore books).

Preschoolers who are beginning to explore books also need books that have familiar content rather than stories about events that are not part of their prior experience. As their teacher, you will be deciding which books will be appropriate. For example, preschoolers living in an urban area would be able to comprehend books about riding on a bus or subway easier than they would books about farm life. Similarly, preschoolers living in a rural area would find books about farm life more understandable than books about riding a subway. For these children, it is also important to select books that have simple illustrations rather than abstract or complex illustrations. You may find it appropriate to provide a few board books for children who have not had experience manipulating books, because the stiff, thick pages are easier to manipulate.

Preschoolers who have had many prior experiences with books and have participated in story book sharing with parents or teachers will be ready for a wider variety of book content as well as more complex storylines and illustrations. Appendix D lists books for children who have had earlier experiences with story books and are ready for more complex stories. They will also be ready for books that involve imaginary characters or events, such as fairy tales. As you observe and interact with the preschoolers in your classroom, you will be able to determine which books are developmentally appropriate.

Provide a wide variety of books. Preschoolers enjoy both fiction (story books) as well as nonfiction (information books). They will also enjoy special feature books, such as pop-up books, flap books, and scratch-and-sniff books; however, these books are more fragile and need gentle handling. Preschoolers are beginning to interact more verbally as they interact with books. For this reason, it is important to have many books in the library center that have been read previously at story time. Their memory for the story and book content provides them with a basis for interacting with the book independently.

You will also want to include books that have diversity represented in the characters and book content. This is important for all children, not only for children from diverse backgrounds. Creating an awareness and appreciation of different cultures, languages, and social settings can be facilitated through including multicultural literature in your library center.

Include book-related props. Preschoolers' involvement with books can also be encouraged by including several book-related props. These include hand- or finger-puppets and stuffed animals that resemble characters in books. You can encourage children's engagement with books by providing different types of child-sized hats, such as a construction hard hat, a floppy-brimmed hat, a baseball cap, or a fireman's hat.

Create a listening post. Another way of encouraging children's interactions in the library center is to provide a listening post, where they can listen to an audiotaped reading of a book while looking at the book. You can provide a tape recorder for children to use independently, and headphones that are easy to put on and take off. Audiotaped children's books are available commercially and often contain background music or story-related sound effects. You can also create your own audiotaped books by recording one of your read-aloud group story times and then placing both the book and the audiotape in the library center for children to enjoy. For preschool children, it is very important that the audiotapes are of familiar story books; therefore, if you select a commercially audiotaped book, be sure that you have read it to your preschoolers first at group story time.

Periodically introduce new books. Children's involvement in the library center can also be enhanced by the inclusion of new books. While you observe and respond to children's interests and book-reading behaviors, you can note the types of books that engage individual children, and use this as a basis for selecting new books for your library center. It is also valuable to introduce new books that are part of the seasonal or thematic focus of your classroom's curriculum. When you add new books to your library center, be sure to either read them to your class at group story time or preview the book at group time so children will be aware of the new book.

Observe and reflect on children's transactions with books. Although your library center is designed to be a time for children to interact with books independently and with their peers, you will want to carefully observe the ways in which children interact and engage in book reading. If you see a child wandering aimlessly in the book center, and you know he is interested in books on trucks and cars, you will want to help him find a book that relates to this topic.

Books in the center can become torn or in need of repair. Talk with the children and ask them to let you know when a book needs to see the "book doctor" to receive "first aid" (Gottshall, 1995). You can provide a special basket for books that need to be repaired. By showing how books are cared for, you are helping children understand the ways in which books can be kept in usable condition. When favorite books become worn-out due to their popularity, replace them and also consider providing multiple copies.

As you observe children's transactions with books and with each other in the library center, you can use your observations to plan which books you will share at the group story time. For example, if several children seem to be interested in books on various forms of transportation, you might plan to share books on that topic during the group story time.

Computer center. By providing a computer center in your preschool classroom, you can support children's literacy transactions in both reading and writing/symbol-making. Reading software packages are available that involve animated stories and story-related activities. Other software involves the use of graphics that can provide the opportunity for children to use pictures, create their own illustrations, and add print. Examples of each type of software are described in Appendix E.

In deciding to include a computer center in your classroom, you will find the following guidelines useful:

Select literacy-related software programs that are developmentally appropriate. This means that the program should be easy for your preschoolers to use independently. The software program should also be interactive so that the preschooler is engaged rather than passive. You will need to thoroughly review the software and be sure that you know how to use each feature in order to support your children's interactions. A format for reviewing literacy-related software programs is provided in Appendix E.

Provide ample space for collaboration. Set up the center to accommodate two children plus space for an adult to assist. This arrangement encourages children to talk about what they are doing as well as to problem-solve.

Introduce the center and each software program to children on an individual or small group basis. Avoid overwhelming children with instructions that they are not yet able to comprehend or follow. As the center is used, you (or your aide/volunteer) will want to remain close by to demonstrate and respond to their questions.

Expect a range of interest in this center. As with other centers in your classroom, children's use of this center should be child-initiated and voluntary. Expect a time of exploration and experimentation with each software program. It is likely that some children will have been introduced to computer use at home or at the local public library. Other children may have not had any experience. You will need to be sensitive to their individual experience levels so that you can support their use of this center.

Creative drama center. This area provides opportunity for children to use their imagination while taking on different roles and communicating through speech, gestures, and symbolic representations. For example, a large empty box might be the setting for a spaceship, train, bus, or cave. As with the other centers described in this section, children's participation in a creative drama center is self-selected, and essentially child-directed. Preschoolers' creative drama may represent their prior experiences at home or in their community or they may portray events from familiar story books. For example, preschoolers may engage in book-related dramatic play, using vocabulary and concepts from familiar books and assuming the role of specific characters (Rowe, 1998). Creative drama provides a setting in which children can try on different roles and act out their understandings of concepts and events, as well as negotiate their participation within a peer group.

Provide props and setting. As you prepare this area for creative drama, keep in mind that the context you create will influence the quality of the children's interactions (Marjanovič-Umek & Musek, 2001). It is important to consider not only the developmental levels of your preschoolers, but also their cultural experiences. For example, in a kitchen/house area, you need to provide the types of objects that are found in your children's homes. Be sure to include clothing items that are culturally appropriate.

The creative drama area needs to be large enough to accommodate several children at once with room for them to move around as they portray different events and actions. While some preschool classrooms have a permanent creative drama area that centers on a child-sized kitchen setting, you may decide to have a creative drama area that is flexible and can be changed to fit different themes, such as a post office, a grocery store, or a doctor's office. Regardless of the type of creative drama center you provide in your classroom, you will need to carefully select the objects and other props that accompany the area. Include actual items, such as wooden kitchen spoons and dishes, as well as more unstructured props, such as blocks or empty boxes (Nourot & Van Hoorn, 1991). Some children will need to have more realistic props, while others may welcome the opportunity to use their imaginations with unstructured props in specific, symbolic ways.

Include literacy-related props. In creating a literacy-rich environment in your preschool classroom, you can also enhance children's opportunities by including props in your creative drama center that involve written language. For example, in a kitchen center, you might include a telephone book, a real telephone, food coupons, and cookbooks, labeled recipe boxes, blank recipe cards, empty food boxes, a notepad, pens, markers, and play money (Neuman & Roskos, 1990). You could also include food ads from a local newspaper. In deciding what type of props to include, you will want to select those that are developmentally appropriate (that is, can it be used safely and naturally by children?). Because literacy objects are cultural tools, it is important to select props that represent real items in preschoolers' homes and community environments (Neuman & Roskos, 1990, 1992). For additional creative drama-center themes and lists of literacy-related props, see further Neuman & Roskos (1990) and Morrow & Rand (1991).

While it is important to include literacy-related props in your creative drama center, you will need to avoid overpopulating a center with literacy props and placing too much emphasis on children's interactions with them (Roskos & Christie, 2001). Your goal is to enrich the center with literacy-related props, using only enough to create interest and provide opportunity to develop new knowledge and understanding within the larger context of the creative drama setting.

Observe, support, and reflect on children's creative drama interactions. In addition to providing the appropriate setting and prompts, you can also enhance children's involvement in creative drama by activating or developing their knowledge for a specific context or event. For example, you might announce to children in the house area, "Today is sister's birthday. Let's have a birthday party. What can we do to get ready for the party?" By creating a setting and asking opening questions, you will activate children's knowledge of this event and support their role playing (Christensen & Kelly, 2003).

You may decide that you want to develop their knowledge for a particular context or event. One way of doing this is to share books at group story time that involve a similar setting (Christensen & Kelly, 2003). For example, you might read *To the Post Office with Mama* (Farrell & Lewis, 1994) to familiarize the children with what happens at a post office.

As you monitor children's creative-drama interactions, look for children's continued active involvement and focus. You may find it necessary to step into the drama as a participant to suggest a way of solving a problem, modeling use of a literacy prop, or to extend their roles or interactions (Christensen & Kelly, 2003; Morrow & Rand, 1991). At the same time, you will want to avoid becoming overly directive or intrusive (Rybczynski & Troy, 1995).

Your observations of preschoolers' language and literacy-related interactions during their creative drama activities will provide you with awareness of their emerging literacy knowledge (Roskos & Christie, 2001). For example, when a three-year-old "picks up a small square of paper, calls it a ticket, and pretends to go to the movies," you can see his transformation of the piece of paper into a symbol (Hatcher & Petty, 2004, p. 79). You may also observe other literacy-related behaviors during preschoolers' creative drama as they make signs, scribble notes, or pretend to read. Preschoolers' literacy-related interactions during creative drama can provide opportunities for assessment of their emergent literacy, but it is important to avoid interrupting their activities for assessment purposes (Roskos & Christie, 2001). It will interfere with the continuity of their involvement and endanger the children's ownership of their dramatic activities.

Additional activities related to creative drama. Creative drama can also be encouraged by providing a small, portable puppet stage, which would accommodate one to two children. You will also want to provide a basket of hand-puppets in an assortment of basic characters (such as animals and people). Another way of encouraging creative drama is to provide a flannel board with story bags that contain the characters and scenery pieces for favorite stories.

Concept centers. Concept centers are designed to encourage children's individual hands-on exploration of objects and simple processes. While children engage in the activities provided in this type of center, they will be developing and refining their concepts and vocabulary.

Decide the focus of the concept center. In setting up a concept center, you will want to pick a topic that relates to children's particular interests or to a current curricular theme. For example, if your curricular theme is "going to the beach" and you have just shared a book at story time involving sea shells, you could then place a collection of different kinds of sea shells and some play dough in the concept center. Children would then explore the different impressions they can make with the shells in the play dough. This would help them experience the different visual and textual features of sea shells, such as wavy, bumpy, and smooth. You could also place two small trays in the concept center, labeled "Small" and "Big." Children could then sort the shells according to their size.

Include a magnifying glass in the center so children can see the details of each sea shell and how they differ from each other.

Include reading, drawing, and writing opportunities. Although a concept center mainly involves exploration, you can also encourage reading, writing, and drawing by including paper and writing/drawing tools for children to record their experiences in the center. In the fall season, you might have a concept center that includes exploring the shapes, textures, and colors of leaves. You can encourage children to draw their observations or trace around the leaves. They could also do a leaf-rubbing by placing a leaf under a sheet of thin paper and rubbing a crayon over the paper. You could also set up small boxes for sorting the leaves by color or shape. Their individual documentations could then be shared at group time or posted on a bulletin board or poster.

Signs and labels that provide directions or storage locations will help preschoolers see the functions of written language. You could include a couple of visors that have "Scientist" written on them for children to wear while they are in this center (Gauthier, 2005). Include a special laboratory apron with the word "Scientist" written on it, too.

Periodically change the focus of the center. To keep children interested, you will need to periodically change the center's focus. Be sure to tie the conceptual focus of the center to other parts of your curriculum, such as books shared at group story time or outdoor activities. This provides reinforcement for concepts learned as well as opportunities to use new vocabulary or skills.

Formally introduce the center. Although the purpose of a concept center is for children's individual and independent exploration, it is important to formally introduce each new center to your preschoolers. You could take a few minutes at the group circle time to show the materials from the center and explain how the materials should be used. It is important to also mention any specific rules that apply to the center, such as putting materials away or limiting the number of children at one time in the center. If you decide to use any signage in the center, such as directions or labels on containers, you can explain these signs during your introduction to the center.

Make prior concept activities available. Some children may be interested in revisiting a particular concept activity, while others need something new. You can arrange an open table space along with a shelf where you store plastic shoeboxes containing the prior concept activities. By storing each concept activity in a plastic shoebox that is labeled and has an identifying picture, children are able to revisit their favorite activities (Sherwood, 2005). These boxes can also be loaned out for children to enjoy at home.

Teacher-Mediated Activities

In the previous section on Independent Activities, the role of the teacher was to prepare the learning environment for preschoolers' explorations and then to observe their interactions while not overtly directing their activities. In this section, the teacher's role is to directly mediate preschoolers' transactions in language and literacy-related activities. The emphasis here is not only on facilitating preschoolers' communication and transactions with written language but also to mediate their transactions in a way that helps them begin to focus on specific features of language and books, such as the beginning sounds of words and vocabulary.

Teacher-mediated activities include large group activities where most, if not all of the preschoolers in your classroom will participate in an activity at the same time, as well as small group activities where you may be interacting with 3–4 children at a time. In each

Effective concept centers provide hands-on experiences that enhance preschoolers' vocabulary development.

Matka_Warlatka

type of group setting, you will be mediating children's interactions during language and literacy-related activities.

Although this type of group activity may be referred to by different names, such as "rug time" or "circle time," the activities generally include an initial segment involving either rhymes, finger plays, or action songs and a longer segment in which a story book is read aloud by the teacher. As with any group activity, the length of the activity will be determined by children's attention span and interest in the activity. Storytelling, story re-enactment, and story dictation are also valuable literacy-related group activities for preschoolers.

Rhymes, finger plays, and action songs. Nursery rhymes and songs that have actions and gestures paired with the words help preschoolers understand the meaning of the words they are saying (Arnold & Colburn, 2005; Bafumo, 2004). For example, in "The Itsy Bitsy Spider" the words *up* and *down* are accompanied by gestures that help children understand those concepts. Finger plays and action songs also contain rhyming words that are emphasized further by melodic patterns and refrains. This emphasis on rhyme helps children develop phonological awareness (Flett & Conderman, 2002; Lombardo, 2005; Neuman, 2004). The rhythmic or melodic pattern of the words also enhances children's memory of the song or finger play (Kenney, 2005; Neuman, 2006). Nursery rhymes, finger plays, and action songs express simple stories or sequences of events that help children to develop a sense of story through their memory for the sequence of actions.

Use as an introductory activity for story book sharing. Because these rhymes and songs are short in duration, they are often used to help children settle into the large group activity of sharing a story book (Armstrong, 2006).

Selecting the rhyme, action song, or finger play. When you select the rhyme, finger play or action song to use, you will want to keep in mind the activity level and the thematic content. If you decide to use an action song to start out your group activity, pick one that does not involve exuberant actions or you will have a more difficult time quieting your group to attend to the story book sharing. You may want to choose a rhyme, finger play, or action song that follows the thematic content of the book you will be sharing at story time. If you are going to read a story book about farm animals, you could select an action

Action songs and finger plays help children develop a sense of story as well as vocabulary.

bikeriderlondon

song such as "Old MacDonald Had a Farm." Resources for children's action songs, finger plays, and rhymes are located in Figure 7.1.

Use repetition. Preschoolers will need to have repeated opportunities to learn a new song, rhyme, or finger play. Try repeating it three times during the first session as well as using the same song, rhyme, or finger play several times in one week. When you are introducing a new rhyme, song, or finger play, expect that you will be "going solo" for a while until children catch on to the words and rhythm. Carefully observe their responses and participation and make any necessary adjustments to the length of the activity or to the type of song, finger play, or rhyme that is shared. Once learned, children will enjoy repeated opportunities to perform their newly learned finger play or action song.

 Figure 7.1 Resources for Preschoolers' Action Songs, Finger Plays, and Rhymes

Hohmann, M. (2002). *Fee, fie phonemic awareness:130 prereading activities for preschoolers.* High/Scope Press. *Literacy activities for circle time: Music and poetry.* (2005). Grand Rapids, MI: School Specialty Publishing.
Newcome, Z. (2002). *Heads & shoulders, knees & toes: And other action counting rhymes.* New York: Candlewick Press.
Orozco, J. (2002). *Diez deditos & other play rhymes & action songs from Latin America.* New York: Penguin.
Silberg, J., & Schiller, P. (2002). *The complete book of rhymes, songs, poems, finger plays, and chants.* Beltsville, MD: Gryphon House.
Schiller, P. (2001). *Creating readers: Over 1000 games, activities, tongue twisters, finger plays, songs and stories to get children excited about reading.* Beltsville, MD: Gryphon House.
Schiller, P., & Moore, T. (1993). *Where is Thumbkin?* Beltsville, MD: Gryphon House.
Schiller, P., & Moore, T. (2004). *Do you know the muffin man?: Literacy activities using favorite rhymes and songs.* Beltsville, MD: Gryphon House.
Simpson, J. (2005). *Circle time poetry: Around the year.* New York: Scholastic.
Stemple, A. (2006). *This little piggy with CD: Lap songs, finger plays, clapping games, and pantomime rhymes.* Cambridge, MA: Candlewick.
Stetson, E. (2001). *Little hands: Finger plays and action songs.* Ideals Publications.

Be enthusiastic. The lively intonations and actions that accompany a song, finger play, or rhyme will be motivating for your preschoolers. This will encourage them to participate in any way that they can. Your enthusiasm will also make this time enjoyable and memorable.

Interactive story book sharing. The sharing of story books provides many important opportunities for children to continue to develop their knowledge of language and literacy. Interactive story book sharing is associated with increases in vocabulary as well as developing phonological awareness, syntactic knowledge, and concepts of print (Allor & McCathren, 2003; Elley, 1989; Isbell et al., 2004; Otto, 1996; Sénéchal, LeFevre, Hudson, & Lawson, 1996; Whitehurst & Lonigan, 2002).

Scheduling group story times. Successful group story times involve more than simply reading a story book to your preschoolers. Rather than using story book sharing to fill in the daily schedule when there is extra time, story book sharing should be a daily routine (Dickinson, 2001), carefully planned and implemented to build on children's developing language and literacy knowledge.

Children who have no prior experience with story book sharing or who are developmentally delayed will need to have more one-on-one or small group experiences with sharing books before they can successfully participate in large group story book interactions (Gottshall, 1995). It is not simply a matter of attention span, but more a matter of comprehension of oral language and prior experiences with books. Small group story sharing also allows preschoolers to participate verbally and increases their involvement in the story sharing (Kragler & Martin, 1998). When teachers attempt to read aloud to a large group of preschoolers who vary in language development and listening comprehension, they may become frustrated because some children are restless and inattentive. As a result, they may cancel the story time, even though they acknowledge the importance of story book sharing (Dickinson, 2001).

To avoid this situation, schedule your group story book sharing when you know there will be no interruptions. It is recommended that in a full-day program you have three story book sharing times of about 15 minutes each (Dickinson, 2001). Also schedule other times when you can share books with children individually or in smaller groups. Make story book sharing a priority in your curriculum. Through careful planning, story book sharing will be a key activity in providing important language and literacy experiences.

Selecting books to share based on your knowledge of your preschoolers. Preschoolers will be interested in story book time when the books that are shared are about familiar topics and events that they have experienced (Gottshall, 1995). You will also want to select books that are at an appropriate level of language and story complexity. Story books that have language and story lines that are too complex will be difficult for children to comprehend and this will lead to their inattention and restlessness. Select books with texts that are only slightly above your preschoolers' level of expressive language. Preschoolers rely on a book's illustrations to provide meaning to the story, so it is important to choose books with large, clear illustrations. Be sure the illustrations can be seen several feet away from the book. Preschoolers also like to participate in the book sharing and find it difficult to simply sit and listen. With this in mind, you will want to select books that have a predictable text or refrain that will encourage children to anticipate upcoming text and chime in.

You may also decide to select books that have specific language features or emphasize certain language concepts, such as phonemic awareness. For example, *Six Sleepy Sheep* (Gordon, 1991), emphasizes the /s/ sound; *More Bugs in Boxes* (Carter, 1990), focuses on the /b/ sound. (See also Yopp, 1995a, for a bibliography of read-aloud books for developing phonemic awareness). Books with rhyming text will also encourage phonological awareness. Dr. Seuss' books, such as *The Cat in the Hat Comes Back* (1958) or *There's a Wocket in My Pocket* (1974, 1996) have been children's favorites for many years. The rhythmic language fascinates children and increases their awareness of sound patterns within words.

Preschoolers will like to have some books read over and over again. As a book becomes increasingly familiar, encourage children to participate more in the reconstruction of the story by anticipating text refrains, rhyming words, or upcoming events. Even though you will want to use these favorite books in response to children's requests, you also will find that preschoolers enjoy hearing new books (Neuman & Celano, 2001). Share your enthusiasm and excitement with your preschoolers as you introduce a new book.

Sharing the book. After you have selected a book to share, you will need to carefully study the text and pictures to determine how you will present the book to your preschoolers. As their teacher, you will not only read the text that is in the book, but you will also need to mediate and scaffold your children's understanding of the book's content (Neuman & Celano, 2001). This mediation and scaffolding occurs in three stages: (a) Introducing the book, (b) reading the book, and (c) discussing the book after you have finished reading (Smallwood, 2002).

1. ***Introducing the book.*** Before reading the book to children, it is important to activate their knowledge of the topic of the book. If the book is about trains, you could first talk about their experiences riding on a train or seeing a train go by. Another way of introducing the book is to go on a "picture walk" (Kragler & Martin, 1998). This involves paging through the book and talking about the pictures and making predictions about story events. Picture walks are especially effective for introducing new books. Books that have been read on previous occasions will be introduced differently by activating children's memory of the story events and characters. As you engage children in these prereading activities, reflect on the knowledge and experiences children share to further determine how you will actually read the text and how you will refer to the illustrations. If you are previewing *The Snowy Day* (Keats, 1962), for example, and children appear unfamiliar with how to make a snow angel, you could then decide to expand on this when you are reading the book (Kragler & Martin, 1998).

2. ***Reading the book.*** When you are reading a book for the first time to your preschoolers, you will need to carefully observe their nonverbal and verbal responses for evidence that they understand the story. If you are concerned they do not comprehend, you will need to simplify book language, refer to the content of illustrations, or use questions to enhance their comprehension and refocus their interest in the story sharing. Children's comprehension can also be enhanced by the way in which you use intonation, tempo, and rhythm in reading the text. It is especially important to read dialogue segments with conversational intonation, creating distinct voices for the different characters. Comprehension is also enhanced when you point to the illustrations and use gestures to indicate actions portrayed in the story.

When you share a familiar story book at group time, you will be using different strategies to keep children interested and to expand on their understanding of the book. If you simplified the book text during the first time you shared the book, you may be able now to include more of the actual vocabulary and text, as well as elaborate on and extend the book language. As children become familiar with a book, they will be eager to help re-create the story. You can encourage this by giving them opportunity to make predictions about upcoming events as well as involving them in discussing the illustrations.

Another way you can engage preschoolers in re-creating the story is to provide linguistic scaffolding. This means that you will read a segment of text and then pause, providing an opportunity for the preschoolers to respond (Cochran-Smith, 1984; Doake, 1981; Otto, 1984). This scaffolding can be used when sharing book texts that have a refrain or repeated phrase. In creating this scaffolding, you might pause within a sentence, leaving off one or more words that complete a phrase. At other times, you might pause after reading a segment of text and ask a question to elicit preschoolers' comments or contributions. You will want to acknowledge children's responses and comments before you continue the story. Participating in this dialogue about the story helps children develop a clearer understanding of the story as well as their ability to engage in a discussion.

3. *Discussing the book.* After you have finished reading the book, you will want to give children an opportunity to talk briefly about the story. You can initiate this discussion with a question or two. Because preschool children have not yet developed inner speech, you may find that your discussion quickly includes other topics. Preschool children say what they are thinking. They cannot yet monitor their thinking and speech so that they focus and speak only on the discussion topic. This is illustrated in the following example of a discussion about the book, *Corduroy* (Freeman, 1968).

Teacher:	(*closes the book*) What a happy ending to the story that was! Corduroy now has a new home. Why was Corduroy sad at the beginning of the story?
Child #1:	He wanted a home.
Child #2:	Mommy says we're gonna have a new home.
Child #3:	Mommy told me I'm gonna get new shoes.
Child #4:	I'm gonna get a new coat.

As a preschool teacher, you should expect that children will easily talk off topic. Gently and patiently guide their discussion back to the topic using questioning and linguistic scaffolding, referring to the story illustrations and content.

This is also the time when you will want to encourage children to raise their hands to be recognized before they start talking as well as to encourage them to listen carefully to what others are saying. With preschool children, this discussion time will be only a few minutes. Then you can provide a transition to other types of activities.

Follow-up activities. The stories and content shared during story time can be extended to other activities in your preschool classroom in several ways. One way of doing this is to be sure that you place the books shared at group time in the library center so that children can enjoy them individually and as often as they want. Another way is to provide topic-related small group activities that are available on a rotating basis for all children in your room. For example, if you have shared a story about apple picking, you might have a small group activity for making applesauce. To be sure that everyone has a chance to participate, you will need to have several small group sessions. The applesauce could then be served at snack-time.

Storytelling. Storytelling, like interactive story book sharing, has been linked to language and literacy development. Storytelling experiences have been associated with positive gains in concept development, vocabulary, visualization, complexity of syntax and morphemes, and story comprehension (Curenton, 2006; Isbell et al., 2004; Malo & Bullard, 2000; Speaker, Taylor, & Kamen, 2004).

Storytelling differs from interactive story book sharing in several ways. First of all, in storytelling, the teacher tells the story without using a book. While this requires more preparation, there are benefits to storytelling. Because there is no book or set text to read, the storyteller is able to create her own dramatic interpretation of a story and focus more on the nonverbal and verbal responses of her audience.

Storytelling involves a transaction between the speaker (teacher) and the audience (preschoolers) (Roney, 1996). In this transaction, the storyteller creates visual images of the story events and characters through her choice of words and the manner in which the story is told, such as through gesture, intonation, movement, or story-related props. The storytelling process requires that the audience listen carefully to the storyteller. Storytelling sessions in preschool are more effective when props, costuming, or puppets are used to provide additional visual referents for story characters or concepts. You could also use a storyboard with cut-outs of cardboard or felt characters to add visual support to the storytelling.

Guidelines. As you plan and engage in storytelling, you will find the following guidelines useful:

- ❖ Choose a story that has a series of events that can be easily portrayed through dramatic dialogue, descriptions, and gestures.
- ❖ Choose a story that relates to children's prior direct or vicarious experiences.
- ❖ Thoroughly read the story and plan your oral rendition of the story to emphasize specific words and phrases that are key to children's understanding and visualization of the story, keeping in mind the oral language vocabulary levels of your preschoolers.
- ❖ Plan the ways in which you will use gestures, actions, costumes, or props to communicate specific aspects of the story.
- ❖ Rehearse until you are very comfortable with the entire sequence of your storytelling performance.
- ❖ As you engage your preschoolers in the storytelling event, carefully observe their responses (nonverbal and verbal) and make any necessary adjustments to your oral story or to your use of gesture or story props so that their interest and comprehension are supported.

Story re-enactment of familiar story books. Another way of engaging preschoolers in books is to involve them in re-enacting a familiar story (Christensen & Kelly, 2003). Children will need to be very familiar with the story so they have the background knowledge and know what the characters say and how they act.

Identifying children's roles. In beginning this activity, you will want to identify the characters needed. Children who do not have character roles will be part of the audience. You will also need to decide what props or costumes will be appropriate for each role. Avoid having too many props because that may create a distraction.

Teacher's role. Your role in mediating and scaffolding this activity is to guide children's participation through narrating and prompting their actions. Occasionally, you may need to take a momentary role in the re-enactment to model a particular action or event. If this is a new activity for your preschoolers, you may find that while they enjoy the acting out of characters' roles, they are hesitant when it comes to giving characters' dialogue. You can support children's participation by initially taking over the verbal roles (with appropriate dialogic intonation). Then as they become more comfortable in this activity, you can use linguistic scaffolding to gradually encourage them to begin to participate in the characters' dialogue.

Story dictation. In story dictation, the teacher serves as the scribe, writing down what children want to have in their story. These stories are based in children's experiences. If it is a group story, it is based on an in-classroom event or a field trip. If the dictation involves an individual child, it is based on his personal experiences.

The process of story dictation provides opportunity for preschoolers to observe the writing process as well as opportunity to have their story permanently recorded on paper. As children see their oral words written down on paper, they develop an awareness of the way in which speech is encoded in print.

Guidelines for group story dictation. Allow about 20 minutes for this activity. To maximize children's memory for their experience, schedule the group dictation shortly after the shared event.

- ❖ Prepare for story dictation by having chart paper available, displayed on a stand or attached to a chalkboard. Have broad, felt-tipped markers available (black or blue ink for best visibility)
- ❖ Seat children on the floor in front of you. Be sure all of the children can see you as well as the chart.
- ❖ Tell your preschoolers that you will be writing a story together. Indicate that your role as teacher is to do the writing. Their role as class members is to decide what they want the story to say.
- ❖ Ask children to remember the special time that they had together, for example, a trip to pick apples, trip to the zoo, walk in the neighborhood. Encourage children to focus on what was seen and the sequence of events.
- ❖ Suggest a simple title for your story and write it at the top of the chart paper, for example, "Our Trip to the Orchard" or "Apple Picking."
- ❖ Begin to elicit children's suggested story text by asking, "What was the first thing we did on our trip to the orchard?" After receiving a response, you then will incorporate it into a sentence and write it down, repeating the words as you write them on the chart paper. For example, "We all got on the bus."
- ❖ Continue with questioning and commenting to elicit children's suggestions for the text. Be sure to write down what the children say, even if it is not in Standard English grammar. Where appropriate, elicit direct quotations or dialogue from children to incorporate into the story.
- ❖ The length of the dictated story will be determined by the interest and attention span of your preschoolers. Your initial attempts at dictated stories may only be several sentences in length.
- ❖ After the story is complete, and "The End" is written to create closure, reread the story aloud, pointing to each word, and encourage interested children to follow along. You may decide to have them echo-read. This means that you read a segment or sentence of the text and then they echo or repeat what you said.

Group-dictated stories can be incorporated into class story books by recopying the story text into a booklike format, adding photographs or children's illustrations, and then binding the pages together. After it is shared in group story time, it can then be placed in the library center for children to enjoy during their independent activity time.

Guidelines for individual story dictation. Taking dictated stories from individual children follows the same type of scaffolding used with the group story dictation. Because the child is referring to his own experience and not a shared experience, you will need to use

Preschoolers who are English language learners will benefit from frequent opportunities for oral communication.

more general questions and prompts than you did with the group story dictation. Be sensitive to culturally linguistically diverse children who may tell a story that does not have a narrative structure. Let each child structure his own story rather than imposing a structure (McCabe, 1997). To better understand children's dictation styles, you may find it beneficial to become familiar with the story structures prevalent in children's home cultures or languages.

Children's individually dictated stories can be directly written down in small booklet formats. Take two sheets of plain paper and one sheet of colored paper (for the cover). Fold them in half and staple on the fold in two places, creating a booklet. Then you are ready for the child's dictation. As you are taking the dictation, allow space on each page for illustrations or photographs to be added later. Be sure you ask the child for the title of his story (either before or after the dictation) and place the child's name on the cover as author. You could include the date of the story's dictation. Some children may want to place their books in the classroom library; others will want to take their books home.

Guidelines for Teachers of English Language Learners (ELLs)

Preschool children who are English language learners will still be developing their home language (Coltrane, 2003). Their knowledge of vocabulary and grammar in their home language is still growing. This means that they are "working toward two milestones at the same time: the full development of their native language and the acquisition of English" (p. 2). Preschool teachers of English language learners need to acknowledge the importance of the home language in the daily lives of these children. It is in this linguistic context that these preschoolers have received their early nurturing and socialization, and have developed their early communication competencies. Teachers who value children's home languages and recognize the need for children to continue to develop their home language along with acquiring English will be providing important support to their development. Specific guidelines for interacting with ELL children in preschool are described in the following sections; a summary chart is provided in Figure 7.2.

Figure 7.2 Guidelines for Teachers of English Language Learners (ELLs) in Preschool

❖ Support continued development of children's home languages

❖ Focus on developing oral language

❖ Activate and build upon children's prior knowledge

❖ Establish predictable routines

❖ Focus on children's strengths

❖ Provide a range of language and literacy-related activities embedded in direct experiences

❖ Encourage parents to engage their children in conversation and language play

Support Continued Development of Children's Home Languages

You can provide support for children's home language by first establishing communication with their families (Coltrane, 2003). By learning a few key phrases in a child's home language, you will be acknowledging the value of the home language for communication as well as the value of becoming bilingual. Key phrases in several different languages are provided in Table 7.1. Check your pronunciation of each language with a native speaker or other resource.

You will also want to make an effort to become more familiar with each child's home culture (De Atiles & Allexsaht-Snider, 2002). By understanding and acknowledging the ways in which literacy is used in their homes, you will be better able to develop learning experiences that draw on children's prior experiences and conceptual knowledge (Ordoñez-Jasis & Ortiz, 2006).

When possible, invite native speakers such as parents or volunteers into your classroom to enhance communication during learning activities. Bilingual paraprofessionals would also help English language learners interact and communicate more effectively. You will also want to provide some story books and information books in your library center that use children's home languages (Ordoñez-Jasis & Ortiz, 2006). By providing these avenues of support, you will be helping children continue to use their home language while they are also developing English competencies.

Focus on Developing Oral Language

As described earlier in this text, oral language provides a basis for the development of literacy. This is no different for English language learners. Additionally, just as a child's first language is learned through social interaction with adults and older siblings, so is a child's second language. For this reason, teachers who have ELL preschoolers need to focus on providing many opportunities for oral communication. These opportunities will involve hearing and speaking in the new language in a variety of contexts and learning activities (Smith, 2003), ranging from informal conversations with you and their peers to interactive story book sharing. Repeating the activity also enhances and solidifies the learning.

Expect English language learners to experience a silent period. It is also important to remember that second language learners will go through a silent period while they are developing their receptive knowledge of English, but are not yet ready to begin to use English to express themselves (De Atiles & Snider, 2002). During this time, you will want to closely observe the ELL child's nonverbal responses and engagement in learning activities. Based on close observations, you will be able to determine if the child is

Table 7.1 Basic Greetings and Expressions in Different Languages

English	Spanish	Gujarati	Urdu	Japanese	Polish
Good morning	Buenos dias	Su prabhatam	As-saalam-u-alaikum	Ohayo-gozaimasu	Dzieńdobry
Good afternoon	Buenas tardes	—	As-saalam-u-alaikum	Kon-nichi-wa	Dzieńdobry
Good evening	Buenas noches	Subh ratri	As-saalam-u-alaikum	Kon-ban-wa	Dobry wieczór
Hi/Hello	Hola	Namaste	Ad-aab *or* Kush-am-deed	Kon-nichi-wa	Cześć/Witam
How are you?	Como está Ud.?	Ta-mai kem Cho?	Kai-se hai aap?	Ogenki desu ka?	Jak się macie?
Thank you	Gracias	a-bhar	Shoo-kri-ya	Arigato gozaimasu	Dziękuję
You are welcome	De nada	—	—	Dou itashimashite	Proszię/Nie ma za co
I'll see you tomorrow	Hasta mañana	Ta-ma-nay ka-lay ma-li-su.	Ka-al mu-la-khat hogi *or* Ka-al mi-len-gai.	Ashifa o-as shimashou	Do jutra
It is very nice to meet you	Es un placer conocerla (*fem.*) Es unplacer concerlo (*masc.*)	Ta-ma-nay mali ne Ba-huuj a-nand . thayo.	Aap se mil kar khu-shi hui.	Oai-dekite ureshii desu	Miło mi was poznać
Please	Por favor	Ma-her-ba-ni karo	Me-herb-a-ni	Onegai shimasu	Proszę
My name is . . .	Mi nombre es—	Maru naam —che.	Mera naam —hai.	Watashi no namae wa—desu	Nazywam się—
What is your name?	Como se llama?	Tamaru naam su che?	Aap-ka naam Kya hai?	O-namae wa nan desu ka?	Jak się nazywacie?

comprehending the content and understanding the nature of the activity. You may find that an ELL preschooler is willing to participate verbally in a one-on-one conversation much earlier than they will participate in responding during group story time. You will want to support this growth by allowing time for individual conversations and small group interactions.

Engage ELLs in interactive shared story book reading. As described in earlier sections of this text, story book sharing provides a context for oral language development as well as an opportunity to begin to develop knowledge of written language. This is no different for second language learners. Thus, it is critically important that English language learners have frequent opportunities to engage in story book sharing.

While you will not want to exclude the preschoolers who are English language learners from large group story times, you may find that they are not able to comprehend the story or participate in the verbal interactions, and thus lose interest and become inattentive.

These behaviors all reflect the need for specific story book sharing that is tailored to meet their individual language development levels. Continue to include them in the larger group story time, but provide additional opportunities for one-on-one or small group story book sharing.

Individual or small group story book sharing with ELLs needs to involve developmentally appropriate books as well as developmentally appropriate interactive strategies. If the English language learner is experiencing a silent period or is at the one-word phase or telegraphic speech phase in English acquisition, you would want to use books that can be shared by labeling and commenting rather than read from books that have a complex storyline. It is also important to choose books that have clear, high-quality, but simple illustrations. Your interaction style would resemble the way in which you would share books with a toddler. Instead of reading the text, use labeling and commenting, and encourage the child to participate in the book sharing. Point to the illustrations frequently as you label and comment. You could also ask questions that the child can answer by pointing to the illustrations.

If you decide to use a book that has been shared at the class story time, you will need to mediate the story text in ways that increase the English language learner's comprehension and interaction. For example, you might use labeling and commenting about the illustrations instead of reading the story text. You might decide to pause more often to encourage children's comments or questions. Although you will be using the same interaction patterns you use with other children, such as eye contact and shared reference, communication loops, questioning, linguistic scaffolding, and mediation, you will be using them in a way that increases comprehension and involvement for English language learners.

Activate and build upon children's prior knowledge. English language learners will become more engaged in learning activities that build upon their prior conceptual knowledge and life experiences (Coltrane, 2003). To determine children's prior knowledge and experiences, gather this information through informal conversations with their parents, community volunteers, and even the children themselves. You will then use this information as you plan your classroom curriculum, for example, the concept centers, creative drama center, and story book activities.

Establish predictable routines. English language learners will benefit from established routines that allow them to predict the sequence of classroom activities or specific steps in participating in an activity (De Atiles & Allexsaht-Snider, 2002). This provides them with a feeling of self-confidence, stability, and security.

Focus on children's strengths. With ELLs, it is important to focus on what they are able to do rather than what they cannot yet accomplish (De Atiles & Allexsaht-Snider, 2002). By using observation notes and samples of their work, you will be able to provide examples of children's language and early literacy development. (See further the upcoming section on Assessment and sample observation forms in Appendix C.)

Provide a range of language- and literacy-related activities embedded in direct experiences. Real-life, hands-on experiences provide opportunities to develop concepts and acquire the related vocabulary. This context-rich learning is particularly important for ELLs. For example, experiences with animals, planting a garden, raking leaves, making applesauce, or taking a walk in the neighborhood all provide opportunities for language- and literacy-related activities.

Encourage parents to engage their children in conversation and language play. Parents who carry on conversations with their children at home and also engage in language play will be strengthening their children's oral language (Ordoñez & Ortiz, 2005). Storytelling, singing, rhymes, and poetry all help ELL children to become more aware of different features of language. Teachers can also encourage parents to use word-less picture books to engage children in labeling and commenting, describing, and sequencing events—all of which are important aspects of beginning literacy.

Guidelines for Teachers of Preschoolers Who Are Language-Delayed

Young children who are language-delayed are likely to have difficulties later on developing literacy competencies (Bogott, Letmanski, & Miller, 1999; Paul, 1993). Language delays may be influenced by physical abnormalities, cognitive impairments, or a lack of social interaction. Some children with language delays will also come from home environments that are low in literacy-related experiences. Children with severe language delays will receive special education services that are targeted to their individual special needs. Children with slight or moderate language delays may not be identified or assessed until they are in a preschool setting. As a preschool teacher, you will want to be aware of children who are language-delayed so that you can make any necessary referrals for further assessment and diagnosis. You will also want to provide additional opportunities for individualized language and literacy-related activities.

Specific strategies have proven beneficial in enhancing language and literacy development among children with a wide range of special needs: cognitive impairment, language impairment, at-risk/poverty level, and other disabilities (Bogott, Letmanski, & Miller, 1999; Crain-Thoreson & Dale, 1999; Genisio & Drecktrah, 1999; Notari-Syverson, O'Connor, & Vadasy, 1996; Perkins & Cooter, 2005; Raver, 2006; Sharif, Ozuah, Dinkevich, & Mulvihill, 2003; Yaden, Rowe, & MacGillivray, 1999). Six general guidelines for interacting with preschoolers who are language-delayed are described in the following sections; Figure 7.3 provides a summary of these guidelines.

Use effective interaction strategies. These strategies include eye contact–shared reference, communication loops, verbal mapping, linguistic scaffolding, and mediation. You will want to place special emphasis on engaging the child as a conversational partner. Throughout these interactions, you will need to pay special attention to providing sufficient wait time for the child to respond. Children who are language-delayed may take longer to respond verbally as well as nonverbally.

Increase one-on-one conversations. Conversations with individual children provide an opportunity to focus on a single child and to encourage verbal and nonverbal responses.

Figure 7.3 Guidelines for Teachers of Preschoolers Who Are Language-Delayed

❖ Use effective interaction strategies

❖ Increase one-on-one conversations

❖ Increase one-on-one or small group interactive book sharing

❖ Increase repetitions of book sharing and other activities to enhance learning

❖ Use shared book content as a theme for other related learning activities

❖ Design concept centers so that children who are language-delayed can engage in self-directed learning

You will also focus the conversation on the child's particular interests and actions. This involves active listening on your part and taking the child's lead in the topic of your conversation.

Increase one-on-one or small group interactive book sharing. Preschoolers who are language-delayed may not be able to remain attentive during a large group teacher read-aloud because the story and language may be too complex for them to comprehend. For this reason, you will need to engage children who are language-delayed in frequent individual or small group book sharings. In this way you will be able to scaffold and mediate their interactions with the books within their individual zones of proximal development. You will also want to select specific story books that reflect their prior experiences, concepts, and listening vocabulary.

Increase repetitions of book reading and activities to enhance learning. Repeated sharing of the same story book will enhance children's memory for the events of the story as well as reinforce the learning of concepts and vocabulary. Be sure to select books that were previously enjoyed. Children's memory for the specific language of the book will be enhanced during these repeated readings. You can also provide opportunities for engaging in related activities in other areas of your curriculum, for example, the concept centers, creative drama, and story re-enactment. These repeated opportunities will strengthen their development and learning.

Use shared book content as a theme for other related learning activities. Preschoolers who are language-delayed will benefit from activities that are related to concepts introduced during story time. For example, after sharing *The Hungry Caterpillar* (Carle, 1971), related activities might include pretending to be caterpillars while crawling on the floor, going on a walk outdoors, or watching a caterpillar that has been brought into the classroom's terrarium. You could serve pieces of fruit at snack time that were mentioned in the book. As you engage children who are language-delayed in these related activities, you will be emphasizing the vocabulary and referring to the events that occurred in the book. This enhances children's language development and provides opportunity to reflect upon book content.

Design concept centers so that children who are language-delayed can engage in self-directed learning. A child who is language-delayed will be able to experiment and practice their developing skills in a relaxed, exploratory setting (Genisio & Drecktrah, 1999; Yaden, Rowe, & MacGillivray, 1999).

Assessment

Preschool teachers who engage in reflective practice also engage in ongoing assessments of children's development and learning. These assessments then inform their curricular decisions. By understanding children's individual developmental levels and needs, teachers can better plan, develop, and implement appropriate learning activities.

When assessing children's emergent literacy development, it is important to remember that literacy development occurs along a continuum (Neuman & Roskos, 2005; also see Chapter 3, Figure 3.2). Each child progresses at his own rate and in his own manner along this continuum. During the preschool years, you can expect to see developmental variations from day to day and week to week. Assessment of preschool children's emergent literacy can be focused on documenting children's behaviors and responses over time so that you will have a comprehensive picture of each child's growth and development in their transactions with literacy.

Preschool children's transactions with literacy involve a complex interaction between their language knowledge, the learning context, and the specific literacy-related task. This complexity cannot be captured by one type of assessment, therefore, teachers need to use a variety of ways to determine children's growth and development in literacy (IRA & NAEYC, 1998; Neuman & Roskos, 2005). Assessments of preschool English language learners should also include a focus on the child's home language and document the child's development in his home language as well.

Key Areas of Emergent Literacy Assessment

Key areas of emergent literacy assessment during the preschool years include the following: (a) Oral language development, (b) phonological awareness and phonetic knowledge, (c) receptive and expressive knowledge of narratives, (d) knowledge of how to read, and (e) knowledge of how to write. Examples of preschool children's knowledge in these areas were described in Chapter 6. Each of these areas has been associated with subsequent success in reading and writing during kindergarten and primary grades. In the paragraphs that follow, key behaviors to look for in each area will be highlighted. The figures accompanying each area provide additional specific questions.

Oral language development. Your observation of a preschooler's oral language development will focus on the following questions:

1. Does the child pay attention when spoken to by an adult?
2. Does the child establish eye contact and shared reference?
3. Does the child participate in a turn-taking dialogue?
4. Does the child pay attention to ongoing or new events in the classroom?
5. What is the child's level of oral language (for example, one word, telegraphic speech, multiword phrases, or sentences)?
6. What is the child's home language? (See Figure 7.4.)

Phonological and phonetic awareness. Your observations in this area will focus on a child's awareness of patterns of sound found in rhyming and alliteration, as well as the child's involvement in word play. You will also want to notice if a child shows awareness of letter–sound associations. (See Figure 7.5.)

Receptive and expressive knowledge of narratives. Children's knowledge of narratives can be observed by focusing on these questions:

1. Does the child comprehend stories when they are told orally or read?
2. Does the child create personal narratives?
3. Does the child create imaginary narratives?
4. When the child reconstructs a story from a familiar story book, are the major events included in an accurate sequence?

(See Figure 7.6.)

Knowledge of how to read. Your assessment of children's knowledge of how to read can occur when they are engaged in a shared reading with you (or another adult) and also when they are engaged in an independent story book reading. When assessing a child's behaviors during a shared reading, you will want to focus on these questions:

1. Does the child establish a shared reference with you and the book?
2. Does the child engage in turn-taking, dialogic participation?
3. How does the child physically interact with the book?

Figure 7.4 Observing a Preschooler's Ways of Communicating

Focus of Observation	Questions to consider:
Attention to adult's speech	1. Does child look to speaker? 2. Does child turn to face the speaker? 3. Does child stop what they are doing and look to see who is talking?
Eye contact, shared reference	1. Does child respond to adult's request to "look"? 2. Does child follow adult's pointing gestures? 3. Does child make eye contact with adult when adult is talking and directly in front of or holding the child? 4. When presented with an object, does child first look at adult and then at object?
Turn-taking/dialogic participation	1. When adult speaks to child and then pauses, does the child respond nonverbally? 2. When adult speaks to child and then pauses, does child respond verbally? 3. Does child "take turns" in listening and responding?
Attention to ongoing events	1. Does child notice a new event in classroom? 2. Does child continue to watch ongoing event?
Level of language	Which level characterizes child's expressive language? 1. one-word (invented and conventional) 2. two- to three-word phrases 3. utterances composed of multiword multiphrases

Home Language: ___Standard English ___Dialect of English ___Other Language

 Figure 7.5 Observation of a Preschooler's Phonological and Phonetic Awareness

Focus of Observation	Questions to consider:
Phonological Awareness	1. Does child show awareness of rhyming words? 2. Does child show awareness of word alliteration? 3. Does child engage in word play?
Knowledge of letter–sound relationships	1. Does child show awareness of sounds associated with individual letters? 2. Does child focus on specific features of letters and discriminate between letters?

4. Does the child indicate a memory for familiar book content?
5. Does the child maintain interest and attention in the shared reading?
6. Does the child appear to enjoy the shared reading?

Additional questions to focus on are located in Figure 7.7.

Observation of preschool children's independent story book interactions will focus on some of the same areas as you observed during the shared book interactions, however, there is more of a focus on the story or "text" created by the child. Specifically, you will be observing the child's reading to determine the source of the story (pictures? print?

Figure 7.6 Observation of a Preschooler's Receptive and Expressive Knowledge of Narratives

Focus of Observation	Questions to consider:
Receptive: Comprehension of oral stories or teacher read-alouds	Does child: 1. Listen attentively to story during teacher read-aloud? 2. Participate in story discussions? 3. Ask questions related to story or book content?
Expressive: Creates personal narratives	Does child: 1. Recount personal events that he or she experienced? 2. Narrate a clear sequence of events in time or cause-and-effect sequence?
Expressive: Creates imaginary narratives	Does child: 1. Create a narrative of imaginary events? 2. Narrate a clear sequence of events?
Expressive: Reconstructs story from familiar story book	Does child's story reconstruction: 1. Include the major events of the story? 2. Include similar sequence of events as in the story?

Figure 7.7 Observation of a Preschooler's Knowledge of How to Read During Shared Book Reading

Child's name: _____   Age: _____

Focus of Observation	Questions to consider: Does child . . .
Shared reference	Follow adult's gestures/pointing?
Turn-taking/dialogic participation	Respond nonverbally? Respond verbally?
Book handling	Touch, pat, or hit book? Attempt to turn pages? Pick up book independently?
Memory for book content	Anticipate book content: Through gestures or facial expression? Through verbal expression?
Attentiveness	Maintain focus on book?
Affective response	Appear to enjoy book sharing? Initiate book-sharing interaction?

both?), the use of labeling, commenting, and sequencing of story events, along with the language style (similar in meaning, verbatim-like, or accurate decoding). (See Figure 7.8.)

Knowledge of how to write. As you observe preschoolers' developing knowledge of writing, you will find the questions useful:

1. Does the child show an interest in adults' writing?
2. Is the child interested in environmental print?
3. Is the child interested in using crayons, markers, and other tools for graphic expression?

Figure 7.8 Observation of a Preschooler's Knowledge of How to Read: Independent Book Reading

Child's name: _____	Age: _____
Focus of Observation	**Questions to consider:** Does child . . .
Book handling	Orient book correctly? Proceed from front to back of book?
Source of story/text	Refer to pictures only? Refer to both pictures and print? Focus on print only?
Story/Text	Use labeling and commenting? Connect series of events? Describe or re-create all major events of original story?
Language style	Create segments of text similar to original in meaning? Re-create verbatim-like text segments? Accurately decode words in book?
Affective response	Appear to enjoy book reading?

4. What forms of graphic expression does the child use (drawing, scribbling, letter-like forms, random letters, or invented spelling)?
5. Does the child attempt to read what he wrote or ask an adult to read it for him?

(See Figure 7.9.)

Examples of more detailed observation forms for each of these key areas of emergent literacy are located in Appendix C. Full-size, reproducible forms are available in the Instructor's Guide.

Contexts of Assessment

Your assessment of children's emergent literacy behavior will occur in two different contexts: (a) Informal observations and (b) elicited tasks. In each context, it is important that you carefully document children's interactions and responses. Most of your assessments of individual children will be informal observations. These observations will be made as children interact during independent activities and as you are implementing teacher-directed activities. The instruments used to make these informal observations include checklists, rating scales, and anecdotal records.

Additional resources for informal observations of children have been developed. For example, the Teacher Rating of Oral Language and Literacy (TROLL) (Dickinson, McCabe, & Sprague, 2001, 2003) is a comprehensive observation tool that focuses on preschool children's listening, speaking, reading, and writing skills. Owocki & Goodman (2002) have also developed extensive observation formats that will assist teachers in documenting preschool children's literacy growth.

At other times you may decide to engage individual children in a more specific assessment of emergent literacy. These assessments directly elicit preschoolers' emergent literacy knowledge through specific reading and writing tasks and related direct questioning, such as "point to the cover of the book." Elicited task assessments are conducted with individual children and therefore require a quiet corner and a time when there are no

Figure 7.9 Observation of a Preschooler's Knowledge of How to Write

Child's name:_____	Age: _____
Behaviors to look for:	**Description of behavior (include dates observed)**
Interest in adult's writing	
Interest in environmental print	
Interest in graphic expression	
Forms of graphic expression (attach artifacts or copies of child's writing)	Drawing? Scribbling? Letter-like forms? Letters? Invented spelling? Prephonemic? Phonemic? Letter-name? Known words?
Meaning attributed to graphic expression	Pretends to "read' drawing? Pretends to "read" scribbling or prephonemic spelling? Attempts to read phonemic, letter name, or known word spelling?

interruptions. For example, Clay's (1993) *Observation Survey of Early Literacy Achievement* assesses preschool children's early literacy knowledge through the following tasks: letter identification, concepts about print, word tests, writing samples, and dictation. Assessment through specific tasks is more systematic and requires set procedures be followed for administration, scoring, and interpretation of the results.

Another type of assessment involves asking preschoolers to "read" a familiar story book. This task elicits children's knowledge of how one goes about interacting with books in sharing the "text" with another person. Sulzby (1985, 1991) developed a technique for eliciting children's story book readings and a classification system for documenting and tracking children's development of emergent literacy (refer to Table 6.2). Preschool teachers will find this form of assessment a useful way to better understand what children know about the reading process.

It is important to remember that these informal assessments are not tests with right or wrong answers. Instead, they are tools for exploring and documenting what children are beginning to understand about reading and writing. After you have used these assessments with many children over a considerable time, you will develop an awareness of which children are progressing and which children may benefit from more intervention and curricular support.

Home–School Connections

Earlier sections of this text have emphasized the important role that home and community contexts have in children's developing literacy as well as the importance of establishing rapport with children's families. The four guidelines for establishing home–school connections introduced at the infant and toddler level are still relevant at the preschool level (see Chapter 5). These guidelines are: (a) Acknowledge home and community language and literacy, (b) share information about classroom learning activities, (c) share information about children's language and emergent literacy, and (d) assist parents in providing literacy materials at home. As you follow these guidelines, you will be helping parents and family members feel that they are in partnership with you in enhancing their children's development. It is also important to provide opportunities for parents to share information about their child's experiences and developmental achievements that have occurred at home. This information provides you with additional awareness of how your classroom activities and mediation can support each child's literacy development.

Another way of strengthening this feeling of partnership is to invite family members to visit your classroom and become familiar with the learning materials and activities. Some family members may be interested in participating in your classroom's learning activities with their children. For example, you might decide to schedule a "family story book" event, opening your classroom to parents and other family members and inviting them to share favorite books with small groups of children.

Developmentally, preschool children are likely to be in the exploration phase of literacy acquisition or the experimentation phase. There may be some children who are starting to read simple texts and write known words. As a preschool teacher, you can encourage parents and family members to support their children's continued development in literacy at home by observing the following five guidelines (Butler, Liss, & Sterner, 1999; Epstein, 2002b; Kassow, 2006; Otto & Johnson, 1996; Partridge, 2004; Sharif, Ozuah, Dinkevich, & Mulvihill, 2003; Ulmen, 2005). (See Figure 7.10 for a summary of these guidelines.)

Create a Lending Library in Your Classroom

Parents may not always have time to stop by the local library to check out books for their preschooler and they may not have the financial resources to buy books to have at home. By creating a lending library in your classroom, you will be making it possible for parents to have appropriate books to share with their preschoolers. You will want to be sure that the lending library books are kept in good repair and reflect the interests and experiences of your preschoolers.

Locating books for your lending library. In building your lending library you may find you can locate books economically by going to garage sales or resale shops. Community organizations and local libraries sometimes sponsor used-book sales of donated or gently used books. It is also a good idea to stock your lending library with multiple copies of books that have become favorites of your preschoolers. Not only will the children already be familiar with the story, but the multiple copies of the book will mean that they will not

 Figure 7.10 Summary of Guidelines for Creating Home–School Connections for Literacy Development

- ❖ Create a lending library in your classroom
- ❖ Help parents understand the many ways that books can be shared
- ❖ Encourage parents to engage children in oral storytelling and mealtime conversations
- ❖ Encourage parents to let their children explore and experiment with visual communication
- ❖ Share ideas and information with parents through short newsletters

have to wait long to take home a favorite book. Be as generous as possible in supplying a variety of attractive, engaging books. You may also be able to obtain support from community service groups in providing books for your lending library.

Provide attractive, child-sized book bags. To add to the interest in taking books home, you could even provide special, simply made, canvas book bags for children. You will want to allow them to decorate their own bags with their personal art and name. This special place for their borrowed books will facilitate carrying books between school and home (see Figure 7.11).

Provide supplementary materials to accompany the books. To add interest to the shared reading at home, provide puppets that represent book characters. For example, a mouse puppet or a teddy-bear puppet will be relevant for many preschool books. In addition, by making packets of writing materials available to accompany books home, you will be encouraging children to share their responses to their home book time with drawing and writing attempts. Each packet need contain only a couple sheets of paper and a small assortment of writing tools (for example, crayons and felt-tip, washable markers). You could also include small pieces of recycled wrapping paper, cut in a variety of shapes to add to children's ways of expressing themselves visually.

Encourage children to share their visual creations and respond with interest when children talk about their reading and writing at home. The importance of their activities can also be acknowledged when you post their creations on a classroom bulletin board.

Parent or community volunteers can help in preparing these supplementary materials. You will also need to replace the materials as they are used. In addition, you will need to expect that sometimes materials will be lost or misplaced.

Help Parents Understand the Many Ways in Which Books Can be Shared

For many parents, reading to their child means that they read while their child sits quietly and listens as each page is read. Preschoolers benefit much more when the book sharing

Figure 7.11 Example of Child's Book Bag for Lending Library

Providing attractive, child-sized book bags adds to children's interest in taking books home.

is more interactive. In fact, the actual book text does not have to be read to be beneficial. Parents can engage their child in looking at the illustrations and talking about the events and objects that are pictured. In this way books can be objects of contemplation and shared conversation. The key part of this shared-book interaction is the dialogue that accompanies the book. It is in this shared meaning-making that children benefit. Even when parents actually read the story text, it is important to stop to ask questions and engage their children in talking about the story or illustrations.

By emphasizing the oral conversations about a book rather than the actual word-by-word reading of a story, you will be encouraging the social interactions that are so important to language and literacy development. You will also be providing ways that parents who have low literacy skills can still enjoy sharing books with their preschoolers.

Routine for shared reading are important. While encouraging your preschoolers' parents to engage their children in shared reading, you can also suggest that parents have a regular time for story sharing. It does not take long to share a book, perhaps only five to ten minutes. Many parents find that story sharing is a good way to help their children relax before bedtime.

Encourage Parents to Engage Children in Oral Storytelling and Mealtime Conversations

As families interact at home at the end of the day, many times there is a recounting or oral reporting of events they experienced during the day. This recounting often resembles an oral story as a sequence of events is remembered and told. These personal narratives of the day's events are often followed by related conversations about those events with family members. Sometimes this occurs at mealtime, other times it occurs as they are traveling home in their car or on the bus. Oral storytelling may also be a way that family members share knowledge about past events specific to their culture or stories handed down through generations.

Both of these events, oral storytelling and conversations, provide opportunities for children to develop oral comprehension of narratives as well as begin to create narratives of their own. It is important to let parents know that this will help their children understand written stories later on when they are reading independently. It also develops vocabulary and other language-related knowledge.

Encourage Parents to Let Their Child Explore and Experiment with Visual Communication

This includes creating messages and interacting with environmental print. Chapter 6 described preschoolers' early symbol-making behaviors as well as their interactions with environmental print. By encouraging parents to support this exploration and experimentation, preschoolers will develop an awareness of the ways that written language is used to get things done. Parents can provide opportunities to let their children observe them reading and writing as they go about their daily activities, for example, reading a recipe, paying bills, using written texts as a part of religious services, reading a newspaper, reading items received in the mail, or using a computer. Parents can also involve their children in interacting with environmental print, such as reading labels on food cartons, helping with the grocery shopping, mailing letters at the post office and noticing signs on the streets/roads. Having a family message-board or posting messages to each other on the refrigerator provides a way for preschoolers to participate in visual communication

Figure 7.12 Sample Newsletter to Parents

Ms. White's Classroom Newsletter
October 2006

Our Lending Library Is Open!

Our classroom's lending library is now open. We have a large variety of books ready for you and your child to check out and enjoy.

Thanks to our classroom volunteers, each child has their own special book bag. Stop in after school and take a moment to pick out a book or two to take home.

Remember:
Open House
November 6, from 5 to 7 p.m.
Refreshments will be served.
Come to see our exciting classroom!

Take your child on a "picture walk":

- Select a new story book to share with your child.
- Instead of reading the text, focus on the pictures.
- Starting with the front cover, talk with your child about the pictures.
- For example, say "Let's look at this book. What do you think it will be about? What's happening on this page? What do you think will happen next?"
- Picture walks help your child develop vocabulary and conversation skills.

with family members through drawing and writing attempts. While you will want to encourage parents to take time to answer preschoolers' questions about print, you will want to emphasize that the preschool years are times of exploration and experimentation, rather than intensive direct teaching.

Share Ideas and Information with Parents via Short Newsletters

One way to share ideas and information with parents is to develop a newsletter. Because parents are busy (and so are you!), each newsletter should be short—only one page. In addition, the articles in the newsletter should be short, with simple sentences. Wherever possible, provide lists or bulleted points rather than detailed paragraphs. Adding graphics and color will also make your newsletter more attractive (and more likely to be read). Avoid using a small font since it will discourage quick reading. A sample newsletter is provided in Figure 7.12.

Chapter Summary

The focus of this chapter was on the ways that teachers can create and implement language and literacy-rich curricula for preschool children. Teachers' reflective decision-making is an important part of creating and sustaining this language and literacy-rich environment. Children's literacy development can be enhanced throughout the preschool curriculum. Informal conversations and procedural activities, such as attendance-taking and interacting with environmental print provide important opportunities for language and literacy interactions. Specific independent activities that benefit literacy development include the following: art/writing center, library center, creative drama center, and concept centers. Preschool children who are ready for small and large group activities will also benefit from specific activities that are directed and mediated by their teacher. These specific activities include: rhymes, finger plays, and action songs; interactive story book sharing; storytelling; story re-enactment of familiar books; and story dictation.

Preschool children who are English language learners are still developing their home language. Teachers can provide support for English language learners by encouraging continued development of their home language competencies and also by focusing on oral language development in the second language at preschool. Interactive story book sharing is an important way of increasing ELL children's oral language and vocabulary. By activating and building on ELL children's prior knowledge, providing direct experiences, and focusing on their strengths, their language and literacy development will be enhanced.

Guidelines for teachers of preschoolers who are language-delayed include: using effective interaction strategies, increasing one-on-one conversations and interactive book sharing, providing book extension activities, providing opportunities for repetition, and creating concept centers that foster self-directed learning.

Assessment of children's development is an integral part of curriculum planning and implementation. Assessment of preschool children's emergent literacy should focus on documenting children's behaviors and responses over time and in varied contexts so that teachers will have a comprehensive picture of each child's transactions with literacy. Key areas of emergent literacy assessment during the preschool years include: oral language development, knowledge of narratives, phonological awareness, phonetic knowledge, knowledge of how to read, and knowledge of how to write.

Home–school connections for fostering preschoolers' literacy development can be facilitated by teachers who create lending libraries in their classrooms and help parents to understand the many ways that books can be shared. In addition, preschool teachers can encourage parents to include their children in oral storytelling and mealtime conversations, as well as exploring ways of communicating through drawing and early writing attempts. Short, attractive newsletters also enhance school–home communication.

Chapter Review

Chart for Review: Summarize the value of each activity to preschool children's literacy development.

Activity	Relationship to Literacy	Guidelines
Informal conversations		
Procedural activities		
Art/writing center		
Library center		

Activity	Relationship to Literacy	Guidelines
Creative drama center		
Concept centers		
Rhymes, finger plays, and action songs		
Interactive story book sharing		
Storytelling		
Story re-enactments		
Story dictation		

Chapter Extension Activities

Observation: Select one of the observation forms located in Appendix E. Conduct an observation of a preschool child based upon the questions in the observation form. Share your observations with your college/university class.

Curriculum Development: Plan and provide the materials for a creative drama center that incorporates literacy-related activities. Prepare your plan using the chart format for independent activities located in Appendix K. Consider the following themes (or develop your own): post office/package service, medical office, grocery store, shoe store. Obtain permission to implement this creative drama center in a preschool classroom. Observe the ways in which children interact in the center. Prepare a reflective essay evaluating the success of your center and suggestions for further development or revision. *Optional:* Select a story book that focuses on the theme of your creative drama center. Describe how reading this story prior to making the center available might influence children's use of the creative drama center.

Research:
1. Observe and reflect upon the ways in which a preschool art/writing center enhances literacy development. Describe the types of materials available and the ways that children were interacting in the center. Describe the manner in which children were expressing themselves visually as well as any writing attempts. If possible, include copies of children's work.
2. Conduct online research on one of the following curriculum models. Prepare a description of the model that focuses on developmentally appropriate literacy-related activities that are embedded in the model. Share your findings with your class.

   a. *The Creative Curriculum®.* http://www.teaching strategies.com/page/about.cfm
   b. *HIGH/SCOPE® Educational Research Foundation* http://www.highscope.org
   c. *Success for All® Foundation Curiosity Corner* http://successforall.com/early/early_curiosity. htm

Chapter 8

Emergent Literacy Among Kindergartners: Signs, Standards, and Assessment

> **A** month before she entered kindergarten, Julie was asked how drawing is different from writing. She replied, "Drawing is like coloring. Writing is writing a note to somebody." Then, when asked if she could write, Julie printed her name.

Children come to kindergarten having had a wide variety of experiences in their preschool years. Like Julie, some children will come to kindergarten being able to distinguish between drawing and writing. Other children will be still exploring the ways in which thoughts are expressed on paper through different graphic forms.

In this chapter we will be focusing on kindergarten children's developing literacy knowledge as it has been documented in various research studies in the field of emergent literacy. While this research was conducted in the late 1970s through the early 1990s and therefore may appear dated, it is important to keep in mind that this research served as a catalyst as well as a foundation for our current understandings of kindergarten children's literacy development. This early research as well as more recent studies has served to inform the development of kindergarten performance standards by professional organizations and agencies at national and state levels. These standards specify the language and literacy expectations for children as they exit kindergarten. Therefore, a second emphasis of this chapter will be on becoming acquainted with kindergarten standards for the language arts. As a kindergarten teacher, you will not only need to be aware of children's level of emergent literacy when they first come to your classroom, you will also need to be aware of the expectations for their literacy development as they move on to first grade. In order to determine kindergartners' levels of emergent literacy and to implement developmentally appropriate curriculum, you will need to use assessment strategies that can assist you in beginning to document kindergartners' literacy development. With this in mind, the last section in this chapter will focus on assessing children's emergent literacy as they begin kindergarten.

Looking for Signs of Emergent Literacy Among Kindergartners

Kindergarten children's emergent literacy behaviors occur as they engage in reading- and writing-related tasks at home, in the community, and at school (for example, Heath, 1983; Sulzby, 1986; Tabors, Snow, & Dickinson, 2001). These signs of emergent literacy do not occur in isolation, nor do they occur universally for all kindergarten children. Instead, these signs of emergent literacy occur within complex and dynamic settings. As a way of understanding these complex and dynamic settings in which kindergartners interact, we will take a closer look at these literacy transactions.

Components of Kindergartners' Literacy Transactions

Children's transactions with literacy that result in meaning construction or meaning-making involve interactions among these three components:

- ❖ what children know about language (oral and written),
- ❖ the texts or literacy-related tasks children encounter, and
- ❖ the contexts in which the literacy events occur.

Additionally, the mediation provided by others (teachers, parents, or older siblings) also affects the transactions. In this mediation, the adult or older peer focuses on the child's transactions, providing linguistic scaffolding and adjusting the learning task so that it is within the child's zone of proximal development. As a teacher, your awareness of each child's knowledge of oral and written language will guide not only the curriculum you implement in your classroom, but also the ways in which you mediate their transactions with literacy. The relationship between these components is represented in Figure 8.1.

Each literacy transaction is unique. While the components in each literacy transaction are the same, each literacy transaction is different because each component will vary in unique and individual ways. For example, no two shared book experiences are exactly the same, even if the same teacher and children are involved in sharing the same book on the two occasions. The teacher may read the text in a slightly different way, and the children may ask different questions or comment on different illustrations. Events

Figure 8.1 Components of Kindergartners' Transactions with Literacy

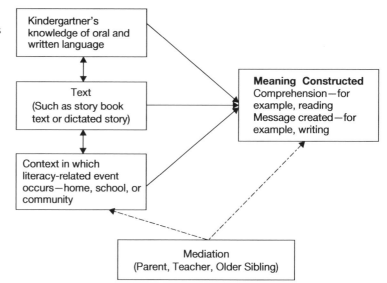

Each time you share books at group story time, children's responses will reflect their prior knowledge and experiences.

Monkey Business Images

preceding the two story book sharing events may differ in ways that influence the book sharing and literacy transaction. By recognizing the uniqueness of each literacy transaction, teachers are able to acknowledge the complex interactions that occur as children participate in reading and writing activities.

School and home settings are the two main contexts in which kindergarten children's transactions with literacy occur. While kindergartners begin to spend more time in a school setting, their home remains an important context for their literacy-related transactions. In each setting, specific factors have been identified that are associated with kindergartners' emergent literacy, as well as specific types of texts or literacy-related events that occur. It is important to remember, however, that the transactions that occur in these contexts are complex and that no simple or universal cause-and-effect relationships have been documented.

Context of kindergarten. When children enter kindergarten, they are entering an educational setting that differs from earlier preschool settings because most kindergartens are part of a larger school setting where there are multiple grade levels and multiple classrooms of the same grade. One of the most dramatic differences is in curriculum. At the kindergarten level there is more emphasis placed on individual student achievement within a more formal learning context. Due to this emphasis, the classroom curriculum is more structured and connects to the total elementary curriculum, that is, the kindergarten curriculum is designed to prepare children to meet the expectations of first grade. There is also a greater emphasis on literacy development.

Traditionally, kindergarten was based upon a "children's garden" approach to learning that combined large blocks of independent play with teacher-mediated activities (Froebel, 1976). The kindergarten year was considered a time for children to transition from home to school. There was an emphasis on nurturing the development of children as they transitioned to formal schooling. The curriculum typically focused on art, music, and play (Nielson, 1996). Reading and writing instruction were not part of the traditional kindergarten curriculum, but were introduced only when children reached first grade.

Today, however, kindergarten is considered the beginning of elementary school. In many states, kindergarten is part of the public school system and is housed in elementary school buildings. Additionally, the kindergarten curriculum is seen as an integral part of the total elementary program, rather than as a separate curriculum.

By recognizing the ways in which the contexts of kindergarten classrooms are different from preschool environments, you can better prepare to welcome children to your kindergarten classroom, begin to look for signs of children's emergent literacy, and provide appropriate learning activities.

Key Signs of Emergent Literacy Among Kindergartners

Since the 1970s researchers have explored kindergartners' interactions with literacy for evidence of children's developing knowledge of reading and writing. Additionally, researchers began to document the relationships between these signs of emergent literacy and later success in becoming fluent readers and writers. In this section, six key emergent literacy behaviors will be described that have been associated with literacy development among kindergartners. These key signs of emergent literacy among kindergartners include:

1. Oral language competencies
2. Interest in literacy-related events
3. Reading and writing for personal purposes
4. Focus on print
5. Metalinguistic knowledge
6. Phonological awareness

Oral Language Competencies

Kindergartners' listening and speaking competencies enable them to comprehend during group story book time and to participate in discussing a book's content. These competencies contribute to later reading comprehension (Gee, 2001). Children with larger listening and speaking vocabularies were also found to have higher reading achievement in the primary grades (Huba & Ramisetty-Mikler, 1995; Roth, Speece, & Cooper, 2002). Kindergarten children's listening vocabularies have also been found to predict their scores on later vocabulary and reading comprehension in fourth and seventh grades (Tabors, Snow, & Dickinson, 2001). Higher vocabulary development and listening comprehension has been associated with the greater exposure to story book sharing experiences (Sénéchal, LeFevre, Hudson, & Lawson, 1996).

Children who start kindergarten with a more extensive vocabulary may also continue to develop their vocabulary at a faster rate than children with less extensive vocabularies (Ewers & Brownson, 1999). In addition, kindergartners who were active participants in story book sharing events increased their vocabularies more than did children who were more passive.

Children's conceptual knowledge and vocabulary may also influence their independent interactions with books and other materials available in school and community libraries. In contrast to middle-income children, children from low-income settings may not have had the opportunities to develop the conceptual knowledge and vocabulary found in books and other literacy materials. For example, low-income children may not have opportunities to visit museums or zoos. This lack of direct experience may have an impact on their conceptual knowledge and vocabulary. This difference in prior knowledge and experience may affect children's interest in books and reading. When low-income and middle-income children's use of public library resources were compared, significant differences were documented in the amount of reading, the purposes for reading, and the complexity of reading materials (Neuman & Celano, 2006). The long-term effect of these differences was a knowledge gap between the low-income and middle-income children. Neuman and Celano concluded that "deficiencies in knowledge not only lead to difficulties in learning to read but also difficulties in acquiring new knowledge" (pp. 197–198). Although low-income children's oral vocabulary may increase from year to year, catching up to their middle- and upper-income peers may not occur (Juel, Biancarosa, Coker, & Deffes, 2003).

Children's vocabulary and listening and speaking competencies have also been found important in the reading achievement of children who are English language learners (Brisk & Harrington, 2000). Oral language competencies in Spanish were related to not only reading scores in Spanish, but also predicted reading scores in English (Miller, Heilmann, Nockerts, Iglesias, Fabiano, & Francis, 2006).

Interest in Literacy-Related Events

Children who are curious about the world around them will actively seek out ways of exploring and experimenting within their environments. This is also true for children's early transactions with literacy. Kindergartners who show an interest in participating in literacy-related events will be actively constructing their knowledge of written language. Their experiences in literacy-related events provide them with an awareness of the power of written language to communicate.

In their study of low-SES kindergarten children, Purcell-Gates and Dahl (1991) concluded that a child's stance as an explorer and experimenter was important and that the amount of experience with written language was more important than social class. Among low-SES children, those who began school with an active approach to exploring and experimenting with literacy were more successful than were kindergartners who were more passive. The active-seekers, having acquired an understanding of the power of literacy, were able to make sense of the reading and writing instruction they received. They also pursued personal transactions with written language outside of the classroom's skill lessons and continued to test their emerging hypotheses about reading and writing. For example, they explored print by attempting "to read names written on workbooks, decipher the print on various posters and displays around the rooms, and copy words from books and bulletin boards" (p. 17).

Engaging in Reading and Writing for Personal Purposes

Another key sign of emergent literacy occurs when children engage in reading and writing for personal purposes. This may occur at school or at home (Bissex, 1980; Clay, 1975; Dyson, 1981, 1985, 1988; Goodman, 1990; Temple, Nathan, Temple, & Burris, 1993). In your classroom, you will see this when children are in the writing center or library center during independent activity time. Their writing may involve exploring how to form print or how to communicate a particular message by using a combination of drawing and graphic forms. You may see children writing lists, signs, notes, one-page stories, or little books. Perhaps they will simply write all of the names or words that they know. If you listen to children's comments to each other as they are engaged in a writing center, you will become aware of their personal purposes for writing. These comments may reveal the content of their stories (for example, "this is a story about a giant") or the format of the story (for example, "this is an alphabet book").

Evidence of children's use of reading and writing for personal purposes may also occur as they engage in creative drama (Goodman, 1990). For example, in the house corner

Conversations at the writing center often focus on children's personal purposes for writing.

Goodluz

they may write down phone messages, use recipe books, clip coupons, or share storybooks with their dolls. In the block area, they may make traffic signs. While playing "store," they may read packages, shopping lists, and write out checks.

Focus on Print: Decoding and Encoding

Conventional reading and writing require that the child focus on the print to figure out the words (decode) and to be able to use letters to make words (encode). Kindergarten is a time when many children begin to focus on print. Some children will come to kindergarten already paying attention to print; others will develop this focus as they engage in literacy-related activities in the classroom.

Decoding. Kindergartners' attempts at decoding print have been documented during independent story book interactions (for example, Sulzby, 1985, 1991) and in their interactions with environmental print (for example, Bissex, 1980). When children begin to focus on the print, they are indicating their awareness that the print carries the message. Some children begin to focus on print during their preschool years and will show this focus when they arrive in kindergarten. Other children may not yet focus on print.

Encoding. Kindergarten children use a range of strategies to put meaning on paper, gradually transitioning to using more print, using invented spelling (prephonemic and phonemic), and conventionally spelled words. In studying kindergartners' initial encoding strategies, researchers have found that children experiment with symbol-making by using random and wavy scribbles, cursivelike script, letter-like forms, and letters, as well as copying environmental print (Dyson, 1981, 1985, 1988, 1990; Sulzby, Barnhart, & Hieshima, 1989).

Although kindergarten children may be aware that letters represent specific sounds, they may continue to use a variety of writing strategies when they are creating their stories, combining scribbling and random letter strings with invented spelling (Bus, Both-deVries, de Jong, Sulzby, de Jong, & de Jong, 2001). By using a variety of strategies, children can communicate their thoughts more fully by using drawing, scribbling to represent unknown words, and letter-like forms to represent unknown letters.

An example of this experimentation with different symbols and letter-like forms is found in Elizabeth's story, shown in Figure 8.2. This story book was created during the third

Figure 8.2 Example of
Kindergartner's Writing Forms
Elizabeth, Age 5½

month of her kindergarten year. Along with illustrations, Elizabeth used letters, letter-like forms, and cursivelike script in creating her storybook. She also clearly positioned her writing in horizontal lines and combined the various forms in different word-like units and sequences.

Metalinguistic Knowledge

Metalinguistic knowledge is a key sign of emergent literacy in kindergarten because participation in teacher-guided literacy activities may directly involve responding to specific language concepts, such as "letters," "sounds," and "words" (Yaden, 1986). For example, when a kindergarten teacher announces that "Today's lesson will be on the letter B," children will need to be able to focus on this concept and differentiate this letter from others, as well as begin to associate a particular sound with the letter. While some kindergartners are beginning to develop a conscious awareness of language and specific language concepts, not all children develop this intuitively (Yaden, 1986).

Figure 8.3 presents several examples of metalinguistic knowledge that were evident during an interview with a young girl that took place one month before kindergarten. In this interview, Julie (5½ years old) responded to questions about words and other specific language concepts.

Now that you have read Julie's interview, let's take a look at some specific instances that provide evidence of her metalinguistic knowledge. First of all, Julie's ability to use

Figure 8.3 Julie's Interview on Words

(1) *Interviewer:*	What is a word?	
(2) *Julie:*	[*no response*]	
(3) *Interviewer:*	What's your favorite word?	
(4) *Julie:*	Red. That was my first word.	
(5) *Interviewer:*	What does it mean?	
(6) *Julie:*	It's a color. Robbie's (*her younger brother*) favorite word is green.	
(7) *Interviewer:*	What's another favorite word?	
(8) *Julie:*	Snack.	
(9) *Interviewer:*	What does it mean?	
(10) *Julie:*	It's a meal you can eat anytime you want.	
(11) *Interviewer:*	(*showing stimulus cards*) Is this a word?	
(12) *Julie:*	No. It's a person.	
(13) *Interviewer:*	Is this a word?	
(14) *Julie:*	No. It's a letter.	
(15) *Interviewer:*	Is this a word?	
(16) *Julie:*	Yes.	
(17) *Interviewer:*	What does it say?	
(18) *Julie:*	I don't know.	
(19) *Interviewer:*	Is this a word?	
(20) *Julie:*	No.	
(21) *Interviewer:*	Is this a word?	
(22) *Julie:*	Yes. It's Robbie.	

language to respond to the interviewer's questions and tasks showed that she was able to use language to communicate and carry on a conversation. Some of the questions asked in the interview focused on identifying examples of certain language concepts. For example, when Julie was asked to identify a favorite word (line 3), she did not hesitate and answered "red," explaining that that was her first word. When asked what "red" meant (line 5), Julie responded that it was a color and then went on to identify her younger brother's favorite color. Julie's ability to respond to a question about a word's meaning indicated that she was conscious that words have specific meanings and that she could reflect on their meanings. This is also seen in her response in line 10 when she defines the word "snack."

Questions that ask children to define linguistic concepts require much more advanced metalinguistic knowledge. For example, in line 1, when asked to define "word," Julie made no response, yet she was able to identify examples of words, such as her favorite word, and reflect on its meaning. As the interview proceeded and Julie responded to several stimulus cards that contained drawing, scribbling, letter-like forms, and her brother's name, it was evident that she was consciously aware of some of the features of words although she was not able to give a definition for a "word." In a follow-up interview, Julie was shown a series of cards and asked to identify whether or not the cards each contained a word. When asked why the cards in the "word pile" were words and those in the "not words" pile were not words, Julie responded, "Pictures can be anything you want but words can't. They have to be letters." Julie's conscious awareness of "word" as a language concept and her ability to focus on the features of words provided evidence that she was beginning to develop metalinguistic knowledge.

Metalinguistic knowledge is also a key sign of emergent literacy among children who are English language learners. In learning a second language at school, children are taught specific language concepts (Cummins, 2003), such as letters, sounds, grammatical structures, punctuation, and spelling. Developing this knowledge involves learning how to think about language and how it is used, that is, metalinguistic knowledge. For ELLs it also involves learning new information that may be similar to the language knowledge of their home language or may be distinctly different.

In order to participate in classroom instruction, children must also be able to verbalize their metalinguistic knowledge. For example, a lesson on identifying rhyming words in English might build on the concept of rhyme that Spanish-speaking children may already have; however, in order to participate in the English classroom, they will need to apply their concept of what rhymes to English words, and be able to participate orally in that lesson.

In fact, researchers have found that ELLs are often more successful in performing metalinguistic tasks (Pang & Kamil, 2004), because the process of second language acquisition requires that they focus on the structures and aspects of both their first and second language in order to successfully communicate.

Phonological Awareness

Another key sign of emergent literacy among kindergartners is phonological awareness, a conscious awareness that words can be separated into distinct sound units such as syllables, initial sounds, and ending sounds. Phonological awareness has been identified as a precursor for both invented spelling and actual reading of print (Foy & Man, 2006; Goswami, 2002; Huba & Ramisetty-Mikler, 1995; Mann & Foy, 2003; Maclean, Bryant, & Bradley, 1987; National Reading Panel, 2000; Roberts, 1998; Silva & Martens, 2003). Children who scored higher on tasks requiring phonological awareness, such as rhyming tasks, also performed at higher levels on early reading and writing measures.

Early readers (those who read before kindergarten) had higher scores on phonemic segmentation and their scores predicted second-grade reading achievement (Huba & Ramisetty-Mikler, 1995).

Research-Based Implications for Kindergarten Curriculum

Emergent literacy research has also contributed to an awareness that literacy development does not begin in first grade with formal reading and writing instruction, but begins earlier as children engage in literacy-related transactions. Not only do children develop emergent literacy, but this emergent literacy is associated with later reading and writing achievement. Research (described in earlier sections of this text) has also created an awareness of the importance of developing basic literacy competencies prior to third grade. In this way, emergent literacy research has contributed to the following general implications for kindergarten:

- ❖ Literacy development is a critical aspect of the kindergarten curriculum.
- ❖ Teachers need to know the signs of emergent literacy.
- ❖ Literacy-related experiences should be provided that are within children's zones of proximal development.

Looking for Signs of Emergent Literacy in Your Kindergarten

Your awareness of each child's emergent literacy provides a strong rationale for the curriculum you develop and implement in your classroom as well as the strategies you use when interacting with each child. In this section, specific behaviors representing each of the key areas of emergent literacy are described. In addition, a class observation form is included that can be used during your observation. It is important to remember that the purpose of these initial observations is to better understand your children's strengths and areas of potential growth so that you can plan instruction to enhance their literacy development.

Oral Language Competencies

Throughout this text, there has been an emphasis on the close relationship between oral language and literacy development. Your observations of your kindergartner's language competencies will occur during the independent activity times in your classroom as well as when you are engaging them in group story times. As you observe, you will be looking for the following language behaviors to be exhibited by each child:

1. Does the child establish eye contact with the speaker? Children who establish eye contact are indicating they are aware of the speaker and that they are attending to what is spoken. This is an essential part of child–teacher interactions. It is also important for you to be aware of cultural settings in which children may not have been encouraged to establish eye contact with adults. This may explain a child's hesitancy to begin to establish eye contact with you.

2. Does the child speak clearly by using complete, coherent sentences? Children who can communicate clearly will be better able to participate in the verbal

interactions that are involved in the social and academic transactions in your classroom.

3. Does the child respond appropriately to one- to two-step oral directions? Many times during the kindergarten day, children are asked to perform certain actions that are involved with specific learning activities or organizational routines. In order to participate fully, kindergartners need to be able to follow simple oral directions.

4. Does the child listen attentively at group story time? Many learning activities from kindergarten on involve group settings. Children who listen attentively are indicating they comprehend the teacher's oral reading. When children are easily distracted it may indicate a less extensive listening vocabulary or an inability to focus on a group activity due to immaturity, fatigue, hunger, or emotional factors. Whatever the reason for the inattentiveness, you will need to be aware of each child's ability to benefit from group story time. You will also want to note if this inattention occurs each time or only on certain occasions and then determine other factors involved in the setting that may be influencing the child's lack of attention.

5. Does the child participate by commenting or asking questions during group story time? This also reflects children's comprehension of the story, as well as their understanding of specific concepts and vocabulary. You may also want to note their use of grammar and complete sentences.

6. Does the child respond to a teacher's questions about the story? Children who respond to questions about a story indicate not only that they are comprehending the story but that they are able to focus on the information asked in the question and participate in the discussion.

7. Does the child remember story content when books are shared repeatedly? When familiar story books are read, children may predict upcoming events, ask related questions, or anticipate specific book language. Memory for story and text will be needed as children begin to read independently.

8. Does the child orally participate in finger plays or action songs during group time? As children participate in these activities, there is opportunity to develop awareness of rhythmic patterns and words that rhyme, which contributes to phonological awareness.

9. Does the child participate in conversations with his or her teacher? Children's oral communication skills provide a foundation for their participation in the instructional dialogues that take place in educational settings.

10. Does the child participate in conversations with peers? Children's ability to engage in conversations with their peers will influence their social and learning interactions in the classroom.

A format for observing each of these listening and speaking competencies is presented in Figure 8.4.

Figure 8.4 Classroom Observation: Oral Language Competencies in Listening and Speaking

					Children's Names					
Does child:										
Establish eye contact with speaker?										
Speak clearly using complete, coherent sentences?										
Respond appropriately to 1–2-step oral directions?										
Listen attentively at group story time?										
Participate by commenting or asking questions during group story time?										
Respond to teacher's questions about story content?										
Remember story content when books are shared repeatedly?										
Orally participate in finger play or action song during group time?										
Participate in conversations with teacher?										
Participate in conversations with peers?										

Symbol code: Option 1: **Y** = yes; **N** = no
                 Option 2: **F** = frequently; **S** = seldom; **N** = not observed

Interest in Literacy-Related Events

Children's curiosity about reading and writing is evident when they seek out opportunities to engage in literacy-related activities and ask questions about reading and writing processes. They are also indicating that they see reading and writing as meaningful activities. This is an important motivational factor that supports children's active involvement in literacy-related events. You can observe your kindergartners' interest in literacy by asking the following:

1. Does the child ask questions about environmental print? Most classrooms will have signs that indicate location of items, directions, or student locker space. Notice whether children pay attention to this environmental print and ask what it means. Once you have explained the print, do they remember the meaning and respond appropriately?

2. Does the child seek out opportunities to interact with books independently? Children do not voluntarily engage in activities that have no meaning or purpose for them. Children who go to the book corner and look at books independently are indicating they find the activity enjoyable and meaningful.

3. Does the child seek out opportunities to use drawing and writing independently? Children's interest in drawing and writing during independent activity time indicates they have an inner motivation to explore and experiment with ways of creating meaning on paper.

4. Does the child attend to the teacher's reading at story book time? When children are inattentive at story book time, it may indicate they do not comprehend the story. Because the story is not comprehended, there is no interest in the book sharing. When this experience is repeated over time, children may develop an aversion to story book sharing time.

5. Does the child incorporate literacy-related events into creative drama? Perhaps you notice that several children are delivering pretend mail and packages around the room. In the block area, you notice that children have made traffic signs. Each of these instances indicates children see how written language is used in meaningful ways.

6. Does the child express pleasure in hearing books read? This pleasure can be observed by noting children's comments and questions during and after story time as well as their nonverbal behaviors (smiling, laughing). Also note if children look forward to group story time and express this anticipation by asking you what book will be read or requesting a favorite book.

7. Does the child express pleasure in drawing and writing attempts? Interest in literacy-related events is also evident when children express their pleasure when drawing or writing by commenting on or sharing with others what they have created. This also shows that they see these activities as valuable and meaningful.

A format for observing children's interest in literacy-related events is presented in Figure 8.5.

Figure 8.5 Class Observation Form: Interest in Literacy-Related Events

	Children's Names									
Does child:										
Ask questions about environmental print?										
Seek out opportunities to interact with books independently?										
Seek out opportunities to use drawing and writing independently?										
Attend to teacher's reading at group story book time?										
Incorporate literacy-related events into creative drama?										
Express pleasure in hearing books read?										
Express pleasure in drawing/writing attempts?										

Symbol code: Option 1: Y = yes; N = no
Option 2: F = frequently; S = seldom; N = not observed

Reading and Writing for Personal Purposes

Children who engage in reading and writing for personal purposes are more active learners and are more motivated. They have a personal orientation to literacy that provides a foundation for later school-based literacy instruction (Purcell-Gates & Dahl, 1991). You can observe children's use of reading and writing for personal purposes by asking yourself the following questions about the children in your kindergarten:

1. Does the child interact with environmental print to determine location or content? Look to see if children use the print in your classroom to locate or store learning materials. Do they know how to find which cubby or locker is theirs by using the name card posted on each locker or cubby?

2. Does the child select and orally "read" specific story books during independent activity time? Children who have favorite story books or who seek out specific books are indicating that they are personally motivated. For example, some children may look only at books that have been shared at group story time. Other children might actively pursue reading books related to their personal interests such as trucks, trains, or dinosaurs.

3. Does the child write emergently about experiences that occurred at home or at school? Children who use writing to share events that happened at home or at school are using writing for personal purposes.

4. Does the child make comments while engaged in drawing or writing about the content or purpose of his or her activity? You can also become aware of children's personal purposes for writing when you listen to their comments: perhaps they are making signs for the block area, or a child may indicate she is making a birthday card for her dad.

5. Does the child connect life experiences to events and information in books? During story time, children may comment that they have had a related experience to what happened in the book, such as, "I went to the zoo yesterday." This connection provides a personal meaning to the story and also provides evidence of the transaction that occurs between child, text, and context.

6. Does the child dictate stories or event sequences about personal experiences? When you provide an opportunity for individual children to dictate to you, you encourage them to create a story or event text that has meaning to them. Because you are the scribe, writing down what they say, it frees the child to focus on the meaning of what they want to say rather than figuring out how to put their thoughts into print. During these times of dictation, note the way in which children use this dictation for personal communication and with whom the dictated story or text is later shared (such as peers or family members).

7. Does the child express personal preferences for books, rhymes, and songs? When children request that specific books be read, or action songs be performed, they are showing their personal interests, motivation, and orientation to literacy. These behaviors may also indicate prior literacy experiences that had personal meaning and enjoyment.

A format for observing children's engagement in reading and writing for personal purposes is presented in Figure 8.6.

Figure 8.6 Class Observation: Reading and Writing for Personal Purposes

Children's Names

Does child:										
Interact with environmental print to determine location or content?										
Select and orally "read" specific story books during independent activity time?										
Write emergently about personal experiences that occurred at home or at school?										
Make comments while engaged in drawing/writing about the content or purpose of his or her activity?										
Connect life experiences to events and information in books?										
Dictate story or event sequence about personal experiences?										
Express personal preferences for books, rhymes, songs?										

Symbol code: Option 1:   Y = yes; N = no
                     Option 2:   F = frequently; S = seldom; N = not observed

Focus on Print

In planning your kindergarten curriculum, you will want to observe which children are beginning to focus on print. Most of your observations will occur during informal, independent activity time; however, you may also see children focus on print during group story time or during group story dictations. In some instances, you might decide to elicit children's knowledge of print directly through specific naming or identification tasks. You will find the following questions useful as you make these observations:

1. Does the child understand that print communicates meaning? This is a basic understanding of the purpose of print. Children who have this knowledge will be able to participate more fully in literacy-related events.

2. Does the child identify by name individual letters of the alphabet? Most children will not arrive in kindergarten knowing the names of each of the 26 letters of the alphabet. It will be useful for you to determine which letter names are known because knowledge of letter names has a strong association with later reading achievement.

3. Does the child attempt to track print when emergently reading a familiar storybook or his or her own writing? To observe this, you will need to closely watch the child's visual tracking as he "reads." You might decide to ask them to point to the print as they read.

4. Does the child write his or her name? For many children the first words they learn to write at home are their names. You may see evidence of this as they are in the writing center. You might also see this as they put their names on their pieces of artwork. You could also encourage children to "sign in" as they arrive in class and then observe the ways in which their name is written.

5. Does the child write other known words, such as the names of family members, friends, or pets? You will also want to note whether children spontaneously write other known words when they are in the writing center. Also note whether they read what they have written.

6. Does the child write individual letters when dictated? Some kindergartners will ask how to spell certain words while they are in the writing center. Notice whether they are able to write the individual letters when you name the letter.

By observing children's focus on print in these different areas, you will be better able to plan learning activities that facilitate and enhance their understanding of print. A format for observing children's focus on print is presented in Figure 8.7.

Metalinguistic Knowledge

Children need to have an awareness of specific literacy-related concepts in order to understand and benefit from classroom learning activities. As you begin the kindergarten year, you will want to determine if your students are aware of specific concepts related to reading. The following questions focus on children's awareness of specific concepts as well as aspects of reading and writing processes:

1. Does the child distinguish the front and back covers of a book and the book title? Knowing these parts of a book allows children to participate more actively during group story time as well as to interact with books independently.

Figure 8.7 Class Observation: Focus on Print

Children's Names

Does child:										
Understand that print communicates meaning?										
Identify by name individual letters of the alphabet?										
Attempt to track print when emergently reading a familiar story book or own writing?										
Write his/her name?										
Write other known words? (for example, names of family members, friends, or pets)										
Write individual letters when dictated?										

Symbol code: Option 1: **Y** = yes; **N** = no
Option 2: **F** = frequently; **S** = seldom; **N** = not observed

2. Does the child distinguish between individual letters and words? Knowing that words are composed of individual letters is necessary not only for reading, but for writing as well. If you do not observe this informally, you may want to specifically ask children to point to a letter and then to point to a word.

3. Does the child indicate that print proceeds from left to right and from top to bottom on each page? When we read in English, we read print from left to right and from top to bottom. Children need to be aware of this and you will need to determine their level of this awareness in order to plan appropriate learning activities.

4. Does the child distinguish between the author and illustrator roles? When books are shared at story time, teachers often refer to the author and illustrator during the introduction to, or discussion of, the story. Children who can distinguish between author and illustrator roles will be better able to participate in shared book interactions.

5. Does the child use spaces between "words" when writing emergently? When spaces are provided in their writing, children are indicating that they know that each group of letters represents a distinct word or idea.

6. Does the child reflect verbally on the reading or writing process? When children express their questions or concerns when reading or writing, they are showing metalinguistic awareness. For example, a child when writing might say, "See how I made the L, one tall line and one short line."

A format for observing children's metalinguistic knowledge is presented in Figure 8.8.

Phonological Awareness

Reading curricula for kindergarten as well as first grade place strong emphasis on phonological awareness because it has been associated with reading achievement in the elementary grades. As you begin your kindergarten year, you will want to observe your children's phonological awareness during group story time and as they interact throughout your curriculum. Use the following questions to guide your observations:

1. Does the child orally identify rhyming words? When you read a rhyming text, such as *There's a Wocket in My Pocket* (Seuss, 1994), pause while reading the text to see if children will predict upcoming rhyming words.

2. Does the child visually identify rhyming words? Children may also identify rhyming words visually when participating in a shared reading of a rhyming text in a big book. This indicates they are aware that words that are spelled with the same endings have the same ending sounds.

3. Does the child identify initial sounds in words? During your shared story book times, you can encourage children to identify initial sounds in words by focusing on specific, high-interest words and asking children to tell you the sound that starts each word. For example, when reading *The Wide-Mouthed Frog* (Faulkner, 1996), you might focus on words starting with an /m/ sound, or a /w/ sound. This will give you an opportunity to see which children respond when you ask them to focus on or identify the beginning sound in a word.

4. Does the child identify two or more words that have the same initial sound (alliteration)? You can observe this by encouraging children to identify words with similar initial sounds when you read stories that feature alliteration. For example, *A Trio of Triceratops* (Most, 1998) contains many phrases of alliteration. When reading this text, you could pause to see if children can identify the repeated initial sounds.

5. Does the child orally identify ending sounds in words? When children identify rhyming words they are focusing on the ending sounds of words. Some children

Figure 8.8 Class Observation: Metalinguistic Knowledge

Does child:	Children's Names									
Distinguish the front cover, back cover, and book title?										
Distinguish between letters and words?										
Indicate that print proceeds from left to right and top to bottom on each page?										
Distinguish between author and illustrator roles?										
Use spaces between "words" when writing emergently?										
Reflect verbally on reading and/or writing process?										

Symbol code: Option 1:   **Y** = yes; **N** = no
Option 2:   **F** = frequently; **S** = seldom; **N** = not observed

may also be able to focus on the ending sounds of words that do not rhyme. For example, ask which of these words have the same last sound: cat, pet, pan? Children usually cannot separate out ending sounds in words until they are able to separate out beginning sounds.

6. Does the child associate individual letters with specific sounds? For example, a child who is looking at an alphabet book might match up the pictured items with the letter of the alphabet on the page, such as "B is for bunny," and "Y is for yogurt." Children may also spontaneously express this awareness as they focus on print in your classroom, such as trying to read the name cards or locker labels of their classmates.

7. Does the child orally create or invent words by substituting sounds in familiar words? Children may spontaneously engage in this type of word play as they interact in your classroom. You could also elicit this word play as you read to them at story time. For example, when reading *There's a Wocket in My Pocket* (Seuss, 1996), you could ask what other words they could make up that would go with "pocket" and then notice which children participate in creating the new nonsense words.

A format for observing children's phonological awareness is presented in Figure 8.9.

 Figure 8.9 Class Observation: Phonological Awareness

Children's Names										
Does child:										
Orally identify rhyming words?										
Visually identify rhyming words?										
Identify initial sounds in words?										
Identify the ending sounds in words?										
Identify two or more words that have the same initial sound (such as alliteration)?										
Associate individual letters with specific sounds?										
Create or invent words by substituting sounds in familiar words?										

Symbol code: Option 1: **Y** = yes; **N** = no
Option 2: **F** = frequently; **S** = seldom; **N** = not observed

Kindergarten Language Arts Standards

As a kindergarten teacher, you will be expected to incorporate your state's learning standards into the curriculum of your classroom and your daily lesson plans. In addition, these standards will be the focus of your assessment of students' progress.

While specific expectations for children's achievement by the end of the kindergarten year have been developed for all areas of the curriculum, this section will focus only on language-arts standards. In most cases, these state standards involve an extensive listing of specific expectations. For example, the state of Texas identifies 67 different expectations for kindergartners in the area of language arts alone (Texas Education Agency, 2006).

Common Areas of Expectations for Kindergartners

Each state's standards are specific to that state; however, there are several common strands across most states. To illustrate this, state language arts standards for kindergarten were reviewed from the following states: California, Florida, Illinois, New York, and Texas. These states were selected because they represent areas of large population in the United States.

Common areas of expectations for kindergartners included the following:

- ❖ Alphabet knowledge: Recognizing and naming all upper- and lower-case letters
- ❖ Phonological awareness: Knowing letter–sound correspondences, blending sounds, identifying beginning and ending sounds, recognizing and producing rhymes and alliteration, isolating sounds
- ❖ Print and book concepts: Understanding that print carries meaning; Understanding that books are read from front to back, and that print is read from left to right, and from the top to the bottom of the page
- ❖ Word recognition: Reading simple one-syllable and high-frequency words
- ❖ Comprehension
  - ❖ Making predictions by using titles, illustrations, prior knowledge, and story segments to anticipate book content
  - ❖ Asking and answering questions during story book sharing
  - ❖ Retelling stories or events in accurate sequences
  - ❖ Connecting book content to life experiences
  - ❖ Distinguishing different literary forms, such as fiction, nonfiction, newsletters, signs, lists
- ❖ Writing
  - ❖ Writing upper- and lower-case letters
  - ❖ Using a variety of strategies for writing including drawing, prephonemic spelling, phonemic spelling, and known words.

Although these common areas of expectations were evident in the review of kindergarten language arts standards from California, Florida, Illinois, and Texas, each state had additional specific standards that were unique to that state. As you prepare your curriculum for kindergarten, you will need to become familiar with the specific standards developed by your state education department (or agency) as well as any other standards developed by your local school district. In most instances, these standards can be obtained from your state department/agency or school district website.

Implementing the Standards

Faced with the extensive number of standards that need to be addressed by teachers in their classrooms, some schools have adopted commercial curriculum that has been designed to meet their specific state's standards. While this may appear to resolve the concern about meeting state standards, it is important for kindergarten teachers (as well as teachers at other levels) to still be concerned that they are providing developmentally appropriate learning activities and experiences for children in their classrooms.

Commercial reading and language arts curricula typically center on group instruction and involve numerous printed materials, such as workbooks, black-line masters, and specially designed readers. At the kindergarten level, this may mean that there is more direct instruction and more seat-work—activities that were formerly part of a first-grade curriculum that are now included as part of kindergarten curriculum. In order to implement this curriculum, kindergarten teachers may find that there is no longer time for independent learning centers or creative drama. Not all kindergarten children may be developmentally ready for this emphasis on direct, group instruction or seat-work.

This increasing emphasis on academic activities and more formal instruction in kindergarten has been accompanied by intense debate among early childhood professionals, school administrators, and parents (Nielson, 1996). Kindergarten teachers may feel that they are caught between following a commercial curriculum that incorporates their state's standards for student learning and meeting the developmental needs of the children in their classroom (Snow, Burns, & Griffith, 1998).

Meeting Kindergartners' Developmental Needs

In order to provide an appropriate literacy curriculum in your kindergarten, you will need to determine the specific developmental needs of the children in your classroom. In most instances, you will not have any prior information on the children entering your kindergarten in the fall. Thus, you will need to plan your initial classroom curriculum and learning activities so that you will have opportunities to informally observe your students' emergent literacy.

Initial curriculum and classroom assessments. As you begin your new school year in the fall, you will want to set up your curriculum to enhance children's transition to kindergarten by incorporating activities that they may have experienced in preschool settings (refer to Chapter 7). This means that you will have large blocks of time for children to independently engage in various learning centers and free-choice activities. You will also have one or two daily group times when you engage your children in story book sharing, finger plays, action songs, or other music. This curriculum setting will provide you with opportunity to become acquainted with the children in your classroom individually and to observe the ways in which they interact with others and in literacy-related events. By making these observations during the first few weeks of your school year, you will then be able to determine each child's zone of proximal development. This will help you determine the types of activities and instructional contexts that will be developmentally appropriate.

Areas of emergent literacy to observe. As you observe your children, you will want to remember that kindergarten children will still show wide variation in their emergent literacy knowledge. In making these initial observations of children in your classroom, you

Through observation and other informal assessments, you can determine each child's zone of proximal development.

dotshock

can use the observation formats introduced earlier in this chapter that focus on these areas of emergent literacy (see Figures 8.4–8.9):

❖ Oral language competencies
❖ Interest in literacy-related events
❖ Reading and writing for personal purposes
❖ Focus on print
❖ Metalinguistic knowledge, and
❖ Phonological awareness

Each of these areas of emergent literacy has been associated with the acquisition of reading and writing competencies in the elementary grades (Foy & Man, 2006; Goswami, 2002; Huber & Ramisetty-Mikler, 1995; Mann & Foy, 2003; Maclean, Bryant, & Bradley, 1987; National Reading Panel, 2000; Roberts, 1998; Roth, Speece, & Cooper, 2002; Silva & Martens, 2003; Snow, Burns, & Griffith, 1998; Tabors, Snow, & Dickinson, 2001; Yaden, 1986). Additionally, these areas are also represented in state kindergarten standards (California State Board of Education, 2006; Florida Department of Education, 2006; Illinois State Board of Education, 2006; New York State Education Department, 2005; Texas Education Agency, 2006).

Once you have become acquainted with your children's emergent literacy, you can better plan and implement a curriculum designed to enhance their literacy development. Strategies and activities for literacy development in kindergarten are presented in Chapter 9.

Ongoing Assessments

Throughout the school year, you will need to engage in ongoing assessment of children's literacy development in order to provide developmentally appropriate learning activities. You may decide to periodically conduct general classroom observations, using the observation formats included in this chapter (Figures 8.4–8.9), or you may decide to use more structured and individualized assessments.

If your school has adopted a specific commercial elementary reading curriculum that includes instructional materials for kindergarten, you will have access to the assessment tools and strategies provided in that commercial curriculum. Such assessments will be designed to document and evaluate children's progress based on the learning experiences provided in the specific commercial curriculum. Many commercial curricula provide tools for periodic assessments that will contribute to the quarterly or midterm report card schedule of most schools. Additional assessments will be described in Chapter 9.

Chapter Summary

Children come to kindergarten with a wide variety of experiences from their preschool years. When these experiences involve interactions with reading- and writing-related events, children's emergent literacy develops. Important components of children's literacy transactions include: what each child knows about language (both oral and written), the texts or literacy-related tasks they encounter, and the contexts in which the literacy events occur. The mediation provided by others, such as parents, older siblings, and teachers, also influences these transactions.

In order to plan developmentally appropriate learning activities, kindergarten teachers need to be able to recognize the signs of emergent literacy. Key signs of emergent literacy among kindergartners include: oral language competencies in listening and speaking, interest in literacy-related events, reading and writing for personal purposes, a focus on print, metalinguistic knowledge, and phonological awareness.

Traditionally, instruction in reading and writing was not part of kindergarten curricula. Instead, reading and writing instruction were begun when children reached first grade. Today, however, kindergarten is considered the beginning of elementary school, with reading and writing instruction now taking place in kindergarten. This change has been accompanied by the development of specific expectations or performance standards in the area of language arts. Kindergarten teachers can use these standards to guide their planning and implementation of learning activities that will prepare children to be successful when they reach first grade. In order to provide appropriate literacy curricula in kindergarten, teachers need to determine the specific developmental needs of their children. This determination can be accomplished through careful observation during the first few weeks of school. Specific formats for these observations have been included in this chapter.

Chapter Review

For each statement, determine whether it is true or false and state your reasoning:

1. The components of children's literacy transactions include the child's knowledge of language, the texts they encounter, and the contexts of the literacy events. ___T ___F

2. All kindergarten-age children can communicate through conventional writing. ___T ___F

3. Once a child begins to attend kindergarten, the home context does not influence the child's learning. ___T ___F

4. There are many similarities between preschool and kindergarten learning contexts. ___T ___F

5. Kindergarten children's listening vocabulary is predictive of reading comprehension in higher elementary grades. ___T ___F

6. Literacy-related activities are an optional component in most kindergarten curricula. ___T ___F

7. The best way to implement language arts standards in kindergarten is to use a commercial curriculum that is based on those standards. ___T ___F

Chapter Extension Activities

Observation: Select one of the observation formats (see Figures 8.4–8.9) to use for observing in a kindergarten classroom. Prepare a summary of your observation to share in your college/university class.

Class or online discussion: Interview a local kindergarten teacher about his or her use of state or district language arts standards. Also focus on the ways in which assessment is used to measure student progress. Share a summary of your interview during class or online discussion.

Research: Acquire and review your state's or district's kindergarten standards for the language arts area. Identify the similarities and differences with the areas of common standards presented in this chapter.

Chapter 9

Enhancing Emergent Literacy and Beginning Reading and Writing in Kindergartners

It's late September in Ms. Gordon's kindergarten room. She has spent the first few weeks observing her kindergartners as they have interacted with the learning centers and group activities she has provided. Ms. Gordon's observations have made her aware of which children know how to write their names. She also knows which children will listen attentively at story time and which children will become restless when a more complex story is shared. She reminds herself that some children who do not participate in the story time discussion are just learning English and may be experiencing a "silent period" before they begin using English orally. Ms. Gordon also is aware of which children are able to follow oral directions and those who need to be reminded of each step.

Ms. Gordon, like many kindergarten teachers, starts each school year with a curriculum that provides opportunities for her to observe her children and determine their strengths and areas of future development. By providing large blocks of time for her new kindergartners to work independently and collaboratively in interest centers along with whole group story times, Ms. Gordon is able to observe how children interact and how they respond to different contexts and tasks. Because she is concerned about her children's orientation to literacy, she is careful to observe how they interact in reading- and writing-related events in her classroom.

Now, after several weeks of observations, Ms. Gordon will use her observations as a basis for beginning to plan learning activities and contexts that will enhance the development of her children's literacy. In planning her literacy curriculum, Ms. Gordon will consider her state's language arts standards for kindergarten as well as her school's adopted commercial curriculum, which covers grades K–6.

As a reflective teacher, Ms. Gordon also realizes the key role she plays as a guide and mediator of children's transactions with literacy. She knows that each child who comes to her classroom is unique in terms of background experiences, prior knowledge, literacy-related experiences, and motivation. She also knows that her responsibility is not simply to teach the curriculum provided by her school district—that would work only if all children were at the same developmental level and entered school with the same prior knowledge.

Ms. Gordon is aware that she needs to use her knowledge of each child, her professional knowledge and skills, and available curricular materials to create a learning environment that is developmentally appropriate for each child.

Additionally, Ms. Gordon realizes the importance of literacy development for both success at school and in adult life. She values the contributions of researchers in identifying key signs of emergent literacy that are associated with later literacy achievement. As she plans her curriculum, she decides which activities and strategies to use based on her awareness of how literacy development will be enhanced.

As you prepare to teach at the kindergarten level, you will want to be aware of strategies and activities that enhance literacy development. The focus of this chapter will be on describing these strategies and activities. It is also important to keep in mind the unique position of kindergarten in children's lives. In the following section, an overview of unique aspects of the kindergarten context and curriculum is presented. This is followed by sections that discuss specific strategies and activities that enhance children's literacy development in kindergarten. Additional sections focus on assessment and the role of families in fostering literacy development.

Kindergarten Context and Curriculum

For many children, the context in which they interact changes when they begin attending kindergarten. They may have not attended preschool, or attended preschool only two or three half-days a week; now they are going to school five days a week. Perhaps they are now attending a full-day kindergarten. Although kindergarten attendance is mandatory in only seventeen states, most children in the United States do attend kindergarten, either in a public or private school setting (Morrison, 2006). Currently, there are about equal numbers of half-day and full-day kindergarten programs; however, the number of full-day programs is increasing.

Kindergarten as perceived by many school administrators, as well as parents, differs from their view of preschool. Kindergarten is considered "real school" and therefore, there are specific expectations for curriculum and for more academic tasks. This stance has been reflected in the development of specific standards for kindergartners' achievement, which were described in Chapter 8.

Kindergarten is characterized by two major changes in children's educational setting: (a) Children are in a more structured school setting for a longer amount of time and (b) kindergarten curriculum is focused on preparing children to meet specific expectations prior to moving on to first grade.

When you teach, it is important that you know not only what strategies or activities to implement, but also why each particular activity or strategy is valuable. It is also important that you consciously determine why that activity or strategy is appropriate for children in your classroom.

Key Areas of an Emergent Literacy Curriculum

The sections that follow describe strategies and activities that enhance development of the key areas of emergent literacy, as previously discussed in Chapter 8 and as shown in Figure 9.1 (see also Beach & Young, 1997; Lesiak, 2000). These areas include:

- ❖ oral language competencies
- ❖ interest in literacy

- ❖ reading and writing for personal purposes
- ❖ focus on print
- ❖ metalinguistic knowledge
- ❖ phonological and phonetic awareness

Each of these key areas can be enhanced through independent, self-guided activities as well as through teacher-guided activities. In several instances, a suggested activity or strategy was first introduced in the preschool chapter (Chapter 7). Keeping in mind the general planning and implementation guidelines introduced in Chapter 7, this chapter will emphasize the ways in which the activity or strategy can be focused on enhancing literacy development at the kindergarten level. As you gain experience in teaching in kindergarten, you will be able to modify as well as extend these basic activities and strategies to meet the specific needs of children in your classroom.

Figure 9.1 Key Areas of an Emergent Literacy Curriculum

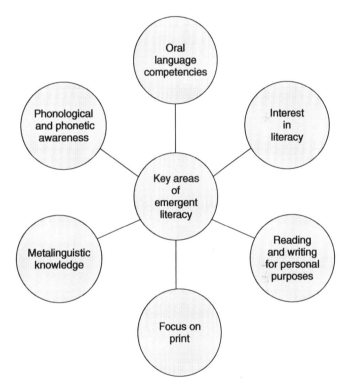

Key Learning Contexts and Activities for Emergent Literacy

As a teacher of young children, the ways in which you demonstrate and share your curiosity for learning about the world motivates and encourages children to explore and learn along with you. This is particularly true when you share your interest in literacy-related activities.

In your kindergarten classroom you will want to build upon and enhance children's interest in reading and writing. The greater their interest in literacy-related activities the more they will seek out opportunities to explore and experiment with reading and writing. Your classroom environment plays an important role in supporting children's literacy development. Environments that provide children with meaningful choices and support children's explorations in literacy are associated with greater motivation and orientation toward literacy (Gutman & Sulzby, 2000). You can motivate children by providing a literacy-rich environment filled with interesting, accessible books and child-centered literacy activities. These motivating activities may occur during their independent learning time as well as during group time.

As you interact with your kindergartners, observing their responses during classroom activities, you will develop an awareness of their individual zones of proximal development and be able to support and mediate their literacy transactions.

Enhancing Literacy Development Through Independent Activities

In kindergarten, children still need to have frequent opportunities for exploratory, self-guided activities. In early childhood settings, this time is often referred to as "free play." During this time, children can choose from a range of activities that are typically exploratory and open-ended. Such opportunities are associated with the development of conceptual knowledge, vocabulary, and communication competencies. The value of play as a context of children's learning is widely accepted and promoted in the field of early childhood education (see further, Dewey in Cuffaro, 1995; Froebel, 1917; Piaget, 1962; Vygotsky, 1976); however, in kindergarten settings the use of the term "play" is often misunderstood by parents and school administrators, who assume that play means children are aimlessly engaged or are involved in recreational activities that have no educational value when compared to a teacher's direct instruction. For this reason, these exploratory, self-directed opportunities for learning are referred to in this text as "independent activities" rather than "free play."

It is important that independent activities be scheduled so there is a sufficient block of time for children to become engaged and to fully participate in one or more areas without being rushed. In the kindergarten classroom, independent activities provide a wide range of opportunities for enhancing children's language and literacy competencies through engagement in the library center, listening center, drawing/writing center, computer center, learning centers, and creative drama.

General Guidelines for Providing Extra Support During Independent Activities

When you have children who are English language learners (ELLs) or children who are developing at a slower pace, you will want to support their language and literacy development during their independent activity time in several general ways:

Take time for one-on-one conversations. Oral language competencies are developed through social interaction. By making a special effort to engage children in conversations, you will be enhancing their language development. Tailor your interactions with children to fit their level of language development. For example, if you know that a child has a limited expressive vocabulary and uses telegraphic speech, do not expect that the child will answer you in complete sentences.

Provide predictable routines and expectations. This will allow children to focus more on the activity and their interactions, rather than being concerned about upcoming events or figuring out what is expected.

Monitor each child's interactions for signs that additional support is needed. If you see a child wandering aimlessly during independent activity time, or looking confused, take time to mediate by simplifying the task or modeling how to interact in that activity area. It is also important to provide linguistic scaffolding that will encourage the child to communicate as she engages in the activity.

Library Center

Your classroom library is probably the most important activity center you will have that will enhance children's interest in reading. This center serves as a major source of ideas, concepts, and meaningful interactions with books.

Enhancing interest in literacy. Because of this center's prominence in promoting children's motivation to explore books, it is important that the books be displayed in an organized and accessible manner. The center should also be stocked with a wide variety of books. Be sure to include nonfiction as well as story books. It is also important to include books with a multicultural focus. Books representing a range of text complexity should also be included, such as books with predictable text, rhyming text, wordless picture books, concept label books, narratives, alphabet books, nonfiction books, and easy-to-read books. Specific book titles for each of these categories are provided in Appendix F.

You also want to stock your library center with books that have eye-appeal because that also increases children's motivation to interact with books. This means that the books you select should have illustrations that support and extend the meaning of the story/text. Remember, children use illustrations to develop an understanding of the book content. Novelty books, such as pop-up books, add further meaning as the characters and events move up or out of the page when the page is turned or manipulated.

As your kindergarten year progresses and you become more aware of your children's interests and emergent literacy, you will know which types of books you need to include. You will also want to keep adding new book titles to further children's interest in literacy. Check with your school library and your local public library for the procedures to follow in borrowing books to include in your classroom library.

Enhancing reading for personal purposes. During independent activity time, kindergartners will read for personal purposes when they are able to locate books that they are interested in. You can facilitate this by first finding out children's interests and locating related books to include in your library center. To make them accessible, group the books in book bins labeled by topic along with a graphic symbol or picture. For example, you could have different book bins for books on transportation, animals, adventure, friends, families, faraway places, and alphabet books.

Not only is the book topic important in enhancing children's reading for personal purposes, but in addition, it is important to have books in your library center that are at the appropriate level of complexity and vocabulary for children in your classroom. For example, you may have several children interested in trucks and other forms of transportation; however, these children may vary in their vocabulary as well as other aspects of emergent literacy. For this reason, you will want to include books in your library center that represent different levels of complexity. *Richard Scarry's Best Word Book Ever* (Scarry, 1991) and *Trucks: Whizz! Zoom! Rumble!* (Hubbell, 2003) are both books that focus on labeling different kinds of transportation, while *The Airplane Trip* (Parent, 2002) and *Take a Ride with Mickey* (Reit, 1991) both have narrative story content along with a focus on transportation.

Enhancing metalinguistic knowledge. The way in which you organize the library center can also enhance children's metalinguistic knowledge. By grouping books according to genre you can encourage children to become aware of the different types of books and texts. By providing book bins or baskets that are labeled for ABC books, wordless books, fairy tales, and information books, the children will learn that there are different types of books and that they have different types of texts. You can also focus on a particular author by providing a special basket or shelf for several books by the same author. You might choose a different author each month and have a special sign indicating, "Author of the Month: Eric Carle." You could also focus on specific illustrators using the same type of activity.

Enhancing phonological and phonetic awareness. Children's awareness of the sound patterns in language can be fostered by including books with texts characterized by rhyming or alliteration. Alphabet books also focus on the relationships between letters and sounds represented in words. Choose books that have clear and relevant illustrations that support phonological and phonetic awareness.

Providing extra support in the library center. Although all children will benefit from the activities just described, you can provide additional support for enhancing children's interest in literacy in these ways:

1. For ELLs, provide books in the library center that are in their home language. Because they have a foundation in their home language, ELLs will initially be more interested in books that represent their home language and culture. Supporting their interest in interacting with books in their home language will also enhance their interest later on in interacting with books in English.

2. Provide books that focus on basic concepts and vocabulary in English as well as in their home language. Because ELLs may not have the same level of listening comprehension in English as do monolingual English speakers, they need to have books that focus on concepts and English vocabulary rather than a complex storyline. To enhance ELLs' interest in reading, you need to be sure that the story book content can be understood.

3. If you have kindergartners who may not have had many experiences with books in their preschool years, you will want to include some books with limited text and high-quality supportive illustrations or photographs. Wordless picture books and nonfiction concept books can capture their interest without appearing to be "baby" books.

4. Provide literacy resources for children to use at home. Children's transactions with literacy can also be enhanced by providing opportunities for them to extend their independent interactions with reading and writing outside of the classroom by creating book and writing take-home bags. This is an especially critical experience for children who may not have these resources at home due to financial constraints or other situations.

To begin this practice, you might select several books, placing each in a specially marked book bag. Be sure to include books with texts in their home languages for ELLs. Children would be expected to return the book bag within several days or at the beginning of the next week. You will need to develop some type of check-out and -in process in order to keep track of the books. After these procedures are established, children can choose their own book from the library center to take home and you could also include a selection of writing materials (such as paper and writing/drawing tools).

Listening Center

In the listening center, children can listen to a familiar story book on tape or CD while looking at the book. In addition to providing commercial story tapes or CDs, you can also provide story book tapes you have made. You might also tape a group story time, so that children can revisit a special shared book along with the accompanying class discussion.

As you observe children in this center, note whether they are progressing through the book in sync with the oral reading on the tape, and whether they appear to be paying any attention to the print.

Enhancing interest in literacy. The listening center encourages children to be interested in books because they do not have to read the text themselves. Be sure children know how to operate the equipment independently because this will empower them to use this area. Interest in using this area and in "reading along" will also be enhanced if you include tapes of books that you have previously read at group story time. By including tapes of your read-alouds, children have their memory of those events to anticipate the story content, and will be able to follow the book and turn the pages at appropriate times. When a child understands a story, he is more likely to show interest in hearing the story again and enjoy hearing other stories. Some children may even "read" along with the familiar story.

Enhancing language development. When children listen to familiar stories on tape they receive repeated exposure to the story events as well as the vocabulary contained in the story. This increases their listening comprehension and vocabulary. Opportunities to listen to stories read by a fluent reader also increase their exposure to "book language" (that is, decontextualized academic English) and contribute to their listening comprehension.

Enhancing phonological awareness. Children's awareness of sound patterns and rhythmic text will be fostered by providing tapes of poetry, rhyming texts, nursery rhymes, and texts with alliteration and rhythmic refrains.

Providing extra support in the listening center. You can provide additional support by encouraging children to partner in the listening center. You will need to have equipment that allows more than one child to listen to the tape at the same time and provide multiple copies of the books on tape. Be sure to include tapes of stories and content that reflect children's prior experiences and community settings.

In addition to providing audiotapes of books shared at group or individual story time, you will want to provide tapes of books in the home languages of your ELLs. Although

Opportunities to interact independently with books enhances kindergartners' interest in reading for personal purposes.

Sergey Nivens

the goal for ELLs is to become fluent in English, you will still want to make story tapes available in their home language. Their interest in literacy and their use of reading for personal purposes will be furthered by opportunities to listen to stories in their home language as well as in English.

Creative Drama

In many kindergarten classrooms, the creative drama center may be crowded out of the curriculum because it is thought to lack any purposeful learning; however, creative drama activities remain an important way for kindergartners to develop language and literacy through social interaction. In setting up this area, you will want to provide a familiar context or theme for the creative drama, such as a kitchen corner, post office, store, or doctor's office. Be sure to include familiar objects, artifacts, and accessories (hats, outer garments, shoes). This allows children to use their prior experiences as a basis for their creative drama. This is especially important for children from diverse cultural backgrounds.

Enhancing oral language. Creative drama opportunities allow children to practice their conversational and problem-solving skills. Creative drama activities also provide opportunities to learn and use new vocabulary and more complex syntactic patterns. Encourage children to talk with each other as they interact in this area. Occasionally, you may need to provide a conversation starter or join in their conversations to model decision-making or even assist with conflict resolution.

Enhancing interest in literacy. You can provide a special focus on reading and writing by including theme-related literacy props. For example, in the kitchen corner you could include a telephone book, blank paper, writing tools, food store ads, recipe books, and envelopes. This encourages children to incorporate reading- and writing-related tasks in their interactions.

If you set up a grocery store area you might want to include empty food packages, shelf labels, store signs, product coupons, store advertisements from newspapers, paper bags, writing tools, and blank pieces of paper (to serve as checks, receipts, or money). Children will be encouraged to use these artifacts and tools as they engage in their collaborative drama.

Providing extra support during creative drama. Additional support for children from diverse linguistic and cultural settings can be provided in the creative drama area by including objects from their cultural settings as well as literacy props that represent their languages and home/community settings. For example, in a grocery-store setting, include food packages that represent items they might have seen at home or at the local grocery store. Provide newspapers and sales flyers in their home language as well. Do not be surprised if you hear ELLs speaking in their home language during creative drama. This should not be discouraged. Instead, realize that they will transition to English as they are able and as they try to communicate with English-only speakers.

Drawing/Writing Center

This center will have the basic set-up and range of drawing and writing materials similar to those found in a drawing/writing center at the preschool level (see Chapter 7). If you find that your kindergartners do not become actively engaged in this area on their own, you may want to take some time to introduce your kindergartners to the resources in this center. This could be done at the group time or with small groups during the independent activity time. You will want to show them the different materials and how the various drawing/ writing and book-making tools are used.

Enhancing interest in literacy. In this center, children are encouraged to explore and experiment with written language. The materials that you include in this center will provide interest and motivation for children. By providing a range of paper with different textures and colors, you will be creating visual interest in producing messages and story texts. Kindergartners will also be interested in using book-making tools, such as a stapler, hole punch, tape, blunt-nosed scissors, glue, and yarn or string. You will want to ensure that this center is set up and implemented so that children have complete autonomy in deciding how they communicate on paper (for example, drawing and forms of emergent writing) (Gutman & Sulzby, 2000).

In the drawing/writing center, interest in literacy can be enhanced by encouraging children to begin to write their names. This is a very personal and meaningful use of written language. To encourage this, you could place a name card for each child in the center. This name card would have their first name on one side and their last name on the back side. On each side, their name would be paired with a special symbol. This allows them to more easily distinguish their card before they are able to remember the letter sequence for their names. An example of a name card is found in Figure 9.2. Instead of a special symbol, you could have a picture of each child on their card.

By providing this set of children's name cards, children have opportunity to focus on their classmates' names as well. To make this activity user-friendly, use a hole punch and attach the cards to a ring holder to keep them together and accessible.

Enhancing focus on print. Children's focus on print can be enhanced in the drawing/ writing center by including specific resources. For example, include a poster with the letters

Figure 9.2 Sample of Name Card, Front and Back

(a)

(b)

of the alphabet written in simple black lines. You could include two or three small magnetic boards and a supply of magnetic letters. To increase interest, you could make a new word with the magnetic letters each day prior to the children's arrival. Then as they begin their independent activities, they might look forward to seeing what word you created. Initially, keep the words short and simple, such as cat, dog, hi, car, you.

Another resource for the writing center could be a "word wall" where special words are posted for children to see and perhaps include in their writing activities. These words would be ones that have been introduced at story time or in other activities.

Enhancing reading and writing for personal purposes. To encourage kindergartners to use writing and drawing for personal purposes, you need to supply this center with a wide range of materials such as plain and decorative papers and assorted trimmings (for example, scraps of ribbon, stickers, and paper doilies). An assortment of small envelopes will also be useful. You can encourage awareness of different types of written communication by including some examples of paper folded into blank books and cards.

You will also want to talk with your kindergartners about the different ways written language is used, such as birthday cards, thank-you cards, invitations, letters, signs, story books, information books, and alphabet books. For example, Isabelle, a five-year-old, created a book about her mom (see Figure 9.3), describing their special relationship. Through her use of invented spelling and conventional spelling, Isabelle used written language for a very personal purpose. As you read what she wrote, note the conventional spelling of many high-frequency words (I, love, mom, in, me, with, on, she, bed, like) and the invented spelling of less familiar words (bekos = because, toks = tucks, taks = takes, boyk = bike). By encouraging kindergartners to write "any way they want" they can focus on the message they are communicating rather than confining their writing to only the words that they can spell conventionally.

You could also occasionally sit down in this area alongside your kindergartners and create you own simple card, sign, or invitation. While doing this, you could "think aloud," sharing your thoughts while you create your special card or message, and further modeling reading and writing for personal purposes.

You might also consider including a tape recorder and blank tapes in this center so children can "read" what they have created. To do this, you will need to establish a procedure for children to identify themselves as they begin their taping and then sign a "tape recording log" for each tape. This way you can periodically review children's reading of their stories and other written communication.

It is important to remember that children's individual purposes for reading and writing will vary. You will need to observe carefully your children's interests as well as talk with them as they engage in these literacy transactions. This will help you better structure their learning environment with the materials and activities that enhance their use of literacy in personally meaningful ways.

Enhancing metalinguistic knowledge. When you are organizing a drawing/writing center in your kindergarten, be sure to arrange seating at a table for several children to be there at the same time. This will encourage conversations among the children about their writing and drawing. As they talk, they may focus on the letters and words they are trying to write, the content of the illustrations they are making, or the features of the book they are creating. Opportunities for conversations about their writing and drawing encourage children to share their conscious awareness of written language and how it is used to communicate, that is, metalinguistic knowledge. As you monitor this area, occasionally join in their conversations as they talk. When appropriate, refer to specific language concepts such as book cover, author, illustrator, page, words, and illustrations.

Figure 9.3 Isabelle's Book About Her Mother

I Love my
mom bekos
she toks me
in to bed.
I olso Love
my mom.
bocos my
mom feds meabox

(a)

I love my
mom bekos
she taks cav
oive me. she
olso tawoks
with me. I
like that To.
she heps me.

(b)

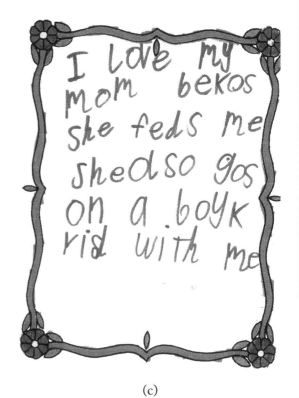

I love my
mom bekos
she feds me
she olso gos
on a boyk
rid with me

(c)

You can expect that children will vary in their conscious awareness of specific language features and concepts. By providing opportunities for children to talk as they are engaged in their independent activities, you will be able to observe the growth of their metalinguistic knowledge.

Enhancing phonetic awareness. Phonetic awareness can be enhanced in the writing center by providing a poster of the alphabet with each letter paired with a sample word and picture of an object that represents that letter sound. You could also include several alphabet books and picture dictionaries for children to use as references for their writing activities.

Providing extra support in the drawing/writing center. Children who are English language learners will benefit from additional support as they work in the drawing/writing center. When they express interest in writing or creating books or cards, encourage them to write "any way they want." When a book is created that has only illustrations, offer to take the child's dictation of the story that goes with his illustrations. Be careful not to impose your idea of story structure on this dictation. Simply write down what is dictated. Then encourage the child to read his story with you using echo or unison reading, pointing to each word as it is read.

You can also enhance ELLs' attention to print by including posters or displays in the writing center that include their home languages. For example, you might develop a poster that has words for hello and good-bye in each of the languages spoken by your ELLs. This is also a beneficial experience for the English-only children and draws their attention to print.

Computer Center

For many kindergartners, becoming involved in using a computer is a highly motivating activity; however, the software and computer set-up need to be developmentally appropriate in order for this experience to be a valuable one for your kindergartners' literacy development.

Setting up a computer center. Most kindergarten classrooms will have only one or two computers. This means that the children will cycle in and out of the computer center as they do the other areas during independent activity time. At each computer, set up two chairs facing the computer with another chair on the side. This encourages two children to work together and provides space for you or your aide to assist when necessary.

Demonstrating and mediating children's use of software. Children's successful use of the computer center and software will depend on the way in which you demonstrate and mediate their interactions. Start by gathering two or three children at a time in the computer center and demonstrating how to start the software, how to control it, and some of the basic activities found on the software. Be sure that children understand they can stop the activity at any time and show them how to exit the program. Provide an illustrated poster to remind children of the basic steps to follow. Initially, you or your aide will need

When you include posters that have the home languages of your English language learners, you encourage them to focus on print.

English	Spanish	Gujarati	Japanese
Hello	Hola	Namaste	Kon-nichi-wa
Thank you	Gracias	A-bhar	Arigato gozaimasu
Please	Por favor	MA-her-ba-ni karo	Onegai shimasu

Beverly Otto

to remain in the area and monitor children's use of the software and to respond to their questions or demonstrate different features.

Choosing software that will motivate and enhance literacy development. When you are selecting software to include in your literacy curriculum, you will want to select software that is easy for you and your students to use. This means you should try out the software thoroughly and use it until you are comfortable before you introduce it in your classroom. Since most kindergartners will still be developing their keyboarding skills, choose software that is controlled by manipulating the mouse (point and click) or a touch-screen feature (Haugland, 1997). Voice-activated technology may also be an option (Mandell, 2000).

Select software that supports your emphasis on one or more areas of emergent literacy, such as oral language, interest in literacy, reading and writing for personal purposes, and phonological and phonetic awareness. A software evaluation guide and a listing of several examples of current software are provided in Appendix E. As a kindergarten teacher you will want to keep current with new developments in literacy-related software. In the sections that follow, general guidelines for enhancing literacy development through the selection of software with specific features are described.

Enhancing interest in literacy. Children's interest in literacy can be fostered by providing software that involves story books or nonfiction text rather than focusing on isolated skill development. To encourage children's literacy transactions in the computer center, select story book and nonfiction software that represents the interests and developmental levels of children in your classroom. For this, you will use some of the same criteria you use when selecting books for your library center.

Electronic versions of books, usually on CD-ROM format, have added sounds, and click-on animation that adds context and action to a story, and may even expand story ideas (Amberg, 2000). In many instances, these additional animation and sound features are beneficial and enhance interest and comprehension; however, depending on the software, the features may actually draw the child's focus away from the main sequence of story events, thus weakening comprehension. This is why you need to thoroughly review software before using it in your classroom.

Enhancing reading and writing for personal purposes. Look for software that allows children to be in control of the interaction with text. For example, choose software that allows children to determine when the pages are turned, the volume of the music or speech, having specific words sounded out, or controlling a sound associated with a picture (for example, a siren sound that accompanies a fire engine picture) (Schrock, 2001).

Also look for software that encourages children to create texts and illustrations, such as the virtual art tools found in Kid Pix®. This type of software allows children to choose the artistic medium as well as combine writing with creating illustrations. Most children will find this highly motivating.

Enhancing phonological and phonetic awareness. Children's awareness of rhyme, alliteration, phonemes, and letter–sound associations can be enhanced with software that presents story books with those features in their texts. Because the story text is read and illustrations are animated to coincide with the text content, children can become aware of the sound patterns of language.

Providing extra support in the computer center. Children who have not had computer experience prior to coming to kindergarten may need to have more mediation and scaffolding for learning how to use the technology. Encourage children to partner when using the computer. ELLs will enjoy opportunities to use software that features their home language.

Be sure the software is developmentally appropriate. Encourage ELLs to collaborate with other ELLs as well as native English speakers when using the computer center. Also consider including software that corresponds to books you have read at group story time. This familiarity will provide a comfort level in using the related software.

Learning Centers

Children's language and literacy can be enhanced by opportunities to become involved in various learning centers, such as a manipulatives table (such as Legos®), a block center, and a concept/discovery center. Learning centers are experiential and are designed to promote particular concepts or cognitive skills, such as problem solving. As you plan and implement each area, you will want to keep two general guidelines in mind. First, make sure each center is supplied with developmentally appropriate and high-interest materials. Second, organize each center to accommodate more than one child.

Enhancing oral language. Encourage children to engage each other in conversations while interacting with the materials in the centers. Don't expect children to work quietly or silently: Conversation and discussion skills are enhanced when children have opportunities to participate in spontaneous peer conversations about concepts or cognitive tasks. This contributes to children's concept development and vocabulary.

By providing collaborative tasks in one or more learning centers, you can encourage children to problem-solve together. For example, you could develop a sorting or matching activity with animal picture cards, other pictured concepts, or graphic designs. When children work together to sort or match the cards, they use oral language to negotiate and make decisions about the tasks. This enhances their speaking competencies.

Enhancing a focus on print. Posting directions or guidelines for using learning centers also encourages children to focus on print; however, you need to introduce children to the posters so that the print is meaningful to them. Environmental print serves no purpose if children are not encouraged to use it or if it has no meaning for them. You could encourage a focus on meaningful print by setting up a learning center that involves matching traffic signs with the specific words, such as the symbol of stop sign with the word "Stop."

Enhancing phonological and phonetic awareness. Phonological awareness can be fostered through learning center activities that involve sorting words by sound. In this activity, children group picture cards by their beginning sound. For example, picture cards with a heart, a house, and a horse would be grouped together and cards with a ball, a banana, and a basket would be grouped together. Picture cards could also be sorted by beginning or ending sounds. A sample of this sorting activity is illustrated in Figure 9.4.

A similar activity can be developed to match pictures that represent things that rhyme. For example: bug, jug, rug, and mug. These learning center activities are often available from companies specializing in early childhood learning materials, or you can create the activity yourself. Be sure to select pictures of items that are easily identified and are part of children's prior experience and vocabulary.

Phonetic awareness can be fostered by developing a learning center that involves matching objects with the letter representing the initial sound of the object's name. For example, the letter A would be matched with a picture of an apple; the letter B would be matched with a picture of a ball.

Providing extra support in learning centers. You can provide extra support in learning centers by including illustrated posters with simple texts that list the steps or guidelines

Figure 9.4 Sample Sorting Activity for Phonological Awareness

for children to follow in using the learning center. Wherever possible, incorporate culturally relevant objects and tasks in the learning centers. By providing this level of familiarity, the children will be able to draw on their prior knowledge and experiences, providing a basis for continued conceptual development and vocabulary growth.

Enhancing Literacy Development Through Teacher-Guided Activities

Teacher-guided activities usually involve a group setting, either a large group encompassing all of the children in the classroom or smaller groupings of two to six students. This setting provides opportunities for the teacher to focus on specific concepts or processes and to provide mediation within children's zones of proximal development. These activities are centered in the group or circle-times when stories are shared, discussed, and re-enacted. Additional activities involve dictated/language experience stories and interactive writing. Teacher-guided activities may also involve using word study and word walls as well as show-and-tell and author's chair. Teacher-guided literacy transactions can also occur during procedural activities.

Procedural Activities

Throughout the school day, you will be engaging in procedural activities such as taking attendance and directing children from one activity to another. You will probably have times when children move from a whole group to smaller groups and back to whole groups. There will also be times when your class has activities in another part of the school building and you need to have children line up before leaving your classroom. These times provide additional opportunities to encourage language and literacy interactions.

Enhancing a focus on print. As you begin your school year, create a name card for each child, with his/her photo attached to the card alongside his/her printed name. Then each day as children arrive they are to pick out their card from a basket labeled "at home" and put it in a basket labeled "at school." As you gather the children at your opening circle-time, you can hold up children's individual cards from the "at school" basket and have children identify their card and the cards of others. You might want to put children's first names on one side of the card and their last names on the back side. This will allow you to focus initially on their first names and then later focus on their last names. (Refer to example in Figure 9.2.)

Later on in the school year, make a new set of name cards without the photos. This will further encourage children to focus on the print. Because of their prior experiences with the cards when the photos were attached, they will better able to now focus on the print and read the names on the cards.

Enhancing phonological and phonetic awareness. As you hold up each attendance card, give clues to help children identify each card. For example, when you hold up Roberto's card, you might point to the R and say, "This person's name begins with an R. /rrr/. Who do we know who has a name that starts with this sound?" You could also cover up the photo portion of the card until children have guessed the identity of the card and then reveal the picture to confirm their responses.

One variation of this activity is to select cards of children whose first names start with the same letter and talk about the ways in which the names are the same and different. Be sure that the print on the name cards is large enough to be seen from a distance.

You can also focus children's attention on the sounds in their names by dismissing them from the various group times during the day by using the sound–symbol relationships. For example, "Now, everyone whose name begins with a /t/ sound can go line up." Then you would follow this in a similar manner using other initial sounds until everyone was lined up for the next activity.

Recognizing that names and other words can be divided into parts or syllables also involves phonological awareness. For example, as you say each child's name, clap once for each syllable. Roberto would be three claps, Ro-ber-to. Scott would be just one clap. Then instead of focusing on initial sounds as you direct students to line up, you might use the number of syllables in their first name, such as "If your first name has two parts, you can line up."

Read-Alouds

Story book read-alouds enhance nearly every area of literacy development; however, the way in which you interact with children during your story book read-alouds will determine how children will specifically benefit from those experiences.

You need to prepare for the read-aloud by thoroughly reading the book and preplanning what illustrations, concepts, words, or events you will emphasize as you read as well as the questions or comments you will make after the book is shared. Be sure to select a book that is large enough so illustrations can be easily seen by everyone. Kindergartners still need illustrations to provide the situational context for the language of the story.

Enhancing oral language. When you read a book to your kindergartners at group time, you can enhance their concept and vocabulary development as well as their ability to comprehend more complex language. It is important for you to select books that have stories or content that build on your children's prior knowledge and experiences as well as their interests. Take time while reading to focus on new vocabulary and to talk about the illustrations.

When you use flannel boards and puppets to accompany your read-alouds, you are providing important visual support for children's listening comprehension. The advantage of puppets or flannel board figures is that they can be manipulated to accompany events occurring in the story. This allows you to dramatize important concepts and events, providing a clear demonstration of specific vocabulary. For example, when presenting a flannel board– or puppet-aided read-aloud of "The Three Billy Goats Gruff," you will be acting out the "trip, trap, trip, trap" of the Billy Goats as they move across the bridge. These additional visual supports demonstrate word meaning and thus increase comprehension.

In most instances, puppets and flannel board figures will be more visible and recognizable from a distance than will book illustrations. This benefits children who may be sitting farther away from you. As you share particular stories on repeated occasions, you can have children help you with the story by assuming responsibility for a particular puppet or flannel board figure. Some children may simply want to provide the actions, while others might also be able to contribute to the verbal dialogue in the story. You could also make these materials available in the children's library corner so that they can re-enact the story during their independent activity time.

Enhancing interest in literacy. Children's interest in literacy can be fostered during read-alouds. Here are some guidelines for you to follow:

1. Select a book with content that builds on children's prior knowledge and experiences. In addition, children will benefit from having books read that are related to other activities within your curriculum. For example, if your curricular theme is "insects," and you have arranged a discovery center focusing on insects, sharing a book about insects will enhance their interest in your read-aloud.

Story book read-alouds enhance nearly every area of literacy development.

XinXinXing

2. Thoroughly review the book and prepare your reading so that you are enthusiastic and expressive. Also plan your gestures and how you will use the illustrations to increase children's comprehension.

3. Provide a brief introduction to the story. This introduction should activate children's prior knowledge and experiences, thus setting up expectations and predictions about the upcoming story. For example, if you have chosen *The Very Lonely Firefly* (Carle, 1999), you might introduce the story by talking about the time you saw a firefly in your backyard in the summer, describing how it quickly darted about and blinked its light. Then you could ask if any of the children have seen a firefly before. You might decide to then explain what the word "lonely" means because that concept is key to understanding the story.

4. As you read aloud, monitor children's nonverbal behaviors for signs of comprehension. If you see children who do not appear to comprehend the story, make adjustments in your reading. You might need to adjust the vocabulary, use less complex sentences, read more expressively, or even move through the story more quickly.

5. Provide opportunities to connect reading with writing and drawing or other artwork. Children's interest in literacy can be enhanced by encouraging them to draw or illustrate a favorite part of a familiar story. You could also focus on the ways in which book illustrations communicate meaning. For example, after reading several of Eric Carle's books, a kindergarten teacher talked with her children about the media used to create the illustrations. This was followed up by a short video on the author/artist and his techniques. Then the children were given an opportunity to create an illustration and write about what they created. This activity extended the read-aloud experience to include writing as well as the use of specific artistic media (scraps of wallpaper).

Figure 9.5 shows the story and illustration Isabelle created during this activity in her kindergarten. As you read her written description of her illustration, you can see the connections she made between her experiences with Eric Carle's books and what she created. Also note that she used a combination of phonemic invented spelling (dro = drew, grene = green, prte = part, move = movie, botrfliy = butterfly, scie = sky; sed = said, grac = grass, wohd = watched) and conventionally spelled words (sun, likes, we, in, it, the, and). During kindergarten, children often use a combination of writing forms to communicate meaning.

Enhancing reading for personal purposes. Read-alouds provide important opportunities for you to demonstrate reading for personal purposes by selecting books that are related to children's interests, to learning-center content, or to other curricular themes.

Enhancing focus on print. Using big books (enlarged versions of story books) is a way of encouraging children to focus on print. Big books may be provided in your commercial reading curriculum or you may have a collection of big books that are independent of a commercial curriculum.

To focus children's attention to print, display the big book on a book stand or easel so that the book will stay open and be at a height where all children can see each page without any obstructions. By displaying the big book in this way, you will then be able to point to the pictures and the print as you read. Start with big books that have only a few words on each page. After you have taken the children on a "picture walk" through the book, begin reading the text while pointing to the words as you read them. It is helpful to use a pointer (ruler or long wand) as you are reading to direct children's attention to the print as well as the illustrations.

Figure 9.5 Isabelle's Illustration and Written Description

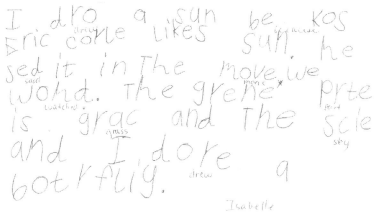

(a)

(b)

Children's interest in literacy can be enhanced by encouraging them to draw or illustrate a favorite part of a familiar story.

Sarawut Chamsaeng

As children become familiar with specific books, encourage them to chime in or echo as you read. When the big book has a predictable text, such as *Polar Bear, Polar Bear, What Do You Hear?* (Martin, 1992), children will be able to anticipate upcoming text. As they respond, point to the words so they can see how speech and print match.

Enhancing metalinguistic knowledge. When you read story books to your kindergartners at group time, you can focus on metalinguistic concepts by referring explicitly to the cover of the book, the book title, illustrator, author, and dedication page. Introduce these concepts over time and refer to them on repeated occasions. After you have demonstrated these concepts for a while, you can have children participate in identifying or locating the book title or author's name, as well as other metalinguistic concepts.

Enhancing phonological and phonetic awareness. Phonological awareness can be enhanced during read-alouds when you focus on the differences and similarities of sounds in words. You can select books for your read-aloud that emphasize phonological awareness through words that rhyme (Flett & Conderman, 2002; Yopp, 1995a). Encourage children to anticipate upcoming rhymes by pausing as you read.

Identifying individual sounds, or phonemes, in words is more complex than recognizing words that rhyme or separating words into syllables. Begin focusing on individual sounds in words by emphasizing the beginning sounds of words. You can do this by reading aloud specific books that are designed to focus on beginning sounds (Allor & McCathren, 2003; Ukrainetz, Cooney, Dyer, Kysar, & Harris, 2000). For example, *My "B" Sound Box* (Moncure, 2001), is a story about a girl who collects objects that have the initial word sound of /b/. Throughout the story text there are over 80 words that begin with that sound. At the end of the story 13 different objects beginning with /b/ have been identified and collected.

You can also use familiar big books to have children identify words that begin with certain letters to foster phonetic awareness. For example, take a particular page in a book, read that page aloud, and then have children come up to point to all of the words that begin with the letter B (or another letter that is used frequently at the beginning of words on the page). As they point to the words, pronounce the words so that children see the relationship between the initial letter and the word's pronunciation.

Providing extra support during read-alouds. At group time, you will want to support English language learners and encourage their interest in literacy in several ways. First, you will want to monitor their responses to your read-aloud for evidence they are attending to the story and comprehending it. Be sure to select books with content that builds on their prior knowledge and experiences.

You could also gather your ELLs in a small group prior to the large group time and engage them in a picture walk of the book you will use at group time. That way they will have an opportunity to become familiar with the book before it is read aloud at group time. This prior knowledge of the book will help them be more interested during story time and will increase their comprehension of the story.

ELL children will also benefit from having the story book you shared at the large group time repeated later as a read-aloud within a small group setting with you or your teaching aide. This will allow them more opportunity to view the illustrations as well as to make comments and ask questions. By increasing their interactions with books, you will be increasing their interest in literacy. It will also contribute to building their vocabulary and their comprehension of English.

Small group time with ELLs can also focus on interacting with concept/label books or story books that have their home language along with English. For example, *Perro Grande ... Big Dog ... Perro Pequeño ... Little Dog* (Eastman, 1982) contains both English and Spanish text throughout the book. By providing this type of language support, children can use their knowledge of their home language to begin to learn English vocabulary and syntax. If you do not speak children's home language, learn the correct pronunciation with the help of a parent or other native speaker. Often, ELLs can provide you with the correct pronunciation as well for specific words in their speaking vocabularies.

Children who are English language learners will benefit from small group and individual opportunities to interact with big books that are shared at the larger group time. You will want to make these books available in your library center as well as plan a special time for you, your aide, or a classroom volunteer to engage ELLs in revisiting the big book, talking about the book content, and focusing on the print as it is read.

You can also provide story and vocabulary props during your small group read-alouds with ELL children. For example, when reading the *Big Dog, Little Dog* book, you could bring in examples of beets and spinach to accompany the page where these foods are pictured. By increasing ELLs' comprehension at shared book time, you will also be enhancing their interest in literacy.

During read-alouds, ELL children will benefit from having additional opportunities to see metalinguistic concepts demonstrated as they participate in small group or one-on-one activities with you, your classroom aide, or volunteer. Provide ELLs with extra opportunities to identify book titles, authors, illustrators, or to observe a teacher's "think aloud."

Circle-Time Discussion

Oral discussions during or after read-alouds provide important opportunities for language and literacy development. By observing children's facial expressions and other nonverbal behaviors, you will be aware of which children are interested in participating in the discussion. Be sure to establish eye contact throughout your group of kindergartners so that everyone feels included in the discussion.

Enhancing oral language. The focus of circle-time discussions is often on story comprehension and vocabulary development. This can occur at various points in the course of reading a story as well as after the story reading is completed. As you plan and prepare for reading aloud to your children, also plan specific questions to use during the circle-time discussion. Include a variety of questions: Many of your questions will focus on the literal understanding of story events and characters, and other questions will encourage children to make inferences. Open-ended questions also are valuable in encouraging children to think of related experiences they have had and to share those experiences orally.

Providing extra support in circle-time discussions. By paying close attention to children's nonverbal and verbal behaviors during story time, you can be alert to children who are not comprehending as well as those who are eager to participate in discussing the book. To encourage children who do not participate frequently, start by providing questions that ask for only short answers of one to two words. This allows children to participate within their zone of proximal development (and comfort).

Book Talks

When you add new book titles to your library center, you can introduce them to your children by providing a "book talk" at group time. For example, you could structure your book talk in the following way:

> I have some special new books that will be in our library center for several weeks. These books are from our city library, so we want to be sure to take good care of them. Before I put them in our library center, I want to give you a peek at the books so you will know what wonderful books they are.

At this point, you would hold up each book so children can see the cover. Give the title of the book and page through it, taking a quick "picture walk," and talking about the story as it is illustrated. You could indicate that you will be reading these books at story time during the next few weeks. Throughout this book talk, be enthusiastic and share your joy in the opportunities to have new book titles in your library center. When you give these book talks, keep in mind children's attention span. In most instances, you will want to keep each book talk limited to one to three new titles. Place these new titles in a special book bin or basket that is labeled "new books" so that children can easily locate them.

Enhancing interest in literacy. Book talks are similar to a "sales pitch" or advertisement. If you have selected new books that correspond to children's areas of interest and experience, your enthusiastic introduction of the new books will generate increased interest in reading.

Story Re-Enactment

This activity encourages oral expression as well as provides a way of showing story comprehension through actions. You will need to gradually introduce this activity, building up to having children provide the story dialogue as well as acting out the events. You will find the following sequence of steps useful in this activity:

1. Select a familiar book that has a series of actions and a number of characters. Children will also participate more readily if the text has a predictable refrain or text pattern. For example, in the Gingerbread Man story, the character repeatedly says, "Run, run, as fast as you can. You can't catch me, I'm the Gingerbread Man."
2. Read the book several times and encourage all of the children to participate as a group in performing the actions or giving a short verbal response.
3. After children are comfortable with responding in a group, you can begin to ask for individual children to take a particular role. Some children who are hesitant to participate verbally may be very comfortable performing a character's actions.
4. You will probably remain the narrator of the story re-enactment; however, as children become more and more familiar with this activity and with a particular story, you may be able to encourage children's narrative participation by asking, "Who can tell us what is going to happen next?"

Throughout the story re-enactment, it is important to focus on children's participation in re-creating the meaning of the story rather than the exact wording or dialogue of the original text. You also want to be sure that everyone feels a part of the re-enactment whether they be the actors, speakers, or members of the audience.

Enhancing oral language. Acting out familiar story books fosters children's oral language development because children use their own words to re-create characters' dialogue and recall story events. Although they may not use the exact wording found in the text, the words they use will capture the main ideas that were in the text. You could also encourage children to extend the stories further by improvisation, portraying events that they think could happen if the story events were continued (Ferguson & Young, 1996).

Providing extra support in story re-enactments. Children who are hesitant to participate in story re-enactments may be encouraged if given parts that involve only gestures, other nonverbal behaviors, or limited speaking. They may also need to have more opportunities to become familiar with the story book prior to participating in a re-enactment.

Dictated Stories and Informational Writing

In these activities, the teacher (or classroom aide) serves as the scribe, writing down what children dictate for the story or informational text. Dictated story and informational writing activities can be used in large groups as well as smaller group or individual settings.

Story dictation is often implemented from a "language experience approach" (Stauffer, 1980). This means that children dictate a text (using their language) about an experience they have had. For example, in Ms. Lyon's classroom the children have just had a visit from the local fire department. The visiting fireman demonstrated how to "stop, drop, and roll" and talked about fire safety. He also showed his firefighting equipment and let several children try on his hat and boots. After the visit was over, Ms. Lyons gathered the children at group time and suggested that they write a story about the fireman's visit. She emphasized the importance of writing down what happened so they could remember this special event. First, she conducted a brief review of what happened during the visit and what the fireman said. Then she began to take the children's dictation, writing what was said on chart paper for all to see.

While most story dictation in kindergarten involves a group story about a shared class experience, it is also important to provide opportunities for individually dictated stories. This can be facilitated more easily if you have a classroom aide or volunteer. Children may choose to focus their dictations on their out-of-school experiences or on a classroom event. The dictation process is the same as for group dictation. While you can use plain sheets of paper for the dictation, it may be more motivating for children if you put their dictation directly into a book format. To do this, take several sheets of paper, fold them together in half, making a book, and staple the folded edge. While the child dictates, write a segment of the dictation on each page. Be sure to ask the child what the title of the book should be and write the child's name as author and illustrator. Then the book is ready for the child to illustrate. You can provide additional interest in this activity by sharing the child's story at group time.

Enhancing oral language. Providing opportunities for children to dictate stories to you also enhances their oral language development and encourages them to use more decontextualized or "book language." When you are taking children's dictation, be sure that you write down exactly what each child says. Not only will this validate their story contributions, but it will provide an opportunity for you to observe how they use language to communicate a sequence of events and describe what happened.

Providing opportunities for dictated stories and 'news' enhances children's awareness of how speech becomes print.

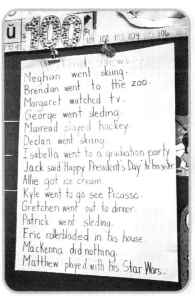

Kathleen Lyons

Enhancing interest in literacy. Providing opportunities for children to dictate stories can also enhance their interest in literacy. Through this dictation, they can see their words become print and they can see how written stories are created. Be sure to use their exact words and review what you have written to confirm what they wanted to say.

You can also increase children's interest in story dictation by incorporating their names into the story. For example, when you first begin story dictation in your kindergarten you can use a format similar to the one in Figure 9.6 to increase children's interest in participating in the group dictation. Seeing their name in the story will be motivating and help them remember what was dictated.

An additional way of using dictation to increase children's interest in literacy is to make the dictated stories into a class book. To do this, you take several sheets of paper (either 8½″ × 11″ or poster size) and write the story in segments so that it continues for several pages. Be sure to include a cover with the title, authors, and date, as well as a back page. You then ask children to provide illustrations for the pages. As they begin to create the illustrations be sure that you have reviewed with them the text on each page. When the illustrations are complete, assemble the book by stapling it together. You may also decide to laminate the pages to increase durability. Once the book is assembled, share the book at group time and show your delight in their class book. You will want to place it in your library center and make it available for children to check out to share at home.

Enhancing personal purposes for writing. Another way of showing specific purposes for writing during group time is to develop a chart or sign to post in your classroom. This chart or sign could remind children of certain rules for working in a learning center. You would use some of the same strategies that you use in story dictation to elicit and write down children's contributions. Here is how such a dialogue might proceed:

Teacher: I have brought this chart paper today so we can think of some rules for us to follow in the block area. After we decide on the rules, I will write them down and then we can put this sign in the block area to help us remember what we need to do.

Let's think about what rules we need. . . . Oh, here's one. Because the block area is not very big, we probably only want to have three people in the block area at one time. So let's make that our first rule. (*Teacher then writes down: 1. Only three people at a time.*) Now, let's think of another rule we need. (*pauses*)

Frankie: (*raises hand; teacher calls on him*) Put blocks away when you go.

Teacher: Yes, that is an important rule. (*Teacher writes down: 2. Put blocks away when you go.*)

Figure 9.6 Example of Group Dictation Incorporating Children's Names

> A Visit from the Fireman to Room 102
> Anolla said, "A fireman came to our room today".
> Brian said, "He brought his big boots."
> Frankie said, "He brought his big coat and special hat."
> Karina said, "He showed how to stop, drop, and roll."
> Jose said, "I got to try on his hat."
> Gretchen said, "There was a fire on my block."
> Eduardo said, "I got to try on his boots. They were so big!"

This interaction continues until there are three to four rules. After the rules are completed, the teacher and children read the rules aloud using echo or unison reading while the teacher points to each word. You may find that it is also helpful to combine pictures or graphic symbols with each rule to support children's comprehension of each rule. (See sample in Figure 9.7.)

After group time, the sign is posted in the block area. Then as children interact in the block area, it is referred to as situations arise when they need to be reminded of the rules.

Enhancing focus on print. Language experience/dictated stories are another way of encouraging children to focus on print. As you write the children's dictation, say each word. Once the sentence is written, you can then reread the sentence and point to each word. After the dictation is completed, you will also want to read the entire story, encouraging the children to echo-read or chime in as you read it.

Enhancing metalinguistic knowledge. When you are writing down children's dictated stories, you will be able to enhance their metalinguistic knowledge by "thinking aloud" as you write. This means that you will share your thoughts as you encode their speech into print. For example, in the dialogue example located in Figure 9.8, the teacher shares her thoughts on specific letter–sound relationships, sentences, and punctuation.

By demonstrating specific language concepts using a think-aloud strategy, children will become familiar with the concepts and the related vocabulary. This provides a foundation for children to refer to metalinguistic concepts later on, when they engage in reading and writing on their own.

Enhancing phonological and phonetic awareness. Interactive writing has developed as a strategy to enhance children's phonological and phonetic awareness. A distinguishing feature of interactive writing is the participation of the children in the actual writing process (Boroski, 2004). Although you may write many of the words during the interactive writing of a group or individual story, children are encouraged to help write specific words that are in the story. As children participate in writing, you will direct their attention to

Figure 9.7 Group Dictated Sign for Block Area

Rules for Block Center

1. Only three people at a time.

2. Put away blocks when you go.

3. No fighting.

4. No grabbing.

Figure 9.8 Example of Kindergarten Teacher's Think-Aloud During Dictation

Setting: Ms. Camacho has engaged her kindergartners in dictating a story about their trip to a local apple orchard.

Ms. C.: Let's start our story by writing a title for it. What shall we call our story?

Sarah: Our trip to the apple orchard

Ms. C.: That's a good title. [*writes "Our Trip to" and begins writing "The" on the chart paper, pauses and says*] The Apple [*pauses*] Hmmm. What sound starts the word apple? /AAA/ Oh, I know, apple starts with the letter A. I'm going to use a capital A to begin apple because it is part of our title. [*writes "Apple" on the chart paper, followed by the word "Orchard"; after writing this she pauses*] Look at the two a's. Here is a big A, a capital A [*pointing to the A in apple*] and here is a little a, here in orchard. Now we're ready to begin telling what happened on our trip. What happened first?

Roberto: We put on our coats and walked out to the bus.

Ms. C.: Oh, I like your sentence Roberto! Roberto said, "we put on our coats and walked out to the bus." That's a long sentence, isn't it? Help me remember the words as I write them on our story chart. [*She repeats the words as she writes them and encourages children to chime in.*] Let's count the words in this long sentence [*points to words as they count them*] one, two, three. . . [*counts eleven words*]. OK, what happened next?

Lisa: Then it started to rain!

Mrs. C.: (laughs) Yes, just as we got on the bus, it started to rain so hard! [*writes, Lisa said, "Then it started to rain" on the chart*] (*pauses*) Hmm. I want to remember how Lisa said her sentence. She was excited, wasn't she? How can I remember this when I read this later? Hmm. Oh, I know. I can use an exclamation point at the end of the sentence. This is what it looks like. [*writes an exclamation point at the end of Lisa's sentence*] Now I will be able to remember how Lisa said her sentence and read it that way again.

analyzing the sounds in words and the letters used to represent those sounds (Brotherton & Williams, 2002). Because you want your children to be successful in this activity, you will need to know which sounds they are ready to begin to encode in print. This requires that you have a clear awareness of children's developmental levels and emergent literacy.

To prepare for interactive writing, you will need to decide on the topic and instructional focus of your interactive writing activity (Boroski, 2004). Perhaps you pick for a topic a recent field trip or decide to use the current theme of study (for example, community helpers). For the focus of your instruction, you might begin with an emphasis on initial consonant sounds. Then as you conduct your interactive writing, you will encourage children to volunteer to write the first consonant sound in certain words that you choose for them. It is important to limit the number of words because the process initially takes time, and if you ask children to participate in writing every word, they will become inattentive. In addition, this lengthy process may decrease children's overall comprehension of the message you are creating.

Once you have gathered your materials, determined the topic of the interactive writing, and chosen the focus of your instruction, you are ready to begin. Here are some basic steps to follow (Boroski, 2004; Wiley, 1999):

1. Start with prompts similar to those you use when beginning language experience/dictated stories. Talk about the event or topic, reviewing what happened and what will be included in the story/text. Then decide on a sentence to start your writing.

2. After you and the children have agreed on a beginning sentence, repeat the sentence slowly. While doing this, hold up one finger for each word in the sentence.

3. Ask the children to repeat the sentence with you slowly and also to count the words by holding up their fingers. This counting process helps children understand that sentences are composed of separate words.

4. Begin writing the sentence on chart paper. When you come to a word that you want the children to help write, pause and think-aloud, eliciting their participation. For example, if your story is going to be about the visit from the fire department, you might have agreed on this beginning sentence: "A fireman came to visit our class today." When you begin to write, you pause and say, "Our first word is A. What letter should we write?" After children indicate the letter A, ask for a volunteer to come up to write an A on the chart paper. Next repeat the sentence. Then say, "Our next word is fireman. Let's think about how we should start writing that word. What is the first sound in fireman?" After children respond with /fff/, you say, "that's right, /fff/. We need to start the word fireman with a letter f. I need to have someone come up and write the letter f. Who would like to do that?"

5. After a child writes the f letter, you then write the rest of the word because your emphasis this time is just on the initial sounds.

6. Next, repeat the sentence again, and decide which additional words you want the children to help you write. Choose words for which the children will be successful in identifying the initial sound. When you start engaging children in interactive writing, you also want to select words that have simple phonetic relationships to the letter name. For example, in the sentence, "A fireman came to visit our class today," you might select *a, fireman, to,* and *today* as words for which you want children to write the first letter. You would not select *came* at this time because the first sound is a "hard c" sound, similar to the letter name for K, and thus has a more challenging letter–sound relationship. Similarly, *visit* and *class* would not be chosen yet because of their more complex letter–sound relationships.

7. Continue this process of deciding what words to write, eliciting student participation in writing parts of the words, and rereading what has been written until the text is completed. However, you need to monitor the interest and comprehension of your students to maintain their attention to this writing process. Starting out, you may decide to have them help only for a short while and then transition back into a dictated story approach, in which you do all of the writing.

Interactive writing is a powerful strategy for enhancing children's phonetic awareness; however, to be successful it needs to be implemented with a clear awareness of your children's levels of literacy development and your understanding of how children acquire phonetic information. By clearly understanding your children's zones of proximal development, you can structure the interactive writing activities to gradually lead them to greater understanding of how speech becomes print and how they can figure out how to spell words they want to write.

Interactive writing can be used with other types of writing. In addition to writing stories or narratives, interactive writing can be used to create informational text, lists, charts, letter writing, recipes, and ABC books. The interactive writing strategy can be extended and elaborated as it is used in first grade through third grade. Additional resources for interactive writing are found in Appendix G.

Group dictation activities in kindergarten encourage children to be aware that important information can be written down and shared.

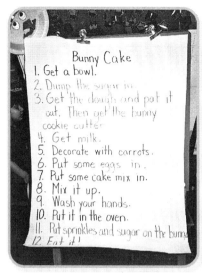

Kathleen Lyons

Providing extra support in dictation activities. By engaging children in a small group story dictation or an individual dictation, you can give them more specific support in mediating their transactions with written language. These individual and small group dictations can represent more directly their prior knowledge and interests. They will also be closer to you so they can see how you are writing down what they say. You may need to provide a story starter as well as further linguistic scaffolding as the dictation proceeds; however, encourage children to participate as much as they can in dictating the text.

After you have finished their dictation, read it and encourage them to either echo what you read or attempt to read along. You may also want to provide several opportunities for children to reread their dictated texts, pointing each time a word is read. Be sure that each child receives a copy of what they have dictated and revisit the dictation, reading it on several occasions. Be sure to give them recognition so all children in your class see their efforts are valued.

Another way to provide more support during dictations is to jointly create a version of a predictable, familiar story. For example, after they become familiar with the book *Brown Bear, Brown Bear, What Do You See* (Martin, 1996), you could create their version of the story book by substituting the names of other animals. To start this process, you may need to provide some of the text and then ask children to suggest words to finish the storyline. You can also support children by involving them in illustrating their individually dictated texts, as well as participating in the illustration of your whole class dictated story books.

As children show interest or as special occasions arise, take time to engage them in dictating greeting cards or notes home. Then encourage them to add their own writing or illustrations. Be sure to let them pick the type of paper and format as well as decide on other embellishments to add to their greetings or notes.

Another way of providing additional support is to reread a group dictated story with a small group of children or one-on-one. As you begin this rereading, remind them what the story was about: This will activate their prior knowledge and support them as they engage in the rereading. Introduce this activity by having them echo-read each sentence or text segment. With additional repetitions, they will be able to read along in unison with you. Continue to point to the print as you read.

Additional support for children's participation in dictated stories and informational texts can be provided by making the topic of the dictation a real object, artifact, picture, or photo related to a prior experience they have had. Before starting the dictation process, engage the child (or children) in talking about the object or photo, describing it and talking about its purpose or their experiences. Then begin the dictation process. By building this contextual support, children's prior knowledge is activated and the dictation process will be facilitated.

Word Study

The goal of word study activities is to develop children's decoding and word recognition competencies so that they gradually develop fluent, conventional reading. Word study involves a direct instructional focus on the features of words. It can be conducted in large group or small group settings; however, small groups will probably be more beneficial because you can better target your instruction to meet the needs of each child and provide more opportunities for each child to participate.

Enhancing metalinguistic knowledge. Word study activities encourage the development of metalinguistic knowledge because the focus is on specific language concepts, such as beginning and ending sounds, letters, sound similarities (rhyming and alliteration), words, and word families. As children participate in word study activities, they are also encouraged to learn the appropriate terminology for the language concepts.

Enhancing phonetic awareness and focus on print. Children's phonetic awareness can be enhanced by engaging them in word study activities (Adams, Foorman, Lundberg, & Beeler, 1998; Johnston, Bear, Invernizzi, & Templeton, 2004). In planning to implement this strategy, you will first select a group of words to be the focus of your lesson. Choose words that have some common features, either in letter–sound relationships or spelling patterns. For example, you might select a word family, such as the -at family. Using word cards and a pocket chart (see Figure 9.9), draw children's attention to the -at pattern in the words as well as the initial consonant letter. Introduce each card separately, putting up the card into the pocket chart and then reading it. When you have introduced all of the cards, read the words aloud again and encourage children to echo-read or read with you.

You can also use word families to encourage children to learn how to separate and substitute sounds. For this you will need a card with the word-family ending, such as -at, along with individual cards for the initial consonant sounds, such as m- and b-. Using your pocket chart, demonstrate how to change the beginning letter to make different words.

Word study can also contribute to children's sight vocabulary. One activity is to use sentence strips from a familiar story or from one of the class' dictated stories (Lenters, 2003).

Figure 9.9 Pocket Chart with Activity on -at Word Family

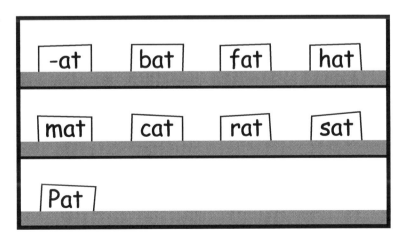

Word study involves a direct instructional focus on the features of words.

Monkey Business Images

Cut up the strips, separating the words. Then focus on each word, identifying the initial sounds represented in the words. Some children may recognize the high-frequency words without effortful decoding. Then have children reassemble the sentences by putting the words in order. As children further develop their sight vocabulary, they will gain confidence in reading as well as fluency.

Using word walls to support word study. Word study activities are frequently supported by a visual display of selected words on a classroom wall or large poster. Each word is written on a separate card and attached to the display by tape or Velcro. The words are grouped alphabetically or by some other categorization, such as word family. Be sure the chart is at a height where children can easily read it and that the words are legible from a distance. Throughout the year, your word wall will reflect your varied word study activities.

Word walls are also used to encourage children to recognize high-frequency words without effortful decoding. **High-frequency words** are those words that appear repeatedly in most texts. For children to become fluent readers, they need to develop a **sight vocabulary** of words that they recognize immediately without effortful letter–sound decoding.

You can provide support for children's developing sight vocabulary in kindergarten by focusing on high-frequency words. For example, *all, to, at, and, the,* and *go* are high-frequency words. Pinnell and Fountas (1998, p. 89; in Tompkins, 2003, p. 148) list the following 24 words that kindergartners need to be able to recognize:

a	at	he	it	no	the
am	can	I	like	see	to
an	do	in	me	she	up
and	go	is	my	so	we

By learning to recognize high-frequency words, children are able to read and write more fluently. Many high-frequency words are difficult to decode because they may have irregular letter–sound relationships (such as the phonemes in *to* and *go,* which differ although the spelling pattern is similar). Many of the high-frequency words are function

To encourage children's acquisition of a sight vocabulary, post high-frequency words on a 'word wall.'

Kathleen Lyons

words (such as conjunctions, prepositions, pronouns, and prepositions), and therefore have meanings that are more difficult to define because their meanings derive from the way in which they are used in sentences.

In addition to providing a visual display of high-frequency words, you can also draw attention to them as you read big books, and engage in dictated stories and interactive writing with your kindergartners.

Providing extra support during word study. When children who are English language learners are developing phonetic awareness of English, there may be instances where the letter–sound relationships in English are confusingly different from their home language. For example, in Spanish the letter J is associated with a sound much different from the letter J in English, such as *Juan* as compared to *John*. In addition, all vowels in Spanish are short sounds, while in English vowels are usually categorized as being either short or long. Thus, ELLs may need additional support in developing phonetic awareness of English. This additional support can be provided by you, your aide, or a classroom volunteer in small group and individual settings. In these settings, ELLs have more opportunity to participate and experience reinforcement of the earlier large group lessons. Specifically, you will want to provide opportunity for repeating word study and word recognition activities that were first experienced in a larger group setting.

Re-Enactment of Children's Stories

When children have participated in creating a dictated/language experience story as part of a group or if they have individually dictated a story, you may decide to encourage them to act out their story. Their stories will come to life as they take on specific roles and create dialogue to accompany their actions (Paley, 1999). In acting out their stories they also will be recalling the sequence of events. As their teacher, you can support their re-enactments by providing linguistic scaffolding and narration.

Enhancing oral language. This dramatization provides children with valuable opportunity to use language and actions to communicate their stories to others. Expect children's story re-enactments to take time to develop because their re-enactment may involve more elaboration than their dictated or written story.

Enhancing reading and writing for personal purposes. Because children are acting out stories that they have created, it validates their perspectives and experiences. By providing repeated opportunities and welcoming their personal stories, children's literacy development is enhanced.

Show and Tell

During show and tell time, children take turns talking in front of the class about an object they want to share. Because kindergartners' attention spans may be relatively short, most teachers find it is better to have only three to five children take their turns each day.

Enhancing language development. You will use linguistic scaffolding to support children's participation by asking questions, using expansion, and commenting as they talk about their object. As you are conducting the show and tell, you will want to observe the ways in which the speakers use their oral language, as well as observe the listening skills of those in the audience.

Providing extra support for show-and-tell. You can encourage children's participation in show-and-tell by increasing your linguistic scaffolding. In addition, you (or your teaching aide) could meet individually with children prior to the show-and-tell, to talk about the object they have brought to share. This would support their participation in the subsequent group setting.

Author's Chair

The author's chair activity resembles show and tell because individual children share their stories and other writing at group time. To make this event special, designate a specific child-sized chair as the "author's chair," attaching a decorated sign and perhaps providing a soft cushion. Place this chair next to yours in front of the group. This provides proximity support to the young author and allows you to be near if you need to provide linguistic scaffolding or help hold the child's story while they read it or talk about the illustrations. The author's chair activity is voluntary and is scheduled when specific children request the opportunity.

Enhancing writing for personal purposes. The author's chair activity encourages children to share their writing and supports their writing for personal purposes. Regardless of the form of emergent writing they have used, children can talk about what they have created and what it "says."

Providing extra support in author's chair activities. Some children may appear interested in sharing what they have written, but become speechless in front of the class. You can provide support by using linguistic scaffolding and giving basic prompts such as: Tell us about your story/pictures. What is happening on this page? Regardless of the length of a child's verbal sharing, be sure to thank them for sharing their story.

Putting It All Together

The activities and strategies described in this chapter focused on developing kindergarten children's emergent literacy in six key areas: oral language, interest in literacy, reading and writing for personal purposes, focus on print, metalinguistic knowledge, and phonological and phonetic awareness. Both independent and teacher-guided activities can be implemented in ways that enhance children's literacy development. As a reflective kindergarten teacher, your focus will be on using your professional knowledge to select the activities that are developmentally appropriate for the children in your classroom. Figure 9.10

Figure 9.10 Putting It All Together: Key Areas of Emergent Literacy with Related Strategies and Activities

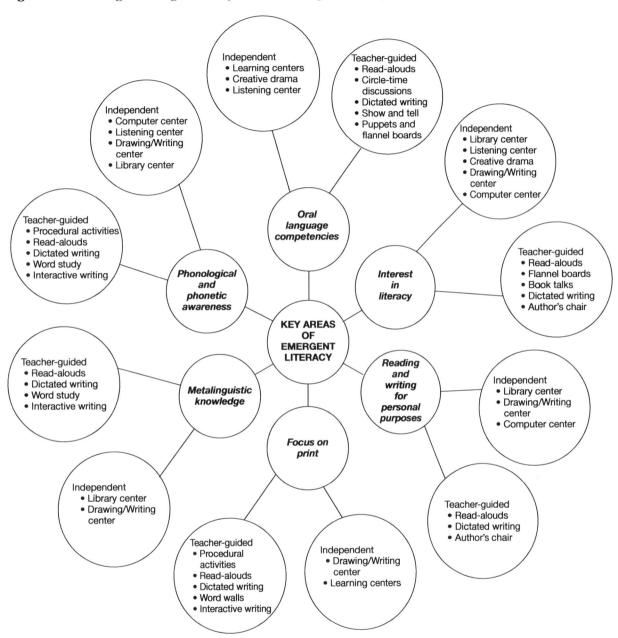

provides an overview of the six key areas of emergent literacy and the various independent and teacher-guided activities that enhance development in each area.

Assessments

Assessing student progress is an important part of your teaching because it provides awareness of children's growth and development. Chapter 8 included several informal observation formats for assessing kindergartners' emergent literacy (see Figures 8.4–8.9). In contrast to the observation formats provided in Chapter 8, the assessments described in this section focus on specific aspects of the reading process and are administered to children individually. The first two assessments, Clay's Observation Survey (1993) and Sulzby's Story book Reading Classification Scheme (1985, 1991) provide a comprehensive assessment of children's literacy interactions. The remaining two, the Yopp-Singer Test of Phonemic Awareness (1995b) and the Dynamic Indicators of Basic Early Literacy Skills/DIBELS (2001) focus on children's phonemic and phonetic awareness during decoding. An overview of each of these assessments follows. In order to appropriately use these assessments, you will need to obtain the original author's work and become thoroughly familiar with the guidelines for using each assessment.

Comprehensive Assessments

Clay's Observation Survey. Marie Clay's Observation Survey of Early Literacy Development (1993) is comprised of several assessments that are useful to kindergarten teachers as they document children's literacy development. In addition to providing guidelines for making systematic observations, Clay describes other assessment tasks. These include letter identification, concepts about print, word tests (for reading high-frequency words), collecting and analyzing a writing sample, and a dictation task. Clay also provides specific directions for administering, scoring, and interpreting each assessment.

Sulzby's Story Book Reading Classification Scheme. Elizabeth Sulzby (1985, 1991) developed a way of assessing children's emergent literacy through observing their independent interactions with familiar story books (refer back to Table 6.2). The assessment instrument is a set of descriptions of eleven subcategories, beginning with picture-governed attempts in which the child labels and comments on the pictures. The highest category describes children reading independently from print. Kindergarten teachers will find this classification scheme useful in describing how children interact independently with story books and documenting how their interactions change over time.

Assessing Phonemic and Phonetic Awareness

The Yopp-Singer Test of Phonemic Awareness. Assessment of children's ability to separate and articulate the sounds of a word in order is the focus of the Yopp-Singer Test of Phonemic Awareness (1995b). It is administered individually and usually takes around five to ten minutes; however, there is no time limit. The test was designed to be used with kindergartners and older children who are not yet reading. In the test, children are asked to break apart the word by its sounds and say each sound at a time in sequence. For example, the correct response for the word *cat* is /k/ /a/ /t/.

The 22-item test includes words that vary in the number of phonemes and words that have **consonant digraphs** and **consonant blends**. No credit is given if a child gives the letter name instead of the sound (phoneme). Research using this instrument has indicated that children's scores on the test were associated with reading and spelling achievement in future grades; however, it is important to remember that phonemic awareness is just one part of the reading process.

Dynamic Indicators of Basic Early Literacy Skills/DIBELS. This is a measure of early literacy skills that is designed to be used with grades K–3. It assesses children's fluency in five areas (Good, Kaminski, Simmons, & Kame'enui, 2001; additional information and assessment materials are available from http://dibels.uoregon.edu/). The areas of the assessment include: recognizing initial sounds in orally presented words, segmenting phonemes in words containing three to four phonemes, decoding nonsense words, and naming letters. Fluency is defined in this assessment as the rapidity of children's responses in each area. Scores in each area are represented in the number of correct responses that occurred during one minute. Thus, this set of assessments captures only what children are able to respond to in a timed setting. The Oral Reading Fluency test involves no assessment of comprehension.

While these two phonemic and phonetic assessments provide specific information about the way a child interacts with the targeted print found in each assessment, it is also important to remember that the narrow focus of such assessments may limit your understanding of a child's transactions with literacy (Goodman, 2006; Johnston & Costello, 2005).

Planning and Using Assessment Information

Throughout this text literacy has been described from a transactional perspective, involving interactions between a child's prior experiences and knowledge of language, the texts they encounter and the contexts in which those events take place. This perspective also is useful in deciding what assessments you will use and how this assessment information will influence your teaching. In making these decisions, you will find the following two questions helpful: What does this specific assessment tell me about this child's reading and writing strategies and knowledge? Where does this assessment information fit in the larger picture of becoming a reader and writer? Because reading and writing cannot be reduced to isolated, separate bits of knowledge or skill, it is important for your assessment plan to incorporate a wide variety of different types of assessments that sample children's literacy interactions. For example, to obtain a thorough understanding of children's literacy development you need to include both informal observations of children's transactions with different types of texts and in different contexts along with more specific, elicited assessments that focus on particular aspects of the reading process, such as letter–sound relationships.

After you have gathered information about your children's literacy development through the use of informal observations and specific, elicited assessments, the way in which you use this information to create an appropriate instructional environment will determine whether or not their literacy development will be enhanced.

For example, perhaps you find that several kindergartners are not yet associating letters with sounds, and then you decide that this means you should put them in a group for targeted, direct instruction using worksheets for 30 minutes a day. Because you have only so much time in your half-day kindergarten program, this small group instruction needs to take place as the other children in the room are engaged in independent activities at the various centers. As a result, the children in this grouping do not have any opportunity to participate in the independent learning centers.

In this situation, it is important to pause and consider the following question: How will this increased emphasis on a specific aspect of literacy fit into children's overall orientation to, and motivation for, reading and writing? Researchers have documented many instances where an emphasis on becoming proficient in a reading subskill does not result in increased comprehension or motivation to read (Flurkey, 2006; Goodman, 2006; Johnston & Costello, 2005; Tierney, 2006). As a kindergarten teacher you have a professional responsibility to plan, use, and interpret assessment information in a manner that enhances children's long-term transactions with literacy. Your goal is to support children's lifelong literacy.

Family Involvement in Kindergartners' Literacy Development

Kindergarten children's literacy development is further enhanced through the teacher's active connections with their families. These connections involve three separate aspects: welcoming families as partners in their child's education, encouraging literacy-related activities at home and in the community, and involving families in school and classroom events.

Welcoming Families as Partners

Children who come to your kindergarten classroom may represent a variety of home settings. It is likely that many will come from homes where both mother and father are present. It is also likely that some children will have families where only one parent is present. You may have children from homes where there are a number of brothers and sisters. Some homes will have extended family members who live in the home or who live close by and have an active role in the family's daily interactions. You may also have children who are living in foster homes or who have been recently adopted. Realizing this diversity in your children's family settings is important as you welcome each family to be partners in their kindergartner's education.

Family involvement in children's literacy-related experiences has a positive effect on their development of reading and writing (Come & Fredericks, 1995; Darling & Westberg, 2004; Purcell-Gates, 1996; Sénéchal & LeFevre, 2002). While this is important for all children in your kindergarten, it is especially important for children who are ELLs as well as other children who may not have had many literacy-related experiences prior to entering your classroom (Burningham & Dever, 2005; Come & Fredericks, 1995; Purcell-Gates, 1996).

As you start your school year, you will want to begin establishing this partnership. You can do this by communicating with family members as they bring their child to school and pick them up after school. Use this time for communicating to briefly share news of classroom activities as well as to learn about home and community experiences. Most schools have an open house during the first month or so each school year. During this time, you can talk with parents and other family members about your classroom literacy activities as well as encourage them to talk about the literacy-related events that occur at home or in their communities. As you listen to parents and family members as they share information

Encourage emergent readers to share their story books with younger family members.

Marcel Mooij

about their kindergartners' experiences and interests, you will be communicating your sincere interest in partnering with them in developing their kindergartners' literacy.

This sharing of information also validates and recognizes children's prior knowledge and experiences as they enter your classroom. It provides you with information about each child's prior transactions with literacy-related events in different contexts. Throughout the kindergarten year, you will want to work to keep the lines of communication open and positively focused on children's development of literacy. Family members can be a valuable resource for information throughout the year as they observe their kindergartner's growth toward becoming a reader and writer.

Encouraging Literacy-Related Activities at Home and in the Community

Kindergartners who have frequent opportunities to engage in literacy-related activities at home and in the community experience greater growth in literacy development (Come & Fredericks, 1995; Jordan, Snow, & Porche, 2000; Purcell-Gates, 1996; Purcell-Gates, L'Allier, & Smith, 1995). You can encourage and support increased reading and writing activities at home by communicating with family members about the types of activities that are beneficial as well as how to engage the young reader and writer in these activities. This communication can occur as you meet with family members and through the periodic newsletters that you send home. Be careful to introduce these activities over several months to avoid overwhelming parents and family members. Instead, you want to gradually encourage families to integrate these activities throughout the year. Even if just one or two activities are integrated into their family's activities, their children will benefit.

By encouraging the following activities and interactions, you can help parents and family members understand the importance of home and community literacy-related activities:

Dinnertime and travel-time conversations. Family conversations that include kindergartners are great opportunities for oral language development and vocabulary enrichment. At dinnertime these conversations may include narratives about the events of the day. Travel-time conversations can focus on events and experiences children have as they ride in a car, bus, or train, or walk with family members.

Shared reading. It is important to emphasize that books can be shared in a number of ways—by looking at the pictures and talking about what is happening in the story, by making up a story to go with the pictures, and by reading part or all of the text. Encourage family members to focus on the meaningful aspect of the book. Also emphasize the importance of encouraging children to participate in reading familiar books by anticipating upcoming text, telling their own version of a story book, recalling specific story events, or echo-reading (Elster, 1994b).

You can encourage children and parents to keep a reading log that records the books shared as well as the dates they were shared (see Figure 9.11). Suggest that parents encourage children to write down the name of the book on the reading log so that children take an active role in recording their reading. Avoid prescribing the number of books to be shared or awarding a prize for the most books read. Instead, encourage parents to use the log as a way of helping their children remember which books have been shared.

Facilitating access to books at home. You can increase children's access to books through a book-lending program in your classroom. By encouraging children to check-out books so that they have them over the weekend you are increasing the chances that the books will be read, because families may have more time than during the work week (Giambo & Szecsi, 2005). You can also provide families with information about the local library, such as how to

Figure 9.11 Sample Kindergarten Reading Log

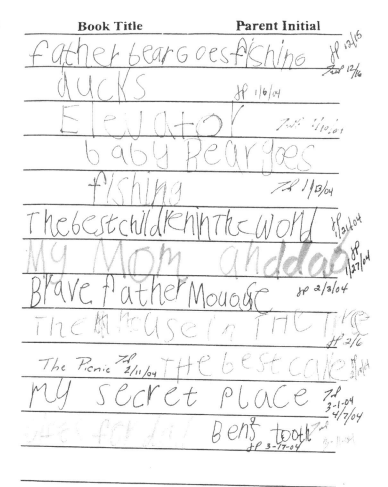

Book Title	Parent Initial
father bear Goes fishing	JP 12/15 / 2nd 12/16
ducks	JP 1/6/04
Elevator	2nd 1/10/04
baby bear goes fishing	2nd 1/13/04
The best children in the world	JP 1/24/04
My Mom and dad	JP 1/27/04
Brave father Mouoge	JP 2/3/04
The Mouse in The Tre	JP 2/6
The Picnic 2nd 2/11/04 The best cake	JP 2/?/04
My secret place	2nd 3-1-04 4/7/04
Ben's tooth	JP 3-17-04 / 2nd 3-11-04

obtain a library card, along with the location and hours the library is open and special library events for children. Families will also appreciate information about school or community book sales, garage sales, or resale shops where gently used children's books can be obtained.

In addition to the shared reading of children's books, families can encourage their kindergartners to participate in reading other types of texts at home, such as recipe books, instructions, newspapers, advertisements, and religious materials.

Participation in community events. Kindergartners will also benefit from participating with their families in community programs and events. These include attending museums and historic sites, as well as hands-on programs available at local parks and nature centers. Children also benefit from participating in sports programs. Each of these activities provides experiences and social interactions that support the development of conceptual knowledge and vocabulary. In addition, these experiences enhance oral language competencies involved in listening and speaking.

Reading in the community. Family members can also encourage kindergartners' literacy development by engaging them in reading and understanding environmental print in their community. This could include traffic signs, storefront signs, billboards, as well as print that is used at the post office, grocery store, restaurants, and other businesses, and during religious services.

Shared writing. Family members can encourage kindergartners' literacy development by including them in writing activities at home. You will want to emphasize the importance of accepting children's writing "any way they want to write" as beneficial to their developing knowledge of written language (Dailey, 1991). Including children in the preparation and sending of greeting cards, letters, and email, as well as communication with family members through notes and signs posted on the family bulletin board, helps children understand the varied purposes of written language. Children's writing at home can be further encouraged when children have their own supply of writing materials that is kept in a special place. This could be a designated drawer in the kitchen, in their room, or perhaps a clear plastic box.

As you encourage family members to include their kindergartners in these activities at home and in the community, it is important to welcome family members' observations, comments, and questions about kindergartners' participation in these literacy-related activities. You want to be sure that they understand that it is not necessary to buy a workbook on phonics or to insist that the child practice reading aloud every night in order to encourage literacy development. Sharing literacy with their kindergartner can encompass many different activities that will fit easily into their family interactions and events.

Involving Families in School and Classroom Events

In addition to encouraging your children's family members to attend open house, holiday programs, and individual conferences, you can provide opportunities for them to participate in your classroom. As you become acquainted with each family, you may find that family members have special hobbies or talents they can share with your class. They may also be able to volunteer to work with individuals or pairs of children for book sharing or story dictation. Parents of ELLs can share with your class the common greetings of their home language, such as hello, good-bye, please, and thank you.

Chapter Summary

Kindergarten is characterized by two major changes in children's educational setting: (a) Children are in a more structured school setting for a longer amount of time and (b) the kindergarten curriculum is focused on preparing children to meet specific expectations prior to first grade. In planning curriculum, kindergarten teachers need to know which strategies and activities will be developmentally appropriate as well as understand how those activities and strategies enhance children's literacy development and meet children's individual needs. Key areas for a literacy curriculum in kindergarten include: oral language development, interest in literacy, reading and writing for personal purposes, focus on print, metalinguistic knowledge, and phonological and phonetic awareness.

Assessing student progress is an important part of teaching because it provides awareness of children's growth and development, and informs curricular planning. By combining informal assessment with more focused, elicited assessments, a comprehensive understanding of children's development is obtained.

Kindergarten children's literacy development is further enhanced by establishing active connections with their families. These connections can be established by welcoming families as partners in their child's education, encouraging literacy-related activities at home and in the community, and involving families in school and classroom events.

Chapter Review

1. Terms to know:

    interactive writing   consonant digraphs

    high-frequency words   consonant blends

    sight vocabulary

2. Why is informal assessment an important part of a kindergarten teacher's curriculum planning as she starts the school year?

3. Why are oral language activities part of a kindergarten literacy curriculum?

4. Describe two activities that can enhance children's interest in literacy. Explain how these activities would be implemented.

5. Describe how you will support ELLs in their reading and writing for personal purposes.

6. Distinguish the differences between story dictation and interactive writing. Explain how each enhances literacy development.

7. In what ways can the attendance-taking process be used to enhance literacy development?

8. Why do children need to develop metalinguistic knowledge?

9. Distinguish between phonological awareness and phonetic awareness. Give an example of an activity for enhancing each type of awareness.

10. Describe three ways kindergarten teachers can encourage families to support literacy development at home.

Chapter Extension Activities

Discussion: Assume that you are a first-year kindergarten teacher and you are welcoming parents to your fall term's open house. You are approached by one parent who asks you why you have so many "play centers" when children need to be learning how to read and write. Describe how you will respond to this parent's concern.

Curriculum Development:

1. Select one of the books listed in Appendix F. Prepare a "book talk" presentation to your college/university class that describes the way in which you would use this book. Use one of the lesson-plan formats provided in Appendix K. Be sure to identify the vocabulary you will emphasize and demonstrate how you will introduce this book and begin reading it to a group of kindergartners. Present your lesson in a kindergarten setting or in your college classroom. Conclude this assignment with a reflective evaluation of your teaching.

2. Develop a lesson plan for reading aloud either a story book or a Big Book. Use one of the lesson-plan formats provided in Appendix K. Present your lesson in a kindergarten setting or in your college classroom. Conclude this assignment with a reflective evaluation of your teaching.

Research: Locate the original source for one of the assessments previewed in this chapter. Thoroughly review the procedures and then administer this assessment to a kindergarten-age child. Submit a written summary of the assessment results and prepare a short presentation for your college or university class.

Chapter 10

Literacy Instruction in First Grade: Becoming an Independent Reader and Writer

> The school bell has just rung to start another day. One by one, Ms. Wetter's 22 first-graders arrive in her classroom. She greets each child as she or he walks in. After they have taken their seats, she again says "Good morning," and then points to the morning message that is written on the chalkboard. It reads,
> "Today is Tuesday. We have gym class today."

Like Ms. Wetter, many first-grade teachers start each day with a morning message activity; however, the way in which they each conduct the activity may differ. As earlier chapters have emphasized, instruction should be planned so that it will meet the specific needs of the children in our classrooms. Although we may use the same activities, the ways in which we use them will depend on our instructional goals, our understanding of students' developmental needs, and the instructional resources we have available. For example, the morning message activity could be used to focus on specific letter–sound relationships or development of sight vocabulary. If the morning message is written with missing words or letters, then students can be encouraged to figure out what is missing using clues and decoding strategies.

This chapter describes specific activities and strategies to support children's literacy development in first grade. First grade is the time when all children are expected to focus on print and begin to read conventionally. It is also the first time that many children will experience being in school for a full day.

Learner Characteristics

Literacy instruction needs to reflect the developmental levels of children in your classroom. You will need to become familiar with each child's level of oral language competency because oral language provides a foundation for literacy development. It is especially important for you to be aware of the oral language competencies of children who may be learning English as their second language.

Many children who come to first grade will have some basic understandings about reading and writing (Beach, 1996). They will have an awareness that words are made up of separate sounds. They may also be able to distinguish between words, letters, and sounds, and can focus on initial letters when trying to figure out a word. Some children will be able to recognize a number of conventional words, such as mom, dad, stop, and go. Not all children will be at the same phase of literacy development. You may find that some children have not yet developed phonemic awareness and are in an early phase of invented spelling. For this reason, you will need to carefully observe your first-graders during the initial weeks of school to determine which learning activities and teaching strategies will be appropriate.

Learning Contexts

The context of first grade is influenced by several factors. This is the first universally required grade of school attendance across the United States. For many children, this is the first experience of attending school all day. Compared to earlier school settings, there is greater emphasis on direct instruction, which requires children to listen and follow directions. Generally, there are fewer opportunities for the exploratory activities that were offered in preschool and kindergarten.

Emphasis on Learning Standards

The context of first grade is also influenced by the expectations for children's learning set forth in state- and district-level learning standards. To view your state's learning standards in reading/language arts, go online to http://www.education-world.com/standards/#state. These standards influence the type of commercial curriculum that are adopted by each school district as well as the other educational resources provided in your school.

The major expectation of children in first grade is that they begin to read and write conventionally. This means that they are expected to develop a sight vocabulary, as well as use phonetic knowledge in decoding words and in their writing. In many ways, this focus on literacy development dominates the first-grade curriculum.

When you begin your teaching position in first grade, you will be given the school-adopted literacy (reading/language arts) commercial curriculum. This will be the foundation of your instruction for children's literacy development; however, it is important to remember that it is not the method or curriculum itself that is the key to children's learning, but instead the ways in which you support and guide children's learning through reflective teaching that makes the difference (Duffy & Hoffman, 1999). In order to teach reflectively, you will be making decisions about how to use the curricular materials and educational resources at your school. It is important to evaluate these resources to determine how they will meet the needs of your students. In the section that follows, specific features of commercial literacy programs are described, as well as ways of looking at the additional literacy-related resources available at your school.

Commercial Literacy Programs

Throughout the past 50 years, commercial curricula for the teaching of reading and writing have been used as a main instructional resource in the elementary grades. During this time, these materials have gradually changed to reflect more current understandings and approaches to reading and writing instruction (Weaver, 2000). The term **basal reading program** has been used to refer to these commercial curricula, denoting their use as a "basic," or main, curriculum. While these basal reading programs previously focused only on reading, many of today's literacy curricula also incorporate listening, speaking, and writing activities. This is a reflection of the current understandings of the many facets of literacy and the interrelationships that exist.

During the past 15 years, the number and variety of instructional materials included in literacy programs have increased dramatically (Weaver, 2000). Where once a basal reading system was composed of students' readers, a teacher's manual, and a workbook, today's literacy programs comprise many different types of materials. These materials are organized around a scope and sequence of specific skills identified as appropriate to a particular grade level. Major publishers of today's basal systems have also developed their curricula to reflect state learning standards. The result is a highly organized, extensive collection of instructional materials for each grade level. The challenge for you is to understand how to select and use the various materials to enhance your students' literacy development. In most instances, there are far more materials and teaching activities than can be used in the time you will have allotted for reading/language-arts instruction. This is especially true if you want to be a reflective teacher, making your choices of materials and strategies to fit the needs of your students. While the large commercial curricular systems for reading and language arts may be designed to provide learning activities for a range of students, only you can decide what is appropriate for the students in your classroom.

In the section that follows, the typical materials included in commercial literacy programs for first-grade level are described. This will provide you with an overview of what you might find in a literacy program adopted by your school.

Main components of a literacy program. The three main components include: specially designed texts, student workbooks, and a teachers' edition/manual.

Specially designed texts. These reading texts are designed to represent specific reading levels. Often, such texts are referred to as **leveled texts**. This means that the "reading materials represent a progression from more simple to more complex and challenging texts" (Brabham & Villaume, 2002b, p. 438). The multiple levels reflect differences in vocabulary, size and layout of print, predictability, illustration support, and complexity of concepts (Rog & Burton, 2002). The very early levels have books with a limited vocabulary of high-frequency words, large print, a small amount of print on each page, predictable or patterned text, illustrations that directly support the text, and simple story lines or nonfiction concepts. Big book versions with leveled texts are included along with personal-sized small books. These leveled texts are to be used in a specific sequence with children based upon each child's level of reading development.

Some systems include **decodable readers**, which have texts composed of words with similar phonological patterns and frequent word repetition, for example, Dan ran to Nan. Dan and Nan ran to see the man. Additional texts which may be included are anthologies, or collections, of well-known stories that have been adapted for developing readers.

Student workbooks. These are paper-and-pencil activities that provide sequenced subskill practice that are coordinated with children's reading of specific stories/texts. Since children at this level learn best from hands-on, authentic literacy experiences, workbooks are best used selectively to provide additional practice. Overuse, such as requiring every sheet be completed, or using them as busy work to keep children working quietly at their desks, may not be beneficial to literacy development and may also decrease student motivation.

Teacher's manual. This contains daily, weekly, and unit lesson plans and directions for using the various materials included in the basal reading program. It usually incorporates a downsized version of children's texts along with margin notes of discussion questions or teaching strategies. Some teachers' manuals provide general guidelines, sequential outlines, or teaching ideas; others are more specific, and actually provide a word-by-word script that the teacher is expected to follow for each lesson.

Additional literacy program materials. A wide variety of additional instructional materials may be included, such as (a) entry, weekly, end of unit, and quarterly assessments; (b) instruction materials: charts, transparencies, and posters; (c) record-keeping forms; (d) additional skill activities using workbooks, card sets, and blackline masters; (e) activities targeted for students who are gifted, struggling, or English language learners, and (f) electronic (CD-ROM) or taped versions of stories/texts included in students' books, as well as additional skill-based activities. Some programs also provide online access to more student materials and teaching resources.

Additional School Resources

Along with becoming familiar with the literacy program adopted by your school, you will also want to become aware of the other school resources that will benefit your students' literacy development. Some of these resources will be located in your classroom. Others will be found in the school library or in schoolwide programs that support literacy.

Classroom library. Literacy-rich classrooms will have a library center or corner that is supplied with a wide range of fiction and nonfiction books in a variety of genres and multicultural titles. Age-appropriate children's magazines and comic books should also be included. This center should accommodate several children at a time in comfortable seating (for example, large pillows, bean-bag chairs). Books should be displayed in a way that encourages interest and accessibility. For example, group books by content and genre rather than alphabetically by author. Shelf labels and signs will help children find books as well as return them to the right location. Book storage bins that are labeled, as well as shelves containing pull-out bins add to the accessibility of books. A sample floor plan of a first-grade library center is shown in Figure 10.1. In Figure 10.2 an example of a user-friendly book display is pictured.

School library. Nearly every elementary school has its own library. In addition to becoming familiar with the depth and breadth of the library's collection of books for students at your grade level, you will want to become familiar with the ways in which your students can use the library. For example, how often will your class visit the library? Will your entire class go to the library at one time, or will smaller groups of children go on different occasions? How many books can each child check out? How long can they keep a book? Can they visit the library individually before or after school? Become familiar with the location of the books that are appropriate to your grade level and find out what assistance the school librarian will provide to children in locating a book. Will your school librarian assist you in locating specific books to enhance your classroom activities? Can you borrow books from the school library to add to your classroom library? What audiovisual and computer resources are available in the library, and which ones can be used in your classroom? Is there support staff to assist you in using computer software in your classroom? All of these considerations will influence your use of the school library as a support for your students' literacy development.

Figure 10.1 Sample Floor Plan of a First-Grade Library Center

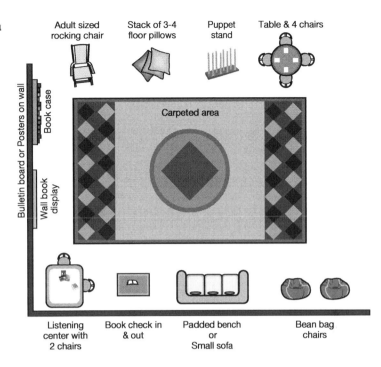

Adult sized rocking chair

Stack of 3-4 floor pillows

Puppet stand

Table & 4 chairs

Bulletin board or Posters on wall

Book case

Wall book display

Carpeted area

Listening center with 2 chairs

Book check in & out

Padded bench or Small sofa

Bean bag chairs

Figure 10.2 Example of a User-Friendly Book Display for First Grade

Schoolwide literacy support. Additional resources to support your students' literacy development may be found in schoolwide programs and policies. For example, is there a reading motivation program in your school? Are book fairs held with a wide variety of low-cost books available? How many field trips are part of each grade-level's curriculum? Is there a lending program with the local public library? Does the school have a parent–teacher organization? What parent–school events are typically held? What procedures are followed for scheduling guest speakers and parent/community classroom volunteers? In asking these questions, you will become aware of the additional avenues of support for your students' literacy development.

Key Areas of Literacy Instruction in First Grade

As you become familiar with your school's literacy curriculum and the other resources that are available, you will want to keep your focus on providing learning activities and instruction that center on five key areas (National Reading Panel, 2000; Center for the Improvement of Early Reading, 2001). These areas include: (a) Phonological awareness, (b) phonetic awareness, (c) comprehension of vocabulary, (d) comprehension of text, and (e) fluency in oral reading and independent silent reading. Phonological awareness and phonetic awareness receive more emphasis in first grade than in later grades. This, however, does not mean that the other areas are not emphasized. It is important to remember that comprehension or sense-making is also a big part of literacy. Phonological and phonetic awareness are important, but they are only important as they contribute to the larger processes of reading and writing. In the next section, learning activities and teaching strategies are described that will enhance children's literacy development in each of these five areas.

Learning Activities and Teaching Strategies

General Guidelines

Expect to use a variety of activities and strategies. Because the children in your first-grade classroom will vary in their literacy development, there is no magic set of activities or instructional method that will guarantee that every child will develop literacy (Bucar, 2002). With each year's class and within each class you teach, you will find that some strategies and activities are more beneficial than others. This awareness informs your reflective teaching. You make decisions about the learning activities and teaching strategies based upon your knowledge of your students and their developmental levels. This means that you will consider your commercial literacy program as a resource rather than the only determinant of your curriculum.

Plan to use different-sized student groupings. Literacy develops through social interactions as well as through adult/teacher mediation and support. For this reason you will want to use a variety of groupings so that students can experience different types of social interaction. This means that you will have times when you engage the whole class in a literacy activity, such as a teacher read-aloud or dictated story. At other times, you may work with a small group of five to seven students. Students may also partner with each other for selected activities. There will be other activities that are individual and independent.

Keep literacy and language connected. Literacy development involves six different facets of language use: listening, speaking, reading, writing, viewing, and visually creating. (See Figure 10.3.) In the course of literacy development, each of these facets plays a part. For example, listening is an important part of the social interactions children have with adults and peers in literacy-related events. In fact, children spend more time listening than they do in any other classroom activity (Jalongo, 1995).

Children's speaking skills also are involved in literacy as they respond to teachers' questions, ask their own questions, and make comments about their literacy transactions.

Figure 10.3 Facets of Literacy Development

	Receptive Language	Expressive Language
Oral Language	Listening	Speaking
Written Language	Reading	Writing
Visual Language	Viewing	Visually Creating

Children's viewing of illustrations in story books also contributes to comprehension of text in their early literacy transactions. Their early writing is often accompanied by drawing and illustrations that add to the meaning of their stories. When teachers welcome children's emergent writing, they encourage children to actively use their language knowledge to communicate. When only reading is emphasized, children may remain passive learners. According to Elbow (2004), "Reading tends to imply, 'sit still and pay attention,' whereas writing tends to imply, 'get in there and *do* something'" (p. 199). When all facets of literacy are recognized and incorporated into your classroom, children will become more active learners.

Practice reflective teaching. As a reflective decision-maker, you will be engaging in active listening and observation of your students as they become involved in your literacy curriculum. You will then use this knowledge to make decisions about which activities and strategies will meet their individual developmental needs. Many of these activities and strategies can be found in the various commercial literacy curricula. By focusing on the six facets of literacy and the five key areas of literacy instruction, you will have a strong foundation for enhancing first graders' literacy development.

Phonological Awareness Instruction

Many children will have developed phonological awareness before they come to first grade. This means that they will be aware that oral words are composed of separate sounds. Since phonological awareness is a precursor to developing knowledge of letter–sound relationships, it is beneficial to start first grade with activities that focus on phonological awareness so that you can identify children who need further experiences. Children who have not developed this awareness will have a more difficult time learning letter–sound relationships (that is, phonetic awareness).

Phonological units: Segments of sound. The development of phonological awareness involves this progression of sound awareness: rhyme, syllable units, onset-rime, and phonemes (Yopp & Yopp, 2000). In observing this progress, you would first want to focus on rhyme awareness, and then move to syllables, onset-rimes, and then phonemes. In this way, you are proceeding from the larger units of sound to the smaller units.

When focusing on words that rhyme, it is important to remember that the emphasis is on the sounds of words, not the spelling patterns. Words that rhyme have the same ending sound but may not have the same spelling. Phonological awareness is not concerned with the spelling of the words, just the sounds of the words. For example, *cuff* and *tough* have the same ending sound, but are not spelled the same.

Syllables are segments of words that influence the way a word is pronounced. Some words have one syllable, such as cat; other words have several syllables, such as *happiness* (3 syllables), *picnic* (2 syllables), *beneficial* (4 syllables). *Onset* refers to the initial consonant or consonant blend in a syllable and **rime** refers to the first vowel in a syllable and the remaining consonants in the syllable. For example, in *cat,* c is the onset and -at is the rime; in *train*, tr is the onset and -ain is the rime. Words with the same rime are in the same **word family**, for example, cat, rat, fat, sat, mat, pat, and hat. A **phoneme** is the individual sound in a word. For example, *cat* has three phonemes, /k/ /a/ /t/.

Enhancing phonological awareness. Phonological awareness can be enhanced during teacher read-aloud when you select books with texts that rhyme or have alliteration (Yopp & Yopp, 2000; see also examples of books in Appendix H). First, share the book by reading the text without focusing explicitly on the rhyming or alliteration. When you read the book again, begin to point out the sound similarities in the words. If you are focusing on rhyming, this means that you will draw children's attention to words that end in the same sound, such as rake, cake, bake, snake. If you are focusing on alliteration, this means that you will draw children's attention to words in the text that begin with the same sounds, such as the /b/ words in the following sentence: The busy bunnies wore beautiful bonnets to the beach and carried baskets of buttered bread.

It is important that children be actively involved in identifying words that have similar sounds, such as rhyming or alliteration. You can encourage children's participation by pausing before a rhyming word to let them fill in the missing word or to suggest another rhyming word.

It is also important to start with the phonological tasks that are easier. For example, children will find it easier to first match sounds than they will to segment or delete sounds from a word (Yopp & Yopp, 2000). For example, asking them whether *kite* and *car* start with the same sound will be an easier task than separating the /k/ sound from the word *kite*.

Phonological awareness activities involve only the oral sounds of words. When printed words are used along with a focus on the sounds in words, the activity then becomes a phonetic awareness activity. For some children, this addition of the visual letters to a focus on sound similarities contributes to their understanding of how speech is represented in print.

Phonetic Awareness Instruction

The goal of phonetic awareness instruction is to provide children with the knowledge and strategies they need to be able to accurately recognize (or decode) words when reading. The teaching of phonics has probably been the most controversial aspect of literacy instruction. Over the years, there have been varied approaches to teaching children the relationships between letters and sounds (Mesmer & Griffith, 2005; Stahl, Duffy-Hester, & Stahl, 1998). Today there are different opinions about how much phonics instruction is needed and what types of learning tasks are most beneficial.

Principles of good phonics instruction. Based on their review of research, Stahl, Duffy-Hester, and Stahl (1998) offer these seven principles of good phonics instruction:

1. Phonological awareness should be developed before instruction focuses on letter–sound relations.
2. Phonics instruction should develop an understanding that letters represent sounds.
3. Phonics instruction should develop a thorough knowledge of the letters by name and identifying both upper- and lower-case.
4. Good phonics instruction is embedded in direct instruction while reading connected texts, rather than in worksheets.
5. Good phonics instruction involves practice reading words in isolation and in stories as well as practice in writing words through dictation or by invented spelling.

6. Good phonics instruction results in automatic word recognition.
7. Phonics instruction is only one part of a literacy program.

Enhancing phonetic awareness. In this section three basic ways of focusing on letter–sound relationships or phonetic awareness will be described. These include (a) guided reading, (b) guided word study, and (c) interactive writing.

Guided reading. Guided reading takes place in a small group format with children who are similar in reading ability and their teacher. The texts used are "leveled" for the ability group. Sometimes these texts are in big book format, but more often each child has her own copy of the story text. The teacher provides scaffolding and mediation to facilitate children's decoding of print. As children attempt to read and come to a word they do not recognize, the teacher's scaffolding and mediation provide guidance so children are able to develop word recognition skills in decoding text. This is where the teacher can anchor word study in meaning (see Juel & Deffes, 2003–2004).

In the example that follows, Juan's teacher, Linda, provides mediation and scaffolding that supports his oral reading (Cole, 2006, p. 450):

> In Linda's first-grade classroom, Juan, a novice reader, decodes a short sentence below a picture in the book he is holding. Just as Juan stumbles on the word *running*, his teacher leans forward to mask the *-ing* with her thumb while prompting, "what's this part?" Juan produces the initial sound /r/ and then stops. "Good start," praises Linda, but she immediately redirects Juan's focus to a picture cue by tapping the image of a boy running. Juan looks up and smiles. "Running!" he responds. Before his success can sidetrack him, Linda moves her finger to the beginning of the sentence, cueing Juan to reread. The novice follows that silent prompt, and this time independently decodes the word *running* and reads on.

In this example, Linda first focused Juan's attention on the initial letter of the word, and then directed him to look at the accompanying illustration. Thus, she used two different cues, a phonetic cue for the initial sound of the word and a semantic (meaning) cue from the accompanying illustration. If instead of giving a meaning cue, she had insisted

During guided reading, teachers focus on observing and supporting children's interactions with print.

that Juan continue to "sound out" each part of the word and then blend the sounds together, it would have probably resulted in less success in recognizing the word.

By using multiple cues in the scaffolding, children are encouraged to see reading as a meaning-making process rather than just "sounding out" words based on letter–sound relations (Goodman, 1993). This emphasis on sense-making in teachers' scaffolding encourages children to monitor their reading so that what they read they also understand.

While there are no set steps for teachers to follow to help young readers when they stumble on a word, cues that focus on letter–sound relations, word parts, or meaning appear to be more immediately useful than asking the young reader to recall a long-past experience or an abstract phonics "rule" (Cole, 2006). The longer the interruption in a child's reading due to difficulty in recognizing a word, the more interruption there is in the comprehension of what they are reading, and the longer it takes to put him or her back "on track" in oral reading. Thus, you will want to use cues that are immediately helpful in moving the child along, as well as helping him or her develop strategies for figuring out unknown words. The scaffolding you will use will vary depending upon the children you are reading with, the texts they are reading, and the words with which they have difficulty. In most instances, you will not know what words will be difficult until your students are actually attempting to read them. At this point, you will develop your scaffolding "on the spot." Your knowledge of the child's prior experiences, his oral vocabulary, and your analysis of a word's specific features will be the basis for the cues you give the reader.

Guided word study. Instruction in letter–sound relationships also takes place during guided word study. This means that there is direct instruction on letter–sound relationships. This may involve working with a small group of students or it may involve the entire class working individually or in pairs. If you work with a small group of students, then you can design the activities to fit the knowledge level of the students. There are many different activities that can be used for word study (see further Johnston, Bear, Invernizzi, & Templeton, 2004).

In word study activities, a group of words is first identified that has specific linguistic features, such as the same initial letter-sound, as in *car, cat, cape, corn*, and *cup*. The activity focuses on that similar linguistic feature in the group of words so that children can learn to recognize the words based on their linguistic features.

Word-building activities focus on rimes and syllables in high-frequency words (Gunning, 1995), and build on children's oral vocabulary of high-frequency words. For example, if you were focusing on the -at rime, you might sequence the lesson as follows:

1. Write -at on the board.
2. After you have students read this, ask them what letter would need to be added to -at to create the word *sat*.
3. Then you would proceed to have them also decide what beginning letters are needed to form other words in the same word family, such as rat, mat, fat, and cat.
4. You can also call attention to the individual sounds in the -at rime and the letter representing the sound.

Different variations of this activity involve using flip charts with the onset and rime on different card sections or using a pocket chart to hold individual onset and rime cards. Students can use card sets at their desk or can write the words on paper or individual chalkboards.

Be sure to provide opportunities for children to read text that has words from the word families they have studied. For example, after focusing on the -at word family, you could read *Cat on the Mat* (Wildsmith, 1982).

Students can use card sets at their desks, arranging words in columns to match the rime category.

Beverly Otto

Some word families represent more complex phonetic knowledge, such as onsets and rimes in words that contain blends (such as *gr* in *great*) and digraphs (two letters having one sound, such as *ph* in *phone*). This means you will want to first focus on word families that are less complex and gradually build up to the more complex onset and rime combinations (Johnston, 1999).

After your students have developed knowledge of word families, you can extend this experience by focusing on more complex word building in a gamelike format (Aiken & Bayer, 2002; Cunningham & Cunningham, 1992). In preparation for this activity, you will need to select a word from their reading text to use as a basis for the word building. Then prepare a separate set of letter cards for each child (or pair of children) based on that word. For example, if your students were reading *The Berenstain Bears We Like Kites* (Berenstain & Berenstain, 2004) story book, you might select the word *string* as your base word and then prepare a set of letter cards for s, t, r, i, n, and g. You will also need a larger set of letter cards for use in front of the class (in a pocket chart or on the ledge of the chalkboard). Then you would introduce the activity in this way:

1. Display your letter cards in random fashion and ask the students to display all of their letter cards in a horizontal line on their desks.
2. Review the letter names and the sounds usually associated with each letter.
3. Start word building with a two-or three-letter word. Prompt them by saying: Let's take two of our letters and make the word *in*. What two letters do we need?
4. After they form the word *in*, then say, "OK, now let's add just one letter and make the word *tin*. What letter will we add?"
5. After the word *tin* is formed, then say, "The next word is a little tricky. Let's take away the *t* and add two other letters to make the word *grin*. What two letters shall we add?
6. This scaffolding continues as you direct students to manipulate the letters to form additional words, such as *rig, ring, rings,* and *sing.*
7. The final step in this word building game is to make a word by using all of the letters, which in this example is the word *string*. After you have used this activity several times, students will begin to anticipate the "mystery" or "big" word, which adds to their interest in the activity.

Figure 10.4 ABC Word Wall
(segment shown)

A	B	C	D	E
apple	ball	cat	dog	egg
ant	boy	car	door	eat
animal	bear	come	dad	end

F	G	H	I	J
frog	goat	hat	i	jam
fly	girl	home	in	jar
fish	go	hill	ice	jump

Word walls. Another way of focusing on letter–sound relationships is to display groups of words on a word wall. For example, you might initially create an ABC word wall that has words that begin with each letter of the alphabet. This could be done interactively with your students by selecting a different letter each day and asking them to help you think of words that begin with the letter of the alphabet. You would write the words on a letter card and place it in a visual display on the front wall of your classroom. A section of an ABC word wall is shown in Figure 10.4.

Word families can also be displayed on a word wall. You would develop this word wall concurrently with your word building activities. By displaying the word families on the word wall, you can use it to visually focus on letter–sound patterns. It also provides a reference point for children's spelling during their independent writing activities. (See photo.)

Interactive writing. By engaging in writing, children are encouraged to use their knowledge of letter–sound relationships (Beach, 1996; Goodman, 1993). Reading is also a part of the writing process, because during the writing process, the writer also rereads what has been written. Interactive writing activities involve students in the actual writing process. This activity can take several forms. Three different forms of interactive writing will be described here: (a) The morning message, (b) narrative writing, and (c) informational writing. Each activity involves using a chart paper and broad-tipped felt markers. You want to be sure that the writing can easily be seen by all children. You may also find it useful to write each sentence in a different color (avoiding pastel colors) because this will help children track the print as they read from left to right. If you have difficulty writing horizontally, use chart paper that is lined.

Word walls provide a reference point for children's writing.

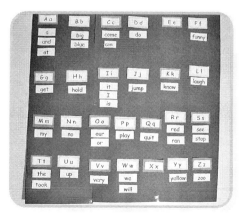

Beverly Otto

Morning message. This activity involves creating a new message every day to share with your students (Beach, 1996; SchifferDanoff, 2001). Your message might focus on a current event, such as new snowfall, or on the upcoming day's schedule of learning activities. Print your message on chart paper, using black or brightly colored markers. Use a letter format with a standard greeting ("Dear Girls and Boys") and closing ("Your teacher, _____"). Early in the year you will need to use simple sentence structure and vocabulary. You may want to start out with only three to five sentences, and then gradually increase this during the school year. It may also be helpful for your initial morning messages to have a similar pattern to the text, such as "Today is (day of the week). It is (cold/rainy/snowy/sunny/windy/cloudy) outside." As the year progresses, your morning messages can become more grammatically complex and use a more varied vocabulary. You may also want to include pictures or drawings as word cues, that is, rebus-style.

In order to use this activity to enhance phonetic awareness, you will need to decide which aspect of phonetic knowledge will be emphasized, for example, initial sounds, word rimes. As you write down your message, leave off specific letters or whole words that correspond to your phonetic emphasis. These missing parts then provide opportunities for children to "share the pen" with you.

The morning message is part of the initial group time as each class day begins. When children arrive in your classroom, they will gather around the chart containing this morning message. As you read the message to or with them, you will stop at the missing parts to encourage children's participation in determining how to finish the words or what words need to be added. After you have discussed each missing part, ask for someone to write in the letter or word. Use contrasting markers for children's contributions. The morning message remains displayed all day and can be used for a follow-up activity the next day.

Narrative writing. Interactive story writing can also provide opportunities to focus on letter–sound associations. You start this activity by first determining the story to be told. Perhaps it is a retelling of a favorite story book (Button, Johnson, & Furgerson, 1996) or a narrative about a recent field trip or classroom visitor. Then as your students dictate the story to you, you will pause at different points to have them participate in writing the story. This means that you need to decide ahead of time which phonetic concept you will

The morning message activity provides opportunities to focus on specific literacy-related concepts.

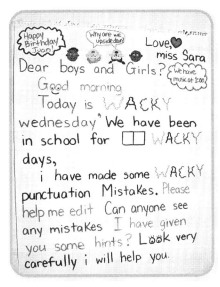

Beverly Otto

focus on. Perhaps you decide that your focus will be on consonant blends such as str-, as in string, street, and strong, or gr-, as in great, group, and green. Each time a word is dictated that starts with a consonant blend, you will stop to have children participate in deciding how that blend is written to start the word. In scaffolding their participation, you will slowly say the target word, stretching it out and encouraging them to listen to the sounds needed for the word, and then deciding which letters represent those sounds. To emphasize the particular phonetic concept, use different-colored markers to circle or draw a box around the letters.

Informational text. Using interactive writing for creating informational text follows many of the same procedures as interactive narrative writing. You will still need to select a phonetic concept for the focus of your interactive writing. The difference is in the format of what is written. For example, if you decide to create an alphabet book together, you will focus on the initial sounds of words representing that letter. You would probably have a separate page for each letter along with several words representing that letter sound on each page. Later during the day, you could provide opportunities for children to add illustrations to go along with the words. The pages could be bound together and the book added to your classroom library.

Independent writing. In addition to teacher-guided activities involving phonetic awareness, first graders also need blocks of time for independent writing. It is during this time that they will continue to explore the relationships between the alphabet letters and the sounds in words. Perhaps some children will have time to use the writing center while others are engaged in guided reading or other learning centers. They may also be involved in independent writing while at their individual desks. Regardless of the location in which they engage in independent writing, the emphasis of this time is on communicating through writing or drawing. It is important to keep the emphasis on the sharing of meaning rather than the product that is created. This means that children's writing is not evaluated for conventional spelling, grammar, or punctuation. While they are writing, allow children to talk with each other. This provides them with an opportunity to talk about what they are thinking while they are composing as well as receive feedback and suggestions from a peer.

Two ways in which independent writing is encouraged involve journaling and story writing. While journaling typically involves writing an entry daily or several times a week, you will need to introduce this activity gradually so that children are not overwhelmed with the expectation for writing. In addition, provide journals that are lined only on half of the page. This reduces the implied expectation for lots of writing and also encourages children to provide illustrations to go with their writing. Many first graders are much more comfortable drawing than they are writing. The purpose of journaling is to motivate children to want to share their thoughts and ideas through writing (and drawing). As you introduce this activity, demonstrate creating a journal entry, first thinking of a topic to write about, then writing what you want to say and illustrating your message. Then talk with children about a range of topics they could focus on when journaling.

Because the focus of journaling is on communication, be sure to provide opportunities for the journals to be shared. As you start journaling, you will want to read their journals so that you can respond to them and be aware of their writing. As the year progresses, you may find it appropriate for children to share their journals with each other, verbally or by writing their responses to each other.

Story writing is also a focus of first graders' independent writing. In this instance, "story" is loosely defined to refer to any type of text created, whether it is oral or written. Children are encouraged to use any format they wish. They may decide to make an actual book or perhaps the story is just one page. Maybe the story is told to the class, accompanied by a drawing, or maybe the story is written with invented spelling. The content may be a recollection of an event that they experienced or it may be an imaginary story. Again, the focus is on communicating a message. Until children are comfortable creating stories, there is no emphasis on including the specific steps in the writing process (that is, prewriting, writing, revising, editing, and publication). In first grade, the emphasis is on motivating children to create stories and other written texts. Placing emphasis on a long process of creating a finished story (through revision and editing) will decrease children's interest in writing. When children develop an interest in story writing in first grade, they are then ready to participate in the specific steps in the writing process in second and third grade (see Chapter 11).

Isabelle's Halloween story (see Figure 10.5) is rich in descriptive details ("I slowly opened the door creak. The door went creak again.") and shows more complex awareness of letter–sound relationships (night = night, stoly = slowly, and scaird = scared). Her illustration adds further meaning and drama. Children's written stories provide teachers with opportunities to informally assess phonetic awareness as well as children's developing sense of narrative. A later section of this chapter will focus on informal assessment of children's writing.

Comprehension of Vocabulary

Comprehension of text depends upon understanding the words in the text. Thus, vocabulary development is a critical part of children's literacy development. A child first develops a **listening vocabulary**. These are words that a child can understand when used by others during conversations and other oral speech. A child's **speaking vocabulary** includes those words the child can use when she is speaking with others. When a child learns to read, she develops a **reading vocabulary**. These are the words she is able to recognize immediately and understand. Children also develop a **writing vocabulary**. These are the words that a child is able to use when writing. Children's reading and writing vocabularies develop from a foundation in their listening and speaking vocabularies.

Enhancing vocabulary development. Effective vocabulary instruction focuses on words as they are used in situational and written contexts (Blachowicz & Fisher, 2006; Juel & Deffes, 2003/2004; National Reading Panel, 2000). This means that you will want to provide activities that focus on vocabulary that accompanies hands-on experiences or vocabulary embedded in a text. In the section that follows, several activities that focus on vocabulary development are described.

Interactive teacher read-alouds. Teacher read-alouds expose children to new vocabulary in the context of a story. When the teacher also explicitly focuses on specific words in the story, explaining their meaning in that context, it adds to children's vocabulary development. You can increase children's engagement in the read-aloud by asking them to help you figure out what specific words mean.

When you are preparing to read a book aloud to your first graders, you will want to identify the words that may be new to them and preplan how you will clarify the meaning of those words. For example, if you are reading *Nilo and the Tortoise* (Lewin, 1999), you might select the following words as your vocabulary focus: volcanoes, lava, adventures, anchored, island, and panga. As you read the story and come to a sentence with one of the words, you would first read to the end of the sentence and then stop for a short talk about the selected word. After reading the sentence that has both *volcano* and *lava* in it, you might say, "Hmm, here are two new words for us to talk about. Volcano. What is a volcano? (take children's responses; one child says that volcanoes explode hot stuff) That's right. Lava is the name of the melted mixture of hot rocks and ash that comes out of a volcano."

Figure 10.5 Isabelle's
Halloween Story

Isabelle 10-19-04
~~the scapy story~~
thair ~~was a~~ wich
on Hallown nigth.
She woct up to
the dore of a
scairy house. I
stoly opind the
dore ckrec. The
dore went ckrec ogen.
I was scaird
Sodinte bats floe
doun the stairs and
out the dore. I

(a)

duad my ked I
ran out the dore
and then a vanpir
came out of the
house. It was
just my frend after all
drest up in a vanpier
costom.

(b)

(c)

If the selected vocabulary words are also supported by the accompanying illustrations, you will want to be sure to refer to the illustrations in your explanations and encourage children to talk about the illustrations. As you share the book with your students and monitor their comprehension of the story, you may find that there are additional word meanings that need to be clarified. After you have finished reading the story, you can then refocus on the selected vocabulary words to make further clarifications and reinforcement.

As you engage in interactive read-alouds, you will want to keep a balance between reading the story and talking about word meanings. Too much dialogue can interfere with the overall comprehension of the story. Because it slows down the unfolding events, it may result in children becoming inattentive and restless.

Story retelling and re-enactment. After you have shared a story book, engaging children in retelling or re-enacting the story provides opportunities to use the vocabulary they have heard as the story was read. Story retelling focuses on recalling the specific events in the story as well as information about the characters and setting (Hoyt, 1999). The general steps in conducting a story retelling are listed in Figure 10.6. Story re-enactment involves children in acting out a story, using dramatic gestures and story dialogue. Basic steps for conducting a story re-enactment were described in Chapter 7. A summary of those steps is provided here in Figure 10.7. Story re-enactments generally require more than one day's planning and preparation, especially if this is a new experience for children in your classroom.

Your role in conducting both the retelling and re-enactment activities is to provide scaffolding that supports children's participation. This scaffolding takes the form of questioning, commenting and prompting, as well as providing any needed narration. As you provide this scaffolding, you can focus your questioning, comments, and prompts on the new vocabulary found in the story text. Additional ways of using story retelling and re-enactments to enhance text comprehension are described in a later section of this chapter.

Computer software. Vocabulary development can also be enhanced by electronic story books presented on CD-ROM and other software programs (for example, *Early Learning* from Tool Factory and *Emergent Reader* from Sunburst). These electronic programs provide features that allow students to click on sound effects, animated graphics, or word definitions (LeFever-Davis & Pearman, 2005). When children are able to use this software independently, it provides additional opportunities for reading and vocabulary development. (See Appendix E for guidelines to follow in selecting software.)

 Figure 10.6 General Steps in Story Retelling

1. Recall setting: After the story has been read, begin the story retelling by asking students to help you remember where the story took place. Did the setting change during the story?
2. Recall characters: Ask who were the characters in this story? What were they like? How old were they? What did each character like? . . . dislike? Which characters were the most active in the story?
3. Recall the main events: Ask children to identify the most important events in the story. What was the sequence of these events?
4. Recall the problem: Ask children to identify the "main problem" of the story. Which of the characters were faced with this problem?
5. Recall the solution: Ask children to describe how the problem was solved. Which of the characters helped to solve the problem?
6. Relate story to personal experiences: Ask children how this story resembles an experience they have had or an experience someone they know has had.

Figure 10.7 General Steps in Story Re-Enactment

1. Select a story that is a favorite or one that you have just shared with your class.
2. Review with students the main events in the story and the characters. If there are many different events, decide which events will be re-enacted.
3. Ask for a volunteer to take each character's role. If there are different events or story segments, different children could be assigned roles to re-enact the varied events or segments.
4. Decide who will be the narrator. If children are just beginning to participate in story re-enactments, the teacher or teacher's aide will need to assume the role of narrator.
5. Decide upon props or simple costumes, such as a hat or an object related to the character's actions. Encourage children to suggest props or costume items.
6. Provide rehearsal time so children have opportunity to practice what they will say. You or your teaching aide will need to monitor and provide scaffolding during this practice time.
7. Schedule the time for the re-enactment to be performed. Be prepared to fill in with narration or with characters' speaking parts in case children forget what they planned to say. Be sure everyone's performance is valued and appreciated regardless of the amount of speaking or the expressiveness in acting out their part.

Vocabulary development can also be enhanced with opportunities to use electronic story books and other software programs.

CristinaMuraca

Concept center. Learning centers that focus on developing concepts through hands-on activities also enhance vocabulary development. For example, you could develop a concept center around *The Very Quiet Cricket* (Carle, 1990). In this center, you could focus on the names of the nine different types of insects that are found in this book, by developing a matching game where the name of each insect is paired up with a picture of the insect. Prior to setting up this learning center, read the book to your class during read-aloud time.

Comprehension of Text

Understanding what is read also requires that readers construct meaning not only at the word level, but also at the sentence, paragraph, and whole-text level. Good readers read with purpose and actively think as they read (Center for the Improvement of Early Reading/

CIERA, 2001). By the time children arrive in first grade, they have typically had more experiences with fiction or narrative texts than with informational or nonfiction text. Recent research indicates that for some children, exposure to informational texts is very low, averaging only about four minutes per day (Duke, 2000). Yet being able to read and comprehend informational text is critical for success in school. In addition, some children will be more interested in nonfiction texts than in stories. For this reason it is important to provide frequent opportunities for first-graders to hear and read informational text (Duke, 2000; Walker, Kragler, Martin, & Arnett, 2003).

Enhancing text comprehension. In this section, guidelines and specific activities are described that will enhance students' comprehension of both fiction and informational texts.

General guidelines for enhancing comprehension. As you engage in teacher read-alouds and guided reading with your first-graders, you will find the following guidelines useful in encouraging them to think about what they are reading:

1. *Develop and use a variety of questions.* Asking students questions about what has been read is a technique that teachers have typically used to determine their comprehension of text. Questioning can also be used to set the purpose for reading and to activate prior knowledge.

The type of questions asked also influences the way in which comprehension is enhanced. There are three basic types of questions. **Literal questions** ask students to locate information directly stated in the text. This type of questioning is also referred to as text-explicit questioning. **Inferential questions** require that students use information from two or more sentences in constructing their answer. **Open-ended questions** ask students to develop an answer based upon their prior knowledge and experience as well as the context in the story. Inferential questions and open-ended questions require higher levels of comprehension because they involve integrating knowledge from multiple sources. As you develop questions to use during story reading and discussion, you will want to include all three types of questions.

2. *Activate students' prior knowledge.* Before starting to read, ask students to think about the title and predict what the book will be about. This will help them comprehend the text better and sets a purpose for reading. Then as you read, you can pause at different points to predict upcoming text.

3. *Encourage students to think of their own questions.* Because we want to encourage students to think about what they are reading, it is beneficial for students to begin to think of their own questions about what they are reading. By modeling the use of the signal words for questions (who, what, where, when, and how), students can begin to formulate their own questions (Stahl, 2004). You could develop a poster such as the one in Figure 10.8 to display in your classroom that will remind students of questions to ask themselves when they read. Introduce the poster first during a read-aloud or guided reading, modeling how to use the question prompts as you read. Then display the poster as a reminder for students to use as they read independently. As you encourage students to think of their own questions as they read, you are also encouraging them to monitor their comprehension of text.

4. *Schedule book talks.* Another way of enhancing comprehension is to have students pick a favorite book and then tell why it is their favorite. You will need to initially demonstrate this for your first graders, sharing with them a favorite book and telling them what you liked, for example, the characters, setting, or events in a story book, or the interesting facts in a nonfiction book. Book talks can be scheduled for a group time that would follow independent reading time.

Figure 10.8 This is a Sample of a Poster that Reminds Students of Questions to Ask Themselves When They Read

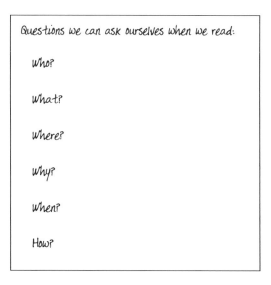

Questions we can ask ourselves when we read:

Who?

What?

Where?

Why?

When?

How?

Guidelines for enhancing comprehension of narrative text. Although some comprehension strategies can be used with both fiction and nonfiction, this section will focus on strategies that are effective when reading fiction. A subsequent section will focus on strategies for nonfiction or informational text.

1. ***Use a Directed Reading-Thinking Activity (DRTA) for narrative texts.*** (Stauffer, 1969, in Stahl, 2004). When using this strategy, you create a scaffold in which students first make predictions about the story. Then they read a segment of the story and verify their predictions. Before reading further they make new predictions about upcoming story events. This sequence continues throughout the reading of the story.

2. ***Encourage students' recall of story events through story retelling and story re-enactment.*** (Refer back to Figures 10.6 and 10.7 for basic steps in conducting each activity.) Through story retelling, students recall the major events and characters and provide a summary of the story. This provides an opportunity for them to use their own language and thoughts in retelling the story. Story re-enactment also involves this recall of events and characters along with acting out the major events of the story. To initiate each activity, provide narrative support to guide the students' retelling or re-enactment. Gradually students will be able to contribute more and your role as narrator can decrease.

Puppets and flannel board characters can also be used to re-enact stories. These activities can enhance oral language competencies and comprehension among English-speaking students as well as with ELLs (Crepeau & Richards, 2003; Ediger, 2000). Children from diverse cultures with a heritage of oral storytelling will also benefit from using puppets and flannel board characters to bring written stories to life (Bennett, 2002; Cobb, 2001; Stanchfield, 1972). Children who are shy or withdrawn generally feel more relaxed when using a puppet or flannel board character during a re-enactment (Ediger, 2000). As much as possible, encourage children to create their own puppets, such as sock puppets, paperbag puppets, or stick puppets.

3. ***Use story mapping.*** Story mapping is a way to graphically represent the major aspects of a story. This enhances students' awareness of story structure (Boyle & Peregoy, 1990). It also provides a way of recalling important aspects of a story. The story map found in

Figure 10.9 Story Map

Where does this story take place?

↓

Who are the characters in this story?
What are they like?

↓

What is the "problem" in the story?

↓

What happens that takes care of the problem?

↓

How does the story end?

Figure 10.9 focuses on setting, characters, problem, solution, and final event or story closure. By using this story map as a postreading activity, you will encourage students to recall significant aspects of the story they just read. Story maps can also be used when comparing two or more stories for similar features or aspects.

4. *Use reader-response journals.* First-graders can begin to respond to stories by drawing or writing in journals. Encourage them to think about the story they have just read and then write or draw, reflecting on the story and relating it to their own experiences. Drawing adds to the way in which their responses to stories can be communicated. You may find that students will need some ideas to start their writing, but keep your prompts general rather than specific, using open-ended questions or incomplete sentences, such as "What character did you like and why?" or "My favorite part of the story was when. . . ." As a follow-up to writing and drawing in their journal, journals can be shared in either a large group setting or with a partner. Writing in journals and verbally sharing their thoughts enhances students' comprehension because it requires that they communicate their ideas through oral and written language.

First graders' text comprehension can be enhanced with opportunities to draw and write in response to what they have read.

Blend Images

Guidelines for enhancing comprehension of informational text. While the purpose of narrative text is to communicate a story, the purpose of informational text is to communicate specific information and facts. This difference in purpose is reflected in the way that informational text is structured. Four different ways in which informational text is structured include (Emmitt, Komesaroff, & Pollock, 2006): (a) Explanations of how something works or how something is formed; (b) procedures/instructions for understanding the steps in a process or sequence; (c) descriptions of an object or entity, its characteristics, features, functions, and how it may differ from other similar objects or entities; and (d) opinions/arguments that state a position and attempt to persuade the reader to adopt that opinion or position. Because of these differences in text structure, you will need to support your students' reading of informational text in different ways from their reading of narrative. Here are some guidelines for using specific strategies:

1. ***Read informational text during read-aloud time.*** It is important for you to model how to read informational text. By reading it to your first-graders at read-aloud time you can support their comprehension of informational text. You can also respond to their questions about the ideas presented in the text. Informational text is not shared the same way that you will share a narrative/story. Instead of reading through the whole book as you do when sharing a story, you probably will read only a segment of an informational book at a time. This is because of the density of concepts and information found in the nonfiction book. You may decide to read portions of the book over a period of several days.

When introducing the book, you will want to activate children's prior knowledge for that topic. This means that you will ask them to recall what they already know or have experienced related to the topic. While this can be done orally, it is also useful to represent students' responses on the chalkboard, chart paper, or overhead transparency using a word web or simple listing. While introducing the book, it is also important to focus on the way in which the book is organized and the types of information found in the book. Perhaps the book is divided into sections that present a series of related concepts. This may be a good time to talk about the table of contents and explain how it is used. Reviewing the illustrations (photographs, drawings) is also a good way to help students comprehend the general information presented in the book.

2. ***Use the K–W–L (Ogle, 1986) strategy to encourage students' active involvement throughout the reading of informational text.*** The K–W–L strategy involves first activating prior knowledge by asking "What do I already **know**?" (the K - part). Then purposes for reading are set by asking "What do I **want** to know?" (the W - part). After the text has been read, a final question is asked: "What have I **learned**?" (the L - part)? Students' responses to these questions are usually recorded on a chart like the one in Figure 10.10. Repeated

Figure 10.10 K–W–L Chart

Our Topic: _____		
What do we already know?	What do we want to know?	What did we learn?

experiences using this strategy in a group setting will encourage students to internalize this approach as they read independently.

3. *Use charts and other graphic forms to show students how to visually organize the information they have read.* In addition to using a K–W–L chart to guide students' comprehension, other formats will also help students to think about and reflect on what they have read (Walker, Kragler, Martin, & Arnett, 2003). The type of format you use will depend upon the type of informational text that you have read with your students. You may decide to make a chart that simply lists new facts students have learned from the informational text or the sequence in which a task is completed. Or if you have read a book about rivers and lakes (such as *Rivers and Lakes*, Morris, 1998), you might use a format like that shown in Figure 10.11.

Another type of format is the word/concept web. In this format the focus is on the way in which concepts are related. Start with the main concept and add related concepts in a web like format, as shown in Figure 10.12. Initially, you will want to have simple word webs and then build up to webs with more levels and related concepts as you read other informational texts. Graphic organizers are only useful if they support students' comprehension and

 Figure 10.11 Comparison Chart on Rivers and Lakes

	Rivers	**Lakes**
What is it?		
Where does the water come from?		
Where does the water go?		
Special words to remember		

Figure 10.12 Example of a Word/Concept Web

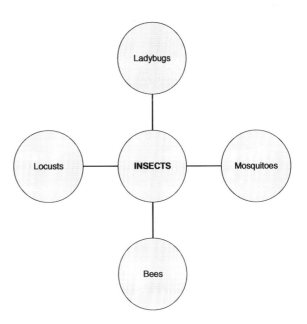

Shared reading allows students to talk about what they are reading and learning.

Thomas M Perkins

memory of text. Therefore, you want to be sure that students can understand the way in which the information is organized in the visual chart or graphic.

4. *Use partner reading and journaling.* First-graders will also benefit from having opportunities to work with a partner in reading a nonfiction text. This shared reading allows students to talk about what they are reading and learning. Their comprehension is further enhanced when they share their thoughts through exchanging their response journals. You could also have each pair share one or two facts they have learned at group time.

5. *Provide opportunity for students to develop mini-reports.* This activity involves first providing a collection of nonfiction, informational trade books on a particular theme or topic, such as animals, the ocean, or mountains. Your students would select one or more of these books to read (and look at) and then create a short report of important facts they have learned from reading the book(s). Encourage children to decide what they think is important or interesting and to write it any way they want, such as using emergent spelling and illustrations.

Sarah, a first grader, created a report on the Pilgrims (see Figure 10.13). In addition to the three pages shown in Figure 10.13, her actual report contained several other pages of text. As you read her report, notice the historical sequence of events: the king's command that they had to attend his church, their secret meetings, the king's spies, alienation from their neighbors ("the Pilgrims neighbors stopped talking to the Pilgrims"), the move to North America, sailing on the Mayflower, wanting a better life, having little food to eat, and enduring the cold and damp. From her mini-report, it is clear that Sarah was able to identify the main events in the Pilgrims' travel to America and was able to express her knowledge through conventional and invented/phonemic spelling.

Fluency: Oral Reading and Silent Reading

Comprehension requires not only that readers decode or recognize the words, but also that their rate of reading be smooth and free of frequent stops. According to Hasbrouck (2006), "When children read too slowly or haltingly, the text devolves into a broken

Figure 10.13 Sarah's Mini-Report on the Pilgrims

Ouns opon a time thar
was a King. And
he comanddid the
Pilgrims to go to
his church. And
the Pilgrims wher
mad. the Pilgrims
wher so mad thay
maid a secert meeting
meetings but the
King sent spies
to woch them
whar ever thay

(a)

whent. whar ever the
Pilgrims went the spes whet
the Pilgrims
neighbors stopt
tocing to the Pilgrims
next doore to them.
And then most of
the Pilgrims movd
awa to North America.
Thay sald the
Mayflower and
thay hope it wood
be a better life
in North Amarica.

(b)

Thay had to
leave thar house
and thar neighbors
and thar relatives.
And then thay
had a trip to
go on. And the
bot was colld
the Mayflower.
And thay had a
littl cosis of food
to eat it was
cold. and damp

(c)

string of words and/or phrases; it's a struggle just to remember what's been read, much less extract its meaning (p. 24)." Nonfluent reading is characterized by word-by-word reading and a lack of varied, expressive intonation. In contrast, fluent reading involves reading accurately and smoothly in meaningful phrases that reflect the grammatical structure of the original text (Hasbrouck, 2006; National Reading Panel, 2000). Fluency is not just quickly recognizing the words in a text, but also reading those words in meaningful phrases using expressive intonation.

While fluency is mainly associated with oral reading, it also applies to silent reading. If word identification is problematic during silent reading, comprehension suffers and motivation to continue reading declines. For this reason, both oral fluency and silent reading fluency should be emphasized in literacy curricula.

Enhancing fluency. At the first-grade level, teaching strategies for enhancing fluency involve developing sight vocabulary, modeling fluent reading, guided oral reading, and repeated reading of texts (Hasbrouck, 2006; National Reading Panel, 2000).

Developing sight vocabulary. Fluent reading requires that most words are recognized automatically without effortful decoding. While phonetic awareness activities enhance children's awareness of patterns of letter–sound associations found in many words, and thus facilitates decoding, some frequently appearing words do not follow those predictable patterns, such as *could, the*, and *down*.

To enhance students' recognition of these high-frequency words, a visual display of these words, or word wall, can be created and used to support word recognition. For this display, words are written on separate cards or paper and placed on a wall in front of the classroom, so that all children can easily see the display. For this initial word wall in first grade, arrange the words in alphabetical order beneath alphabet letter cards to designate each grouping. A high-frequency word wall will be built slowly, introducing around five words per week (Hall & Cunningham, 1999). Select the words for the word wall from the reading materials children use in your guided reading groups. Then be sure to refer to the word wall as you engage students in interactive writing, dictated stories, and independent writing.

Another strategy for enhancing word recognition is to use sentence strips and word cards. This provides an opportunity for repeated reading of familiar text in a teacher-mediated setting. The steps for conducting this activity are listed in Figure 10.14.

You may want to repeat this activity on successive days to increase students' fluency in reading the sentences as well as their accuracy and speed in re-assembling the sentences. This sentence-building activity can be continued by adapting it for a learning center. Put

 Figure 10.14 Steps in Using Sentence Strips and Word Cards to Enhance Word Recognition

1. Select several sentences from a familiar text, such as a favorite story book or class-dictated story.
2. Then print each sentence on a long strip of lightweight cardboard.
3. At group time, introduce the sentence strips and ask students to read them with you.
4. This is followed by having individual students or pairs of students read the sentences again.
5. You can also ask students to locate individual words on the sentence strips.
6. After students have accurately read the sentence strips, cut the strips apart at the word level.
7. For each sentence, place the words on your pocket chart or chalkboard ledge in random order.
8. Ask students to help you figure out how to put each sentence back together again. This is accompanied by reading the words repeatedly and deciding if the words are in the correct order.

When you read aloud in your classroom, the way in which you read contributes to students' awareness of what fluent reading sounds like.

Robert Kneschke

the cards for each sentence in separate envelopes with the sentence written on the outside. Students can practice reading and re-assembling the sentences in the learning center during independent work time. This could also become a "take-home" activity as well.

Modeling fluent reading. When you read aloud in your classroom, whether it is fiction or nonfiction, the way in which you read contributes to students' awareness of what fluent reading sounds like. Be sure to read with expression and use phrasing that contributes to the meaning of the text.

By using Big Books that have large print, students are able to follow along as you read aloud. You may also want to have students echo-read. This means that you will read a phrase or short sentence, pause, and then the students will repeat what you have read. This helps them understand that fluent reading is not word-by-word reading, but involves reading phrases and other groups of words and then pausing. By using this large-format book (Big Book), you can also encourage them to see the words as you read and where you pause by pointing to the print.

Guided oral reading. When you are engaged in guided reading with a small group of students, you can encourage fluency by having students reread a sentence or phrase after they have stopped to decode a particular word. This provides additional practice in reading the difficult word as well as focusing on comprehension of the whole sentence or phrase.

Fluency is not possible if students are repeatedly struggling to recognize words when they read. This means that you need to be sure that the texts they read are at the appropriate level of difficulty. There are three levels of difficulty (Tompkins, 2007): (a) Easy—when the text is read with 96–100 percent accuracy accompanied by strong comprehension, (b) just right—when the text is read with 90–95 percent accuracy and good comprehension, and (c) too hard—when the text is read with less than 90 percent accuracy and poor comprehension. For guided reading activities, students should be reading texts that are "just right." Avoid giving students texts that are too hard because they will have difficulty decoding and comprehension will be impaired.

If you discover that a text is too difficult for a child when you are with a guided reading group, provide scaffolding that allows the child to echo-read with you or to take turns reading with you. Do not insist that they continue to read alone at this level of frustration.

Before the next guided reading experience with that child, you will need to find a more appropriate text. Your awareness of each child's reading level will help you select appropriate texts; however, the only way you can accurately determine whether a text is at the right level for any student is to have the student attempt to read the text.

Opportunities for repeated reading. Fluency can also be enhanced through opportunities for repeated reading (Samuels, 1997). By reading the same text several times, word recognition becomes easier because a child's memory for what has been read helps them to predict the words in the text.

One way of encouraging repeated reading is to provide a recording center in your classroom where students can tape-record their reading. Be sure that each child has their own cassette tape and that you show them how to control the recording of their reading and how to play it back so they can listen to themselves. You probably will need to have earphones so that they can record and listen to themselves without distracting other students who are working nearby. Also show them how to rerecord their reading so that they can start over if they decide that is necessary. Most students will find this very motivating because they are able to hear themselves reading, practice reading independently, and decide on their own to start over or to continue reading. Students' taped readings are also an effective way to show development of fluency over time.

Another strategy for encouraging repeated readings is to have students partner with each other and read together. Be sure that they have read the text previously during guided reading. Suggest that they take turns reading short segments of several sentences or a paragraph. You will also want to talk with your students so that they know how to be a good partner by listening attentively and helping their partner only when asked.

Independent reading times. Children who read more generally become better readers. Providing time in your classroom for children to read independently can enhance their silent reading fluency; however, you will need to be sure that the books they read are at an appropriate level for their independent reading. This means that you will need to help them learn how to pick out books that are at an "easy" level so that their word recognition is accurate and comprehension of text is high. One way to do this is to suggest they follow these steps (Reutzel & Cooter, 2004):

1. Select a book that they think might be interesting.
2. Begin reading on any page that has quite a few words on it.
3. For each word they cannot immediately recognize, hold up a finger. If they encounter more than five words on the page they do not know, it means that they should pick another book.

Time that is set aside for independent reading has been referred to as Sustained Silent Reading (SSR) as well as Drop Everything and Read (DEAR). Typically 15–20 minutes are set aside for SSR/DEAR time at the first-grade level. It is important that this time be intrinsically motivating for your students and not just another thing they "have to do." You can increase their motivation to read independently in these ways (Gambrell, 1996):

1. Encourage students to read with a friend. This provides opportunity for social interactions and changes the context of the reading. Partners' verbal interactions may also increase comprehension of text.
2. Stock your classroom library with a wide variety of interesting books at a range of reading levels. Be sure to include informational books as well as narrative story books. Multicultural books also will appeal to students from diverse settings, as well as increase all students' awareness of other cultures.

3. Read your own book while children are reading independently. This indicates that you enjoy reading and value it as a worthwhile personal activity.

4. Provide time after SSR or DEAR for students to gather together and share comments about what they have read. If you find that you don't have enough time for everyone to share their comments, you could have students take turns on different days.

5. Provide incentives that are related to reading, such as bookmarks and free books to take home and keep. You can collect gently used books from garage sales, library sales, and flea markets for this purpose. You might also be able to have books donated to you from the school's parent association or other community service groups. By rewarding students for reading at school with books they can choose and keep, they learn to value books and are more likely to read at home.

Strategies for Working with ELLs and Struggling Readers

Early on in your school year, you will notice students who are not able to keep up with the rest of the class. They may begin to withdraw from classroom activities or they may act out and become disruptive. It is important that you carefully observe their responses to the learning activities and interactions as well as draw on the social and instructional supports provided by your school to address the needs of children who are at-risk. Difficulties in first grade rarely go away on their own. Instead, patterns of behavior and disinterest in learning may carry over into future years.

In this section, guidelines and strategies for enhancing literacy transactions with two groups of children who may be at-risk for later learning difficulties are described. These two groups include English language learners and struggling readers (who are native English-speakers). Both groups may experience difficulties in learning to read which then may affect their success in learning activities at later grades. As you interact with children who are struggling, you will want to keep your focus on supporting each child to be an active, curious learner. Among children who are at-risk, "the less students respond, the less they learn, and the more likely they are to acquire skill deficits" (Kamps, Wills, Greenwood, Thorne, Lazo, Crockett, Akers, & Swaggart, 2003, p. 221).

Welcome all students into your classroom community. The social interactions in your classroom are an important part of your learning community. This is especially critical for children who are out of your room for part of the day. Whether children are pulled out of your classroom for ELL, special education, or other resource assistance, you will want to be sure that they feel a part of your classroom community.

One way to communicate your value of each student in your learning community is to emphasize each student's strengths and use positive feedback. This is especially important for students who are at-risk (Cooter & Cooter, 2004). By providing opportunities for students to work with others during specific activities and encouraging students to also focus on each other's strengths and unique qualities, you can create a classroom where everyone feels valued and respected.

Cooperative/collaborative projects. Thematic units that incorporate collaborative or cooperative groupings involving two to three children for small projects can provide opportunities for each to contribute in different ways to the completion of the project. For example, one student might create a drawing or a 3-D model or diorama while another might write important facts on a poster.

Paired reading during SSR. Children who have difficulty reading may not benefit from having independent reading time (Hasbrouck, 2006). Encouraging them to read with a friend may provide them with the needed social and linguistic support they need when interacting with books (Griffim, 2002).

Home–school connections. Regardless of the literacy development level of each of your students, positive home–school connections are critical for all students. General guidelines for developing home–school connections have been described in earlier chapters. Two additional guidelines will be described here:

1. Emphasize the importance of students' families as part of your classrooms' learning community (Gray & Fleishman, 2004–2005; Ortiz & Ordoñez-Jasis, 2005). Welcome students' families (including extended family members) into your school and classroom by providing a variety of opportunities at different times of the week and day throughout your school year. Encourage students to share news and photographs about family interests and cultural events.

2. Encourage literacy-related activities at home and in the community. It is important for you to communicate to your students' families that literacy is more than simply learning to read and write at school. Literacy is embedded in many daily activities and cultural events. By actively involving their children in the literacy-related events at home and in their community they are helping their children become lifelong readers and writers. For example, involving children when reading the newspaper, writing a letter to a relative, making a birthday card, or writing a shopping list, or encouraging them to read a story book to a younger brother or sister all contribute to their child's literacy development.

Guidelines for Interacting with English Language Learners

Most schools will have pull-out programs for English language learners. These programs are designed to help ELLs develop English competencies with an emphasis on oral language. While these programs are beneficial, you should not assume that the pull-out program will take the place of instructional activities in your classroom (Mohr, 2004). You will need to focus on keeping ELLs actively engaged in the learning activities in your

Sharing books with younger siblings provides opportunities to develop reading fluency and confidence.

Tania Kolinko

classroom and not passively waiting for their pull-out program time. ELLs' time in your classroom is just as important as their time in a pull-out program. An ESL teacher may not have strong background in reading, so time in an ESL classroom may lack the focus on reading and writing that a regular classroom would offer.

You will also want to consider the time of the day when the ELLs are out of your room. If it always takes place during your reading/language arts time, you will need to be sure that the children are able to develop language arts knowledge at other times in your room. For many classrooms, the content that is shared during reading/language arts time becomes the "common knowledge" base for other related activities in the classroom. When ELLs miss out on this time, they are also missing out on developing this shared knowledge.

Emphasize vocabulary development. Each area of vocabulary development is important for ELLs: listening, speaking, reading, and writing. ELLs may have more difficulty with comprehension for two reasons: (a) Their limited proficiency in English and (b) their prior knowledge/experiences that may not relate to the content found in texts used in school (Boyle & Peregoy, 1990).

Focus on vocabulary in context. In supporting ELLs' vocabulary development, you will want to provide hands-on experiences that enhance conceptual knowledge as well as vocabulary. It is also important to provide opportunities to see and hear the vocabulary used in the context of oral conversations as well as books (Gersten & Geva, 2003; Mohr, 2004). Teacher read-alouds provide important opportunities for introducing new vocabulary within the context of a narrative or informational text. To avoid overwhelming ELLs with a high volume of new vocabulary, segment the text you are reading into 200–250 word sections and read the book over several days (Hickman, Pollard-Durodola, & Vaughn, 2004). Sequencing your read-aloud provides an opportunity to focus on a smaller number of new vocabulary each day and to engage in a review of the previous day's vocabulary before continuing the story or informational text.

A series of teacher read-alouds on a common topic (for example, animals) allows children to experience the same vocabulary used across different books. Thematic units that combine literacy instruction with social studies, science, or mathematics also provide a context for vocabulary development (Mohr, 2004).

Use visual aids and gestures to provide context for vocabulary. In addition to focusing on vocabulary in the context of oral conversations and written texts, you can further enhance vocabulary development by using visual aids and gestures when you are interacting with ELLs (Gersten & Geva, 2003; Gray & Fleishman, 2004–2005). These visual aids would include illustrations, photographs, and actual objects.

Use questions that request completion, not generation (Gray & Fleishman, 2004–2005). When you engage ELLs in instructional dialogue, you can provide a supportive scaffold by asking them to choose an answer from a list in a multiple-choice format or by completing a sentence. Without this supportive scaffold, they may not attempt to participate in the instructional dialogue.

Provide multicultural literature. By providing a range of multicultural literature in your classroom library and literacy curriculum, children from diverse cultures and languages will be able to use their prior knowledge and experiences as they engage in reading and writing activities. They will be better able to relate to characters and story events that are similar to their prior experiences (Drucker, 2003).

Provide supportive contexts for oral reading. Because ELLs are in the process of developing their English, they need to have supportive contexts for their oral reading. You can provide this support through choral- and echo-reading while using Big Books. As you read aloud, point to where you are reading and encourage students to read with you (choral reading) or to echo what you read. Taped books also provide a supportive context for reading because once a child is familiar with the story, he can read along with the tape (Drucker, 2003). You could also tape your read-aloud to the whole class, and then place the tape and the book in your class listening center for ELLs to use during independent work time.

Guidelines for Interacting with Struggling Readers

Children who are native English speakers and show signs of difficulty in beginning reading will also need additional support and mediation in your classroom. Many of the activities and strategies described earlier in this chapter (as well as those in Chapter 9) will benefit struggling readers, for example, encouraging active involvement in learning through hands-on activities, teacher read-alouds, buddy reading, developing oral vocabulary (Cooter & Cooter, 2004; Griffin, 2002) and repeated readings (Wood, 2005); however, additional supportive scaffolding and individual attention should be provided as these activities are implemented. You may need to work closely with struggling readers to assist them in locating books to read during SSR/DEAR time. Be sure also to provide books that reflect their individual interests and prior knowledge.

Focus on phonological and phonetic awareness. Children who are having difficulty in beginning reading often do not seem to understand the relationship between speech and print (Snow, Burns, & Griffin, 1998). Thus, they may need to have more explicit and focused instruction in phonological awareness and phonics (Carlisle, 2004; Juel & Minden-Cupp, 2000; Paratore, 2002). This means you will want to have more time with them in small group lessons or one-on-one. Although you will use some of the same types of activities that you used with regular achieving students, you will use more repetition and review to be sure students are grasping the concept or skill before you move on to new concepts or skills (Cooter & Cooter, 2004).

Emphasize reading as a meaning-making process. Although struggling readers will benefit from explicit instruction, it is still important to emphasize reading as a meaning-making process. Too much emphasis on decoding and isolated word recognition may result in decreased motivation to read. In addition, if children are given experiences reading only leveled texts that are not interesting (Meyerson & Kulesza, 2006; Wood, 2005), or if their choices during independent reading time are overly restricted, motivation for reading will also decline (O'Donnell & Wood, 2004).

Be knowledgeable of special resources and programs. As you become more aware of children in your first-grade classroom who are falling behind in literacy development, you will need to seek out information about programs and resources that could provide additional support to at-risk learners.

Reading Recovery. One program that is available in many schools is Reading Recovery. It is an early intervention program for first graders who are experiencing difficulty learning to read. The Reading Recovery program was developed by Marie Clay, an educator and researcher, in New Zealand in the 1970s. This program involves one-on-one tutoring for 30 minutes a day for 12 to 20 weeks with a specially trained teacher. Reading Recovery teachers receive extensive, year-long training in an apprenticeship prior to their appointment as well as continued professional development (Askew, Pinnell, Fountas, Schmitt, & Lyons, 2000). Based on the diagnostic assessment of each child, the daily tutoring session typically involves reading a familiar story, writing a story, sentence building using cut-up sentences, and reading a short new book (Department of Education, Office of Research, 2007). Each child's responses during the daily tutoring session are carefully documented and serve as a basis for the next day's lesson.

Since a school's Reading Recovery program may not be supported by either federal or state funds, school districts may need to provide all of the financial resources for teacher training and program implementation. Since it was introduced in the 1980s, Reading Recovery has been widely and successfully used in the United States, serving more than 1.6 million first graders (Reading Recovery Council of North America, 2007). Ongoing and extensive data collection documents the success of this program in terms of the cost benefits as well as the impact on individual children's reading achievement (see http://www.readingrecovery.org/sections/ reading/index.asp).

Informal Assessment Strategies

Assessment of children's development of literacy provides a basis for instructional planning and implementation. As a part of your interactions with your first-grade students, you will be informally observing which students are developing literacy competencies and which ones are struggling. As a reflective teacher, you will also determine the progress of your classroom of students using periodic assessments. Many commercial reading curricula include specific assessment tools to be used at different points in the school year. For example, the Houghton Mifflin Reading curriculum (2006) for first grade includes the following assessment materials: Baseline Group Test, Benchmark Progress Tests, Emerging Literacy Survey, Integrated Theme Test, Phonics/Decoding Screening Test, Leveled Reading Passages Assessment Kit, Teacher's Assessment Handbook, Theme Skills Test, and Weekly Skills Tests. You will want to become familiar with the assessment materials available at your school and then decide which ones will be beneficial to you and your students.

Analyzing Readers' Miscues

When you are listening to children read, it is useful to notice the types of reading miscues they are making. By calling children's errors in reading "miscues" the emphasis is on examining the way in which the reader "missed one or more language cues: graphic (word, letter pattern, and letter cues), syntactic (grammar cues), and/or semantic (meaning cues)" (Weaver, 2002, p. 120). By analyzing the types of miscues young readers make, you can better understand the ways in which you can mediate and support their literacy development.

Types of miscues. In this section, four types of miscues are described (see further Clay, 2000; Goodman, 1993). These types include: substitution, insertion, omission, and mispronunciation.

Substitution. When a student substitutes a different word for one in the text, you need to determine the relationship of the substituted word to the original word in the text. This will give you an idea of the nature of the miscue. There are three different kinds of substitution miscues: semantic, syntactic, and visual. For example, if a student read *home* instead of *house,* the miscue would have semantic similarity. *House* and *home* also have visual similarity because they both begin with *ho* and end with an *e. House* and *home* also have syntactic similarity because they are both nouns. For additional examples of substitution miscues see Table 10.1.

Insertion. A reader may insert an additional word into the text when she reads it. Sometimes this reflects a reader's anticipation of what would be grammatically appropriate. For

Table 10.1 Analyzing Substitution Miscues

Analysis of Miscue Similarity to Word in Text

Miscue	Text word	Syntactic	Semantic	Visual
wiggly	webbed	Yes, both are adjectives	no	Yes, both start with *w*
around	beside	Yes, both are prepositions	Yes, both denote nearness	no
road	river	Yes, both are nouns	No. Does not fit with story	Yes, both start with *r*

example, in the text sentence, "the ducklings swam in the pond" a reader might say, "the ducklings swam *around* in the pond."

Omission. When a student omits a word when reading, you will want to note the word that was skipped and determine whether having skipped the word will impact comprehension of the text. For example, in the sentence "he went to the town," omitting the word *the* may not have any impact on comprehension of the text.

Mispronunciation. Miscues that result in mispronouncing a word may indicate that the word is not part of the child's oral vocabulary or they may indicate that there was a miscue related to letter–sound relationships; for example, saying /kity/ for the word *city*.

Summative analysis. After you have listened to a student read and noted what types of miscues were made, you can further analyze their miscues by answering the following questions: (a) What types of miscues were made? (b) Was there a predominance of one type of miscue? (c) Did the student self-correct any of the miscues? (d) Did the miscues interfere with comprehension of the text? Because reading is a meaning-making process, miscues that impair comprehension are a concern. In addition, readers who do not make any self-corrections may not be focusing on the meaning of what they are reading.

Documenting miscue analysis. Experienced teachers find that they can analyze students' miscues on the spot and provide mediation that will help students read more accurately. Novice teachers may find that they need to practice analyzing readers' miscues by taping students' reading first and then conducting the analysis later when reviewing the taped reading. By using a format for documenting students' miscues, such as the format found in Figure 10.15, you will be able to thoroughly review the types of miscues a student has made during oral reading.

Informal Assessment of Children's Writing

The focus of this informal assessment is to develop an understanding of what a child knows about writing as shown in his or her independent writing. This assessment provides information about the child's zone of proximal development and serves as a basis for planning future learning activities.

An annotated checklist that can be used for informally assessing children's written stories is presented in Figure 10.16. This checklist focuses on three areas: children's concepts of print, spelling, and narrative text. The specific concepts of print include the use of spaces between words, capitalization of proper nouns and at the beginning of each sentence, punctuation, and directionality of print (from left-to-right and top-to-bottom). Spelling is assessed for the presence of conventionally spelled words and invented

Figure 10.15 Format for Documenting and Analyzing a Student's Reading Miscues

Miscue	Text	Substitution/ Semantic	Substitution/ Syntactic	Substitution/ Visual	Omission	Insertion	SC[1] Y/N	Comp[2] Y/N
Totals								
Percent								

[1] SC = Was miscue self-corrected?
[2] Comp = Did miscue interfere with text comprehension?

Figure 10.16 Annotated Checklist for Informal Assessment of Children's Written Stories

Child's name: _____ Written story: _____ * Date: _____

Feature:	Consistent	Inconsistent	Not present	Your notes
Concepts of print				
Spaces between words				
Capitalized proper nouns and at the beginning of each sentence				
Uses appropriate punctuation				
Left-to-right and top-to-bottom directionality				
Spelling				
Conventional				
Conventional spelling only of high-frequency words				
Transitional spelling				
Phonemic spelling				
Prephonemic spelling				
Scribbling				
Uses only drawing				
Narrative Text				
Complete sentences				
Descriptive words (adverbs, adjectives)				
Setting described				
Characters identified				
Problem or goal stated				
Sequence of linked story events				
Story titled				

*Attach copy of child's story.

spelling. The features of narrative text that are focused on include the use of complete sentences and descriptive words; the identification of a setting, characters, problem, or goal statement; a series of linked events; and a story title. More formal assessments of children's writing are often provided in language arts and literacy curriculum programs.

Revisiting the Transactional Perspective: Comprehensive Literacy Instruction in First Grade

First graders' transactions with literacy reflect their knowledge of language, the texts they encounter, and the contexts of their reading and writing. A wide range of texts are typically encountered in first grade: trade books, leveled books, student anthologies, Big Books, workbooks, journals, fiction, and nonfiction. The contexts of literacy also vary and may include large group read-alouds, guided reading in small groups, partner reading, interactive writing, choral- and echo-reading, and concept centers. As a first-grade teacher, your awareness of students' knowledge of language, the texts they encounter, and the contexts of their literacy events will influence the ways in which you interact with students to mediate their learning and literacy development. Your interactions will reflect your observations of students' learning and your awareness of their zones of proximal development. Additionally, your interactions will be influenced by your professional knowledge, the instructional resources you have, and the decisions you make. The interrelationships between these components are represented in Figure 10.17.

Figure 10.17 Comprehensive Literacy Instruction in First Grade

Chapter Summary

First grade is a time when many children experience full-day school for the first time. In addition, there is more emphasis on direct instruction. The major expectation of first grade is that children will begin to read and write conventionally. As a result, the focus on literacy development dominates the first-grade curriculum. In most schools, a commercial curriculum for literacy is adopted and teachers are expected to follow this curriculum. The challenge for you, as a reflective teacher, is to understand how to use a commercial curriculum as well as other instructional resources to provide activities and strategies that will enhance literacy development for all of your students. The five key areas of literacy instruction in first grade include: phonological awareness, phonetic awareness, comprehension of vocabulary, comprehension of text, and fluency in oral reading and independent silent reading. As you implement learning activities in each of these areas, you will want to focus on using a variety of activities and strategies to keep students engaged. In addition, using different-sized groupings will contribute to learner involvement. By keeping literacy and language connected in your first grade curriculum, you are recognizing the ways in which listening, speaking, reading, writing, viewing, and visually representing interact and contribute to children's lifelong literacy development.

Chapter Review

1. Terms to know:

basal reading program	listening vocabulary
leveled texts	speaking vocabulary
decodable readers	reading vocabulary
onset	writing vocabulary
rime	literal questions
word family	inferential questions
phoneme	open-ended questions

2. Why is phonological awareness a prerequisite for phonics instruction?

3. In what ways can Big Books be used to enhance phonetic awareness?

4. How do word-building activities enhance phonetic awareness?

5. What is the value of including a focus on reading nonfiction text in first grade?

6. How does the K–W–L strategy enhance comprehension of informational text?

7. How does fluency contribute to comprehension of text?

8. In what ways do a student's reading miscues reflect their reading strategies? How can a reflective teacher use the analysis of a student's miscues to enhance literacy development?

Chapter Extension Activities

Curriculum Review: As a small group activity or independently, review a commercially prepared literacy curriculum for a first grade using the format provided in Appendix I. Present your findings in class.

Curriculum Development: Using a format provided in Appendix K for K–4 grades, develop a lesson plan for a first-grade classroom for one of the following activities:

a. Interactive writing
b. Read-aloud
c. Guided word study
d. Story mapping
e. Informational text read-aloud and K–W–L Chart

Online or In-Class Discussion: Locate software designed for beginning readers at your university or public library. Thoroughly explore how to use the software. Identify which areas of literacy development are included in the activities found in this software. Share your experiences in an online or in-class discussion.

Research:

1. Locate your state's reading/language-arts standards for first grade. Analyze the relationship of these standards to the five key areas of literacy instruction identified in this chapter. Prepare a poster summarizing your findings. Present your poster in class.

2. Read and prepare a written review of a professional journal article on one of the following topics: Reading Recovery, struggling readers, phonics instruction, English language learners' literacy development, or interactive writing.

Chapter 11

Literacy Instruction in Second and Third Grade: Transitioning to Fluent Reading and Writing

It is 9:30 in the morning. Mr. Thomas' second-grade class is actively involved in their literacy block of learning activities. Seated around a small table, Mr. Thomas is conducting a guided reading group with six children. At the end of the guided reading activity, he gives them a task to complete during their independent work time. Today their assignment is to add five new words to their personal dictionary from the story they just read, along with a synonym for each word. He also reminds them where the picture thesauruses and illustrated dictionaries are located in the classroom. Then he calls for the next reading group to gather at the table.

While he conducts each guided reading group, the rest of the class is involved in other small group or independent learning activities. There are several options from which to choose. Some children are in the writing center, creating their own storybooks and talking quietly about their stories. Several children are at learning centers that focus on word study or specific science concepts. Two children are at the computer, involved in sharing an electronic story book. Still others are in the classroom library, silently reading self-selected books. After all children have met with Mr. Thomas for guided reading, the entire class gathers for an interactive read-aloud.

As you read this vignette, you might have asked yourself these questions: Why are there so many activities going on at once? Wouldn't it be better and less confusing to have the whole class doing the same thing at the same time? What is the purpose of the small group and independent activities? Are children really learning something in those activities or are they just keeping busy and quiet until they can meet with Mr. Thomas for guided reading?

Responses to these questions are based in our current understandings of literacy development and the transactional perspective. In this perspective, literacy transactions occur through interactions between what learners know about language (oral and written), the texts which they encounter, and the contexts in which the literacy events take place. This means that each literacy transaction is unique and that each learner is unique. This also means that the process of literacy development is dynamic and complex. In Mr. Thomas' classroom, the varied activities provide a range of contexts and texts for children's literacy transactions. As a reflective teacher, Mr. Thomas' awareness of the components of literacy transactions and the complexity of the interactions provides him with an awareness of the importance of providing learning activities and instructional scaffolds that support individual children's literacy development. The focus of this chapter is on describing the ways in which you can provide second- and third-grade children with opportunities to continue their literacy development across a range of different types of texts and learning contexts.

Learner Characteristics

During second and third grade, children continue to build on their understandings of reading and writing. Most children will enter second grade with a sight vocabulary of about 100 words, can read simple texts accurately using their phonetic knowledge to decode new words, and can write using both conventional and invented spelling.

There will also be variability among the children: for example, differences in the size of children's listening vocabularies as well as sight vocabularies. You may have children in your classroom who are English language learners or who have other special learning needs. In working with ELLs you will want to know their prior language experiences, such as the language spoken at home and how long they have resided in the United States. Children whose families are recent immigrants and/or who do not speak English at home will need to have learning activities adapted to fit their zones of proximal development. You will also want to be aware of children who experienced low achievement in first grade. Because of these differences among children in typical second- and third-grade classrooms, it is necessary to provide a range of learning contexts and literacy materials to address their individual needs.

Learning Contexts

The context of literacy development in second and third grade is influenced by the commercial curriculum adopted by each school as well as other instructional resources at the school. This context is also influenced by specific state standards for student achievement in literacy. These standards are often integrated into the commercial curriculum, serving as guides for lesson planning and assessment. As a reflective teacher, you have a very important role in using the available curriculum materials and state standards to establish learning contexts that enhance literacy development of all children. In this section, you will learn general guidelines for creating a literacy-rich classroom at the second- and third-grade level. Subsequent sections of the chapter focus on specific strategies for enhancing key areas of literacy development.

Guidelines for Creating a Literacy-Rich Classroom

Provide a range of formal and informal contexts. Children this age benefit from having both direct teaching and informal or self-guided literacy experiences. In direct teaching, a teacher introduces and/or demonstrates the skill or concept to be learned (Rooperine & Johnson, 2005). This is followed by guided practice during which time the teacher mediates and supports children's use of the concept or skill. During direct teaching, you will probably have children grouped by their common instructional needs. For example, in the opening vignette, Mr. Thomas' guided reading groups were composed of children who were at the same level of oral reading.

An important part of the learning process involves giving children opportunities to apply what they have learned through informal, self-directed activities. These activities may involve working with a peer or working independently. For example, the groupings of children that occurred while Mr. Thomas was engaged with a guided reading group varied according to the specific activity.

Nurture a literacy community perspective through interactive read-alouds. Throughout your school day, you will be grouping children in various ways for different instructional purposes. To create a feeling of classroom community, you will want to have several times during the day when everyone in your classroom is engaged in a joint activity. This feeling of community can be nurtured through interactive read-alouds.

Language and literacy develop through social interaction. Simply because children are beginning to read on their own does not mean that you should discontinue reading aloud to them. By gathering your second and third graders together for a read-aloud, you are inviting them to sit back and enjoy hearing someone else read (Fisher, Flood, Lapp, & Frey, 2004). Reading for personal enjoyment is a major motivation for many readers. You are also modeling fluent reading and creating a setting for the sharing of interesting text. It is important that you not simply read aloud, but that you read interactively, involving your children in active listening and responding to what you read. Interactive read-alouds foster the creation of a literacy community in several ways: (a) Developing shared knowledge among your children, (b) valuing all children's responses to read-aloud texts, and (c) increasing literacy-focused social interactions.

Developing shared knowledge. When you read stories and information books aloud to your class at circle time, you are fostering a shared knowledge of concepts, vocabulary, and story events. This shared knowledge becomes a frame of reference for them and provides a focus for their conversations and interactions. You are also showing them the ways in which reading adds meaning to our experiences and life events. It is very important that all children be present for your read-aloud times so that they do not miss out on building this shared knowledge. By reading multicultural literature, you will be tapping into the funds of knowledge of your diverse students (Gonzalez, Moll, Floyd-Tenery, Rivera, Rendon, Gonzales, & Amanti, 1993; Gonzalez, Moll, & Amanti, 2005) as well as enhancing the knowledge of your nonminority students (Laier, Edwards, McMillon, & Turner, 2001). This will contribute further to the shared knowledge of your learning community. Be sure to select multicultural literature that authentically represents the culture and language and is free of stereotypes (Diamond & Moore, 1995).

The way in which you read aloud also impacts the development of this shared knowledge. As you read, pause to focus on new vocabulary and talk about specific events or situations. In addition, varying your intonation and volume and using meaningful gestures and facial expressions contributes to children's comprehension of text and development of shared knowledge.

Valuing all children's responses. In a literacy community, each child's response to what is read is valued and recognized as a reflection of the literacy transaction that has occurred. When children listen to a text being read, their comprehension and understanding of the text will reflect their prior knowledge, the text being read, and how it is being shared. During your read-aloud, you will use questioning to first activate children's prior knowledge and to predict book content. Then during and after reading you could elicit children' comments and questions to predict or reflect on book content. As you do this, be sure that each child has an opportunity to participate in this sharing of thoughts and respond to what was read. Your goal is to have wide participation from students. You can encourage this wide participation by following these guidelines:

1. Be sure to maintain frequent eye contact with your children so that you can monitor their non-verbal as well as verbal responses to what you read.
2. Provide 3–4 seconds of wait time before you call on someone. This will discourage students from quickly waving their arms wildly and will encourage more thoughtful responses as well as responses from more children.
3. As you elicit responses from students, encourage them to stay focused on story as well as the on-going discussion.
4. Remind students that everyone needs a chance to talk.
5. Use a variety of questions to encourage participation from all students. For example, ask some questions that involve only a word or two response, as well as other questions that elicit a more elaborate explanation or encourage students to relate story content to their own experiences.

To encourage all children's responses, it is also helpful to give students guidelines for their participation in a discussion. These can be developed through a group discussion and then recorded on chart paper or a poster to be displayed in the classroom. Figure 11.1 lists five example guidelines for students to follow.

Increasing literacy-focused social interactions. Stories shared at read-aloud time can become the focus of story re-enactments and story extensions. When everyone in your class is familiar with the original story, there will be greater participation and involvement as the story is re-enacted or extended. You could also segment the story into parts and have a different group of children create a puppet show for their particular segment of the story. These shared experiences build a sense of community among your children.

Provide well-stocked classroom library. Classroom libraries are a critical component of a literacy-rich classroom (Routman, 2003; Sanacore, 2006). Classroom libraries increase accessibility to books and that encourages children to engage in more voluntary reading (Young & Moss, 2006). This is especially important for children who may not have access to books outside of your classroom. You will also want to provide a "suggestion box" for children to let you know what types of books they would like to see added to the

 Figure 11.1 Student Guidelines for Participation in Class Discussion

Remember to:
1. Be a good listener.
2. Raise your hand to be called on.
3. Focus on the current topic of discussion.
4. Respect others' personal space when seated on the rug area.
5. Take turns participating.

Figure 11.2 Checklist for a Well-Stocked Classroom Library

☑ Reading materials representing a variety of reading levels
☑ Multicultural books reflecting a wide range of diversities
☑ Nonfiction books reflecting interests of children in class
☑ Sufficient numbers of books (approximately 8 to 10 per child)
☑ Developmentally appropriate children's magazines and comic books
☑ Comfortable seating for several children
☑ Materials clearly organized for easy access and return to display
☑ All materials in good condition.
☑ Range of fiction: realistic fiction, modern fantasy, folktales, historical fiction
☑ Range of nonfiction: biography, science, social science, how things work, how-to books, hobbies, crafts, sports
☑ Poetry
☑ Books with audiotapes
☑ Clear directions for check-out and return of materials/books for at-home reading

classroom library. By providing a wide range of book titles and other printed materials (such as children's magazines, poetry, and comic books), you will be able to increase children' motivation to read. This is particularly important for children who are experiencing difficulty in learning specific reading skills. Additional criteria for a well-stocked library are included in the checklist located in Figure 11.2. A listing of suggested fiction and nonfiction books is provided in Appendix L.

In addition to providing a well-stocked library, you need to be sure that all children have equal opportunities to use the classroom library. If children can use the classroom library only after they have finished all of their other work, children who are struggling or who spend time out of the room for resource assistance will not have the same opportunities as others to use the classroom library. It is important that they become engaged with books for personal purposes, as well as during direct instruction. Increased access to books in classrooms is associated with more positive attitudes about reading as well as higher reading comprehension and achievement (Young & Moss, 2006).

Provide a range of text types throughout literacy activities. The types of texts that your children read also contribute to the literacy context of your classroom. In addition to making sure your classroom library has a wide range of text types, that is, different genres, you will want to be sure that the other literacy activities also are characterized by different types of text. For example, if the guided reading sessions use only narrative text, children will miss out on learning how to read and comprehend informational text. Similarly, if poetry is not included as text during guided reading, children may not develop strategies for reading and comprehending poetry.

Strategies for Enhancing Key Areas of Literacy

Literacy instruction in second and third grade is focused on supporting children in becoming independent readers and writers. In reading instruction, four areas are emphasized:

❖ decoding/word recognition,
❖ vocabulary,
❖ text comprehension, and
❖ fluency

Writing instruction emphasizes two areas: the writing process and spelling. In this section, strategies for enhancing these key areas of literacy are described. Some of these strategies were introduced at the first-grade level; however, in second and third grade these strategies are focused on more complex literacy transactions.

Decoding and Word Recognition

In second grade and third grade the emphasis on decoding and word recognition focuses on word structure and figuring out unknown words by looking at the entire word, not only the beginning and ending sounds. Now the focus will include supporting children's decoding of words that have more complex letter–sound relationships, such as consonant blends (*str* in *street*), digraphs (*ph* in *phone*), silent consonants (*k* in *know*), and diphthongs (*oi* in *foil*), as well as letters that are associated with multiple sounds (*g* in *giant, gum,* and *gym*) (Rycik & Rycik, 2007). Other word analysis strategies emphasized in second and third grade include using base words, prefixes, and suffixes, and recognizing compound words (Fox, 2004; Mountain, 2005; White, 2005). Children are also encouraged to learn how to divide words into parts (syllables) as a strategy for figuring out words they do not immediately recognize. Guided reading and word study are two main instructional strategies for enhancing decoding and word recognition.

Guided reading. In guided reading, a teacher meets with a small group of children, usually four to six children, who are at the same reading level. The texts that are used in guided reading are at the "just right" level (Tompkins, 2007), where the text is read with 90 to 95 percent accuracy and good comprehension. This means that the children will be able to read most of the words, but still need support for decoding some words that they are not able to recognize. As they take turns reading orally, the teacher provides scaffolding and support.

As you are interacting with children during guided reading, you want to help them know how to figure out words that they do not know. Rather than just telling them what the word is, you want to give them cues and strategies for figuring out words. Some of your cues may focus on the letter–sound relationships and word parts, such as syllables and base words; other cues may focus on the meaning implied in the rest of the sentence (Brown, 2003). Your cues will vary with the target word and with the way in which the word is used in the text. Weaver (2002) suggests the following prompts to support children' decoding and word recognition:

❖ Look at the picture. Does it give you a clue to the mystery word?
❖ Look at the first letter(s) in the word. What word might fit here that would make sense?
❖ Read to the end of the sentence. What word would make sense here?
❖ Look at the parts of the word. Do these give you clues to the mystery word?
❖ Back up and read the sentence over. What would make sense here?

As you use these prompts during guided reading, children will begin to internalize these prompts so they can use them during independent reading. You could also display these prompts on a classroom poster or on bookmarks for children to keep at their desks.

Word study. Decoding and word recognition strategies are also the focus of guided word study. This means that the teacher selects a group of words that have the same phonetic characteristics and directs children' attention to the ways in which these words are structured. Words may be selected that have the same consonant or vowel letter–sound pattern, or represent the same rime pattern (Fox, 2004). You will want to select the group words

During word study, teachers focus children's attention on the ways words are structured and how sounds are represented in print.

Beverly Otto

for study from the children's text. This is because you want children to have practice recognizing these words in meaningful text and not only in isolation.

After you have selected the words to be studied, write each word on a separate 4" × 6" card or piece of paper, using a black or dark-blue marker. During group time, display the word cards on a pocket chart and begin your instruction.

Perhaps you decide you want to focus on the sounds associated with the letter S (Fox, 2004) and you have selected words representing these sounds from your children' reading texts. Your word cards might include the following (p. 233):

> sack, salt, save, saw
> bass, boss, bus, chase
> amuse, arise, as, cause

With the words displayed on a pocket chart, you first point to each word, pronounce it, and ask your children to say the word. Then you say, "let's think about the sounds made in these words by the letter S." As you then read each word again, stretch out the sounds so that children can begin to identify the different sounds associated with the letter S. At this point, you can have children help you sort the words into groups according to the S sound in the word. After you have concluded your lesson, place the word cards on the word wall so children can refer to them as they read and write. This activity can be extended by providing individual sets of word cards so each child can be involved in sorting the words while gathered in a small group activity (see photograph page 279).

Word walls can serve as a major focal point in your word study activities. Throughout the year, your word wall may be organized in various ways, depending on how you are using it. Word walls are also used to display high-frequency words that are hard to spell and decode,

Differences in vocabulary among children begin to have a significant impact on reading comprehension and academic performance in second and third grade.

Monkey Business Images

such as *they, said, have,* and *because,* as well as contractions, common compound words, and common prefixes (*dis-, un-, in-*), and frequently misspelled words found in children's writing (Hall & Cunningham, 1999). A word wall can also help children to study words that are part of a particular thematic unit, such as "Animals in the Forest" or "Famous People."

Vocabulary

Vocabulary development is important at each developmental level. Differences in vocabulary among children begin to have a significant impact on reading comprehension and academic performance in second and third grade, and if not addressed continue to have an impact in the upper grades. Because reading materials now are more complex and use a wider vocabulary, the size of children's vocabulary becomes more critical (Chall, 1996).

Impact of vocabulary differences. Dramatic differences in the vocabulary size of second and third graders have been reported by researchers. In some instances children "begin school knowing 1,000 to 3,000 fewer words than their peers" (Brabham & Villaume, 2002, p. 264). Biemiller and Slonim (2001, in Biemiller, 2003) found that among second graders, children with the most extensive vocabularies averaged 7,100 base words and children with the least extensive vocabularies averaged 3,000.

If you were teaching in a classroom with a wide disparity in vocabulary size, you would notice significant differences in children's comprehension of text as well as their ability to contribute in oral discussion of stories and other texts. Not only would you need to adapt your lessons to support the children with reduced vocabulary, you would need to make vocabulary development a priority for these children so that they do not fall further behind. Follow-up research by Biemiller and Slonim (Biemiller, 2003) of children with less extensive vocabularies found that by fifth grade they still had not reached the vocabulary size reached by the high-vocabulary children three years earlier. Thus, second and third grade is a time when vocabulary development is a major focus in the literacy curriculum. Vocabulary development is especially important for second- and third-grade children who are English language learners, as well as other children who are not reading at grade level.

"Knowing" a word. Vocabulary development involves much more than simply memorizing a definition or identifying the correct definition in a multiple-choice question. In order for a word to be "known," a reader has to not only understand the word's core meaning, but also must understand that the meaning may change depending on the context in which the word is used (Osborn & Armbruster, 2001). Awareness of how context changes a word's meaning is enhanced by encountering the word in a variety of texts. For example, the word *run* has multiple meanings and is used in many different contexts. As you read through the following sentences, note the different meanings for the word *run:*

> Orlando can run fast.
> Susan went on a run around the park.
> Susan decided to run to the store for a gallon of milk.
> Mr. Jones decided to run for Congress.
> When you put too much paint on the wall, it will begin to run.
> Marco hit a home run in the ball game.
> Don't give me the run-around.

In addition to learning that the meaning of words will vary depending on the context in which the words are used, children also need to develop more abstract understandings of conceptual relationships between words. For example, the words *drizzle* and *shower* are conceptually closer than are *drizzle* and *volcano*. Drizzle and shower both describe a form of precipitation, while volcano does not.

Understanding the ways in which words relate to other words provides a way of grouping words into useful categories that can contribute to comprehension. For example, some words have opposite meanings, such as *hot* and *cold*. These are referred to as **antonyms**. Other words have similar meanings, such as *happy* and *joyful*, and are referred to as **synonyms**.

Enhancing vocabulary development. Most children learn about 3,000 to 4,000 new words each year: however, only about 300 to 500 of those words are directly taught (Osborn & Armbruster, 2001). This means that much of children's vocabulary growth occurs during independent reading and other related activities. While independent reading appears to be associated with greater vocabulary growth, direct vocabulary teaching provides children with strategies and understandings that will support this vocabulary growth as they read independently (Brabham & Villaume, 2002). As you engage children in focusing on vocabulary, remember that you are setting the atmosphere for their learning. Your enthusiasm for learning new words sets the stage for your children's learning (Cunningham, 2006).

Provide opportunities for hands-on, direct experiences. Vocabulary develops through direct and vicarious experiences. Direct experiences are those in which a student is involved as a participant, for example, riding on the subway or riding on a horse. Vicarious experiences are those that occur while reading a book, watching a video, or hearing someone else speak about an event. These two types of experiences develop the conceptual knowledge that is then represented by specific vocabulary words (see Figure 11.3). Because children in second and third grade are in the concrete operations stage of cognitive development (as described by Piaget, see Flavell, 1996), they still need to have direct experiences connected to their vocabulary development. Because of this, you will want to incorporate real experiences as much as possible into your curriculum when you focus on vocabulary development. This can be done through field trips and guest speaker demonstrations,

Figure 11.3 Experiential Basis of Vocabulary Development and Comprehension

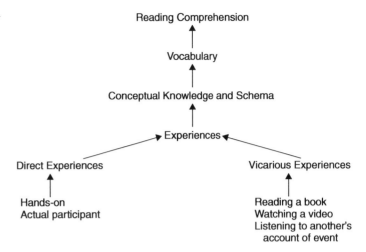

and by incorporating realia and other artifacts into your vocabulary emphasis. These experiences are especially important for children who may not have had opportunities for such experiences at home or in their community. Be sure to focus on key vocabulary words that are related to these direct experiences.

Use both teacher-guided vocabulary instruction and opportunities for independent vocabulary experiences. Because you cannot provide direct experiences for all of your vocabulary instruction, you will use teacher-guided vicarious experiences that involve reading, listening, and viewing, as well as provide opportunities for children to read interesting books independently. Teacher-guided vocabulary activities occur during interactive read-alouds, guided reading, and guided word study. Osborn and Armbruster (2001) offer these guidelines:

❖ Select words to teach that reflect grade-level content areas and literacy curricular materials. Children will remember them better if the words they are studying are also encountered when reading in class. In this way the guided word study facilitates those later literacy transactions.

❖ Encourage children to connect new words to words they already know. These connections help children to remember the words better and understand how the new words relate to previously known words.

❖ Provide multiple opportunities to focus on the same words in meaningful activities that incorporate both oral and written language. Reading the same new words in multiple texts as well as using them when writing and speaking reinforces the new vocabulary.

❖ Teach parts of words that contribute to meaning, such as prefixes, suffixes, and base words. Children can use these meaningful parts as clues to understanding new vocabulary.

As you engage children in directly focusing on vocabulary during interactive read-alouds and guided reading, you can demonstrate strategies they can then use when they are reading by themselves. When children ask about the meaning of a particular word, show them ways to use the context to narrow down the meaning of the word before stopping their reading to look the word up in a dictionary. There are two main reasons this is beneficial. First of all, the literal dictionary meaning may not match the way in which the word is used in the text. In addition, when a reader stops to look up a word in the dictionary, the time it takes to locate the word in the dictionary and then determine how that applies to the use of the word in the text interrupts comprehension of the text. Instead, encourage children to use the following two strategies: synonym search and looking inside the word.

1. *Synonym search.* When children come to a word they do not understand, suggest that they first read to the end of the sentence and think of a word that would make sense. Then, ask them to write the unknown word down on a slip of paper or sticky note along with their guess as to what it might mean or a word that they think is similar in meaning. Then they should reread the entire sentence, substituting in their guess. If they think of another word that would make sense, they can also write that down on the sticky note or slip of paper. After they have finished reading, they can look up the unknown words in a dictionary or thesaurus and confirm or revise their notes. It is also useful to transfer the new words to a notebook so they can refer to them later on.

2. *Looking inside the word.* Encourage children to look "inside" words for familiar base words, prefixes, or suffixes that give clues to meaning. **Prefixes** are morphemic units that are added to the beginning of base words to change meaning. At the second-grade level you will focus first on the four prefixes that appear most frequently: *un-* (undone), *re-* (redo), *in-* (incomplete), and *dis-* (disagree) (Fox 2004). Then you can gradually include other prefixes as well.

Suffixes are morphemic units that are added to the end of base words. There are two main types of suffixes: inflectional and derivational. **Inflectional suffixes** are added to the end of base words to show plurality (bush*es* or cat*s*), verb tense (walk*ed*, walk*ing*), or make comparisons (fast, fast*er*, fast*est*). **Derivational suffixes** change the grammatical function of the base word. For example, by adding *-or* to the verb *instruct*, it becomes a noun, *instructor*. Knowledge of common prefixes and suffixes helps children "look inside the word" for meaning clues when they are reading.

Provide developmentally appropriate dictionaries, glossaries, and thesauruses. When you are selecting vocabulary reference aids for your classroom, select those that reflect the reading level of your children. Avoid selecting dictionaries that have pronunciation guides with diacritical markings for second or third graders. Illustrated dictionaries also provide visual support for the definitions. In addition, the illustrations make finding the words in the dictionary easier. Children's use of these reference aids will increase if they each have a small paperback dictionary or thesaurus at their desks. You will want to demonstrate how to use the guide words located at the top of each page as well as any abbreviations or coding notations.

Use interactive read-alouds to enhance children's listening vocabulary. Vocabulary development of all children is enhanced when interesting and high-quality literature is shared during interactive read-alouds (Osborn & Armbruster, 2001). Reading aloud increases exposure to the rich language found in good literature (Brabham & Villaume, 2002). In second and third grade, children will have texts that are leveled for reading difficulty. While this is necessary to provide children with texts that they can read without becoming frustrated, it also means that the words in the texts are controlled with respect to the number of syllables per word as well as the number of new words introduced in each selection. Leveled texts also may not have the rich vocabulary or literary devices such as similes, metaphors, or poetic language found in trade books (Dzaldov & Peterson, 2005). For this reason, your read-alouds provide important exposure to more complex vocabulary (Blachowicz & Obrochta, 2005). As you read to your children, focus on new vocabulary before, during, and after reading the text. When children understand new vocabulary encountered during read-alouds, they then have a foundation for recognizing and understanding the words when the words appear in their reading texts.

Avoid vocabulary materials that are unrelated to children's reading texts. Many different commercial materials are available that focus on vocabulary development. Generally these materials have a format in which a certain number of words are designated for each lesson and a series of activities are prescribed for using those words, such as writing the definition from a dictionary, using the word in sentences, completing fill-in-the-blank exercises, or crossword puzzles, followed by a test before moving on to the next unit of new words. While these materials may provide vocabulary activities that children can work on independently, they are not as effective as activities that involve vocabulary drawn from the texts that children are reading. Adding vocabulary from current reading encourages children to incorporate the new vocabulary into their existing schema and conceptual knowledge (Brabham & Villaume, 2002).

Use graphic displays of words. Word webs provide a visual representation of word meaning and how words are related to each other (Laframboise, 2000). Initially you will develop word webs as a part of your direct vocabulary instruction. Children can contribute to a class word web and then develop their own. Here are several steps you can follow in creating a word web:

1. Select a word that is commonly known and used by children as your focus for this demonstration. Perhaps you select a word that is commonly overused, such as *happy* or *good*. Prepare a poster or piece of chart paper with the word written in the center.
2. Brainstorm with your children for other words that are similar to the target word. Limit this brainstorming to a minute or so. Add several responses to your chart paper.
3. Divide your class into groups of two to three children and have them continue thinking of words that are related to the target word children.
4. After a short time (10 to 15 minutes), reconvene your entire class and ask children to share their responses.
5. Add their responses to your class word web, discussing the variations of meaning represented in each word.

A sample word web for the word *happy* is found in Figure 11.4.

Another graphic organizer that is effective for showing word relationships is a semantic word map (Rupley, Logan, & Nichols, 1998/1999). This format provides a way of showing how words are related. This activity could follow your read-aloud of an informational text, such as a book on weather. The first step in developing a semantic word map is to brainstorm with your children about the topic or main concept, generating a list of related words. Then you can demonstrate how the words can be grouped into different categories, asking

Figure 11.4   Example of a Word Web

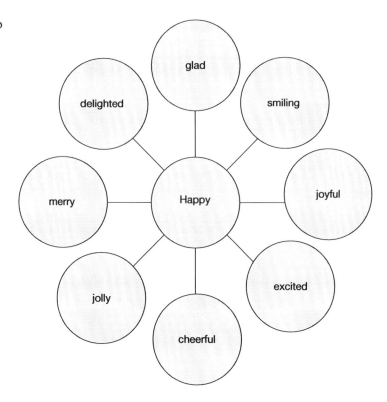

children to suggest which words might fit in a specific category. Figure 11.5 shows the list of words generated by children, and how the words were organized in a semantic word map.

Provide opportunities for independent reading.   Vocabulary is also enhanced when children read interesting books on their own. You will want to be sure to have books in your classroom library that reflect students' interests and prior experiences, as well as books that appeal to their intellectual curiosity.

By also providing books in the library center that have been shared at group story time, children's comprehension and enjoyment of the text will be enhanced. Audiotapes of familiar books also provide additional support for vocabulary development. Adding audiotapes to your lending library provides further opportunities to enjoy favorite stories and strengthens vocabulary development through repetition.

Providing extra support.   Because vocabulary development is critical to comprehension, you will need to provide additional support for children who appear to have limited listening and reading vocabularies. While each of the activities described earlier in this section is beneficial for all children, you may need to provide additional support through one-on-one or small group activities.

It is also important to encourage parents to read to their children at home. If parents are not fluent in reading English, they can be encouraged to share books by talking about the illustrations. To encourage children's reading at home, provide a lending library in your classroom of easy-reading fiction and nonfiction books with quality illustrations or photos.

English language learners.   The vocabulary of English language learners in second and third grade can be enhanced by (1) making connections to their first language, (2) making connections to real objects and prior experiences, (3) providing dual language as well

Figure 11.5 Semantic Word Map for Vocabulary Study

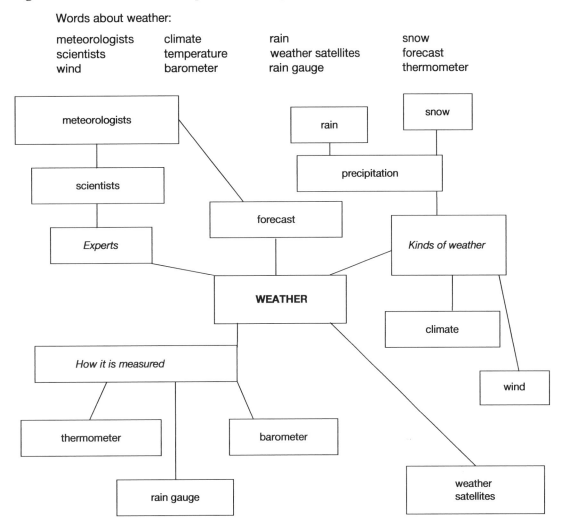

Words about weather:

meteorologists	climate	rain	snow
scientists	temperature	weather satellites	forecast
wind	barometer	rain gauge	thermometer

as illustrated reference materials, and (4) providing opportunities for repeated exposure to new vocabulary through meaningful texts.

1. *Make connections to cognates in their first language.* A **cognate** is a word that has a similar form and meaning to a word in another language (Harris & Hodges, 1995). Not all languages will have cognates; however, for languages that have cognates with English, it is beneficial to emphasize these similarities as it creates a tie between their home language and English. In the following list, English words and their Spanish cognate are listed (Cappellini, 2005, p. 277–278):

English	*Spanish*
predict	predecir
connect	conectar
describe	describir
author	autor

city	ciudad
islands	isles
rivers	rios
number	numero

By focusing on cognates, ELLs are encouraged to use their knowledge of their home language to learn new English vocabulary (Au, 2002b). This is especially helpful in content areas such as science, social science, and math. You could also create a word wall or chart of the related words in both languages (Cappellini, 2005).

2. ***Make connections to real objects and prior experiences*** (**Cunningham & Allington, 2007**). As much as possible, provide real objects that represent new vocabulary, as well as using visuals, such as charts or illustrations. Before ELLs read a text, encourage them to read the pictures, going on a "picture walk" to activate prior knowledge and related vocabulary. Having children "act out" new vocabulary is also beneficial; for example, acting out "curious" or "nervous." You can create a word card–picture matching activity by using photographs, clip art, pictures from magazines, or simple illustrations. This activity can be placed in a learning center.

3. ***Provide dual-language reference materials.*** By providing dual-language dictionaries and glossaries, ELLs can use their home language as a basis for acquiring English (Blachowicz & Fisher, 2006). You will need to have a dual-language dictionary for each language represented in your classroom. You can also encourage ELLs to make their own dual-language glossary or dictionary of words they know and are learning. They can also add illustrations to their definitions as a way of visually representing word meaning. Providing dual-language reference materials also encourages English-only students to learn words in another language, which can deepen the students' understanding of diversity within your learning community.

4. ***Provide opportunities for repeated exposure to new vocabulary through meaningful texts*** (**Meyerson & Kulesza, 2006**). By choosing reading selections that follow a certain theme or topic, children are more likely to encounter the same new vocabulary across different texts. Repeated exposures are also needed to learn words that have more than one meaning.

Struggling readers. Children who are reading below grade level will also benefit from vocabulary activities that incorporate real objects and draw on their prior experiences (Cunningham, 2006). As you use an object to introduce new vocabulary, engage children in describing the object, such as its size, shape, color, function, and similarity to other objects. You could encourage children to develop their own questions about the object using a version of the 20-questions game. You might decide to summarize your discussion by creating a word web or semantic word map. Additional beneficial activities include word card–picture matching games, acting-out of new vocabulary words, and access to high-interest, easy-reading texts for independent reading.

Recognizing and knowing the meaning of words is an important part of comprehension; however, being able to pronounce the words and know the meaning of individual words alone does not lead to text comprehension. Some children can decode words and accurately pronounce them, but do not yet fully comprehend the meaning of the text. In the next section, the focus is on enhancing children's comprehension of narrative and informational texts.

Comprehension

Difficulties in comprehending text may occur as second- and third-grade children encounter literacy program materials with a wider vocabulary and more complex grammatical structures. Comprehension also becomes more critical as they begin to use reading to learn in the content areas (for example, science, social studies, and math). In addition to needing support for comprehending more complex text structures, children also need to be supported in understanding the more complex ideas presented in these texts. Because children in second and third grade are still in the concrete operations stage of cognitive development, as described by Piaget (Flavell, 1996), it is important to remember that they will need to have visual representations (photographs, illustrations, or drawings), actual objects, or hands-on, direct experiences to support their understanding of abstract concepts presented in content area texts (DeCorse, 2001).

Primary goal: Nurturing independent readers. The primary goal of reading instruction is to support children's development as independent readers who comprehend what they are reading and can use reading to learn across the curriculum. Comprehension does not simply involve knowing what is stated literally in the text, but also involves making inferences and connecting the text to prior knowledge and experiences. According to Pardo (2004), "meaning emerges only from the engagement of that reader with that text at that particular moment in time" (p. 272). Effective comprehension involves thinking about the ways in which you are reading and monitoring your understanding of the text. This self-monitoring involves a conscious awareness of how you read as well as an awareness of comprehension difficulties.

Teachers support children' development as independent readers by demonstrating how to consciously use comprehension strategies across a range of text types (Barton & Sawyer, 2003/2004). This involves whole group direct instruction along with guided practice in small groups. Through this demonstration and support, children learn to monitor their own comprehension and know how to fix it when comprehension is problematic. Gradually children internalize these strategies so they can then use them during independent reading.

Strategies for enhancing children's comprehension of texts. As you begin to demonstrate strategies for children to use in comprehending texts, you will want to focus on strategies that are easily remembered as well as effective.

STAR Technique. The STAR technique developed by Marcell (2006), provides an example of an easily remembered, but effective way of encouraging children to actively think about what they read. This technique incorporates four main strategies that enhance comprehension: visualizing, predicting, asking questions, and connecting. The STAR acronym represents the following steps that readers can follow in comprehending text:

> S = See it in your mind's eye.
> T = Think about what's going to happen next.
> A = Ask questions.
> R = Relate the story to your life. (pp. 66–67)

When introducing this technique, prepare a chart or overhead transparency with thought bubbles representing each step. Then as you are reading with the whole class in an interactive read-aloud, you can pause to refer to each thought bubble, providing sample responses and eliciting responses from your children. When you use this technique again, provide each student with laminated thought bubbles and a marker so they can respond individually. As children become more independent in using this technique, provide them with laminated bookmarks to help them remember each step. Examples of thought bubbles are displayed in Figure 11.6.

Figure 11.6 Thought Bubbles to Encourage Comprehension Using the STAR Strategy

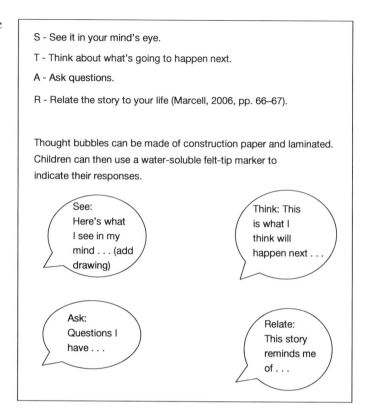

Students can also be encouraged to use this technique by providing them with a STAR bookmark, such as the one shown in Figure 11.7. You can also encourage children to design their own bookmarks.

Teacher think-alouds. The STAR technique also illustrates the importance of teacher think-alouds in demonstrating the comprehension process. "Think alouds make invisible mental processes visible to children" (Wilhelm, 1999, p. 1). Think-alouds model the transaction or "meaning-making" process that occurs between reader, text, and context (Pressley, 1999). This means that as you read aloud to children, you pause and verbally share what you are thinking about the text, your feelings, your questions, prior experiences, and predictions of upcoming text. Through frequent teacher think-alouds, children learn how effective readers transact with text, and not simply decode or recognize individual words. Children then begin to internalize this process of active thinking while they read, benefiting their comprehension of text. Children can then apply the various strategies when reading independently.

Self-monitoring comprehension: Before, during, and after reading. Effective readers monitor their comprehension of text (Duke & Pearson, 2002). This monitoring takes place as they begin to interact with a text, while they are reading, and after reading the text. As you encourage children to self-monitor their comprehension you can focus on the following questions:

- ❖ Before reading: What do I think this book will be about? What do I know about this topic?
- ❖ During reading: Do I understand what is being described in the text? Does this make sense? What do I think will be next?

Figure 11.7 Example of STAR Bookmark

Be a Star!

S - See it in your mind.

T - Think about what's going to happen next.

A - Ask questions.

R - Relate the story to your life.

❖ After reading: What can I remember about this book? Think of the 5 Ws and 1 H: who, what, where, when, why, and how?

In addition to focusing on comprehension at these three times when reading, you can encourage children to use a checklist as they are reading, such as the one in Figure 11.8. First introduce this checklist during a guided-reading session, with the checklist displayed

Figure 11.8 Comprehension Check Poster

Questions to ask when I read:
Does it make sense?
☐ Yes: Keep on reading!
☐ No:

    ❖ Look at the illustrations for clues.
    ❖ If there is an unknown word, spell it aloud to yourself. Try to guess the identity of the word.
    ❖ Reread the sentence. Can you guess at the meaning of the new word(s)?
    ❖ Reread the paragraph, looking for new information.
    ❖ Read ahead several sentences and then go back to reread, focusing on the meaning of the text.

on a poster. After children are familiar with the checklist, provide them with individual bookmarks containing the checklist so they can refer to it when they are reading. This will help them think about what they are reading and give them a way of dealing with comprehension problems (Massey, 2003).

Peer-group conversations about texts. Another way of enhancing children's comprehension involves providing opportunities for discussion with their peers about stories or texts read to them at group time or read independently. Through interactive discussions, children "learn to comprehend beyond decoding the words" (Hammerberg, 2004, p. 655). By viewing reading as a transaction between a reader, the text, and the context, thus welcoming readers' multiple perspectives, answers, and interpretations, children's comprehension of text extends beyond decoding and word recognition. It also encourages children to connect texts with their individual lives and experiences as well as connecting with the perspectives of their peers (Leal, 1993).

You may find it useful to start peer discussions between dyads of children rather than larger groupings. Dyad groups will encourage more active participation by each child. You may also find that you need to provide some starter questions for children to use in discussing the text. After a short time for peer discussion, gather your whole class together for a sharing of thoughts and interpretations that were expressed in the dyads.

Children can also share their thoughts about what they have read through dialogue journals with a peer (Bode, 1989; Cooper & Kiger, 2006). To start children in this sharing, each child needs to have a spiral notebook. You may need to provide them with general topics such as, "Here's what I liked about the story . . ." or "This story reminded me of . . . ." Children then exchange journals to share what they have drawn or written. Each partner then responds by writing or drawing in the shared journal. Because dialogue journals are not evaluated by the teacher for spelling and grammar, children can focus on meaning rather than form when they write or draw in their journals (Peyton, 1993). Dialogue journals have been found to be very beneficial to English language learners (Peyton, 1993; Reyes, 1995).

Strategies for comprehending specific types of text. Comprehension of different types of texts involves different ways of reading. Narrative texts generally involve characters who are involved in a sequence of events. In contrast, informational texts are structured in a number of different ways, such as descriptive, cause and effect, and comparisons. Specific strategies are needed to successfully comprehend both narrative and informational text.

Narrative text. Children's comprehension of narrative text can be enhanced by strategies that focus on making inferences, story structure, and characterization.

1. *Making inferences.* **Inferencing** requires a reader to search within a text for related information and combine it to come to a conclusion or to make a prediction (Wilhelm, 1999). As you engage in interactive read-alouds of narrative texts, you can model inferencing through thinking-aloud and sharing your thoughts, predictions, and conclusions. You can also encourage children's inferencing during guided reading by asking questions that go beyond what is stated in the text, requiring them to combine facts and predict what will happen or to reflect on characters' motivations and the significance of story events.

2. *Focusing on narrative structure by using story maps.* Using story maps is an effective way of showing how stories have common elements, for example, setting, characters, problem, goal, action, outcome, resolution, and theme (Pearson, 1981 in Duke & Pearson, 2002). Children who have had experience with using story maps in first grade may be ready for story maps that are more complex (see Figure 11.9). Adding this visual support during story discussion provides children with a framework for comprehension and for remembering significant events and structural elements of a story. It is important to remember that the focus of story mapping is on increased understanding of the story, rather than just the creation of the story map (Hammerberg, 2004).

3. *Focusing on characterization.* Children's comprehension of narrative text is also enhanced by strategies that focus on the characters. This may involve describing a character's personality, motivations, feelings, and actions (Barton & Sawyer, 2003/2004; Bluestein, 2002; Shanahan & Shanahan, (1997). Characterization requires that children interact with text at a deeper level of comprehension.

As you focus children's attention on characters in a narrative, your questions might include the following (Bluestein, 2002):

1. What words describe this character?
2. Do you agree with the character's actions? Why or why not?
3. What do you think the character will do next? Why?
4. Why do you think this character has this problem?
5. How do you think this character feels? Have you ever felt this way?

Figure 11.9 Story Map

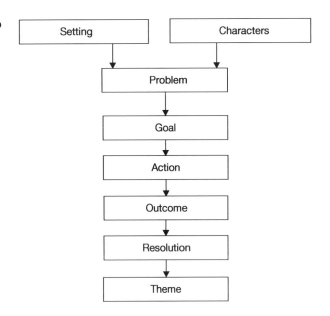

As you engage children in characterization, you may find that charts and other graphic organizers are useful in providing a way of focusing children's attention as well as sharing and remembering information. The format of the graphic organizer you use will depend upon the way in which you are thinking about the characters. It may take the form of a word web, with the character's name in the center, surrounded by words that describe the character. Or you may decide to create a character continuum (Barton & Sawyer, 2003/2004) that shows how a character changes throughout a story. If you decide to compare the similarities and differences between two characters you might use a Venn diagram or a simple two-column chart.

Informational text. Comprehension strategies for understanding informational text are emphasized in second and third grade as a way of preparing children for interacting with increasing amounts of informational text in upper elementary grades (Hall, Sabey, & McClellan, 2005). Four strategies that enhance comprehension of informational text include:

1. Activating prior knowledge and setting purposes for reading
2. varying reading speed to reflect the purpose for reading
3. using book features to anticipate content
4. reviewing and summarizing expository text by creating graphic organizers.

As you use these strategies with your children, you will first demonstrate them in a whole-class setting and then provide opportunities for children to begin to apply the strategies as they engage in guided and independent reading of informational texts.

1. *Activating prior knowledge and setting purposes for reading.* Comprehension of informational text is enhanced when prior knowledge of the topic is activated. By using the first two steps in the K-W-L strategy (described in Chapter 10; Ogle, 1986), children first recall what they already know about a topic and then list what they would like to know. This then sets a purpose for reading. Based on the oral discussion that occurs during the beginning steps of a K-W-L, you could also develop a study guide or list of general questions for children to answer as they read. Overuse of study guides, however, contributes little to learning because it discourages children from setting their own purposes for reading (Palmer & Stewart, 2005).

2. *Varying reading speed to reflect the purpose for reading.* Informational text is not read the same way as narrative text. Depending on the purpose set for reading informational text, it may be read at different speeds and in different ways. Reutzel and Cooter (2004) describe three different speeds of reading: skimming, scanning, and previewing. **Skimming** involves silently reading the print quickly, focusing on key words such as nouns, verbs, and adjectives. Skimming provides a reader with a general idea of text content. **Scanning** involves quickly looking through a text for specific pieces of information, such as dates or names. **Previewing** is a way of obtaining an overview of an extended amount of informational text, such as a chapter or a nonfiction trade book, in a short amount of time. The initial step involves reading the first two paragraphs of the text. Then only the first sentence of each following paragraph is read. The last step is to read the section summary or conclusion, if provided in the text. If there is no such designated summary, then the last two paragraphs of the selection are read. With this overview, a reader can then return to the beginning of the informational text and read with increased comprehension.

3. *Using book features to anticipate content.* Encourage your children to preview informational text by reading the table of contents and page titles. Skimming the glossary and index along with looking at the illustrations are additional ways of anticipating book content.

4. *Review and summarize information text by creating graphic organizers.* Graphic organizers are an effective way to enhance children's comprehension of informational text because the process of creating a graphic organizer requires that a reader review what was read and represent that knowledge in a graphic format.

Using graphic organizers in this way requires that you first have a thorough understanding of the informational text that your children have read. This will provide you with an awareness of the type of graphic organizer that will best illustrate the relationships among the concepts presented in the text (Merkley & Jefferies, 2000/2001). For example, *Mountains* (O'Mara, 1996) is a descriptive text that focuses on the different types of mountains. A graphic organizer for reviewing and remembering information from this book could be a chart of the types of mountains and their characteristics, or it might be a semantic web of related concepts (see Figures 11.10 and 11.11).

Figure 11.10 Graphic Organizer in Chart Format

Types of Mountains

	How formed	Examples
Folded mountains	When the earth's crust folds	Rocky Mountains Appalachian Mountains Alps
Faulted mountains	When big areas of rocks pull or break away from each other	Grand Tetons Sierra Nevada Mountains
Volcanic mountains	When volcanoes erupt to form a cone-shaped mountain	Mount Rainier Vesuvius in Italy
Dome mountains	When magma pushes up into a dome shape and then hardens back into rock	Black Hills Adirondack Mountains

Figure 11.11 Graphic Organizer in Web Format

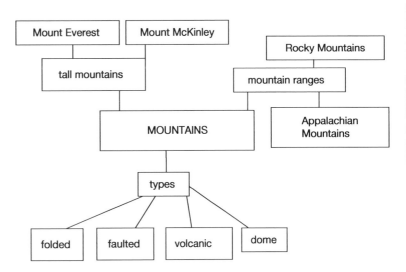

The format of the graphic organizer is determined by the concepts you want to emphasize and the relationship between those concepts. When you compare Figure 11.10 and 11.11, you can notice that each format represents and summarizes the information differently. A graphic organizer might focus on only a part of the book, depending upon the purpose for reading the text.

After you have decided on the appropriate format for the graphic organizer, place the format of the graphic organizer on a large chart, chalkboard, or overhead transparency. Fill in only the major headings or categories to start. Then use this graphic organizer as you scaffold your children' recall of the informational text they have read, filling in the other areas based on student comments and responses.

Fluency

During second and third grade, children's increased word recognition and vocabulary contribute to the development of comprehension as well as to their fluency in oral and silent reading. Fluency does not simply mean that a reader can recognize and pronounce words rapidly; a fluent reader also reads with meaningful intonation and phrasing.

Fluency is a critical development in second and third grade because children are beginning to transition from learning to read to reading to learn. Fourth-grade curriculum, especially in the content areas of science and social studies, expects that children will have oral- and silent-reading fluency, so that they can use written texts as sources of learning. Slow, word-by-word reading means that a reader has to spend much more time reading than his classmates who are reading at a level of fluency appropriate to their grade level (Rasinski, 2000). Slow readers quickly fall behind. Poor comprehension and low overall reading performance are also associated with slow reading (Armbruster, Lehr, & Osborn, 2001). Slow, effortful reading often leads to frustration. Frustrated readers then avoid reading whenever possible.

Strategies for enhancing fluency. As a second- or third-grade teacher, you will want to provide opportunities for your children to continue developing fluency as well as provide additional support for children who are struggling with oral- and silent-reading fluency. The strategies for enhancing fluency initially described in Chapter 10 for first-grade classrooms are also appropriate for second and third grade. These include developing sight vocabulary, modeling fluent reading, guiding oral reading, and providing opportunities for repeated reading and independent reading (see also Pikulski & Chard, 2005).

In this section several additional strategies that are effective for enhancing fluency in second- and third-grade classrooms are described. These strategies include:

- ❖ Readers' Theatre
- ❖ Poetry performances
- ❖ Paired reading
- ❖ Reading with audio books

Readers' Theatre. This strategy involves creating a script from a familiar story for children to read expressively. It resembles a dramatic performance but does not have costumes, props, or sets. The focus is on orally reading a script in an expressive and effective manner. Through the dramatic reading, children use "their voices to bring characters to life" (Martinez, Roser, & Strecker, 1998/1999, p. 326). In addition, children do not memorize their lines; instead they practice their lines with the goal of reading expressively and "in character." Readers' Theatre contributes to fluency because participation requires that children practice their parts so that they can read expressively. The social aspects of this

Opportunities for independent reading can enhance reading fluency and motivation to read.

wavebreakmedia

shared performance in re-creating a story are also motivating for children. Because parts can be assigned to fit children's reading levels, all children can participate.

Guidelines for conducting a Readers' Theatre are located in Figure 11.12. After you have used this activity with your children several times, you might decide to have them participate in writing a script.

To engage them in writing a script, begin by reviewing the main events in the story as well as the specific characters involved. You will then follow a format similar to what you

During silent reading, young readers will benefit from opportunities to read with a friend.

wavebreakmedia

Figure 11.12 Guidelines for Readers' Theatre Strategy

1. Select a story book that has a clear series of events and several characters engaged in direct dialogue.
2. Read the book to your class during interactive read-aloud time. Talk about the story events and characters.
3. Prepare a script that includes short narrative segments along with the dialogue between the characters. Keep the script at an appropriate level of reading for your children. Include parts that have different levels of reading.
4. Determine which children will participate in this Readers' Theatre and their specific roles. Decide if you are going to have multiple groups of children reading the same story script or if you will divide the script into sections so multiple groups can take part in the Readers' Theatre at different points in the story. The more children who can participate, the more will benefit from this practice in oral reading.
5. Provide two copies of the script for each child. One copy is kept at school; the other copy goes home so that the child can practice reading at home.
6. Schedule times during your class day when children can practice their scripts independently or with a peer. You will probably need to plan for several days of practice before scheduling the performance. Also include time when the performance group can meet to practice together.
7. Invite guests to come to the performance. This may include your school principal, librarian, nurse, or another class.
8. Celebrate your children's success. Consider audiotaping their performance and placing the tape in your classroom library/listening center.

do during story dictation, by asking for suggestions about which character is speaking, what is to be said, and what event is taking place. For this group activity in generating a script, you will need to be writing down their contributions on chart paper, just as you would a story dictation, adding in the characters' names beside their speaking parts. You may need to continue generating this script over several days. When it is complete, make copies of the script so that each participant has their own copy. With repeated opportunities to engage in this joint script generation, children may show an interest in creating their own scripts in small collaborative groups.

It is also important for everyone in your class to be involved in Readers' Theatre. This is why you will need to have scripts that include parts written for a range of reading levels. Specific resources for locating Readers' Theatre scripts and additional guidelines are provided in Appendix L.

Poetry performances. Like Readers' Theatre, children's oral reading of poetry also can contribute to fluency because it involves repeated practice and expressive reading (Rasinski, 2000). Additionally, the phrasing of poetry allows for children to have "turns" that vary in length.

You will want to select poetry that relates to a curricular theme or student interests. Resources for locating poetry are found in Figure 11.13. The poetry you select should also reflect your commitment to respecting and valuing each child, as well as multicultural diversity. For example, while many of Shel Silverstein's poems are appropriate for use in class poetry performances, some of his poems also have elements of violence, bias, and ridicule of others that you will want to avoid using. In addition to using poems selected from collections of poetry, you could also use story book texts that are written in poetic form, such as *The Cat in the Hat* (Seuss, 1957), *Green Eggs and Ham* (Seuss, 1960), *This is the House That Jack Built* (Taback, 2004), and *Over in the Meadow* (Keats, 1999).

Figure 11.13 Resources for Poetry Performances

Franco, B. (2004). *The great big book of thematic poetry*. New York: Teaching Resources.
Prelutsky, J., & Lobel, A. (2000). *The Random House book of poetry for children: A treasury of 572 poems for today's child*. New York: Random House.
Prelutsky, J., & Sis, P. (2006). *Scranimals*. New York: HarperColllins.
Silverstein, S. (1981). *A light in the attic*. New York: Harper & Row.
Silverstein, S. (2004). *Where the sidewalk ends. 30th Anniversary Special Edition*. New York: HarperCollins.
Tiedt, I. (2002). *Tiger lilies, toadstools, and thunderbolts: Engaging K–8 children with poetry*. Newark, DE: International Reading Association.

Once you have selected the poetry you will use, you will need to make copies for each child to have, as well as copy the poetry on a class poster or chalkboard. Specific steps for implementing a poetry performance to enhance reading fluency are located in Figure 11.14.

Paired reading. During silent reading (SSR or DEAR time), slow and struggling readers will benefit from opportunities to read with a friend (Lee-Daniels & Murray, 2000; Rasinski, Padak, Linek, & Sturtevant, 1994). Be sure that you have a variety of high-interest reading materials that are at children's independent reading levels. Providing independent reading time is not beneficial unless children are interested in reading, have materials that capture their interest, and can read independently without becoming frustrated or discouraged. For this reason you will want to provide a wide range of reading materials and closely observe children's interest in reading. Be sure to provide informational texts as well as narratives. It is also important to provide reading materials that have abundant illustrations (Vardell, Hadaway, & Young, 2006) to support comprehension and interest. Taped books that children can use during independent reading time and can share with their reading partner also support children's fluency and comprehension. By reading along with the taped book, children's expressive reading is enhanced.

Cross-grade reading partnerships can also enhance fluency (Cunningham & Allington, 2007; Rasinski, 2000). For example, you might pair third graders with second or first graders. In this instance, the third grader would select (with a teacher's help) a first- or second-grade–level book to share with the younger child. After the third grader has repeated practice reading the story aloud, he or she would pair up with the younger reader

 Figure 11.14 Steps to Follow in Planning and Implementing a Poetry Performance

1. Select a poem that relates to a curricular theme or children's interests.
2. Write the poem on a large chart.
3. Read it aloud to your class. Talk about phrasing and expression. Discuss with children why it was read that way, why you paused at a particular point, and how your voice variations influenced their comprehension of the poem. Have children read in unison with you. Point to the words as you read and indicate the pauses you made in reading.
4. Hand out individual copies of poem. Break class into small groups and assign individual parts within each group. Provide practice time over several days.
5. Have a poetry performance day.
6. Repeat this strategy, using multiple poems so that each small group has a different poem. Invite another class, other teachers, or administrators to your poetry performance. Celebrate your children's success.

and share the story book by reading the text and talking about the story. This sharing might also involve echo reading or having the two readers take turns reading the text.

Writing Process

Knowledge of written language develops throughout children's literacy-related experiences in early childhood settings. Opportunities to engage in writing provide important experiences to apply the language knowledge they are developing as well as continuing to explore and learn more about using written language to express meaning (Hughes & Searle, 2000). Phonetic knowledge is involved in figuring out how to use alphabet letters to encode the words they want to use. Semantic knowledge is used in figuring out which words will represent the meaning they intend. As they structure their text at the sentence and paragraph level to express their intended meaning, they use syntactic knowledge. Morphemic knowledge is used when prefixes, suffixes, and other word endings are added to base words to refine or alter word meaning. Knowing how to write for a particular purpose, such as writing a fairy tale or a persuasive letter, involves pragmatic knowledge.

These opportunities to engage in writing must be accompanied by children's motivation to write for their personal communication of ideas and stories, not simply to please the teacher or to receive a grade in writing. Therefore you will want to enhance children's interest in writing along with their development of competencies in using written language.

Levels of support for children's writing. Earlier chapters have described children's involvement in writing activities that are embedded in reading activities as well as in independent writing. These activities involve a range of support from the teacher. Tompkins (2004) describes this range of support as including the following levels:

- ❖ *Modeling writing*: Teacher composes and writes, demonstrating the writing process. *Example:* Morning message
- ❖ *Shared writing*: Teacher writes on chart paper or overhead while encouraging children to help compose the text. *Example:* Dictated language experience story
- ❖ *Interactive writing*: Teacher encourages children to help write the words in the group's dictated text. *Example:* Class version of favorite story book
- ❖ *Guided writing*: Teacher provides a format or structure for children to use in creating a text. *Example:* Fill-in-the-blank page format for a class ABC book. (See Figure 11.15.)

Figure 11.15 Page Format for Class ABC Book

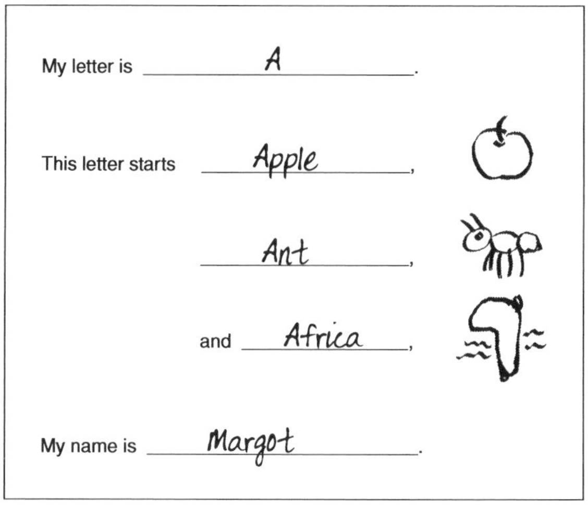

My letter is _____ A _____.

This letter starts _____ Apple _____,

_____ Ant _____,

and _____ Africa _____,

My name is _____ Margot _____.

❖ *Independent writing:* Children compose and write on their own. *Examples:* Response journals, stories, signs, lists

Providing these varied levels of support is still important in second and third grade. Although children will now be able to write more independently, they will still benefit from having you provide a supportive framework through modeled writing, shared writing, interactive writing, and guided writing. It is also important that you demonstrate new strategies and language concepts related to the writing process.

The writing process. During second and third grade, children are introduced more directly to the different steps in the "writing process." The focus is on encouraging children to think about what they are writing and how they are writing it. You can enhance children's interest in writing by emphasizing their role as authors in deciding what they want to write about. Children's positive orientation to writing as a form of personal expression is key to continued writing development.

The process of writing has been described as having these five stages (Hoffman, 2000; Piazza, 2003; Tompkins, 2004): prewriting, drafting, revising, editing, and publishing. In this section each of these stages will be described along with ways of enhancing children's engagement in writing.

Prewriting. This is the "idea" stage when writers decide on the topic or content of what they are going to write. Children should be encouraged to select any topic they want. You can support this stage by engaging children in discussions of their ideas as a group or individually. You could also show them how to use a simple graphic organizer, or idea sheet, such as the examples shown in Figures 11.16 and 11.17. You might find it useful to have children keep a writing folder to contain their prewriting ideas so that they can refer to them later.

Figure 11.16 Graphic Organizer for Prewriting Information Text

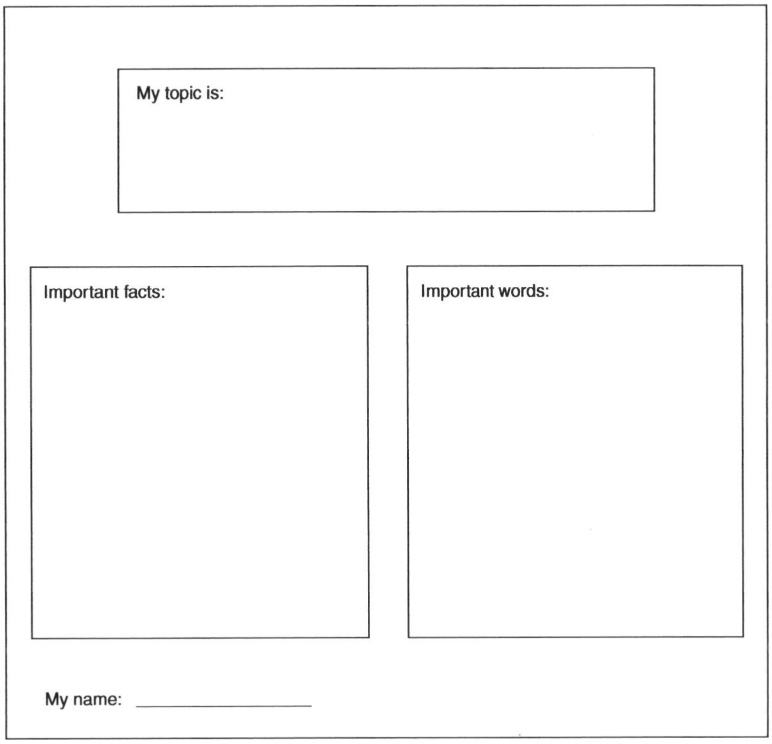

My topic is:

Important facts:	Important words:

My name: _____

Figure 11.17 Prewriting: Idea Sheet for Story Writing

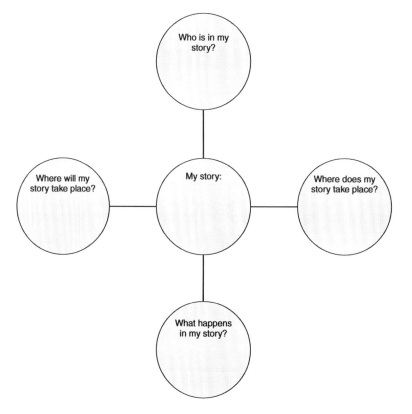

Drafting. In this stage, writers put their ideas down on paper. The focus is on composing a text, so spelling, punctuation, and capitalization are not a concern. In addition to using invented spelling, children can also be encouraged to use a blank line to indicate a word that they do not know how to spell. Second and third graders may also find it helpful to include illustrations as part of their draft. It is also useful to encourage children to write the word "draft" on their writing papers so parents will be aware that the writing is "in progress" and not a finished piece (Piazza, 2003).

Revising. This stage could also be called "reflecting and revising" because writers now read back over what they have written and decide if they want to make any changes. For many children, this is a difficult task. If their initial writing was especially effortful and difficult, they may not be interested in considering any changes whatsoever. You can support children in this stage by talking with children individually. During these conferences, you will first have the child read to you what was written. Then you can ask questions that guide the child to think about what was written and whether they want to change anything. Perhaps a change might involve including a word to complete a thought. A new sentence might be added to clarify an event that took place. Maybe another word will be substituted or perhaps deleted. This reflection and revision encourages children to be proactive in the writing process, taking ownership of what changes they want to make rather than passively making the corrections that are identified by their teacher. Accept each child's decision as to what changes are to be made. You want to keep the ownership of the writing with the child as author. This is a major difference from the way in which writing instruction occurred previously. In this writing process approach, the teacher no longer edits children's writing with a red pen and requires them to recopy the work until it is "acceptable."

You can demonstrate and provide guided practice for this reflection and revision phase by developing written tasks that involve reading a short paragraph and making revisions. For example, in her second-grade class, Mrs. Main provided guided practice with a writing activity that involved first revising several sentences that all began with the same three words. In this example, the first three words of each sentence were "At my school. . . " After the children had changed them so that there were different beginning phrases, she asked them to write their own short paragraph about school. After they had written their paragraphs, they were asked to underline the first three words. In response to this assignment, Amanda, one of Ms. Main's students, wrote the paragraph shown in Figure 11.18. As you read this, note the different way she begins each sentence.

By providing this guided practice in revising short examples of text, children begin to learn how to look for text features that can be revised to make a text more interesting.

Editing. This stage in the writing process involves making the written piece ready to share with a wider audience. It is at this time that attention is paid to spelling, punctuation, grammar, and capitalization. This stage is only experienced if the writing is to be published for others to read. Most children will need significant support for this stage. Teacher demonstration along with guided practice in editing examples of writing will help children understand how to edit their own work. For example, you could demonstrate editing by recopying a class-dictated story and purposely misspelling several words. Display this version and ask your students to be "word detectives" by finding the misspelled words and correcting them. Encourage children to "think aloud" as they are participating in this editing activity.

Publishing. This is the time when the written piece is shared with a larger audience. It may involve children making a final copy in a booklike format and placing it in the classroom library or school library. Perhaps the written piece will be published in a classroom newspaper or placed on a classroom bulletin board.

Figure 11.18 Amanda's Paragraph about Her School

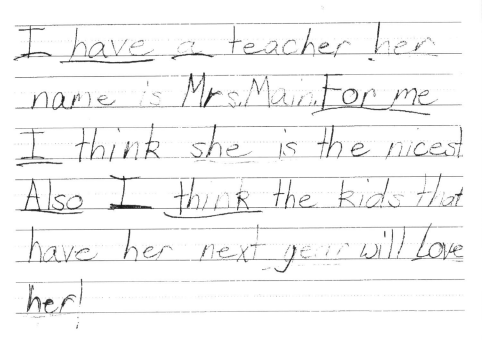

While these stages are described sequentially, it is important to remember that each piece of children's classroom writing will not end up at the publishing stage. For those written pieces that are published, there may be repeated cycles of the revising and editing stages—and perhaps the revisions may involve going back to the prewriting stage to gather more ideas. It is also important to remember that there is no set timeline for progressing through the various stages of the writing process (Hoffman, 2000). Each child needs the flexibility to progress at his own pace through the different stages of writing.

The writing workshop. Enhancing children's growth as writers through the different stages in the writing process requires a flexible and child-centered approach rather than a set sequence of writing tasks in which all children are doing the same thing at the same time (Dahl & Farnan, 1998). Because of this need for flexibility and individualized attention, the "writing workshop" has developed as a way to engage children in the writing process (Calkins, 1983; Calkins & Harwayne, 1987; Routman, 1991).

Although there are different variations of the writing workshop, this approach generally involves the following activities: teacher-guided mini-lessons, teacher–student conferences, and a block of time for children's independent writing. To implement a writing workshop in second and third grade, you will need to designate about 40 minutes for this activity.

The writing workshop time usually starts with a short mini-lesson that focuses on a specific aspect of one of the stages of the writing process and involves the entire class (Calkins & Harwayne, 1987). Teachers determine the focus of their minilessons based on their knowledge of student needs and interests. This lesson may last only a few minutes, but generally involves demonstrating the new concept or strategy and providing guided practice. After the minilesson, the students work on their individual pieces of writing. During this time, the teacher holds conferences with individual students or circulates among the students, monitoring their writing activities. At the end of the writing workshop time, there is a whole class meeting where the teacher and children respond to several students' in-progress pieces.

Teachers have found it useful to keep track of each student's writing workshop activities by using a "state-of-the-class" chart. This chart contains all of the students' names and records which workshop activities they are engaging in each day of the week. An example of this chart format is provided in Figure 11.19.

Spelling

Throughout the writing workshop, teachers can expect children to have questions about spelling, because spelling is a necessary part of writing. According to Hughes and Searle (2000), "writing challenges children to use their knowledge of print to express their thoughts on paper. Writers may spell correctly or incorrectly, but they cannot avoid spelling" (p. 203). Writing also supports spelling development because in preparing to share their writing with others, children develop a sense of audience. In order for their writing to be "reader-friendly," conventional spelling is necessary. In this section, strategies for enhancing children's spelling development are described.

In earlier chapters of this text, writing activities were described that encouraged young children to create their own stories and other texts using invented spelling and drawing. In contrast to earlier years of school, children in second and third grade are expected to begin to spell more words conventionally.

Approaches to teaching spelling. Traditionally, spelling has been taught as a separate "subject." Each week, a prescribed list of words is given to students (Bloodgood, 1991; Matz, 1994). This is followed by using the words in a different spelling activity each day.

Figure 11.19 State-of-the-Class Chart Format for Writing Workshop

Student	Monday	Tuesday	Wednesday	Thursday	Friday

Activity codes:[1]

P = prewriting   SE = self-editing
D = drafting   FE = final editing
R = reflection and revision   FC = final copy before publishing
C = conference with teacher

[1] Other codes can be added as needed for further detail

These activities might involve writing each word a number of times, looking up each word in a dictionary and copying down the meaning, completing fill-in-the-blank or word puzzle exercises, using the words in sentences, and taking a practice test. Friday is typically the day for the "real test." Students performing poorly on the Friday test are often assigned to write the words they had missed multiple times to ensure that they then learn the correct spelling. This approach, however, has not been associated with long-term spelling achievement. Even when students are able to do well on the Friday test, they may go on to misspell those same words the following week in written assignments or independent writing (Schlagal, 2002). In many instances the spelling activities have been totally isolated from the rest of the language arts/literacy curriculum.

Another approach to spelling began during the time the Whole Language approach was popular. This approach, referred to as the incidental approach, does not use any spelling books or formal spelling curriculum, but instead incorporates spelling minilessons in reading and writing workshops as the need arises (Schlagal, 2002). This approach assumes that children learn conventional spelling through reading a variety of texts and meaningful writing. This approach has not proven successful for all children. Researchers have begun to discover the benefits of combining guided word study with reading and writing activities to enhance spelling development across the literacy curriculum (Bloodgood, 1991;

Butyniec-Thomas & Woloshun, 1997; Gentry, 2004; Goddard & Heron, 1998; Heald-Taylor, 1998; Hughes & Searle, 2000; Matz, 1994; Schlagal, 2002; Templeton, 1991).

Guidelines for enhancing spelling development. In this section, research-based guidelines are presented for you to keep in mind as you focus on spelling throughout your literacy curriculum.

Encourage children to read with word awareness. As you read-aloud and reread dictated stories with your class, focus children's attention on spelling patterns found in the words used in the text. With these experiences, children will be more likely to transfer this awareness to their own reading.

Provide frequent opportunities for children to write for meaningful purposes. When children are engaged in writing for personal purposes and have ownership of the writing process as "authors," and anticipate sharing their writing with an audience, they are more likely to care about correct spelling because they want their writing to be read and understood by others.

Encourage children to self-monitor their spelling. The goal of spelling instruction is to foster children's ability to figure out how to spell words conventionally on their own. Encourage children to refer to the classroom word wall, grade-appropriate dictionaries, and other reference aids. You can also encourage them to use their memory when they encounter specific words as they read in story books or other written materials. For example, Alice, a second grader, described the way she used her memory for reading a particular word as a source of spelling information (Hughes & Searle, 2000):

> Suppose this is the book page and here we have "The girl jumped over the fence." So I read this and when I'm writing about a fence, I'd remember back to a book with "fence," or I'd close my eyes or something, but I just see it in my head. (p. 205)

Take advantage of opportunities for incidental teaching. As you engage children in minilessons and student conferences during writing workshop, be alert for opportunities to point out spelling similarities between words or important letter–sound relationships. As you focus on specific words, use a "think-aloud" strategy to share how you are focusing on a particular spelling pattern.

Engage children in guided word study of spelling patterns. Although spelling development involves visual memory, it is not simply memorizing how each word is spelled (Bloodgood, 1991). Instead, spelling development involves an awareness of letter patterns and morphemic patterns (word parts, prefixes, and suffixes).

For example, you could develop word sort activities where children sort word cards according to the similar sounds and letter patterns, such as sorting words for short A and long A (Bear, Invernizzi, Templeton, & Johnston, 2004). First you would write the following list of words randomly on an overhead, chart, or chalkboard: cap, cape, chain, gas, came, rain, back, name, pail, and so on. After reading the words together, ask students what spelling patterns they notice and what sounds are associated with the letter *a*.

Select a spelling program that groups words by morphemic or orthographic features. If you decide to use a spelling book or basal that has a different list of words to be learned each week, look for word lists that have words grouped by morphemic or spelling patterns. In this way, children's awareness of spelling patterns is fostered.

Select spelling words from content-area texts. Spelling is not a matter of simple memorization; spelling needs to become part of long-term memory and this requires more meaningful and extensive exposure to using the new words in writing as well as in reading. When you select spelling words from social studies, science, or health textbooks, your students will be focusing on the spelling of words that they will use in the reading and writing activities of these other curricular areas.

Strategies for Teacher–Parent Partnerships

Throughout this text, there has been an emphasis on developing partnerships with parents that support children's literacy development. These partnerships continue to be important in second and third grade.

Establish and Maintain Frequent Communication

A key part of creating partnerships with parents is to establish and maintain avenues for frequent communication. You may decide to do this through a weekly or biweekly newsletter. You might also develop a classroom Webpage which describes current classroom activities, topics, and upcoming events. Many teachers also provide an email address so parents can leave messages or clarify assignments. Once you have established this routine, be consistent so that parents can count on receiving classroom information in a timely manner.

Share Ideas for Supporting Children's Literacy Development at Home

In your communication with parents you will want to provide them with ideas for supporting second and third graders' literacy development at home. Here are some ideas you might share with parents:

Read to and with your child. Shared-book reading increases your child's listening and reading vocabulary. When you read with your child, you also show that you value reading and find it enjoyable. Shared stories and informational texts also build a bond of knowledge and experiences between you and your child. Additional opportunities to read at home also enhance reading fluency.

Shared reading can take several different forms (Morrow, Kuhn, & Schwanenflugel, 2006; Rasinski, 2000). You can echo-read with your child. This means that you will read a line or long phrase and have your child repeat the same phrase or line. Point to where you are reading and, over time, gradually increase the length of the segments that are echo-read. Choral reading, where you and your child read in unison, is also beneficial. Taking turns reading is another option. This means that you read one sentence and your child reads the next sentence. With time, this turn-taking can gradually build up to involve multiple sentence segments. Repeatedly reading the same book within a few days or week's time is also beneficial in enhancing fluency.

To encourage parents to try out these various ways of reading, you could demonstrate them at an open house or play a video or audiotape you have made of your use of these different ways of reading with the students in your class. You could also incorporate brief descriptions of each in a parent newsletter.

Show interest in your child's school day. Talk with your child about their day at school using open-ended questions that elicit more than a yes or no answer. For example: "What did you read at school today? Tell me about the story. Who was your favorite character? Why?"

Reduce TV viewing in favor of hands-on experiences. Most TV viewing is a passive experience. Instead, encourage activities that involve more engagement and interaction: Cook together in the kitchen, make something in the garage together, work in the garden, or play ball or a game of soccer in the park or backyard. Show your child that you enjoy non-TV activities, such as reading the newspaper or magazines and engaging in hobbies. When your child watches TV, sit with him and talk about the program content as you would if you were enjoying a book together.

Provide a quiet area for reading and studying. This area needs to be well-lit with a small table or desk and comfortable chair. Be sure there are sufficient supplies, such as paper, a stapler, hole-puncher, tape, and writing tools.

Make frequent visits to public library. Show your child how to find interesting books. Check out books or other materials for yourself as well. Children need to see their parents enjoying reading. This gives children a wider orientation to literacy. They learn that adults read for pleasure and that reading is not just something you do for school.

To encourage parents to use the local library, you may find it useful to provide information to parents on the location and hours of the library. Also provide them with information about obtaining a library card. You might consider planning a class field trip to the local library and obtaining library card applications for your children at the same time.

Provide ways for developing your child's personal library. Books make wonderful birthday and holiday gifts. A subscription to a children's magazine, such as *Ranger Rick*, gives children something to look forward to each month. Inexpensive books can be obtained at garage sales, resale shops, and used-book sales.

Show your child that you are still curious about the world. Share news events, talk about new science discoveries, and use maps to find locations that are in the news. As you show your curiosity, you will also be modeling lifelong learning.

Encourage activities that enhance vocabulary. Take your child on trips to museums, or historic sites. Talk about what you see and read the exhibit signs with your child. Becoming involved in sports or hobbies also enhances the development of specialized vocabulary related to that activity. Talking with your child about these experiences provides opportunity to use the new vocabulary.

Assessment and Literacy Portfolios

Assessment of children's reading development in second and third grade takes a variety of forms. If you are using a commercial literacy curriculum, you will probably use the assessments provided in that curriculum. These may include informal, observational assessments and various skills tests, along with assessments involving leveled-reading passages. Children who are experiencing difficulty may be referred for additional evaluation by the school's reading specialist.

In many states, third grade is the time when standardized achievement testing is mandated for all public schools. Reading comprehension and various reading subskills are a major part of such testing. While these achievement tests provide accountability for schools, the time lag in obtaining results of these tests prohibits teachers from using the results to guide instruction or to provide additional support to struggling readers. In addition, standardized tests may assess only a small part of children's literacy behaviors.

As a reflective teacher, you will want to engage in assessment that provides a comprehensive look at children's literacy development throughout the school year so that you can use the assessment information to guide your lesson planning and instructional interactions. Using portfolios as a way to gather documentation and reflect on children's literacy development has been a recommended practice since the early 1990s (Cohen & Wiener, 2003; Valencia, 1990).

Literacy Portfolios

Portfolios provide a way of collecting a range of different assessments related to each child's literacy development. This provides teachers with an opportunity to document children's literacy growth using both formal and informal assessments.

Guidelines for developing and using literacy portfolios. The process of using portfolios allows considerable flexibility because the ways in which portfolios are used reflects each individual classroom and grade level. You, the teacher, are the designer of your portfolio system. The guidelines that follow focus on the role each teacher has in deciding how the portfolio process will contribute to awareness of their children's literacy development.

Decide what types of documentation will be included. Teachers must decide what aspects of the reading process they are going to document, how it will be documented, why this assessment is important, how it fits into their total curriculum, how this information will be useful, and how it will be shared with children's parents.

For example, you may decide to have children's oral reading audio- or videotaped on a periodic basis. You might also include children's reading logs that document what books or other materials they read during independent reading times. Anecdotal notes you take during guided reading groups might also be added as documentation (Manning & Manning, 1994; Schwartz, 2005). Including children's responses to questionnaires about their reading interests might also be a valuable addition to their literacy portfolios (see example in Figure 11.20).

When you are just beginning to use portfolios in assessing children's literacy development, it is better to start off with only one or two types of assessments per child. Above all, your literacy portfolio process needs to be manageable and useful. It can quickly become overwhelming if you do not phase in assessments gradually.

Set aside time to review individual portfolios. Using portfolios does not mean that you simply collect a variety of children's work samples and other assessments in individual folders or notebooks. For portfolios to be useful, you need to take time to reflect on the contents of individual children's portfolios on a regular basis. One way of doing this is to select a number of children's portfolios to review each week (for example, five or six). By doing this, you will have reviewed all of the portfolios every month or so.

Decide how you will involve children and their parents. Children's awareness of their development and learning increases when they are allowed to help decide what documents are included in their portfolios. Allowing them to include items from outside school shows what they value, how they see themselves as readers and writers, and what they want to share (Hansen, 1992). It is also important to encourage parents to add artifacts of their child's literacy development. Not only does this increase a teacher's understanding of literacy events in children's homes, but it also provides parents with a wider understanding of children's literacy development (Paratore, DiBiasio, & Sullivan, 1993).

Figure 11.20 Student Interest Questionnaire

What are your interests?

Your name: _____

1. What do you like to do when you are not in school?

2. What do you like to talk with your friends about?

3. What places do you like to visit?

4. Check the things that you like best:

_____ sports (list the sports you like _____)

_____ drawing   _____ science

_____ pets/animals   _____ space/stars

_____ puzzles   _____ music

_____ jokes   _____ making things

_____ cooking   _____ computers

_____ art/drawing   _____ nature

5. What is your favorite book? _____

6. What is your favorite type of book?

_____ information   _____ story

Children benefit from opportunities to talk about their portfolios with their teacher. You will want to schedule these conferences after you have reviewed the portfolio. During these conferences, start the conversation with some general questions (Winograd & Arrington, 1999), such as "What is your favorite part in your portfolio? Why?" or "Tell me why you decided to include this in your portfolio." Allow the child to do most of the talking, using follow-up questions to clarify or extend your understanding of the child's response.

Literacy portfolios can serve as a basis for sharing children's progress during parent–teacher conferences. Parents benefit from seeing and hearing examples of their children's reading and reading-related activities. As you prepare for these conferences, identify key examples of each child's work that you will share.

Decide on an organizational format that is simple, yet accessible. There is no one best way to organize your literacy portfolios. Whether you decide to use accordion-pocket folders, plastic containers, cardboard boxes, or file cabinets, you will want to adopt a format that is simple and easily accessible for you as well as your children. The scope of your documentation will influence the storage format of your literacy portfolios. If many artifacts are to be included in each child's portfolio, you will need a system that

Individual conferences provide opportunity for children to talk about the items in their portfolio.

Business plus

accommodates this volume. Space may become an issue in classrooms that have 25 or more children. Each portfolio should be clearly labeled with the child's name.

Some teachers create a separate system of files for collecting more confidential assessments, such as tests and anecdotal observations. They then also have another system of files for student's work samples. Only the work-sample files are accessible to children. At conference time, the teacher reviews both the confidential file and the work sample file.

Most teachers find that the way in which they organize portfolio assessment evolves as they gain experience in managing this process. Only you can decide which organizational format will work for you (Manning & Manning, 1994).

Chapter Summary

Children in second and third grade are continuing to build on their understandings of reading and writing. Literacy-rich classrooms are characterized by providing a range of formal and informal contexts for literacy-related activities, developing a community of learners, providing a well-stocked classroom library, and providing engagement in a range of text types throughout all literacy activities. Key areas of reading instruction in second and third grade include: decoding and word recognition, vocabulary development, text comprehension (narrative and informational) and fluency (oral and silent). Writing instruction emphasizes the writing process and spelling. In each of the key areas, instruction focuses on demonstrating specific strategies, providing guided practice, and then encouraging children to use the strategies during independent reading and writing. Teacher–parent partnerships are facilitated by establishing and maintaining frequent communication. Teachers can also share with parents ideas for supporting children's literacy development at home. Assessment of children's literacy development informs teachers' lesson planning and interactions with students. Literacy portfolios allow teachers to develop an assessment system that reflects the formal and informal ways children's literacy development is documented.

Chapter Review

1. Terms to know:

antonyms	cognate
synonyms	inferencing
prefixes	skimming
suffixes	scanning
inflectional suffixes	previewing
derivational suffixes	

2. How is "learning to read" different from "reading to learn"? What are the implications of this difference for curriculum in the second and third grades?

3. Why are direct teaching activities and informal, self-guided literacy activities both included in second- and third-grade classrooms?

4. Why is it important for informational texts to be included in the reading materials for second and third graders?

5. What are the benefits of having a classroom library?

6. Develop several guidelines for using dictionaries in second- and third-grade classrooms.

7. Explain the value of using graphic organizers to enhance comprehension of informational texts.

8. Why is it important for children to develop reading fluency?

9. What areas of language knowledge are involved in writing?

10. In what ways does process writing encourage children to take ownership of their writing?

11. Why should children be encouraged to self-monitor their spelling?

Chapter Extension Activities

Curriculum Development:

1. Select an informational trade book appropriate for second or third grade. Thoroughly review the book. Develop a lesson plan for reading this book aloud and using a graphic organizer to enhance children's comprehension of this book. Use a lesson plan format from Appendix K. Present this to your college class. Describe how you developed the specific format of the graphic organizer.

2. Select a story book appropriate for second or third grade. Thoroughly review the book. Develop a lesson plan for reading this book aloud and creating a story map to enhance children's awareness of narrative text structure and story comprehension. Use a lesson plan format from Appendix K. Present your story map to your college class on a poster or overhead transparency. Describe how you would use this in a second- or third-grade classroom.

3. With a small group of your peers, prepare a Readers' Theatre script based on a children's story book. Present this in your college class. Describe the process of creating your script. Explain the value of this activity for enhancing children's oral fluency.

4. With a small group of your peers, prepare a poetry performance. Select a poem from one of the sources in Figure 11.13. Present your performance in your college class. Describe how your group decided to assign reading parts and how this activity enhances oral fluency.

5. Using a format from Appendix K, develop a lesson plan that focuses on one of the following stages in the writing process: prewriting, drafting, reflecting and revising, or editing. Your plan should include a demonstration as well as guided practice. Present your plan in your college class.

Research and Development: Develop a Webpage or newsletter appropriate for a second- or third-grade classroom. Include information about your (hypothetical) current classroom events and tips for parents. Present your Webpage or newsletter in your college class. Explain the steps you used in developing the Webpage or newsletter.

Research: Review several different children's dictionaries. Decide which dictionary is best suited for use by second and third graders. Explain your reasoning. Present your conclusions to your college class. Bring in the dictionaries to demonstrate the differences that you saw that contributed to your decision.

Chapter 12

Transitioning to Fourth Grade—Reading and Writing to Learn

Ms. Lopez's fourth-grade class has just come back from lunch. It's now time for science. They are beginning a unit on the solar system. She has placed a K-W-L chart in front of the class. For the next few minutes, she encourages students to tell what they already know about the solar system and what they would like to know. Then she points to a library cart filled with a variety of trade books on the solar system. "Here are some exciting books for you to use. Your job is to select and read one or more books from this collection. Keep in mind the questions about the solar system we've been talking about. Then you will develop a poster that shares what you have learned. You can work alone or with a partner."

Although Ms. Lopez's class has a science textbook, she has decided to open the study of the solar system with this poster activity for several reasons. First of all, Ms. Lopez is aware that her students' literacy transactions involve interactions between what they already know, the texts they read, as well as the context in which their reading occurs. By having students talk about what they already know about the solar system, she is activating their prior knowledge. By encouraging them to think about what they would like to know, she is helping them set a purpose for their reading. Creating a context for their literacy transactions that involves working with a partner and selecting their own reading materials provides additional motivation to students. Ms. Lopez plans to have the poster activity followed by a preview of their science text's chapter on the solar system. Only then will students be assigned segments of the chapter to read.

This final chapter focuses on fourth grade. While most states and the National Association for the Education of Young Children/NAEYC define early childhood in terms of infancy through third grade, there are other states that include fourth grade as part of their early childhood teaching certification. Therefore, we have tried to be as inclusive as possible. In addition, all primary teachers need to be aware of the context and academic expectations of fourth grade in order to appropriately prepare their students for success. Finally, third-grade teachers who have students who are academically talented will also want to be aware of ways to challenge these students with more complex literacy experiences.

The content of this chapter is presented in three major sections. The first section provides an overview of literacy transactions in fourth grade, highlighting the three components of literacy transactions: the learner, the context and the text. This is followed by a section that describes strategies for enhancing literacy development in fourth grade. The final section of the chapter focuses on ways to provide extra support for struggling readers and writers.

Literacy Transactions in Fourth Grade

Children's literacy transactions in fourth grade are characterized by increasing complexity. This is particularly evident in the contexts in which they read and write, as well as in the texts that they encounter. Another aspect of this complexity is each learner's prior experiences and knowledge as well as their orientation to learning and school.

Learners

When children arrive in fourth grade, they bring with them their experiences and knowledge from their prior years of interaction in home, school, and community settings. Academic development does not occur apart from the other facets of development. Social, emotional, and cultural experiences also contribute to each child's self-concept as a learner (Erickson, 1963, 1972; McDevitt & Ormrod, 2004). For example, has a child's effort in learning at school resulted in feelings of competence and success? Did his hard work and persistence pay off? Or does the child feel that even when he tries hard he cannot meet parents' or teachers' expectations? As a fourth-grade teacher, you will want to be sensitive to children's need to experience feelings of competence and industry. This is particularly important because the context of fourth grade differs in several significant and challenging ways from the context of learning in earlier grades.

Contexts

Fourth grade is a year of transition between the elementary grades and middle school. It is a time when students are expected to have mastered the basic skills associated with decoding, word recognition, text comprehension, and fluency (Snow, Burns, & Griffin, 1998). Students are also expected to be able to orally discuss and write in response to what they have read. These expectations were evident in Ms. Lopez's class when she gave the independent reading and poster assignment. The way in which she began the new unit of study also showed Ms. Lopez's awareness that some initial mediation was needed to activate students' prior knowledge and develop purposes for reading content-area materials.

Fourth grade is also a time when students are expected to further develop a wide range of reading and writing strategies that will be used as they interact with more complex narrative and informational texts (Blake, 1990). In fourth grade, reading and writing are used as tools for learning in science, social studies, health, and mathematics. The instructional materials in these content areas include both trade books and text books. Being able to read, comprehend, and write about what was read is required in each of the subject areas. Knowledge of the symbol system used in mathematics, for example, is required in addition to being able to read and understand mathematical problems.

When faced with these increased expectations, some students who have progressed at a regular pace during the primary years may experience a "slump" in achievement in fourth grade (Chall, Jacobs, & Baldwin, 1990; Chall, 1996; Chall & Jacobs, 2003; Snow, Burns, &

Griffin, 1998). If this is not addressed, it may start a decline in academic achievement. Reading is a critical issue in fourth grade because children cannot learn from books that they cannot read and comprehend (Allington, 2002b).

Texts

Range of text types. Students in fourth grade encounter a wide range of instructional materials. In reading, teachers are more likely to use both basal and trade books than only a basal system or only trade books (Coley & Coleman, 2004). Within a basal system, there may also be a variety of texts, including leveled readers and anthologies. Different types of narrative texts such as historical fiction, realistic fiction, informational texts, and poetry are often included. In the content areas, students encounter grade-level textbooks and trade books. Some commercial curricula in the content areas also provide leveled readers for that area (for example, social studies and science). Content-area study may also involve using newspapers and magazines.

Characteristics of grade-level fiction. Compared to earlier grades, commercial reading materials developed for fourth-grade-level reading have a greater variety of new vocabulary and more complex sentence structures. Grade-level trade books also show more complexity. The narratives are longer and divided into chapters. They also have more complex plots and characters. These text characteristics require students to remember the story from day to day and integrate the new events with what happened previously in the book. Because there are generally fewer illustrations, readers need to be able to visualize the story events and characters on their own.

Characteristics of informational texts. Books in the content areas of science, social studies, health, and math are characterized by texts that are dramatically different from the texts encountered in reading curricula. These differences include:

1. *Concept density.* Because the purpose of informational text is to explain concepts, ideas, and phenomena, informational texts have a greater density of concepts. This means that throughout the text, new concepts are introduced. Mathematics textbooks have been found to have the greatest concept density (Barton, Heidema, & Jordan, 2002).

2. *New vocabulary.* Content-area texts are designed to expose students to new knowledge. The vocabulary of the content-area texts centers on new vocabulary (and concepts) that may be unfamiliar to students, especially children from diverse backgrounds (Chall & Jacobs, 2003), for example, *solar radiation, atmosphere*, and *ozone layer.*

3. *Specialized vocabulary.* Each content area has a specialized vocabulary. This vocabulary is interconnected. For example, in math, the terms "numerator" and "denominator" refer to the two parts of fractions. In science, *mineral, igneous, sedimentary,* and *metamorphic* each refer to a type of rock, and also relate to each other in specific ways.

This specialized vocabulary may refer to abstract concepts. The concepts represented by this vocabulary may not involve concrete objects but represent ideas that must be conceptualized cognitively or visualized based on a written description, such as the concept of "interdependence" among organisms in a rain forest ecosystem.

4. *Different text structures.* The most common types of informational text structures include: cause-effect, descriptive (concepts and definitions), procedural, compare-contrast, and problem-solution (Frey & Fisher, 2007). Within these text types, signal words may cue

the reader to look for a particular structure in the way the information is presented. For example, in texts that focus on cause and effect, the following signal words are often found: "*if . . . then, since, because, as a result*" (p. 10).

5. *Specific text features.* Informational texts are characterized by specific organizational features such as paragraph headings, picture captions, margin notes, table of contents, glossary, index, and graphic aids (for example, charts, diagrams, and illustrations) (Frey & Fisher, 2007, p. 10). While these features are designed to support comprehension, readers need to know how to use these features in order for comprehension to be enhanced. If a text has several of these features on each page, students may be confused as to how the text should be read (directionality of reading). For example, on pages with margin notes, should the margin notes be read before the rest of the text on the page or after the page is read, or at some point when reading the page?

These five characteristics of informational text may make reading in content-area textbooks confusing as well as overwhelming to some students. This is especially true for students who may not have had much prior experience reading and comprehending informational texts, as well as students who experienced reading difficulties in earlier grades.

Enhancing Literacy Development in Fourth Grade

In this section, specific strategies for enhancing literacy development for all students in fourth grade are described. Some strategies focus on the contexts of learning; others focus on providing specific types of texts, and still other strategies focus on the ways in which students interact with text and context.

Create a Literacy-Rich Environment

As with other grade levels, the classroom learning environment sets the stage for students' engagement in learning activities. This engagement is influenced by the learning materials that are available and the ways in which students are actively involved in using those materials. A literacy-rich environment can be created by providing a wide range of written materials and by creating a setting where students are engaged as active learners.

Multitext classroom. In many classrooms, textbooks are the only type of reading material provided in the content areas; however, students and their teachers often report that the textbooks are too hard or not interesting to read (Ivey, 2002). This may lead to a lack of motivation and interest in content-area learning. Teachers are encouraged to develop a collection of "real" books and content-rich materials (in addition to textbooks) (Ivey, 2002). When a wide range of materials is provided, such as trade books (fiction and nonfiction), newspapers, children's magazines, poetry, photo essays, historical fiction, and journals/ diaries, the curricular focus becomes concept-centered rather than centered on just what is provided in one textbook. Students then develop a broader perspective from reading multiple texts on one topic. Trade books and photo essays also provide more visual support for understanding concepts (Billman, 2002). By providing a range of different types of content-rich reading materials, students can use texts with which they are most comfortable. This often results in increased motivation and interest in content-area study.

Active learning environment. Students benefit from a learning environment that encourages them to be active learners rather than passive recipients of instruction. According to Allington (2002a), effective teachers provide students with choices in assignments. This

Collaborative projects can integrate all of the facets of literacy: listening, speaking, reading, writing, viewing, and visually representing.

does not mean the students have unlimited choices, but are able to select among a variety of tasks or topics centered on a particular theme or concept. Providing for such choices engages students more actively because they have selected a personally purposeful topic or task.

Interdisciplinary units. Another way of creating an active learning environment is through integrated or interdisciplinary units of study (Barton & Smith, 2000; Shanahan, 1997). Integrated, curricular units of study combine reading and writing with one or more content areas, such as social studies, science, and/or math (Anders & Pritchard, 1993; Karnes & Collins, 1997; Muth, 1997; Nesbit & Rogers, 1997). Within each unit there is a combination of fiction and informational texts. For example, a unit on Pioneer Life could integrate social studies and science with reading and writing. For this unit, a collection of trade books would be selected that included both firsthand and fictional accounts of daily pioneer life, factual descriptions of life on the prairie and traveling in a wagon train, frontier cookbooks, and ABC books. A listing of books for such an interdisciplinary unit is found in Figure 12.1.

Literacy-related tasks might involve writing a letter to a relative back East, creating a timeline, participating in a Readers' Theatre, or creating a travel brochure highlighting the benefits to homesteading out West.

Cooperative learning. Opportunities for cooperative learning also contribute to students' active engagement in the content areas. Although there are different forms of cooperative learning, all of the forms involve small groups of students working together to learn and complete tasks (Slavin, 1991). The groups are usually heterogeneous. Key aspects of cooperative learning include (Marr, 1997): (a) A clear and attainable group goal or task, (b) each member is responsible for his part as well as in contributing to the group's success, and (c) members self-evaluate their effective participation in the group. When these aspects are part of cooperative learning groups, positive gains in literacy as well as content knowledge have been documented (Hendrix, 1999; Marr, 1997).

Figure 12.1 Trade Books for a "Pioneer Life" Unit in Fourth Grade

Bryant, J. (2003). *Wagon train*. Calgary, AB: Weigl Publishers.
Downie, M., & Gerber, M. (2005). *A pioneer ABC*. Plattsburgh, NY: Tundra.
Foran, J. (2003). *Homesteading*. Calgary, AB: Weigl Publishers.
Hermes, P. (2002). *Westward to home: Joshua's Oregon Trail diary, Vol 1*. New York: Scholastic.
Johmann, C., Rieth, E., & Kline, M. (2000). *Going west!: Journey on a wagon train to settle a frontier town*. Nashville, TN: Ideals Publications, Kaleidoscope Kids Books.
Kamma, A., & Watling, J. (2003). *If you were a pioneer on the prairie*. New York: Scholastic.
MacLachlan, P. (1987). *Sarah, plain and tall*. New York: HarperCollins.
McMullan, K. (2003). *For this land: Meg's prairie diary*. New York: Scholastic.
Walker, B., & Williams, B. (1989). *The Little House cookbook: Frontier foods from Laura Ingalls Wilder's Classic Stories*. New York: HarperCollins.
Wilder, L., & Williams, G. (2004). *Little house on the prairie*. New York: HarperCollins.

Encourage Reading for Personal Purposes

While emphasis is placed on reading to learn from fourth grade on, it is important to remember that the long-term goal for literacy development is for children to become readers who engage in reading outside of school as well as in school. Reading is not something that is done only to get through school. Instead, reading becomes an enjoyable part of daily living. According to Gambrell (1996), the "central and most important goal of reading instruction is to foster the love of reading" (p. 14). This is especially important for children who experience difficulty learning to read.

For this reason, fourth grade is a critical time for enhancing children's enjoyment of reading for personal purposes. By setting aside time in your daily class schedule for students' independent reading of self-selected materials you will be setting the stage for students to become motivated to read for their own enjoyment (Biancarosa, 2005; Biancarosa & Snow, 2004; Gardiner, 2005; Krashen, 2005).

It is also important to ensure that there are books and other reading materials that reflect students' interests. You can use reading interest questionnaires (refer to Figure 11.20) or make a suggestion box available for students to use in communicating their interests to you. Be sure to also include multicultural titles that represent students' social-cultural experiences and ethnicities. While all students will benefit from having access to reading materials that reflect their interests, it is particularly important for those who may be experiencing difficulty in reading. Students who are low-level readers need to have high-interest materials that keep them engaged and motivated to read for personal purposes.

Provide time for independent reading. Time set aside for independent reading has been referred to as Sustained Silent Reading (SSR) and Drop Everything and Read (D.E.A.R. time). The main focus of each of these approaches is to provide a block of time, usually 15 to 30 minutes, in which students select their own reading materials and read for enjoyment. Because the focus is to read for enjoyment, there are no related assignments such as filling out a book report or writing in a response journal that is graded by the teacher. The focus is entirely on reading for pleasure and personal purposes.

Provide a wide selection of reading materials. To encourage all students to become engaged in reading for personal purposes, you will need to have a wide selection of reading materials with respect to content, format, and reading levels. Be sure to make an assortment of children's magazines available that reflect the interests of your students

(See Appendix J). You will want to help students know how to pick out appropriate reading materials. One way of doing this is to brainstorm with students about how to select something to read. By welcoming their suggestions as well as offering your own, you can provide students with strategies they can use in selecting materials to read. It is also helpful to make a list of these guides for selecting reading materials on a poster or an overhead, or on the chalkboard. You could also make bookmarks with the guidelines.

Support struggling readers. Simply providing readers with time for independent reading does not automatically result in successful reading experiences. You need to be sure that you provide the appropriate level of materials for your students. This means that you need to be sensitive to the needs of readers who are struggling and who are also concerned about their classmates' perceptions of their reading difficulties. Struggling fourth graders do not want to be seen reading the "baby" or "easy" books (especially when the books have been color-coded by reading levels). Yet when they try to read grade-level books independently, they become frustrated (Fielding & Roller, 1992). For this reason, you will want to provide a wide range of different formats in addition to narrative storybooks, such as children's magazines, poetry, and high-quality, illustrated informational trade books. Fourth graders may also enjoy specific sections of a daily newspaper, such as the sports or comics section.

You will want to also discuss with students how these different formats are read. For example, when reading a magazine, it is not read from the first page to the last in succession; instead, a reader picks out specific articles he wants to read and may read an entire article or just a portion. Books of poetry also are read in a similar manner. It is also important to provide opportunities for all students (especially struggling readers) to read with a partner. This allows students to support each other's reading and comprehension.

Monitor students' independent reading. Although initial approaches to implementing independent reading time in elementary classrooms specified that teachers should also read for enjoyment and not interact with students, more recent reports of successful independent reading times have described teachers taking a more active role in monitoring and mediating students' transactions with literacy (Block, 2004; Taberski, 1998). This change has come in response to teachers' observations that some students became distracted, unengaged, or wandered from book to book. Teachers now are encouraged to circulate during independent reading time to help students who are struggling to find the "right" book as well as students who are experiencing difficulty with a particular word.

Avoid associating independent reading with extrinsic rewards. In an effort to encourage independent reading both in and out of school, many schools have adopted motivational reading programs that provide rewards for high-volume reading. Perhaps the reward is seeing the principal dressed as a story book character or maybe the reward is a pizza party. Other schools have adopted a commercial, independent reading program that is accompanied by computer-administered tests on each book read. After reading each book, students take the related test. The computer software keeps track of who has read what, the scores, and the number of books read. This data then is often factored into students' report cards.

Do these programs increase the volume of students' reading? Yes, probably so. Many schools report that their incentive reading programs have resulted in increases in the number of books read (Manning, 2005). Do these programs increase students' enjoyment of reading and foster lifelong reading? That question is more difficult to answer because there is a scarcity of longitudinal research in this area. One recent study reported that even though the number of books read and test scores remained unchanged, students' attitudes toward reading became less positive (Stanfield, 2006).

When tangible rewards are paired with independent reading, the focus often is the number of books read or the points earned rather than the enjoyment of reading for personal purposes. In such programs, students may figure out that reading a skinny book counts as much as a "fat" book or conclude that reading is enjoyable only because there will be a pizza party at the end of the incentive program. Other students may consciously select books that have large print or are amply illustrated because they know that it would still count as "reading a book." While not all incentive programs end up this way, Manning (2005) offers these reasons why reward programs should receive careful consideration:

❖ The competitiveness encouraged by reading-reward programs places slow readers at a disadvantage. Realizing they cannot keep up with the faster readers, these struggling readers may develop negative attitudes toward reading.

❖ Requiring that students read books only in their "level" limits the free choice that is important in enhancing reading enjoyment. It becomes just another school assignment. In addition, categorizing books according to reading levels may not reflect students' interests, prior knowledge, or the individual factors that influence what each reader can gain from interacting with a specific book.

Provide opportunities for students to talk about their independent reading. One way of enhancing students' enjoyment of independent reading is to set aside time for them to talk with each other about what they have read (Gambrell, 1996). This sharing not only increases enjoyment but also comprehension since the readers tell what they have read using their own words (Leeser, 1990). You may find that daily sharing sessions become routine and decrease in value; instead, you may find that two or three sharing sessions per week provide the motivating peer interaction that contributes to reading enjoyment.

Encourage Students' Personal Responses to Texts

An important aspect of literacy development involves responding to what is read. This is directly stated in the third standard of the National Council of Teachers of English and the International Reading Association's Standards for the English Language Arts (1996). It states:

> Students apply a wide range of strategies to comprehend, interpret, evaluate, and appreciate texts. They draw on their prior experience, their interactions with other readers and writers, their knowledge of word meaning and of other texts, their word identification strategies, and their understanding of textual features (for example, sound–letter correspondence, sentence, structure, context, graphics). (p. 31)

One way of encouraging students' personal responses to text is to provide sharing sessions at the end of independent reading. Two additional ways of encouraging students' personal responses are literature circles and dialogue journals.

Literature circles. Literature circles are small discussion groups of readers who have read the same story (Daniels, 1994). As students participate in literature circles, they share their thoughts and feelings about what they have read. They make connections between what they have read and their own life experiences. They become more aware of others' literacy transactions and learn to consider multiple perspectives.

In planning for literature circles, the classroom teacher selects a group of books that reflect curricular themes or goals as well as the independent reading levels of her students.

Figure 12.2 Suggested Books for Fourth-Grade Literature Circles

Adler, D. (2004). *The Babe & I.* Fort Worth, TX: Harcourt Children's Books.
Atwater, R. (1992). *Mr. Popper's penguins.* New York: Little, Brown & Company.
Blume, J. (2003). *Tales of a fourth grade nothing.* New York: Penguin.
Byars, B. (1997). *Tornado.* New York: HarperCollins.
Byars, B. (2004). *Little horse on his own.* New York: Henry Holt.
Cleary, B. (2000). *Dear Mr. Henshaw.* New York: HarperCollins.
Danziger, P. (1996). *Amber Brown goes forth.* New York: Scholastic.
DiCamillo, K. (2001). *Because of Winn-Dixie.* Cambridge, MA: Candlewick Press.
Gardiner, J. (1983). *Stone fox.* New York: HarperCollins.
Gipson, B. (1990). *Old Yeller.* New York: HarperCollins.
Konigsburg, E. (2002). *From the mixed-up files of Mrs. Basil E. Frankweiler.* New York: Simon &
    Schuster.
Naylor, P. (2000). *Shiloh.* New York: Simon & Schuster.
Park, B. (2006). *Rosie Swanson: Fourth-grade geek for president.* New York: Random House.
Paterson, K. (1977). *Bridge to Terabithia.* New York: HarperCollins.
Spinelli, J. (1993). *Fourth grade rats.* New York: Scholastic.
Spinelli, J. (1999). *Maniac Magee.* New York: Little, Brown & Company.
Spinelli, J. (2003). *Loser.* New York: HarperCollins.

Most of the time, novels are used for literature circles. Nonfiction books, picture books, and newspaper articles also can be used successfully (Brabham & Villaume, 2000; Lin, 2002). Students then indicate their individual choices from those provided by the teacher. A listing of suggested books for fourth-grade literature circles is presented in Figure 12.2. It is important to remember that as their classroom teacher, only you can decide which books will be appropriate choices for your students to read in their literature circles.

Literature circles are formed as students self-select what they will read. Group sizes are kept relatively small (four to six children) in order to maximize opportunities for individual students to participate in the discussions (Long & Gove, 2003/2004). As a result, there may be two or more groups reading the same book.

Students prepare for their literature circle discussions by first reading the assigned section of the book. Within each literature circle, students assume different roles. These roles are identified and assigned by the classroom teacher. This provides structure to the literature circle, providing specific tasks for students that contribute to the sharing of their individual responses to what they have read. For example, one student might be the discussion leader and another might develop questions to be discussed. Additional roles might involve identifying and defining new vocabulary or providing illustrations to represent events in the story. Prior to participating in their literature circle, students will have prepared specifically for the role they have been assigned. This preparation may involve taking notes, adding sticky-notes to pages they want to discuss, or completing an assignment sheet designed for their specific role (for example, a list of discussion questions or a list of interesting or new vocabulary) (Brabham & Villaume, 2002).

Need for gradual implementation. The implementation of literature circles requires a gradual introduction of the procedures and expectations for student participation. Because literature circles are student-directed, you will want to be sure that your students are able to work cooperatively and productively in a small group setting, with only limited monitoring on your part. You might decide to introduce the various group roles one at a time (Brabham & Villaume, 2000). This would involve having each member of a literature

Student-led discussion groups provide opportunity to share personal responses to texts.

Nadya Lukic

circle develop discussion questions or a list of vocabulary words. With each member experiencing the same role at the same time, they are able to share their experiences in assuming the specific role. Then, later on, each member can assume a separate role.

Students also will need to have had experience in sharing their personal responses to literature as well as responding to other students' comments and questions. For this reason, you may decide to first read aloud to your class, followed by a whole-class discussion. Then you would divide the class into small group for discussion, providing a series of open-ended questions. By creating this structure you are supporting students' gradual transition to participating successfully in a peer-led discussion.

Dialogue journals. Journaling is a way of encouraging students to share their responses to what they are reading. It is not meant to be a written response to teacher-generated questions. Instead, the focus of journaling is on readers' unique transactions with text. In a way, it is like a "think-aloud," but written down. Students are encouraged to write down what they are thinking about when they read. This may involve making predictions about what will happen next, what advice they would give a specific character, or how the characters and/or events relate to their own personal experiences (Hancock, 1993). Dialogue journals often are used as an alternative to small group discussions in literature circles.

Dialogue journaling involves written conversations between the journal writer and his partner. Initially, the classroom teacher serves as the dialogue partner for each student. This provides guided practice for students in expressing their personal responses to texts. Later on, students will be able to partner with a classmate for their dialogue journals.

When you read and respond to your students' journal entries, you engage in a written conversation with them about what they have expressed. The focus is entirely on the thoughts that are shared rather than the grammar or spelling of what was written. Your role is to encourage and facilitate students' thinking and personal responses.

Implementing dialogue journals does require that you have time to respond in writing to each student's journal. You may find that collecting and responding to students' journals each day results in having time to write only limited comments. Only you can decide the best way to implement this strategy. As you work out how you will implement dialogue journals, it is important to keep in mind that the goal of the activity is to encourage students' personal responses to what they have read.

Fourth grade is a time when students are encouraged and expected to use writing as a tool for learning.

Ermolaev Alexander

Encourage Students to Become Strategic Writers

Fourth grade is a time when students are encouraged and expected to use writing as a tool for learning—to record their thoughts and questions, to share what they have learned about a particular topic, to share a story that they have created, and so on. This is also a time when students are encouraged to begin to "take charge" of their writing through monitoring how what they write meets the requirements of the task at hand. This means they are taking on a **metacognitive** role as a learner, reflecting on their thought processes and how they go about learning. You can encourage this by focusing on specific strategies for students to use during the writing process and writer's workshop as well as in monitoring their spelling.

Emphasize students' roles as "authors." In each stage of the writing process, students are encouraged to consciously focus on what they are writing and how they are expressing their thoughts and ideas (see Chapter 11 for a description of each stage). If students have had prior experiences in the writing process, they will now be ready to focus in more detail on each stage.

Prewriting and drafting. In the prewriting stage, you can encourage them to select a particular genre, such as poetry, a play script, or a persuasive letter. For informational writing, you can suggest they conduct research to learn more about their topic. Provide access to reference aids and other materials for students' research. Be sure to emphasize students' role as decision-makers in their selection of the topic, genre, and content of their writing.

Some students may find using a **storyboard** a good way to plan their narrative or sequence of segments in an informational text. Storyboards resemble the format of comics: essentially, a series of illustrations that show the actions or events taking place. Originally, storyboards were used to plan videos, films, or write scripts (Farbman, 2005), but now are also used during the prewriting phase of the writing process (Harrington, 1994). A sample storyboard format is found in Figure 12.3. If your students have not used a storyboard prior to fourth grade, provide one that has only about 6 to 8 frames. As

Figure 12.3 Example Format for a Storyboard

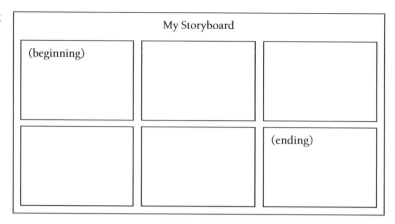

their stories or texts become more complex, encourage them to include more frames in their storyboard planning sheet.

As with other strategies, you will need to first demonstrate how to use storyboards at group time, followed by guided practice in pairs or individually. Then students can be encouraged to use this technique independently.

Since the storyboard format is used in the prewriting phase, encourage students to simply sketch the story, using simple drawings and stick figures to indicate the events and actions. If illustrations are to be part of the final version, they can be added during the publication stage. Dialogue or thought bubbles can be added to indicate character inter-actions. Narrative phrases or short sentences can also be added to the storyboard.

In using the storyboard, encourage students to think through the beginning and end-ing of their stories first (Harrington, 1994). Once those two points are decided, the points in between will fall into place easier. After the storyboard is complete, it provides a struc-tural framework for writing the story or informational text.

Students can also use their storyboards to share their prewriting with others. It is help-ful for students to "talk out" their stories with their peers because this may help them to realize where there are missing parts or unnecessary details. There may also be less resis-tance to changes because their stories are not yet committed to written form.

Reluctant writers may also be more motivated to develop a story using this technique because they can use art to express their ideas. Then the storyboard could be used as a basis for a dictated story or a shared/joint writing project involving several children.

Revision and editing. Once students are comfortable with the prewriting and drafting stages, you will be able to focus more attention on strategies students can use during revi-sion and editing. Revision focuses on the content of the writing and editing focuses on the mechanics of writing (spelling, punctuation, and grammar). Both revision and edit-ing require writers to step back and look at their drafts from a reader's perspective.

You can support students' efforts in revising their work by encouraging them in the following ways (Brady & Jacobs, 1988; Calkins, 1981; Dahl & Farnan, 1998; Graves, 1994; Sowers, 1988; Tompkins, 2004; Walshe, 1981):

1. Remind students to read their drafts aloud to themselves. As they read their draft aloud, they can hear how their words and sentences fit together. When they read and think about what they have written, they may become aware of changes they want to make to clarify the sequence of events or to describe an event or character.

Figure 12.4 Example Questions Teachers Can Use during Individual Student Conferences

1. What did you write about?
2. What part do you like the best? Read it to me. Why do you like this part?
3. What is going to happen next?
4. I'd like to know more about this part. . . .

2. Plan individual conferences with each student. During this time the student will read all or part of their draft and you will respond with questions and comments. Focus your questions and comments on the content of the student's draft. While the questions and comments will differ with each conference, there are several general questions that teachers have found useful. These questions are listed in Figure 12.4.
3. Demonstrate and model ways to share writing and provide feedback to others. To do this, you need to create a draft of your own writing. Read this aloud to your students and encourage them to listen carefully and reflectively to what you read. Then model for them how as listeners they can make positive comments and ask questions about an author's draft.
4. Provide opportunities for students to share their drafts with the class. In this setting, you can encourage students to think about their writing as well as the writing of others in specific ways. In planning for this group sharing, the focus should be on creating a setting where students feel comfortable sharing what they have written. In doing this you will want to consider the guidelines provided in Figure 12.5. The emphasis is on providing positive feedback to the writer. Typically, this involves only 3 to 4 students sharing their work each day.

To encourage and support the editing process, you will also need to demonstrate in a group setting how editing is done by displaying a final draft on the overhead, chalkboard, or chart paper. To provide a focus on spelling, capitalization, grammar, or punctuation, be sure that the draft contains the features to be edited. First, read the draft together and ask for suggestions of what needs to be changed. As each suggestion is made, circle or highlight the location in the text of the item to be changed. Then discuss with students how they can determine whether a change should be made and how it should be changed. Your goal in this editing demonstration is to help students begin to look carefully at a written draft, determine areas that may need editing, and then know how to decide if changes are actually needed. It is also useful to explain to students that while the editing process may "mess up a draft" with cross-outs, insertions, and deletions, it is all part of the process of making a final draft ready for others to read.

As students edit their own work, it may also be useful to have them circle the words or features they think need to change and then show it to a classmate to receive their input on the change(s).

Encourage Students to Become Strategic Readers

Effective reading requires that readers monitor their own comprehension (Janzen, 2003). A proficient reader not only determines that what is read makes sense, he also is aware of what to do when comprehension is problematic (Bossert & Schwantes, 1995–1996; Paris, Lipson, & Wixson, 1994). Because students in fourth grade are encountering a wider

Figure 12.5 Steps and Guidelines for Sharing Students' Drafts at Group Time

1. **Setting the stage.** Ask for several students to volunteer to take turns reading their drafts. You will probably only have 3 to 4 students share each day. Determine who wants to go first, second and so on. Then briefly review the process for sharing, focusing on the roles of the writer/author and the listeners.
2. **Writer reads.** Before the first student reads, remind students in the audience that their job is to listen carefully to the reader. While they are listening they should be thinking about compliments and questions they have for the writer.
3. **Listeners comment.** After each draft is read, the listeners offer their comments and questions. The comments should focus on the strengths of the draft. For example, "I like the way you. . ." or "It was interesting when . . ." or "I'd like to know more about . . ."
4. **Writer comments and questions.** In this step, the writer asks questions of the listeners about his draft. For example, "I'm not sure about this part . . ." or "Could you picture this happening when I read it?"
5. **Listeners respond to writer's comments and questions.** Encourage listeners to word their suggestions in a way that recognizes the author's role in deciding what will be changed. For example: "You might consider doing this . . ." "You could try this . . ." "When you read that part, I wondered about . . ."
6. **Writer makes plan for revision.** This part takes place after the group sharing, as the teacher follows up with each writer who has shared their draft at group time. Because it may take some time for writers to think about the suggestions offered during the group time, you will want provide time for this reflection before having your follow-up conference with each writer. During this conference, you could ask questions such as: Was the group sharing helpful for you? What ideas did you receive from the audience? What are your plans for continuing to work on your draft?

range of texts in different learning activities, they need to be able to apply different strategies to enhance comprehension (Barton & Sawyer, 2003).

Focus on essential comprehension strategies. Barton and Sawyer (2003) identified 10 comprehension strategies that are effective and can be applied to a range of different text types. These include: "locating details, sequencing, comparing and contrasting, summarizing, envisioning character change, drawing conclusions, determining cause and effect, making predictions, making thematic connections, and taking multiple perspectives" (p. 337).

Provide explicit strategy instruction. Students' use of specific comprehension strategies is enhanced by teachers' explicit instruction (Allington, 2002a). This instruction focuses on teaching students to use specific strategies as they read different text types and how specific strategies can be used to "fix" problems in comprehension that they may experience. Strategy instruction occurs in a variety of contexts: whole class, small groups, and one-on-one. The strategy is first demonstrated by the teacher. This is followed by guided practice where the teacher supports students' use of the strategy by providing graduated scaffolding. After the guided practice, opportunities to use the strategy during independent reading are provided.

Demonstrate the strategy. When demonstrating a particular comprehension strategy, you are focusing on a thought process involved in reading. For this reason, your demonstration involves thinking aloud. For example, as you read aloud to your students, you stop to model the ways in which you are thinking about what you are reading. Perhaps you are demonstrating how to compare and contrast two characters. Your think-aloud comments would share with students how you are going about comparing and contrasting the two characters' actions and personal attributes. Laminack and Wadsworth (2006) caution teachers to avoid making excessively detailed or lengthy think-aloud comments: "Too much commentary may take away the need for readers and listeners to think independently and may even reduce the extent to which they are able to engage with the story" (p. xi). The focus is to demonstrate thinking for students, not to think for them.

Think-alouds can be used to focus awareness on a wide range of specific strategies that enhance comprehension (Baumann, Jones, & Seifert-Kessell, 1993; Block & Israel, 2004), such as selecting a book to read, activating prior knowledge, focusing on characters and setting, identifying with characters or events in the book, predicting upcoming events, figuring out vocabulary from context and word analysis, and applying the text content to one's life.

As you are demonstrating a particular strategy by using a think-aloud, you may also find it beneficial to use a graphic that provides a visual summary of your comments (Barton & Sawyer, 2003/2004). In demonstrating a sequencing strategy, you might use a time line with the major events noted. When comparing and contrasting characters, you might use a Venn diagram or a two-column chart.

Provide guided practice. After you have demonstrated the strategy, provide students with the opportunity to work with each other in pairs or small groups in using the target strategy by reading a segment of text (Barton & Sawyer, 2003/2004; Baumann, Jones, & Seifert-Kessell, 1993; Laminack & Wadsworth, 2006). In this setting, you may decide to read aloud the segment of text, have students read to each other, or have each student read silently. Then direct students to share with their peer(s) what they were thinking when the text segment was read that relates to the target strategy. You will initially need to circulate in your classroom to monitor this sharing and to provide redirection, answer questions, and provide support. After the small group/paired sharing occurs, engage the whole class in talking about the strategy and how it was used to enhance comprehension. Working with peers in this guided practice is beneficial in helping students internalize the strategy. You may find that students need to have multiple opportunities for guided practice before they are comfortable using the strategy on their own.

Provide opportunity for independent practice. The goal for strategy instruction is for students to be able to use the new strategy when they are reading independently. Thus, guided practice needs to be followed by independent practice in using the target strategy. Even though this is "independent," it is important for teachers to monitor students' success in using the target strategy when reading by themselves. Students who are not yet able to use the strategy independently may need to have it demonstrated again as well as more guided practice.

Focus on Strategies for Comprehending Informational Text

Informational texts require readers to use different strategies than when narrative texts are read. This is because informational texts are characterized by concept density, new and specialized vocabulary, as well as different text structures and text-based features.

Vocabulary strategies. Vocabulary is an important part of content area instruction because many content words represent complex concepts (Harmon & Hedrick, 2000). For example, in social studies, new vocabulary involves the names of famous people, places, events, and geographic areas, and the ways in which these concepts interrelate. Vocabulary in science also represents complex concepts that have specific relationships to other concepts. For example, studying the tropical rain forest would involve learning many new concepts and their specific terminology, as well as the ways in which the concepts interrelate. Thus, for students to come to "know" a new vocabulary word in social studies, health, science, or math they need to develop knowledge that is specific to that word as well as the relationship of that word (and concept) to other concepts.

Preteach vocabulary. Before students are expected to read a selection that has new vocabulary, it is beneficial to preteach the vocabulary. Blachowicz and Fisher (2006) suggest teachers follow these steps in preteaching vocabulary:

1. Identify words in the text that are new to students or that have unfamiliar meanings.
2. Place the words on a poster, overhead transparency, or chalkboard.
3. Discuss each word with students and elicit their understanding of the words.
4. Provide students with new meanings of the words as used in the selection to be read.
5. Encourage students to develop questions related to the concepts represented in the selected words as well as their prior knowledge of the topic.
6. Read the text.
7. Ask students to respond in writing to the questions in step 5.
8. Guide students in clustering or grouping the information and new vocabulary they have learned.

Focus on word structure. Encourage students to "look inside" a word for clues to its meaning. Prefixes, suffixes, base words, and compound words can provide information about a word's meaning. For example, think about the ways in which the following words can be examined for meaning clues: unsaturated, longitude, quadrilateral, mudslide, aftershock, headwaters, magnetic, nonmagnetic, recycling, pollution.

You can encourage ELLs to focus on word structure by creating an awareness for cognates, or words that have a similar spelling pattern and meaning in their home language as well as in English. For example, many vocabulary words in the content areas have cognates in Spanish. Spanish cognates in the area of geography include these (Cappellini, 2005, p. 278):

English	Spanish cognate
city	ciudad
state	estado
nation	nación
islands	isles
lakes	lagos
rivers	rios
oceans	océanos
latitude	latitud
longitude	longitud

By making these connections between students' home language and English, their vocabulary development is enhanced.

Use visuals and graphic organizers. By creating graphic representations of concepts and their related vocabulary, you can help your students visualize and understand the relationships between concepts. The way in which you represent vocabulary in these visual supports will depend upon the specific concept and its relationship to other concepts. You may decide to use word webs, semantic maps, charts, or Venn diagrams. Engage your students in creating the visuals rather than presenting them with a completed visual. The process of creating the visual and representing the concepts graphically engages students in higher levels of comprehension.

Textbook previewing. Fourth grade is often a time when students are faced with a content-area textbook that is comprehensive and lengthy. You can help students become more comfortable with their textbooks if you encourage them to preview the text prior to beginning to read. Manz (2002) describes a strategy for previewing content-area textbooks that provides a thorough overview of a chapter's contents. The steps in this preview form the acronym THIEVES, which represents the idea that in previewing the text, readers are "sneaking into the chapter" for information before reading the chapter. These steps for previewing include:

T = **Title:** Focus on the title of the chapter for an idea of the chapter's focus.

H= **Heading:** Look at the headings throughout the chapter to become familiar with the specific topics included in the chapter.

I = **Introduction:** Read the introduction to find out the general focus of the chapter.

E = **Every first sentence in a paragraph:** By reading the first sentence in each paragraph, students become more aware of the sequence of concepts presented in the chapter.

V = **Visuals and vocabulary:** Look at the photos, charts, graphs, maps, and diagrams along with the accompanying captions. Look for highlighted words that identify new vocabulary. Think about what you already know about the words.

E = **End of chapter questions:** Most content-area textbooks will have a series of comprehension questions at the end of the chapter. By skimming these questions, a reader can determine what information is emphasized in the chapter.

S = **Summary:** Read the summary provided at the end of the chapter. Summaries generally focus on the big ideas of a chapter. By reading the summary ahead of time, readers are more aware of the major points or ideas they will find when they read the chapter.

Each of these steps helps readers begin to anticipate content found in a chapter as well as activate their prior knowledge of the topics included. When introducing this strategy to your fourth-grade students, you might decide to introduce one step at a time, gradually building up to all seven steps. It would also be beneficial to have the steps displayed on a poster or wall chart so students can refer to it as they use the strategy.

Active reading strategies. As a reflective teacher, you will want to help students become aware of strategies they can use that will help them monitor their comprehension and understanding of informational text. Because literacy transactions are unique to each reader, some students may find specific strategies more useful than others. Only by trying out the various strategies will readers be able to determine which strategies work for them. In this section, three strategies for comprehending informational text are described. The first two strategies involve readers in specific ways in actively thinking before they begin reading, while they are actively reading the text, and after they have finished reading. The last strategy involves writing in learning logs in response to reading informational texts. Encouraging students to begin to use these strategies first involves demonstration of each strategy, followed by guided practice and then independent practice.

TWA. This strategy encourages students to focus on their thinking prior to reading informational text, while they read and after reading (Mason, Snyder, & Kedem, 2006). The first step, "Think before reading," involves activating prior knowledge, thinking about the author's purpose, and setting a purpose for your reading. The second step, "Thinking while reading," focuses on linking the text to your own knowledge, varying rereading speed (skimming, scanning), and rereading parts to clarify comprehension. After the text is read, the third step, "Thinking after reading," involves stating the main idea in your own words, summarizing the information, and retelling or reflecting on what you learned.

SQRQCQ. Solving word problems in math class requires that students be able to read the problem as well as determine the mathematical question. Students also have to be able to know what information found in the word problem is needed to solve the problem and which information may be extraneous (Adams, 2003; Barton, Heidema, & Jordan, 2002). Many word problems are constructed in a storylike format and end with a question to be answered based upon mathematical computation. Story problems often require multiple readings before it is clear which information is relevant and which mathematical operations are required. The SQRQCQ strategy was developed to provide a process for students to use when reading and solving word problems in math (Fay, 1965). It involves these six steps:

> S = **Survey**. Read through the problem quickly to get a general idea of the scope and nature of the problem.
> Q = **Question**. Ask yourself what information is needed to begin solving the problem.
> R = **Read**. Carefully read through the problem, noting the pieces of information needed for solving the problem.
> Q = **Question**. Ask yourself what type(s) of computation will be needed, for example, addition, subtraction, multiplication, or division.
> C = **Compute**. Perform the needed computation(s).
> Q = **Question**. Ask yourself if the solution you came up with fits the original question. You may need to reread the story problem to be sure.

When you demonstrate this strategy for your students, you may find it helpful to display these steps on a poster, bulletin board, or overhead projector, as well as providing bookmarks for students to keep in their math textbooks. Then during guided practice and independent practice they can easily refer to the specific steps in this strategy.

Learning logs. Learning logs are notebooks that students use to record their thoughts and ideas while reading informational text (Blake, 1990; Moss, 2005). Students' entries in their learning logs can take a variety of formats, such as "questions about content, reflections on what students have learned, webs, charts, diagrams of processes or events" (p. 50). Learning logs provide an opportunity for students to use writing as a way of taking information that was read and restating it in their own words or creating a graphic to represent their understanding of the concepts. Learning logs can also be used as a prereading strategy for making predictions and activating prior knowledge (Blake, 1990; Knipper & Duggan,

2006). For example, at the first social studies class of the school year, one teacher asked students to respond in their learning logs to this question: "What is social studies?" (Chard, 1990). The responses she received indicated a wide range of knowledge and awareness as shown in the following examples (p. 62):

Angela: It's a book you can study with at school. Sometimes you have to use it if you need it or not.

Susan: It teaches you a lot about space, what we live on. It teaches the solar system, map, and globe. It shows where we live, about what people do, and different kinds of people.

Kelly: Social studies is things that you learn about: history, the future, animals, people and the world. It's where you learn about the states. And about your country and a lot of other things. You learn about people.

From these learning log entries, the teacher became aware of students' prior knowledge as well as their expectations for what would be part of social studies. She then was able to use that information in planning and structuring how she would begin her social studies curriculum.

When you introduce learning logs, you may find that students need to have some general prompts to get started. These prompts should be open-ended rather than questions that simply ask for facts related to their reading. Encourage students to think of their learning logs as a place to write down their thoughts and questions. You will need to collect their learning logs periodically so you can be aware of their perceptions and questions. You might also have students think of discussion questions to share. Then you could have students meet in small groups to talk about their questions or have them exchange their learning logs with a partner and then have the partner write a response to the questions. By having students develop their own questions from their reading of informational text, students are encouraged to think of the major points or facts. In this way their comprehension of informational text is enhanced.

A word of caution. It is important to keep strategy instruction focused on students' effective comprehension of text and not to emphasize strategy steps so much that meaningful reading is lost. Strategies are useful only if they increase students' comprehension and reading satisfaction. "Prolonged use of imposed strategies and scaffolds seems intrusive and cumbersome as does excessive use of . . . think-alouds and reflections" (Villaume & Brabham, 2002, p. 676). In addition, strategies that involve multiple, detailed steps or imply that the steps must be followed rigidly may not be useful as long-term strategies for independent reading. Strategy instruction is beneficial when readers are able to use the strategies for independent reading. As their teacher, you can demonstrate and provide guided practice and opportunities for independent application of the strategies used by proficient readers, but it is up to your students whether they each will find the strategies useful in their literacy transactions.

Providing Extra Support for Struggling Readers and Writers

Fostering children's success in learning is an important consideration for each teacher in each grade level; however, because of the changes in the learning context and learning tasks in fourth grade, teachers at this level need to be especially sensitive to children who may be struggling. Students who experience difficulty in fourth grade may represent three different groups: those who experienced difficulty learning to read and write in the primary grades and have not yet achieved grade-level standards; those who were successful in the primary grades, but find the challenges of fourth grade problematic; and ELLs, who are faced with these same challenges and are also acquiring new knowledge and skills in a new language (English). This decrease in academic performance has been referred to as "the fourth-grade slump" (Chall, 1996; Chall, Jacobs, & Baldwin, 1990; Snow, Burns, & Griffin, 1998).

Factors associated with the "fourth-grade slump." Several factors appear to be associated with this decline in academic performance in fourth grade. These include: (a) More complex instructional materials and learning tasks, (b) the increasing importance of students' prior conceptual knowledge and vocabulary in comprehending content-area texts, and (c) decreasing motivation to learn.

More complex instructional materials and learning tasks. Fourth grade is characterized by a dramatic increase in exposure to informational text as well as an increase in teacher-directed learning (Hedrick, Harmon, & Wood, 2005; Salinger, 2003). In addition, there may be an increase in the amount of teacher-talk as direct instruction takes place. As described earlier in this chapter, informational text differs dramatically from narrative text because it has greater concept density and new and specialized vocabulary, as well as different and more complex text structures. When this change in learning materials is accompanied by increasing expectations for students to read and comprehend with limited contextual support, reading becomes a more difficult task.

Increasing importance of students' prior conceptual knowledge and vocabulary. By their very nature, content-area texts are filled with new concepts as well as more precise vocabulary. Comprehension of such texts appears to be influenced by students' prior related knowledge (Best, Floyd, & McNamara, 2007). When children have prior experiences and related vocabulary that provide a foundation for acquiring more precise vocabulary and advanced concepts, comprehension of content-area texts is facilitated. For example, children who have had prior experiences with the concepts of prairies, hills, creeks, streams, rivers, and mountains will have a foundation for understanding social studies texts that describe the pioneers' movement westward. Children without this foundational knowledge may be overwhelmed with all of the unfamiliar concepts and vocabulary in their social studies text. The role of prior knowledge in contributing to text comprehension is also evident when children encounter science textbooks.

Decreasing motivation to learn. Children who are experiencing difficulty at school become aware that they are not keeping up with others in their classroom. Because they do not understand why learning is more difficult for them, they may feel powerless (Taylor, Harris, Pearson, & Garcia, 1995). This is often accompanied by low self-esteem, decreasing motivation, and avoiding reading-related activities (Rasinski & Padak, 2004; Salinger, 2003). The nature of the curriculum and the learning context in fourth grade makes avoidance of reading-related activities impossible. Fourth-grade teachers have a critical role in providing extra support for students who are struggling. Without this support, academic achievement may begin a downward spiral that quickly manifests itself in other negative and disruptive behaviors (Salinger, 2003).

Strategies and guidelines for supporting struggling readers. In the fourth grade, struggling readers differ from more capable readers in three ways: their vocabularies are less developed, they lack reading fluency, and they experience difficulty in comprehending grade-level texts (Kuhn & Morrow, 2005). As a result, strategies for providing support for struggling readers involve these three areas: fluency, vocabulary, and comprehension

Figure 12.6 Strategies for Supporting Struggling Readers

Enhancing Fluency

❖ Continue group time read-alouds as a way of modeling fluent reading for all students.

❖ Show students how to "read" punctuation as a guide for phrasing and intonation.

❖ Provide access to taped readings of familiar stories as well as informational texts, including assigned content-area textbook chapters.

❖ Provide opportunities for partner reading, Readers' Theatre, and poetry performances as a way to encourage repeated readings and expressive reading.

❖ Emphasize word-recognition strategies. Avoid assuming that students who have trouble decoding words need more phonics instruction at the level of letter–sound associations. Instead focus on word study that involves meaningful clusters of letters (prefixes, suffixes, base words) and high-frequency words.

Enhancing vocabulary

❖ Build students' listening and speaking vocabularies in meaningful ways through read-alouds and opportunities to talk in large and small group settings.

❖ Talk about the meanings of idioms, metaphors, and colloquial expressions that are used orally and in texts.

❖ Demonstrate and provide guided practice with reference materials such as dictionaries and thesauruses.

❖ Focus students' attention on the small differences in words that have big differences in meaning, for example, cap–cape, friend–fiend, horse–house, whether–weather, than–then, and scare–score.

Enhancing Comprehension

❖ Provide direct and focused strategy instruction, such as KWL, SQRQCQ, and think-alouds. Talk with students about the ways these strategies can enhance their comprehension.

❖ Preteach vocabulary in content area texts so students can anticipate how these words will be used in their assigned reading.

❖ Emphasize the importance of self-monitoring comprehension.

❖ Provide contextual support for comprehension through use of realia and hands-on experiences.

❖ Provide graphic organizers as a way of focusing on the main points in a text and relationships between concepts.

❖ Encourage previewing assigned content area reading before actually reading the assigned sections/pages.

❖ Provide opportunities to talk about what was read and how it relates to what they know and what experiences they have had.

Sources: Chall & Jacobs, 2003; de Leon, 2002; Salinger, 2003; Taylor, Harris, Pearson, & Garcia, 1995).

(Chall & Jacobs, 2003; Salinger, 2003). In each of these areas, there is also an emphasis on developing students' metacognitive awareness. This means that students are encouraged to consciously think about the way they go about reading and comprehending. Struggling readers need to develop ways of increasing their fluency, vocabulary, and comprehension of assigned texts. Figure 12.6 provides an overview of specific strategies that focus on supporting fluency, vocabulary, and comprehension. Because these strategies were

Figure 12.7 Strategies for Supporting Struggling Writers

❖ Provide a full range of support as needed, such as modeled writing, shared writing, and interactive writing.

❖ Demonstrate how specific genres of text are structured and encourage students to use storyboards and other graphic organizers in planning their writing.

❖ Empower students as authors and decision-makers in the writing process. This provides a sense of ownership and motivation.

❖ Encourage students to read their own writing aloud. This builds their fluency and confidence as readers and writers.

❖ Focus the writing process on prewriting and drafting phases. Students need to be comfortable with these two phases before they can consider revisions and editing.

❖ When conferencing with students during prewriting and drafting, focus on content rather than mechanics of writing.

❖ Encourage students to use word processing and spell-/grammar-check software for the editing and publication phases.

❖ Be sure writing is shared with peers because having an audience provides motivation for "real" communication.

❖ Provide opportunity to work in pairs for composing as well as illustrations to accompany text. In this way students can support each other and talk about the composing process.

Sources: Harrington, 1994; Kuhn & Morrow, 2005; Rasinski & Padak, 2004; Salinger, 2003; Scala, 2001; Tompkins, 2004.

introduced in earlier chapters of this text, specific steps or guidelines are not included in this chapter. Instead, refer to the descriptions in previous chapters.

Strategies and guidelines for supporting struggling writers. Students who are struggling writers need opportunities to write within a supportive and positive learning community. The workshop approach to writing provides a setting where there is an expectation that students will work at their own pace (Roller, 1996). Struggling writers may show a reluctance to write based upon their prior experiences in writing (Salinger, 2003). Thus, they will need to have additional support to be motivated to write. Specific strategies and guidelines for supporting struggling writers are highlighted in Figure 12.7.

Chapter Summary

Fourth grade is a year of transition between the elementary grades and middle school. It is a time when students are expected to have mastered the basic skills associated with decoding, word recognition, text comprehension, and fluency. In fourth grade, reading is used as a tool for learning in science, social studies, health, and mathematics. Textbooks in the content areas are dramatically different from the texts encountered in the reading and language-arts areas. These informational texts are characterized by concept density, new and specialized vocabulary, different text structures, and specific text features.

Children's literacy development in fourth grade can be enhanced by creating a literacy-rich environment, encouraging reading for personal purposes, encouraging students' personal responses to texts, encouraging students to become strategic readers and writers, and focusing on specific strategies for comprehending informational texts. Providing extra support for struggling readers and writers is critical in the fourth grade in order to prepare students for continued success in school. Factors associated with the "fourth-grade slump" include the increased complexity of instructional materials and learning tasks, the increased importance of students' prior conceptual knowledge and vocabulary, and students' decreasing motivation to learn. Strategies for supporting struggling readers focus on increasing their fluency, vocabulary, and comprehension. Strategies for supporting struggling writers are centered in a workshop approach to the writing process, along with emphasizing the role of the student as author and decision-maker.

Chapter Review

1. Terms to know:

   metacognitive   storyboard

2. In what ways does the context of fourth grade differ from earlier grades?

3. Why do students need specific strategies for comprehending informational texts?

4. How does an active learning environment enhance literacy development in fourth grade?

5. In what ways does independent reading time enhance literacy development in fourth grade?

6. How is the think-aloud strategy used in providing explicit instruction in comprehension?

7. How can visuals and graphic organizers be used to focus on vocabulary in informational texts?

8. In what ways can interdisciplinary units incorporate literacy development in the content areas?

9. What is the rationale behind an emphasis on "empowering students as authors"?

10. What is the role of metacognition in the writing process?

11. Why is it important for students to have an "audience" for their writing?

12. Why should teachers be concerned about the "fourth-grade slump"?

Chapter Extension Activities

Curriculum Development:

1. Select an informational trade book appropriate for fourth grade. Read through the book, identifying five to six key vocabulary words. Using a format provided in Appendix K, develop a lesson plan to preteach the vocabulary words. Follow the steps outlined in this chapter. Present your lesson plan to your college class.

2. Locate a fourth-grade social studies or science textbook. Using a lesson plan format provided in Appendix K, develop a lesson plan that involves creating a word web or semantic map that would enhance students' comprehension of a specific chapter. Present your plan and the graphic to your college class. Explain how you developed this graphic.

3. With a group of two to three classmates, read one of the books listed in Figure 12.2. Assign roles among your group members and participate in a literature circle discussion. Share your experiences with your college class.

4. Develop a class poster and individual bookmark to use in encouraging students to use either the THIEVES or SQRQCQ strategy. Display your poster and bookmark in your college class.

Research:

1. Review two commercial basal programs for fourth grade. Compare and contrast the two programs with respect to (a) materials provided, (b) skills emphasized, and (c) theoretical perspective/instructional approach. Share your conclusions with your college class.

2. Review a commercial curriculum for fourth grade in science, social studies, health, or math. Analyze the curriculum for the literacy skills that are part of the learning activities. Share your findings with your college class.

Online or In-Class Discussion: Do you find reading informational texts more challenging than narrative texts? Why? What strategies do you use in reading informational texts that enhance your comprehension and learning?

Glossary

Academic English Specialized form of English that is used in educational settings as well as the fields of commerce, business, law, science, and government

Academic register *See* academic English

Anecdotal records Written observations describing children's interactions and behaviors

Antonym A word that has the opposite meaning of another word

Basal reading program Commercial curriculum for reading that serves as a basis for classroom instruction

Basic Interpersonal Communication Skills (or BICS) Refers to the development of conversational English by second language learners.

Bottom-up process Belief that reading occurs when a person first processes discrete pieces of visual information, such as letters and letter–sound associations

Cognitive Academic Proficiency Skills (or CALPS) Refers to the development of academic English and related language skills by second language learners

Caption books Picture books created by using photographs of a child's favorite people and objects accompanied by captions naming each person or object

Cognate A word that has similar spelling and meaning to a word in different language

Compound word Formed when two separate words are joined or hyphenated and considered one unit of meaning

Comprehensible input Level of language that a teacher uses that can be comprehended by an English language learner

Consonant blend A cluster of two or more consonants in a syllable that when pronounced are distinguishable, for example, *gr* in *great*

Consonant digraph A cluster of two consonants representing a sound not associated with the individual letters, for example, *ch* in *chair*

Contingent reinforcement Reinforcement that is determined by a child's preceding verbal or nonverbal behavior

Curriculum A written set of specific instructional plans for teaching children at a particular level of development

Decodable readers Texts for beginning readers that are composed of words with similar phonological patterns and frequent word repetition

Decoding The ability to recognize and comprehend written words

Decontextualized language Language that is used to communicate events and concepts that are not present in the current context of interaction

Developmentally appropriate practice Instructional interactions based on the belief that the learning environment and learning tasks should be directly related to the developmental level of each child rather than his or her chronological age

Derivational suffix Morphemic unit added to the end of a base word that changes the grammatical function and meaning of the word

Dialects Variations of a language that develop within a specific population or geographic region

Dialogic reading A form of shared reading with children that involves a turn-taking, conversation-like interaction, characterized by asking questions about illustrations, asking open-ended questions, and expanding on children's responses

Early phonemic spelling Form of invented spelling in which letters are used to represent part of the sounds in a word

Echolalic babbling Reflects the intonation and rhythm of the speech of adults in the infant's environment

Emergent literacy Gradual development of literacy knowledge among young children prior to formal instruction in reading and writing

Encoding The ability to use the alphabetic system to communicate through writing

Environmental print The ways in which written language is used to communicate in home and community settings; for example, newspapers, business letters, advertisements, magazines, road signs, business signs, product logos and labels, personal correspondence, and shopping lists

Expressive language A child's use of language to communicate

Genre Type of text categorized by form or content, for example, fairy tale, mystery, fiction, and informational text

Grammar A system of rules for putting words together in phrases and sentences

High-frequency words Words that appear repeatedly in most texts

Idiomorphs A child's invented, wordlike units of speech

Inferential questions Require students to use information from two or more sentences in constructing their answers

Inferencing Text comprehension that requires a reader to search within a text for related information and combine it to come to a conclusion or to make a prediction

Inflectional suffix Morphemic unit added to the end of a base word to show plurality, verb tense, possession or make comparisons

Interactive writing A shared writing activity in which the teacher and children jointly write a group story

Invented spellings Children's early attempts to write words that involve their own versions of specific words; considered to be evidence of children's developing phonetic knowledge

Letter-name spelling Form of invented spelling in which the sounds are represented by the name of the letter, for example, *LADE* for *lady*

Leveled texts Students' readers that have been specifically designed for different reading levels

Linguistic scaffold An adult's use of questioning, expansion, and repetition to support a child's participation in conversation and other verbal interactions

Listening vocabulary Words that a child can understand when used by others during conversations and other oral speech

Literacy Competency in using written language to communicate with others and in acquiring new knowledge and skills

Literal questions Ask students to locate information directly stated in the text

Literate register *See* academic English

Mediation Parent or adult adapts the literacy event to fit their child's developmental level

Metacognitive Reflecting on one's own thought processes as he/she goes about learning

Metalinguistic knowledge Conscious awareness of specific features of language including its structure and how language units (sounds, words, text segments) can be manipulated

Morphemic Aspect of language that refers to knowledge of word structure and meaningful word parts

Narratives Stories expressed orally or in writing

Onset The initial consonant or consonant cluster in a syllable

Open-ended questions Ask students to develop an answer based upon their prior knowledge and experience as well as the context of the story or informational text

Oral cloze A strategy used by adults for eliciting a child's verbal participation in story sharing by reading a segment of text, stopping at a predictable part, and encouraging the child to fill in the gap

Phoneme Smallest unit of meaningful sound in a language

Phonemic awareness Awareness that speech units can be separated into distinct sounds

Phonemic spelling Form of invented spelling in which multiple phonemes in words are represented by letters or letter clusters

Phonetic awareness Awareness that alphabet letters represent specific sounds and are combined to create words

Phonics The teaching of relationships between alphabet letters and the sounds associated with the letters and letter clusters

Phonological awareness Awareness of the general sound structure of language; includes awareness of phonemes, syllables, and other segments of sounds in words

Pragmatic Aspect of language that focuses on the way in which language is used differently in different settings

Prephonemic spelling Invented spelling that has no phonetic relationship between the letters and the sounds in the words when "read" by the child

Prefix Morphemic unit added to the beginning of a base word that changes the meaning

Previewing Quickly skimming the different parts of an informational text (for example, table of contents, first two paragraphs, conclusion) to obtain an overview

Reading readiness Belief that specific, isolated subskills are required before a child is ready to learn to read

Reading vocabulary Words a child is able to recognize immediately and understand; also known as sight vocabulary

Receptive language A child's comprehension of others' speech

Reflective practice Instructional decisions based on a conscious consideration of professional knowledge, observation of students' learning, personal intuition, and curricular resources

Rime The first vowel in a syllable and the remaining consonants in the syllable

Scaffolding Verbal and nonverbal support provided by adult to child during book sharing to elicit and sustain child's engagement in the literacy event

Scanning Reading by quickly looking through a text for specific pieces of information, such as dates or names

Sensorimotor stage Stage of cognitive development described by Piaget in which infants (birth to 18 months) experience their environment and learn through their senses, movements, and manipulation of objects they encounter

Sight vocabulary Words that a reader recognizes immediately without effortful letter–sound decoding

Simultaneous bilingualism Children who learn two languages concurrently, generally prior to age 3

Skimming Silently reading the print quickly, focusing on key words such as nouns, verbs, and adjectives to get a general idea of text content

Speaking vocabulary Words the child uses when speaking with others

Storyboard A sequential arrangement of illustrations that show the setting, actions, and events in a story or narrative; used in the idea or pre-writing stage of the writing process

Suffix A morphemic unit that is added to the end of a base word

Synonym A word that has a similar meaning to another word

Syntax A system of rules, or grammar, for putting words together in phrases and sentences

Tag question A form of questioning used by adults that restates what the child said and adds a question that asks for confirmation

Telegraphic speech A child's speech that resembles a telegram because it includes only content words; no conjunctions, articles, prepositions, or inflectional word endings are used

Top-down process Belief that reading is meaning-driven and process begins with nonvisual information, such as prior knowledge of language, conceptual knowledge, and past experiences

Transactional perspective Belief that reading and writing involve transactions that occur between the reader's knowledge of language and concepts, the texts encountered, and the contexts in which the literacy event occurs

Transitional spelling *See* phonemic spelling

Vicarious experiences Experiences in which the actual event is not directly participated in, but is experienced through reading a book, watching a video, or hearing someone tell a story

Whole language approach Emphasizes immersing children in authentic reading and writing activities rather than direct instruction involving isolated skills

Word family A group of words with the same rime

Writing vocabulary Words a child is able to use when writing

Zone of proximal development The area of potential growth between what a child can do independently and what the child can do with adult mediation

Appendix A

Recent Reading-Related Initiatives in the United States

Professional Organizations

Association for the Education of Young Children (ACEI)
http://www.acei.org

Education Commission of the States
http://www.ecs.org

International Reading Association (IRA)
http://ira.org

National Association for the Education of Young Children (NAEYC)
http://www.naeyc.org

National Council for Teachers of English
http://www.ncte.org

Publications

Center for the Improvement of Early Reading Achievement (CIERA) (2001). *Putting reading first: The research building blocks for teaching children to read.* Jessup, MD: National Institute for Literacy, U.S. Department of Education.

Department of Education (2005), Analysis of State K–3 Reading Standards and Assessments.
http://www.ed.gov/print/rschstat/eval/other/reading/state-k–3reading.html

Gottlieb, S. (2001). A review of state reading and language arts standards. ERIC Digest. ED456425
http://www.ericdigests.org/2002–2)state.htm

Learning First Alliance (2000). *Every child reading: A professional development guide.* Baltimore, MD: Association for Supervision and Curriculum Development.

Mid-continent Research for Education and Learning (2006). *Content knowledge standards and benchmarks.* Retrieved 1/1/2007. http://www.mcrel.org/standards-benchmarks/docs/purpose.asp

National Association for the Education of Young Children (1998). Learning to read and write: Developmentally appropriate practices for young children. *Young Children, 53*(4), 30–46.

National Commission on Excellence in Education (1983). *A nation at risk: The imperative for educational reform.* Washington, DC: U.S. Department of Education.
http://www.ed.gov/pubs/NatAtRisk/title.

National Council of Teachers of English (NCTE) & International Reading Association (IRA) (1996). *Standards for the English language arts.* Urbana, IL: National Council of Teachers of English.

National Institute for Early Education Research (2007). *Language arts standards for early education.* Retrieved 1/1/2007. http://nieer.org/resources/facts/index/php?FastFactID=4

National Institute for Literacy (2001). *Put reading first: The research building blocks for teaching children to read.* Jessup, MD: National Institute for Literacy.

National Institute for Literacy (2006). Public Law 102–73, the National Literacy Act of 1991. Retrieved 2/21/2006. http://www.nifl.gov/public-law.html

National Reading Panel (2000). *The report of the National Reading Panel: Teaching children to read.* Washington, DC: National Institute of Child Health and Human Development.

National Reading Panel (2006). About the National Reading Panel (NRP) and Charge to the National Reading Panel. Retrieved January 27, 2006. http://www.nationalreadingpanel.org

No Child Left Behind Legislation, Washington, DC: U.S. Government. http://www.ed.gov/print/nclb

Scott-Little, C., Kagan, S., & Frelow, V. (2003). Creating the conditions for success with early learning standards: Results from a national study of state-level standards for children's learning prior to kindergarten. *Early Childhood Research & Practice, 5*(2), 27 pgs. Retrieved 1/1/2007. http://ecrp.uiuc.edu/v5n2/little.html

Whitmore, K., & Goodman, Y. (1995). Transforming curriculum in language and literacy. In S. Bredekamp & T. Rosegrant (Eds.), *Reaching potentials: Transforming early childhood curriculum and assessment, volume 2.* Washington, DC: National Association for the Education of Young Children.

Appendix B

Literacy Resources for Infants and Toddlers

Songs, Finger Plays, and Rhymes for Infants and Toddlers

Chupela, D. (1998). *Once upon a childhood: Fingerplays, action rhymes, and fun times for the very young*. Lanham, MD: Rowman & Littlefield.

Collins, B., & Calmenson, S. (1991). *The eentsy, weentsy spider: Fingerplays & action rhymes*. New York: HarperCollins.

Feierbend, J. (2000). *Book of tapping and clapping: Infants and toddlers*. West Hartford, CT: GIA Publications.

Feierbend, J. (2000). *Book of wiggles and tickles*. West Hartford, CT: GIA Publications.

Newcome, Z. (2002). *Heads & shoulders, knees & toes: And other action counting rhymes*. New York: Candlewick Press.

Orozco, J. (2002). *Diez deditos & other play rhymes & action songs from Latin America*. New York: Penguin.

Public Domain Staff. (2000). *My first action rhymes*. New York: HarperCollins Children's Books.

Random House, & Brannon, T. (Illus.) (2002). *Pat-a-cake & other first baby games*. New York: Random House.

Random House, & Croll, C. (Illus.) (2001). *Finger plays and songs for the very young*. New York: Random House.

Schiller, P., Lara-Alecio, R. & Irby, B. (2004). *The bilingual book of rhymes, songs, stories and fingerplays*. Beltsville, MD: Gryphon House.

Schiller, P. (2006). *And the cow jumped over the moon*. Beltsville, MD: Gryphon House.

Silberg, J., & Schiller, P. (2002). *The complete book of rhymes, songs, poems, fingerplays and chants*. Beltsville, MD: Gryphon House.

Stemple, A. (2006). *This little piggy with CD: Lap songs, finger plays, clapping games and pantomime rhymes*. Cambridge, MA: Candlewick.

Stetson, E. (2001). *Little hands: Fingerplays and action songs*. Nashville, TN: Ideals Publications.

Wilmes, L., & Wilmes, D. (1994). *2's experience: Fingerplays*. New York: Building Blocks Publications.

Yolen, J. (2006). *This little piggy: Lap songs, fingerplays, clapping games, and pantomime rhymes*. New York: Candlewick Press.

Books for Infants and Toddlers: Observers and Explorers

Board Books

Brown, M. (1994). *Big red barn board book*. New York: HarperFestival.

Cox, P. (1999). *Find the puppy*. London: Usborne Publishing.

Dorling Kindersley (2001). *Farm animals*. New York: Doring Kindersley Publishing.

Fleming, D. (1992). *Lunch*. New York: Henry Holt and Company, LLC.

Hague, M. (1993). *Teddy bear, teddy bear*. New York: Tupelo Books, William Morrow & Co.

Koeppel, E. (2004). *The garbage truck*. New York: Scholastic.

Lionni, L. (1993). *Let's play*. New York: Alfred A. Knopf.

McFarlane, S. (2004). *On the farm: What's that sound?* Markham, Ontario: Fitzhenry & Whiteside.

Miller, M. (2001). *Peekaboo baby*. New York: Little Simon, Simon & Schuster.

Patricelli, L. (2005). *Blankie*. Cambridge, MA: Candlewick Press.

Scarry, R. (1963, 2004). *I am a bunny*. New York: Random House.

Scarry, R. (1963, 2004). *The rooster struts*. New York: Random House.

Schofield, J. (2005). *Animal babies in mountains*. Boston, MA: Kingfisher, a Houghton Mifflin Company imprint.

Wells, R. (1998). *The itsy-bitsy spider*. New York: Scholastic.

Special Feature Touch-and-Feel Books

Boynton, S. (1998). *Dinosaur's binkit*. New York: Simon and Schuster Children's Publishing.

Boynton, S. (2003). *Fuzzy fuzzy fuzzy!: A touch, skritch, & tickle book*. New York: Simon & Schuster Children's Publishing.

Davies, E. (2001). *Pat the bunny*. (Touch and Feel Books). New York: Golden Books.

Hathon, E. (2000). *Night, night baby: A touch & feel book*. New York: Grosset & Dunlap.

McDonald, J. (2006). *Pat-a-cake*. New York: Scholastic.

Page, J. (2006). *Hey diddle diddle*. New York: Scholastic.

Priddy, R. (2003). *Fuzzy bee & friends*. New York: St. Martin's Press.

Priddy, R. (2003). *Squishy turtle & friends*. New York: St. Martin's Press.

Schwartz, B., & Turner, D. (2000). *What makes a rainbow?: A magic ribbon book*. New York: Intervisual Books, Inc.

Watanabe, K. (2003). *Sweet dreams: My first taggies book*. New York: Scholastic.

Other Favorites

Cabrera, J. (1999). *Over in the meadow*. New York: Holiday House.

Hoban, T. (1991). *All about where*. New York: Greenwillow Books.

Hoban, T. (1992). *Look up, look down*. New York: Greenwillow Books, William Morrow and Company.

Hoban, T. (1997). *Look book*. New York: Greenwillow Books, William Morrow and Company.

Hubbell, P. (2003). *Trucks: Whizz! zoom! rumble!* Tarrytown, NY: Marshall Cavendish.

Kraus, R. (1967, 2005). *The happy egg*. New York: HarperCollins.

Munari, B. (1963, 2005). *Bruno Munari's zoo*. San Francisco, CA: Chronicle Book.

Polushkin, M. (1978, 2005). *Mother, mother, I want another*. New York: Knopf.

Scarry, R. (1991). *Richard Scarry's best word book ever*. Racine, WI: Western Publishing Company, Inc.

Stevenson, R. (2005). *Block city*. New York: Simon & Schuster.

Bilingual Books for Infants and Toddlers

Ada, A. (1997). *Gathering the sun: An alphabet in Spanish & English*. New York: Lothrop, Lee & Shepard Books.

Ada, A. (2004). *The lizard and the sun/La lagartija y el sol*. New York: Doubleday.

Beaton, C. (2003). *Toys*. New York: Barron's Education Services.

Beinstein, P. (2003). *Dora's book of words/Libro de palabras de Dora*. New York: Simon Spotlight, Simon & Schuster.

Carle, E., & Iwamura, K. (2003). Where are you going? To see my friend. (English–Japanese). London: Orchard Books.

DePaola, T. (2003). *Marcos counts: One, two, three/Uno, dos, tres*. New York: G. P. Putnam & Sons.

Doring Kindersley (2004). Los colores/*Colors*. New York: DK Publishing.

Escardó I Bas, Mercé. (2006). *The three little pigs/Los tres creditos*. San Francisco, CA: Chronicle Books.

Hoppey, T. (2005). *Tito, the firefighter/Tito, el bombero*. Green Bay, WI: Raven Tree Press.

Pfister, M. (2006). *Rainbow fish opposites: Opuestors*. New York: North–South Books.

Websites for Bilingual Books

Cooperative Children's Book Center
    School of Education, University of Wisconsin-Madison
      http://www.education.wisc.edu/ccbc/books/detailListBooks.asp?idBookLists=102
Innovative Educators
      http://innovative-educators.com/area/asp?area=Spanish+%26+Bilingual
Just for Kids
      http://www.just-for-kids.com/BABYLABI.HTM
      (includes bilingual books featuring French, German, Italian, and Spanish)
Language Lizard (40 different languages available)
      http://www.LanguageLizard
Mantra Lingua Ltd. (20+ different languages available)
      http://www.mantralingua.com

Appendix C

Preschool Observation Forms

C–1 Observation of a Preschooler's Ways of Communicating

Child's name:_____ Age:_____ Date(s) observed:_____

Focus of Observation	Questions to consider:	Consistently	Occasionally	Not at this time
Eye contact, shared reference	1. Does child respond to adult's request to "look"? 2. Does child follow adult's pointing gestures? 3. Does child make eye contact with adult when adult is talking and directly in front of, or nearby? 4. When presented with an object, does child first look at adult and then at object?			
Turn-taking/ dialogic participation	1. When adult speaks to child and then pauses, does the child respond nonverbally? 2. When adult speaks to child and then pauses, does child respond verbally?			
Level of language	Which level characterizes child's expressive language? 1. one-word (invented and conventional) 2. two- to three-word phrases (telegraphic speech) 3. utterances composed of multi-word multiple-phrases			
Social interaction	1. Does child initiate conversations with peers? 2. Does child initiate conversations with adults?			

Home Language: _____Standard English _____Dialect of English _____Other Language

C–2 Observation of a Preschooler's Phonetic Knowledge

Child's name:_____ Age:_____

Focus of Observation	Questions to consider:	Date: Context:	Date: Context:	Date: Context:
		Descriptive example:	Descriptive example:	Descriptive example:
Phonological awareness	1. Does child show awareness of rhyming words? 2. Does child show awareness of word alliteration? 3. Does child engage in word play?			
Knowledge of letter–sound relationships	1. Does child show awareness of sounds associated with individual letters? 2. Does child focus on specific features of letters and discriminate between letters?			

C–3 Observation of a Preschooler's Knowledge of Narratives

Child's name:_____ Age:_____

Focus of Observation	Questions to consider:	Date: Context:	Date: Context:	Date: Context:
		Descriptive example:	Descriptive example:	Descriptive example:
Comprehension of oral stories or teacher read-alouds	Does child: 1. Listen attentively to story during teacher read-aloud? 2. Participate in story discussions? 3. Ask questions related to story or book content?			
Creates personal narratives	Does child: 1. Recount personal events that he/she experienced? 2. Narrate a clear sequence of events in time or cause and effect sequence?			
Creates imaginary narratives	Does child: 1. Create a narrative of imaginary events? 2. Narrate a clear sequence of events?			
Reconstructs story from familiar storybook	Does child's story reconstruction: 1. Include the major events of the story? 2. Include similar sequence of events as in the story?			

C–4 Observation of a Preschooler's Knowledge of How to Read During Shared Book Reading

Child's name:_____ Age:_____

Focus of Observation	Questions to consider:	Date: Book:	Date: Book:	Date: Book:
		Descriptive example:	Descriptive example:	Descriptive example:
Shared reference	Follows adult's gestures/pointing?			
Turn-taking/ dialogic participation	Responds nonverbally? Responds verbally?			
Book handling	Touches, pats, or hits book? Attempts to turn pages? Picks up book independently?			
Memory for book content	Anticipates book content: Through gestures or facial expression? Through verbal expression?			
Attentiveness	Maintains focus on book?			
Affective Response	Appears to enjoy book sharing? Initiates book sharing interaction?			

C–5 Observation of a Preschooler's Knowledge of How to Read: Independent Book Reading

Child's name:_____ Age:_____

Focus of Observation	Questions to consider:	Date: Book:	Date: Book:	Date: Book:
		Descriptive example:	Descriptive example:	Descriptive example:
Book handling	Orients book correctly? Proceeds from front to back of book?			
Source of story/text	Refers to pictures only? Refers to both pictures and print? Focuses on print only?			
Story/Text	Uses labeling and commenting? Connects series of events? Describes or recreates all major events of original story?			
Language style	Creates segments of text similar to original in meaning? Re-creates verbatimlike text segments? Accurately decodes words in book?			
Affective Response	Appears to enjoy book reading?			

C–6 Observation of a Preschooler's Knowledge of How to Write

Child's name:_____ Age:_____

Behaviors to look for:	Description of behavior (include dates observed):
Interest in adult's writing	
Interest in environmental print	
Interest in graphic expression	

Forms of graphic expression (Attach artifacts or copies of child's writing)	Drawing?
	Scribbling?
	Letterlike forms?
	Letters?
	Invented spelling?
	   Prephonemic?
	   Phonemic?
	   Letter-name?
	Known words?

Meaning attributed to graphic expression	Pretends to "read" drawing? Pretends to "read" scribbling or prephonemic spelling? Attempts to read phonemic, letter name, or known word spelling?

Appendix D

Suggested Story Books for Preschoolers

Carle, E. (1977). *The grouchy ladybug*. New York: Crowell.

Crews, D. (1998). *Night at the fair*. New York: Greenwillow.

Eastman, P. D. (1960). *Are you my mother?* New York: Random House.

Eastman, P. D. (1961). *Go dog, go!* New York: Random House.

Ehlert, L. (1989). *Eating the alphabet: Fruits and vegetables from A to Z*. San Diego, CA: Voyager Books Harcourt, Inc.

Ehlert, L. (1997). *Cuckoo: A Mexican Folktale/Cucu: un cuento folklorico mexicano*. Translated by G. Andujar. San Diego, CA: Harcourt Brace.

Ehlert, L. (1997). *Moon rope: A Peruvian folktale/Un lazo a la luna: Una Leyenda Peruana*. Translated by Amy Prince. San Diego, CA: Harcourt Brace.

Fleming, D. (2005). *The first day of winter*. New York: Henry Holt and Company.

Freeman, D. (1968). *Corduroy*. New York: Viking.

Freeman, D. (1978). *A pocket for Corduroy*. New York: Viking.

Keats, E. (1962). *Snowy day*. New York: Viking.

Keats, E. (1967). *Peter's chair*. New York: Harper & Row.

Khan, R., & Kyong, Y. *Silly chicken*. New York: Viking.

Krauss, R., & Johnson, C. (2005). *The happy egg*. New York: HarperCollins.

Krauss, R., & Sendak, M. (2005). *Bears*. New York: HarperCollins.

Levenson, G. (2004). *Bread comes to life: A garden of wheat and a loaf to eat*. Berkeley, CA: Ten Speed Press/Tricycle.

Lionni, L. (1992). *Swimmy*. New York: Random House.

Mayer, M. (1976). *There's a nightmare in my closet*. New York: Penguin.

McCloskey, R. (1999). *Make way for ducklings*. New York: Penguin.

Medearis, A., & Ransome, J. (1997). *Rum-a-tum-tum*. New York: Holiday House.

Most, B. (1990). *The cow that went OINK*. San Diego, CA: Harcourt Brace.

Munari, B. (2005). *Bruno Munari's zoo*. San Francisco, CA: Chronicle.

Norac, C. (2004). *My daddy is a giant*. New York: Clarion.

Viorst, J. (1972). *Alexander and the terrible, horrible, no good, very bad day*. New York: Atheneum.

Weeks, S. (2002). *My somebody special*. New York: Gulliver Books.

Wildsmith, B. (1970). *Circus*. New York: Watts.

Yolen, J. (1995). *Henry and Mudge and the best day of all*. New York: Scholastic.

Zion, G. (2002). *Harry the dirty dog*. New York: HarperCollins.

Appendix E

Enhancing Literacy Development with Computer Software

Criteria for Evaluating CD-ROM Storybooks for Young Children

Name of CD-ROM Storybook:_____ Targeted age:_____

Key Criteria	Questions to Ask:	Yes/No	Notes
Literary Merit	1. Well-structured story? 2. Rich vocabulary? 3. Interesting content or storyline?		
Text Characteristics	1. Appropriate font size? 2. Appropriate amount of text on each screen? 3. Appropriate sentence length?		
Child controls	1. Forward and backward? 2. Pausing? 3. Restarting? 4. Activating media features?		
Media Features	1. Highlighted oral reading? 2. Music? 3. Sound? 4. Animation?		
Embedded reading subskills	1. Rhyming? 2. Syllabication? 3. Letter–sound relationships? 4. Word recognition? 5. Vocabulary?		
Directions and operation	1. Options given both in pictures and verbally? 2. Mouse- or touch-screen controlled?		
Installation	1. Quick start-up? 2. Clear directions?		
Final Evaluation:			

Source: Adapted from Shamir, A., and Korat, O. (2006, March). How to select CD-ROM storybooks for young children: The teacher's role. *The Reading Teacher, 59* (6), 532–543.

Examples of Software for Preschool-Kindergarten

Animated Stories and Story-Related Activities

Reading Blaster Ages 4–6. Knowledge Adventure.
Jump Start Kindergarten. Knowledge Adventure.
Stickybear. Optimum Resource.
Every Child a Reader and *Emergent Reader*. Sunburst.
Tumble Book Library. Source of e-books by subscription for schools; an online collection of animated, talking picture books. http://www.tumblebooks.com/library/asp/about_tumblebooks.asp

Graphics Software

KidPix. The Learning Company. This software provides a variety of different modes for creating graphics: painting, chalk, pencil, crayons, markers. You can also modify pictures and create animations. Spanish support is also available.
Storybook Weaver. Riverdeep. This software provides story starters, an extensive collection of graphics (including multicultural images), and a variety of graphic tools. Bilingual/Spanish text-to-speech feature.

Suggested Categories and Specific Titles for the Kindergarten Library Corner

Predictable Text

Anderson, L. (1998). *Tick-tock*. New York: Farrar, Straus & Giroux.

Burningham, J. (1983). *Mr. Gumpy's motor car*. New York: Puffin.

Carle, E. (1973). *Have you seen my cat?* New York: Scholastic.

Carle, E. (2000). *Does a kangaroo have a mother too?* New York: HarperCollins.

Fox, M. (1986). *Hattie and the fox*. New York: Bradbury.

Hutchins, P. (2002). *We're going on a picnic*. New York: Greenwillow.

Mayer, M. (1985). *Me too!* Racine, WI: Western.

Tolstoy, A. (1968). *The great big enormous turnip*. London: Heinemann.

Rhyming Text

Erhardt, K. (2006). *This jazz man*. New York: Harcourt.

Keats, E. (1971). *Over in the meadow*. New York: Scholastic.

London, J. (2001). *Park beat: Rhymin' through the seasons*. New York: HarperCollins.

Martin, B. (1996). *Brown bear, brown bear, what do you see?* New York: Henry Holt.

Martin, B. (2000). *Chicka chicka boom boom*. Bibra Lake, WA, Australia: Alladin Paperbacks.

Martin, B. (2004). *Chicka chicka 1, 2, 3*. New York: Simon & Schuster.

Seuss, Dr. (Geisel, T.) (2003). *Tooth book*. New York: Random House.

Shaw, N. (1997). *Sheep in a jeep*. Boston, MA: Houghton Mifflin.

Wadsworth, O. (2003). *Over in the meadow*. San Francisco, CA: Chronicle Books.

Wordless Picture Books

Anno, M. (1977). *Counting book*. New York: HarperCollins.

Carle, E. (1995). *Do you want to be my friend?* New York: HarperCollins.

Crews, D. (1991). *Truck*. New York: HarperCollins.

Crews, D. (1993). *School bus*. New York: HarperCollins.

DePaola, T. (1978). *Pancakes for breakfast*. New York: Harcourt.

Hutchins, P. (1971). *Changes, changes*. New York: Simon & Schuster.

Mayer, M. (1997). *Frog goes to dinner*. New York: Dial.

Mayer, M. (2003). *A boy, a dog, & a frog*. New York: Dial.

McCully, E. (2003). *Picnic*. New York: HarperCollins.

McCully, E. (2005). *School*. New York: HarperCollins.

Concept Label Books

Brown, M. (1990). *The important book*. New York: HarperCollins.
Davis, K. (2004). *Who hoots?* San Diego, CA: Harcourt.
Hoban, T. (1987). *I read signs*. New York: HarperCollins.
Hoban, T. (1988). *Look! look! look!* New York: Greenwillow.

Narratives

Brett, J. (2005). *Honey . . . honey . . . lion!* New York: Putnam's.
Freeman, D. (1976). *Corduroy*. New York: Penguin.
Khan, R. (2005). *Silly chicken*. New York: Viking.
Marshall, J. (2000). *George and Martha*. Boston, MA: Houghton Mifflin.
Most, B. (1990). *The cow that went OINK*. San Diego, CA: Harcourt Brace & Company.
Slate, J. (2001). *Miss Bindergarten gets ready for kindergarten*. New York: Penguin.
Wells, R. (2000). *Noisy Nora*. New York: Penguin.

Alphabet Books

Agard, J. (1989). *The Calypso alphabet*. New York: Henry Holt.
Doering, A. (2005). *Homes around the world ABC: An alphabet book*.
    Mankato, MN: Capstone Press.
Doubilet, A. (1991). *Under the sea from A to Z*. New York: Crown.
Ehlert, L. (1989). *Eating the alphabet: Fruits & vegetables from A to Z*. San Diego,
    CA: Voyager Books, Harcourt Brace & Company.
Feldman, J. (1991). *The alphabet in nature*. San Francisco, CA: Children's Press.
Ferguson, D. (1992). *Winnie the Pooh's A to Zzzz*. New York: Scholastic.
Herzog, B. (2004). *H is for home run: A baseball alphabet*. Chelsea, MI: Sleeping Bear Press.
Lluch, A. (2005). *Zoo clues animal alphabet*. San Diego, CA: Wedding Solutions.
Magee, D., & Neuman, R. (1990). *All aboard ABC*. New York: Cobblehill.
Ryden, H. (1989). *Wild animals of Africa ABC*. New York: E.P. Dutton.

Easy-to-Read Books

Berenstain, S. (2004). *We like kites*. New York: Random House.
Bonsall, C. (1997). *Mine's the best*. New York: HarperCollins.
Buck, N. (1998). *Oh cats!* New York: HarperCollins.
Cohen, C. (2000). *How many fish?* New York: HarperCollins.
Karlin, N. (1999). *I see, you saw*. New York: HarperCollins.
Lobel, A. (1970). *Frog and toad are friends*. New York: Harper and Row.
Rylant, C. (1996). *Henry and Mudge and the happy cat*. New York: Simon & Schuster.
Seuss, Dr. (Geisel, T.), (1968). *The foot book*. New York: Random House.

Nonfiction

Fleming, D. (1995). *In the tall, tall grass*. New York: Holtzbrinck.
Fleming, D. (1998). *In the small, small pond*. New York: Holtzbrinck.
Hoban, T. (1995). *26 letters and 99 cents*. New York: HarperCollins.
Hoban, T. (1997). *Exactly the opposite*. New York: HarperCollins.

Levenson, G. (2004). *Bread comes to life: A garden of wheat and a loaf to eat.* Berkeley, CA: Ten Speed Press/Tricycle.

Morris, A. (1992). *Houses and homes.* New York: HarperCollins.

Morris, A. (1998). *Tools.* New York: HarperCollins.

Prince, A. (2006). *What do wheels do all day?* Boston, MA: Houghton Mifflin.

Robbins, K. (2005). *Seeds.* New York: Atheneum.

Appendix G

Resources on Interactive Writing

Bickel, D., Holsopple, S., Garcia, P., Lantz, M., & Yoder, D. (1999). Relationship of interactive writing to independent writing in kindergarten and first grade. ERIC ED 432015.

Button, K., Johnson, M., & Furgerson, P. (1996). Interactive writing in a primary classroom. *The Reading Teacher, 49*(6), 446–454.

Fountas, I., McCarrier, A., & Pinnell, G. (1999). *Interactive writing: How language & literacy come together, K–2*. Portsmouth, NH: Heinemann.

Tompkins, B., & Collom, S. (2004). *Sharing the pen: Interactive writing with young children*. Upper Saddle River, NJ: Merrill/Prentice Hall.

Appendix H

Books for Enhancing Phonological Awareness

Cauley, L. (2001). *Clap your hands*. New York: Penguin Young Readers.

Doudna, K. (2000). *Mm: See it. Say it. Hear it*. Edina, MN: ABDO Publishing.

Ellwand, D. *Emma's elephant*. New York: Dutton.

Flanagan, A. (2000). *Play day: The sound of long A*. Chanhassen, MN: The Child's World, Inc. Wonder Books.

Flanagan, A. (2000) *I like bugs: The sound of long B*. Chanhassen, MN: The Child's World, Inc. Wonder Books.

Hanson, A. (2005). *Nan and Nick: A rebus reader*. Edina, MN: ABDO Publishing.

Janovitz, M. *Bowl patrol!* New York: North-South.

Janovitz, M. (2007). *Look out bird*. New York: North-South.

Jonas, A. (1997). *Watch Willima walk*. New York: Greenwillow.

Kirk, D. (1998). *Miss Spider's ABCs*. New York: Scholastic.

Kirk, D. (2006). *Miss Spider's tea party*. New York: Scholastic.

Klingel, C., & Noyed, R. (2000). *Rusty Red: The sound of R*. Chanhassen, MN: The Child's World, Inc. Wonder Books.

Leaney, C. (2004). *Just lazy Luke*. Bethany, MO: Fitzgerald Books.

Medearis, A. *Rum-a-tum-tum*. New York: Holiday House.

Moncure, J. (2001). *My "B" sound box*. Chanhassen, MN: The Child's World, Inc. Wonder Books.

Moncure, J. (2002). *Word bird makes words with cat*. Chanhassen, MN: The Child's World, Inc. Wonder Books.

Molter, C. (2003). *-ake as in cake*. Edina, MN: ABDO Publishing.

Most, B. (1990). *Four & twenty dinosaurs*. San Diego, CA: Harcourt Brace.

Most, B. (1991). *Pets in trumpets and other word-play riddles*. San Diego, CA: Harcourt Brace.

Most, B. (1998). *A trio of triceratops*. San Diego, CA: Harcourt Brace.

Most, B. (1999). *Z-Z-Zoink!* San Diego, CA: Harcourt Brace.

Nichols, G. (1997). *Asana and the animals*. Cambridge, MA: Candlewick.

Rau, D. (2007). *Look for ladybugs*. New York: Children's Press.

Reiser, L. (1996). *Beach feet*. New York: Greenwillow.

Roberts, B. (1996). *Camel caravan*. New York: Tambourine.

Roza, G. (2002). *Lots of leaves: Learning the L sound*. New York: The Rosen Publishing Group's PowerKids Press.

Vaughan, M., & Hutchinson, S. (1994). *Snap!* New York: Scholastic.

Appendix I

Format for Evaluation
of a Commercial Literacy Program

Name of Program Reviewed:_____

Copyright date:_____ Publisher:_____

Grade levels:_____

1. List the separate materials available in this program.

2. Examine the type of literature used in this program with respect to diverse cultures and languages. What diversity is represented?

3. Are both fiction and nonfiction included? Explain.

4. Examine the Instructor's Manual. Describe the level of detail in the instructions provided.

5. Identify the theoretical approach to reading that is present in this program. Explain your answer with examples from the materials provided and the activities recommended.

6. Describe the technology needed to use this reading program effectively.

7. Does this reading program emphasize each of the five cueing systems/aspects of language knowledge (phonetic, semantic, syntactic, morphemic, and pragmatic)? Give examples.

8. What evidence is there that comprehension is taught rather than just assessed? Give examples.

9. What type(s) of assessment of student progress is incorporated into this program?

10. What resources are available for students who are English language learners? Struggling readers? Gifted readers?

11. Would you select this program to use in your classroom (assuming you are teaching at this level)? Explain your reasoning.

Appendix J

Magazines for K–4 Students

Appleseeds. www.Cobblestonepub.com

Ask. www.Cobblestonepub.com

Boy's Quest. www.boysquest.com

ChickaDEE: Discover a World of Fun. www.owlkids.com

Creative Kids: The Magazine by Kids for Kids. P.O. Box 8813, Waco, TX 76714–8813

Cricket. Carus Publishing Company, Cricket Magazine Group, 315 Fifth Street, Peru, IL 61354

Humpty Dumpty's Magazine. Children's Better Health Institute, P.O. Box 567, 1100 Waterway Blvd., Indianapolis, IN 46206

National Geographic Kids. National Geographic Society, P.O. Box 63001, Tampa, FL 33663–3001

Ranger Rick. National Wildlife Federation, 11100 Wildlife Center Drive, Reston, VA 20190–5362

Spider: The Magazine for Children. Carus Publishing Company, Cricket Magazine Group, P.O. Box 9304, 315 Fifth Street, Peru, IL 61301–9800

Your Big Backyard. National Wildlife Federation, P.O. Box 2038, Harlan, IA 51593–2017

U.S. Kids. Children's Better Health Institute, P.O. Box 420235, Palm Coast, FL 32142

Appendix K

Lesson Plan Templates and Examples

Overview

This appendix provides several formats for developing lesson plans that you can use in your curriculum coursework, field experiences, and student teaching. Each of these formats requires a detailed description of your plan for instruction. Detailed lesson plans are a necessary step in providing developmentally appropriate instruction as well as in determining future learning activities. Different formats are provided for independent activities as well as teacher-guided activities at different developmental/age/grade levels. As you use these formats you will find it necessary to expand each format to include the information necessary for a detailed plan.

An important part of lesson planning is engaging in self-reflection after you have implemented each lesson plan. Focus your reflection on determining whether your lesson was successful in meeting the learning objectives and the response(s) of the child(ren) to your instruction. Use your reflective evaluation to think of how you might teach the lesson again as well as what type of learning activities would build upon the lesson you just taught.

Chart Format: Independent Activities

Class: _____ Focus: _____			Teacher: _____ Date: _____	
Activity Area	*Emergent Literacy Objective*	*Description of Activity*	*Teacher's Interaction Strategies*	*Materials Needed*
(1)				
(2)				
(3)				
Reflective Evaluation: (What responses from children did you observe? What changes in materials, procedures, or guidance need to be made before planning this activity again?)				

Example of Chart Format: Independent Activities

Class: <u>Older Toddler Room</u>

Focus: <u>Emergent Literacy</u>

Teacher: <u>Sarah T.</u>

Date: <u>April 5</u>

Activity Area	Emergent Literacy Objective	Description of Activity	Teacher's Interaction Strategies	Materials Needed
Library Center	Interest in literacy	Opportunity to explore board books and soft cloth books	Monitor child's use of books, eye contact, nonverbal and verbal communication	Small bin containing familiar board books, soft cloth books
Drawing Center	Interest in writing	Opportunity to use writing tools to communicate	Observe child's nonverbal and verbal expression as writing tools are used; respond to child's questions and comments using linguistic scaffolding	Assorted washable felt-tip markers, large sheets of unlined paper, taped to table top
House Area	Oral Communication: Listening and speaking	Imaginative play and communication with peers	Observe verbal and nonverbal communication. Support and extend interaction by limited participation in suggesting events or actions, or assuming role of participant	Kitchen utensils and furniture; recipe book; telephone; telephone book; paper and washable markers

Reflective Evaluation:

Library Center: Several children wanted books about trains and trucks. Go to public library to find more books.

Drawing/Writing Center: Active interest in this area from seven children today. Post today's writing sheet on wall. Provide new sheet for tomorrow's writing center.

House Area: Limited verbal interactions today. Maybe more literacy-related and realia/props are needed. Plan to bring in empty food cartons; be sure to bring in some Asian and Hispanic food cartons. Also bring in cloth bags for carrying groceries.

Chart Format: Infant-Toddler

Teacher-Guided Activity

Class: _____	Teacher: _____
Language/Literacy Focus: _____	Date: _____
Activity: _____	Grouping: _____

Description/Sequence:	Behaviors to observe:

Reflective evaluation:

Example Chart Format: Infant-Toddler

Teacher-Guided Activity

Class: _Toddler Room_	Teacher: _Noemi_
Language/Literacy Focus: _Listening Vocabulary_	Date: _October 23_
Activity: _The Big Red Barn (Brown, 1989)_	Grouping: _Individual_

Description/Sequence:	Behaviors to observe:
Share board book with a toddler: • Look at cover and pictures in book, eliciting child's responses to what is seen by questioning and linguistic scaffolding • Focus on these concepts/words: barn, pig, horse, hay, sheep, donkey, scarecrow, butterfly, rooster, bird, cow	• Eye contact and shared reference • Nonverbal responses • Verbal comments and utterances • Book handling • Page turning • Pointing to pictures

Reflective evaluation: Shared book with Cassandra (2½ yrs). She eagerly pointed to each of the animals and said each name when asked what the animal was. She particularly liked the butterfly. She wanted to hold the book and turn the pages. We read this in the morning. Later in the day I saw her looking at the book, pointing to the pictures, and saying the animals' names aloud. Next time: Read/adapt portions of the story text and include more vocabulary.

Chart Format: Preschool

Teacher-Guided Activity

Class: _____	Teacher: _____
Language/Literacy Focus: _____	Date: _____
Activity: _____	Grouping: _____
Related State Standard(s): _____	

Activity Description/Sequence:	Behaviors to observe:

Adaptations for diverse students (for example, ELLs, children with learning delays):

Reflective evaluation:

Example of Chart Format: Preschool

Teacher-Guided Activity

Class: *4-year-olds*	Teacher: *Jackie*
Language/Literacy Focus: *Listening comprehension*	Date: *April 9*
Activity: *The Very Quiet Cricket (Carle, 1990)*	Grouping: *Whole class*
Related State Standard(s): *Predict what will happen next using pictures and content; retell information from a story; respond to simple questions about reading material (Illinois Early Learning Standards for 3 to 4 year olds 2006).*	

Activity Description/Sequence:	Behaviors to observe:
• Hold up book for all to see. Ask what insect is on the cover. Has anyone seen a cricket before? What noise do they make? • Take a "picture walk" through the book. Talk about each new insect, naming it and also locating the cricket on the page. Focus on the cricket's meeting with other insects.	• What were children's responses to questions? • Were children able to name any other insects? • Did children anticipate upcoming text and events? • Did children respond to questions about events in the book?

- Read the text, pausing to talk more about the pictures and asking questions to check comprehension. After the second set of pages, the repeated pattern of the text will cue children to upcoming events. Pause before reading the repeated words and ask children what is going to happen next. Continue this for the remainder of the book.
- After the book is read, go back and have children tell the story from looking at the pictures.

- Were children able to retell the events based on the pictures?

Adaptations for diverse students: Reduce word-for-word reading of text if needed to fit children's comprehension and questions. Some children may not be familiar with all of the different insect names. Encourage unison responses to predicting upcoming repetitions in text.

Reflective Evaluation: Children seemed fascinated with learning the names of the different insects. Several children (Matt, Jamie, and Sasha) quickly picked up on the repeated refrain in the text. Soon others followed and by the end of the book, many were involved in predicting upcoming text as well as the insects they would see. The picture walk really seemed to help them anticipate the content when I then read the story. Many also participated in the story retelling. Later on during independent activity time, Liz, Tiffany, Brandon, and Marcus took turns "reading" the book to themselves. I think I'll use the "picture walk" and "retelling activity" again-soon.

Chart Format #1: K–4 Grades

Topic of Lesson: _____   Length of lesson: _____

Developmental level/Grade level: _____   Date: _____

Grouping: _____

Literacy Development Objective(s):

Related State Learning Standard(s):

Procedures: (describe what you will do in each part)	Oral Directions and Guidance given to children:	Materials/ Supplies Needed
Introduction: Learning Activity: Conclusion:		

Adaptations for diverse learners:

Assessment of learning objectives and state standards: (explain how you will determine whether this lesson has achieved the learning objectives and related state standards)

Post-lesson reflective evaluation: (After teaching this lesson, evaluate your effectiveness as a teacher; also include your ideas for a future lesson to build upon this lesson's learning activity and outcome)

Narrative Format #2: K–4 Grades

Topic of Lesson: _____ Length of lesson: _____

Developmental level/Grade level: _____ Date: _____

Grouping: _____

Literacy Development Objective(s): _____

Related State Learning Standard(s): _____

Procedures: (what the teacher does in steps, along with directions or guidance given to children)
Introduction:

Learning Activity:

Conclusion:

Materials needed:

Adaptations for diverse students:

Assessment:

Post-lesson reflective evaluation:

Chart Format #3: K–4 Grades

Topic of Lesson: _____

Developmental level/Grade level: _____

Grouping: _____

Literacy Development Objective (s): _____

Related State Learning Standard (s): _____

Teacher: _____

Date: _____

Lesson Length: _____

Procedures: (describe what you will do)	Time allotted:	Oral Directions and Guidance given to children:	Materials/Supplies Needed
Introduction:			
Learning Activity:			
Conclusion:			
Adaptations for diverse learners:			
Assessments:			
Post-lesson Reflective Evaluation:			

364

Example of Chart Format #3

Topic of Lesson: _Making a poster for the Block Area_	Teacher: _Ms. Lyons_
Developmental Level/Grade level: _Kindergarten_	Date: _4/9/07_
Grouping: _Whole class_	Lesson length: _approx. 20 min_

Literacy Development Objective (s): _Children will develop an awareness of the relationships between speech and print. Children will participate in dictating rules for the Block Area. Children will participate in echo and unison reading of the completed poster._

Related State Learning Standard(s): _Understand that print carries meaning; understand that print is read from left to right and from top to bottom of each page; recognizing one-syllable and high-frequency words[2]_

Procedures: (describe what you will do)	Time allotted:	Oral Directions and Guidance given to children:	Materials/Supplies Needed
Introduction: _Tell purpose of poster activity_	_3–5 minutes_	_Let's get settled so everyone can see this poster. Today we are going to think of some rules for us to follow in the block area. After we decide on the rules, I'll write them down on this poster. Then we can put this up in the block area to help us remember what we need to do._	_Easel, chart paper and felt-tip marker_
Learning Activity: _Engage children in thinking up rules and dictating the wording for each rule. Write each rule on the poster, numbering each. Engage children in echo and unison reading. Ask children to locate and read high-frequency words._	_15 minutes_	_Let's think about what rules we need.... Oh, here's one._ _Because the block area is not very big, we probably only want to have three people in the block area at a time. So let's make that our first rule. (write rule on poster) (Follow this with eliciting other rules; when there are 3–4 rules, ask the children to echo read; follow this with unison reading, pointing to each word that is read)_ _Now, let's be word detectives and look for words that we know. (pick several high frequency words that have been used in the rules and ask individual children to come up to point to the words and read the target word)_	_Pointer to use during reading of chart_
Conclusion: _Thank children and display poster in block area_	_1–2 minutes_	_Thank you for helping me make this poster for our block area. It will help us remember how we need to work in the block area. (take sign to block area and mount on wall or bulletin board)_	_Tape or hook for mounting poster in block area_

Adaptations for diverse learners: _Encourage children to come up to point to words in pairs. If words are too complex, ask children to point to specific letters; perhaps letters that begin their names._

Assessments: _Observe children's focus on print during echo and unison reading. Note whether children were able to identify high-frequency words._

Post-lesson Reflective Evaluation: _Children were eager to help make up the rules. I need to do this more often so more children can participate in locating words (as well as letters). Pairing up the ELLs to come to find letters seemed to work well. They seemed to like being called "detectives." Next time: Have children "sign" their names to the poster to show that they agree to the rules. That may make the poster's rules more "real" to them if they have signed their names to it._

[2] California State Board of Education (2006).

Chart Format #4: 1–4 Grades—Strategy Instruction

Topic of Lesson: _____   Teacher: _____

Developmental level/Grade level: _____   Date: _____   Lesson Length: _____

Grouping: _____

Literacy Development Objective(s): _____

Related State Learning Standard(s): _____

Procedures: (describe what you will do)	Time allotted:	Oral Directions and Guidance given to children:	Materials/Supplies Needed
Introduction and Strategy Demonstration:			
Guided Practice:			
Independent Practice and Conclusion:			
Adaptations for diverse learners:			
Assessments:			
Post-lesson Reflective Evaluation:			

Example Chart Format #4: 1–4 Grades—Strategy Instruction

Topic of Lesson: _Vocabulary, Base words and Suffixes_	Teacher: _Adriene_
Developmental level/Grade level: _4th grade_	Date: _March 20_ Lesson Length: _40–45 minutes_

Grouping: _Whole class_

Literacy Development Objective(s): _Learn to use suffixes (for example, inflectional morpheme-ed for past tense verbs) as a way of determining word meaning and enhancing comprehension_

Related State Learning Standard(s): _Use word structure such as roots, prefixes, and suffixes to determine meaning[3]_

Procedures: (describe what you will do)	Time allotted:	Oral Directions and Guidance given to children:	Materials/Supplies Needed
Introduction and Strategy Demonstration: (This lesson follows a teacher read-aloud of the first five pages of the book.) Write the selected words on chart paper in front of the room. For each word, demonstrate underlining the base or root word (for example, yell, point . . .) and circling the word ending (-ed)	5 min.	Today we are going to be word detectives, looking inside words for clues to their meaning. We're going to look at for words that show action (verbs). Then we're going to look at the word endings that also help create meaning. Here are some action words with special endings that were on the first two pages of the story: yelled, pointed, looked, beckoned, shouted, worried, hesitated. Let's look inside these words to figure out what they mean. (Identify base word and ending for each example)	Individual copies of Tornado by Byers (1996); chart paper on easel with felt-tip marker, or use overhead transparency or chalkboard
Guided Practice: Pass out list of words. Students work individually or in pairs to identify base word, word ending and word meaning	15–20	Here are some other action words that were in the pages we read together: helped, worried, ducked, pulled, smelled, listened, bowed, cleared, teased, settled. Work by yourself or with a partner to underline the base word and circle the ending. Then find the words in the story text and write a clue as to what each word means.	Handout with target words written in a column on the left side of the page.
Independent Practice and Conclusion: Assign next chapter to be read. Students need to identify the action verbs ending in -ed, writing them in their learning logs.	20 min.	Now, I want you to try this on your own. Read Chapter 2 and look for the action words that end in -ed. Write them in your learning logs, underline the base word and circle the ending. Then write a clue to each word's meaning.	Students' learning logs

Adaptations for diverse learners: Option to work with a partner during guided practice, as well as during independent practice.

Assessments: Monitor students during guided practice and independent practice. Were students able to identify the base words, the word endings, and give meanings of the words? Review students' learning logs that showed their independent practice. Re-teach or provide additional strategy experience if appropriate.

Post-lesson Reflective Evaluation: Most students could quickly locate the base word and were able to define the words. I found that I needed to clarify the words that did not follow a regular pattern of just adding the -ed, such as teased and settled, because only a -d is added to the base word. Also with worried—the y changes to i and the -ed is added. Need to plan for similar opportunities for students to focus on word structure and vocabulary.

[3] New York State Education Department, (2005).

367

Appendix L

Literacy Resources
for Second and Third Grades

Suggested Books for the Library Corner and Read-Alouds

Fiction

Adler, D. (2000). *Young Cam Jansen and the pizza shop mystery*. New York: Viking.

Armstrong, J. (1997). *Lili the brave*. New York: Random House.

Blumenthal, D. (2005). *The pink house at the seashore*. New York: Clarion Books.

Byers, B. (2004). *Little horse on his own*. New York: Henry Holt.

Bunting, E. (1999). *I have an olive tree*. New York: HarperCollins.

Cameron, A. (1988). *The most beautiful place in the world*. New York: Random House.

Castaneda, O. (1993). *Abuela's weave*. New York: Lee and Low Books.

Christopher, M. (2000). *Hat trick*. Boston: Little, Brown & Company.

Daly, N. (2004). *Jamela's dress*. New York: Farrar, Straus & Giroux.

Esterl, A. (1995). *Okino and the whales*. San Diego, CA: Harcourt.

Fitz-Gibbon, S. (2005). *On Uncle John's farm*. Allston, MA: Fitzhenry & Whiteside.

Gordon, S. (1989). *Play ball, Kate*. New York: Troll Communications, Scholastic.

Kenah, K. (2005). *The best seat in second grade*. New York: HarperCollins.

Kinsey-Warnock, H. (1992). *Wilderness cat*. New York: Penguin Young Readers.

Krensky, S. (2001). *Arthur and the best coach ever*. Boston: Little, Brown & Company.

McBrier, P. (2001). *Beatrice's goat*. New York: Simon & Schuster.

McDermott, G. (1993). *Raven: A trickster tale from the Pacific Northwest*. San Diego, CA: Harcourt.

McGovern, A. (1992). *. . . If you lived in colonial times*. New York: Scholastic.

Medearis, A. (1997). *Rum-a-tum-tum*. New York: Holiday House.

Monjo, F. (1993). *The drinking gourd*. New York: HarperCollins.

Parrish, P. (1996). *Play ball, Amelia Bedelia*. New York: HarperCollins.

Priceman, M. (1994). *How to make an apple pie and see the world*. New York: Knopf.

Rossi, J. (1995). *The gullywasher*. Flagstaff, AZ: Northland Publishing.

Shank, N. (1999). *The Sanyanasin's first day*. New York: Marshall Cavendish.

Tsubakiyama, M. (1999). *Mei Mei loves the morning*. Morton Grove, IL: Albert Whitman.

Informational/Nonfiction

Anderson, C. (2003). *Daddylonglegs*. Chicago, IL: Heinemann Library.

Brusca, M. (1991). *On the pampas*. New York: Henry Holt.

Cooper, J. (2007). *High tide, low tide*. Vero Beach, FL: Rourke Publishing.

Dunphy, M. (1999). *Here is the African savanna*. New York: Hyperion.

Gordon, S. (2006). *At home on the farm*. New York: Marshall Cavendish Benchmark.

Hartley, L. (1996). *Hermit crab moves house*. Ada, OK: Garrett Educational Corporation.

Harvey, M. (1999). *Look what came from India*. New York: Scholastic.

Haydon, J. (2001). *Journey to Antarctica*. Barrington, IL: Rigby.

Hutchings, A. (2006). *Pets at the vet*. New York: Scholastic.

Lewis, A. (2005). *I grew up on a farm*. Warwick, NY: Moo Press.

Lincoln, M. (1992). *Amazing boats*. New York: Alfred A. Knopf.

Miller, M. (2006). *Dogs and puppies.* Irvine, CA: QEB Publishing.

Royston, A. (1992). *Ships and boats.* New York: Macmillan.

Stone, L. (1996). *The prairie.* Vero Beach, FL: Rourke.

Wallace, K. (2003). *A trip to the zoo.* New York: DK Publishing.

Wolfman, J. (2004). *Life on an apple orchard.* Minneapolis, MN: Lerner Publishing.

Wright, A. (1999). *At home in the tide pool.* Watertown, MA: Charlesbridge Publishing.

Resource Books for Readers Theatre

Barchers, S. (2000). *Multicultural folktales: Readers theatre for elementary students.* Englewood, CO: Teacher Ideas Press.

Barchers, S. (2006). *More readers theatre for beginning readers.* Englewood, CO: Teacher Ideas Press.

Laughlin, M. (1990). *Readers theatre for children: Scripts and script development.* Englewood, CO: Teacher Ideas Press.

Shepard, A. (2003). *Folktales on stage.* Olympia, WA: Shepard Publications.

Shepard, A. (2005). *Stories on stage: Children's plays for readers theatre.* Olympia, WA: Shepard Publications.

Wolfman, J. (2004). *How and why stories for readers theatre.* Englewood, CO: Teacher Ideas Press.

Worthy, J. (2005). *Readers theatre for building fluency.* New York: Scholastic.

References

Adams, M. (1990). *Beginning to read: Thinking and learning about print*. Urbana: Center for the Study of Reading. University of Illinois at Urbana-Champaign.

Adams, T. (2003). Reading mathematics: More than words can say. *The Reading Teacher, 56*(8), 786–795.

Adams, M., Foorman, B., Lundberg, I., & Beeler, T. (1998). *Phonemic awareness in young children: A classroom curriculum*. Baltimore, MD: Brookes.

Aiken, A., & Bayer, L. (2002). They love words. *The Reading Teacher, 56*(1), 68–74.

Alexander, P., & Fox, E. (2004). A historical perspective on reading research and practice. In R. Ruddell & N. Unrau (Eds.), *Theoretical models and processes of reading* (5th ed.) (pp. 33–68). Newark, DE: International Reading Association.

Allington, R. (1982, November). Content coverage and contextual reading in reading groups. Paper presented at the Annual Meeting of the National Council of Teachers of English, Washington, DC. ERIC ED 228 604.

Allington, R. (2002a). What I've learned about effective reading instruction from a decade of studying exemplary elementary classroom teachers. *Phi Delta Kappan, 83*(10), 740–747.

Allington, R. (2002b). You can't learn much from books you can't read. *Educational Leadership, 60*(3), 16–19.

Allor, J., & McCathren, R. (2003, November). Developing emergent literacy skills through storybook reading. *Intervention in School and Clinic, 39*(2), 72–79.

Altwerger, B., Edelsky, C., & Flores, B. (1989). Whole language: What's new? In G. Manning & M. Manning (Eds.), *Whole language: Beliefs and practices, K–8* (pp. 9–23). Washington, DC: National Education Association.

Amberg, E. (2000, August). Software focus on reading/language development. *T H E Journal, 28*(1), 62–66.

Anders, P., & Pritchard, T. G. (1993). Integrated language curriculum and instruction for the middle grades. *The Elementary School Journal, 93*(5), 611–624.

Anderson–Yockel, J., & Haynes, W. (1994). Joint book-reading strategies in working-class African American and white mother-toddler dyads. *Journal of Speech and Hearing Research, 37*(3), 583–603.

Armbruster, B., Lehr, F., & Osborn, J. (2001). *Put reading first: The research building blocks for teaching children to read*. Jessup, MD: National Institute for Literacy and Center for the Improvement of Early Reading Achievement (CIERA).

Armbruster, B., Lehr, F., & Osborn, J. (2003, Spring). *A child becomes a reader: Birth through preschool*. Portsmouth, NH: RMC Research Corporation.

Armstrong, L. (2006, February). Number rhymes for story times. *Library Media Connection*, p. 26.

Arnold, R. (2005, July). Charming the next generation: A strategy for turning toddlers into readers. *School Library Journal, 51*(7), 30–32.

Arnold, R., & Colburn, N. (2005, August). Sound advice. *School Library Journal, 51*(8), 33.

Askew, B., Pinnell, G., Fountas, I., Schmitt, M., & Lyons, C. (2000). A review of reading recovery. In R. Robinson, M. McKenna, & J. Wedman (Eds.), *Issues and trends in literacy education* (2nd ed.) (pp. 204–207). Boston: Allyn & Bacon.

Association for Childhood Education International. (2003). Elementary Education Standards. Retrieved 1/2/2007. http://www.udel.edu/bateman/acei/ncateinf.htm

Au, K. (1997). A sociocultural model of reading instruction: The Kamehameha elementary education program. In S. Stahl & D. Hayes (Eds.), *Instructional models in reading* (pp. 181–202). Mahwah, NJ: Lawrence Erlbaum.

Au, K. (2002a). Balanced literacy instruction: Addressing issues of equity. In C. Roller (Ed.), *Comprehensive reading instruction across the grade levels: A collection of papers from the Reading Research 2001 Conference* (pp. 70–87). Newark, DE: International Reading Association.

Au, K. (2002b). Multicultural factors and the effective instruction of students of diverse backgrounds. In Farstrup & S. J. Samuels (Eds.), *What research has to say about reading instruction* (3rd ed.) (pp. 392–414). Newark, DE: International Reading Association.

Bafumo, M. (2004). Rhymes and Reasons. *Teaching PreK–8, 34*(7), 8.

Baghban, M. (1984). *Our daughter learns to read and write: A case study from birth to three*. Newark, DE: International Reading Association.

Baghban, M. (2007). Scribbles, labels, and stories: The role of drawing in the development of writing. *Young Children, 62*(1), 20–26.

Barbe, W., Lucas, V., & Wasylyk, T. (Eds.). (1984). *Handwriting: Basic skills for effective communication*. Columbus, OH: Zaner-Bloser, Inc.

Bardige, B., & Segal, M. (2005). *Building literacy with love: A guide for teachers and caregivers of children from birth through age 5*. Washington, DC: Zero to Three Press.

Barton, M., Heidema, C., & Jordan, D. (2002). Teaching reading in mathematics and science. *Educational Leadership, 60*(3), 24–28.

Barton, J., & Sawyer, D. (2003/2004). Our students *are* ready for this: Comprehension instruction in the elementary school. *The Reading Teacher, 57*(4), 334–347.

Barton, K., & Smith, L. (2000). Themes or motifs? Aiming for coherence through interdisciplinary outlines. *The Reading Teacher, 54*(1), 54–63.

Baumann, J., Jones, L., & Seifert-Kessell, N. (1993). Using think-alouds to enhance children's comprehension monitoring abilities. *The Reading Teacher, 47*(3), 184–193.

Beach, S. (1996). "I can read my own story!"—Becoming literate in the primary grades. *Young Children, 52*(1), 22–27.

Beach, S., & Young, J. (1997). Children's development of literacy resources in kindergarten: A model. *Reading Research and Instruction, 36,* pp. 241–265.

Beals, D. (2001). Eating and reading: Links between family conversations with preschoolers and later language and literacy. In D. Dickinson & P. Tabors (Eds.), *Beginning literacy with language* (pp. 75–92). Baltimore, MD: Paul H. Brookes.

Bear, D., Helman, L., Templeton, S., Invernizzi, M., & Johnston, F. (2007). *Words their way with English learners: Word study for phonics, vocabulary, and spelling instruction.* Upper Saddle River, NJ: Pearson Merrill Prentice Hall.

Bear, D., Invernizzi, M., Templeton, S., & Johnston, F. (2004). *Words their way: Word study for phonics, vocabulary, and spelling instruction* (3rd ed.). Upper Saddle River, NJ: Pearson Merrill Prentice Hall.

Ben Zeev, S. (1977). The influence of bilingualism on cognitive strategy and cognitive development. *Child Development, 48,* 1009–1018.

Bennett, R. (2002, May). Teaching reading with puppets. In B. Barnaby & J. Reyhner (Eds.), *Indigenous languages across the community. Proceedings of the 7th Annual Conference on Stabilizing Indigenous Languages.* Toronto, ON (pp. 151–159). Flagstaff, AZ: Northern Arizona University.

Berenstain, S., & Berenstain, J. (2004). *The Berenstain Bears we like kites.* New York: Random House.

Berk, L., & Winsler, A. (1995). *Scaffolding children's learning: Vygotsky and early childhood education.* Washington, DC: National Association for the Education of Young Children.

Best, R., Floyd, R., & McNamara, D. (2007). Understanding the fourth-grade slump: Comprehension difficulties as a function of reader aptitudes and text genre. Retrieved 4/22/2007. http://csep/psyc.memphis.edu/mcnamara/pdf/bestetal.pdf

Biancarosa, G. (2005). After third grade. *Educational Leadership, 63*(3), 16–22.

Biancarosa, G., & Snow, C. (2004). *Reading Next—A vision for action and research in middle and high school literacy: A Report to the Carnegie Corporation of New York* (2nd ed.). Washington, DC: Alliance for Excellent Education.

Biemiller, A. (2003). Vocabulary: Needed if more children are to read well. *Reading Psychology, 24,* 323–355.

Billman, L. (2002). Aren't these books for little kids? *Educational Leadership, 60*(3), 48–51.

Bissex, G. (1980). *GYNS AT WRK: A child learns to read and write.* Cambridge, MA: Harvard University Press.

Bissex, G. (1985). Watching young writers. In A. Jaggar & M. T. Smith-Burke (Eds.), *Observing the language learner* (pp. 99–114). Newark, DE: International Reading Association.

Blachowicz, C., & Fisher, P. (2006). *Teaching vocabulary in all classrooms* (3rd ed.). Upper Saddle River, NJ: Pearson Merrill Prentice Hall.

Blachowicz, C., & Obrochta, C. (2005). Vocabulary visits: Virtual field trips for content vocabulary development. *The Reading Teacher, 59*(3), 263–268.

Blair-Larsen, S., & Williams, K. (1999). *The balanced reading program: Helping all students achieve success.* Newark, DE: International Reading Association.

Blake, M. (1990). Learning logs in the upper elementary grades. In N. Atwell (Ed.), *Coming to know: Writing to learn in the intermediate grades*

(pp. 53–60). Portsmouth, NH: Heinemann.

Block, C. (2004). Research-based effects of trade book reading. *Illinois Reading Council Journal, 32*(4), 3–8.

Block, C., & Israel, S. (2004). The ABCs of performing highly effective think-alouds. *The Reading Teacher, 58*(2), 154–167.

Bloodgood, J. (1991). A new approach to spelling instruction in language arts programs. *The Elementary School Journal, 92*(2), 203–211.

Bloodgood, J. (1999). What's in a name? Children's name writing and literacy acquisition. *Reading Research Quarterly, 34*(3), 342–367.

Bluestein, N. A. (2002). Comprehension through characterization: Enabling readers to make personal connections with literature. *The Reading Teacher, 55*(5), 413–434.

Bode, B. (1989). Dialogue journal writing. *The Reading Teacher, 42,* 568–571.

Bogott, T., Letmanski, J., & Miller, B. (1999). Improving student language and literacy skills through vocabulary development and phonemic awareness. Unpublished Master's Action Research Project, Chicago, IL: Saint Xavier University. ED 438 548.

Bond, G., & Dysktra, R. (1967). The cooperative research program in first-grade reading instruction. *Reading Research Quarterly, 2,* 5–142.

Bond, G., & Dykstra, R. (1997). The cooperative research program in first-grade reading instruction. *Reading Research Quarterly, 32*(4), 348–427.

Booth, K., Walter, L., & Waters, G. (1999). What is a top-down reading model? LinguaLinks Library, SIL International. Retrieved 6/1/2006. http://www.sil.org/lingualinks/literacy/ReferenceMaterials/glossaryofliteracyterms/WhatIsA

Boroski, L. (2004). *An introduction to interactive writing.* In G. Tompkins & S. Collom (Eds.), *Sharing the pen: Interactive writing with young children* (pp. 1–4). Upper Saddle River, NJ: Pearson Merrill Prentice Hall.

Bossert, T., & Schwantes, F. (1995–1996, Winter). Children's comprehension monitoring: Training children to use rereading to aid comprehension. *Reading Research and Instruction, 35,* 109–121.

Boyle, O., & Peregoy, S. (1990). Literacy scaffolds: Strategies for first- and second-language readers and writers. *The Reading Teacher, 44*(3), 194–200.

Brabham, E., & Villaume, S. (2000). Continuing conversations about literature circles. *The Reading Teacher, 54*(3), 278–80.

Brabham, E., & Villaume, S. (2002a). Vocabulary instruction: Concerns and visions. *The Reading Teacher, 56*(3), 264–268.

Brabham, E., & Villaume, S. (2002b). Leveled text: The good news and the bad news. *The Reading Teacher, 55*(5), 438–441.

Brady, S., & Jacobs, S. (1988). Children responding to children: Writing groups and classroom community. In T. Newkirk & N. Atwell (Eds.), *Understanding writing: Ways of observing, learning and teaching K–8* (2nd ed.). (pp. 142–152). Portsmouth, NH: Heinemann.

Bredekamp, S. (Ed.). (1986). *Good teaching practices for 4- and 5-year-olds: A position statement.* Washington, DC: National Association for the Education of Young Children.

Bredekamp, S. (1997). Developmentally appropriate practice: The early childhood teacher as decisionmaker. In S. Bredekamp & C. Copple (Eds.), *Developmentally appropriate practice in early childhood programs* (Revised ed.) (pp. 33–52). Washington, DC: National Association for the Education of Young Children.

Bredekamp, S., & Copple, C. (1997). *Developmentally appropriate practice in early childhood programs.* Revised edition. Washington, DC: National Association for the Education of Young Children.

Briggs, C., & Elkind, D. (1977). Characteristics of early readers. *Perceptual and Motor Skills, 44*(3), 1231–1237.

Brisk, M., & Harrington, M. (2000). *Literacy and bilingualism: A handbook for all teachers.* Mahwah, NJ: Lawrence Erlbaum.

Britto, P., Brooks-Gunn, & Griffin, T. (2006). Maternal reading and teaching patterns: Associations with school readiness in low-income African American families. *Reading Research Quarterly, 41*(1), 68–89.

Bronfenbrenner, U. (1979). The ecology of human development: Experiments by nature and design. Cambridge, MA: Harvard University Press.

Bronfenbrenner, U. (1989). Ecological systems theory. In R. Vasta (Ed.), *Annals of child development.* Volume 6. (pp. 187–251). Greenwich, CT: JAI Press.

Bronfenbrenner, U., & Evans, G. (2000). Developmental science in the 21st century: Emerging questions, theoretical models, research designs and empirical findings. *Social Development, 9*(1), 115–125.

Bronfenbrenner, U. (2005). Ecological systems theory. In U. Bronfenbrenner (Ed.), *Making human beings human: Bioecological perspectives on human development* (pp. 3–15). Thousand Oaks, CA: Sage Publications. (Original work published in 1992.)

Brotherton, S., & Williams, C. (2002, Spring). Interactive writing instruction in a first-grade Title I literacy program. *Journal of Reading Education, 27*(3), 8–19.

Brown, K. (2001). Read and rise: Preparing our children for a lifetime of success. New York: National Urban League, Inc. ERIC ED 462526.

Brown, K. (2003). What do I say when they get stuck on a word? Aligning teachers' prompts with students' development. *The Reading Teacher, 56*(8), 720–733.

Bruck, M., & Genesee, F. (1995). Phonological awareness in young second language learners. *Journal of Child Language, 22*(2), 307–324.

Bruer, J. (1999). *The myth of the first three years.* New York: The Free Press.

Bruner, J. (1990). *Acts of meaning.* Cambridge, MA: Harvard University Press.

Brynildssen, S. (2002). Recent reading initiatives: Examples of national, state, and professional organizations'

efforts. ERIC Digest. ED469927. First Search, retrieved on 1/27/2006.

Bucar, D. (2002). Teaching reading in first grade: Ideas from a nine-patch reading quilt. *Young Children, 57*(1), 72–79.

Bunting, E. (1994). *A day's work.* Boston, MA: Houghton Mifflin.

Burningham, L., & Dever, M. (2005, September). An interactive model for fostering family literacy. *Young Children,* 87–94.

Bus, A. (2002). Joint caregiver-child storybook reading: A route to literacy development. In S. Neuman and D. Dickinson (Eds.), *Handbook of early literacy research* (pp. 179–191). New York: The Guilford Press.

Bus, A., van IJzendoorn, M., & Pellegrini, A. (1995). Joint book reading makes for success in learning to read: A meta-analysis on intergenerational transmission of literacy. *Review of Educational Research, 65*(1), 1–21.

Bus, A., Both-deVries, A., de Jong, M., Sulzby, E., de Jong, W., & de Jong, E. (2001). Conceptualizations underlying emergent readers' story writing. Ann Arbor, MI: Center for the Improvement of Early Reading Achievement. ERIC ED458 616.

Butler, D., & Clay, M. (1979) *Reading begins at home.* Portsmouth, NH: Heinemann.

Butler, J., Liss, C., & Sterner, P. (1999, Winter). Starting on the write foot: Helping parents understand how children learn to read and write. *Texas Child Care,* 2–9.

Button, K., Johnson, M., & Furgerson, P. (1996). Interactive writing in a primary classroom. *The Reading Teacher, 49*(6), 446–454.

Butyniec-Thomas, J., & Woloshyn, V. (1997). The effects of explicit-strategy and whole language instruction on students' spelling ability. *Journal of Experimental Education, 65*(4), 293–302.

Cabrera, J. (1999). *Over in the meadow.* New York: Holiday House.

California State Board of Education. (2006). Kindergarten English-language arts content standards.

Sacramento, CA: California State Board of Education. Retrieved 4/1/2007. http://www.cde.ca.gov/be/st/ss/engkindergarten.asp

Calkins, L. (1981). Writing taps a new energy source: The child. In R. Walshe (Ed.), *Donald Graves in Australia—"Children want to write . . ."* (pp. 45–54). Rozelle, NSW, Australia: Primary English Teaching Association.

Calkins, L. (1983). *Lessons from a child: On the teaching and learning of writing.* Portsmouth, NH: Heinemann.

Calkins, L. (2000). Let the words work their magic. *Instructor, 110*(3), 25–28.

Calkins, L., & Harwayne, S. (1987). *The writing workshop: A world of difference.* Portsmouth, NH: Heinemann.

Campbell, R. (2001). Learning from interactive story readings, *Early Years, 21*(2), 97–105.

Cappellini, M. (2005). *Balancing reading and language learning.* Portland, ME: Stenhouse Publishers.

Carle, E. (1990). *The very quiet cricket.* New York: Philomel Books.

Carle, E. (1999). *The very lonely firefly.* New York: Philomel Books.

Carlisle, J. (2004, July). Meeting the literacy needs of struggling readers in the early elementary years. Presentation for the Summer Institute. Ann Arbor: University of Michigan. Retrieved 1/28/07. http://www.ciera.org/library/presos/2004/csi/jfcarl.pdf.

Carlson, L., & Bricker, D. (1982). Dyadic and contingent aspects of early communicative intervention. In D. Bricker (Ed.), *Intervention with at-risk and handicapped infants: From research to application* (pp. 291–308). Baltimore: University Park Press.

Carter, D. (1990). *More bugs in boxes.* New York: Simon and Schuster.

Cary, S. (2000). *Working with second language learners: Answers to teachers' top ten questions.* Portsmouth, NH: Heinemann.

Casbergue, R. (1998). How do we foster young children's writing development? In S. Neuman & K. Roskos (Eds.),

Children achieving: Best practices in early literacy (pp. 198–222). Newark, DE: International Reading Association.

Cassidy, J., & Wenrich, J. (1998). Literacy research in practice: What's hot, what's not and why. *The Reading Teacher, 52*(4), 402–406.

Center for the Improvement of Early Reading/CIERA. (2001). *Putting reading first: The research building blocks for teaching children to read.* Jessup, MD: National Institute for Literacy.

Chall, J. (1996). *Stages of reading development* (2nd ed.). Fort Worth, TX: Harcourt Brace.

Chall, J., Jacobs, V., & Baldwin, L. (1990). *The reading crisis: Why poor children fall behind.* Cambridge, MA: Harvard University Press.

Chall, J., & Jacobs, V. (2003). Poor children's fourth-grade slump. *American Educator, 27*(1), 14–15.

Chamot, A., & O'Malley, J. (1994). Instructional approaches and teaching procedures. In K. Spangenberg-Urbschat & R. Pritchard (Eds.), *Kids come in all languages: Reading instruction for ESL students* (pp. 82–107). Newark, DE: International Reading Association.

Chard, D., & Kame'enui, E. (2000, Spring). Struggling first-grade readers: The frequency and progress of their reading. *Journal of Special Education, 34*(1), 28–39.

Chard, N. (1990). How learning logs change teaching. In N. Atwell (Ed.), *Coming to know: Writing to learn in the intermediate grades* (pp. 61–68). Portsmouth, NH: Heinemann.

Christensen, A., & Kelly, K. (2003). No time for play: Throwing the baby out with the bath water. *The Reading Teacher, 56*(6), 528–530.

Clark, E. (1978). Awareness of language: Some evidence from what children say and do. In A. Sinclair, R. Jarvella, & W. Levelt (Eds.), *The child's conception of language* (pp. 17–44). New York: Springer-Verlag.

Clark, H., & Clark, E. (1977). *Psychology and language.* New York: Harcourt Brace Jovanovich.

Clay, M. (1966). Emergent reading behavior. Unpublished doctoral dissertation, University of Auckland Library.

Clay, M. (1975). *What did I write?* Portsmouth, NH: Heinemann.

Clay, M. (1979). *Reading: The patterning of complex behavior* (2nd ed.). Auckland: Heinemann.

Clay, M. (1982). *Reading begins at home.* Exeter, NH: Heinemann Educational Books.

Clay, M. (1985). *The early detection of reading difficulties.* Portsmouth, NH: Heinemann.

Clay, M. (1987). *Writing begins at home.* Portsmouth, NH: Heinemann.

Clay, M. (1991). *Becoming literate: The construction of inner control.* Portsmouth, NH: Heinemann.

Clay, M. (1993). *An observation survey of early literacy achievement.* Portsmouth, NH: Heinemann.

Clay, M. (1998). *By different paths to common outcomes.* York, Maine: Stenhouse.

Clay, M. (2000). *Running records for classroom teachers.* Portsmouth, NH: Heinemann.

Cobb, J. (2001). The effects of an early intervention program with preservice teachers as tutors on the reading achievement of primary grade at-risk children. *Reading Horizons, 41*(3), 155–173.

Cochran-Smith, M. (1984). *The making of a reader.* Norwood, NJ: Ablex.

Cohen J., & Wiener, R. (2003). *Literacy portfolios: Improving assessment, teaching and learning* (2nd ed.). Upper Saddle River, NJ: Pearson Merrill Prentice Hall.

Cole, A. (2006). Scaffolding beginning readers: Micro and macro cues teachers use during student oral reading. *The Reading Teacher, 59*(5), 450–459.

Coley, R., & Coleman, A. (2004). *The fourth-grade reading classroom: Policy information report.* Princeton, NJ: Educational Testing Service.

Collier, V. (1995). Acquiring a second language for school. *Directions in language and education, 1*(4), 3–14. ERIC ED 394301.

Collins, P. (1990). Bridging the gap. In N. Atwell (Ed.), *Coming to know: Writing to learn in the intermediate grades* (pp. 17–34). Portsmouth, NH: Heinemann.

Collom, S. (2004). The writing continuum: Levels of teacher support. In G. Tompkins & S. Collom (Eds.), *Sharing the pen: Interactive writing with young children* (pp. 5–8). Upper Saddle River, NJ: Pearson Merrill Prentice Hall.

Coltrane, B. (2003). Working with young English language learners: Some considerations. ERIC Digest. ED 481 690.

Come, B., & Fredericks, A. (1995). Family literacy in urban schools: Meeting the needs of at-risk children. *The Reading Teacher, 48*(7), 566–570.

Condon, W., & Sandler, L. (1974). Neonate movement is synchronized with adult speech: Interactional participation and language acquisition. *Science, 183*, 99–101.

Cooper, J. D., & Kiger, N. (2006). *Literacy: Helping children construct meaning.* Boston, MA: Houghton Mifflin.

Cooter, K. (2006). When mama can't read: Counteracting intergenerational illiteracy. *The Reading Teacher, 59*(7), 698–702.

Cooter, R., & Cooter, K. (2004). One size doesn't fit all: Slow learners in the reading classroom. *The Reading Teacher, 57*(7), 680–684.

Corcoran, C., & Leahy, R. (2003, Fall). Growing professionally through reflective practice. *Kappa Delta Pi Record, 40*(1), 30–33.

Cox, B., & Hopkins, C. (2006). Building on theoretical principles gleaned from Reading Recovery to inform classroom practice, *Reading Research Quarterly, 41*(2), 254–267.

Cox, B., Fang, Z., & Otto, B. (1997). Preschoolers' developing ownership of the literate register. *Reading Research Quarterly, 32*(1), 34–53.

Cox, P. (1999). *Find the puppy.* London: Usborne Publishing.

Crago, M., & Crago, H. (1983). *Prelude to literacy: A preschool child's encounter with picture and story.* Carbondale: Southern Illinois University Press.

Crain-Thoreson, C., & Dale, P. (1999). Enhancing linguistic performance: Parents and teachers as book reading partners for children with language delays. *Topics in Early Childhood Special Education, 19*(1), 28–39.

Crepeau, I., & Richards, M. (2003). *A show of hands: Using puppets with young children.* St. Paul, MN: Redleaf Press.

Cuffaro, H. (1995). *Experimenting with the world: John Dewey and the early childhood classroom.* New York: Teachers College Press.

Cummins, J. (1979). Linguistic interdependence. *Review of Educational Research, 49*, 222–251.

Cummins, J. (1981). Age on arrival and immigrant second-language learning in Canada: A reassessment. *Applied Linguistics, 2*, 132–149.

Cummins, J. (1994). The acquisition of English as a second language. In K. Spangenberg-Urbschat & R. Pritchard (Eds.), *Kids come in all languages: Reading instruction for ESL students* (pp. 36–61). Newark, DE: International Reading Association.

Cummins, J. (2003). Reading and the bilingual student: Fact and fiction. In G. Garcia (Ed.), *English learners: Reaching the highest level of English literacy* (pp. 2–33). Newark, DE: International Reading Association.

Cunningham, P. (2006). What if they can say the words but don't know what they mean? *The Reading Teacher, 59*(7), 708–711.

Cunningham, P., & Allington, R. (2007). *Classrooms that work: They can all read and write* (4th ed.). Boston, MA: Allyn & Bacon.

Cunningham, P., & Cunningham, J. (1992). Making words: Enhancing the invented spelling-decoding connection. *The Reading Teacher, 46*(2), 106–115.

Curenton, S. (2006, September). Oral storytelling: A cultural art that promotes school readiness. *Young Children*, 78–90.

Curenton, S., & Justice, L. (2004). African American and Caucasian preschoolers' use of decontextualized language: Literate language features in oral narratives. *Language, Speech, and Hearing Services in Schools, 35*, pp. 240–253.

Dahl, K., & Farnan, N. (1998). *Children's writing: Perspectives from research.* Newark, DE: International Reading Association.

Dahl, K., & Freppon, P. (1994). A comparison of inner-city children's interpretations of reading and writing instruction in the early grades in skills-based and whole language classrooms. ERIC ED 370075.

Dailey, K. (1991, Spring). Writing in kindergarten: Helping parents understand the process. *Childhood Education*, 170–175.

Daniels, H. (1994). *Literature circles: Voice and choice in one student-centered classroom.* Portland, ME: Stenhouse.

Daniels, J. (2004). *Literate behaviors in African-American Head Start families: A multiple literacies perspective.* Unpublished dissertation, University of Maryland, College Park, MD.

Darling, S., & Westberg, L. (2004). Parent involvement in children's acquisition of reading. *The Reading Teacher, 57*(8), 774–776.

Davis, S. (1991). Three reading groups: An American educational tradition. Literacy Research Report No. 8. Dekalb: Northern Illinois University, Curriculum and Instruction Reading Clinic. ERIC ED 311 005.

De Atiles, J., & Allexsaht-Snider, M. (2002). Effective approaches to teaching young Mexican immigrant children. ERIC Digest. ED 471 491.

DeCasper, A., & Fifer, W. (1980). Of human bonding: Newborns prefer their mothers' voices. *Science, 208*, pp. 1174–1176.

DeCorse, C. (2001). Children reading meaning in their stories and lives: Connecting with student response. In P. Schmidt & A. Pailliotet (Eds.), *Exploring values through literature, multimedia, and literacy events: Making connections* (pp. 10–19). Newark, DE: International Reading Association.

DeLoache, J. (1984, April). What's this? Maternal questions in joint picture book reading with toddlers. Presented at the Annual Meeting of the American Educational Research Association, New Orleans, LA.

DeLoache, J., & DeMendoza, O. (1985, December). Joint picture book interactions of mothers and one-year-old children. Technical Report No. 353. Center for the Study of Reading, University of Illinois at Urbana-Champaign, Champaign, IL.

Delpit, L. (1988). The silenced dialogue: Power and pedagogy in educating other people's children. *Harvard Educational Review, 58*(3), 280–298.

Delpit, L. (1990). Language diversity and learning. In S. Hynds & D. Rubin (Eds.), *Perspectives on talk and learning* (pp. 247–266). Urbana, IL: National Council of Teachers of English.

Delpit, L. (1992). Acquisition of literate discourse: Bowing before the master? *Theory Into Practice, 31*(4), 296–302.

Delpit, L. (2002). No kinda sense. In L. Delpit & J. Dowdy (Eds.). *The skin that we speak: Thoughts on language and culture in the classroom* (pp. 33–48). New York: The New Press.

Department of Education. (2005). Executive summary: Analysis of state K–3 reading standards and assessments. http://www.ed.gov/print/rschstat/eval/other/reading/state-k3-reading.html

Department of Education, Office of Research (2007). Reading Recovery. Retrieved 1/29/2007. http://www.ed.gov/pubs/OR/ConsumerGuides/readrec.html

Diamond, B., & Moore, M. (1995). *Multicultural literacy: Mirroring the reality of the classroom.* White Plains, NY: Longman.

Diaz, R. (1985). The intellectual power of bilingualism. ERIC ED 283 368.

Dickinson, D. (2001). Large group and free play times: Conversational settings supporting language and literacy development. In D. Dickinson & P. Tabors (Eds.), *Beginning literacy with language* (pp. 223–256). Baltimore, MD: Brookes.

Dickinson, D., McCabe, A., & Sprague, K. (2001). Teacher rating of oral language and literacy (TROLL): A research-based tool. CIERA Report. Ann Arbor, MI: Center for the Improvement of Early Reading Achievement. ERIC ED 468 087.

Dickinson, D., McCabe, A., & Sprague, K. (2003). Teacher rating of oral language and literacy (TROLL): Individualizing early literacy instruction with a standards-based rating tool. *The Reading Teacher, 56*(6), 554–564.

Dickinson, D., & Smith, M. (1994). Long-term effects of preschool teachers' book reading on low-income children's vocabulary and story comprehension. *Reading Research Quarterly, 29*(2), 104–122.

Dickinson, D., & Sprague, K. (2002). The nature and impact of early childhood care environments on the language and early literacy development of children from low-income families. In S. Neuman & D. Dickinson (Eds.), *Handbook of early literacy research* (pp. 263–280). New York: The Guilford Press.

Dickinson, D., & Tabors, P. (Eds.). (2001). *Beginning literacy with language.* Baltimore, MD: Paul H. Brookes.

Diener, M., Wright, C., Julian, J., & Byington, C. (2003). A pediatric literacy education program for low socioeconomic, culturally diverse families. *Journal of Research in Childhood Education, 18*(2), 149–159.

Dixon-Krauss, L. (1996). *Vygotsky in the classroom: Mediated literacy instruction and assessment.* White Plains, NY: Longman.

Dinsmore, K. (1988, April). Baby's first books: A guide to selection of infant literature. *Childhood Education, 64*(4), 215–219.

Doake, D. (1981). Book experience and emergent reading behavior in preschool children. Unpublished doctoral dissertation, University of Alberta, Canada.

Doake, D. (1986). Learning to read: It starts in the home. In D. R. Tovey & J. E. Kerber (Eds.), *Roles in literacy learning* (pp. 2–9). Newark, DE: International Reading Association.

Dodici, B., Draper, D., & Peterson, C. (2003, Fall). Early parent–child interactions and early literacy development. *Topics in Early Childhood Special Education, 23*(3), 124–136.

Dorling Kindersley (2001). *Farm animals.* New York: Dorling Kindersley Publishing.

Dreher, M., & Zenge, S. (1990). Using metalinguistic awareness in first grade to predict reading achievement in third and fifth grades. *Journal of Educational Research, 84*(1), 31–21.

Drucker, M. (2003). What reading teachers should know about ESL learners. *The Reading Teacher, 57*(1), 22–29.

Duffy, G., & Hoffman, J. (1999). In pursuit of an illusion: The flawed search for a perfect method. *The Reading Teacher, 53*(1), 10–16.

Duke, N. (2000). 3.6 minutes per day: The scarcity of informational texts in first grade. *Reading Research Quarterly, 35*(2), 202–224.

Duke, N., & Pearson, P. D. (2002). Effective practices for developing reading comprehension. In A. Farstrup & S. J. Samuels. (Eds.), *What research has to say about reading instruction* (3rd ed.) (pp. 205–242.) Newark, DE: International Reading Association.

Durkin, D. (1966). Children who read early: Two longitudinal studies. (ERIC Document Reproduction Service No. ED019107).

Dynamic Indicators of Basic Early Literacy Skills (DIBELS) (2001). Accessed 11/17/2006. http://dibels.uoregon.edu/

Dyson, A. (1981). Oral language: The rooting system for learning to write. *Language Arts, 58*(7), 776–784.

Dyson, A. (1985). Puzzles, paints, and pencils: Writing emerges. *Educational Horizons, 64,* 13–16.

Dyson, A. (1988, March). Appreciate the drawing and dictating of young children. *Young Children,* 25–32.

Dyson, A. (1990). Symbol makers, symbol weavers: How children link play, pictures, and print. *Young Children, 45*(2), 50–57.

Dyson, A. (2003). *The brothers and sisters learn to write: Popular literacies in childhood and school cultures.* New York: Teachers College Press.

Dzaldov, B., & Peterson, S. (2005). Book leveling and readers. *The Reading Teacher, 59*(3), 222–229.

Early Childhood Today (2001). Activities that build a love of books. *Early Childhood Today, 16*(2), 20.

Early Childhood Today (2004). Book-sharing activities. *Early Childhood Today, 18*(4), 26.

Eastman, P. D. (1960). *Are you my mother?* New York: Random House.

Eastman, P. D. (1982, 1973). *Perro grande . . . Big dog . . . Perro pequeño . . . Little dog.* Translated into Spanish by P. de Cuenca & I. Alvarez. New York: Random House.

Edelsky, C., Altwerger, B., & Flores, B. (1991). *Whole language: What's the difference?* Portsmouth, NH: Heinemann.

Ediger, M. (2000, Fall). Speaking activities and reading. *Reading Improvement, 37*(3), 137–146.

Education Commission of the States (2006). At-Risk: Dropouts. Denver, CO: Education Commission of the States. Retrieved 1/30/2006. http://www.ecs.org/html/issue.asp?issueid=13&subIssueID=74

Edwards, C., & Willis, L. (2000). Integrating visual and verbal literacies in the early childhood classroom. *Early Childhood Education Journal, 27*(4), 259–265.

Eisenberg, R. (1976). *Auditory competence in early life: The roots of communicative behavior.* Baltimore: University Park Press.

Elbow, P. (2004, October). Writing first! *Educational Leadership, 62*(2), 8–13.

Elley, W. (1989). Vocabulary acquisition from listening to stories. *Reading Research Quarterly, 24*(2), 174–187.

Elster, C. (1994a). Patterns within preschoolers' emergent readings. *Reading Research Quarterly, 29*(4), 403–418.

Elster, C. (1994b, March). "I guess they do listen": Young children's emergent readings after adult read-alouds. *Young Children, 49*(3), 27–31.

Elster, C. (1998). Influences of text and pictures on shared and emergent readings. *Research in the Teaching of English, 32*(1), 43–78.

Ely, R., Gleason, J., MacGibbon, A., & Zaretsky, R. (2001). Attention to language: Lessons learned at the dinner table, *Social Development, 10*(3), 355–373.

Emmitt, M., Pollock, J., & Komesaroff, L. (2003). *Language and learning: An introduction to teaching* (3rd ed.). New York: Oxford University Press.

Emmitt, M., Pollock, J., & Komesaroff, L. (2006). *Language and learning: An introduction for teaching* (4th ed.), New York: Oxford University Press.

Epstein, A. (2002a). Good beginnings in reading for infants and toddlers in High/Scope programs. High/Scope Educational Research Foundation. Retrieved 5/11/2006. http://www.highscope.org/NewsandInformation/PositionPapers/infanttoddler.htm.

Epstein, A. (2002b, Summer). Helping preschool children become readers: Tips for parents. *High/Scope ReSource,* 4–6.

Erikson, E. (1963). *Childhood and society* (2nd ed.). New York: Norton.

Erikson, E. (1972). Eight ages of man. In C. Lavatelli & E. Stendler (Eds.), *Readings in child behavior and child development.* San Diego, CA: Harcourt.

Evans, J. (1978). Increasing toddlers' vocabularies through picture-reading. Austin: Southwest Educational Development Lab. ERIC ED 207 682.

Ewers, C., & Brownson, S. (1999). Kindergartners' vocabulary acquisition as a function of active vs. passive storybook reading, prior vocabulary, and working memory. *Journal of Reading Psychology, 20,* 11–20.

Faltis, C. (1998). *Joinfostering: Teaching and learning in multilingual classrooms* (3rd ed.). Upper Saddle River, NJ: Merrill/Prentice Hall.

Farbman, M. (2005). Tickets, please. *Instructor, 115*(2), 59–61.

Farrell, S., & Lewis, R. (1994). *To the post office with Mama.* Toronto, ON, Canada: Annick Press.

Farris, P., Fuhler, C., & Walther, M. (2004). *Teaching reading: A balanced approach for today's classrooms.* Boston, MA: McGraw Hill.

Faulkner, K. (1996). *The wide-mouthed frog.* New York: Dial Books for Young Readers.

Fay, L. (1965). Reading study skills: Math and science. In J. Figural (Ed.), *Reading and inquiry* (pp. 93–94). Newark, DE: International Reading Association.

Felton, R., & Wood, F. (1992). A reading level match study of nonword reading skills in poor readers with varying IQ, *Journal of Learning Disabilities, 25*(5), 318–326.

Ferguson, D. (1992). *Winnie the Pooh's A to Zzzz.* New York: Disney Press.

Ferguson, P., & Young, T. (1996). Literature talk: Dialogue improvisation and patterned conversations with second language learners. *Language Arts, 73,* 597–600.

Ferreiro, E. (1986). The interplay between information and assimilation in beginning literacy. In W. Teale and E. Sulzby (Eds.), *Emergent literacy: Writing and reading* (pp. 15–49). Norwood, NJ: Ablex.

Fielding, L., & Roller, C. (1992). Making difficult books accessible and easy books acceptable. *The Reading Teacher, 45*(9), 678–685.

Fisher, D., Flood, J., Lapp, D., & Frey, N. (2004). Interactive read-alouds: Is there a common set of implementation practices? *The Reading Teacher, 58*(1), 8–17.

Fitzgerald, J. (1999). What is this thing called "balance"? *Reading Teacher, 53*(2), 100–107.

Fitzgerald, J., & Cunningham, J. (2002). Balance in teaching reading: An instructional approach based on a particular epistemological outlook. *Reading & Writing Quarterly, 18,* 353–364.

Flavell, J. (1996). Piaget's legacy. *Psychological Science, 7*(4), 200–203.

Fletcher, K., & Jean-Francois, B. (1998). Spontaneous responses during repeated reading in young children from "at risk" backgrounds. *Early Child Development and Care, 146,* pp. 53–68.

Flett, A., & Conderman, B. (2002, March). 20 Ways to promote phonemic awareness. *Intervention in School and Clinic, 37*(4), 242–245.

Florida Department of Education (2006). Grade level expectations for the Sunshine State standards: Language arts grades K–2. Retrieved 11/8/2006. www.myfloridaeducation.com

Flurkey, A. (2006). What's "normal" about real reading? In K. Goodman (Ed.), *The truth about DIBELS: What it is, What it does* (pp. 40–49). Portsmouth, NH: Heinemann.

Focus Adolescent Services (2000). Youth who drop out. Retrieved 1/30/2006. http://www.focusas.com/Dropouts.html

Fox, B. (2004). *Word identification strategies: Phonics from a new perspective.* Upper Saddle River, NJ: Pearson Merrill Prentice Hall.

Fox, B., & Saracho, I. (1990). Emergent writing: Young children solving the written language puzzle. *Early Child Development and Care, 56*, 81–90.

Foy, J., & Mann, V. (2006). Changes in letter sound knowledge are associated with development of phonological awareness of preschool children. *Journal of Research in Reading, 29* (2), 143–161.

Freeman, D. (1978). *Pocket for Corduroy.* New York: Viking Press.

Freeman, F. (1954). *Teaching Handwriting.* Washington, DC: National Education Association.

Freppon, P. (1993, April). Making sense of reading and writing in urban classrooms: Understanding at-risk children's knowledge construction in different curricula. Final Report. Paper presented at the Annual Meeting of the American Educational Research Association, Atlanta, GA. ERIC ED 361 433.

Frey, N., & Fisher, D. (2007). *Reading for information in elementary school: Content literacy strategies to build comprehension.* Upper Saddle River, NJ: Pearson Merrill Prentice Hall.

Froebel, F. (1917). *Pedagogics of the Kindergarten.* New York: D. Appleton.

Froebel, F. (1976). *Mother's songs, games, and stories.* New York: Arno.

Fromkin, V., & Rodman, R. (1998). *An introduction to language* (6th ed.). Fort Worth, TX: Harcourt Brace College Publishers.

Froese, V. (1996). Introduction to whole-language teaching and learning. In V. Froese (Ed.), *Whole language: Practice and theory* (pp. 1–21). Boston, MA: Allyn & Bacon.

Gambrell, L. (1996). Creating classroom cultures that foster reading motivation. *The Reading Teacher, 50*(1), 14–25.

Garcia, G. (2003). Bilingual children's reading. In M. Kamil, P. Mosenthal, & P. D. Pearson (Eds.), *Handbook of reading research*, Vol. 3 (pp. 813–834). Mahwah, NJ: Lawrence Earlbaum Associates.

Gardiner, S. (2005). A skill for life. *Educational Leadership, 63*(3), 67–70.

Gauthier, G. (2005, November/December). The Early Years: What do your science learning centers look like? *Science and Children, 43*(3), 20.

Gee, J. (2001). Reading as situated language: A sociocognitive perspective. *Journal of Adolescent & Adult Literacy, 44*(8), 714–725.

Genesee, F., Tucker, G., & Lambert, W. (1975). Communication skills of bilingual children. *Child Development, 46*, 110–114.

Genisio, M., & Drecktrah, M. (1999). Emergent literacy in an early childhood classroom: Center learning to support the child with special needs. *Early Childhood Education Journal, 26*(4), 225–231.

Gentry, J. R. (1982). An analysis of developmental spelling in *GYNS at WRK. The Reading Teacher, 36*(2), 192–200.

Gentry, J. R. (2000). A retrospective on invented spelling and a look forward. *The Reading Teacher, 54*(3), 318–332.

Gentry, R. (2004). *The science of spelling: The explicit specifics that make great readers and writers (and spellers!).* Portsmouth, NH: Heinemann.

George, M., Raphael, T., & Florio-Ruane, S. (2003). Connecting children, culture, curriculum, and text. In G. Garcia (Ed.)., *English learners: Reading the highest level of English literacy* (pp. 308–332). Newark, DE: International Reading Association.

Gersten, R., & Geva, E. (2003). Teaching reading to early language learners. *Educational Leadership, 60*(7), 44–48.

Giambo, D., & Szecsi, T. (2005). Parents can guide children through the world of two languages. *Childhood Education, 81*(3), 164–165.

Gilliam, R., McFadden, B., & van Kleeck, A. (1995). Improving narrative abilities: Whole language and language skills approaches. In M. Fey, J. Windsor, & S. Warren (Eds.), *Language intervention: Preschool through the elementary years* (pp. 145–182). Baltimore, MD: Paul Hl Brookes.

Glaubman, R., Kashi, G., & Koresh, R. (2001). Facilitating the narrative quality of sociodramatic play. In A. Göncü & E. Klein (Eds.), *Children in play, story, and school* (pp. 132–160). New York: Guildford Press.

Glazer, S. (2004). Reflective teachers. *Teaching PreK–8, 34*(4), 90–91.

Goddard, Y., & Heron, T. (1998). Please, Teacher, help me learn to spell better teach me self-correction. *Teaching Exceptional Children, 30*(6), 38–43.

Goldenberg, C. (2002). Making schools work for low-income families in the 21st century. In S. Neuman & D. Dickinson (Eds.), *Handbook of early literacy research* (pp. 211–231). New York: The Guilford Press.

Gonzalez, N., Moll, L., & Amanti, C. (2005). *Funds of knowledge: Theorizing practices in households and classrooms.* Mahwah, NJ: Lawrence Erlbaum.

Gonzalez, N., Moll, L., Floyd-Tenery, M., Rivera, A., Rendon, P., Gonzales, R., & Amanti, C. (1993). *Teacher research on funds of knowledge: Learning from households.* Santa Cruz, CA: University of California, Center for Research on Education, Diversity & Excellence.

Good, R., Kaminski, R., Simmons, D., & Kame'enui, E. (2001). Using Dynamic Indicators of Basic Early Literacy Skills (DIBELS) in an outcomes-driven model: Steps to reading outcomes.

Oregon School Study Council, 44(1), 2–24.

Goodman, K. (1965). Cues and miscues in reading: A linguistic study. *Elementary English, 4*(6), 635–642.

Goodman, K. (1967, May). Reading: A psycholinguistic guessing game. *Journal of the Reading Specialist,* 126–135.

Goodman, K. (1993). *Phonics Phacts.* Portsmouth, NH: Heinemann.

Goodman, K. (2006). A critical review of DIBELS. In K. Goodman (Ed.), *The truth about DIBELS: What it is, what it does* (pp. 1–39). Portsmouth, NH: Heinemann.

Goodman, K., & Goodman, Y. (1979). Learning to read is natural. In L. Resnick & P. Weaver (Eds.), *Theory and practice of early reading,* Vol. 1 (pp. 137–154). Hillsdale, NJ: Erlbaum.

Goodman, Y. (1986). Children coming to know literacy. In W. Teale and E. Sulzby (Eds.), *Emergent literacy: Writing and reading* (pp. 1–14). Norwood, NJ: Ablex.

Goodman, Y. (1990). *How children construct literacy: Piagetian perspectives.* Newark, DE: International Reading Association.

Goodman, Y. (2002). Foreword. In R. Meyer, *Phonics exposed: Understanding and resisting systematic direct intense phonics instruction* (pp. ix–xii). Mahwah, NJ: Lawrence Erlbaum.

Goodz, N., Legare, M., & Bilodeau, L. (1987). The influence of bilingualism in preschool children. *Canadian Psychology, 28,* 218.

Gopnik, A., Meltzoff, A., & Kuhl, P. (1999). *The scientist in the crib.* New York: William Morrow.

Gordon, J. (1991). *Six sleepy sheep.* New York: Puffin Books.

Goswami, U. (2002). Early phonological development and the acquisition of literacy. In S. Neuman & D. Dickinson (Eds.), *Handbook of early literacy research* (pp. 111–125). New York: The Guilford Press.

Gottlieb, S. (2001). Review of state reading and language arts standards. ERIC Digest. ED456425.

Gottshall, S. (1995). Hug-a-book: A program to nurture a young child's love of books and reading. *Young Children, 50*(4), 29–35.

Gough, P. (1972). One second of reading. In J. Kavanagh & I. Mattingly (Eds.), *Language by ear and by eye* (pp. 331–358). Cambridge, MA: The MIT Press.

Grant, L., & Rothenberg, J. (1981, April). Charting educational futures: Interaction patterns in first and second grade reading groups. Paper presented at the Annual Meeting of the American Educational Research Association, Los Angeles, CA. ERIC ED 200 902.

Grant, R. (1995). Meeting the needs of young second language learners. In E. Garcia & B. McLaughlin (Eds.), *Meeting the challenge of linguistic and cultural diversity in early childhood education* (pp. 1–17). New York: Teachers College Press.

Grant, R., & Wong, S. (2003). Barriers to literacy for language-minority learners: An argument for change in the literacy education profession. *Journal of Adolescent & Adult Literacy, 46*(5), 386–394.

Graves, D. (1994). *A fresh look at writing.* Portsmouth, NH: Heinemann.

Graves, M. (1994). *A fresh look at writing.* Portsmouth, NH: Heinemann.

Graves, M., & Watts-Taffe, S. (2002). The place of word consciousness in a research-based vocabulary program. In A. Farstrup & S. J. Samuels (Eds.), *What research has to say about reading instruction* (pp. 140–165). Newark, DE: International Reading Association.

Gray, T., & Fleishman, S. (2004 December/2005 January). Successful strategies for English language learners. *Educational Leadership, 62*(4), 84–85.

Green, C. (1998). This is my name. *Childhood Education, 74*(4), 226–31.

Greenspan, S. (1997). *The growth of the mind: And the endangered origins of intelligence.* Reading, MA: Perseus Books.

Greenspan, S. (1999). *Building healthy minds: The six experiences that create* intelligence and emotional growth in babies and young children. Cambridge, MA: Perseus Books.

Griffin, J. (1987, July 31). Dropout rate tied to early failures: Lack of reading ability top factor. *Chicago Tribune,* p. 1.

Griffin, M. (2002). Why don't you use your finger? Paired reading in first grade. *The Reading Teacher, 55*(8), 566–773.

Groth, L., & Darling, L. (2001). Playing "inside" stories. In A. Göncü & E. Klein (Eds.), *Children in play, story, and school* (pp. 220–240). New York: The Guilford Press.

Gunn, B., Simmons, D., Kameenui, E. (2006). Emergent literacy: Synthesis of the research. National Center to Improve the Tools of Educators. Retrieved 5/11/2006. http://idea.uoregon.edu/~ncite/documents/techrep/tech19.htm1

Gunning, T. (1995). Word building: A strategic approach to the teaching of phonics. *The Reading Teacher, 48*(6), 484–488.

Gutman, L., & Sulzby, E. (2000, Winter). The role of autonomy-support versus control in the emergent writing behaviors of African American kindergarten children. *Reading Research and Instruction, 39*(2), 170–184.

Hall, D., & Cunningham, P. (1999). Multilevel word study: Word charts, word walls, and word sorts. In I. Fountas & G. Pinnell (Eds.), *Voices on word matters: Learning about phonics and spelling in the literacy classroom.* Portsmouth, NH: Heinemann.

Hall, K., Sabey, B., & McClellan, M. (2005). Expository text comprehension: Helping primary-grade teachers use expository texts to full advantage. *Reading Psychology, 26,* 211–234.

Hammerberg, D. (2004). Comprehension instruction for socioculturally diverse classrooms: A review of what we know. *The Reading Teacher, 57*(7), 648–658.

Hammond, W. D. (1999). A balanced early literacy curriculum: An ecological perspective. In

W. D. Hammond and T. Raphael (Eds.), *Early literacy instruction for the new millennium* (pp. 113–135). Grand Rapids, MI: Michigan Reading Association.

Hancock, M. (1993). Exploring and extending personal response through literature journals. *The Reading Teacher, 46*(6), 466–474.

Haney, M. (2002). Name writing: A window into the emergent literacy skills of young children. *Early Childhood Education Journal, 30*(2), 101–105.

Hansen, J. (1992). Literacy portfolios: Helping students know themselves. *Educational Leadership, 49*(8), 66–68.

Harlin, R., Lipa, S., & Lonberger, R. (1991). *The whole language journey*. Markham, Ontario: Pippin Publishing, Ltd.

Harmon, J., & Hedrick, W. (2000). Zooming in and zooming out: Enhancing vocabulary and conceptual learning in social studies. *The Reading Teacher, 54*(2), 155–160.

Harries, R., & Yost, M. (1981). *Elements of handwriting: A teacher's guide*. Novato, CA: Academic Therapy Publications.

Harrington, S. (1994). An author's storyboard technique as a prewriting strategy. *The Reading Teacher, 48*(3), 283–286.

Harris, T., & Hodges, R. (Eds.) (1995). *The literacy dictionary: The vocabulary of reading and writing*. Newark, DE: International Reading Association.

Hart, B., & Risley, T. (1995). *Meaningful differences in the everyday experience of young American children*. Baltimore: Paul H. Brookes.

Hasbrouck, J. (2006, Summer). Drop everything and read—but how? *American Educator*, 22–31.

Hatcher, B., & Petty, K. (2004, November). Seeing is believing: Visible thought in dramatic play. *Young Children*, 79–82.

Haugland, S. (1997). How teachers use computers in early childhood classrooms. *Journal of Computing in Childhood Education, 8*(1), 3–14.

Haussler, M. (1985). A young child's developing concepts of print. In

A. Jagger & M. T. Smith-Burke (Eds.), *Observing the language learner* (pp. 73–81). Newark, DE: International Reading Associaton.

Haynes, W., & Saunders, D. (1999, Spring). Joint book-reading strategies in middle-class African American and white mother-toddler dyads: Research Note. *Journal of Children's Communicative Development, 20*(2), 9–17.

Heald-Taylor, B. C. (1998). Three paradigms of spelling instruction in grades 3–6. *The Reading Teacher, 51*(5), 404–413.

Heath, S. (1983). *Ways with words: Language, life, and work in communities and classrooms*. New York: Cambridge University Press.

Hedrick, W., Harmon, J., & Wood, K. (2005). From trade books to textbooks: Helping bilingual students make the transition. In R. McCormack & J. Paratore (Eds.), *After early intervention, then what? Teaching struggling readers in grades 3 and beyond* (pp. 190–207). Upper Saddle River, NJ: Pearson Merrill Prentice Hall.

Henderson, E. (1986). Understanding children's knowledge of written language. In D. Yaden, Jr., & S. Templeton (Eds.), *Metalinguistic awareness and beginning literacy: Conceptualizing what it means to read and write* (pp. 65–78). Portsmouth, NH: Heinemann.

Hendrix, J. (1999). Connecting cooperative learning and social studies. *Clearing House, 73*(1), 57–61.

Herrell, A., & Jordan, M. (2006). *50 Strategies for improving vocabulary, comprehension, and fluency: An active learning approach* (2nd ed.). Upper Saddle River, NJ: Pearson Merrill Prentice Hall.

Hickman, P., Pollard-Durodola, S., & Vaughn, S. (2004). Storybook reading: Improving vocabulary and comprehension for English-language learners. *The Reading Teacher, 57*(8), 720–730.

Hiebert, E. (1993). Early literacy experiences at home and school. In S. Yussen & M. Smith (Eds.), *Reading*

across the lifespan (pp. 33–55). New York: Springer-Verlag.

Hiebert, E. (1999). Every child a reader: At work in a first-grade classroom. In W. D. Hammond and T. Raphael (Eds.), *Early literacy instruction for the new millennium* (pp. 23–48). Grand Rapids Michigan Reading Association.

Hiebert, E. (2002). Standards, assessments, and text difficulty. In A. Farstrup & S. J. Samuels (Eds.), *What research has to say about reading instruction* (3rd ed.) (pp. 337–369). Newark, DE: International Reading Association.

Hill, E. (1980; 2000). *Where's Spot?* New York: Putnam.

Hoban, T. (1983). *I read symbols*. New York: Greenwillow Books.

Hoban, T. (1997). *Look book*. New York: Greenwillow Books.

Hoffman, J. (2000). Process writing and the writer's workshop. In R. Robinson, M. Mckenna, & J. Wedman (Eds.), *Issues and trends in literacy education* (2nd ed.) (pp. 312–315). Boston, MA: Allyn & Bacon.

Holdaway, D. (1982, Autumn). Shared book experience: Teaching reading using favorite books. *Theory Into Practice, 21*, 293–300.

Honig, A. (2001, October). Building language and literacy with infants and toddlers. *Scholastic Early Childhood Today, 16*(2).

Honig, A., & Brophy, H. (1996). *Talking with your baby: Family as the first school*. Syracuse, NY: Syracuse University Press.

Honig, A., & Shin, M. (2001). Reading aloud with infants and toddlers in child care settings: An observational study. *Early Childhood Education Journal, 28*(3), 193–197.

Houghton Mifflin Reading (2006). Grade 1 Products. Retrieved 1/29/2007. http://www.eduplace.com

Huba, M., & Ramisetty-Mikler, S. (1995). The language skills and concepts of early and nonearly readers. *Journal of Genetic Psychology, 156*(3), 313–331.

Hubbell, P. (2003). *Trucks: Whizz! zoom! rumble!* Tarrytown, NY: Marshall Cavendish.

Hughes, M., & Searle, D. (2000). Spelling and "the second 'R'." *Language Arts, 77*(3), 203–208.

Hyson, M. (2001, May). Reclaiming our words. *Young Children,* 53–54.

I Dioscuri (1992). *En vacances: dictionnaire multilingue.* Paris: PML Editions.

Ianco-Worrall, A. (1972). Bilingualism and cognitive development. *Child Development, 43,* 1390–1400.

Illinois State Board of Education, Division of Early Childhood Education (2002). *Illinois Early Learning Standards.* Springfield: Illinois State Board of Education.

Im, J., Parlakian, R., & Osborn, C. (2007, January). Stories: Their powerful role in early language and literacy. *Young Children, 62*(1), 52–53.

Innes, R. (2002). There's more than mythology to California's reading decline. *Phi Delta Kappan, 84*(2), 155–156.

International Reading Association (2005). *Literacy development in the preschool years: A position statement of the International Reading Association.* Newark, DE: International Reading Association.

International Reading Association & National Association for the Education of Young Children (1998, July). Learning to read and write: Developmentally appropriate practices for young children: A joint position statement of the International Reading Association and the National Association for the Education of Young Children. *Young Children, 53*(4), 30–46.

Isbell, R., Sobol, J., Lindauer, L., & Lowrance, A. (2004). The effects of storytelling and story reading on the oral language complexity and story comprehension of young children. *Early Childhood Education Journal, 32*(3), 157–163.

Ivey, G. (2002). Getting started: Manageable literacy practices. *Educational Leadership, 60*(3), 20–23.

Jalongo, M. (1995). Promoting active listening in the classroom. *Childhood Education, 72*(1), 13–18.

Janzen, J. (2003). Developing strategic readers in elementary school. *Reading Psychology, 24,* 25–55.

Jensen, P., Williams, W., & Bzoch, K. (1975, November). *Preference of young infants for speech. Nonspeech stimuli.* Paper presented to the annual American Speech and Hearing Association Convention, Washington, DC.

Johns, J., & Elish-Piper, L. (1997). *Balanced reading instruction: Teachers' visions and voices.* Dubuque, IA: Kendall/Hunt.

John-Steiner, V., & Panofsky, C. (1992). Narrative competence: Cross-cultural comparisons. *Journal of Narrative and Life History, 2,* 219–234.

Johnston, F. (1999). The timing and teaching of word families. *The Reading Teacher, 53*(1), 64–75.

Johnston, F., Bear, D., Invernizzi, M., & Templeton, S. (2004). *Word sorts for letter name-alphabetic spellers.* Upper Saddle River, NJ: Pearson Merrill Prentice Hall.

Johnston, P., & Costello, P. (2005). Principles for literacy assessment. *Reading Research Quarterly, 40*(2), 256–267.

Jordan, G., Snow, C., & Porche, M. (2000). Project EASE: The effect of a family literacy project on kindergarten students' early literacy skills. *Reading Research Quarterly, 35*(4), 524–546.

Jordan-Davis, W. (1984). The cry for help unheard: Dropout interviews. Austin, Texas: Austin Independent School District, Office of Research and Evaluation. ERIC ED248413.

Joyner, R., & Ray, E. (1987, May). Reading behavior in infancy: Developmental and attitudinal implications. Paper presented at the Meeting of the Association for Childhood Education International, Omaha, Nebraska.

Judge, S. (2005). The impact of computer technology on academic achievement of young African American children. *Journal of Research in Childhood Education, 50*(2), 91–101.

Juel, C., Biancarosa, G., Coker, D., & Deffes, R. (2003). Walking with Rosie: A cautionary tale of early reading instruction. *Educational Leadership, 6*(7), 13–18.

Juel, C., & Deffes, R. (2003–2004) Making words stick. *The Best of Educational Leadership 2003–2004.* 27–31.

Juel, C., & Minden-Cupp, C. (2000). Learning to read words: Linguistic units and instructional strategies. *Reading Research Quarterly, 35*(4), 458–492.

Just, M., & Carpenter, P. (1980). A theory of reading: From eye fixations to comprehension. *Psychological Review, 87*(4), 329–355.

Kaderavek, J., & Sulzby, E. (2000). Narrative production by children with and without specific language impairment: Oral narratives and emergent readings. *Journal of Speech, Language, and Hearing Research, 43*(1), 34–49.

Kamii, C. (1985). Leading primary education toward excellence. *Young Children, 40*(6), 3–9.

Kamps, D., Wills, H., Greenwood, C., Thorne, S., Lazo, J., Crockett, J., Akers, J., & Swaggart, B. (2003). Curriculum influences on growth in early reading fluency for students with academic and behavioral risks: A descriptive study. *Journal of Emotional and Behavioral Disorders, 11*(4), 211–214.

Kantor, R., Miller, S., & Fernie, D. (1992). Diverse paths to literacy in a preschool classroom: A sociocultural perspective. *Reading Research Quarterly, 27*(3), 184–201.

Karmiloff, M., & Karmiloff-Smith, A. (2001). *Pathways to language: From fetus to adolescent.* Cambridge, MA: Harvard University Press.

Karnes, M., & Collins, D. (1997). Using cooperative learning strategies to improve literacy skills in social studies. *Reading & Writing Quarterly,* 13(1), 37–52.

Karrass, J., & Braungart-Rieker, J. (2005, March). Effects of shared parent–infant book reading on early language acquisition. *Journal of Applied Developmental Psychology: An International Lifespan Journal,* 26(2), 133–148.

Kassow, D. (2006). Parent–child shared book reading: Quality versus quantity of reading interactions between parents and young children. Seattle, WA: Talaris Research Institute. Retrieved 8/30/2006. http://www.talaris.org/test/research sharedbook.htm

Keats, E. (1962). *The Snowy Day.* New York: Viking.

Keats, E. (1999). *Over in the meadow.* New York: Penguin.

Kenney, S. (2005, Fall). Nursery rhymes: Foundation for learning. *General Music Today,* 19(1), 28–31.

Kirk, E., & Clark, P. (2005, Spring). Beginning with names: Using children's names to facilitate early literacy learning. *Childhood Education,* 81(3), 139–144.

Knipper, K., & Duggan, T. (2006). Writing to learn across the curriculum: Tools for comprehension in content area classes. *The Reading Teacher,* 59(5), 462–470.

Kragler, S., & Martin, L. (1998, January/February). Early book sharing: What teachers should know. *Reading Horizons,* 38(3), 163–169.

Kragler, S., Walker, C., & Martin, L. (2005). Strategy instruction in primary content textbooks. *The Reading Teacher,* 59(3), 254–261.

Krashen, S. (1981). *Second language acquisition and second language learning.* London: Pergamon Press.

Krashen, S. (1982). *Principles and practice in second language acquisition.* New York: Pergamon Press.

Krashen, S. (1995). Bilingual education and second language acquisition theory. In D. Durkin (Ed.), *Language issues: Readings for teachers* (pp. 90–115). White Plains, NY: Longman.

Krashen, S. (1997). Why bilingual education? ERIC Digest. ERIC ED 403101.

Krashen, S. (2002). Whole language and the great plummet of 1987–92. *Phi Delta Kappan,* 83(10), 748–753.

Krashen, S. (2003a). *Explorations in language acquisition and use.* Portsmouth, NH: Heinemann.

Krashen, S. (2003b). Three roles for reading for minority- language children. In G. Garcia (Ed.), *English learners: Reading the highest level of English literacy.* Newark, DE: International Reading Association.

Krashen, S. (2005, February). Is in-school free reading good for children? Why the National Reading Panel Report is (still) wrong. *Phi Delta Kappan,* 444–447.

Kuhn, M., & Morrow, L. (2005). Taking computers out of the corner: Making technology work for struggling intermediate-grade readers. In R. McCormack & J. Paratore (Eds.), *After early intervention, then what? Teaching struggling readers in grades 3 and beyond* (pp. 208–216). Upper Saddle River, NJ: Pearson Merrill Prentice Hall.

LaBerge, D., & Samuels, S. (1974). Toward a theory of automatic information processing in reading. *Cognitive Psychology, 6,* 293–323.

Labov, W. (2003). When ordinary children fail to read. *Reading Research Quarterly,* 38(1), 128–131.

Labov, W. (2004). Academic ignorance and Black intelligence. In O. Santa Ana (Ed.), *Tongue-tied: The lives of multilingual children in public education* (pp. 134–151). Lanham, MD: Rowman & Littlefield.

Laframboise, K. (2000). Said webs: Remedy for tired words. *The Reading Teacher, 53,* 540–546.

Laier, B., Edwards, P., McMillon, G., & Turner, J. (2001). Connecting home and school values through multi-cultural literature and family stories. In P. Schmidt & A. Pailliotet (Eds.), *Exploring values through literature, multimedia, and literacy events: Making connections* (pp. 64–75).

Newark, DE: International Reading Association.

Laminack, L., & Wadsworth, R. (2006). *Reading aloud across the curriculum.* Portsmouth, NH: Heinemann.

Lamme, L., & Packer, A. (1986). Bookreading behaviors of infants. *The Reading Teacher,* 39(6), 504–509.

Latham, A. (1998, November). The advantages of bilingualism. *Educational Leadership,* 56(3), 79–80.

Lazo, M., Pumfrey, P., & Peers, I. (1997). Metalinguistic awareness, reading and spelling: Roots and branches of literacy. *Journal of Research in Reading,* 20(2), 85–104.

Leal, D. (1993). The power of literary peer-group discussions: How children collaboratively negotiate meaning. *The Reading Teacher,* 47(2), 114–120.

Learning First Alliance (2000). *Every child reading: A professional development guide. A companion to every child reading: An Action Plan.* Washington, DC: Learning First Alliance.

Lee-Daniels, S., & Murray, B. (2000). DEAR me: What does it take to get children reading? *The Reading Teacher,* 54(2), 154–156.

Leeser, J. (1990). USSR and USA. *The Reading Teacher,* 43(6), 429.

LeFever-Davis, S., & Pearman, C. (2005). Early readers and electronic texts: CD-ROM storybook features that influence reading behaviors. *The Reading Teacher,* 58(5), 446–454.

Lenters, K. (2003). The many lives of the cut-up sentence. *The Reading Teacher,* 56(6), 535–536.

Lenters, K. (2004). No half measures: Reading instruction for young second-language learners. *The Reading Teacher,* 58(4), 328–336.

Lesiak, J. (2000). Research-based answers to questions about emergent literacy in kindergarten. In R. Robinson, M. McKenna, & J. Wedman (Eds.), *Issues and trends in literacy education* (2nd ed.) (pp. 213–236). Boston, MA: Allyn & Bacon.

Lewin, T. (1999). *Nilo and the tortoise.* New York: Scholastic.

Lin, C. (2001). Early literacy instruction: Research applications in the classroom. ERIC Digest. ED 459 424.

Lin, C. (2002). Literature circles. ERIC Digest. ED 469 925.

Liston, M. (1980). Early readers: Preschool children who learn to read at home. ERIC ED197297.

Literacy Partners of Manitoba. (1999). *Let's talk about literacy.* http://www.literacy.ca/litand/5.htm Retrieved 8/30/2006.

Lombardo, M. (2005, January). Rhythmic reading and role playing. *Library Media Connection,* 38–39.

Long, T., & Gove, M. (2003). How engagement strategies and literature circles promote critical response in a fourth-grade, urban classroom. *The Reading Teacher, 57*(4), 350–361.

Lopshire, R. (1988). *Put me in the zoo.* New York: Random House.

Loughner, S. (1993). A comparison of mothers' and fathers' verbal interactions with their children during picture-book reading. Unpublished manuscript. Evanston, IL: National Louis University.

Lu, M. Y. (1998). Language learning in social and cultural contexts. ERIC Digest. ED423531.

Lucas, T., Henze, R., & Donato, R. (2004). The best multilingual schools. In O. Santa Ana (Ed.), *Tongue-tied: The lives of multilingual children in public education* (pp. 201–213). Lanham, MD: Rowman & Littlefield.

Lujan, M., & Wooden, S. (1984). An exploration of environmental correlates of early childhood literacy. (ERIC Document Reproduction Service No. ED258696).

Lyons, C. (2003). *Teaching struggling readers: How to use brain-based research to maximize learning.* Portsmouth, NH: Heinemann.

Maclean, M., Bryant, P., & Bradley, L. (1987). Rhymes, nursery rhymes, and reading in early childhood. *Merrill-Palmer Quarterly, 333,* 255–281.

Magee, M., & Sutton-Smith, B. (1983, May). The art of storytelling: How do children learn it? *Young Children,* 4–12.

Makin, L. (2006, October). Literacy 8–12 months: What are babies learning? *Early Years: Journal of International Research & Development, 26*(3), 267–277.

Malo, E., & Bullard, J. (2000, July). Storytelling and the emergent reader. Paper presented at the International Reading Association World Congress on Reading, Auckland, New Zealand.

Mandell, P. (2000, July). CD-ROM: Language Arts. *School Library Journal, 46*(7), 57.

Mann, V., & Foy, J. (2003). Phonological awareness, speech development and letter knowledge in preschool children. *Annals of Dyslexia, 53,* 149–173.

Manning, M. (2005). Coaxing kids to read. *Teaching PreK–8, 35*(6), 80–81.

Manning, G., & Manning, M. (1989). *Whole language: Beliefs and practices, K–8.* Washington, DC: National Education Association.

Manning, M., & Manning, G. (1994). Teaching reading and writing: managing literacy portfolios. *Teaching PreK–8, 24*(7), 84–86.

Manning, M., & Underbakke, C. (2005). Spelling development research necessitates replacement of weekly word list. *Childhood Education, 81*(4), 236–238.

Manz, S. (2002). A strategy for previewing textbooks: Teaching readers to become THIEVES. *The Reading Teacher, 55*(5), 434–436.

Manzo, K. (2005). Dropouts identifiable by 6th grade factors. *Education Week, 24*(29), 9.

Marcell, B. (2006). Comprehension clinchers. *Teaching PreK–8, 36*(8), 66–67.

Marjanovič-Umek, L., Kranjc, S., & Fekonja, U. (2002). Developmental levels of the child's storytelling. Paper presented at the annual meeting of the European Early Childhood Education Research Association, Lefkosia, Cyprus.

Marjanovič-Umek, L., & Musek, P. (2001). Symbolic play: Opportunities for cognitive and language development in preschool settings. *Early Years, 21*(1), 55–64.

Marr, M. (1997). Cooperative learning: A brief review. *Reading & Writing Quarterly, 13*(1), 7–21.

Martens, P. (1999). "Mommy, how do you write 'Sarah'?": The role of name writing in one child's literacy. *Journal of Research in Childhood Education, 14*(1), 5–15.

Martin, B., Jr. (1992). *Polar bear, polar bear, what do you hear?* New York: Holt, Rinehart, & Winston.

Martin, B., Jr. (1996). *Brown bear, brown bear, what do you see?* New York: Holt, Rinehart, & Winston.

Martin, L., & Reutzel, D. R. (1999, Fall). Sharing books: Examining how and why mothers deviate from the print. *Reading Research Quarterly, 39*(1), 39–69.

Martinez, M., Roser, N., & Strecker, S. (1998/1999). "I never thought I could be a star": A Readers' Theater ticket to fluency. *The Reading Teacher, 52,* 326–334.

Mason, L., Snyder, K., & Kedem, D. (2006). TWA + PLANS Strategies for expository reading and writing: Effects for nine fourth-grade students. *Exceptional Children, 73*(1), 69–89.

Massey, D. (2003). A comprehension checklist: What if it doesn't make sense? *The Reading Teacher, 57*(1), 81–83.

Matson, B. (1996). Whole language or phonics? Teachers and researchers find the middle ground most fertile. The great reading debate. *Harvard Education Letter, 12*(2), 1–5.

Matz, K. (1994). 10 things they never taught us about spelling. *Education Digest, 59*(7), 70–72.

McCabe, A. (1992). All kinds of good stories. Paper presented at the Annual Meeting of the National Reading Conference, San Antonio, TX. ERIC ED 355474.

McCabe, A. (1997). Cultural background and storytelling: A review and implications for schooling. *The Elementary School Journal, 97*(5), 453–473.

McCaleb, S. (1994). *Building communities of learners: A collaboration among teachers, students, families and community.* Mahwah, NJ: Lawrence Erlbaum.

McDevitt, T., & Ormrod, J. (2004). *Child development: Educating and working with children and adolescents* (2nd ed.). Upper Saddle River, NJ: Pearson Merrill Prentice Hall.

McGee, L., & Richgels, D. (2000). *Literacy's beginnings: Supporting young readers and writers* (3rd ed.). Boston: Allyn & Bacon.

McIntyre, E. (1996). Strategies and skills in whole language: An introduction to balanced teaching. In E. McIntyre & M. Pressley (Eds.), *Balanced instruction: Strategies and skills in whole language* (pp. 1–20). Boston, MA: Christopher-Gordon.

McKechnie, L. (2006). Observations of babies and toddlers in library settings. *Library Trends, 55*(1), 190–201.

McNeill, J., & Fowler, S. (1996, Summer). Using story reading to encourage children's conversations. *Teaching Exceptional Children, 43–47.*

Menig-Peterson, C., & McCabe, A. (1977). Structure of children's narratives. Paper presented at the Biennial Meeting of the Society for Research in Child Development, New Orleans. ERIC ED 138 376.

Merkley, D., & Jefferies, D. (2000/2001). Guidelines for implementing a graphic organizer. *The Reading Teacher, 54*(4), 350–357.

Mesmer, H., & Griffith, P. (2005). Everybody's selling it—but just what is explicit, systematic phonics instruction? *The Reading Teacher, 59*(4), 366–376.

Meyerson, M., & Kulesza, D. (2006). *Strategies for struggling readers and writers: Step by step.* Upper Saddle River, NJ: Pearson Merrill Prentice Hall.

Miller, J., Heilmann, J., Nockerts, A., Iglesias, A., Fabiano, L., & Francis, D. (2006). Oral language and reading in bilingual children. *Learning Disabilities Research & Practice, 21*(1), 30–43.

Miller, M. (2001). *Peekaboo baby.* New York: Little Simon, Simon & Schuster.

Moats, L. (2000). Whole language lives on: The illusion of "balanced" reading instruction. Washington, DC: Thomas B. Fordham Foundation. ERIC ED449465.

Moerk, E. (1974). Changes in verbal child–mother interactions with increasing language skills of the child. *Journal of Psycholinguistic Research, 3*(2), 101–106.

Mohr, K. (2004). English as an accelerated language: A call to action for reading teachers. *The Reading Teacher, 581,* 18–26.

Moll, L., & González, N. (2004). Beginning where children are. In O. Santa Ana (Ed.), *Tongue-tied: The lives of multilingual children in public education* (pp. 152–156). Lanham, MD: Rowman & Littlefield.

Moncure, J. (2001). *My "B" sound box.* Chanhassen, MN: The Child's World, Inc. Wonder Books.

Morris, N. (1998). *Rivers and lakes.* New York: Crabtree.

Morrison, G. (2000). *Fundamentals of Early Childhood Education* (2nd ed.). Upper Saddle River, NJ: Merrill Prentice Hall.

Morrison, G. (2006). *Fundamentals of Early Childhood Education* (4th ed.). Upper Saddle River, NJ: Merrill Prentice Hall.

Morrow, L. (2001). *Literacy development in the early years: Helping children read and write* (4th ed.). Boston, MA: Allyn & Bacon.

Morrow, L., & Asbury, E. (1999). Best practices for a balanced early literacy program. In L. Gambrell, L. Morrow, S. Neuman, & M. Pressley (Eds.), *Best practices in literacy instruction* (pp. 49–67). New York: The Guilford Press.

Morrow, L., & Rand, M. (1991). Promoting literacy during play by designing early childhood classroom environments. *The Reading Teacher, 44*(6), 396–402.

Morrow, L., Kuhn, M., & Schwanenflugel, P. (2006). The family fluency program. *The Reading Teacher, 60*(4), 322–333.

Moss, B. (2004). Teaching expository text structures through information trade book retellings. *The Reading Teacher, 57*(8), 710–718.

Moss, B. (2005). Making a case and a place for effective content area literacy instruction in the elementary grades. *The Reading Teacher, 59*(1), 46–55.

Most, B. (1998). *A trio of triceratops.* San Diego, CA: Harcourt Brace & Company.

Mountain, L. (2005). ROOTing out meaning: More morphemic analysis for primary pupils. *The Reading Teacher, 58*(8), 742–749.

Muñoz, M., Gillam, R., Peña, E., & Gulley-Faehnle, A. (2003, October). Measures of language development in fictional narratives of Latino children. *Language, Speech, and Hearing Services in Schools, 34*(4), 332–342.

Murphy, C. (1978). Pointing in the context of a shared activity, *Child Development, 49,* 371–380.

Muth, D. (1997). Using cooperative learning to improve reading and writing in mathematical problem solving. *Reading & Writing Quarterly, 13*(1), 71–83.

National Association for the Education of Young Children (NAEYC) (1996, January). NAEYC position statement: Responding to linguistic and cultural diversity—recommendations for effective early childhood education. *Young Children,* 4–16.

National Association for the Education of Young Children (NAEYC). (1997). Developmentally appropriate practice in early childhood programs serving children from birth through age 8. In S. Bredekamp & C. Copple (eds.), *Developmentally appropriate practice in early childhood programs* (Rev. ed.) (pp. 3–30). Washington, DC: NAEYC.

National Association for the Education of Young Children (NAEYC). (1998). Learning to read and write: Developmentally appropriate practices for young children. *Young Children, 53*(4), 30–46.

National Council of Teachers of English (NCTE) & International Reading Association (IRA) (1996). *Standards for the English Language Arts.* Urbana, IL: NCTE and Newark, DE: IRA.

National Institute of Child Health and Human Development. (2000). *Report of the National Reading Panel: Teaching children to read: An evidence-based assessment of the scientific research literature on reading and its implications for reading instruction. Reports of the subgroups* (NIH Publication No. 00-4769). Washington, DC: U.S. Government Printing Office.

National Institute for Literacy. (2001). *Put reading first: The research building blocks for teaching children to read.* Jessup, MD: National Institute for Literacy.

National Institute for Literacy. (2006). Public Law 102–73, the National Literacy Act of 1991. Retrieved 2/21/2006. http://www.nifl.gov/public-law.html

National Reading Panel/NRP. (2000). *The report of the National Reading Panel: Teaching children to read.* Washington, DC: National Institute of Child Health and Human Development.

National Reading Panel (2006). About the National Reading Panel (NRP) and Charge to the National Reading Panel. http://www.nationalreadingpanel.org Retrieved January 27, 2006.

Nesbit, C., & Rogers, C. (1997). Using cooperative learning to improve reading and writing in science. *Reading & Writing Quarterly, 113*(1), 53–71.

Neuharth-Pritchett, S., Hamilton, C., & Schwanenflugel, P. (2005, Spring). Revisiting early literacy practices for pre-kindergarten children: Systematic strategies that promote preliteracy skills. *ACEI Focus on Pre-K & K, 17*(3), 1–7.

Neuman, J. (1985). Insights from recent reading and writing research and their implications for developing Whole Language curriculum. In J. Neuman (Ed.), *Whole language: Theory in use* (pp. 7–36). Portsmouth, NH: Heinemann.

Neuman, S. (1999). Books make a difference: A study of access to literacy. *Reading Research Quarterly, 34*(3), 286–311.

Neuman, S. (2004). Learning from poems and rhymes. *Scholastic Parent & Child, 12*(3), 32.

Neuman, S. (2006, January/February). Speak up! *Early Childhood Today, 20*(4), 12–13.

Neuman, S., & Celano, D. (2001). Access to print in low-income and middle-income communities: An ecological study of four neighborhoods. *Reading Research Quarterly, 36*(1), 8–26.

Neuman, S., & Celano, D. (2006). The knowledge gap: Implications of leveling the playing field for low-income and middle-income children. *Reading Research Quarterly, 4*(2), 176–201.

Neuman, S., & Roskos, K. (1990). Play, print, and purpose: Enriching play environments for literacy development. *The Reading Teacher, 44*(3), 214–221.

Neuman, S., & Roskos, K. (1992). Literacy objects as cultural tools: Effects on children's literacy behaviors in play. *Reading Research Quarterly, 27*(3), 202–225.

Neuman, S., & Roskos, K. (2005, July). Whatever happened to developmentally appropriate practice in early literacy? *Young Children, 60*(4), 22–26.

New York State Education Department (2005). *English language arts core curriculum: Prekindergarten–Grade 12.* Albany: The University of the State of New York & The State Education Department. http://www.emsc.nysed.gov/ciai/ela/elacore.htm

Nielson, D. (1996). Effects of literacy environment on literacy development of kindergarten children. *Journal of Educational Research, 89*(5), 259–272.

Ninio, A., (1980). Picture-book reading in mother–infant dyads belonging to two subgroups in Israel. *Child Development, 51,* 587–590.

Ninio, A., & Bruner, J. (1978). The achievement and antecedents of labeling. *Journal of Child Language, 5,* 1–15.

Nord, C., Lennon, J., Liu, B., & Chandler, K. (1999). Home literacy activities and signs of children's emerging literacy, 1993–1999. National Center for Education Statistics, U.S. Department of Education.

Notari, A. (1996). Preparing young children with disabilities for reading instruction: An investigation of effects of early instruction in phonemic awareness. Project Report HO23N20011, U.S. Department of Education. ERIC ED 461 194.

Notari-Syverson, A., O'Connor, R., & Vadasy, P. (1996). Facilitating language and literacy development in preschool children: To each according to their needs. Paper presented at the Annual American Educational Research Association Meeting, New York. ERIC ED 395 692.

Nourot, P., & Van Hoorn, J. (1991, September). Symbolic play in preschool and primary settings. *Young Children, 46*(6), 40–50.

Novick, R. (1999–2000, Winter). Supporting early literacy development: Doing things with words in the real world. *Childhood Education, 76*(2), 70–75.

Nurss, J. R., & McGauvran, M. (1986). *Metropolitan readiness tests* (5th ed.). San Antonio, TX: Psychological Corporation.

O'Donnell, M., & Wood, M. (2004). *Becoming a reader: A developmental approach to reading instruction* (3rd ed.). Boston: Allyn & Bacon.

O'Flahavan, J., & Seidl, B. (1997). Fostering literate communities in school: A case for sociocultural approaches to reading instruction. In S. Stahl & D. Hayes (Eds.), *Instructional models in reading* (pp. 203–220). Mahwah, NJ: Lawrence Erlbaum.

O'Mara, A. (1996). *Mountains.* Mankato, MN: Capstone Press.

Ogbu, J. (1999). Beyond language: Ebonics, proper English, and identify in a Black-American speech community. *American Educational Research Journal, 36*(2), 147–184.

Ogle, D. (1986). K-W-L: A teaching model that develops active reading of expository text. *The Reading Teacher, 39*(6), 564–570.

Ordoñez-Jasis, R., & Ortiz, R. (2006, January). Reading their worlds: Working with diverse families to enhance children's early literacy development. *Young Children,* 42–48.

Ortiz, R., & Ordoñez-Jasis, R. (2005). Leyendo juntos (reading together): New directions for Latino parents' early literacy involvement. *The Reading Teacher, 59*(2), 110–121.

Osborn, J., & Armbruster, B. (2001). Vocabulary acquisition: Direct teaching and indirect learning. In A. Poliakof, (Ed.), *Reading: Phonemic awareness, vocabulary acquisition, teaching and intervention* (pp. 11–15). Washington, DC: Council for Basic Education. ERIC ED 458 565.

Otto, B. (1979). A child's awareness of language. Unpublished manuscript. Evanston, IL: Northwestern University.

Otto, B. (1979–1982). Unpublished research notes. Evanston, IL: Northwestern University.

Otto, B. (1984). Evidence of emergent reading behaviors in young children's interactions with favorite storybooks. Unpublished dissertation. Evanston, IL: Northwestern University.

Otto, B. (1986–87). Unpublished research notes. Chicago, IL: Northeastern Illinois University.

Otto, B. (1990). Structural features in stories created by academically able young children. Paper presented at the National Reading Conference, Miami, FL.

Otto, B. (1991). Developmentally appropriate literacy goals for preschool and kindergarten classrooms. *Early Child Development and Care, 70,* 53–61.

Otto, B. (1994). Unpublished research notes. Chicago, IL: Northeastern Illinois University.

Otto, B. (1996, April). It's storytime: Reading together with infants and toddlers. Presented at the Annual Conference of the Midwest Association for the Education of Young Children, Lincoln, NE.

Otto, B. (1997, August). When does literacy acquisition begin? Taking a look at infants and toddlers. Presented at the 10th European Reading Conference, Brussels, Belgium.

Otto, B. (2002). *Language development in early childhood.* Upper Saddle River, NJ: Pearson Education.

Otto, B. (2006). *Language development in early childhood* (2nd ed.). Upper Saddle River, NJ: Pearson Education.

Otto, B., & Johnson, L. (1996, January). Let's read together: Parents and children in the preschool classroom. *Teaching PreK–8, 56*–57. ERIC ED 383 425.

Owens, R. (2005). *Language development: An introduction* (6th ed.). Boston, MA: Pearson Education.

Owocki, G. (1999). *Literacy through play.* Portsmouth, NH: Heinemann.

Owocki, G. (2001). *Make way for literacy! Teaching the way young children learn.* Portsmouth, NH: Heinemann.

Owocki, G., & Goodman, Y. (2002). *Kidwatching: Documenting children's literacy development.* Portsmouth, NH: Heinemann.

Palardy, J. (1991). Four "teachable" readiness skills. *Reading Improvement, 28*(1), 57–60.

Paley, V. (1981). *Wally's stories.* Cambridge, MA: Harvard University Press.

Paley, V. (1990). *The boy who would be a helicopter.* Cambridge, MA: Harvard University Press.

Paley, V. (1999). *The kindness of children.* Cambridge, MA: Harvard University Press.

Palmer, R., & Stewart, R. (2005). Models for using nonfiction in the primary grades. *The Reading Teacher, 58*(5), 426–434.

Pang, E., & Kamil, M. (2004). Second-language issues in early literacy and instruction. Publication Series No. 1. Stanford, CA: Stanford University.

Paratore, J. (2002). Designing reading instruction to optimize children's achievement. Boston, MA: Boston University. Retrieved 1/28/2007.

http://www.wera-web.org/links/Best Practice 2002.ppt

Paratore, J., DiBiasio, M., & Sullivan, K. (1993, December). Learning from home literacies: Inviting parents to contribute to literacy portfolios. Paper presented at the Annual Meeting of the National Reading Conference, Charleston, SC.

Pardo, L. (2004). What every teacher needs to know about comprehension. *The Reading Teacher, 58*(3), 272–280.

Parent, N. (2002). *The airplane trip.* Temple Terrace. FL: Paradise Press.

Paris, S., Lipson, M., & Wixson, K. (1994). Becoming a strategic reader. In R. Ruddell, M. Ruddell, & H. Singer (Eds.), *Theoretical models and processes of reading* (4th ed.) (pp. 788–811). Newark, DE: International Reading Association.

Parsons, M., & Stephenson, M. (2005). Developing reflective practice in student teachers: Collaboration and critical partnerships. *Teachers and Teaching, 11*(1), 95–116.

Partridge, H. (2004). Helping parents make the most of shared book reading. *Early Childhood Education Journal, 32*(1), 25–30.

Pasternicki, J. (1987). Paper for writing: Research and recommendations. In J. Alston & J. Taylor (Eds.), *Handwriting: Theory, research and practice* (pp. 68–80). New York: Nichols Publishing.

Patterson, J. (2002). Relationships of expressive vocabulary to frequency of reading and television experience among bilingual toddlers. *Applied Psycholinguistics, 23,* 493–508.

Paul, R. (1993, March). Language outcomes in late-talkers: Kindergarten. Paper presented at the Biennial Meeting of the Society for Research in Child Development, New Orleans, LA. ED 356 091.

Pearson, P. D. (2001). Life in the radical middle: A personal apology for a balanced view of reading. In R. Flippo (Ed.), *Reading researchers in search of common ground* (pp. 78–83). Newark, DE: International Reading Association.

Pearson, P. D., & Raphael, T. (1999). Toward an ecologically balanced literacy curriculum. In L. Gambrell, L. Morrow, S. Neuman, & M. Pressley (Eds.), *Best practices in literacy instruction* (pp. 22–33). New York: The Guilford Press.

Pearson, P. D., & Stephens, D. (1994). Learning about literacy: A 30-year journey. In R. Ruddell, M. Ruddell, & H. Singer (Eds.), *Theoretical models and processes of reading* (4th ed.) (pp. 22–42). Newark, DE: International Reading Association.

Perkins, J., & Cooter, R. (2005). Evidence-based literacy education and the African American child. *The Reading Teacher, 59*(2), 194–198.

Peterson, C., Jesso, B., & McCabe, A. (1999). Encouraging narratives in preschoolers: An intervention study. *Journal of Child Language, 26,* 49–67.

Peyton, J. (1993). Dialogue Journals: Interactive writing to develop language and literacy. Washington, DC: ERIC Clearinghouse on Languages and Linguistics. ED 354 789.

Phillips, J. (1990, November–December). Creating a disabled reader: A father's perspective. Paper presented at the Annual Meeting of the National Reading Conference, Miami, FL. ERIC ED 326 840.

Piaget, J. (1955). *The language and thought of the child.* New York: World.

Piaget, J. (1962). *Play, dreams and imitation in childhood.* New York: W.W. Norton.

Piazza, C. (2003). *Journeys: The teaching of writing in elementary classrooms.* Upper Saddle River, NJ: Pearson Merrill Prentice Hall.

Pikulski, J., & Chard, D. (2005). Fluency: Bridge between decoding and reading comprehension. *The Reading Teacher, 58*(6), 510–519.

Piper, T. (1998). *Language and learning: The home and school years* (2nd ed.). Upper Saddle River, NJ: Merrill Prentice Hall.

Potter, G. (1986). Early literacy development. *The Reading Teacher, 39*(7), 628–631.

Potter, C., & Haynes, W. (2000). The effects of genre on mother–toddler interaction during joint book reading. *Infant-Toddler Intervention: The Transdisciplinary Journal, 10*(2), 97–105.

Prelutsky, J., & Lobel, A. (2000). *The Random House book of poetry for children: A treasury of 572 poems for today's child.* New York: Random House.

Prelutsky, J., & Sis, P. (2006). *Scranimals.* New York: HarperCollins.

Pressley, M. (1998). *Reading instruction that works: The case for balanced teaching.* New York: Guilford.

Pressley, M. (1999). Self-regulated comprehension processing and its development through instruction. In L. Gambrell, L. Morrow, S. Neuman, & M. Pressley (Eds.), *Best practices in literacy instruction* (p. 997). New York: The Guilford Press.

Pressley, M., Roehrig, A., Bogner, K., Raphael, L., & Dolezal, S. (2002, January). Balanced literacy instruction. *Focus on Exceptional Children, 34*(5), 1–14.

Puckett, M., & Black, J. (2001). *The young child: Development from prebirth through age eight* (3rd ed.). Upper Saddle River, NJ: Merrill Prentice Hall.

Purcell-Gates, V. (1996). Stories, coupons, and the "TV Guide": Relationships between home literacy experiences and emergent literacy knowledge. *Reading Research Quarterly, 31*(4), 406–428.

Purcell-Gates, V. (2002). ". . . As soon as she opened her mouth!" In L. Delpit & J. Dowdy (Eds.), *The skin that we speak* (pp. 121–141). New York: The New Press.

Purcell-Gates, V., & Dahl, K. (1991). Low SES children's success and failure at early literacy learning in skills-based classrooms. *Journal of Reading Behavior, 23*(1), 1–34.

Purcell-Gates, V., L'Allier, S., & Smith, D. (1995). Literacy at the Arts' and the Larsons': Diversity among poor, innercity families. *The Reading Teacher, 48*(7), 572–578.

Ramos-Sánchez, J., & Cuadardo-Gordillo, I. (2004). Influence of spoken language on the initial acquisition of reading/writing: Critical analysis of verbal deficit theory. *Reading Psychology, 25,* 149–165.

Rasinski, T. (2000). Speed does matter in reading. *The Reading Teacher, 54*(2), 146–152.

Rasinski, T. (2003). Parental involvement: Key to leaving no child behind in reading. *The New England Reading Association Journal, 39*(3), 1–5.

Rasinski, T., & Padak, N. (2004). *Effective reading strategies: Teaching children who find reading difficult* (3rd ed.). Upper Saddle River, NJ: Pearson Merrill Prentice Hall.

Rasinski, T., Padak, N., Linek, W., & Sturtevant, E. (1994). Effects of fluency development on urban second-grade readers. *Journal of Educational Research, 87,* 158–165.

Raver, S. (2006, Summer). Using embedded learning opportunities during cooking for preschoolers with special needs. *ACEI Focus on Inclusive Education, 3*(4), 1–6.

Read, C. (1978). Children's awareness of language, with emphasis on sound systems. In A. Sinclair, R. Jarvella, & W. Levelt (Eds.), *The child's conception of language* (pp. 65–82). New York: Springer-Verlag.

Reading Recovery Council of North America (2007). What is Reading Recovery? Washington, OH: Reading Recovery Council of North America. Retrieved 1/29/2007. http://www.readingrecovery.org/sections/reading/index.asp

Reich, P. (1986). *Language development.* Upper Saddle River, NJ: Prentice Hall.

Reimer, M., & Smink, J. (2005). *Information about the school dropout issue: Selected facts & statistics.* National Dropout Prevention Center/Network. Retrieved 1/30/2006. http://www.dropoutprevention.org/stats/

Reit, S. (1991). *Take a ride with Mickey.* New York: Disney Press.

Reutzel, D. R., & Cooter, R. (2004). *Teaching children to read: Putting the pieces together* (4th ed.). Upper Saddle River, NJ: Pearson Merrill Prentice Hall.

Reutzel, D. R., & Cooter, R. (2005). The essentials of teaching children to read: What every teacher needs to know. Upper Saddle River, NJ: Pearson Merrill Prentice Hall.

Reutzel, D. R., & Fawson, P. (2002). Changing the face of reading instruction: Recommendations of six national reading reports. *Reading Horizons, 42*(4), 235–70.

Reyes, M. de la L. (1995). A process approach to literacy using dialogue journals and literature logs with second-language learners. In O. Garcia & C. Baker (Eds.), *Policy and practice in bilingual education: A reader extending the foundations. Bilingual Education and Bilingualism 2 Series.* Bristol, PA: Multilingual Matters, Ltd. ERIC ED 384251.

Risko, V., Roskos, K., & Vukelich, C. (2002, Winter). Prospective teachers' reflection: Strategies, qualities, and perceptions in learning to teach reading. *Reading Research and Instruction, 41*(2), 149–175.

Roberts, R. (1998). "I no evrethenge": What skills are essential in early literacy? In S. Neuman & K. Roskos (Eds.), *Children achieving: Best practices in early literacy* (pp. 38–55). Newark, DE: International Reading Association.

Roberts, J., Jurgens, J., & Burchinal, M. (2005). The role of home literacy practices in preschool children's language and emergent literacy skills. *Journal of Speech, Language and Hearing Research, 48*(2), 345–359.

Rocklin, J. (2000). Inside the mind of the child: Selecting literature appropriate to the developmental age of children. *Yearbook of the Claremont Reading Conference,* pp. 110–122. Claremont, CA: Claremont Graduate University.

Rog, L., & Burton, W. (2002). Matching texts and readers: Leveling early reading materials for assessment and instruction. *The Reading Teacher, 55*(4), 348–356.

Roller, C. (1996). *Variability not disability: Struggling readers in a workshop classroom.* Newark, DE: International Reading Association.

Roller, C. (2002). Afterword. In C. Roller (Ed.), *Comprehensive reading instruction across the grade levels: A collection of papers from the Reading Research 2001 Conference* (pp. 161–165). Newark, DE: International Reading Association.

Roney, C. (1996, Winter/Spring). Storytelling in the classroom: Some theoretical thoughts. *Storytelling World, 9,* 7–9.

Roopnarine, J., & Johnson, J. (2005). *Approaches to early childhood education.* Upper Saddle River, NJ: Pearson Merrill Prentice Hall.

Rosenblatt, L. (1978). *The reader, the text, the poem: The transactional theory of the literacy work.* Carbondale, IL: Southern Illinois University.

Rosenblatt, L. (1983). *Literature as exploration* (4th ed.). New York: Modern Language Association. (Original work published in 1938).

Rosenblatt, L. (1994). The transactional theory of reading and writing. In R. Ruddell & N. Unrau (Eds.), *Theoretical models and processes of reading* (5th ed.) (pp. 1363–1398). Newark, DE: International Reading Association.

Rosenquest, B. (2002, Summer). Literacy-based planning and pedagogy that supports toddler language development. *Early Childhood Education Journal, 29*(4), 241–249.

Roskos, K., & Christie, J. (2001, May). On not pushing too hard: A few cautionary remarks about linking literacy and play. *Young Children,* 64–66.

Roskos, K., & Neuman, S. (2002). Environment and its influences for early literacy teaching and learning. In S. Neuman & D. Dickinson (Eds.), *Handbook of early literacy research* (pp. 281–292). New York: The Guilford Press.

Roskos, K., Christie, J., & Richgels, D. (2003, March). The essentials of early literacy instruction. *Young Children,* 52–62.

Roth, F., Speece, D. & Cooper, D. (2002). A longitudinal analysis of the connection between oral language and early reading. *Journal of Educational Research, 95*(5), 259–273.

Routman, R. (1991). *Invitations: Changing as teachers and learners K–12.* Portsmouth, NH: Heinemann.

Routman, R. (2003). *Reading essentials: The specifics you need to teach reading well.* Portsmouth, NH: Heinemann.

Rowe, D. (1998). The literate potentials of book-related dramatic play. *Reading Research Quarterly, 33*(1), 10–35.

Rowe, D., & Harste, J. (1986). Metalinguistic awareness in writing and reading: The young child as curricular informant. In D. Yaden & S. Templeton (Eds.), *Metalinguistic awareness and beginning literacy* (pp. 235–256). Portsmouth, NH: Heinemann.

Rubin, R., & Carlan, V. (2005). Using writing to understand bilingual children's literacy development. *The Reading Teacher, 58*(8), 728–739.

Rubinstein-Avila, E. (2006, February). Connecting with Latino learners. *Educational Leadership, 63*(5), 38–43.

Ruddell, M. (1994). Vocabulary knowledge and comprehension: A comprehension-process view of complex literacy relationships. In R. Ruddell, M. Ruddell, & H. Singer (Eds.), *Theoretical models and processes of reading* (4th ed.) (pp. 414–447). Newark, DE: International Reading Association.

Ruddell, M. & Unrau, N. (2004). Reading as a meaning-construction process: The reader, the text, and the teacher. In R. Ruddell & N. Unrau (Eds.), *Theoretical models and processes of reading* (5th ed.) (pp. 1462–1523). Newark, DE: International Reading Association.

Ruddell, R., & Speaker, R. (1985). The interactive reading process: A model. In H. Singer & R. Ruddell (Eds.), *Theoretical models and processes of reading* (3rd ed.) (pp. 751–793). Newark, DE: International Reading Association.

Rumelhart, D. (1985). Toward an interactive model of reading.

In H. Singer & R. Ruddell (Eds.), *Theoretical models and processes of reading* (3rd ed.) (pp. 864–894). Newark, DE: International Reading Association.

Rumelhart, D. (1994). Toward an interactive model of reading. In R. Ruddell, M. Ruddell, & H. Singer, (Eds.), *Theoretical models and processes of reading* (4th ed.) (pp. 864–894). Newark, DE: International Reading Association.

Rupley, W., Logan, J., & Nichols, W. (1998/1999). Vocabulary instruction in a balanced reading program. *The Reading Teacher, 52*, 336–346.

Rush, K. (1999). Caregiver-child interactions and early literacy development of preschool children from low-income environments. *Topics in Early Childhood Special Education, 19*(1), 3–14.

Rybczynski, M., & Troy, A. (1995). Literacy-enriched play centers: Trying them out in "the real world." *Childhood Education, 72*(1), 7–12.

Rycik, M., & Rycik, J. (2007). *Phonics and word identification: Instruction and intervention, K–8.* Upper Saddle River, NJ: Pearson Merrill Prentice Hall.

Sachs, J. (1989). Communication development in infancy. In J. Berko Gleason (Ed.), *The development of language* (2nd ed.) (pp. 35–58). Upper Saddle River, NJ: Merrill/Prentice Hall.

Salinger, T. (2003). Helping older, struggling readers. *Preventing School Failure, 47*(2), 79–85.

Samuels, J. (1997). The method of repeated readings. *The Reading Teacher, 50*(6), 376–381.

Sanacore, J. (2004). Genuine caring and literacy learning fro African American children. *The Reading Teacher, 57*(8), 744–753.

Sanacore, J. (2006, Fall). Nurturing lifetime readers. *Childhood Education, 83*(1), 33–37.

Santa Ana, O. (2004). Introduction: The unspoken issue that silences Americans. In O. Santa Ana (Ed.), *Tongue-tied: The lives of multilingual children in public education* (pp. 1–8). Lanham, MD: Rowman & Littlefield.

Santos, R., & Ostrosky, M. (2002). Understanding the impact of language differences on classroom behavior. ERIC ED 481 990.

Santrock, J. (2001). *Child development.* Boston: McGraw Hill.

Saracho, O. (2001). Exploring young children's literacy development through play. *Early Child Development and Care, 167*, 103–114.

Saracho, O., & Spodek, B. (1995). Preparing teachers for early childhood programs of linguistic and cultural diversity. In E. Garcia & B. McLaughlin (Eds.), *Meeting the challenge of linguistic and cultural diversity in early childhood education.* New York: Teachers College Press.

Savin, H. (1972). What the child knows about speech when he starts to learn to read. In J. Kavanagh & I. Mattingly (Eds.), *Language by ear and by eye* (pp. 319–326). Cambridge, MA: The MIT Press.

Scala, M. (2001). *Working together: Reading and writing in inclusive classrooms.* Newark, DE: International Reading Association.

Scarry, R. (1972). *Hop aboard, here we go!* Racine, WI: Western Publishing.

Scarry, R. (1991). *Richard Scarry's best word book ever.* New York: Western Publishing.

Schickedanz, J. (1981, November). "Hey! This book's not working right." *Young Children*, 18–27.

Schickedanz, J. (1986). More than the ABCs: The early stages of reading and writting. Washington, DC: National Association for the Education of Young Children.

SchifferDanoff, V. (2001). *Beyond the morning message.* New York: Scholastic.

Schlagal, B. (2002). Classroom spelling instruction: History, research, and practice. *Reading Research and Instruction, 42*(1), 44–57.

Schön, D. (1983). *The reflective practitioner: How professionals think in action.* New York: HarperCollins Basic Books.

Schrock, K. (2001, March/April). LeapPad. *Library Talk, 14*(2), 35.

Schwartz, J. (1981, July). Children's experiments with language. *Young Children, 36*(5), 16–26.

Schwartz, R. (2005). Decisions, decisions: Responding to primary students during guided reading. *The Reading Teacher, 58*(5), 436–443.

Schwartz, W. (1996). School dropouts: New information about an old problem. ERIC Digest. Retrieved 1/30/2006. http://www.ericdigests.org/1996-2/dropouts.html

Scott, J. (1995). The King case: Implications for educators. In D. Durkiin (Ed.), *Language issues: Readings for teachers.* (pp. 273–280). White Plains, NY: Longman.

Self, T. (1985). Dropouts: A review of literature. Project Talent Search. Monroe: Northeast Louisiana University. ERIC ED 260 307.

Selman, R. (2001, May). Talk time: Programming communicative interaction into the toddler day. *Young Children*, 15–18.

Sendak, M. (1963). *Where the wild things are.* New York: Harper & Row.

Sénéchal, M. (1997). The differential effect of storybook reading on preschoolers' acquisition of expressive and receptive vocabulary. *Journal of Child Language, 24*, 123–138.

Sénéchal, M., Cornell, E., & Broda, L. (1995). Age-related differences in the organization of parent–infant interactions during picture-book reading. *Early Childhood Research Quarterly, 10*(3), 317–337.

Sénéchal, M., LeFevre, J., Hudson, E., & Lawson, E. (1996). Knowledge of storybooks as a predictor of young children's vocabulary. *Journal of Educational Psychology, 88*(3), 520–539.

Sénéchal, M., Thomas, E., & Monker, J. (1995). Individual differences in 4-year-old children's acquisition of vocabulary during storybook reading. *Journal of Educational Psychology, 87*(2), 218–229.

Sensenbaugh, R. (1996). Phonemic awareness: An important early step in learning to read. ERIC Digest. ED 400 530.

Serafini, F. (2003). Enlarging our vision of balanced reading. *Arizona State Reading Journal, 29*(2), 18–23.

Seuss, Dr. (Geisel, T.) (1957). *The cat in the hat.* New York: Random House.

Seuss, Dr. (Geisel, T.) (1958). *The cat in the hat comes back.* New York: Random House.

Seuss, Dr. (Geisel, T.) (1960). *Green eggs and ham.* New York: Random House.

Seuss, Dr. (Geisel, T.) (1963). *Dr. Seuss's ABC.* New York: Random House.

Seuss, Dr. (Geisel, T.) (1974, 1996). *There's a wocket in my pocket: Dr. Seuss's book of ridiculous rhymes.* New York: Random House.

Shanahan, T., & Shanahan, S. (1997). Character perspective charting: Helping children to develop a more complete conception of story. *The Reading Teacher, 50*(1), 668–677.

Sharif, I., Ozuah, P., Dinkevich, E., & Mulvihill, M. (2003). Impact of a brief literacy intervention on urban preschoolers. *Early Childhood Education Journal, 30*(3), 177–180.

Shatz, M. (1994). *A toddler's life: Becoming a person.* New York: Oxford University Press.

Sherwood, I. (2005). The early years. *Science and Children, 43*(3), 20–23.

Shiro, M. (1995). Focus on research: Venezuelan preschoolers' oral narrative abilities. *Language Arts, 72*(7), 528–537.

Silva, C., & Martens, M. (2003). Relations between children's invented spelling and the development of phonological awareness. *Educational Psychology, 23*(1), 3–16.

Silverstein, S. (1981). *A light in the attic.* New York: Harper and Row.

Silverstein, S. (2004). *Where the sidewalk ends.* 30th Anniversary Special Edition. New York: HarperCollins.

Sinclair, A., & Golan, M. (2002). Emergent literacy: A case-study of a two-year-old. *Early Child Development and Care, 172,* 555–572.

Skinner, B. (1974). *About behaviorism.* New York: Knopf.

Slavin, R. (1991). Synthesis of research on cooperative learning. *Educational Leadership, 48*(5), 71–81.

Smallwood, B. (2002). Thematic literature and curriculum for English language learners in early childhood education. ERIC Digest. ED 470 980.

Smith, C. (2003). Oral language and the second language learner. ERIC Research Summary. ED 482 403.

Smith, F. (1988). *Understanding reading* (4th ed.). Hillsdale, NJ: Lawrence Erlbaum.

Smith, F. (1997). *Reading without nonsense* (3rd ed.). New York: Teachers College Press.

Smullin, M. (1989). Working and playing with literacy. In L. Bird (Ed.), *Becoming a whole language school: The Fair Oaks story* (pp. 64–78). Katonah, NY: Richard C. Owen.

Snow, C. (1983). Literacy and language: Relationships during the preschool years. *Harvard Educational Review, 53*(2), 165–189.

Snow, C., Burns, M., & Griffin, P. (1998). *Preventing reading difficulties in young children.* Washington, DC: National Academy Press.

Soundy, C. (1997, Spring). Nurturing literacy with infants and toddlers in group settings. *Childhood Education, 73,* 149–153.

Sowers, S. (1988). Reflect, expand, select: Three responses in the writing conference. In T. Newkirk & N. Atwell (Eds.), *Understanding writing: Ways of observing, learning and teaching K-8* (2nd ed.) (pp. 130–141). Portsmouth, NH: Heinemann.

Speaker, K., Taylor, D., & Kamen, R. (2004). Storytelling: Enhancing language acquisition in young children. *Education, 125*(1), 3–14.

Spiegel, D. (1999). The perspective of the Balanced Approach. In S. Blair-Larsen & K. Williams (Eds.), *The balanced reading program: Helping all students achieve success* (pp. 8–23). Newark, DE: International Reading Association.

Stadler, M., & Ward, G. (2005, October). Supporting the narrative development of young children. *Early Childhood Education Journal, 33*(2), 73–80.

Stahl, K. (2004). Proof, practice, and promise: Comprehension strategy instruction in the primary grades. *The Reading Teacher, 57*(7), 598–609.

Stahl, S., Duffy-Hester, A., & Stahl, K. (1998). Everything you wanted to know about phonics (but were afraid to ask). *Reading Research Quarterly, 33*(3), 338–355.

Stanchfield, J. (1972, May). Success in first-grade reading. Paper presented at the Annual Convention of the International Reading Association, Detroit, MI. ERIC ED 063 600.

Stanfield, G. (2006). Incentives: The effects on reading attitude and reading behaviors of third-grade students. ERIC ED 494 453.

Stanovich, K. (1993–1994). Romance and reality. *The Reading Teacher, 47*(4), 280–291.

Stauffer, R. (1980). *The language-experience approach to the teaching of reading* (2nd ed.). New York: Harper & Row.

Stevenson, C. (2006). The rules of reading: How to engage baby and toddler. Retrieved 5/11/2006. http://babiestoday.com/articles/2229.php?wcat=12.

Stewart, J., & Mason, J. (1989). Pre-school children's reading and writing awareness. In J. Mason (Ed.), *Reading and writing connections* (pp. 219–236). Boston: Allyn & Bacon.

Stice, C., & Bertrand, N. (1990). Whole language and the emergent literacy of at-risk children: A two-year comparative study. Nashville: Tennessee State University-Nashville. Center of Excellence: Basic Skills. ERIC ED 324 636.

Stoel-Gammon, C. (1998). Role of babbling and phonology in early linguistic development. In A. Wetherby, S. Warren, & J. Reichle (Eds.), *Transitions in prelinguistic communication.* Baltimore: Paul H. Brookes.

Storch, S., & Whitehurst, G. (2001, Summer). The role of family and home in the literacy development of children from low-income backgrounds. *New Directions for Child and Adolescent Development, 92,* pp. 53–71.

Straub, S. (1999, January). Books for babies: An overlooked resource for working with new families. *Infants and Young Children, 11*(3), 79–88.

Strickland, D. (1996). In search of balance: Restructuring our literacy programs. In J. Johns & L. Elish-Piper (Eds.), *Balanced reading instruction: Teachers' visions and voices* (pp. 1–6). Dubuque, IA: Kendall/Hunt.

Strickland, D. (2002). Early intervention for African American children considered to be at risk. In S. Neuman & D. Dickinson (Eds.), *Handbook of early literacy research* (pp. 322–323). New York: The Guilford Press.

Strickland, D. (2004, September). Working with families as partners in early literacy. *The Reading Teacher, 58*(1), 86–88.

Strickland, D., & Riley-Ayers, S. (2006). *Early literacy: Policy and practice in the preschool years.* Preschool Policy Brief. New Brunswick, NJ: National Institute for Early Education Research.

Strommen, L., & Mates, B. (1997, October). What readers do: Young children's ideas about the nature of reading. *The Reading Teacher, 51*(2), 98–107.

Sulzby, E. (1985). Children's emergent reading of favorite storybooks: A developmental study. *Reading Research Quarterly, 20,* 458–481.

Sulzby, E. (1986). Writing and reading: Signs of oral and written language organization in the young child. In W. Teale & E. Sulzby (Eds.), *Emergent literacy: Writing and reading* (pp. 50–89). Norwood, NJ: Ablex.

Sulzby, E. (1991, March). Assessment of emergent literacy: Storybook reading. *The Reading Teacher, 44*(7), 498–500.

Sulzby, E. (1994). Children's emergent reading of favorite storybooks: A developmental study. In R. Ruddell, M. Ruddell, & H. Singer (Eds.), *Theoretical models and processes of reading* (4th ed.) (pp. 244–280). Newark, DE: International Reading Association.

Sulzby, E., Barnhart, J., & Hieshima, J. (1989). Forms of writing and rereading from writing: A preliminary report. In J. Mason (Ed.), *Reading and writing connections* (pp. 31–64). Boston, MA: Allyn & Bacon.

Swick, K., & Williams, R. (2006). An analysis of Bronfenbrenner's bio-ecological perspective for early childhood educators: Implications for working with families experiencing stress. *Early Childhood Education Journal, 33*(5), 371–378.

Taback, S. (2004). *This is the house that Jack built.* New York: Scholastic.

Taberski, S. (1998). What's your role during independent reading? *Instructor-Primary, 107*(5), 32–35.

Tabors, P. (1997). *One child, two languages: A guide for preschool educators of children learning English as a second language.* Baltimore, MD: Paul H. Brookes.

Tabors, P., & Snow, C. (2002). Young bilingual children and early literacy development. In S. Newman & D. Dickinson (Eds.), *Handbook of early literacy research* (pp. 159–178). New York: The Guilford Press.

Tabors, P., Snow, C., & Dickinson, D. (2001). Homes and schools together: Supporting language and literacy development. In D. Dickinson & P. Tabors (Eds.), *Beginning literacy with language: Young children learning at home and school* (pp. 313–334). Baltimore, MD: Paul H. Brookes.

Tager-Flusberg, H. (1997). Putting words together: Mophology and syntax in the preschool years. In J. Berko Gleason (Ed.), *The development of language* (4th ed.). Boston: Allyn & Bacon.

Taylor, B., Harris, L., Pearson, P. D., & Garcia, G. (1995). *Reading difficulties: Instruction and assessment.* New York: McGraw Hill.

Taylor, D. (1983). *Family literacy: Young children learning to read and write.* Portsmouth, NH: Heinemann.

Taylor, D., & Dorsey-Gaines, C. (1988). *Growing up: Learning from inner-city families.* Portsmouth, NH: Heinemann.

Teale, W. (1986). Home background and young children's literacy development. In W. Teale & E. Sulzby (Eds.), *Emergent literacy: Writing and reading* (pp. 173–206). Norwood, NJ: Ablex.

Teale, W., & Sulzby, E. (1986). Introduction: Emergent literacy as a perspective

for examining how young children become writers and readers. In W. Teale & E. Sulzby (Eds.), *Emergent literacy: Writing and reading* (pp. vii–xxv). Norwood, NJ: Ablex.

Temple, C., Nathan, R., Temple, F., & Burris, N. (1993). *The beginnings of writing* (3rd ed.). Boston, MA: Allyn & Bacon.

Templeton, S. (1991). Teaching and learning the English spelling system: Reconceptualizing method and purpose. *The Elementary School Journal, 922,* 185–201.

Texas Education Agency. (2006). Chapter 110. Texas essential knowledge and skills for English language arts and reading, Subchapter A. Elementary. Austin: Texas Education Agency. Retrieved 11/8/2006. http://www.tea.state.tx.us/rules/tac/chapter110/ch110a.html

The Early Years. (2005, November/December). Resources and conversation on PreK to 2 Science, *The Early Years, 43*(3), 20–23.

Throne, J. (1988). Becoming a kindergarten of readers? *Young Children, 43*(6), 10–16.

Thurber, D. (1984). *D'Nealian manuscript: A continuous stroke approach to handwriting.* Novato, CA: Academic Therapy Publications.

Tiedt, I. (2002). *Tiger lilies, toadstools, and thunderbolts: Engaging K–8 students with poetry.* Newark, DE: International Reading Association.

Tierney, R., & Thome, C. (2006). Is DIBELS leading us down the wrong path? In K. Goodman (Ed.), *The truth about DIBELS: What it is, What it does* (pp. 50–59). Portsmouth, NH: Heinemann.

Tindall, E., & Nisbet, D. (2004, Summer). Second language learners: Wellsprings of learning for teachers. *Kappa Delta Pi Record,* 170–174.

Tompkins, G. (2003). *Teaching reading and writing in pre-kindergarten through grade 4.* Upper Saddle River, NJ: Merrill Prentice Hall.

Tompkins, G. (2004). *Teaching writing: Balancing process and product* (4th ed).

Upper Saddle River, NJ: Pearson Merrill Prentice Hall.

Tompkins, G. (2005). *Language arts: Patterns of practice* (6th ed.). Upper Saddle River, NJ: Pearson Merrill Prentice Hall.

Tompkins, G. (2006a). *Literacy for the 21st century: A balanced approach* (4th ed.). Upper Saddle River, NJ: Pearson Merrill Prentice Hall.

Tompkins, G. (2006b). *Language arts essentials.* Upper Saddle River, NJ: Pearson Merrill Prentice Hall.

Tompkins, G. (2007). *Literacy for the 21st century: Teaching reading and writing in prekindergarten through grade 4.* Upper Saddle River, NJ: Pearson Merrill Prentice Hall.

Tompkins, G., & Collom, S. (2004). *Sharing the pen: Interactive writing with young children.* Upper Saddle River, NJ: Pearson Merrill Prentice Hall.

Trawick-Smith, J. (2003). *Early childhood development: A multicultural perspective* (3rd ed.). Upper Saddle River, NJ: Merrill Prentice Hall.

Trawick-Smith, J. (2006). *Early childhood development: A multicultural perspective* (4th ed.). Upper Saddle River, NJ: Merrill Prentice Hall.

Ukrainetz, T., Cooney, M., Dyer, S., Kysar, A., & Harris, R. (2000). An investigation into teaching phonemic awareness through shared reading and writing. *Early Childhood Research Quarterly, 15*(3), 331–355.

Ulmen, M. (2005, November). Hey! Somebody read to me! Ten easy ways to include reading every day. *Young Children,* 96–97.

U.S. Department of Education. (2001a). Executive Summary of the No Child Left Behind Act of 2001. http://www.ed.gov/print/nclb/overview/intro/execsumm.html Retrieved January 27, 2006.

U.S. Department of Education. (2001b). Fact sheet on No Child Left Behind Act of 2001. http://www.ed.gov/print/nclb/overview/intro/factsheet.html Retrieved January 27, 2006.

U.S. Department of Education. (2006). National assessment of adult literacy.

Retrieved 4/1/2007. http://nces.ed.gov/NAAL/index.asp?file=KeyFindings/Demographics/Overall.asp&PageId=16

Valdes, G. (1998). The world outside and inside schools: language and immigrant children. *Educational Researcher, 27*(6), 4–18.

Valencia, R., & Solórzano, D. (2004). Today's deficit thinking about the education of minority students. In O. Santa Ana (Ed.), *Tongue-tied: The lives of multilingual children in public education* (pp. 124–133). Lanham, MD: Rowman & Littlefield.

Valencia, S. (1990). A portfolio approach to classroom reading assessment: The whys, whats, and hows. *The Reading Teacher, 43*(4), 338–340.

Vardell, S., Hadaway, N., & Young, T. (2006). Matching books and readers: Selecting literature for English learners. *The Reading Teacher, 59*(8), 734–741.

Vanderslice, R. (2004, Fall). Risky business: Leaving the at-risk child behind. *The Delta Kappa Gamma Bulletin,* 15–21.

Vernon-Feagans, L., Hammer, C., Miccio, A., & Manlove, E. (2002). Early language and literacy skills in low-income African American and Hispanic children. In S. Neuman & D. Dickinson (Eds.), *Handbook of early literacy research* (pp. 192–210). New York: The Guilford Press.

Vukelich, C. (1990, Summer). Where's the paper? Literacy during dramatic play. *Childhood Education,* 205–209.

Vygotsky, L. (1976). Play and its role in the mental development of the child. In J. Bruner, A. Joy, & K. Sylva (Eds.), *Play: Its role in development and evolution.* New York: Basic Books.

Vygotsky, L. (1978). *Mind in society: The development of higher psychological processes* (M. Cole, V. John-Steiner, S. Scribner, & E. Souberman, Eds.). Cambridge, MA: Harvard University Press.

Vygotsky, L. (1981). The genesis of higher mental functions. In J. Wertsch (Ed.), *The concept of activity in Soviet psychology* (pp. 144–188). Armonk, NY: Sharpe.

Vygotsky, L. (1986). *Thought and language* (A. Kozulin, Ed.). Cambridge, MA: MIT Press.

Wade, L. (1995). *Organic chemistry* (3rd ed.). Upper Saddle River, NJ: Prentice Hall.

Walker, C., Kragler, S., Martin, L., & Arnett, A. (2003, Spring). Facilitating the use of informational texts in a 1st grade classroom. *Childhood Education,* 152–159.

Walker, D., Greenwood, C., Hart, B., & Carta, J. (1994). Prediction of school outcomes based on early language production and socioeconomic factors. *Child Development, 65,* 606–621.

Walsh, R., & Blewitt, P. (2006). The effect of questioning style during storybook reading on novel vocabulary acquisition of preschoolers. *Early Childhood Education Journal, 33*(4), 273–278.

Walshe, R. (1981). *Donald Graves in Australia—"Children want to write . . ."* Rozelle, NSW, Australia: Primary English Teaching Association.

Walton, S. (1989, July). Katy learns to read and write. *Young Children, 44*(5), 52–57.

Wang, M., & Cameron, C. (1996). Children's narrative expression over the telephone. Paper presented at the Biennial Meeting of the International Society for the Study of Behavioral Development, Quebec, Canada. ERIC ED 400959.

Watson, J. (1924). *Behaviorism.* New York: Norton.

Weaver, C. (2000). The basalization of America: A cause for concern. In R. Robinson, M. McKenna, & J. Wedman (Eds.), *Issues and trends in literacy education* (2nd ed.) (pp. 165–174).

Weaver, C. (2002). *Reading process & practice* (3rd ed.). Portsmouth, NH: Heinemann.

Weigel, D., Martin, S., & Bennett, K. (2005). Ecological influences of the home and the child-care center on preschool-age children's literacy development. *Reading Research Quarterly, 40*(2), 204–233.

Weitzman, E., & Greenberg, J. (2002). *Learning language and loving it: A guide to promoting children's social, language, and literacy development in early childhood settings* (2nd ed.). Toronto: The Hanen Centre.

Wells, G. (1986). *The meaning makers: Children learning language and using language to learn.* Portsmouth, NH: Heinemann.

Werner, H., & Kaplan, B. (1963). *Symbol formation: An organisimic approach to language and the expression of thought.* New York: Wiley.

White, T. (2005). Effects of systematic and strategic analogy-based phonics on grade 2 students' word reading and reading comprehension. *Reading Research Quarterly, 40*(2), 234–255.

Whitehurst, G., & Lonigan, C. (2002). Emergent literacy: Development from prereaders to readers. In S. Neuman & D. Dickinson (Eds.), *Handbook of early literacy research* (pp. 11–29). New York: The Guilford Press.

Whitehurst, G., Falco, F., Lonigan, C., Fischel, J., DeBaryshe, D., Valdez-Menchaca, M., & Caulfield, M. (1988). Accelerating language development through picture book reading. *Developmental Psychology, 24*(4), 552–559.

Wildsmith, B. (1987). *Cat on the mat.* Cambridge, MA: Oxford University Press.

Wilhelm, J. (1999). Think-alouds boost reading comprehension. *Instructor, 111*(4), 26–28.

Wilkinson, C., & Spinelli, F. (1981). Peers' requests and responses in third-grade reading groups. Madison: Wisconsin Center for Education Research. ERIC ED 214 119.

Wiley, B. (1999). Interactive writing: The how and why of teaching and learning letters, sounds, and words. In I. Fountas & G. Pinnell (Eds.), *Voices on word matters: Learning about phonics and spelling in the literacy classroom* (pp. 25–36). Portsmouth, NH: Heinemann.

Williams, K., & Blair-Larsen, S. (1999). Introduction. In S. Blair-Larsen & K. Williams (Eds.), *The balanced reading program: Helping all students achieve success* (pp. 1–7). Newark, DE: International Reading Association.

Winograd, P., & Arrington, H. (1999). Best practices in literacy assessment. In L. Gambrell, L. Morrow, S. Neuman, & M. Pressley (Eds.), *Best practices in literacy instruction* (pp. 210–244). New York: The Guilford Press.

Wolff, P. (1969). The natural history of crying and other vocalizations in early infancy. In B. Foss (Ed.), *Determinants of infant behavior, IV* (pp. 81–109). London, Methuen.

Wong Fillmore, L. (1991). When learning a second language means losing the first. *Early Childhood Research Quarterly, 6*, 343–346.

Wong Fillmore, L. (1999). Reading and academic English learning. Paper presented at the 1999 Regional Conference of Improving America's Schools, Chicago, IL.

Wood, C. (2002). Parent-child pre-school activities can affect the development of literacy skills. *Journal of Research in Reading, 25*(3), 241–258.

Wood, M. (2005). Progress with pleasure: Success with struggling beginning readers. *The New England Reading Association Journal, 41*(2), 30–36.

Wren, S. (2001). What does a "balanced literacy approach" mean? Topics in early reading coherence. Austin, TX: Southwest Educational Development Laboratory. ERIC ED 458 555.

Wright, K., Stegelin, D., & Hartle, L. (2007). *Building family, school, and community partnerships* (3rd ed.). Upper Saddle River, NJ: Merrill Prentice Hall.

Yaden, D. (1986). Reading research in metalinguistic awareness: A classification of findings according to focus and methodology. In D. Yaden & S. Templeton (Eds.), *Metalinguistic awareness and beginning literacy* (pp. 41–62). Portsmouth, NH: Heinemann.

Yaden, D., Rowe, D., & MacGillivray, L. (1999). Emergent literacy: A polyphony of perspectives. CIERA Report. Ann Arbor, MI: Center for the Improvement of Early Reading Achievement. ERIC 447 410.

Yopp, H. (1995a). Read-aloud books for developing phonemic awareness: An annotated bibliography. *The Reading Teacher, 48*(6), 538–542.

Yopp, H. (1995b). A test for assessing phonemic awareness in young children. *Reading Teacher, 49*(1), 20–29.

Yopp, H., & Singer, H. (1994). Toward an interactive reading instructional model: Explanation of activation of linguistic awareness and metalinguistic abilities in learning to read. In R. Ruddell, M. Ruddell, & H. Singer (Eds.), *Theoretical models and processes of reading* (4th ed.) (pp. 381–390). Newark, DE: International Reading Association.

Yopp, H., & Yopp, R. (2000). Supporting phonemic awareness development in the classroom. *The Reading Teacher, 54*(2), 130–143.

Young, T., & Moss, B. (2006, Summer). Nonfiction in the classroom library: A literacy necessity. *Childhood Education, 82*(4), 207–212.

Zeichner, K., & Liston, D. (1996). *Reflective teaching: An introduction.* Mahwah, NJ: Lawrence Erlbaum.

Zentella, A. (2005). Premises, promises, and pitfalls of language socialization research in Latino families and communities. In A. Zentella (Ed.), *Building on strength: Language and literacy in Latino families and communities* (pp. 13–30). New York: Teachers College Press.

Author Index

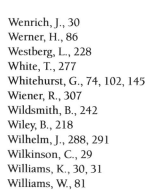

Subject Index